S0-AFA-571

PC/Computing Guide to Quicken 5.0

PCComputing

PC/Computing Guide to Quicken 5.0

Michael E. Kolowich

Ziff-Davis Press
Emeryville, California

Development Editor	Lyn Cordell
Copy Editor	Kate Hoffman
Technical Review	Bruce Gendron
	Maryann Brown
Project Coordinator	Sheila McGill
Proofreaders	Pat Mannion
	Bill Cassel
Cover Design	Michael Yapp
Book Design	Laura Lamar/MAX, San Francisco
	Stephen Bradshaw
Word Processing	Howard Blechman
	Kim Haglund
Technical Illustration	Cherie Plumlee Computer Graphics & Illustration
Page Layout	Bruce Lundquist
	Stephen Bradshaw
	Sidney Davenport
Indexer	Valerie Roberts

This book was produced on a Macintosh IIfx, with the following applications: FrameMaker®, Microsoft® Word, MacLink®*Plus*, Aldus® FreeHand™, and Collage Plus™.

Ziff-Davis Press
5903 Christie Avenue
Emeryville, CA 94608

Copyright © 1992 by Ziff-Davis Press. All rights reserved.

Printed and manufactured in the United States of America.

PC/Computing is a registered trademark of Ziff Communications Company. Ziff-Davis Press, ZD Press, and PC/Computing Guide To are trademarks of Ziff Communications Company.

All other product names and services identified throughout this book are trademarks or registered trademarks of their respective companies. They are used throughout this book in editorial fashion only and for the benefit of such companies. No such uses, or the use of any trade name, is intended to convey endorsement or other affiliation with the book.

No part of this publication may be reproduced in any form, or stored in a database or retrieval system, or transmitted or distributed in any form by any means, electronic, mechanical photocopying, recording, or otherwise, without the prior written permission of Ziff-Davis Press, except as permitted by the Copyright Act of 1976 and except that program listings may be entered, stored, and executed in a computer system.

THE INFORMATION AND MATERIAL CONTAINED IN THIS BOOK ARE PROVIDED "AS IS," WITHOUT WARRANTY OF ANY KIND, EXPRESS OR IMPLIED, INCLUDING WITHOUT LIMITATION ANY WARRANTY CONCERNING THE ACCURACY, ADEQUACY, OR COMPLETENESS OF SUCH INFORMATION OR MATERIAL OR THE RESULTS TO BE OBTAINED FROM USING SUCH INFORMATION OR MATERIAL. NEITHER ZIFF-DAVIS PRESS NOR THE AUTHOR SHALL BE RESPONSIBLE FOR ANY CLAIMS ATTRIBUTABLE TO ERRORS, OMISSIONS, OR OTHER INACCURACIES IN THE INFORMATION OR MATERIAL CONTAINED IN THIS BOOK, AND IN NO EVENT SHALL ZIFF-DAVIS PRESS OR THE AUTHOR BE LIABLE FOR DIRECT, INDIRECT, SPECIAL, INCIDENTAL, OR CONSEQUENTIAL DAMAGES ARISING OUT OF THE USE OF SUCH INFORMATION OR MATERIAL.

ISBN 1-56276-023-8
10 9 8 7 6 5 4 3 2

For Katharine, who has blessed me with one remarkable set of twins, two ferociously competitive ballplayers, and the 15 most fulfilling years of my life.

CONTENTS AT A GLANCE

TABLE OF CONTENTS

FOREWORD

When I first heard that a new book project was underway for Quicken, my first reaction, frankly, was to groan. I'd become disillusioned with software books that were little more than knock-offs of the product manuals. Then I found out that Ziff-Davis would be publishing it, and I was intrigued. When I learned that Michael Kolowich would write it, I knew we were in for something very valuable and different.

I got to know Michael as a first-rate business strategist, before either of us got involved in the computer industry. His launch and expansion of *PC/Computing* as a top-circulation monthly computer magazine is one of the most impressive accomplishments in computer publishing in years. So we invited Michael inside the development process of Quicken 5.0. We shared with him our research and seven years of customer testing, he shared his ideas, some of which we have incorporated into Quicken 5.0.

One result of this collaboration is that Michael understands Quicken in ways that most people never have. In *PC/Computing Guide to Quicken 5.0*, he starts with a look at the financial decisions and problems most Americans face, and then shows how Quicken tackles them. Most importantly, he tailors the financial management experience to his readers and guides them directly to the parts of Quicken that will help them most.

Michael is able to offer this unique approach because he understands that most Americans have a problem. Every household and every business in America must pay bills every month, without fail. Yet there's hardly a person on this planet who actually *likes* to pay bills.

The problem gets worse. Many people don't feel in command of their finances. Others know that lost tax deductions and errors are costing them money. But the distaste for personal financial management is nearly as universal as the need for it.

That's the picture Tom Proulx and I faced in 1983 when we decided to address the drudgery of personal finance with the unique new capabilities of the personal computer. The very things that make bookkeeping so tedious are the things that make it perfect for a PC: it involves the manipulation, storage, and organization of numeric data and plenty of recurring transactions—often with the same data, month after month. Pretty boring for people, but a task that computers are great at.

This was not, mind you, a novel thought. There were already 35 personal finance programs on the market when we started. So what was so different about Quicken that it could eventually become the top-selling software program of any kind? From the start we decided to relentlessly and single-mindedly focus on tailoring the technology to fit precisely the needs and tastes of real people. We used extensive research to understand the things that people don't like about personal financial management. Things like the time it consumes, the worries it creates, the family disagreements it can trigger. We also needed to understand people's tastes and habits. Our design goals were simple: do everything possible to help people save time, save money, and get better control of their personal financial lives without forcing them to change their habits.

The result was, our customers tell us, a product that is as natural to use as a checkbook. A product that eliminates an entire class of clerical work. A product that offers people instant insight into their personal financial situation.

We keep improving Quicken by talking to 10,000 customers every year. We even follow some of them home from the store (with their permission, of course) to make sure we learn how to improve the new user's experience. Quicken 5 is the culmination of that passionate quest for feedback.

Eight years after we got started, and with over 2 million copies sold, Quicken has made a visible dent in the way Americans manage their finances. If, for each customer, we can save 30 minutes a month, help justify one more tax deduction a year, lend one insight that will lead to smarter financial management, or defuse one family financial disagreement, we will have paid back manyfold the investment that that customer made. And though Quicken may not make personal bookkeeping downright fun, it at least can eliminate the pain of a task we'll have to do without fail for the rest of our lives.

Now, by combining the innovative features of Quicken 5.0 with the unique and practical approach that Michael brings in *PC/Computing Guide to Quicken 5.0*, users can enjoy an entirely new experience in financial management. At Intuit, we welcome bright new ideas like Michael's.

Scott Cook
President and Founder, Intuit
Menlo Park, California
September 1991

ACKNOWLEDGMENTS

I wrote this book because I once needed it myself, pure and simple. As good as the Quicken reference manual is, it's limited by the fact that, being a software manual, it must focus on the software itself, systematically covering every menu, feature, and quirk. What's missing are some of the real-world concerns of personal finance—a focus on the everyday problems and decisions we all face in getting control of our personal financial lives.

The leadership of Intuit, creators of Quicken, deserve credit for acknowledging this gap, and for supporting this project as vigorously as they did. The founding team of Scott Cook, Eric Dunn, and Tom Proulx all contributed ideas, encouragement, and support throughout the project. Mari Laterell-Baker was a weekly correspondent, making sure that our readers benefitted from the very latest information as Quicken 5 evolved through the development process. All of these people made me feel very much a part of the team during the creation of a very special product, and allowed my suggestions to leave a footprint or two in the design of the software.

From coast to coast quite literally, my colleagues at Ziff Communications lent exceptional levels of support. *PC/Computing*'s technical editor Dale Lewallen encouraged me to take on the project, and executive editor Chris Shipley helped me hone it. At Ziff-Davis Press, Cindy Hudson and Harry Blake were willing to take the risk on a first-time author, and Lyn Cordell and Kate Hoffman helped me turn my thoughts into polished prose. At the office, my assistants Anne Bala and Lili McGirr preserved a sense of calm at the eye of the storm. Ultimately, though, it is my mentor Bill Ziff who blessed me with opportunity—to build *PC/Computing*, to write this book, and to pursue a professional dream I could barely imagine entertaining four years ago.

Most importantly, though, we have Rebecca Curzon to thank for making it all happen. The demands on my time are myriad and intense, and Rebecca, as my editorial associate, kept the book on track so that it could be available at the same time as the shipment of Quicken 5. Her creativity and vivid imagination are visible in the form of many of the characters and case studies you'll meet in this volume; what's less visible is the personal sacrifice she endured in the name of quality and completeness.

INTRODUCTION

The recent recession serves to remind us of something we've always known but rarely keep in the front of our minds: The line between prosperity and struggle, comfort and adversity is very thin indeed. It's far too easy to be caught unprepared by recession, by sudden unemployment, by dramatic changes in the market, by an unexpected inheritance, and by abrupt fluctuations in our personal cash flow. Such events call for quick choices, and it seems we never have enough data to support the decisions we need to make.

This guide is about being prepared for changes and supporting with facts the decisions they force us to make. It also addresses the routine of managing daily financial life: paying bills, organizing tax information, regulating spending, and managing investments. In most instances, a personal computer can actually help you save time and money on these routine tasks; laying the groundwork for crucial decisions is a bonus!

Intuit's Quicken, the top-selling personal finance program in the world, is central to this book. Especially coupled with useful accessories—an electronic payment service, a tax preparation package, a spreadsheet, and an online information service—Quicken can form the hub of a personal financial management system that would be the envy of many businesses.

In the tradition of *PC/Computing,* this guide will advance your understanding of all the benefits Quicken has to offer and help you harvest the complete potential of Quicken and its related tools.

How to Use This Book

No two people use a software package in exactly the same way. That's particularly true for something as individual as a personal financial management package. Everyone approaches this software with unique motivations and priorities, as well as a different set of terms and level of sophistication. What's special about Quicken is that it accommodates such a range of users. The *PC/Computing Guide to Quicken 5.0* is designed not only to adapt to this variety but also to encourage it. The book organizes Quicken's vast array of features not by menu structure but by the results you want to achieve.

The Preliminaries section, "Lay the Groundwork for Managing Your Finances," invites you to set your objectives in using Quicken. It anticipates the kinds of results you might want to derive from Quicken and asks you how much time you're willing to invest in achieving those results. Armed with this insight, you will then develop a plan for learning to use Quicken in a manner tailored to your particular situation.

The main body of the book is divided into two parts and twelve "levels," each of which focuses on a different set of practical problems and solutions. Together, the levels move logically through typical financial management chores—from the most basic to the most sophisticated. After reading "Lay the Groundwork," you'll be able to decide which levels are most relevant to your financial picture. Part 1, "Learn Quicken," consists of Levels 1 through 5, which familiarize you with Quicken basics. Part 2, "Make Quicken Work for You," includes Levels 6 through 12, which help you manipulate the software to achieve more sophisticated results. Again, the preliminary section, "Lay the Groundwork for Managing Your Finances," will help you decide which levels to tackle.

In addition to the commentary, tutorials, and examples, two other valuable features characterize each level:

- *Plan Ahead*   This feature, located at the beginning of each level, helps you identify and consider the important decisions you'll need to make at each level of use. Look to the Plan Ahead feature to ensure you have all the necessary materials at hand, and to find out what preliminary steps you should have completed before you undertake the new material.

- *Building Blocks*   Each level concludes with a review of the principal new techniques, terms, and concepts covered in the text. Look to the Building Blocks feature when you want to refresh your memory on the central components of each level.

Throughout the book, you'll also find *Toolkits*—charts, tables, and other devices designed to help you customize Quicken and use it more effectively. Each Toolkit provides a practical means of applying what you've just learned to your own situation.

If you're using Quicken for the first time, read "Lay the Groundwork for Managing Your Finances" carefully to plan your strategy for using the rest of the book. If you're a Quicken veteran who's recently upgraded to version 5, you'll want to skim "Lay the Groundwork" and Part 1, and spend more time with Part 2. Version 5 introduces substantial changes in Quicken's user interface (mouse and SAA menu support), in reporting, and in budgeting—not to mention more subtle changes in categorization, memorized transactions, and file maintenance. These innovations build on the introduction of investment tracking and electronic payments in Quicken version 4. Check the "What's New" section of your upgrade manual, and then consult the appropriate sections of this book.

Preliminaries: Lay the Groundwork for Your Finances

Familiarize Yourself with the Tools

Choose When to Start

Ask Yourself Two Key Questions

Adopt a Routine

TO MANY COMPUTER USERS, THE ARRIVAL OF A NEW SOFTWARE PACKAGE poses an irresistible challenge. Experienced users can't wait to strip off the shrink wrap, find Disk 1, type **INSTALL**, start the program, and see how far they can get before finally turning, reluctantly, to the manual. Some people use software for years without ever opening the documentation.

Quicken 5 offers just such a temptation. The software is seductively easy to use, holds your hand through the installation process, and uses metaphors (checks and checkbook registers) that are comfortable and intuitive. Quicken also offers a rich array of valuable features, tools, and shortcuts. Its designers have provided plenty of clever safety nets that minimize the risk of mistakes.

You should, however, avoid at all costs the temptation to leap into Quicken before looking. After all, your personal finances—and your valuable time—are at stake. We sound this note of caution because Quicken differs from most software applications in a crucial way. From your first session with Quicken, you are building a *system* for monitoring and managing your personal finances—a system under which you'll be working for a very long time. While you can change most of the initial decisions you make setting up Quicken, over time it will be increasingly difficult to do so. It's likely that you'll find yourself becoming more and more "invested" in the way you first set up the program.

This chapter will help ensure that your investments of time and energy into Quicken are sound, and that your priorities for Quicken are clear from the outset.

Familiarize Yourself with the Tools

Quicken can certainly be used very effectively on its own. It's designed to be a self-contained application software program; over the last few years its developers have added capabilities to ensure that it isn't necessary for you to use other software along with it. Still, you may find that Quicken is complemented very well by several other software programs and services. Together, these applications constitute an exceptionally strong platform for managing your personal finances.

The Engine: Quicken 5

At the hub of the system, of course, is Quicken itself. This personal financial management package operates with a system of accounts—paralleling standard accounts such as bank accounts, charge card accounts, and investment accounts—and uses familiar metaphors such as checks and checkbook registers to track account activity and pay bills. The software is also a powerful analytical tool, capable of providing overviews of your financial picture by consolidating account activity into customized income and expense categories.

Developed in 1984, Quicken was initially sold principally by banks to customers who wanted to apply their PCs to personal finance. Later, Intuit began selling the software through retail stores with such success that, during some months, large chains sold more copies of Quicken than of any other software program.

The fifth major release of Quicken—Quicken 5—appeared on store shelves in late 1991. It offers a number of innovative improvements, including additional interface options (the mouse and pulldown menus that comply with industry standards), a new budgeting module, new report customization capabilities, more ways to categorize your transactions, and many minor improvements throughout the program.

Valuable Accessories

You may want to complement Quicken with several accessories—software programs and services which work with Quicken to extend its capabilities:

- *An Electronic Payment Service*   While the capability to produce completed checks on your printer is built into Quicken, new services have recently emerged which completely eliminate the need to prepare and send a paper check. The leading service in this area is CheckFree, from CheckFree Corporation in Columbus, Ohio. Intuit has made arrangements with CheckFree to tightly link Quicken's payment preparation methods to CheckFree's electronic transactions system. While the interface is nearly seamless, the companies are still very separate—a point both companies take great pains to remind the user of when they describe their customer support obligations and policies.

- *A Tax Preparation Package*   Quicken will collect and categorize your tax information, but will not help any further when it comes time to file your tax returns. Tax preparation packages (such as MECA's TaxCut or Chip-Soft's TurboTax) have improved dramatically in the last several years, to the point that they can give advice, handle moderately exotic tax situations, and laser print forms that look exactly like those supplied by the Internal Revenue Service. Some of these programs allow for importing Quicken's data, so you can avoid reentering your tax data.

- *A Spreadsheet and Quicken's Transfer Utility*   Quicken provides some very simple analytical tools to help you make informed personal financial decisions. More sophisticated analysis—particularly investment analysis—sometimes requires that you supplement Quicken with a spreadsheet (such as Lotus 1-2-3, Borland's Quattro Pro, or Microsoft's Excel). Intuit offers a transfer utility, sold separately, that facilitates the transfer of data from Quicken into your favorite spreadsheet program, but it's not particularly difficult to import Quicken reports into a spreadsheet without the transfer utility.

- *An On-line Information Service*   If you use the investment management features of Quicken and own a stock portfolio that contains more than six publicly traded securities, you may want to consider using an on-line information service (such as CompuServe or ZiffNet) to update Quicken with the latest prices for that portfolio. Using a good communications program and Quicken's import feature, you can update portfolios containing a hundred stocks and bonds in less than three minutes, for around two dollars.

- *A Payroll Processing Utility*   If you'll be using Quicken to assist in bookkeeping for a small business, and you'll be paying more than one or two employees, you should consider using a payroll-processing utility. Quick-Pay, sold separately by Intuit, is designed to link closely to your Quicken data and to provide many of the check formats and reports you'll need.

Throughout this book, we'll be explaining how these programs can exchange data with Quicken to accomplish important tasks that Quicken can't do alone. You'll find information on how to obtain these accessories in Appendix B of this book.

Choose When to Start

The high sales of Quicken and similar programs in late December and early January each year suggest that personal financial management heads the list of a great number of New Year's resolutions. There are some advantages in starting your Quicken records at the beginning of the year, but doing so is by no means necessary to derive full benefit from the product.

If you start using Quicken at the beginning of the year, you'll see several advantages, two of which are tax related:

- Your tax information for the year will be complete. In contrast, starting midway through the year will force you to consult your paper checkbook and other records for taxable income and deductible expenses which may have occurred before you started recording them.

- Your year-end investment decisions—the timing of which is typically motivated by tax considerations—will be supported by complete information on how those decisions will affect your total capital gains and losses for the year.

- If you plan to use the budgeting features of Quicken—for either now or next year—you'll find that the calendar year is the most convenient interval for planning. Even if you don't plan to start budgeting till the next calendar year, it's useful to have a full year of data on your income and spending patterns to support your budget planning for the year.

However, any time of year is fine for getting Quicken up and running. Even if you buy Quicken in the middle of the year, and plan to start right away, you'll get valuable information on your spending that will help you plan for next year, and you may be inspired to enter historical data back to the beginning of the current calendar year.

If you do start mid-year, there are two areas where you may want to take the time to enter information for the entire year:

- If you'll be using Quicken for tax preparation purposes, you should enter all your tax-related transactions for the year. This way, you won't have to scramble in April for your tax-receipt shoebox to find deductible expenses; they'll all be in one place on your Quicken reports.

- If you'll use Quicken for investment purposes, you'll want to enter not only all your buy, sell, dividend, and interest transactions back to the start of the year for tax purposes, but also the purchase dates and amounts for every security you currently hold in your portfolio.

Ask Yourself Two Key Questions

Now is the time to formulate an approach to personal financial management that fits your particular needs. Before you enter your first check, ask yourself two key questions:

- Why are you using personal finance software?

- How much time are you willing to invest, given the benefits you expect to realize?

The answers to these questions should directly determine which features you use within Quicken, the level of detail you record, and the accessories you use alongside Quicken.

Why Are You Using Quicken?

Properly and diligently applied to your personal finances, Quicken can deliver a wide variety of benefits. These benefits fall into three general categories: saving time, saving money, and taking control of your personal finances. As you begin considering these potential benefits, you can refer to the Set Your Priorities Toolkit later in this chapter. The Toolkit lists a variety of benefits you may realize as you use Quicken—all described in a moment— and lets you rate them in terms of their importance to you. As you weigh these benefits using the Toolkit, you'll begin to identify patterns that will suggest the best direction for you to take with Quicken and this book.

Using Quicken to Save Time

Quicken's name suggests that it's designed to save time, and the program makes good on the pledge once you've learned and customized it. Quicken can significantly reduce the time you spend on several common tasks:

- *Paying and mailing bills* By remembering names, addresses, and transaction details from one session to the next, Quicken can shave time off your bill paying sessions. When combined with CheckFree, an electronic bill paying service, bill paying time can be cut by at least 75 percent.

- *Reconciling your checking account* You can fully reconcile a personal checking account in less than three minutes. Quicken helps you effectively spot errors and make corrections, too. Though easy to avoid or put off in a paper-based system, reconciliation becomes a breeze when it's so easily completed on your PC.

- *Organizing tax data* By collecting and categorizing your payments, you'll find at tax time that locating charitable contributions, mortgage interest, and other deductible items is a snap. Quicken's investment features track capital gains and losses—data you need but won't get out of most brokerage tax reports.

- *Evaluating investment portfolios* Quicken offers the fastest way to get a detailed picture of your personal investments. When combined with an online information service such as CompuServe or Prodigy, Quicken can evaluate even complex portfolios of hundreds of stocks and bonds in a couple of minutes, requiring only a few keystrokes.

- *Preparing credit applications* Whenever you're required to supply a personal statement of net worth—such as for a bank credit application—Quicken can supply you with one in a couple of minutes. While a lender won't always allow you to merely attach the computer generated report, Quicken saves time by keeping vital asset and liability balances current and available.

Using Quicken to Save Money

Less obvious, but no less significant, are the ways Quicken can save you money:

- *Detecting errors* Whether an error is your own or a bank's, vendor's, or credit card company's, Quicken invisibly compares your cash balances to the recorded transactions to help highlight errors that could cost you money.

- *Avoiding minimum balance fees* If your checking or savings account requires you to maintain a minimum balance in order to avoid bank charges, you can use Quicken to ensure you stay above the minimum balance threshold.

- *Optimizing float*   Quicken can hold large bill payments till the last possible moment before they are due, saving interest expense on the float. While its system of prompts and reminders is good, this capability should be used carefully, lest a slip-up cost you more in late charges than you save in interest.

- *Tracking tax deductions*   Not merely a timesaver, tax categories can be used to ensure that no potential deduction slips through the cracks. Since you're recording every significant transaction in Quicken, you can categorize any payment as a deductible expense.

- *Cutting professional tax preparation time*   If you pay by the hour for tax preparation, you'll find that the better organized you are, the more efficiently your tax preparer uses his or her time. A neatly printed tax category report from Quicken is always better than a shoebox full of receipts, no matter how well organized.

- *Managing business expense accounts*   If you travel on a business expense account, you may occasionally lose reimbursable business expense receipts. By recording credit card detail, you will have a tool to check the expenses you submitted against the expenses you actually paid, allowing you to catch forgotten expense items.

- *Tracking the tax cost basis for your home*   Any improvements you make on your home, from carpeting to a new deck, can be added to your home's tax cost basis, on which you base calculations of capital gains when you sell the property.

- *Detecting fraud or forgery*   Again, the reconciliation process helps you discover irregularities in your bank or investment accounts that may be the result of fraud, forgery, or embezzlement. By making reconciliation quick and painless, Quicken helps you detect these problems before you might otherwise do so.

- *Managing small businesses*   For very small businesses—particularly businesses operated out of your home—Quicken is a perfectly capable simple bookkeeping program. By integrating the process of writing business checks with keeping the books, you can save considerable money on accountants or bookkeepers.

Using Quicken to Take Control of Your Finances

The hardest set of benefits to measure—but often the most vital to your financial well-being—are those associated with gaining control of your personal finances:

- *Coordinating joint checking accounts*   Couples have always been haunted by the two-checkbook problem posed by a joint checking account: there is simply no easy way to maintain an accurate running bank balance when two active checkbooks are drawing on the same account. Quicken offers a way of addressing this problem by keeping a register which consolidates all checkbooks drawing on a single account.

■ *Managing cash flow*   Even in the best of economic times, we sometimes run tight on cash. At these times, Quicken can help project cash needs, show the effect of adjusting the timing of payments to match cash inflows, and indicate investments and other liquid assets which might be applied to cash shortfalls.

■ *Setting personal priorities and translating them into a budget*   Quicken's budgeting capabilities can assist you in setting personal financial priorities well in advance of day-to-day spending decisions. Quicken also helps you meet your spending goals by letting you track spending against budgets. This proactive approach is critical to staying in control of your personal finances.

■ *Getting a quick view of your savings rate*   Quicken's many standard reports are informative and easy to set up, providing insight into your current financial profile in seconds.

■ *Supporting year-end tax decisions*   As the end of the year approaches, Quicken's reports make it possible to estimate your tax liability for the year. By accumulating taxable income, deductible expenses, and unrealized capital gains and losses in one place, Quicken can support those last minute decisions to sell securities or to defer (or accelerate) either income or expenses.

■ *Strengthening investment decisions*   While it can't give you advice on how to play the stock market, Quicken can help evaluate the relative performance of all the investments you've made. Grouping and tracking investments by account, type, and investment objective is the first step to ensuring that every component of your investment portfolio is meeting your expectations.

■ *Organizing for an IRS audit*   Just as Quicken reports are better than piles of receipts for your tax preparer, they can be a lifesaver when you're facing an IRS audit.

■ *Aiding better business decision-making*   Quicken isn't just for keeping your personal or small business books. Its database structure can adapt to many different business situations, helping you make better decisions no matter how big your company is.

Toolkit: Set Your Priorities

If you attempt to realize all Quicken's benefits at once, with equal vigor, you'll find yourself sinking into a dizzying and confusing morass of features. To help direct your first efforts at using Quicken, we've provided a Quicken Toolkit that will help you determine what's most important to you.

In the left column, the Toolkit lists the benefits described earlier. Think about each one as it relates to your reasons for using Quicken and decide where it falls on the scale of importance. Circle the appropriate number next to each benefit. Then list the four most important benefits on the blank lines at the bottom. Finally, check which levels pertain to your chosen benefits, and write the levels next to each one.

TOOLKIT   Set Your Priorities

Why Am I Using Quicken?	Level(s)	Unimportant			Very important
To Save Time:					
Paying and mailing bills	1, 3, 4	1	2	3	4
Reconciling my checking account	2	1	2	3	4
Organizing tax data	2, 5, 10	1	2	3	4
Evaluating investment portfolios	8	1	2	3	4
Preparing credit applications	6, 9	1	2	3	4
To Save Money:					
Detecting errors	2	1	2	3	4
Avoiding minimum balance fees	2	1	2	3	4
Optimizing float	3	1	2	3	4
Tracking tax deductions	2, 5, 10	1	2	3	4
Cutting professional tax preparation time	10	1	2	3	4
Managing business expense accounts	5, 12	1	2	3	4
Tracking the tax cost basis for your home	5, 9, 10	1	2	3	4
Detecting fraud or forgery	2	1	2	3	4
Managing small businesses	11	1	2	3	4
To Take Control of My Finances:					
Coordinating joint checking accounts	2	1	2	3	4
Getting a quick view of my savings rate	2, 9	1	2	3	4
Managing cash flow	2, 5, 6	1	2	3	4
Setting personal priorities and translating them into a budget	6,7,9	1	2	3	4
Strengthening investment decisions	8	1	2	3	4
Supporting year-end tax decisions	10	1	2	3	4
Organizing for an IRS audit	10	1	2	3	4
Assisting in doing my job better	12	1	2	3	4

The four most important benefits I want to get out of Quicken (and their levels) are:

1. _____ Level: _____

2. _____ Level: _____

3. _____ Level: _____

4. _____ Level: _____

How Much Time Are You Willing to Invest?

Once you've prioritized the benefits you want to get out of Quicken, you should determine how much time it will cost you to realize those benefits. Presumably, you have already put money into the project by buying Quicken, but even if you paid the full retail price, that investment pales in comparison to the value of your time.

You can invest three types of time in Quicken: setup and learning time, maintenance time, and analysis time.

More than most other software, you'll find that investing time in learning and customizing Quicken to your needs will pay off handsomely by reducing maintenance and analysis later. Every new user should count on spending around three hours getting Quicken up and running. Then, plan on investing another one to two hours of setup and learning time for each new area of Quicken that you decide to explore.

The amount of maintenance time—keeping accounts current and performing routine tasks—can vary from as little as 30 minutes a month to as much as 30 minutes a day, depending on how busy you are, how much time you stand to save, and how much you value intangible benefits such as increased control, confidence, and peace of mind.

For example, when gauging your commitment to maintenance time, consider how much time you've already spent paying bills, gathering tax information, and adding up your investments on the back of an envelope. These times should shrink dramatically. Then, consider how much time it's worth to save $500 on your tax preparation bill, find a $60 error once a year on your credit card statement, or know with confidence that you won't overdraw your checking account at the end of the month. Finally, realize that despite initial time investments, hectic lives can become easier to manage with Quicken's advanced features. Armed with an understanding of your priorities, you'll be able to focus on advanced features that are most useful to you, spending just enough time to keep them working on your behalf.

If you have a financial life of average complexity, consider setting aside 30 minutes a week for maintaining Quicken. As you gain experience with both the software and the routine it encourages, you'll almost certainly depart from this starting point, more or less depending on your priorities.

If you placed a high priority on getting control of your finances, you'll want to allocate additional time for analyzing the data Quicken provides and to make the kinds of budget, investment, and spending decisions it so readily supports. Again, the amount of time you decide to spend will vary according to how sophisticated your work with Quicken becomes.

Armed with your priorities and a sense of what kind of setup, maintenance, and analysis time you're willing to invest, think about how you'll want to be using Quicken six months from now. Here are three general approaches to using Quicken. Your priorities will almost certainly vary over time, but you may find elements of these approaches that suit your own circumstances.

The Dabbler: Quicken on 30 Minutes a Month

Dale Scott has a rather simple financial picture—a basic savings and checking account and no major investments other than an Individual Retirement Account invested in a government securities fund. He doesn't itemize deductions and lives a frugal life—never spending more than what he has, never too close to the minimum balance on his checking account.

Dale's priority is to use his PC to pay bills and balance his checkbook as quickly and painlessly as possible, so he can get on with the pleasant things in life like going out to the Metrodome to watch the Minnesota Twins. He's interested in occasionally surveying what he spends—just to make sure he's not letting anything get out of line.

Dale can get by investing a small amount of setup time, and then using Quicken as little as 30 minutes a month, purely to automate his bill paying chores and balance his checkbook. He'll want to use the *PC/Computing Guide to Quicken* to get up to speed and to discover every shortcut the product has to offer.

- In Level 1 ("Get Started with Quicken"), he'll set up his accounts and learn fundamentals such as entering checks, navigating the Register, and printing reports.

- In Level 2 ("Track Your Spending and Income"), he'll complete a monthly cycle of entering his payments and deposits, balancing his checkbook, and obtaining the reports he needs for his "quick look" every year.

- In Level 3 ("Write Checks with Quicken"), he'll learn to automate the tiresome chore of check writing and printing—often directing bills to be paid with two or three keystrokes.

- He might pursue Level 4 ("Make Payments Electronically") as an alternative to Level 3, especially if his first priority is saving time. Level 4 describes CheckFree, an electronic bill paying service which, when used with Quicken, lets you pay bills in less than one minute.

With 30 minutes a month, Dale will barely scratch the surface of Quicken's capabilities, but he's likely to accomplish his goal of saving time and reducing the drudgery (if not the pain) of bill paying. He'll be able to check his spending patterns periodically, comparing them against his priorities and making adjustments as needed. In addition, the full extent of Quicken's capabilities will be available to him should the complexity of his financial picture ever demand it.

The Tracker: Quicken on 30 Minutes a Week

Maria Lombardi's financial picture suddenly became more complicated when she married Luke Fielding, bought a house, and started a family. As the couple confronted the chore of maintaining a joint checking account, they also discovered how easily they could lose track of their spending. They began accumulating modest investments, Luke dabbling in stocks, Maria trying her hand at mutual funds. With two paychecks and a raft of new tax deductions, they agreed to track more carefully expenditures that could lower their taxes. Maria drew the job of paying the bills and managing the family finances.

Maria's decided that her first priority is saving time paying bills. At the same time, though, she must acquire better command of the family's financial situation. If they spend their money sensibly, they will have enough left over to pay for the children's education and develop a nest egg for retirement.

Maria can probably accomplish her objectives by spending the usual setup time and then a moderate amount of time maintaining the family's Quicken accounts, averaging 30 minutes a week. She'll not only automate her bill paying, but coordinate with confidence the family's checking and savings accounts. She'll be constantly aware of the family's spending patterns and how they change over time. At year's end, she'll have the data at her fingertips to complete their joint tax return. She will also be more efficient at finding the data for filing payroll tax returns for the domestic help she hires to take care of the children while she and Luke are at work.

Maria will want to learn the basics and shortcuts offered by Levels 1 through 4, as did Dale. She'll also want to learn more advanced approaches to Quicken—capturing more detail in her transactions, reconciling Luke's expense accounts, and tracking the value of the family's investment portfolio.

- In Level 5 ("Handle Sophisticated Transactions"), she'll learn more advanced techniques for setting up asset accounts and handling common transactions such as mortgage payments and paychecks, and will also discover how to accomplish more using Quicken's built-in reports.

- Level 6 ("Apply Advanced Tracking Methods") will show her how to track credit card and cash accounts, design custom reports to provide the information she needs, and set up Quicken to track simple payroll needs, such as paying her child care worker.

- She'll skip to Level 8 ("Evaluate and Manage Your Investments") for guidance on setting up investment accounts, tracking the value of these accounts over time, and evaluating the performance of these investments—relative to each other and to the performance of the market as a whole.

- Maria should spend time on Level 10 ("Plan, Organize, and Complete Your Taxes") to learn strategies for both collecting the data and using it with PC-based tax preparation software to produce ready-to-file tax returns.

- Meanwhile, Maria's husband Luke will find many new and surprising ideas in Level 12 ("Use Quicken in Any Business Setting") which he can immediately use at the office.

Maria's 30 minutes a week taps much—but by no means all—of Quicken's power. Without investing much more time than they currently spend paying bills, Maria and Luke will quickly develop a far richer understanding of their financial affairs than would be possible if they spent the same time on manual analysis.

The Commander: Quicken on 30 Minutes Twice a Week

Larry Milner manages his personal finances as crisply and tightly as he runs his business. "I have a plan" is his creed, so he adheres closely to his personal budget. Larry has set one-year, five-year, and ten-year objectives for his net worth and freely trades his investments with every turn of the market. His wife Susan recently started a freelance design business, and Larry has agreed to help her maintain her books.

Larry's principal objective is controlling his finances. He relishes the myriad decisions his financial situation demands; the complexity of both his investment portfolio and tax returns reflects that enjoyment. The more data Larry can muster to support his decisions, the more pleased he is. Until now, Larry has relied on information from his broker and his personal accountant, keeping records in both manual and electronic form. This piecemeal approach has been adequate, enabling him to make sound decisions, although it has consumed more time than he would like.

Larry can get by with two half-hour sessions a week, but he's likely to spend even more time exploring and tuning his Quicken files. He must learn to use Quicken very efficiently, simply to avoid being buried by the workload. When he approaches Quicken and the *Guide,* he'll start with the shortcuts that Dale learned and the more advanced tracking methods that Maria picked up. In addition, Larry will want to explore budgeting, net worth planning, and small business accounting more fully.

- Level 7 ("Manage Your Finances According to a Budget") will support Larry's development of a monthly, quarterly, and yearly budget for the household.

- Level 9 ("Ascertain and Forecast Your Net Worth") will help him plot a path to achieve his goals for increasing his net worth.

- Finally, Level 11 ("Keep the Books for Your Small Business") will provide him all the tools he needs to help Susan with the financial aspects of running her fledgling company.

Larry will come as close as one can to exercising all the features of Quicken 5. While he'll be investing more time than he might currently be spending paying his bills, he'll be making important personal financial decisions armed with data that simply would not be available to him under any manual system.

Adopt a Routine

The single most important step you can take toward effectively using Quicken is developing a routine for entering bill payments, recording other transactions, pricing investments, and reconciling your accounts. There is a special rhythm to good personal financial management—one that has weekly, monthly, quarterly, and annual cycles.

Here, for example, is a routine that Larry Milner, our "commander" from earlier in this section, might have adopted.

Every Week

- Open bills and enter bill payments

- Transmit payments to CheckFree

- Enter checks and deposits from Larry's and Susan's paper check registers

- Enter deposit information from weekly paycheck stub

- Update prices in investment portfolio

- Evaluate investment decisions and enter purchases or sales

- Make weekly backup disk

Every Month

- Execute regular monthly transactions—mortgage, car lease, cable TV bill

- Reconcile savings, checking, and brokerage account transactions

- Enter detail from credit-card accounts and reconcile them

- Make monthly backup disk

Every Quarter

■ Review income and tax deduction reports to prepare quarterly estimated tax payments

■ Review budget reports and revise the budget as necessary

■ Prepare quarterly payroll tax filings for domestic workers

■ Review relative performance of investments by security type and investment objective

Every Year

■ Review tax reports in preparation for year-end tax decisions

■ Review investment reports for unrealized capital gains and losses

■ Plan next year's personal budget

■ Make annual backup disk

■ Transfer tax information to tax preparation program

■ Compress old data files, as required

Of course, at first you'll probably use Quicken less aggressively than Larry does with his hour-a-week program. At whatever level of sophistication you use Quicken—even if it's only to pay monthly bills out of a single checking account—you should adopt a routine to make sure nothing slips through the cracks.

To help you build and keep track of your routine, we've included a special Toolkit: your Maintenance Checklist, which is bound inside the back cover of this book. To use the checklist, indicate in the left-hand column those items you want to complete as part of your regular procedure; then check the items off as you complete them.

Having a routine doesn't mean you should create an atmosphere of obligation and drudgery around your work with Quicken. Always keep your three objectives in mind—saving time, saving money, and taking charge of your personal finances. If you review these objectives frequently and test your routine against them, the time you spend each week and month with Quicken will be both satisfying and rewarding.

1

Learn Quicken

PLAN AHEAD

DECISIONS

Note. Read the Preliminaries chapter of this book if you haven't yet done so. It contains very important information you should consider before you start Quicken for the first time.

When Should You Start?

It might seem sensible that you postpone learning Quicken until the next logical calendar break—for instance, the start of a new financial year. Don't put it off. Instead, begin immediately; even if you start late in the year, you'll quickly begin developing a picture of your finances that will be invaluable later. The more you discover now about both Quicken and your spending and income patterns, the more effective you'll be at budgeting and planning your expense-tracking habits in the new year.

If you haven't read "Choose When to Start" in the Preliminaries section of this book, now is a good time to do so, because that section discusses the pros and cons of waiting, starting immediately, or even going back to fill in historical data.

What Account Should You Use?

If you have more than one bank account, start with the checking account that you use most frequently to pay your household bills. If you use a joint checking account for your routine bills, start with that one: joint accounts are notoriously difficult to manage and are fertile ground for Quicken's ability to coordinate multiple sources of input.

Eventually, of course, you'll want to bring all your checking and savings accounts under the Quicken umbrella. For now, it's best to limit your work to a single account and build from there.

MATERIALS

Bank Statement

Examine the latest bank statement for the account you've chosen. Note the details your bank lists on its statement. Does it provide the payee for each check? Does it list the date the check was written or the date it was posted to your account? Where does your bank report the interest and bank charges? You'll need all these facts on hand when you begin recording your checks and reconciling your bank statements.

Canceled Checks

Even if your bank lists every payee, you should probably have your canceled checks on hand, too. Most of us scribble a brief note on each check we write to remind us what we were paying for (was it Randy's tuition or Suzanne's?). Banks are notorious for miskeying payee detail and sometimes merely write

"Payee detail not processed" where you expect to see "American Express." Also, because most bank statements list the posting date rather than the date on the check, you might want to refer to the canceled check for a more accurate date—perhaps to document all those deductible contributions you make on December 31st that only clear the bank in January.

Checkbook Register

Another good source of memos and notes is your checkbook register. In fact, you'll find your checkbook register a virtual necessity if you don't have access to your canceled checks.

PRELIMINARIES

Set Aside Adequate Time

Before you start your first Quicken session, make sure you have at least two uninterrupted hours to spend—no telephones, no visitors. That will give you a better chance to explore the software and end the session with a genuine sense of accomplishment.

Read the Installation Notes

Look at the installation notes in Appendix A before you start—particularly if your computer is not a "plain vanilla" machine. You'll find valuable information about printers, pointing devices, your communications modem, and registration.

Install the Software

You can't use Quicken straight off the floppy disk without running the INSTALL program. That's because the program files are compressed to fit on two floppy disks. Even if you're using a floppy disk system, you must decompress these files by running Quicken's installation procedure.

Appendix A shows you how to install Quicken and helps you answer the questions the INSTALL program will ask along the way.

Start Quicken for the First Time

Note. If you don't see the First Time Setup window (Figure 1.1) when you first start Quicken, you may navigate there on your own. Type **T** to choose Use Tutorials/Assistants from the Quicken Main Menu, and choose First Time SetUp from the Use Tutorials/Assistants menu.

In most cases, you start Quicken by typing the letter **Q** and then pressing the Enter key. If this doesn't work (if, for example, Borland's Quattro Pro spreadsheet—which has the same starting instructions—overwrites your startup file), you may have to begin with a two-step process. Appendix A explains how to start Quicken in these special circumstances.

The first time you start Quicken, you may elect to follow Quicken's automated setup process, tailored to the needs of new Quicken users. By the time you're done, you have created your first bank account. To take this route, indicate that you're a new user in the Welcome to Quicken 5.0 window at the New user assistance blank (Figure 1.1). Select option 3, "Set up my own Quicken data."

It's a good idea to take advantage of the assistance offered by option 3, even if you have used past versions of Quicken. Intuit has made several important changes to Quicken since version 4, and this new user introduction helps highlight these changes.

Figure 1.1   **First Time Setup window**

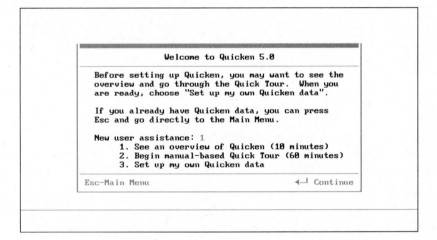

Learn How Quicken Is Organized

Before you dive deeper into the installation process, take a moment to understand how Quicken organizes your data. Quicken's four important building blocks are files, accounts, transactions, and categories. We'll cover a fifth building block—classes—in Level 6 of this book.

Files

At the most general level, Quicken collects data in *files* (called "Account Groups" in earlier versions), each of which represents the financial picture of an individual or a company. You'll probably need only one file to handle all your personal bank accounts, credit cards, and investment portfolios. If you're organizing both your personal finances and those of a separate small business, you might have two files. If you're bookkeeping for many clients, you may have as many files as you do clients.

Accounts

A file is really a collection of *accounts.* Accounts represent the principal entities through which we conduct our business: checking accounts, savings accounts, charge accounts, loan accounts, and investment accounts. To assess your financial health, you note the value of your major accounts and monitor the changes in those account values over time.

Transactions

Changes in an account are the consequence of *transactions*. A transaction might be a check, a deposit, a credit purchase, or a sale of stock. A transfer between bank accounts generates an equivalent (but opposite) transaction in each account. Every time money or assets flow into or out of an account, a transaction occurs.

Categories

Quicken's *categories* represent the way we describe transactions so that we can understand changes in our financial picture. There are two kinds of categories: income categories (such as salaries and dividends) and expense categories (such as mortgage interest, utilities, and food). You can choose to apply the same categories across all the accounts in a file. For example, whether you deposit your paycheck into your checking or savings account, it still belongs to the salary category. You assign all transactions to a category, except those that are transfers from account to account.

How They Work Together

Figure 1.2 shows a sample file called MYMONEY. This file has three accounts and six categories (one income and five expense categories).

Ten transactions are numbered here—eight are categorized and two indicate a transfer between accounts.

Transactions 2 through 8 are expense transactions from a checking account. Each is associated with both an account and an expense category.

Transactions 2 and 4 are food purchases deducted from the same checking account and therefore appear in the same cell. Transactions 5 and 6, both day-care expenses, are handled the same way. Transaction 1 is an income transaction, direct-deposited to the checking account.

Figure 1.2   **How accounts, transactions, and categories are related**

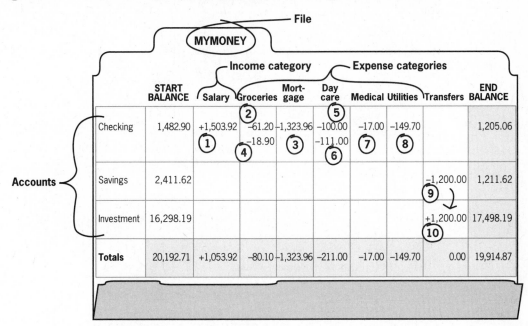

Transactions 9 and 10 represent a transfer of funds from the savings account to an investment account. The transaction that adds $1,200 to the investment account is directly offset by a $1,200 deduction from the savings account.

Quicken constantly balances each account as you enter transactions (see the Totals across the bottom). It also summarizes the transactions within each category (see the End Balance column on the right).

Keep this picture in mind as you begin to use Quicken's powerful system of accounts, transactions, and categories.

Create a Data File

Press Enter several times to move through the diagrams of Quicken's main elements. You'll encounter two quiz questions—which, frankly, you'll probably find to be rather inane. Answer 2 to both questions to fly through them. Then you will see the Set Up a File window (Figure 1.3). Here, you'll name your file and designate the directory where you want to store your data files.

Figure 1.3   **Set Up a File window**

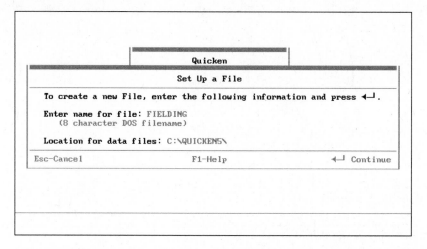

Complete the window as follows:

Note. Remember, DOS file names may contain any combination of eight letters, numbers, and any other characters except the following: . , " / \ [ ] < > + = ; : |

1. Name your data file. Quicken chooses a file name derived from the user-name you entered during setup. You may change the file name to any eight-character DOS file name you wish (MYMONEY, for instance). To change the name, type over Quicken's suggestion, or press Ctrl-Back-space (that is, press the Control key and Backspace together) to clear the field before you type. Press Enter to move on to the Location for Data Files field.

Note. If you want to store your data in a file other than your Quicken program directory, make sure you create it in DOS before starting Quicken. The DOS command MD C:\QUIKDATA will, for example, create a directory called QUIKDATA on the C drive.

2. Specify a data file location. Quicken will suggest that your data be stored in the same place as the program files. Unless you've got a good reason to change it (if, for example, you're keeping your data files on a logical D drive), leave the file location field alone. If you want to store your data elsewhere, you must specify a subdirectory that already exists.

Press Enter to continue on to the Select Standard Categories screen.

Choose Default Categories

Quicken offers a collection of standard income and expense categories that cover many typical income and spending patterns for home and business. As we mentioned earlier, it is these categories that enable Quicken to group your spending and income transactions together with others of a similar nature. Some examples of home and business default categories are shown in the Select Standard Categories window (Figure 1.4). You'll find a full listing of default categories in Level 2.

Figure 1.4   **Select Standard Categories window**

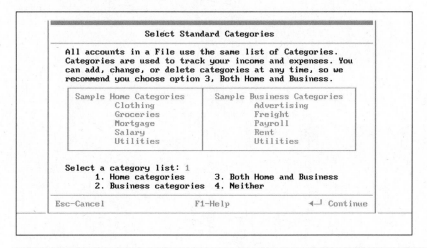

The standard categories are only a starting point. You can easily modify Quicken's category structure later, as you'll discover in Level 2.

At this stage, we recommend that you limit your choice to either home categories (option 1) or business categories (option 2), depending on your initial needs. Quicken allows you to add default categories later if, for instance, you start a home-based business.

Once you've chosen your standard categories, press Enter to tell Quicken you're ready to set up an account.

Set Up the New Account

Once you've specified the name and location of the file and set up the categories you'll use, Quicken displays the Set Up an Account window (Figure 1.5), where you can set up the first account in the file.

Figure 1.5   Set Up an Account window

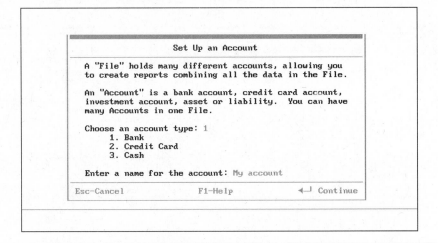

Begin by deciding the kind of account it should be—an easy choice this time, because we're starting with a bank account. Conveniently, Quicken's default choice is Bank account, indicated by the 1 in the "Choose an account type" blank. Accept this choice by pressing Enter, which will move the cursor to the next blank.

Now you can name your bank account. In selecting a name, follow these three guidelines:

- The account name should be no longer than 15 characters.

- The name may contain any combination of letters, numbers, and characters except these four: / : [ ].

- The name you choose should be comprehensible to whoever will see your reports, because it will appear on the reports you produce. (Nonetheless, like most things in Quicken, you can easily change the account name later.)

Usually, the name of the bank will suffice (for example, "Harbor Bank"). If you have multiple accounts at the same bank, append a unique identifier to the bank name, such as an abbreviation of purpose ("Harbor Bk

Note. Quicken will often suggest the choice that is most common in a given situation. Pressing Enter accepts the choice, while typing over the suggestion and pressing Enter inserts another choice and moves the cursor to the next blank.

Joint"), the initials of the account holder ("Harbor Bk LF"), or even the last few digits of the account number ("Harbor Bk 3652").

Once you've named your account, press Enter to bring up the Account Balance and Date window (Figure 1.6).

Figure 1.6   Account Balance and Date window

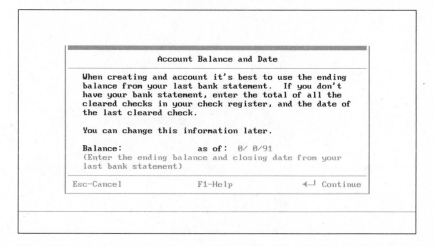

```
                    Account Balance and Date

     When creating and account it's best to use the ending
     balance from your last bank statement.  If you don't
     have your bank statement, enter the total of all the
     cleared checks in your check register, and the date of
     the last cleared check.

     You can change this information later.

     Balance:            as of:  0/ 0/91
     (Enter the ending balance and closing date from your
     last bank statement)
    ─────────────────────────────────────────────────────────
     Esc-Cancel              F1-Help              ←┘ Continue
```

Note. If you make a mistake after moving to the next blank on the screen, you can back up to the previous blank by holding down the Shift key while you press Tab.

Note. Enter dates with a slash between each part (2/7/92). As soon as you type a slash, Quicken moves the cursor to the next part of the date, even if you've only typed one digit in the previous part.

The final information Quicken needs is the starting balance of your account and the date of that balance. Pull out your latest bank statement and, for now, type the opening balance listed there. Pressing Enter will move the cursor to the next blank on the screen.

After you confirm your input, you'll see today's date displayed after "as of:". Here you'll change Quicken's suggestion. Choose a date that is safely before the dates of any of the checks you'll be recording, by typing over the suggested date (for example, for an October 1991 bank statement type **10/1/91**), and then press Enter.

Quicken's Data File Assistant now takes over, automating the process of creating your new data file and your first bank account. Press Enter when you are prompted to continue. You'll be a spectator for the next minute or so, although Quicken will pause at critical moments to show you what it's doing.

Eventually, Quicken will complete the automated process and let you return to the main menu. Again, it's best to start with a single account. You will have plenty of opportunities to add new accounts later.

Choose from the Main Menu

Every time you start Quicken from now on, you'll see the Main Menu (Figure 1.7). The Main Menu is like the central intersection of a large city: while there are many shortcuts for getting around, the least confusing way to move from one place to another is through the Main Menu.

Figure 1.7   Quicken Main Menu

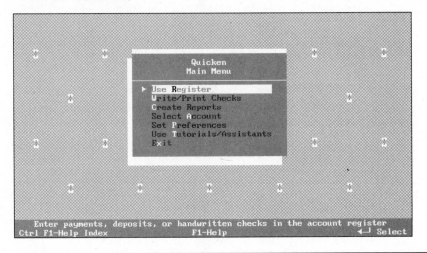

From the Main Menu, you can choose to perform one of six functions or to exit the program. The options are

Note. Pressing the Escape key repeatedly at any place in the program will eventually return you to the Main Menu.

- *Use Register*   Like your check register, this is where you record deposits, transfers, interest and fees, and checks that were not written or electronically paid through Quicken. The Register is a journal listing all the transactions in each account–even those that don't involve checks per se. When you use Quicken, you'll probably spend most of your time working with the Register.

- *Write/Print Checks*   This is the electronic analog of your checkbook, where you'll write checks that Quicken will print or pay electronically.

- *Create Reports*   Unlike any paper analog, this option enables you to obtain a remarkable variety of standardized or custom digests of your spending and income patterns.

■ *Select Account*   In later levels, when you're handling multiple bank, port-folio, and asset accounts, this function will let you choose a specific account to work with. When you're through, it automatically invokes the Register.

■ *Set Preferences*   This function allows you to change from one file to another and also to set up new files. In addition, it lets you manipulate general settings such as screen colors and a password for your files.

■ *Use Tutorials/Assistants*   This option, new to Quicken 5, offers a series of scripted guide paths through certain procedures such as creating new files and accounts or setting Quicken up for payroll.

■ *Exit*   This choice terminates the program, saving your files and offering you the opportunity to make a backup copy of your data.

Choose the Write/Print Checks option from the Main Menu by pressing W. After a moment, Quicken displays a screen laid out like a blank check.

Note. There are two ways to make menu selections from the keyboard in Quicken. Use the arrow keys to move the cursor to the selection you want and press Enter, or press the highlighted letter corresponding to the selection desired.

Record Your First Checks

The Write Checks screen (Figure 1.8) contains all the essentials for issuing printed checks. Your account name is also displayed at the lower-left corner of the screen, and your starting bank balance appears at the lower-right corner. If you write checks against several accounts, the Write Checks screen always displays the account you used most recently.

Figure 1.8   **Write Checks screen**

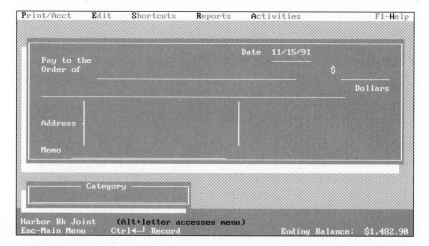

Before you begin entering checks, pick up your bank statement and mark the first ten checks listed on it. If your bank statement doesn't list the payees for each check and the date the check was written, pull out the ten corresponding canceled checks.

Enter Data on the Write Checks Screen

Now, fill out the Write Checks screen just as you would a paper check, pressing Enter to move to the next field. Here are the steps:

1. Type the date the check was written (simply overwrite today's date, which will already be displayed).

2. Specify to whom the money was paid (you have up to 40 characters).

3. Fill in the amount of the check. Quicken instantly protects the check by spelling out the dollar amount on the next line as soon as you press Enter.

4. Skip the address field for now by simply pressing Enter.

5. Write a one-line memo to yourself, describing the transaction (such as "Flowers for Maria's birthday").

6. Press Enter again to return to the Category box.

Categorize the Transaction

Up till now, you have merely duplicated what you previously did by hand. If all Quicken could do was faithfully record manual input to your checkbook, it wouldn't be very useful. However, as you know, Quicken provides categories that let you group similar transactions together, and that give you the basis for tracking the nature of your spending over time.

Press Ctrl-C to bring up the Category and Transfer list (Figure 1.9). This screen displays the standard categories—home, business, or both—that you asked Quicken to install when you set up your file.

Take a moment to peruse the entire list. Because the check you wrote represents a withdrawal from a bank account, Quicken assumes you want to assign the check to one of the expense categories in the list and highlights the first choice. Explore the other categories, using the Up and Down Arrow keys and the Home and End keys to move through them.

The list begins with income categories such as salary, bonus, and dividend income. Further down the list you'll see expense categories, such as clothing, groceries, insurance, and five types of taxes. You'll almost certainly want to modify and augment this list later, but for now try working with it as is.

Note. If you make a mistake, don't forget that Shift-Tab will bring you back to the previous blank. Then just type over the old information, or press Ctrl-Backspace to clear the blank and start over.

Note. Ctrl-C is an example of a shortcut or *quick key*, which quickly moves you from place to place in the program. As you progress through this book, you'll learn other ways of invoking Quicken's features.

Figure 1.9   Category and Transfer list

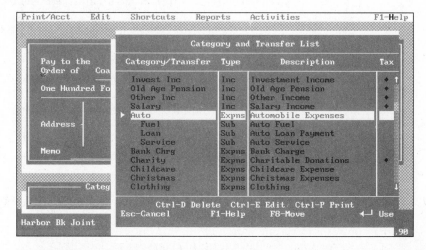

Use the Up and Down Arrow keys to find the category that most closely describes the first check you entered. When this category is highlighted, press Enter. Quicken returns you to the check screen which is now completed (Figure 1.10).

Figure 1.10   Completed Write Checks screen

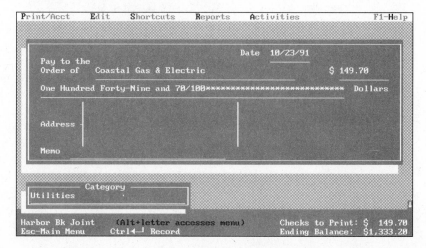

The amount of the check has not been deducted from the account balance at the lower-right corner of the screen, because you haven't recorded the check yet. When you record the check, you must tell Quicken that this transaction is accurate and complete and that the amount should now be deducted from your running balance. Quicken merges each new transaction with all your previous transactions, arranging them first by date and then by transaction number, if any.

To record the check, you can use one of three methods:

- Press Ctrl-Enter.

- Press the F10 function key.

- Press Enter and be prepared to press Enter a second time to confirm your entry.

Note that the disk drive activates when you record your check. Quicken saves your work as you go, so you won't lose much work if your computer's power is interrupted or your laptop's batteries expire.

As it records the check, Quicken scrolls it off the top of the screen and presents a new blank check in its place. In the lower-right corner, Quicken also shows an updated balance and the amount of money represented by checks waiting to be printed. For now, bring the check you just wrote back onto the screen by pressing PgUp.

Now press Ctrl-R (another quick key) to show an entirely different view of your check on the Register screen. Again, this is very similar to the register you might use in a paper-based checkbook.

Examine the Bank Account Register

The Register screen (Figure 1.11) is the primary work area of the Quicken environment. All the data you entered on the Write Checks screen appears here in much more compact form. So does the opening fixed-balance transaction that was created when you set up your bank account. Quicken keeps a running account balance down the rightmost column. Note also the column headed "C", which you'll use later to mark checks that have cleared the bank.

Whenever you work in the Quicken Register, one transaction is current, and Quicken highlights that entire transaction. When you press the Down or Up Arrow key, the highlight moves to the next or previous transaction and makes it current. Within a transaction, you can press Enter or Tab to move to the next field and press Shift-Tab to move to the previous one—just as you navigated through the Write Checks screen.

Note. Throughout this book, we'll use the Ctrl-Enter notation to record a transaction or close a window.

Note. Quicken strings together the checks you write end to end, as if they were on a continuous roll. You can press PgUp to scroll backward on this "roll," or press PgDn to see the next check.

Figure 1.11   **Register screen**

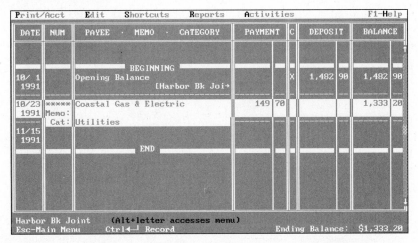

Switch Between the Write Checks and Register Screens

The Write Checks screen offers the advantage of familiarity and simplicity; it looks just like a paper check. It also provides space for the payee's address, however, which will be useful when you print checks for mailing.

The Register screen offers the advantage of more information; it displays at least six transactions at a time, as well as showing interest and deposits. The more experienced you become with Quicken, the more likely you are to spend most of your time working in the Register and skipping the Write Checks screen altogether. Try switching back and forth between the Write Checks screen and the Register by alternately pressing the quick keys Ctrl-W and Ctrl-R.

A second way to move between these screens is to press Escape until you reach the Main Menu. You can select either Write/Print Checks or Use Register from the Main Menu.

Quicken's pull-down menus offer a third way to navigate. The bar across the top of the screen describes the choices you can invoke by pressing the Alt key and the first letter of the command. From the Register, press Alt-A to access the Activities menu, which will drop down from the menu bar (Figure 1.12).

Among the other choices on the Activities menu, you'll find the option of moving to the Write Checks screen. Either type **W** or highlight your choice and press Enter, and you're in business.

Back at the Register, notice that a row of asterisks appears in the NUM column next to the transaction you just entered. This column usually contains check numbers; the asterisks show that you haven't entered a check number

Note. Quicken offers two alternative ways to access its menu bar—the Alt key method and the Function key method. This book uses the Alt key method throughout.

yet. Quicken lets you write checks during any number of work sessions and delay printing them until they are actually due. You date each check according to its due date; its check number is determined later when you actually print it onto valid prenumbered bank checks.

Figure 1.12   **Activities menu**

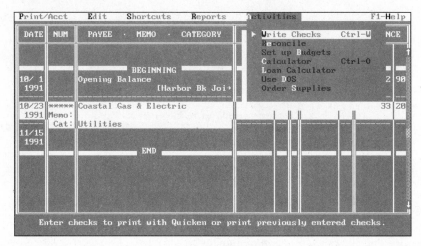

In this case, the check that you entered already has a number. You can enter it in the Register screen, as follows:

1. Use the Up or Down Arrow key to highlight your first check transaction. Press Enter or Tab to move to the NUM field (or press Shift-Tab if you must move backward).

2. Type the proper check number.

3. Press Ctrl-Enter to record the changes.

Note. In the Register, pressing Ctrl-Home moves you to the first transaction, and pressing Ctrl-End moves you to the last one.

Enter Your Remaining Checks Through the Register

Press the Down Arrow key to reach the blank entry at the end of the Register. You will now enter each of the remaining nine checks via the Register view. When you're finished, your screen will list several numbered transactions and give you a running balance, as shown in Figure 1.13. To enter a check via the Register, follow the steps below, pressing Enter or Tab to complete each.

Figure 1.13 **Checks listed in the Register**

```
 Print/Acct    Edit    Shortcuts    Reports    Activities           F1-Help
┌──────┬─────┬──────────────────────────────────┬─────────┬─┬─────────┬─────────┐
│ DATE │ NUM │  PAYEE  ·  MEMO  ·  CATEGORY      │ PAYMENT │C│ DEPOSIT │ BALANCE │
├──────┼─────┼──────────────────────────────────┼─────────┼─┼─────────┼─────────┤
│10/28 │1307 │Wanda Milasz                      │ 100 00  │ │         │1,109 15↑│
│1991  │     │              Childcare           │         │ │         │         │
│10/28 │1308 │Bright Eyes Day Care Center       │ 111 00  │ │         │  998 15 │
│1991  │     │              Childcare           │         │ │         │         │
│10/28 │1309 │Newstime Magazine                 │  19 95  │ │         │  978 20 │
│1991  │     │              Subscriptions       │         │ │         │         │
│10/30 │1310 │Community Health Plus             │  14 00  │ │         │  964 20 │
│1991  │     │              Medical             │         │ │         │         │
│10/30 │1311 │Matt's Wine & Spirits             │  32 15  │ │         │  932 05 │
│1991  │     │              Entertain           │         │ │         │         │
│10/30 │     │                                  │         │ │         │         │
│1991  │Memo:│                                  │         │ │         │         │
│      │Cat: │                                  │         │ │         │         │
└──────┴─────┴──────────────────────────────────┴─────────┴─┴─────────┴─────────┘
 Harbor Bk Joint      (Alt+letter accesses menu)
 Esc-Main Menu     Ctrl◄─┘ Record                    Ending Balance:   $932.05
```

Note. Quicken offers more short-cuts when working in a date field. Type **T** for today's date, **M** for the beginning of the month, **H** for the end of the month, **Y** for the first of the year, and **R** for the last of the year.

Note. As you begin to learn the category names, you can use this shortcut: In the Category blank, simply type the first few letters of the category and press Enter. If Quicken recognizes the category name you've started, it will automatically complete the category name in the blank.

1. The date of the last check is already entered in the Register. If your next check has the same date, simply press Tab or Enter to move to the next blank. If it's one or two days later, use the grey + key to increase the date by one day (the grey − key moves back one day). You can also type over the date that's already there.

2. Enter the check number in the next blank. As with dates, if this check number is one greater than the previous one, press the grey + key once.

3. Type the payee's name in the next field.

4. Enter the check amount in the next column. If it's an even dollar amount, don't worry about typing the decimal portion.

5. Skip the C (cleared) field for now.

6. Type any memo you need to make about the transaction.

7. Press Ctrl-C to bring up the categories list and choose a category. To move through the alphabetized list quickly, type the first character of the category you want; Quicken will move to the first category that begins with the letter you typed.

8. Press Ctrl-Enter to record your check.

Quicken sorts the Register first by date and then, for checks written on the same day, by check number.

Obtain Help

You may not always have your user manual or this guide on hand when you have a question about Quicken. Fortunately, Quicken has a well-organized, extensive help system designed to answer many of your questions. You can access the system from anywhere in Quicken.

To call for help, simply press the F1 function key. Quicken's help system is "context-sensitive," which means it tries to determine what kind of help you need by observing where you are in the program. For example, Figure 1.14 shows what you see when you call for help from the Register.

Figure 1.14   **Help screen for the Register**

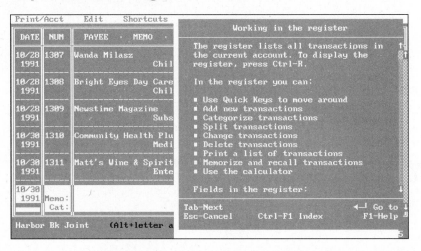

If Quicken guesses wrong about the kind of help you need, press Ctrl-F1 to call up the Help Index (Figure 1.15). If you want to access the Help Index directly, without a context-sensitive help guess, press Ctrl-F1 rather than F1 to call for help.

In the Help Index, use the Up and Down Arrow keys, along with the PgUp and PgDn keys, to move the highlight pointer to the topic you want. Then press Enter to see the help for that topic. Some topics fill more than one screen, so you may need to use the PgDn key to see a whole topic.

In addition, many help screens identify related help topics, and these are highlighted for easy recognition. You can always use the arrow keys to find the related topic of your choice, and then press Enter to jump to that topic.

To exit help, just press the Escape key.

Note. If you want a hard copy of any help screens, make sure your printer is connected and on-line, and then press Shift-PrtSc.

Figure 1.15   Quicken Help Index

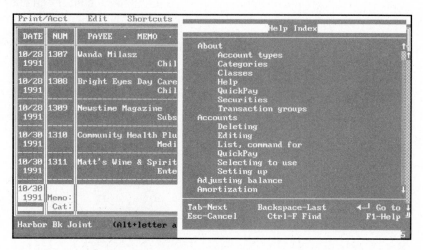

You're already working in the Register, so try this example to obtain some basic information about how to move within the current transaction:

1. Press the F1 function key. Because you're in the Register, Quicken displays the Working in the Register help screen.

2. Press F1 again to see the Table of Contents, which lists general topics covered in Help.

3. To get a few reminders on using the Write Checks screen, type **W**. The highlight moves to Writing and printing checks, the first—indeed, the only—topic that begins with the letter *W*.

4. To see the screen on that topic, press Enter.

5. When you're through using Help, press Escape to return to the Register.

Correct Your Mistakes

If you discover an error in the amount of a check you've recorded, it's easy to correct. Simply use the arrow keys to move to the field that contains the error; then do any of the following:

- Press Ctrl-Backspace to erase the field before typing new information. (This method works best when you're correcting anything beyond a mere typographical error.)

- Start typing at the beginning of the field you need to correct. Unless you start typing over or immediately next to the preexisting number, Quicken will blank out everything to the left of the decimal point and will accept the new number. Don't forget the digits to the right of the decimal point; if you don't change them by typing a decimal followed by two digits, the cents will be retained from the incorrect entry.

- If you need to change only a single character or two, use the arrow keys to move to the digit you wish to change, and then type over the old digit.

To change a typographical error in any of the text fields, just press Tab until you reach the field, use the arrow keys to find the error, and then type over it. To insert text at the cursor, press the Insert key before you begin typing. To erase a text line and start over, press Ctrl-Backspace to clear the blank.

For example, suppose you typed "Millton Grower's Mart" as the payee and then realized it should be "Milltown Farmer's Market." With your cursor in the DATE field, follow these steps to edit the PAYEE field:

1. Press Tab twice to move to the PAYEE field.

2. Use the Right Arrow key to move to the *n* in *Millton*. To insert the *w*, first press the Insert key. Note that the cursor enlarges to indicate it's in insert mode. Type **w**, and then press the Insert key again to turn off insert mode.

3. Use the Right Arrow key to move to the word *Grower's*. To replace the word, simply type **Farmer's**. The new characters will replace the old ones, because insert mode is turned off.

4. Use the Right Arrow key to move to the *t* in *Mart*. To delete the last character, press the Delete key once. Then type the letters **ket** to complete the entry.

5. To record the edited transaction, press Ctrl-Enter.

To change the category designation, highlight the transaction and press the quick key Ctrl-C. When the category screen pops up, simply choose a new category.

Remember, after you've finished making corrections, you must press Ctrl-Enter to record the revised transaction.

If you need to delete an entire transaction from the Register, position the cursor anywhere in the transaction and press Ctrl-D. Alternatively, you may use the Edit menu (press Alt-E) and choose Delete Transaction. Since all the records for this transaction will be erased, Quicken always asks you to verify that you really want to proceed.

Try the Calculator

In case you need to perform quick calculations before entering a number, Quicken provides a simple built-in calculator, reminiscent of a four-function paper-tape adding machine. Press Ctrl-O at any time in Quicken to call up the Calculator (Figure 1.16). If you prefer to use the pull-down menus to activate the Calculator, you'll find it on the Activities menu (Alt-A).

Figure 1.16   Pop-up Calculator

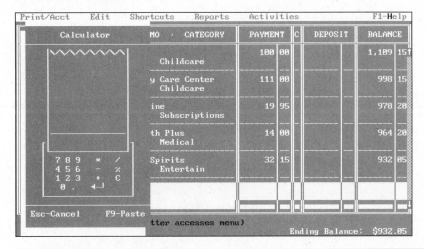

If the cursor is in a number field when you call up the Calculator, that number is automatically entered into the Calculator. Otherwise, the Calculator starts with a fresh balance of zero. Quicken automatically engages the Num Lock function of your keyboard when the Calculator comes up.

Before you begin using the Calculator, always type **C** to clear it. You can enter numbers using the numeric keypad or the number keys across the top of your keyboard. To enter arithmetic operators, use the +, –, *, and / keys. Press Enter to obtain the result. If you're entering a chain of transactions, Quicken will display subtotals along the way as you enter each operator.

For example, suppose you're about to write a check to the local university to pay tuition for a 3.5-credit course on film production. The cost per credit hour is $185. You can use the Calculator to determine the total payment by following these steps:

1. Type **C** to clear the Calculator.

Note. You may add a percentage to any amount by typing +, the percentage number, and the % key. Then press Enter. Subtract a percentage by typing – and following the same procedure.

2. Enter the number **3.5**, using the numeric keypad or the numbers across the top of your keyboard.

3. Type * as the arithmetic operator for multiplication.

4. Type the number **185**, and press Enter to obtain the result.

5. Press F9 if you want Quicken to paste automatically the calculated results into the Register field in which you're working. If you don't want the result to be pasted, press Escape to return to the Register.

Record a Deposit

Locate a deposit on your bank statement—preferably, a deposit such as a paycheck that represents income from a single source. Enter the deposit just as you would a check, in the blank entry at the bottom of the register (Figure 1.17).

Figure 1.17   Entering a deposit in the Register

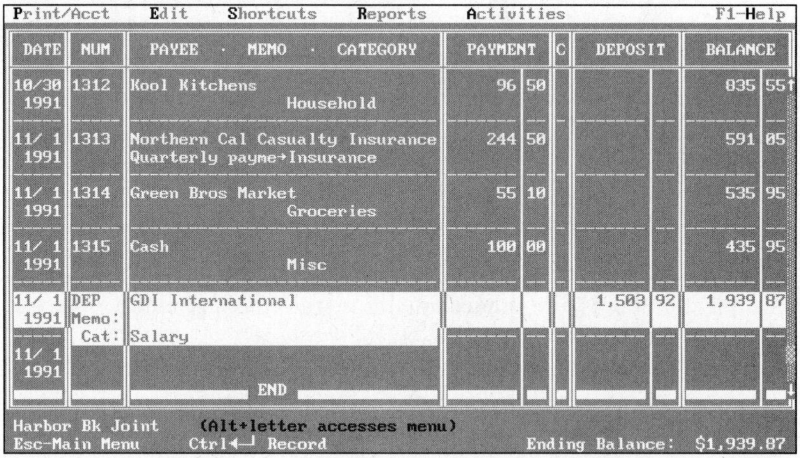

```
Print/Acct    Edit    Shortcuts    Reports    Activities              F1-Help

DATE  NUM   PAYEE  ·  MEMO  ·  CATEGORY    PAYMENT  C   DEPOSIT     BALANCE

10/30 1312 Kool Kitchens                    96 50                    835 55↑
1991                       Household

11/ 1 1313 Northern Cal Casualty Insurance 244 50                    591 05
1991       Quarterly payme→Insurance

11/ 1 1314 Green Bros Market                55 10                    535 95
1991                       Groceries

11/ 1 1315 Cash                            100 00                    435 95
1991                       Misc

11/ 1 DEP  GDI International                           1,503 92     1,939 87
1991  Memo:
      Cat: Salary

11/ 1
1991
                        END

Harbor Bk Joint      (Alt+letter accesses menu)
Esc-Main Menu    Ctrl◄┘ Record              Ending Balance:  $1,939.87
```

1. Since there's no check number to enter, type **DEP** in the number field.

2. For the payee, type the source of the deposit—for a paycheck, this might be the name of your company.

3. To record the dollar amount of the deposit, skip the PAYMENT field and record it in the DEPOSIT field. This will cause the running account balance to increase rather than decrease when the deposit is recorded.

4. Press Ctrl-C to bring up the category list, and choose the income category that is most appropriate to the deposit. Because the transaction is in the DEPOSIT field, Quicken highlights the first income category. If you chose to enter a paycheck, use the Salary category for now. We'll work on splitting your paycheck into its various tax and payroll deduction components in Level 2.

5. Press Ctrl-Enter to record the deposit, and the running balance increases.

Create Your First Report

Most of what you've seen in Quicken so far looks very much like the checkbook you carry around in your pocket or purse. Categories were the first major departure from what you're accustomed to. As you'll see in this section, it's in reports that categories become really useful.

Quicken offers a wide variety of standard reports, such as Profit and Loss, Cash Flow, and Net Worth. You'll find examples of these reports in Appendix D. In addition, Quicken provides a set of custom report design tools that enables you to create almost any kind of report you could ever want.

Follow this simple procedure to create your first Quicken report:

1. Choose the Reports menu from the menu bar (or press Alt-R), and then choose Personal Reports from the pull-down menu.

2. From the list of personal reports, choose the Cash Flow report. A report settings window will pop onto the center of your screen, as in Figure 1.18.

Figure 1.18   Cash Flow Report settings window

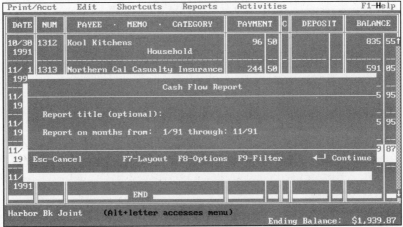

3. Enter a name for your report if you wish (you can use up to 39 characters), and press Enter.

4. If the date range displayed in the window spans the eleven transactions you've just entered, leave it alone. Otherwise, adjust the range to include all the transaction dates you've used.

5. Press Enter to start the report-generation process.

Within seconds, Quicken's Cash Flow report (Figure 1.19) will appear on your screen. Inflows (such as your deposit and your opening balance) are listed first by income category, followed by the categorized expenses you entered.

Figure 1.19   **Cash Flow report**

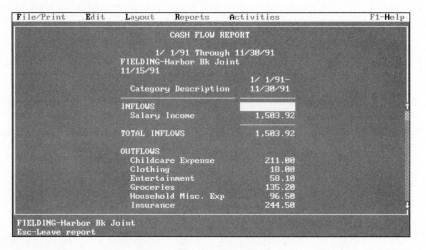

If your printer is installed (see Appendix A) and ready, you can print the report by choosing File/Print from the menu bar (or pressing Alt-F) and selecting Print Report. Ignore the Print Report settings windows for now, and press Enter. Your report should begin printing within seconds. (If nothing happens, review the installation process.) The printed report should resemble the Cash Flow report shown in Figure 1.20.

You may also obtain a printed copy of your check register. From the Register screen, choose Print/Acct (Alt-P) from the menu bar, and then Print Register from the pull-down menu. (Ctrl-P is a quick key for this two-step process.)

Figure 1.20 **Printed Cash Flow report**

```
                              CASH FLOW REPORT
                         1/ 1/91 Through 11/30/91
FIELDING-Harbor Bk Joint                                              Page
11/15/91
                                              1/ 1/91-
                           Category Description  11/30/91

                      INFLOWS
                        Salary Income          1,503.92

                      TOTAL INFLOWS            1,503.92

                      OUTFLOWS
                        Childcare Expense        211.00
                        Clothing                  18.00
                        Entertainment             58.10
                        Groceries                135.20
                        Household Misc. Exp       96.50
                        Insurance                244.50
                        Medical & Dental          14.00
                        Miscellaneous            100.00
                        Subscriptions             19.95
                        Water, Gas, Electric     149.70

                      TOTAL OUTFLOWS           1,046.95

                      OVERALL TOTAL              456.97
```

The Print Register window (Figure 1.21) offers suggestions about the time frame, printer destination, and sorting of the Register. Change what you need to, moving from blank to blank by pressing Enter or Tab. Check to be sure the paper is lined up in your printer, and then press Ctrl-Enter to start printing the Register. You'll soon see a listing that resembles Figure 1.22.

Figure 1.21 **Print Register window**

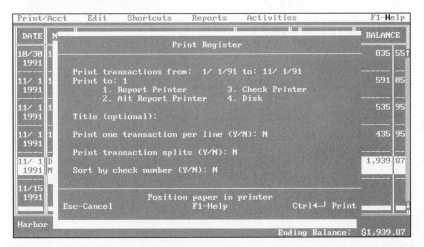

Figure 1.22   Register Transactions report

```
                           Check Register
Harbor Bk Joint                                              Page 1
11/15/91

  Date  Num            Transaction            Payment  C  Deposit    Balance
 -----  ----- ----------------------------------- ----------  -  ----------  ----------

 10/ 1         Opening Balance                             X   1,482.90   1,482.90
 1991 memo:
       cat: [Harbor Bk Joint]

 10/23 1302   Coastal Gas & Electric          149.70                   1,333.20
 1991 memo:
       cat: Utilities

 10/24 1303   Green Bros Market                61.20                    1,272.00
 1991 memo:
       cat: Groceries

 10/26 1304   Pioneer Cleaners                 18.00                    1,254.00
 1991 memo:
       cat: Clothing

 10/26 1305   Green Bros Market                18.90                    1,235.10
 1991 memo:
       cat: Groceries

 10/26 1306   Top Hat Video                    25.95                    1,209.15
 1991 memo:
       cat: Entertain

 10/28 1307   Wanda Milasz                    100.00                    1,109.15
 1991 memo:
       cat: Childcare

 10/28 1308   Bright Eyes Day Care Center     111.00                     998.15
 1991 memo:
       cat: Childcare

 10/28 1309   Newstime Magazine                19.95                     978.20
 1991 memo:
       cat: Subscriptions

 10/30 1310   Community Health Plus            14.00                     964.20
 1991 memo:
       cat: Medical

 10/30 1311   Matt's Wine & Spirits            32.15                     932.05
 1991 memo:
       cat: Entertain

 10/30 1312   Kool Kitchens                    96.50                     835.55
 1991 memo:
       cat: Household
```

```
                           Check Register
Harbor Bk Joint                                              Page 2
11/15/91

  Date  Num            Transaction            Payment  C  Deposit    Balance
 -----  ----- ----------------------------------- ----------  -  ----------  ----------

 11/ 1 1313   Northern Cal Casualty Insurance  244.50                     591.05
 1991 memo: Quarterly payment
       cat: Insurance

 11/ 1 1314   Green Bros Market                55.10                      535.95
 1991 memo:
       cat: Groceries

 11/ 1 1315   Cash                            100.00                      435.95
 1991 memo:
       cat: Misc

 11/ 1 DEP    GDI International                              1,503.92   1,939.87
 1991 memo:
       cat: Salary
```

Back Up Intelligently

Quicken saves data every time you record a transaction. This protects your records from power failure or most other problems during your Quicken session. But this safety net is no substitute for a proper backup regimen.

The sad fact is that hard-disk drives crash, and floppy disks get dropped on the floor or snatched by well-meaning two year olds. If there were a fire in your house, your valuable purchase records could be destroyed at the very time you needed them most. Backing up your work will save you time and avoid losses that could be absolutely devastating.

Unlike earlier versions, Quicken 5 provides an automatic backup procedure. It also offers a way of disabling that feature. Unless you enjoy life on the high wire, be sure to leave one of the automatic backup options in place.

Establish a Backup Routine

Here is an effective backup routine that protects you not only against disk crashes but also against more dramatic disasters (the diagram in Figure 1.23 summarizes the routine):

1. If you followed the installation procedure recommended in Appendix A, you've set the automatic backup option to Daily. This ensures that you'll be offered the opportunity to back up at the end of each session. If you didn't do this, select Set Preferences from the Main Menu, choose File Activities and then Set Backup Frequency, and change the Backup Reminder Frequency to Always (type 2).

2. Prepare four backup disks by formatting them and labeling them Session, Odd Months, Even Months, and Annual (199X). After you've been using Quicken for some time, your files may be large enough to require a second backup disk for each set.

3. As you exit each session, you'll see the Automatic Backup window (Figure 1.24). Insert the Session disk into your floppy-disk drive, type the drive letter, and press Enter. If your data files are very large, Quicken will request a second disk.

4. At the start of your first session each month, use one of your Month disks to back up your files as of the end of the previous month. You can force a backup without exiting by pressing Alt-P to select Print/Acct from the Main Menu bar. Then choose Back Up File from the pull-down menu. Be sure to store the Month disks in a safe location until you need them. This way, you can always reconstruct your records to the time of the last monthly backup.

Figure 1.23   Backup routine

	How:	Keep disks:
To end each session: Session	At the Automatic Backup window, insert disk and type drive letter.	On hand for each session
To begin each month: 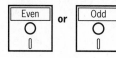Even or Odd	In the Register or Write Checks screen, select Print/Acct (Alt-P), and choose Back Up All Accounts. Insert the appropriate disk.	In a safe place
To end each year: 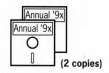Annual '9x Annual '9x **(2 copies)**	In the Register or Write Checks screen, select Print/Acct (Alt-P), and choose Back Up All Accounts. Make a copy of the disk.	One on hand, one in a safe place

Figure 1.24   Automatic Backup window

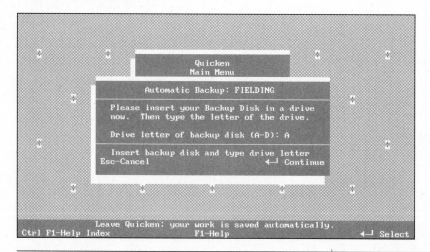

5. Before you take any action to compress or rearrange files at the end of the year, back up your files onto the appropriate Year disk. You may want to make two copies of your Year disk: one to store in a safe place

and one to have on hand for detailed information on previous years' activities, which may not be available in the main data file.

If Murphy Strikes . . .

If you're faithful about using the daily backup routine, your Session disk should contain the most recent data files. To accommodate large files that could spill over onto a second disk, Quicken actually combines several data files into a single file with the extension .BAK. Consequently, backup files cannot be simply copied onto the Quicken directory or used directly off the backup disk; they must first be restored with Quicken.

To restore a file,

1. Insert the backup disk into your disk drive.

2. Select Set Preferences from the Main Menu.

3. Select File Activities and Restore File from the subsequent menus to view the Select drive to restore from window (Figure 1.25).

Figure 1.25 **Restore Data File window**

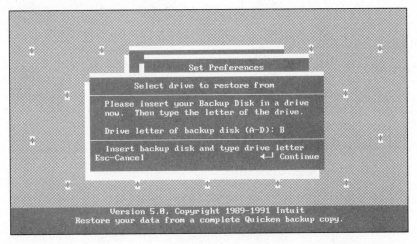

4. Type the letter of the disk drive from which you'll be restoring the data file, and press Enter.

If your Session disk is lost or corrupted, you'll have to resort to one of the monthly backups. You will, of course, have to reenter any work you completed between the date of the backup and the time of the failure.

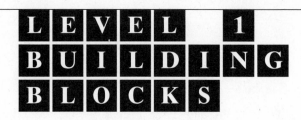

LEVEL 1 BUILDING BLOCKS

Level 1 introduced Quicken's essential concepts and procedures, which allow you to take the first steps toward personal financial management.

TECHNIQUES AND PROCEDURES

■ The Register lists all transactions in order by date and then by transaction number. Add and edit transactions in the Register—indeed, most of your time is spent there. To display the Register, select Use Register from the Main Menu, or press Ctrl-R. Print the Register either by pressing Ctrl-P, or by displaying the Print/Acct menu (Alt-P) and selecting Print Register.

■ The Write Checks screen is like a blank check. Fill it out when you want to write and print checks with Quicken (or pay them electronically, as you'll see later). Any checks that you write will automatically appear in the Register, although they will remain unnumbered until you number them upon printing.

■ You categorize your transactions by entering a category into the appropriate blank in the Register or the Write Checks screen. If you type the first few characters of an existing category and press Enter, Quicken will complete the category for you. Alternatively, press Ctrl-C to display the category list, and then pick a category from it.

■ Reports provide on-screen and printed summaries of the activity in your accounts. The Cash Flow report, for instance, presents a straightforward view of inflows and outflows for any time period. In Levels 5 and 6 you'll see how to get more out of standard reports and how customized reports can reveal hidden details. To call up the Reports menu, press Alt-R.

■ The pop-up Calculator is a tool for handling miscellaneous calculations. It appears when you press Ctrl-O. If the cursor is on a number when you press Ctrl-O, that number will appear in the Calculator. You can paste calculated results into the Register or the Write Checks screen.

■ Need help? Access Quicken's context-sensitive help system by pressing F1. Press F1 again to see the Table of Contents. If you want to bypass the context-sensitive help and go directly to the Help Index, press Ctrl-F1.

TERMS

■ Quicken organizes your transactions—debits and deposits—into *accounts*, which resemble your traditional checking, savings, and charge accounts. Quicken's accounts can also track assets that don't currently reside in accounts per se, such as cash, loan payments, and the value of your home.

■ All related accounts are grouped into a *file*. Most people need only one file. However, if you have clusters of accounts that you must track separately—if, for example, you are self-employed or handle multiple clients or contracts—you will need more than one file.

■ Each change to an account is a *transaction*. Some changes—your paycheck, for example—have an external source. Other transactions might be internal transfers, which cause one account balance to increase while another decreases.

■ *Categories* describe transactions that you can track and analyze your financial patterns. With categories you can track your contributions to a local charity or monitor the money you've spent on Crosby, your golden retriever. All the accounts in a file share a set of categories. Quicken's standard categories provide a good beginning, but you can easily add a "Crosby" category or any others that you need to personalize the list. (In Level 2, you'll see how subcategories can help you fine-tune your categories while Level 6 shows how classes can give you a broader view of your finances.)

■ *Quick keys* are shortcuts around Quicken. A quick key is always a combination of the Control key and a letter (usually one that is easily associated with the effect of pressing the quick key). For example, Ctrl-R takes you to the Register, and Ctrl-W to the Write Checks screen. See Appendix C for a list of the quick keys.

IMPORTANT IDEAS

■ If you know it to be accurate, you can use the balance in your own checkbook as the starting balance for a new account. Alternatively you can use the closing balance on your last bank statement, but then you'll need to enter any checks that haven't yet been cleared by the bank. If you're unsure what to use for an opening balance, enter 0 (zero) to start with. You can always correct the opening balance later by moving to this transaction in the Register (it is usually the first transaction).

■ What transactions should you categorize? To take full advantage of Quicken's ability to group items by categories, you should assign a category to every transaction. But never fear: anything you do can be changed later. As you become more conscious of your financial habits you will get a feel for how closely to track them, and your categories will evolve to reflect your personal approach to financial management. Items that you now subdivide into categories might later be grouped under miscellaneous. As you proceed through this book, you'll discover how detailed your tracking can be and how helpful Quicken's categories really are.

2

Track Your Spending and Income

PLAN AHEAD

DECISIONS

How Will Quicken Drive Decision Making?

Quicken does a good job of automating the preparation and recording of checks; however, if Quicken only replicated manual processes, it would hardly be worth the effort. It's when you decide to use Quicken to inform your day-to-day and year-to-year financial decisions that the program really pays off.

At this point, anticipating the kinds of decisions you'll be supporting with Quicken will help you determine how you categorize your financial transactions and how much detail you ought to track. In later levels, knowing your personal decision-making requirements will influence the way you use accounts and reports as well.

You'll want to consider two broad classes of decisions: operating decisions and tax decisions. Operating decisions might include setting budget priorities, choosing when to buy and sell stocks, managing cash flow, determining personal loan requirements, planning your retirement, and resolving whether to stick with or dismiss your broker. Tax decisions might include deferring or accelerating taxable income and deductible expenses, choosing to take capital losses or gains at the end of the year, and making your charitable contributions in December or January.

Although your view of these important decisions will evolve over time, keep them in mind as you set up your categories and decide on detail today.

How Should You Categorize Your Income and Spending?

The way you categorize your income and spending should follow directly from the preliminary decisions you make. In devising categories, follow this simple rule of thumb: make categories as detailed as necessary to give a full picture and to support your data and decision-making needs, but avoid dividing your categories so minutely that they only increase work and confusion.

For example, if you're planning your budget priorities for the year, would you budget a single amount for Entertainment, or would you divide this category into Dinner Parties, Movies, Video Rentals, Sporting Events, and Children's Birthday Parties? There's no right or wrong here, just appropriate levels of detail. Too much detail creates unnecessary work, wastes paper, and hinders decision making; too little detail is simply not useful.

If you're using Quicken as a tax preparation and decision-making aid, you should choose a level of detail that matches your tax return needs. A category called Tax-Deductible Expenses is generally insufficient if you itemize your deductions; you'll want to make sure you separate investment interest, tax preparation fees, charitable contributions, and home office expenses into individual categories that map onto lines of your 1040 and supporting tax forms.

Early in this level, you'll learn how to build a personalized category structure, based on both the default structure you created when you installed your first data file and on a broader list of categories drawn from your personal experience.

Should You Require Transactions to Be Categorized?

Quicken allows you to leave transactions uncategorized if you want to. Alternatively, you may set up the program to require that you enter a category for each income or expense transaction. Uncategorized transactions end up being reported as "Other" in your reports.

While there will always be transactions that might be considered Miscellaneous or "Other" transactions, it's a good practice to explicitly assign a transaction to a Miscellaneous category when it belongs there. When entering information, it's easy to inadvertently skip the category field. To avoid that, set up Quicken to require categorization, so the program will remind you to categorize each transaction if you neglect to do so.

To turn on the force-categorization setting, select Set Preferences from the Main Menu, choose Transaction Settings from the submenu, and type **Y** after "Require a category on transactions."

Should You Use Subcategories?

One way to provide detail to a category without losing its aggregating power is to use subcategories. For example, an umbrella category—henceforth known as a *parent* category—called Utilities might be broken into subcategories called Water, Electric, Gas, and Sewer. You might want to budget your spending on the entire Utilities category (as in, "We plan to spend $2,300 on utilities this year—five percent more than last year"). But when it's time to diagnose why you're overbudget, subcategories can prove very handy (as in, "Why are we overspending our utilities budget? Oh, it's the Gas subcategory. Of course, we've had such a cold winter.").

Occasionally, you may want to use more than one level of subcategory. Quicken 5 allows you to break subcategories into even finer subcategories. When it comes time to build reports, you may choose to print all the subcategory levels or to collapse the detail into a single category line.

Plan to use subcategories liberally where you anticipate the need for finer detail within a category.

MATERIALS

Bank Statement

You'll want to have on hand the bank statement you used in Level 1. This time, we'll be entering the rest of the statement and reconciling an entire month's transactions. If you've already decided to enter several months of history at once into Quicken, you may want to start with the earliest bank statement whose transactions you want to record. It's relatively easy to add historical data later, so for now start with reasonably recent data—no further back than the start of the current year.

Canceled Checks or Check Register

Once again, your canceled checks or check register will be important for identifying payees, check dates, and memo notes.

PRELIMINARIES

Complete Level 1

You should have installed Quicken, created a data file, built your first bank account, and installed a set of default categories before continuing Level 2.

Identify All Your Money Accounts

Tracking income and expenses is relatively easy if you always work from a single checking account. In real life, however, a family typically uses several checking, savings, and money market accounts. Identify any other bank accounts you have and gather together the statements for these accounts, too. In Level 2, you'll want to tell Quicken about these accounts so it can accommodate the transfer of funds from one account to another.

Start Quicken and Choose Your Main Bank Account

You should have Quicken up and running, and be looking at the Register for your main bank account. If your main bank account isn't identified in the lower-left corner of the Register screen, press the quick key Ctrl-A (for Select/Setup Account, which is also a command on the Print/Acct menu) and choose your main bank account from the list.

Establish Your Own Category Structure

Until now, you've worked within the default category structure provided by Quicken. Since everybody's needs are different, it's important to begin customizing your category structure. The more closely Quicken's category structure is tailored to your needs, the better it can support your financial decision making.

Design a Category List

On the next few pages, you'll find a tool called the Quicken Category Builder that will help you establish your personal list of categories. The Category Builder lists a large number of personal and business categories you may want to apply to your own category structure and also provides space for you to add categories that are unique to your situation. Follow these steps to take full advantage of this tool:

1. Take note of the default categories, which are identified by an entry in the "Default Set" column. Cross out all the categories that are irrelevant to your situation. Be aggressive in pruning categories: if it doesn't support your decision making or data requirements, cross it out. Unnecessary categories clutter your lists and waste memory.

2. Look at the additional categories that are not included in the default list. Again, eliminate anything that isn't relevant to your financial situation.

3. Edit the remaining category names to make them meaningful to you. For example, you might think of tuition and learning costs as Tuition instead of Education. You can change the default categories freely to make the category names memorable and natural to you.

4. Write in any categories specific to your situation that are not covered by the default category list or the expanded list in the Category Builder. We've left plenty of blank spaces for your own ideas.

5. Look at each category and consider whether it warrants further subcategorization. For example, should your Tuition category be further broken down into Suzanne and Maria? When you think subcategories would enhance the level of detail without creating unnecessary work, write the subcategory names in the Potential Subcategories column of the Category Builder. (You'll find some suggested subcategories already in this column.)

6. Look for opportunities to group separate categories together under a parent category. For example, you might include Medical and Dental, Fitness Club (fees and equipment), and Vitamins under a parent category named Health.

7. Review your category names to be sure they are easy to access. Because you can identify a category by typing the first few characters and letting Quicken complete the category automatically, make sure your categories begin with distinctive two- or three-letter combinations. Keep in mind that Quicken's reports sort alphabetically. If you want your categories to be arranged differently, you can place numbers in front of the category names to establish your own order of preference.

8. Consider installing a "placeholder" category to handle transactions that will be categorized later. Particularly with a joint checking account, you won't always know exactly what your partner bought and how to classify it. You might create a category named "?" and described as "Unclassified" for anything that you can't classify, and then plan to sit down together every so often to sift through all the "?" transactions—some very interesting discussions may result!

Again, it's always possible to rename a category later—from Housewares to Household, for example. It's also easy to add new categories; however, subdividing categories later may require some tedious recoding of past transactions if you want an accurate history. For example, deciding after the fact to split the Auto Fuel category into two subcategories for Volvo and Toyota would require some time-consuming rechecking of receipts and checks. That's why it's wise to spend a little bit of time now to come up with a category structure you can work with.

TOOLKIT   A Quicken Category Builder

INCOME CATEGORIES

Category	Description	Default Set	Potential Subcategories
Bonus	Bonus Income	Home	
Canada Pension	Canadian Pension	Home	
Capital Gain	Capital Gains		LT Distribution, ST Distribution, Realized
Car Allow	Car Allowance		
Commission Inc	Commissions Earned		
Consult Inc	Consulting Fees		
Div Income	Dividend Income	Home	Money Market, Stocks
Gift Received	Gift Received	Home	
Gross Sales	Gross Sales	Business	
Int Inc	Interest Income	Home	Loan, Bank Account, Investments
Invest Inc	Investment Income	Home	Interest, Dividends
Old Age Pension	Old Age Pension	Home	
Other Inc	Other Income	Business	
Other Inc	Other Income	Home	
Rent Income	Rental Income	Business	
Royalty Inc	Royalty Income		
Salary	Salary Income	Home	
Trust Inc	Trust Income		
UnrCapGain	Unrealized Capital Gain		

EXPENSE CATEGORIES

Category	Description	Default Set	Potential Subcategories
Ads	Advertising	Business	
Auto	Automobile Expenses	Home	Fuel, Loan, Service
Bad Debts	Bad Debt Expenses		
Bank Chrg	Bank Charge	Home	Account Fees, Credit Card Fees, Penalties
Benefits	Employee Benefits		
Books	Books		
Business Exp	Reimbursable Bus Exp		
Cable TV	Cable TV Subscriptions		
Car	Car & Truck	Business	
Charity	Charitable Donations	Home	
Childcare	Childcare Expense	Home	Babysitters, Day Care, Nanny
Christmas	Christmas Expenses	Home	
Cleaning	Cleaning/Laundry		
Clothing	Clothing	Home	
Commission	Commissions	Business	
Computer	Computer Expenses		
Cost of Goods	Cost of Goods Sold		
Depreciation	Depreciation Expense		
Dining	Dining Out	Home	
Dues	Dues	Home	Clubs, Professional
Education	Education	Home	Books, Adult Education, Tuition
Entertain	Entertainment	Home	
Freight	Freight	Business	
Furnishings	Home Furnishings		
Gifts	Gift Expenses	Home	
Groceries	Groceries	Home	
Heating Oil	Heating Oil		
Home Rpair	Home Repair & Maint.	Home	Cleaning, Landscape, Repair
Household	Household Misc. Exp	Home	
Housing	Housing	Home	Rent
Insurance	Insurance	Home	Homeowners, Life, Medical
Int Exp	Interest Expense	Home	Investment, Personal

EXPENSE CATEGORIES

Category	Description	Default Set	Potential Subcategories
Int Paid	Interest Paid	Business	
Invest Exp	Investment Expense	Home	
Late Fees	Late Payment Fees	Business	
L&P Fees	Legal & Prof. Fees	Business	
Medical	Medical and Dental	Home	Insured, Not Covered
Misc	Miscellaneous	Home	
Mort Int	Mortgage Interest Exp	Home	
Mort Prin	Mortgage Principal	Home	
Moving	Moving Expenses		
Office	Office Expenses	Business	
Other Exp	Other Expenses	Home	
Payroll	Payroll Expense		Gross, Comp FICA, Comp FUTA, Comp MCARE, Comp SUI
Personal	Personal Expenses		
Pets	Pet Food & Maintenance		
Photo	Film and Processing		
Political	Political Contributions		
Postage	Postage		
Professional	Professional Fees		
Recreation	Recreation Expense	Home	
Rent Paid	Rent or Lease	Business	Machin & Equip, Busi Property
Repairs	Repairs	Business	
Returns	Returns & Allowances	Business	
RRSP	Reg Retirement Sav Plan	Home	
Stationery	Stationery & Office Supp		
Subscriptions	Subscriptions	Home	Business, Personal
Supplies	Supplies	Home	
Tax	Taxes	Home	Fed, FICA, Other, Prop, State
Tax	Taxes & Licenses	Business	Fed, State, Prop, Licenses
Telephone	Telephone Expense	Home	Cellular, Regular, Long Distance
Toys	Toys		
Travel	Travel & Entertainment	Business	Travel, Meals, Entertainment

EXPENSE CATEGORIES

Category	Description	Default Set	Potential Subcategories
UIC	Unemploy. Ins Commission	Home	
Utilities	Water, Gas, Electric	Home	Electric, Gas, Water
Vacation	Vacation Travel		
Wages	Wages & Job Credits	Business	

Note. If your computer has a pointing device such as a mouse, you can use it to make menu choices, select transactions, and scroll through lists. Appendix A explains how to use a mouse with Quicken 5.

Make Changes to the Category List

If you used the Category Builder, you'll probably want to enter all your changes now, so that Quicken will be structured the way you want it when you begin entering significant amounts of data. Of course, you can also add categories anytime you're entering transactions. But editing and deleting categories are tasks more easily completed in a single effort, given the restructuring you're probably doing to the category hierarchy.

You add, change, and delete categories through the Category and Transfer List window (Figure 2.1). Access this window at any time by pressing the quick key Ctrl-C, or by choosing Categorize/Transfer from the Shortcuts menu (Alt-S).

Figure 2.1   **Category and Transfer list**

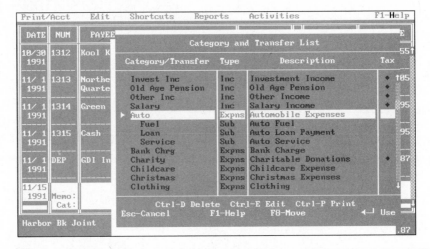

Add Categories

To add a category to the Category and Transfer list,

Note. You can use any combination of letters, numbers, and any characters in category names, except for : / [and]. (These characters are used to designate subcategories, transfers, and classes).

1. Move the cursor to the top of the list by pressing Home (or pressing PgUp as many times as necessary). At the top of the list, select the <New Category> entry by pressing Enter. This will open a Set Up Category window (Figure 2.2).

2. Name the category. Make the name as short (15 or fewer characters), memorable, and distinctive as possible. Consider how easy the category is to enter rather than how it will appear on reports. Normally, it's the longer description (see step 5) that shows up on reports.

3. Identify the category as an income (I) or an expense (E) category. (We'll cover subcategories shortly.)

Figure 2.2   Set Up Category window

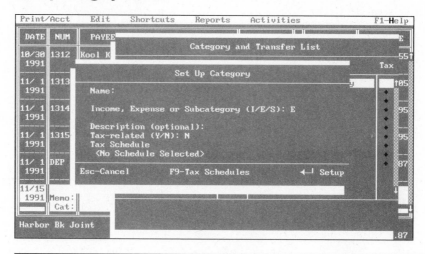

Note. Quicken offers a way to associate a category with line items on federal tax return schedules. Invoke this by Pressing F9 in the Set Up Category window.

4. Describe the category as you want it to appear on your reports, but remember, you only have 25 characters here.

5. Identify whether the category contains tax-related items (such as interest income or charitable contributions). Figure 2.3 shows a complete Set Up Category window.

Figure 2.3   Completed Set Up Category window

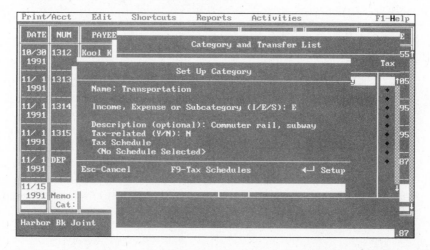

6. Press Enter and the Category and Transfer list reappears. You may have to press PgDn to see the new category in its place.

Add Subcategories

Every subcategory must be associated with a parent category or subcategory. For example, Investment Interest and Bank Interest might fall under the parent category Interest Income. When you create a subcategory, always make sure you've created its parent category first.

To create a subcategory, follow the Add Categories procedure just described, specifying subcategory (S) in step 3. When you complete the Set Up Category window, the Category and Transfer list (Figure 2.4) reappears, showing the new subcategory at the top.

Figure 2.4   New Subcategory in the Category and Transfer list

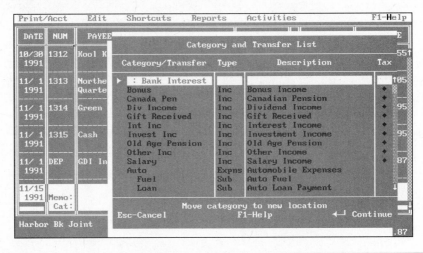

As you press the Up or Down Arrow key to highlight different parent categories, the new subcategory appears next to each possible parent in turn. Use the cursor to select the parent category, and press Enter to finish creating the subcategory. From then on, the new subcategory will appear indented beneath its parent on the Category and Transfer list, as shown in Figure 2.5. The notation "Sub" appears in the Type column in the list. Later, in the Register or Write Checks screen, the syntax *Category:Subcategory* will show the relationship, as in Int Inc:Bank Interest.

Figure 2.5   Subcategory in Category and Transfer list

```
 Print/Acct     Edit     Shortcuts     Reports     Activities           F1-Help
┌────┬─────┬──────────────────────────────────────────────────────────────────E─┐
│DATE│ NUM │PAYEE│                                                            55↑│
│    │     │     │              Category and Transfer List                       │
│10/30│1312│Kool K│                                                               │
│1991│     │     │  Category/Transfer   Type        Description         Tax      │
│11/ 1│1313│Northe│  <New Category>            Set up a new category         105 │
│1991│     │Quarte│  Bonus               Inc   Bonus Income              ♦       │
│    │     │     │  Canada Pen          Inc   Canadian Pension          ♦       │
│11/ 1│1314│Green │  Div Income          Inc   Dividend Income           ♦    95 │
│1991│     │     │  Gift Received       Inc   Gift Received             ♦       │
│    │     │     │  Int Inc             Inc   Interest Income                    │
│11/ 1│1315│Cash  │► Bank Interest      Sub                               95 │
│1991│     │     │  Invest Inc          Inc   Investment Income          ♦       │
│    │     │     │  Old Age Pension     Inc   Old Age Pension            ♦       │
│11/ 1│DEP │GDI In│  Other Inc          Inc   Other Income               ♦    87 │
│1991│     │     │  Salary              Inc   Salary Income              ♦       │
│    │     │     │  Auto                Expns Automobile Expenses                │
│11/15│     │     │    Fuel             Sub   Auto Fuel                       ↓ │
│1991│Memo:│                                                                     │
│    │Cat: │        Ctrl-D Delete   Ctrl-E Edit   Ctrl-P Print                  │
│    │     │     Esc-Cancel      F1-Help       F8-Move           ↵ Use         │
│Harbor Bk Joint│                                                               │
│                                                                          .87  │
└───────────────────────────────────────────────────────────────────────────────┘
```

Delete Categories and Subcategories

You should delete a category or subcategory if you decide that it's redundant or that it generates extraneous detail. For example, you might realize that subdividing the Transportation category into Subway and Commuter Train expenses is splitting hairs.

To delete a category or subcategory,

Note. Quicken sorts categories alphabetically within the classifications income, expense, and accounts. Subcategories are listed under their appropriate category.

1. Find the category or subcategory you wish to delete in the Category and Transfer list by moving the cursor up and down through the list or by typing the first letter of the category repeatedly till you arrive at the right entry.

2. Press Ctrl-D to delete the category.

3. In response to the prompt, confirm the deletion.

Note. Even if you have the force-categorization setting on, Quicken will not notify you of blank category fields resulting from deleting a category unless you edit the transaction.

While you can delete categories with abandon when you first start using Quicken, you'll want to exercise more caution later on, because Quicken blanks out the category line of any transaction that was categorized under a deleted category.

Change Categories or Subcategories

Change a category or subcategory whenever you need to make the category name or description more useful or if the tax status of the category changes. For example, a salesman named Craig Blakely has a dog named Travis. When he started using Quicken, Craig grouped all pet expenses in a Travis category, but as he soon realized, that category conflicted with his Travel category when he tried to use autocompletion. Simply changing the Travis category to Pet Expenses solved this problem and made Quicken work much more efficiently for Craig.

To change any of the information in a category,

1. Highlight the name of the category in the Category and Transfer List window, and press Ctrl-E (for Edit) to open the Edit Category window (Figure 2.6).

Figure 2.6   **Edit Category window**

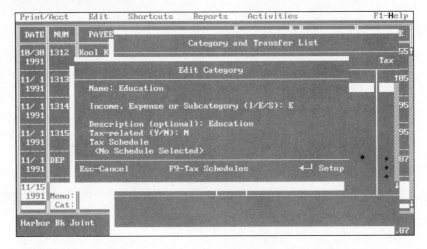

2. Press Tab until you reach the field you want to change.

3. Erase the field with Ctrl-Backspace before typing new information, or move the cursor to the first character you want to overtype.

4. Press Enter to move through the remaining fields and complete the edit.

You won't have to change all your transaction records to accommodate an edited category; Quicken will automatically go through the Register of each account in your file, updating categories for you.

Change the Category Hierarchy

Occasionally, you'll want to change the position of categories and subcategories in the category hierarchy. For example, you might want to convert the Groceries and Dining Out categories into subcategories, grouped together under a new category called Food. To do this,

1. Create the new Food category (see "Add Categories" above).

2. Select the Groceries category from the Category and Transfer List (Ctrl-C) and press Ctrl-E to bring up the Edit Category window.

3. Change its designation to subcategory, and press Ctrl-Enter to leave the window.

4. Highlight the Food category from the list as the new parent for Groceries, and press Enter.

Occasionally, you may want to flatten the category hierarchy, promoting a subcategory to a full-fledged category. To promote a subcategory,

Note. If you promote a subcategory that has one or more subcategories of its own, the sub-subcategories will be carried along with the promotion, and will become first-level subcategories to the new category.

1. Select the subcategory you want to promote from the Category and Transfer List (Ctrl-C), and then press Ctrl-E to call up the Edit Category window.

2. Substitute for the Subcategory designation either I (Income) or E (Expense), as appropriate. The previous relation to a parent category will be dissolved and your selection will rise to the top level of the category hierarchy.

Print Your Category List

It's a good idea to keep a current copy of your category list handy as you're entering checks in Quicken's Register. Even though you can always call a current list to the screen, you will save yourself a lot of extra keystrokes by keeping a current category list (Figure 2.7) on hand for easy reference.

Print your current category list by displaying it (Ctrl-C) and pressing Ctrl-P (the quick key for Print).

Set Up Additional Bank Accounts

Once you've identified your bank accounts, it's very easy to create matching accounts for them in Quicken. The quick key Ctrl-A will always bring you to the Select Account to Use window (Figure 2.8). From the top of the scrolling Account List, choose <New Account>, and enter the information Quicken requests in the Set Up New Account window. For bank accounts, the account type is 1.

You'll want to make sure that your newly created accounts are synchronized with your primary bank account—especially if you frequently transfer funds among your bank accounts. To accomplish this, choose the same time frame for your new bank accounts as you did for your first bank account; if you're starting with October 1991 in your checking account, use the opening balance from October 1991 in your savings account.

Figure 2.7   Printed category list

Category and Transfer List   Page

FIELDING
11/25/91

Category	Description	Tax Rel	Type	Budget Amount
Bonus	Bonus Income	*	Inc	
Div Income	Dividend Income	*	Inc	
Gift Received	Gift Received		Inc	
Int Inc	Interest Income	*	Inc	
Bank Interest			Sub	
Invest Inc	Investment Income	*	Inc	
Other Inc	Other Income	*	Inc	
Salary	Salary Income	*	Inc	
Luke	Luke's Salary		Sub	
Maria	Maria's Salary		Sub	
Auto	Automobile Expenses		Expns	
Fuel	Auto Fuel		Sub	
Loan	Auto Loan Payment		Sub	
Service	Auto Service		Sub	
Bank Chrg	Bank Charge		Expns	
Charity	Charitable Donations	*	Expns	
Childcare	Childcare Expense		Expns	
Babysitting	Misc babysitting		Sub	
Bright Eyes			Sub	
Wanda Milasz			Sub	
Christmas	Christmas Expenses		Expns	
Clothing	Clothing		Expns	
Crosby	Pet expenses		Expns	
Dues	Dues		Expns	
Entertain	Entertainment		Expns	
Books			Sub	
Music			Sub	
Video			Sub	
Food			Expns	
Dining	Dining Out		Sub	
Groceries	Groceries		Sub	
Lunches			Sub	
Gifts	Gift Expenses		Expns	
Health			Expns	
Health Club			Sub	
Medical	Medical & Dental		Sub	
Vitamins			Sub	
Home Rpair	Home Repair & Maint.		Expns	
Household	Household Misc. Exp		Expns	
Insurance	Insurance		Expns	
Auto	Auto Ins		Sub	
Home	Homeowner's Ins		Sub	
Int Exp	Interest Expense	*	Expns	
Invest Exp	Investment Expense	*	Expns	
Kids	Toys, etc.		Expns	
Misc	Miscellaneous		Expns	
Mort Int	Mortgage Interest Exp	*	Expns	
Other Exp	Other Expenses	*	Expns	
Recreation	Recreation Expense		Expns	
Reimb Biz Exp	Reimbursable Business Exp		Expns	

Figure 2.8   Select Account to Use window

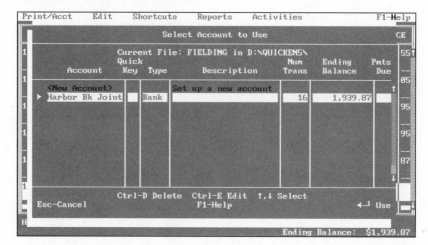

Enter Your First Month's Transactions

In contrast to Level 1's getting-acquainted exercise, this time we'll complete an entire month's worth of transactions. Display the Register screen for your primary bank account by pressing the quick key Ctrl-R. Check the account name in the lower-left corner to make sure you're in the right place. If the wrong account name is showing, press Ctrl-A to call up the Select Account window, and use the cursor to select the correct account.

Change Your Opening Balance

If you completed Level 1 and are merely planning to complete the month from which you selected ten checks for the exercise, you won't need to change the opening balance.

   If you're now recording an earlier month's checks, you should first change the starting balance, the first transaction in the register. You can edit this transaction like any other, simply by highlighting it and typing a new amount. Choose a new starting balance from a bank statement sufficiently before the checks you plan to enter.

Record Checks via the Register

Start entering your checks, following the procedure outlined in Level 1. When working in the Category field of each transaction, keep these procedures in mind:

■ *Category autocompletion*   Type a combination of characters that belong uniquely to one category, and Quicken will automatically complete the category entry for you when you press Enter. Sometimes when using auto-completion, you'll see the following message:

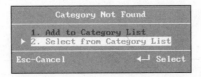

This doesn't necessarily mean that there's no category starting with the letters you typed; it can also indicate more than one match. To proceed, highlight Select from Category List. The Category and Transfer List will appear, and you can pick the category you want.

- *Subcategory assignments*   When you assign a transaction to a subcategory, separate the parent category from the subcategory by a colon (for example, Food:Groceries). You can also press Ctrl-C; when you select a subcategory from the list, Quicken automatically inserts the entire parent:subcategory phrase. Autocompletion works here, too: after using autocompletion to insert the parent, type a colon and then use autocompletion to insert the subcategory.

- *Funds transfers*   If you're moving cash to or from another account, enter the name of the account in the category field (autocompletion works here, too). You'll see the account name appear in square brackets (such as, [Bay Cities]), indicating an interaccount transfer rather than an income or expense transaction (Figure 2.9).

Add New Categories on the Fly

Inevitably, new types of expenses will crop up in your life, and you'll want to expand your category list. You can add categories on the fly, as you're entering a check in your Quicken register. When you reach the Category field, type a new category name. Quicken responds with the Category Not Found window, from which you should choose Add to Category List and fill in the details on the new category.

One caution: always think carefully before you add a new category. Is the category consistent with the level of detail you've worked to achieve across the rest of your category hierarchy? Does it actually represent an asset transfer rather than an expense or income item?

At this level, fine distinctions between expenses and asset transfers aren't that crucial. Some transactions, however, such as the purchase of a Certificate of Deposit, a Treasury Bill, or real estate, would introduce large distortions to your financial picture if you classified them as expenses. In this case, you should set up an Other Asset Account by pressing Ctrl-A, choosing

<New Account>, and following the instructions in the Set Up New Account window. When it comes time to enter the asset transfer transaction, simply put the asset account name under Category, and Quicken will enter offsetting transactions in both accounts.

Figure 2.9　　**Transfer in Register**

Print/Acct	Edit	Shortcuts	Reports	Activities		F1-Help

DATE	NUM	PAYEE · MEMO · CATEGORY	PAYMENT	C	DEPOSIT	BALANCE
11/ 2 1991	1316	Golden State Telephone Telephone	72 30			2,930 49↑
11/ 2 1991	1317	Reeva's Italian Eatery Food:Dining	60 00			2,870 49
11/ 3 1991	1318	San Francisco Daily Subscriptions	14 00			2,856 49
11/ 4 1991	1319	Bright Eyes Day Care Center Childcare:Brig→	111 00			2,745 49
11/ 4 1991	1320	Wanda Milasz Childcare:Wand→	100 00			2,645 49
11/ 5 1991	1321	Bay Cities Fund Group Memo: Cat:[Bay Cities]	500 00			

Harbor Bk Joint　　(Alt+letter accesses menu)
Esc-Main Menu　　Ctrl↵ Record　　　　　　　　Ending Balance: $2,645.49

Transaction showing a transfer (annotation pointing to the Bay Cities Fund Group row)

Split Transactions Among Multiple Categories

Frequently, you'll need to assign a transaction to more than one category. For example, a department store bill of $213.50 might include $64.00 worth of clothing, $37.00 of gifts, and $112.50 of household items. In Quicken's parlance, this is called a *split transaction*.

To record the split transaction just described, you would follow this procedure:

1. Enter the transaction as usual. In this instance, the department store is the payee, and $213.50 is the amount. You can complete any or all of the fields before splitting the transaction. It is useful to enter data at least up to the amount.

2. From any field, press Ctrl-S (for Split), or select Split Transaction from the Edit menu (Alt-E). The Split Transaction window appears. If you've already entered a category name in the Category field—say, Clothing for one portion of the total expenditure—that name will appear in the first line of the Category column. The amount you typed (if any) will appear in the first line of the Amount column.

3. If you need to enter the first category, type it or press Ctrl-C and select it from the Category list; then press Enter.

4. In the Description column, type an optional memo—for example, "New jacket"—as an explanation of that part of the split transaction. This is simply your record of why you split the transaction the way you did. Press Enter.

5. Type the amount related to the first category over any existing amount placed there from the transaction you entered. In this case, you'd type 64.00, the cost of the jacket, over the existing 213.50. When you press Enter, Quicken subtracts the amount you entered from the total transaction amount already in the Register and places the balance—149.50—in the next line of the Amount column, as shown in Figure 2.10. (Typing over the original amount doesn't affect what's displayed in the Register.)

Figure 2.10   **Split Transaction window**

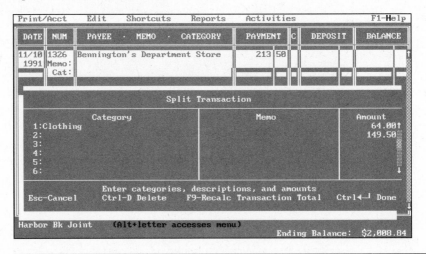

6. Continue entering the remaining portions of the split transaction—37.00 for Gifts and 112.50 for Household. When you enter the last category, the balance opposite it in the Amount column should equal the amount you planned to enter for that portion of the split, as it does in Figure 2.11. If it doesn't, check the amounts you've assigned to each category.

7. When you have finished, press Ctrl-Enter to leave the Split Transaction window. In the Register, the notation SPLIT in the NUM column identifies the split transaction. The first category you entered in the Split Transaction window appears in the Category field (Figure 2.12).

Note. To repeat the category, description, or amount from the previous line of the split transaction, position the cursor in the data you wish to repeat and press the Ditto (") key.

Figure 2.11   Completed Split Transaction window

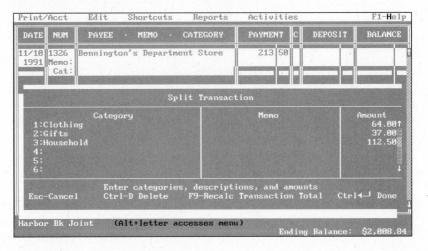

Figure 2.12   Split transaction in the Register

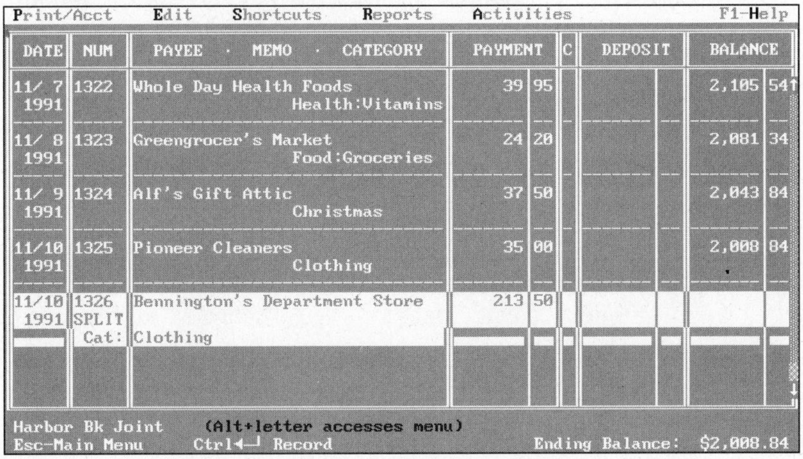

8. Record the completed transaction as usual by pressing Ctrl-Enter.

Sometimes, when you don't know exact amounts for a split, you may want to divide a transaction into percentages. Version 5 of Quicken has a new feature that makes these percentage allocations easier to enter. In the Split Transaction window, simply type percentages rather than dollar amounts into the Amount column. For example, assume you have purchased two items of clothing at a "Buy One, Get Another for a Dollar" sale, intending to give one away as a gift. In this case, you would enter the full amount in the Payment field, and then split the transaction. Then you would type **50%** next to Clothing Expense and **50%** next to Gifts, and the properly allocated dollar amounts would appear automatically.

Record Your Deposits

Recording deposits can sometimes be tricky. Often, you'll want to deposit several checks from different sources at once. On most bank statements, these separate checks are aggregated and reported as a single deposit.

There are two ways to record a multicheck deposit:

- Create a single deposit transaction and enter the check-by-check detail via the Split Transaction window (Figure 2.13).

- Alternatively, enter each check separately, showing the source of the check in the PAYEE field (Figure 2.14). This method has the distinct advantage of pinpointing the exact sources of income at reporting time (when split detail is often abbreviated or suppressed).

Record Bank Machine Withdrawals

You may use a 24-hour banking machine to withdraw money from your account. Each time you do this, a withdrawal transaction appears on your bank statement. Typically, your bank will group these automated teller machine (ATM) transactions on your statement. You need to record these transactions to ensure an accurate account balance.

Record each ATM transaction as though it were a check you wrote to yourself. In the check number column, enter "ATM" so that these transactions will be clustered together on your reports.

Cash machine withdrawals are notoriously challenging to categorize. We'll discuss various methods for keeping track of cash in Level 6. In the meantime, you can create a category called Miscellaneous Cash Expenses as a catch-all petty cash category; for now, categorize these cash machine withdrawals more precisely only if you are withdrawing a large sum of money for a specific purpose.

Enter Bank Fees and Charges

On your bank statement each month, you'll find one or more items related to maintaining the account itself. Usually these fall into one of four categories: bank account fees, interest charges, interest earned, or charges for printing new checks. These charges are easy to overlook, because there are no canceled checks and no manual register entries to remind you of them. Therefore, you should make it a point to find these amounts on your bank statement and enter them each month when you reconcile your account.

Figure 2.13   Split Transaction window for a deposit

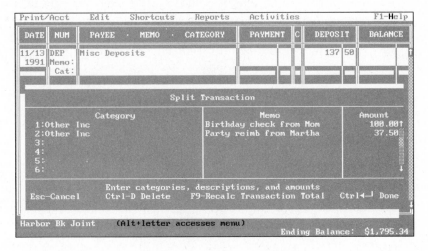

Figure 2.14   Register showing several deposits

Deposits
itemized

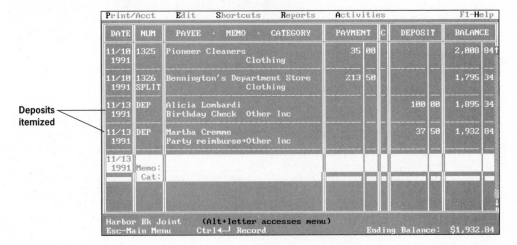

During the reconciliation step, which we'll cover later in this level, Quicken reminds you to enter the bank service charges and the interest you've earned. There is no reminder for interest expenses that might be associated with automatic overdraft protection. If you have such expenses, you'll want to generate an expense transaction categorized as interest expense. New check fees may be categorized in a variety of ways, depending on

Note. If your bank accrues interest earned and pays it the following month, there will always be a transaction on your next statement reflecting the interest credit.

whether you want to isolate those costs: Bank Charges, Misc., or in a separate category, New Checks.

When you enter interest income, be sure to distinguish between the interest paid and the interest accrued. You want to enter the amount actually paid into your account in any given month. Some banks let your account accrue interest during the month and then pay that interest at the beginning of the following month. On your statement, they may report the accrued (but not yet paid) interest, rather than the amount actually deposited, which reflects the previous month's accrual.

Manage Repetitive Transactions

As we've said before, the more you need Quicken, the less time you have to use it. Busy, complicated lives tend to generate the complex financial pictures Quicken manages best. It's absolutely essential, then, that you take advantage of every timesaving shortcut Quicken offers. Among the most important such timesavers is the memorized transaction.

You might be surprised to realize how often you write checks to the same people and companies. To illustrate, look at the transactions in your checking account during a recent month. It's likely that a large percentage of these transactions duplicate others from recent months. Memorized transactions let you enter these transactions using fewer than a dozen keystrokes.

Think of memorized transactions as a stack of partially filled-out checks, already addressed to the department stores, the oil companies, the utilities, and the grocery stores with whom you do business all the time (see Figure 2.15). For Quicken's purposes, they're precategorized, too. All you have to do is pick up the check, write the date and the amount (if you didn't memorize it), and you're done with it.

Figure 2.15   **Sample check with memorized fields**

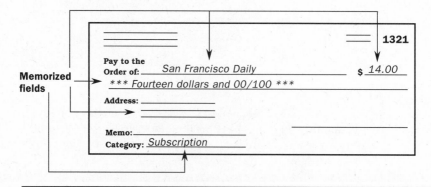

Another subtle benefit of using memorized transactions is that it keeps payee and category names consistent. This is important because it allows you to look at transactions grouped by payee. It's all too easy to record a payment to Shell Oil Company as "Shell" one month, "Shell Oil" the next, and "Shell Oil Co." the month after that. Quicken would list these payments under three different payees in a report. By drawing on a consistent database of memorized transactions, Quicken can improve your access to important facts about your financial picture.

Memorize a Transaction

Every time you enter a new transaction, ask yourself two questions:

- Is this a one-time transaction, or am I likely to be entering more transactions just like this in the future?

- If it isn't a one-time transaction, have I memorized a transaction to this payee in the past?

If this transaction is likely to be repeated but you haven't yet memorized it, then you should do so now.

You can memorize transactions you've already entered, or you can create new memorized transactions to be used later. To memorize a transaction that's already been entered in your register, merely use the cursor keys to highlight the transaction and type Ctrl-M. Quicken highlights the information it will memorize—everything except the date and the check number—and informs you that it's about to memorize the transaction (Figure 2.16). Press Enter to confirm.

To create a new memorized transaction you can use now or later, follow these steps:

1. Press Ctrl-T (Transactions) and choose <New Transaction> from the Memorized Transactions list. The Edit/Setup Memorized Transactions window will appear (Figure 2.17).

2. Enter the information that will be repeated every time you use this memorized transaction. If the transaction will always be the same amount, for example, make sure you enter the amount to be memorized; otherwise, leave the PAYMENT column blank so you'll be prompted for the amount when you apply the memorized transaction later.

3. Enter category information if it won't change each time you use the memorized transaction. You may split the transaction (Ctrl-S) among multiple categories if you wish.

Note. Memorizing an old transaction saves every field except the date and check number. To eliminate one of the saved items (such as amount), use the techniques discussed in "Change a Memorized Transaction," later in this section.

Note. In some cases, you should leave the category blank on a memorized transaction. This might be the case if you repeatedly write a check to the same payee (like a department store) but classify the transaction differently each time.

Figure 2.16   Existing transaction about to be memorized

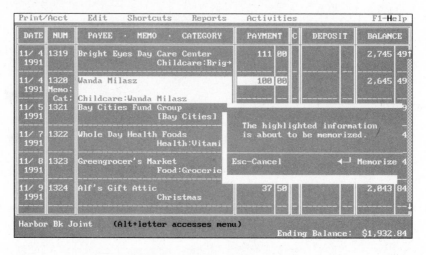

Figure 2.17   Edit/Setup Memorized Transaction window

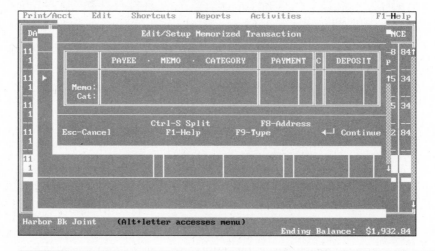

4. For paper checks that you'll be mailing, you may memorize the address to be printed on the check. Press F8 to display the address window, which has room for five lines of text (Figure 2.18). This window also contains a message blank, into which you can type additional account information or any other message you want printed on the check.

Figure 2.18   Address window

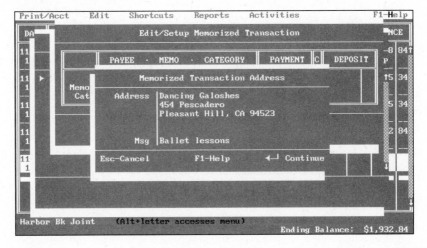

5. You can distinguish between payment type—whether a payment (manual check), check, electronic payment, or deposit—by pressing F9 from the Edit/-Setup Memorized Transactions window and choosing the appropriate option.

6. Press Ctrl-Enter when you're done, and Quicken will memorize the transaction for later use.

A very useful new feature of Quicken 5 is its ability to memorize percentages to apply to a split amount, rather than explicit dollar figures. For example, if you always attribute 75 percent of the cost of a second telephone line to Reimbursable Business Expense and 25 percent to Personal Telephone, Quicken can memorize this transaction and split it automatically each time you enter the amount. To accomplish this,

1. Prepare all the information you want to memorize as above, but enter the payment amount as 100.

2. Open the Split Transaction window (Ctrl-S), and enter the categories and percentages as whole numbers in the AMOUNT column. These amounts should, of course, add up to 100. Press Ctrl-Enter to leave the window.

3. Press Ctrl-Enter to leave the Edit/Setup Memorized Transactions window. At this point, you see the following message:

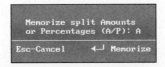

4. Type **P** next to Memorize split Amounts or Percentages. When you do this, you see 100% as the amount for the transaction in the Memorized Transactions list.

Occasionally, you'll want to memorize more than one transaction to the same payee. For example, you may have the same insurance company for both your automobile insurance and your homeowner's insurance and want to distinguish them for categorization purposes. That's no problem; memorize both transactions, and Quicken will let you choose between them when the time comes.

Later, if you decide to use Quicken for printing paper checks that are ready for mailing, you'll want to memorize the payee's address in addition to the name and category information. You can imagine how important memorized transactions become in this instance, because they save many extra keystrokes. You'll learn how to memorize addresses in Level 3.

Apply a Memorized Transaction

By far the quickest way to apply a memorized transaction is to use a form of autocompletion. Suppose Quicken memorized a transaction for paying your subscription bill to an arts journal, the *New Frisco Arts Weekly*. Assuming there is only one memorized transaction for that company, you would apply the memorized transaction like this:

1. Go to the blank transaction at the end of the Register, or press Ctrl-Insert to insert a blank transaction in the middle.

2. Enter the appropriate date for the subscription payment.

3. Type as much of the payee's name as necessary to uniquely identify it (in this case, you could try New) and press Ctrl-E (which stands for Entry here, although in other instances it stands for Edit) to automatically complete the entry. If the characters you entered uniquely identify the *New Frisco Arts Weekly* memorized transaction, Quicken will complete the payee field and fill in the remaining fields with the memorized data.

4. If you haven't typed enough of the payee's name to identify it uniquely—for example, if "New" identifies both *New Frisco Arts Weekly* and *Newstime Magazine*—or if you've entered more than one transaction to this payee, the Memorized Transactions list shown in Figure 2.19 will appear, and Quicken will highlight the first transaction on the list that matches your partial entry. If you want to use a memorized transaction other than the one highlighted, move the cursor to the one you prefer, and press Enter to apply the highlighted transaction.

Figure 2.19   **Memorized Transactions list**

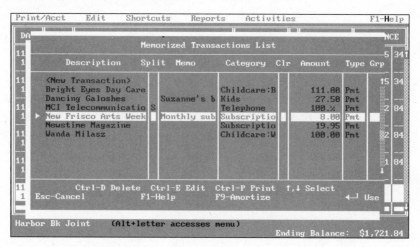

5. Fill in any other information that is missing in the transaction—amount, category, or memo.

6. Press Ctrl-Enter to record the transaction.

    While the autocompletion method is by far the quickest way to apply a memorized transaction, you may simply want to recall a memorized transaction from a list. From a blank Register line, press Ctrl-T or select Recall Transaction from the Shortcuts menu (Alt-S). Then pick the entry you want from the Memorized Transactions list, and press Enter to use it.

Change a Memorized Transaction

Occasionally, you'll need to change a memorized transaction. For example, your monthly subscription price might increase, or you might change your category structure and want to assign certain transactions to a new subcategory.
    To edit a memorized transaction,

1. From the Register or Write Checks screen, call up the Memorized Transactions list by pressing Ctrl-T.

2. Scroll to the memorized transaction you want to edit, and press Ctrl-E (for Edit).

3. Move to the field you want to edit, and make your change.

4. Press Ctrl-Enter when you're done editing.

Note. In a scrolling list, typing a letter will scroll the list quickly to the first entry that starts with that letter. You can type the same letter repeatedly to scroll through additional transactions starting with that letter.

5. Press Escape to leave the Memorized Transactions list.

To delete a memorized transaction,

1. From the Register or Write Checks screen, call up the Memorized Transactions list by pressing Ctrl-T.

2. Scroll to the memorized transaction you wish to delete.

3. Press Ctrl-D (for Delete).

4. Verify that you wish to delete the transaction by pressing Enter when Quicken prompts you.

Master the Register

Because so much of your work is done in the Register, you should get to know some techniques for moving around the Register quickly and for finding transactions that you might want to examine, change, or delete.

Move Quickly Through the Register

The easiest way to move around the Register is to use the cursor keys: the Up and Down Arrow keys to scroll up and down the Register and Left and Right Arrow keys to move within a transaction itself. When a transaction is current, Quicken displays three lines in the PAYEE-MEMO-CATEGORY area, one for each of these fields. Pressing the Up or Down Arrow key twice causes the cursor to move up or down two lines within the current transaction. After that, the Up and Down Arrow keys move from transaction to transaction. (Transactions that aren't current are displayed on two lines with the Memo and Category fields abbreviated.)

The arrow keys may work fine when only a single month's transactions are in the Register, but after a couple months, using them can become tedious.

There are three ways to move rapidly to other parts of the large, complicated Register you'll have assembled in a few months: the Register navigation keys, the Find command, and two types of Go To commands.

Register Navigation Keys

Register navigation keys may be used in the Register at any time. However, if you're in the middle of editing or entering a transaction, Quicken may ask whether to record your changes before moving to another location in the Register.

Table 2.1 shows a complete list of the Register navigation keys.

Table 2.1   **Register Navigation Keys**

Key or Key Combination	Action
PgUp, PgDn	Moves up or down one screen (six transactions) at a time
Home, End	First press of Home (or End) moves to beginning (or end) of current field; second press moves to beginning (or end) of current transaction; third press moves to the first (or last) transaction in the Register
Ctrl-PgUp, Ctrl-PgDn	Moves to the first transaction of the previous month or the next month
Ctrl-Home, Ctrl-End	Moves to the beginning or end of the Register

Find Command

While the navigation keys will move you around quickly, the Find command is often the fastest way to find specific transactions in the Register. The Find command will locate all the transactions that match a pattern you provide.

You can build a pattern based on the contents of any single field or on a combination of fields. For example, if you wanted to find out when you last paid your $244.50 quarterly auto insurance bill to Northern Cal Casualty Insurance, you could choose one of the following strategies:

- Look for transactions that match the name of the company: Northern Cal Casualty Insurance.

- Look for transactions that match the category Auto Insurance.

- Look for transactions in the amount of $244.50.

You don't need to be in a particular place in the Register to begin a Find operation; you can specify the direction of the search. Follow these steps to build a pattern and to find the transaction you want:

1. From the Register, press Ctrl-F (for Find) to open the Transaction to Find window (Figure 2.20) or select Find Transaction from the Shortcuts menu. The Transaction to Find window looks like a blank Register line, without the date and balance columns.

2. Move the cursor to the field whose contents you will use as a matching pattern. Type the contents. Note that you can't use autocompletion to finish entering a partial category name, as you would in a regular Register entry. But you can accomplish the same thing by using the key-word matching techniques described in the next section.

Figure 2.20 **Transaction to Find window**

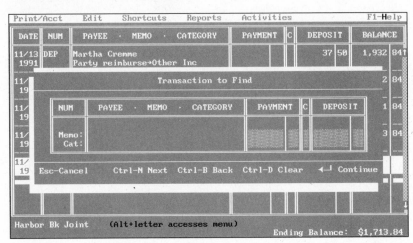

3. If you want to match on two fields—such as the Auto Insurance category and the amount $244.50—press Enter or Tab to move to the other field and type the second criterion.

4. When your search criteria are set, press Ctrl-N (for Next) to search forward from the current transaction, or Ctrl-B (for Backward) to search backward from the current transaction. If you want to be sure that you find the most recent occurrence of the transaction in the Register, regardless of the current transaction, press Ctrl-End to move to the end of the Register, and then press Ctrl-B.

5. When Quicken finds the first matching transaction—or if it finds no match—it returns you to the Register. Continue to press Ctrl-N or Ctrl-B repeatedly until you find the transaction you want.

Finding memorized transactions is even easier, and this is one more reason to use them. Just follow these steps:

1. From the Register, press Ctrl-F to bring up the Transaction to Find window.

2. Press Ctrl-T to bring up the Memorized Transactions list.

3. Locate the transaction you want by pressing the first letter of the payee name repeatedly or by using the arrow keys. Press Enter to drop the memorized information into the Find Transaction window.

4. Find the transaction by pressing Ctrl-N or Ctrl-B, as described in step 4.

Remember, if you've recently edited a memorized transaction, you won't be able to use the new version to find older transactions. To use a new memorized transaction as a search pattern for older entries in the Register, clear the recently edited field after it appears in the Find Transaction window (press Ctrl-Backspace to clear it). Then execute the search by pressing Ctrl-F or Ctrl-B.

Key-Word Matching

Note. In version 4 and earlier versions of Quicken, the matching rules are quite different. Refer to the user manual if you're using an old version.

To save keystrokes, or if you recall only part of the text in the field of a transaction you want to find, you can use a technique called *key-word matching*. When you type text in a field and press Ctrl-N or Ctrl-B, Quicken will find any transaction that contains the text you've typed in the field you're searching. For example, to find a check written to the University of California, you could type only **univ** or **cal**, or any sequence of letters within the phrase without regard for their location.

Quicken also allows you to use a form of wildcards. Type two consecutive periods (..) to represent a missing portion of a text field. For example, instead of typing **Northern Cal Casualty Insurance**, you could simply type **Nor..** as shown in Figure 2.21. Inserting an equal (=) sign before the text indicates that you want to find transactions containing exactly that text and nothing else. Hence, =Mobil will match checks to Mobil but not to Mobil Oil Corporation.

Note. Key-word matching doesn't work with numbers in amount fields. You must search for precise numeric values.

Figure 2.21   **Key-word matching**

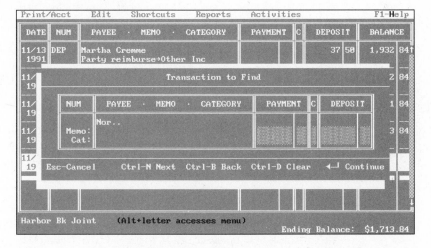

Using key-word matching is naturally less precise than typing the entire text, but it usually saves a great deal of time. You'll find the transactions you want, but sometimes you may have to skip through undesired transactions to do so. Table 2.2 shows four ways you might use the .. characters to find a target transaction, as well as a few other transactions you might find along the way.

Table 2.2   **Key-Word Matching Examples**

If you type:	You will match:
Nor	Northern Cal Casualty Insurance, Nordstrom, Norcross Avenue School of Dance, Connor Pharmacy
Nor..	Northern Cal Casualty Insurance, Nordstrom, Norcross Avenue School of Dance
..ance	Northern Cal Casualty Insurance, Café Dorrance, Norcross Avenue School of Dance
Nor..ance	Northern Cal Casualty Insurance, Norcross Avenue School of Dance
=Nor	(no matches; would match only checks written to Nor)
..Casual..	Northern Cal Casualty Insurance, Marin Casual Wear

Go To Commands

Two other quick keys can rapidly take you where you want to go:

Note. Remember, transfer transactions are distinguished in the Register by the account name appearing in brackets in the category field.

- *Go to Date*   Press Ctrl-G (or select Go to Date on the Edit menu) to bring up the Go to Date window (Figure 2.22). Type the date that you're searching for, using slashes (/) or spaces between the parts of the date; then press Enter. Quicken finds the first transaction recorded for that date, if it's a forward search, or the last transaction recorded for that date, if it's a backward search.

- *Go to Transfer*   When you enter a transfer transaction—recording the movement of funds from one account to another—you're actually entering two transactions: one in each affected account. To jump from one transfer transaction to the offsetting transaction in another account, press the quick key Ctrl-X (or choose Go to Transfer on the Edit menu).

Insert a Transaction

Sometimes it's not convenient to go all the way to the end of the register in order to create a new transaction. If you need to insert a transaction at the point where you're working in the register, simple press Ctrl-Insert, and a blank transaction will appear immediately before the transaction you're currently working with.

Figure 2.22 **Go to Date window**

```
 Print/Acct    Edit    Shortcuts    Reports    Activities          F1-Help
┌──────┬─────┬──────────────────────────────────┬─────────┬──┬────────┬────────┐
│ DATE │ NUM │ PAYEE · MEMO · CATEGORY          │ PAYMENT │C │ DEPOSIT│ BALANCE│
├──────┼─────┼──────────────────────────────────┼─────────┼──┼────────┼────────┤
│11/13 │DEP  │Martha Cremme                     │         │  │  37 50 │1,932 84↑│
│1991  │     │Party reimburse→Other Inc         │         │  │        │        │
│11/13 │1327 │Wanda Milasz                      │  100 00 │  │        │1,832 84│
│1991  │     │                                  │         │  │        │        │
│11/13 │1328 │Bright Ey┌──────────────────────────────────┐ │1,721 84│
│1991  │     │         │          Go to Date             │ │        │
│11/15 │1329 │New Frisc│                                  │ │1,713 84│
│1991  │     │Monthly s│   Date to find: 11/15/91         │ │        │
│11/15 │     │         │                                  │ │        │
│1991  │Memo:│         │ Esc-Cancel  F1-Help ←┘ Continue  │ │        │
│      │Cat: │         └──────────────────────────────────┘ │        │
│      │     │                                  │         │  │        │        │
│      │     │                                  │         │  │        │       ↓│
├──────┴─────┴──────────────────────────────────┴─────────┴──┴────────┴────────┤
│ Harbor Bk Joint      (Alt+letter accesses menu)                              │
│                                         Ending Balance:  $1,713.84           │
└──────────────────────────────────────────────────────────────────────────────┘
```

The new transaction will adopt the date of the transaction which follows it; if you change the date, you should expect that the transaction will move within the register to maintain the general date ordering of any account register.

Delete and Void Transactions

Note. You can prevent groups of transactions from being inadvertently deleted by protecting them with a password. From the Quicken Main Menu (press Escape repeatedly), type **P** (Set Preferences), **W** (Password Settings), and **T** (Transaction Password).

Occasionally, you'll want to void a transaction or delete it altogether. While both have the same effect on the category totals and account balances, voiding a transaction preserves a permanent record in your register that the transaction was made and later neutralized.

For example, you might have mistakenly entered an ATM transaction twice. There is no need to keep a record of this error, so you can delete it as follows:

1. Move to the transaction you want to delete.

2. Press Ctrl-D (for Delete) or select Delete Transaction from the Edit menu.

3. In response to the confirmation box, select Delete Transaction.

Voiding is necessary on occasions when you've actually written an unnecessary check. For example, a scuba enthusiast named Tom Spalone wrote a check to Wet Water Enterprises to cover the cost of a scuba diving course, but subsequently decided to enroll in another outfit's class. Tom destroyed the valid check, but wanted to keep a record of it in the Register. If you find yourself in a similar situation, and need to void a transaction, proceed as follows:

1. Move to the transaction that you want to void.

2. Press Ctrl-V (for Void) or select Void Transaction from the Edit menu.

3. Quicken asks you for confirmation. Press Enter or type **1** to select Void transaction.

4. Quicken places the notation VOID before the payee and places an X in the Cleared column.

5. Record the transaction by pressing Ctrl-Enter. Your screen should resemble Figure 2.23.

Figure 2.23   **Voided transaction in the Register**

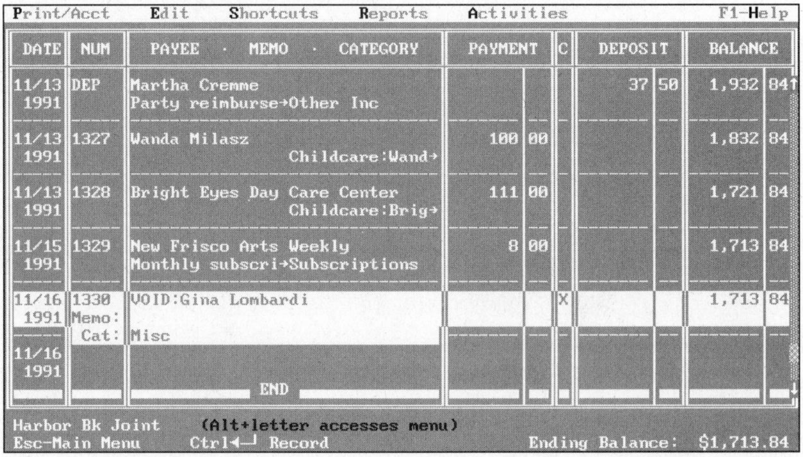

```
 Print/Acct    Edit    Shortcuts    Reports    Activities              F1-Help

 DATE  NUM   PAYEE ·  MEMO  ·  CATEGORY   PAYMENT  C  DEPOSIT     BALANCE

11/13 DEP   Martha Cremme                              37 50     1,932 84↑
1991        Party reimburse→Other Inc

11/13 1327  Wanda Milasz                    100 00              1,832 84
1991                       Childcare:Wand→

11/13 1328  Bright Eyes Day Care Center      111 00              1,721 84
1991                        Childcare:Brig→

11/15 1329  New Frisco Arts Weekly             8 00              1,713 84
1991        Monthly subscri→Subscriptions

11/16 1330  VOID:Gina Lombardi                      X           1,713 84
1991  Memo:
      Cat: Misc
11/16
1991                          END

 Harbor Bk Joint      (Alt+letter accesses menu)
 Esc-Main Menu      Ctrl↵  Record                  Ending Balance:  $1,713.84
```

Postdate Transactions

In certain cases, you may want to record some future income or expense. This is particularly common when you begin writing checks and scheduling electronic payments well in advance of the actual due date. Quicken displays postdated transactions in two locations. First, these transactions appear below a double line in the Register, which represents today's date (see Figure 2.24). Also, the date is emphasized on some monitors for easy visibility (depending on your screen display, it may be in bold letters or in a different color).

Second, Quicken distinguishes two account balances which appear at the lower-right corner of the Register screen: the Current Balance, which is the account balance as of today, before postdated transactions are deducted; and the Ending Balance, which takes into account both current and postdated transactions.

Figure 2.24   Postdated transaction in the Register

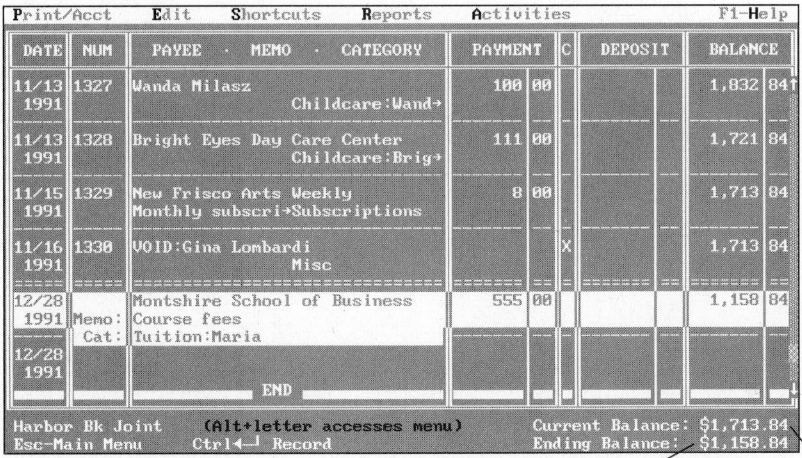

Double line separates past from postdated transactions

Balance as of today

Balance after postdated transactions

Reconcile Your First Bank Statement

It's important that you reconcile your bank account—in other words, balance your electronic checkbook—when you receive your statement each month. Reconciling your account serves several critical purposes:

- It detects errors the bank may have made in handling your account.

- It detects errors you may have made (entry errors and omissions) when entering transactions in your account.

- It identifies checks that have not been cashed and deposits that have not been received by the bank.

The procedure behind reconciliation is relatively simple. It's worthwhile to keep this four-step overview in mind:

1. First you supply the opening and closing balances of your bank account. Quicken compares the opening balance with last month's closing balance to make sure they match. From then on, it works with the closing statement balance you entered.

2. Next, you electronically check off (or, in Quicken parlance, *clear*) the transactions in your Quicken Register that match the transactions reported by the bank in its statement. As you mark transactions,

Quicken keeps a *cleared balance*—that is, a running total of all Register items that have been processed by the bank.

3. Quicken constantly compares the bank statement ending balance to the cleared balance. If they are identical, reconciliation is complete. If they are not, you must begin the process of looking for bank errors, missing Register items, and entry errors, continuing until the two numbers match. (As you find errors, Quicken constantly monitors the narrowing gap and tells you when you've achieved a balance.)

4. Once the Register and statement balance, you should finally review old uncleared transactions, looking for checks and deposits that your bank, your merchants, or the mailman might have lost.

If you've always dreaded the task of reconciliation, remember that Quicken will now do much of the work for you. Previously undetected errors may surface the first time you reconcile your bank statement using Quicken, thus the process may take longer than it ever will again. Don't be discouraged, though; even that first session is likely to be much easier than manual reconciliation, and when you've finished reconciling your account, you can be confident that your Quicken account and your bank's view of your account status agree.

First Steps to Reconciliation

To reconcile your account, be sure you have your bank statement in hand and are looking at the Register for the account you're reconciling (change the current account, if necessary, by pressing Ctrl-A and choosing the account you want to use). Then select Reconcile from the Activities menu (Alt-A). You'll see the Reconcile Register with Bank Statement window, shown in Figure 2.25.

If you've reconciled your bank statement before, some of the information will be carried over from your previous reconciliation session. Specifically, the ending balance you entered last month becomes this month's opening balance, and all the dates are advanced by one month. Enter the following information to set up your reconciliation session:

1. *Bank Statement Balances*   Quicken places the balance you gave when you opened the account next to "Bank Statement Opening Balance." You should enter the ending balance directly from your bank statement. These balances are critical, because the difference between the two numbers must precisely match the transactions in your Quicken account register that have cleared through the bank. If the opening balance carried over from the ending balance of your last reconciliation session is different from the one on your statement, alarm bells should sound. In this case, see the section entitled "Special Reconciliation Procedures" in Level 6 before proceeding.

Figure 2.25 **Reconcile Register with Bank Statement window**

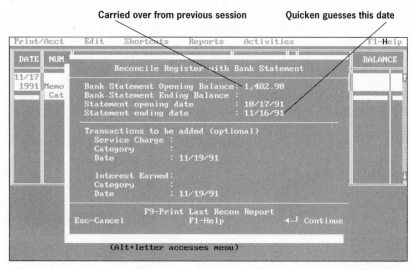

Carried over from previous session   Quicken guesses this date

```
 Print/Acct    Edit    Shortcuts    Reports    Activities         F1-Help
┌──────┬─────┬─────────────────────────────────────────────────┬─────────┐
│ DATE │ NUM │                                                 │ BALANCE │
├──────┼─────┤        Reconcile Register with Bank Statement    │         │
│11/17 │     │                                                 │         │
│ 1991 │Memo │ Bank Statement Opening Balance : 1,482.90       │         │
│      │ Cat │ Bank Statement Ending Balance  :                │         │
│      │     │ Statement opening date         : 10/17/91       │         │
│      │     │ Statement ending date          : 11/16/91       │         │
│      │     │                                                 │         │
│      │     │ Transactions to be added (optional)             │         │
│      │     │   Service Charge :                              │         │
│      │     │   Category       :                              │         │
│      │     │   Date           : 11/19/91                     │         │
│      │     │                                                 │         │
│      │     │   Interest Earned:                              │         │
│      │     │   Category       :                              │         │
│      │     │   Date           : 11/19/91                     │         │
│      │     │                                                 │         │
│      │     │          F9-Print Last Recon Report             │         │
│      │     │ Esc-Cancel          F1-Help        ◄─┘ Continue │         │
│      │     │                                                 │         │
│      │     └─────────────────────────────────────────────────┘         │
│             (Alt+letter accesses menu)                                  │
```

2. *Statement Dates*   Enter the opening and ending dates of your bank statement. Quicken doesn't use the opening date other than in titling reconciliation reports; however, the ending date is used to select the transactions Quicken shows you during the reconciliation process.

3. *Service Charges and Interest Earned*   If you haven't added the bank service charges to the Register as a separate transaction, Quicken will create this transaction for you. Type the amount and the appropriate category, and verify the date for these transactions (Quicken guesses that service charges and interest earned are credited on the same day every month and therefore fills in dates one month later than those used in last month's reconciliation). Press Ctrl-Enter to complete this form, and you'll see the Reconciliation Register (see Figure 2.26).

Note. Transactions with letters—such as ATM—in the NUM field are considered unnumbered transactions for sorting purposes.

Mark Cleared Transactions

The Reconciliation Register lists all transactions in the current account that you have not cleared in a previous reconciliation session, and that are dated no later than the bank statement ending date you provided. Deposits are at the top of the list, followed by unnumbered expense transactions (sorted by date), followed in turn by numbered checks (sorted by number). In the Amount field, deposits show up as positive numbers and payments as negative numbers. This is a scrolling list: pressing the Up and Down Arrow keys will make more transactions appear.

Figure 2.26   **Reconciliation Register**

As you select
transactions they
will be marked in
the C column

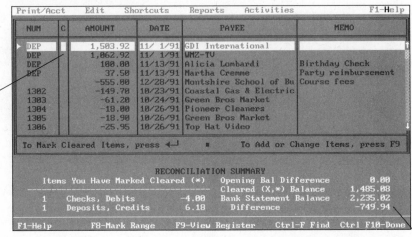

Successful reconciliation cuts this to zero

In the lower-right corner, you'll see a comparison of the cleared Quicken Register balance with the bank statement ending balance, along with the amount of difference between them. As you clear transactions in the Reconciliation register, this difference should be reduced to zero.

To mark a transaction as cleared, use the Up and Down Arrow keys to highlight the item, and then press Enter. An asterisk (*) will appear in the cleared column (marked C), and the highlight will move to the next item. (Alternatively, you can simply press the spacebar and the highlight will stay where it is.) To unmark a transaction you've already marked, highlight the transaction and press the spacebar or Enter again; the asterisk will disappear.

Work systematically from your bank statement to mark off all the items that appear on your statement—deposits, checks, ATM withdrawals, account fees, and interest items. Check the amounts as you go along to save work later; you may detect incorrect entries, duplicate entries, or missing items. Here's how to respond to these situations:

■ If you find an incorrect entry, you can edit the transaction without leaving the reconciliation process. Highlight the transaction and press F9. The Register will appear, as shown in Figure 2.27. Correct the field that needs adjusting, press Ctrl-Enter to record the change, then press F9 to return to the reconciliation list.

Figure 2.27   Editing transactions in the Reconciliation register

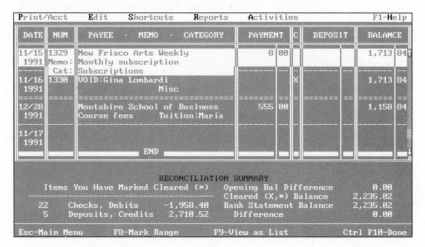

- If a bank statement item is missing from your Register, you can easily enter a new item. Press F9 to see the Register, and move to the end of it. Enter the transaction as usual, and press Ctrl-Enter to record it. Press F9 to return to the reconciliation list.

- If you've entered the same item twice, you can delete the duplicate item from the Register by pointing to it and pressing Ctrl-D.

Balance and Troubleshoot the Account

If you've cleared your transactions methodically, checking for accuracy along the way, the difference between the statement balance and the cleared balance should be zero. If it is, congratulations; you may go to the next step by pressing Escape. If it isn't, then try these troubleshooting techniques:

- Double-check the ending balance on your bank statement. On some statements, you can easily pick up the incorrect number.

- Look for charges against your bank account that may be buried in less than obvious places. Aside from the usual suspects of account fees and interest paid, this might include ATM withdrawals and usage fees, direct deposits to and direct deductions from your account, and bank debit card transfers. If you have a brokerage account connected to your bank account, watch for transfers associated with purchases and sales of stock or with dividends on stock held in your account.

- Look for a transaction amount in your bank statement and in your Reconciliation register that exactly matches the difference displayed in the lower-right corner. If there is a single mistake, you'll often catch it this way.

- Look for mistakes in signs—in other words, deposits that are entered as payments and payments that are entered as deposits. In your Reconciliation register, deposits should show up as positive numbers and withdrawals as negative numbers.

- If you have an interest-bearing checking account, check to be sure that you entered the interest paid rather than the interest earned. Sometimes the earned amount is not actually paid until the following month.

- Look for old checks that predate the start of your Register but have only now found their way out of someone's bureau drawer and into the bank. Enter these as new expenses.

- Look for transposed digits in the Register or bank statement. These errors are quite common, but they can be difficult to find.

As a last resort, Quicken provides a way to close gaps that you can't find, but you should avoid using this unless there is absolutely no alternative—the balancing error is in there somewhere! Moreover, if the imbalance is over 50 cents and you're using Quicken for personal tax accounting purposes, you can no longer be completely confident of your data's integrity and ability to withstand scrutiny.

Still, sometimes the error is just a few cents and simply isn't worth the time it would take to track down. To force a reconciliation before your account balances, follow these steps:

1. Press Escape from within the Reconciliation register. The Reconciliation Is Not Complete window, shown in Figure 2.28, appears, offering you the chance to continue or leave your work. Type **1** to continue.

2. Since your account doesn't balance in this case, a problem window will appear (see Figure 2.29), suggesting some common reasons for the imbalance. The troubleshooting guide in this section is much more comprehensive, so assuming you've already been through that, you can simply press Enter to adjust for the difference.

3. A third window will appear—the Adding Balance Adjustment Entry window shown in Figure 2.30. Type **Y** (yes) when you are asked whether to add an adjusting entry to the Register, and then categorize the transaction (you can use a Miscellaneous category).

To balance the account, Quicken generates a balancing transaction to close the gap. You can also choose to print a reconciliation report; type **Y** next to the prompt. Quicken also performs the final step of updating cleared trans-actions, changing all asterisks in the Register's C column to X's. Figure 2.31 shows how the balancing entry looks in your Register.

Figure 2.28 **Reconciliation Is Not Complete window**

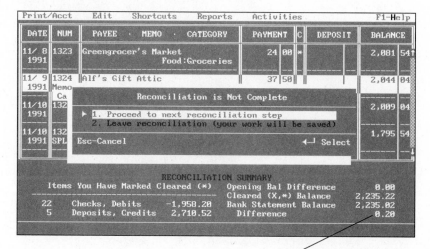

Register is out of balance by 20 cents

Figure 2.29 **Reconciliation Imbalance window**

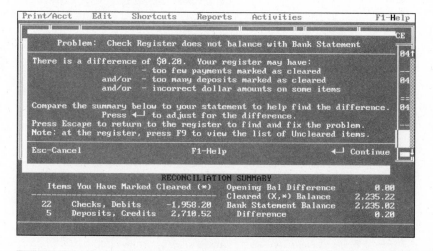

Figure 2.30   Adding Balance Adjustment Entry window

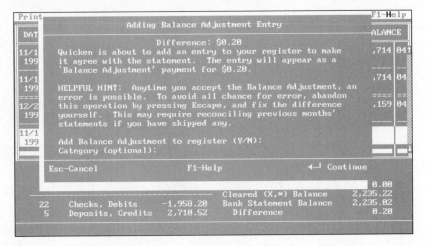

Figure 2.31   Reconciliation Balancing Entry in Register

DATE	NUM	PAYEE · MEMO · CATEGORY	PAYMENT	C	DEPOSIT	BALANCE
11/16 1991	1330	VOID:Gina Lombardi Misc		X		1,714 04↑
11/16 1991	Memo: Cat:	Balance Adjustment Misc	0 20	X		1,713 84
11/19 1991		Service Charge Bank Chrg	4 00	X		1,709 84
11/19 1991		Interest Earned Int Inc:Bank I→		X	6 18	1,716 02
12/28 1991		Montshire School of Business Course fees Tuition:Maria	555 00			1,161 02
11/17 1991						
		END				

Harbor Bk Joint   (Alt+letter accesses menu)   Current Balance: $1,716.02
Esc-Main Menu   Ctrl◂┘ Record   Ending Balance: $1,161.02

With all the troubleshooting tools that you can use to diagnose balancing errors, you stand the best chance of finding balancing errors during the reconciliation process. If you choose to force a balance and later find the error, you can correct the erroneous transaction and then eliminate the balance adjustment transaction.

Occasionally, you may need to edit fields of a transaction that has been cleared through reconciliation. You may want to change the category, the payee name (if you're fixing it for consistency, perhaps), or the split transaction categories and amounts. Use extreme caution in those rare instances when you must edit a cleared transaction amount; you must offset any change in the amount of a cleared transaction with an equal and opposite change in another cleared transaction. Otherwise, Quicken will not be able to guarantee that the integrity of your account balance will be maintained. Quicken will issue the following warning whenever you try to edit a cleared transaction:

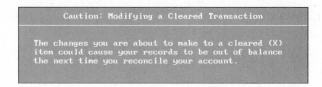

To be safe, you might consider entering the corrections as separate transactions, rather than editing cleared transactions themselves.

Complete the Reconciliation and Obtain a Report

Once you've marked the transactions that make your bank statement balance match your cleared transactions balance, you may complete reconciliation by pressing Ctrl-F10. The Congratulations window, shown in Figure 2.32, verifies that your account balances and offers to print a reconciliation report.

Figure 2.32   **Reconciliation Successful screen**

It's a good idea to keep a printed reconciliation report along with your canceled checks and bank statement. This represents a complete record not only of what happened at the bank but also of how you entered the information into Quicken.

Quicken offers two types of reconciliation reports: a summary and a full report. The Summary report on cleared transactions resembles the summary on your bank statement; it lists total debits, total credits, and an ending balance which should match your bank statement's ending balance. The summary report also totals uncleared transactions and postdated ones, generating an ending balance for your Register. In addition, it prints all uncleared transactions in the account up to the reconciliation date.

The Full report begins with the same cleared and uncleared summaries, but it goes on to print all cleared and uncleared transactions, grouping those transactions dated before the reconciliation date and those dated after it.

To obtain a reconciliation report,

Note. Before you begin printing, you can direct the output to one of four places: to your primary report printer, to your alternate report printer, to your checks printer, or to a disk, which prints an ASCII file.

1. Type **Y** at the prompt to indicate that you want to print a report. You'll see the Print Reconciliation Report window.

2. Type **1** to select your primary report printer. (If during installation you didn't specify a report printer, you may not be able to print now. In this case, review Appendix A. Level 6 also covers printing in some detail.)

3. Enter the report settings in the window. Quicken will supply today's date as the reconciliation date. Press Enter to accept and move past the date. You can then enter an optional report title if you wish.

4. Finally, type **S** for Summary or **F** for Full report, and then press Enter to begin printing.

Run Standard Reports

Quicken has a wonderfully rich and flexible built-in report generator. In fact, you can customize a wide range of reports to support your decision-making needs. Designing these custom reports is a major focus of Level 6.

Quicken has an impressive inventory of standard reports, however, and you'll want to put some of them to work right away. You'll find a complete gallery of Quicken's standard reports in Appendix D. For now, it's enough to reacquaint yourself with the Cash Flow report and learn the Itemized Categories report.

Cash Flow

As you saw in Level 1, the Cash Flow report summarizes by category the cash flowing into and out of your money accounts. The bottom line represents the increase or decrease in your personal liquidity.

Decreases in cash (which the report calls *Outflows*) typically result from either expense payments or purchases of assets (such as a CD or real estate). Increases in cash (which the report calls *Inflows*) typically result from income deposits or sale of assets.

To obtain a standard Cash Flow report,

1. Press Alt-R to see the Reports menu; then select Personal Reports and Cash Flow.

2. Enter an optional report title.

3. Adjust the range of months to represent the period for which you want to see a Cash Flow report. Press Enter to begin generating the report, which should resemble Figure 2.33.

Figure 2.33   Cash Flow report

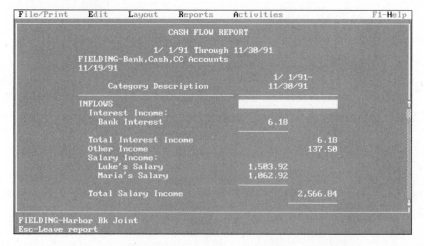

The Cash Flow report you create here will differ from the simpler one you produced earlier by virtue of the presence of more bank accounts, transfers between accounts, and a customized category structure that shows the detail of your income and expenses. Quicken shows you the inflows on top of the report, with income categories sorted alphabetically. Outflows—expenses— appear at the bottom of the report. The Overall Total line, which you can see by pressing PgDn, shows the net change in your accounts over the period.

Seeing the first Cash Flow report for your new category structure might reveal subtle ways you could change your categories to make them more use-ful. For example, you might decide that the Software subcategory is an unnecessary distinction under the PC category. Such adjustments are easy to make when you return to the Register.

Itemized Categories

Another important standard report is the Itemized Categories report, which gives you the detail behind each category and subcategory, transaction by transaction, subtotaling each category along the way. You might want to run this report periodically and scan it to ensure that you're categorizing items consistently over time.

To obtain a copy of the Itemized Categories report,

1. From the Reports menu on the Main Menu bar, select Personal Reports and then Itemized Categories.

2. Enter an optional report title.

3. Again, adjust the time period if necessary, then press Enter. Figure 2.34 shows a portion of the expense categories listed in an itemized categories report.

Figure 2.34   **Itemized Categories report**

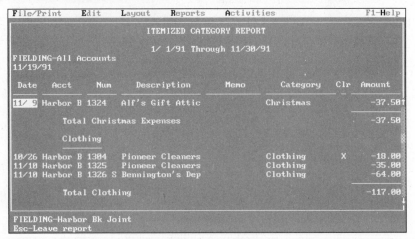

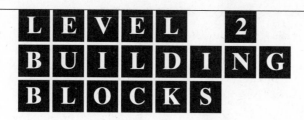

LEVEL 2 BUILDING BLOCKS

In Level 2, you have mastered the techniques for recording and analyzing income, expenses, and transfers of funds to and from your bank accounts.

TECHNIQUES AND PROCEDURES

■ Enhance your category structure by adding and deleting categories, editing them, and changing their relative positions within the hierarchy. Display the Category and Transfer list by pressing Ctrl-C. Add a category by selecting the New Category entry and completing the window that appears. Delete a category with Ctrl-D. Edit a category name or type (income, expense, or subcategory) by pressing Ctrl-E and changing the information in the window. After you designate a subcategory, select its parent from the list that appears.

■ Manage repetitive transactions by memorizing them. Press Ctrl-M as or after you enter the transaction; Quicken will only memorize information that would remain constant over time. To retrieve the memorized transaction, press Ctrl-T, and Quicken will drop it into the Register.

■ Even in registers with hundreds of transactions, you can find buried transactions easily. Press Ctrl-G (for Go to Date, also on the Edit menu) to locate a transaction by its date. Press Ctrl-F (for Find) to locate transactions that match specific patterns of text or numbers. To find similar elements, use keyword matching: replace characters with .., which can represent any number of characters at the beginning, middle, or end of a pattern. To find an exact match, precede the text with =.

■ Standard reports—Cash Flow and Itemized Categories—are useful tools for getting a bird's-eye view of your financial picture.

TERMS

■ A *split transaction* is a single transaction representing amounts assigned to different categories. To split a transaction, press Ctrl-S; then enter the categories and corresponding amounts into the window.

■ A *transfer* is a transaction amount deducted from one account and credited to another. A transfer might be a payment written from your checking account to your savings account, or the purchase of a bank CD or treasury security. To avoid distortions in your income and expense accounts, treat these transactions as transfers rather than as expenses.

■ A *memorized transaction* is a kind of template for a check. Quicken memorizes the repetitive information—the payee, the category, the address (if you plan to print the check), and possibly the amount, if it doesn't vary from payment to payment. When you retrieve a memorized transaction, it is already partially completed; you only need type what is unique for this particular payment.

IMPORTANT IDEAS

■ Reconciliation is so easy with Quicken that you have less reason to avoid it than ever. The first time may be the most difficult, because you may find errors that you had missed before. If you have to accept a discrepancy, let Quicken make the adjustment and then adopt a regular reconciliation routine.

■ Your category structure mirrors your financial activities—indeed, it reflects much of your daily life. Work with categories as you work with Quicken. Refine them so they are easy to use and remember, and so the reports you produce make sense to you. As you'll see, categories can help you make decisions and prioritize, and even change the way you do things so that you have more control over your personal finance.

3

Write Checks
with Quicken

PLAN AHEAD

Enter Your Checks

Memorize Transactions for Check Writing

Use Billminder to Best Advantage

Print Checks for the First Time

Advance to Painless Check Printing

BUILDING BLOCKS

PLAN AHEAD

DECISIONS

Should I Print Checks with Quicken?

You *can* use Quicken solely as a bookkeeping program and be perfectly satisfied that the time you invest is well spent. However, if you first write checks by hand and later record them in Quicken, you're actually wasting time by taking an extra, unnecessary step. When you use Quicken not only to record checks but also to print them, you can eliminate a step and save a significant amount of time. In fact, by using the Memorize Transactions feature, you can reduce some check-writing transactions to just a few keystrokes.

If saving time and making bill paying more convenient are among your key objectives, you should make your payments directly through Quicken, rather than merely recording transactions that you've already completed manually.

Which Payment Method Should I Choose?

Quicken offers two ways to make payments and record them in a single step. You can issue paper checks from your laser or dot matrix printer, or you can make your payments electronically through CheckFree, an independent electronic bill paying service. While you certainly could use both methods for paying bills, it's best to pick one system and stick with it.

Paper checks offer the advantages of simplicity, familiarity, cost-effectiveness, and the shortest interval until a payment is actually received. Electronic payments are quicker and more convenient to issue than paper checks, and they don't require a printer. You can go through a stack of bills and pay them electronically in minutes without licking a single stamp or envelope; however, electronic payments don't reach payees as quickly as paper checks.

If you think you might be interested in CheckFree, read the "Plan Ahead" section in Level 4, which contains a more complete discussion of the advantages and disadvantages of paying bills electronically. Even if you plan to sign up for CheckFree, it's worthwhile to read about and try some of the techniques introduced in this level. You'll save considerable time preparing electronic payments by learning how to enter checks, memorize them, and use transaction groups.

How Much of My Check Writing Should Quicken Handle?

If you're using Quicken to manage your personal finances, it's almost impossible to write all your checks with Quicken. After all, you won't have your PC with you every time you write a check at the grocery store or cash a check on vacation. In all probability, though, the majority of your checking transactions will be bill payments and other checks you write at home. The more payments you make through Quicken, the more time you'll save by eliminating extra recording steps.

While Quicken is certainly capable of printing a single transaction, you'll save the most time by batching many transactions to do at once. By adopting a disciplined weekly or biweekly bill paying routine such as the one recommended in the Preliminaries chapter of this book, you can get in the habit of grouping your check-writing transactions into very efficient sessions.

Should I "Play the Float"?

Quicken facilitates—and even encourages—the postdating of checking transactions. That is, if you're sitting down on December 1st to pay a bill that's not due until the 20th, Quicken allows you to specify that a check be dated the 15th and perhaps not even printed until that date. This practice of paying bills just before they're due is often called "playing the float."

Over time, playing the float can save significant money. For example, if your money earns 7.5 percent in a bank or money market account, every week that you can delay a $2,500 mortgage payment is worth about $3.65. It may not sound like much, but over 12 months it could buy you dinner for two or next year's version of Quicken.

You may also be forced to play the float because of cash flow problems. If you've received a mortgage bill on the 10th and won't have the money to cover it until you're paid on the 30th, you'll definitely want to use Quicken's postdating facility. Unlike a checkbook, Quicken can help you synchronize your payment dates with your expected cash inflow dates.

Playing the float poses some dangers, too. If you postdate checks for later printing, but fail to print them before the bill is due, your vendors can slap you with late charges and interest fees. Often, these penalties far exceed the interest benefits of playing the float. For example, suppose your bank imposes a late charge of 3 percent on any payment that is more than 15 days late. That means a $75 charge on a late payment of your $2,500 mortgage bill. If you forget to print your postdated mortgage check on time, you might earn three extra weeks interest (about $11 at 7.5 percent) but you'll pay $75 in late charges. Clearly, you'll want to avoid this situation.

Delaying payments may also mean that you give up early payment discounts offered by some businesses. Whenever you see the opportunity to save two percent by paying within ten days, you should take the discount—at almost any reasonable rate of return your money might earn elsewhere, paying early is still a better deal.

The bottom line on playing the float is that you should do so sensibly. Don't bother postdating small checks, and make sure you're sufficiently disciplined in your routine to avoid costly mistakes on large transactions.

What Kind of Checks Should I Use?

Quicken supports a variety of sizes and formats for checks, which are obtainable both from Intuit and from other sources. When you are deciding which kind you'd like to use, the basic considerations are

■ *Size*   Your options are standard, payroll/voucher, or wallet-sized checks. Choose payroll/voucher checks ($8^{1}/_{2}$-by-$3^{1}/_{2}$ inches) if you need to attach a stub to each check that records payment information and even how you categorized the transaction. Wallet checks ($2^{5}/_{6}$-by-6 inches, plus a record stub) are designed to fit into small bill envelopes without folding and are the least expensive alternative. Otherwise, order standard checks ($8^{1}/_{2}$-by-$3^{1}/_{2}$ inches).

■ *Printer support*   Continuous-feed or laser checks are available. Continuous checks are for tractor-fed printers, such as most dot-matrix models. Laser checks are stacked as single sheets, suitable for laser printers and many other sheet-fed printers. While standard laser checks cost about the same as continuous-feed checks, you'll pay a 20 to 25 percent premium for laser payroll/voucher checks compared to their continuous counterparts.

■ *Color*   You can choose either blue, green, or maroon checks. Take your pick—they all cost the same. Other colors and styles (such as "antique") may be available, sometimes for more money.

■ *Copies*   One-part, duplicate, or triplicate checks are available. If you're using continuous-feed checks with an impact (that is, dot-matrix) printer, you may want copies of your checks. Order duplicate (two-part) checks for carbonless copies of every check you write. Duplicate checks cost 35 to 45 percent more than one-part checks.

■ *Envelopes*   You may or may not want to use compatible envelopes. If you do order compatible envelopes, the address of each payee will show through a window on the envelope. At 1991 prices, envelopes cost from four to ten cents each from Intuit.

How Should I Number My Quicken Checks?

When you order your Quicken checks, you'll have to specify a starting number for the check series. Most banks now require that the check number appear in special magnetic ink at the bottom of each check, so the check numbers must be preprinted by the check printer. You should choose a starting point well separated from the numbers you use for your manual checks. For example, if your current checkbook shows 1125, you may want to start your Intuit series with the number 3001. With this starting number, you could use 15 handwritten checks per month (plus, of course, additional printed checks from Quicken), which equals 180 per year. This would allow a ten-year gap between the two batches of checks—probably a comfortable margin for you.

MATERIALS

Bills

Accumulate a week or two of household bills, and gather them together for your first check-writing session. Group any bills that are from the same vendor for the same account.

Spend a few moments looking over each bill. If a bill shows an unpaid balance from an earlier billing period, you may want to check your records to see if you've paid the previous balance. Circle the amount that should be paid—it may be the "New Charges" line rather than the "Amount Due."

While you may want to discard the extraneous advertising material that accompanies your bills, do save the envelope. Even if you use Quicken's window envelopes to mail your payments, you'll need the mailing address for your Quicken records. The proper mailing address does not always appear on the bill itself.

Blank Checks

You will need a sufficient number of Quicken checks for your session. Order these checks well ahead of time, using the procedure described later under "Know How to Order Supplies."

PRELIMINARIES

Complete Levels 1 and 2

By now, you should have set up your own account and category structure and become comfortable recording transactions, reconciling bank statements, and running standard reports. In addition, you should know how to memorize and split transactions.

Know How to Order Supplies

At least two weeks before you begin, you should order blank check forms. The most convenient way to do this is through Intuit, the company that developed and now supports Quicken. However, you may want to consult *PC/Computing* and other leading magazines for ads from forms companies that manufacture checks compatible with Quicken.

You can order checks and supplies electronically if you have a modem connecting your computer to a telephone line. Otherwise, Quicken will print an order form that you can use for mailing or telephoning to Intuit's order line. Select Contact Intuit from the Activities menu on the menu bar, and choose Order Supplies from the submenu that appears. You'll find detailed instructions on how to order supplies in Appendix B.

Enter Your Checks

There are some small but important differences between the way you enter checks for printing and the way you enter them for mere recording, as you have done till now. Chief among these is the fact that you may wish to use the Write Checks screen rather than the Register screen when entering your checks.

The Check Screen Method

Only the Write Checks screen allows you to enter addresses and more than one memo line on a transaction. If you're using window envelopes or want to include additional memo information on the check, you'll need to use the Write Checks screen rather than the Register to enter the information.

Set Up an Additional Memo Line

A second memo line is particularly useful for displaying account numbers, which are necessary on your checks but which you may not want to see next to the Memo field in the Register. Save the Memo field for notations that have some meaning for you, such as "Quarterly family membership fee."

To add a second memo line to your checks,

1. From the Main Menu, choose Set Preferences, followed by Checks and Reports Settings. The Checks and Reports Settings window shown in Figure 3.1 will appear.

Figure 3.1   Checks and Reports Settings window

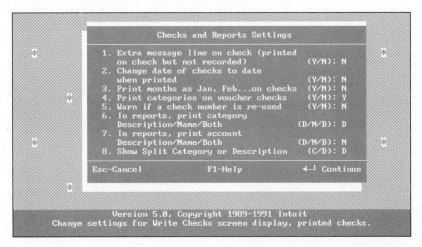

2. For the first setting—Extra message line on check—type **Y** for Yes.

3. Press Ctrl-Enter to leave the window, and then press Escape to return to the Main Menu.

The new memo field will appear on the check as "Msg."

Write Checks

Having gathered your current household bills for this Quicken session, you can settle in to write some checks. Although the information you'll be typing varies a bit from what you've entered in the Register, the entry process should feel somewhat familiar by now.

To write a check that will be printed later,

1. From the Main Menu, select Write/Print Checks, or from the Register, press Ctrl-W (for Write checks). The Write Checks screen will appear (see Figure 3.2).

Figure 3.2 **Write Checks screen**

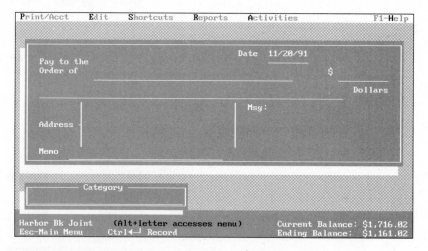

2. Make sure Quicken identifies your main checking account as the current account at the lower-left corner of the screen. If you need to change accounts, press Ctrl-A and choose the correct account from the list.

3. Be sure that an address field, rather than the words "Electronic Payment," appears in the middle of the check on your screen. If you do see "Electronic Payment," you've set up your checking account to work with

Note. Hold down the + and – keys for a moment to change the date several days at a time. You don't have to use the Shift key to get a + symbol; in the Date field, Quicken treats the unshifted = key in the same way as the + key.

Note. The maximum transaction amount Quicken allows is $9,999,999.99. If you are fortunate enough to be entering a seven-figure transaction, however, don't use commas; the maximum transaction with commas is $999,999.99.

CheckFree. Press F9 to indicate that you wish to write paper checks, and the address field will appear.

4. The date on the check will default to today's date. If you want to change it—perhaps to postdate a transaction—you can either type over the date or use the + or – key to change the date one day at a time.

5. Fill in the blanks for payee and amount. Quicken automatically spells out the amount on the next line.

6. If you're using window envelopes, type the payee's name and address in the address block. The payee line doesn't show through the window, so you'll have to repeat it in the address block. To save time, place the cursor on the first line of the address, and press the ditto (") key to automatically repeat the payee name on that line. (The apostrophe (') key also works for this purpose.)

7. After you enter the payee name, press Tab or Enter to move to the Msg field, where you type information that will help the payee identify the payment. This might be an account number, an invoice number, or your social security number in the case of an income tax payment. You're allowed 24 characters for this memo.

8. After completing the Msg field, press Tab or Enter to return to the address and complete it. Your screen should resemble Figure 3.3.

Figure 3.3 **Check with a mailing address**

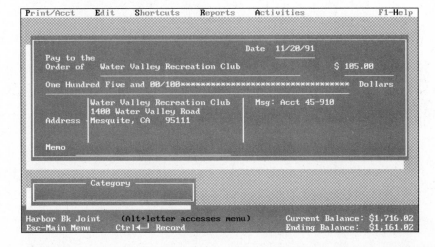

9. In the Memo field, type any notation that will later help you identify the check. As you enter memo items on the transaction, remember that they will actually appear on the printed check; private notes to yourself like "Pain treatment from that quack in the valley" won't be appreciated by the payee.

Note. If you're using a mouse with Quicken, clicking on the Cat: label will display the Category list; you may point to the category of your choice. For complete mouse instructions, see Appendix A.

10. Use the Category field just as you would if you were entering transactions through the Register screen. Either choose from a list, which you call up by pressing Ctrl-C (for Category), or type part of the category name, and then press Enter to automatically complete the entry. Press Ctrl-S (for Split) to split the transaction among several different categories.

11. Press Ctrl-Enter at the end of the check form to record the check. It will scroll off the top of the screen.

Try bringing the check you entered back to the screen by pressing the PgUp key. The screen should resemble Figure 3.4. You can make changes and corrections by pressing the Tab and Ctrl-Tab keys to move from field to field, by pressing Ctrl-Backspace to blank the field before retyping, or by positioning the cursor with the arrow keys and typing over the existing entries.

Figure 3.4   **Completed check**

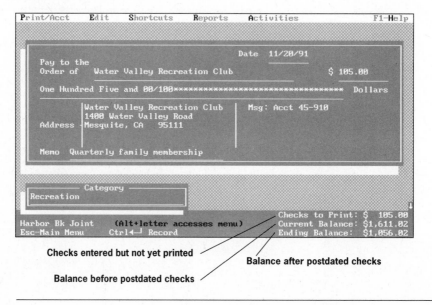

Checks entered but not yet printed

Balance after postdated checks

Balance before postdated checks

Note the numbers in the lower-right corner of the screen. If you post-dated this check—or any previous check in the Register—these three amounts will be displayed:

■ *Checks to Print*   This amount is the total of all the checks you've entered but have not yet printed. It will also include any unprinted checks from previous sessions.

■ *Current Balance*   This amount shows the balance in this account before all postdated checks have been deducted.

■ *Ending Balance*   This amount shows the balance in the account after all postdated transactions have been deducted.

Press Ctrl-R (for Register) to view the Register screen and the new transaction (see Figure 3.5). Note that a line of asterisks appears in the NUM column next to the transaction. The program will assign the check number when you print the checks. Note, too, that the Address and Msg fields do not appear in the Register. Quicken stores the contents of these fields until you print the checks, and then discards the information unless you tell it to memorize the transaction.

Figure 3.5   **Register showing a transaction entered via the Write Checks screen**

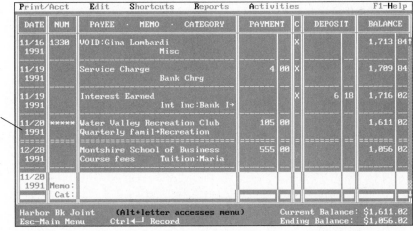

Unprinted check

Register Method

If you don't need to enter an address and message, you may find it easier to enter checks from the Register. Simply enter the information as you did when you entered historical transactions into your Register in Level 2, but with one difference: Type an asterisk (*) into the NUM (check number) column, and that field will instantly fill with asterisks, identifying the current Register entry as a paper check to be printed. Enter the rest of the information as usual and press Ctrl-Enter to record the transaction. If you then want to examine your work on the Write Checks screen, you may do so by pressing Ctrl-W (for Write checks).

Memorize Transactions for Check Writing

Level 2 demonstrated the tremendous amount of time that memorizing transactions can save you when you are entering preexisting transactions. Those time savings are magnified manyfold when you apply them to check writing.

What Memorization Does for You

Quicken can memorize all the details of a transaction except the check number and date. In the case of a printed check with a complicated address block, this can amount to more than a hundred keystrokes. Having memorized a check, you can apply the memorized transaction in just a few keystrokes the next time you write a check to the same payee.

Identify any payee you're likely to be paying again anytime in the future. Even someone you'll only pay once a year is a prospect for a memorized transaction.

Another form of memorization—the *transaction group*—can be used to automate payments that are made at regular intervals for a consistent amount of money each time. Using a transaction group, you can identify all the bills that are due at the beginning of the month—mortgage, car loan, cable TV, and so on—and pay them all automatically with just a few keystrokes. Clearly, this is another way Quicken can save you quite a bit of time.

Memorize Check Transactions

When you memorize a transaction, Quicken stores a copy of that transaction in a special list from which it can later be recalled and applied. The copy should contain any data that is likely to remain constant over time, including the amount. For the memorized transaction to include the address and message lines, you must memorize it in the Write Checks screen.

To enter and memorize a new transaction in the Write Checks screen,

1. Press Ctrl-W to move to the Write Checks screen.

2. Enter the check you want to memorize, excluding the information that won't remain constant over time—the account or category, for example.

3. Press Ctrl-M (for Memorize). You can also select Memorize Transaction from the Shortcuts menu on the Main Menu bar.

4. Quicken informs you that it is about to memorize the transaction and highlights the data that will be memorized (see Figure 3.6).

Figure 3.6   **Write Checks screen about to be memorized**

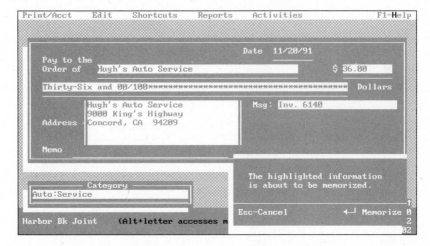

5. Press Enter to confirm that Quicken should memorize the transaction.

6. Press the Ctrl-Tab key to move back and fill in the Amount field for the transaction you're entering (assuming you left it blank).

7. Press Ctrl-Enter to record the transaction.

As is the case when you are memorizing historical transactions, you may sometimes want to leave the Category field empty before you memorize a transaction. For example, if you repeatedly write a check to the same payee—such as a credit card company—but need to split the transaction differently each time, you should leave the Category field blank.

To memorize checks that you've already entered and recorded,

1. In the Register, press PgUp or PgDn to review your transactions and decide which ones you want to memorize.

2. Move to the first transaction you want, and press Ctrl-M (for Memorize). You can also select Memorize Transaction from the Shortcuts menu on the Main Menu bar.

3. Quicken informs you that it's about to memorize the transaction and highlights the data that will be memorized.

4. Press Enter to confirm that Quicken should memorize the transaction.

Setting Up a Transaction Group

If you have regular payments that are always the same amount—particularly monthly payments that are all due on the same day—a transaction group is the most efficient way to handle them.

A transaction group consists of recurring transactions that are all due on the same schedule. Once you inform Quicken of this schedule, it reminds you when these payments are supposed to be made and lets you enter all these checks in a single operation. You can have up to twelve transaction groups, so you may even want to use some single-entry transaction groups to remind you when certain payments are due each month.

To set up a transaction group, you must already have memorized the transactions you want to be part of the group. If you want the transaction group to produce checks that include addresses and message lines, you must memorize each transaction on the Write Checks screen.

To set up a transaction group,

1. Make sure the transactions you want to include are memorized. If they are not, memorize them now.

2. Select Transaction Groups from the Shortcuts menu (Alt-S), or press Ctrl-J. The Select Transaction Group to Execute screen shown in Figure 3.7 appears.

Figure 3.7   Select Transaction Group to Execute screen

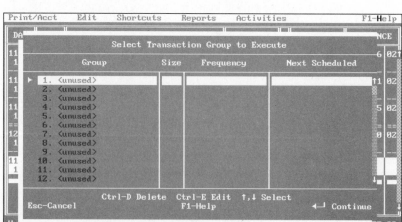

3. Select the first <unused> group by pressing Enter.

4. The Describe Group 1 window will appear (see Figure 3.8). Type a descriptive name for the transaction group, such as "Auto loans," and press Enter.

Figure 3.8   **Describe Group 1 window**

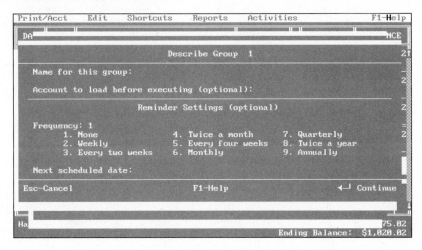

5. You now have the option of specifying the account Quicken should use to execute this group. If you wish to do so, type the account and press Enter.

6. If you need to enter a number representing the frequency of payments for this group, do so.

7. Type the date for the next scheduled payment, and press Enter. The Assign Transactions to Group 1 window appears, as shown in Figure 3.9.

8. Using the Up and Down Arrow keys to move among the transactions, press the spacebar to mark each one that you want to include in this transaction group. For each marked transaction, Quicken places the number of the transaction group in the Group column. Press Enter when you've marked them all.

9. As a final confirmation, Quicken tells you how many transactions are in the group, their frequency, and the next scheduled payment date. Press Escape to return to the Register screen.

Figure 3.9   **Assign Transactions to Group 1 window**

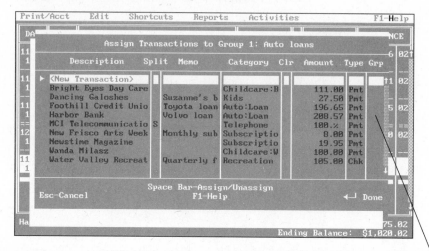

Marking transactions will place group number here

Remember that the next scheduled date should be the day when you want to print the check, not the day the payment is actually due. You must allow time to print the check, mail it, and have it credited to your account.

The payments that you want to include in the transaction group may be historical transactions that you created in the Register that don't include addresses. If you need to add an address to a transaction before including it in a group, follow these steps:

1. Memorize the transaction as usual, by pressing Ctrl-M.

2. Press Ctrl-W to move to the Write Checks screen; then press PgDn to display a blank check.

3. Press Ctrl-T to display the list of memorized transactions. Select the transaction that you just memorized to bring it into the Write Checks screen.

4. Press Enter or Tab to move to the address and to the message line, if necessary.

5. Memorize the modified transaction by pressing Ctrl-M. Quicken will notify you that it is about to memorize the information. Press Enter.

6. When Quicken tells you that the transaction has been memorized, select Replace.

7. Press Ctrl-D (for Delete) to delete the transaction from the Write Checks screen.

Memorized Transactions in Your Check-Writing Routine

The quickest way to apply memorized transactions is to begin typing the payee's name and then press Ctrl-E (for Entry). If you've uniquely identified a memorized transaction, Quicken will enter all the memorized data into the Write Checks screen. If the match fails, you'll see the Memorized Transactions list, from which you can pick the appropriate transaction.

Several days before a transaction group is due, Quicken begins alerting you that the due date is approaching. This reminder takes the form of a warning notice that appears at the bottom of the screen when you first load Quicken (see Figure 3.10).

Note. You may set the number of days in advance that you want to be warned of scheduled transaction groups. For instructions, see the discussion of Billminder later in this level.

Figure 3.10 **Transaction group due warning**

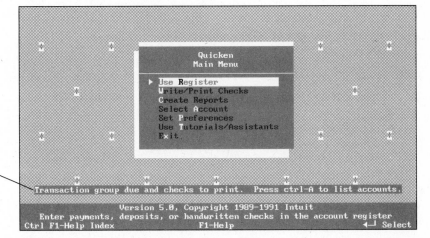

Warning appears here

To apply a transaction group,

1. From the Write Checks screen or the Register, press Ctrl-J, or select Transaction Groups from the Shortcuts menu (Alt-S). The Select Transaction Group to Execute window shown in Figure 3.11 appears, listing all the transaction groups you have set up.

2. Select the group you want to execute by highlighting it and pressing Enter.

3. Quicken displays the due date for the transaction group. This is the date that is printed on the checks. Edit it if necessary, and then press Enter.

Figure 3.11   **Select Transaction Group to Execute window**

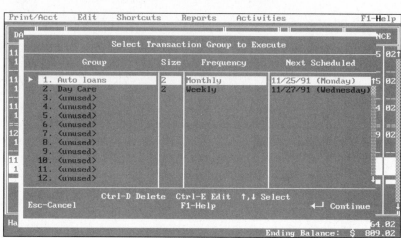

4. Quicken records the transactions and displays the following message reminding you to check the new transactions in the Register:

Press Enter to display the Register.

Note. If no asterisk appears in the Register's NUM column next to a transaction that was part of a group, it means you memorized the transaction in the Register rather than the Write Checks screen. Edit the memorized transaction to place an asterisk (*) in the NUM column.

The new transactions show all the information you memorized except the addresses and any second memo lines, which are only displayed in the Write Checks screen. Asterisks appear in the NUM column. This is the time to add any missing amounts and otherwise edit the transactions as necessary. You can always move to the Write Checks screen to see the address and memo lines. To do so, place the cursor on the transaction and press Ctrl-W.

Once you've made transaction groups part of your regular routine, you may wonder how you survived without them; however, for transaction groups to be effective, you must use Quicken regularly enough to ensure that you receive warnings of impending due dates well in advance. If you are reminded of a payment for the first time *after* the payment is due, you should either use Quicken more frequently, reduce the time until the next scheduled transaction date, or lengthen the warning period before a transaction group comes due.

Use Billminder to Best Advantage

If you use Quicken less frequently than twice a week, you may want to install an auxiliary program called Billminder into your AUTOEXEC batch file—the program which is run each time you start your computer. Intuit supplies Billminder with Quicken, and if you followed the installation suggestions in Appendix A, it was added to your AUTOEXEC file when you installed Quicken.

Every time you start your computer, Billminder checks for pending transaction groups and for checks that must be printed soon. If any of these fall within the warning period you've set, Billminder issues a warning notice, which you'll see before you begin working in a file.

The key is to set the number of days for the warning period to exceed either the maximum number of days you'll go between Quicken sessions, or the maximum number of days you'll go without rebooting your computer, whichever is fewer.

To set the warning period for pending transaction groups and printed checks,

1. Select Set Preferences from the Main Menu; then select Automatic Reminder Settings. You'll see the screen shown in Figure 3.12.

Figure 3.12   Automatic Reminder Settings screen

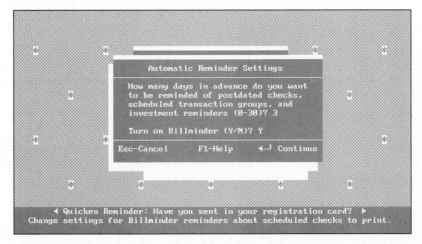

2. Change setting 5, Days in advance to remind yourself of postdated checks and scheduled groups. Type a number between **0** and **30** to indicate how much advance notice you want, and then press Enter.

3. Type **Y** to activate Billminder.

4. Press Ctrl-Enter to return to the Set Preferences window and then Escape to return to the Main Menu.

Unlike many programs in your AUTOEXEC.BAT file, Billminder is not a memory-resident program. Therefore, you don't need to worry about it interfering with other programs. Should you ever need to remove it from your computer's start-up routine, you may do so by deleting the line containing Billminder from your AUTOEXEC.BAT file with any text editing program.

Print Checks for the First Time

Because no one is likely to keep a printer loaded with checks all the time, Quicken's designers had to come up with an easy, reliable way to load checks into the printer and align those checks for very predictable printed results.

Before you use Quicken to print checks for the first time, you should print some samples and give Quicken a chance to adapt to your printer.

Set Up the Printer

Unless you've changed the settings during the installation process, Quicken expects you to be using a tractor-feed printer, set to print characters at ten per inch and connected to a parallel printer port (LPT1). If this matches your configuration, make sure the printer is on and that it is securely connected to your computer's parallel port.

If you have a laser printer or if your printer is connected to a port other than LPT1 (such as a serial port), check the installation notes for proper setup procedures. In any case, be sure the printer is on and securely connected.

You'll also want to check and adjust the settings for printing your checks. To do so, press Escape repeatedly until you reach the Main Menu, then choose Set Preferences, followed by Checks & Reports Settings. The Checks and Reports Settings window shown in Figure 3.13 will appear, offering the following choices:

■ *Extra message line on check*   This choice is normally set to N for No. Type **Y** (for Yes) if you want an extra message block to be printed on your checks to the right of the address block. This can be used for extra memo material that will print with your checks, but will not be recorded.

Figure 3.13   Checks and Reports Settings screen

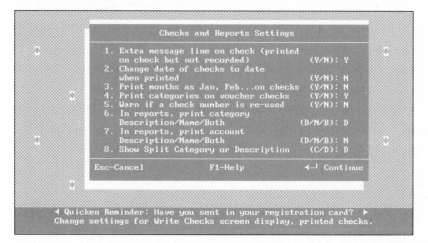

- *Change date of checks to date when printed*   This setting is normally N. Choose **Y** if you always want Quicken to use the current date on checks when they're printed, rather than the date you designated when you entered the checks. If you don't answer Y, you'll have to change the date of postdated checks manually if you decide to pay earlier than expected.

- *Print months as Jan, Feb ... on checks*   Type **Y** to print dates as Jan 15, 1992 rather than 01/15/92.

- *Print categories on voucher checks*   This is normally set to Y, which means your personal categorization scheme will be exposed for all the world (or at least your payees) to see. Individuals may prefer to omit categories, but for small businesses, they may be necessary, especially if Quicken is being used to print payroll checks.

- *Warn if a check number is reused*   This is normally set to N. Answer **Y** if you want a helpful safety net against entering check numbers twice. If you're using Quicken over a number of years, however, natural overlaps in check numbers may occur, and this feature would then become a bother.

- *In reports, print category Description/Name/Both*   This is normally set to D. Type **N** if you want reports to show only the category name, or **B** to show both.

■ *In reports, print account Description/Name/Both*   This setting is usually set to N. Type **D** for reports to show any account description instead of the name; **B** results in both being printed.

■ *Show Split Category or Description*   This is usually set to D. Type **C** if you want reports to show category assignments for split transaction detail.

The remaining set-up option is for use with reports. For now, press Ctrl-Enter to complete the window and return to your work.

Load the Checks

Remove the paper currently in your printer, and replace it with the sample standard checks that Intuit supplies with Quicken. Make sure your printer is on-line. Load the paper exactly as you would if you were about to print a document starting on the first page. Mark the printer (perhaps with a small piece of tape) to show the correct alignment for the top of the paper. This will help you load the paper consistently each time, which is the key to aligning checks precisely the same from session to session.

If you're using a laser printer, you can still use the sample checks supplied with Quicken even though they're designed as continuous-feed checks. Simply remove the tractor-hole strips on each side and separate the checks into groups of three; three checks will fit in your paper tray just as though they were standard sheets of 8½-by-11-inch paper.

In either case, be sure your printer is on-line and ready to print.

Print a Sample

Quicken uses an alignment process so innovative that Intuit has patented its design. The process requires you to print at least one sample check the first time you use a particular printer with Quicken. After making some simple adjustments, you can begin printing valid checks. The procedure differs, however, for continuous-feed and laser checks.

To print a sample of continuous-feed checks,

1. View the Write Checks screen by pressing Ctrl-W (for Write checks).

2. Press PgUp if necessary to view a check that is ready to print. If no checks are ready to print, record a blank check for the purpose of printing a sample.

3. Press Ctrl-P (for Print) to tell Quicken that you want to print checks. The Print Checks window shown in Figure 3.14 will appear.

4. You shouldn't need to change any of the settings in this window to print a sample; they will be set to print standard checks on the check printer you specified when you installed Quicken. If you don't have any standard

checks for printing a sample, you can change the check size by specifying a new check type.

5. Press F9 to print a sample check; then press Enter to move past the message that appears. Don't worry if the text doesn't fall exactly where you expect it to; you're about to tell Quicken how to reposition the text lines on your next check.

Figure 3.14 **Print Checks window**

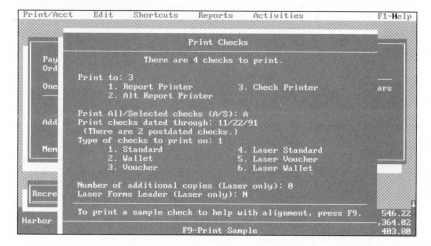

6. The screen now displays the Type Position Number window shown in Figure 3.15. Without moving the printed check or adjusting the printer in any way, examine the voided sample check, which should resemble Figure 3.16. If the printed text sits just above the lines and the check looks good to you, press Enter to tell Quicken that printing was successful. If your check printed correctly, you are now finished with the sample routine and ready to print checks.

7. If the printed text is too high or too low, note where the pointer line arrow falls on the vertical scale along the edge of the checks. The number the arrow points to is the *position number*.

8. Enter the position number in the window on your screen and press Enter. Quicken will print another check, which should be precisely aligned vertically. If the check needs any further vertical adjustment, repeat this step.

Figure 3.15 **Type Position Number window**

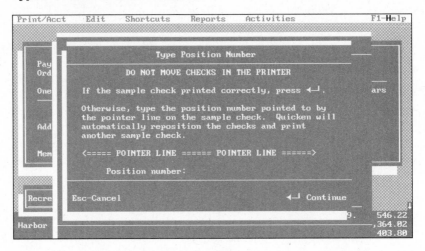

Figure 3.16 **Sample check**

9. If necessary, adjust the horizontal alignment by moving the tractor sprockets on your printer to the left or right. If you readjust these for some other application later, you'll want to mark their current position so you can load your Quicken checks without printing another sample.

10. Make adjustments and print samples until you're satisfied; then, without entering a number at the position number blank, press Enter to exit the sample-printing routine. You're now ready to print checks.

Laser checks require a slightly different approach, because laser printers are prealigned.

To print a sample check on a laser printer,

Note. It's easy to forget which way to load checks into your laser printer (face down or face up, head or foot first?). Once you've determined the correct orientation, draw a picture on the laser check box.

1. Display the Write Checks screen by pressing Ctrl-W (for Write checks).

2. If you have no checks ready to print, record a blank check for the purpose of printing a sample.

3. Press Ctrl-P (for Print) to tell Quicken you want to print checks. The Print Checks window, shown previously in Figure 3.14, will appear.

4. Be sure Quicken is set up to print standard checks on your laser printer.

5. Press F9 to print a sample check.

6. Because a laser printer is designed for consistent alignment, your sample check should print correctly without further adjustment. If it doesn't, check the installation notes in Appendix A to verify that your printer is set up properly.

Once you've printed samples and entered the alignment numbers, you shouldn't need to print samples again unless you change printers.

Advance to Painless Check Printing

Now that you've given Quicken the information it needs to produce consistent results, printing is quite straightforward. Just follow the five simple steps outlined in this section.

Set Up the Printer and Load the Checks

The first step in printing is always to verify that your printer is ready and waiting, loaded with your checks. To accomplish this,

1. Note the preprinted number of the first check. You'll need to enter this check number later on.

2. Load your checks into the printer. If you're using continuous checks, make sure you follow the alignment marks (both vertical and horizontal) that you made while printing your sample checks. If you're using laser checks, stack the check pages as you would stack letterhead stationery.

3. Make sure the printer is turned on, securely connected to the proper printer port, and on-line.

Choose the Checks to Print

If you've entered several checks in the Write Checks screen, you probably won't want to print them all during one session. Of course, Quicken *can* print the entire batch, but it's easy to be selective; you can mark the checks you want to print on a list, or you can specify a cut-off date, as follows:

1. From the Write Checks screen, press Ctrl-P (for Print) to bring up the Print Checks window. Check that the proper printer is selected.

2. If you want to pick and choose among the checks that are ready to print, type **S** (selected) in the blank marked Print All/Selected Checks; then press Enter. The Select Checks to Print window appears, displaying a list of all pending checks (see Figure 3.17). The right-most column indicates that Quicken has preselected for printing all checks dated through the date on the Print Checks window, which should be the current date. Use your cursor keys to move up and down through the list, using the space-bar to select or deselect the checks you want to print. When you're satisfied with the list of specific checks to be printed, press Enter.

Figure 3.17   Select Checks to Print window

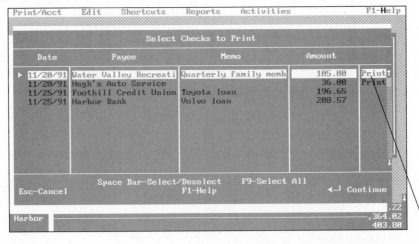

Selecting a check displays the word "Print" here

3. Alternatively, to select a series of checks for printing, type **A** after Print All/Selected Checks. If you have any postdated checks, Quicken will prompt you for a cut-off date. Any checks with dates after the date you specify will not be printed in this session.

4. Be sure you have the proper type of check selected. (If you're using wallet or laser wallet checks, Quicken may warn you that the current print style is too big for these smaller checks.) Press Enter to complete the Print Checks window.

Start Printing

Quicken has no way of knowing what check you have loaded in the printer. You must provide the check number before you can begin to print.

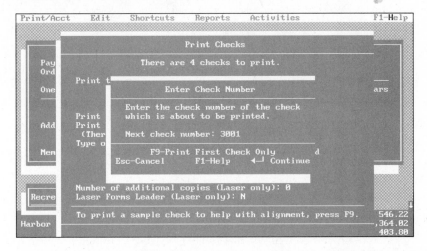

Note. You can adjust the check number easily by using the + and − keys.

After you've completed the Print Checks window, Quicken will request the number of the check that is about to be printed (remember, your checks will be prenumbered). Quicken prompts you with the next check number it expects you to use, as shown in Figure 3.18.

Figure 3.18   **Enter Check Number window**

```
 Print/Acct    Edit    Shortcuts    Reports    Activities            F1-Help
┌──────────────────────────────────────────────────────────────────────┐
│                              Print Checks                              │
│  Pay            There are 4 checks to print.                          │
│  Ord                                                                   │
│  One    Print t┌────────────────────────────────────────┐       ars   │
│                │           Enter Check Number            │             │
│                │  Enter the check number of the check    │             │
│  Add    Print  │  which is about to be printed.          │             │
│         Print  │                                         │             │
│         (Ther  │  Next check number: 3001                │             │
│         Type o │                                         │             │
│  Mem           │         F9-Print First Check Only       │d            │
│                │  Esc-Cancel      F1-Help   ◄─┘ Continue │             │
│                └────────────────────────────────────────┘             │
│         Number of additional copies (Laser only): 0                   │
│  Recre  Laser Forms Leader (Laser only): N                            │
│                                                                        │
│         To print a sample check to help with alignment, press F9.  546.22 │
│  Harbor                                                              ,364.02 │
│                                                                     403.80 │
└──────────────────────────────────────────────────────────────────────┘
```

Note. Some printers store as much as a page of information in advance of printing it and will continue printing even after you press the Escape key. To save valuable check paper, you may want to turn off the printer's power to stop the printing immediately.

If you're confident that your printer alignment is properly set up, press Enter to print the whole series of checks. Otherwise, press F9 to print only the first check in the series.

If the checks jam while printing or if anything else goes wrong, press the Escape key to stop the flow of data to the printer. Pressing Escape again will cancel the printing process, and Quicken will return to the Print Checks screen.

Examine Your Checks

Once the printer stops, Quicken will ask if the checks have been printed correctly (see Figure 3.19). Before you respond, examine each check carefully to be certain both the information and the alignment are correct. If all the checks have been printed properly, press Enter to complete the process. If any have not, you'll need to reprint them.

Figure 3.19   Did Checks Print OK? window

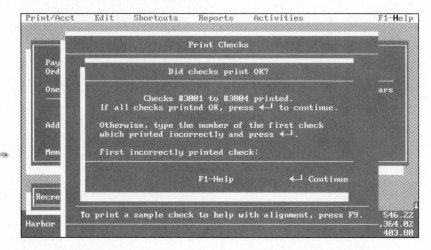

Reprint if Necessary

In the event of a printing mishap, Quicken can immediately reprint the checks you specify. Follow these steps to print:

Note. When you reprint a bad check, a new number is assigned to it. The bad check number will be forever missing from your check series.

1. Type the number of the first check that either did not print or did not print correctly.

2. Tear up and discard the bad check, plus any others that were printed after it. Quicken restores the check you indicated, plus all subsequent checks, to unprinted status.

3. Correct the problem.

4. Follow the procedure for printing checks again; be sure you identify the correct starting check number.

Note. Remember that the address block disappears from the record once you've printed a check. Unless you memorized it, you must reenter the address.

If you ever need to reprint a check—for example, if you drop one in a puddle and want a clean copy to send—you may do so by finding the transaction in the Register, typing an asterisk in the NUM (check number) column, opening the Write Checks screen, and printing the check as usual. If you need a record of the original transaction, you should void the original check by pressing Ctrl-V and then Enter and print an entirely new one. This might be necessary, for example, if a payee loses a check and you stop payment. In this case, it's essential that you keep track of the original transaction, so you need to issue a new check with a new number.

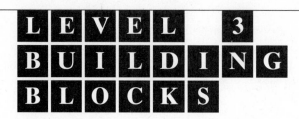

LEVEL 3 BUILDING BLOCKS

In Level 3, you explored writing checks in Quicken and began printing checks.

TECHNIQUES AND PROCEDURES

■ Enter checks in the Write Checks screen if you want to include the address and second memo line. If you prefer to enter checks in the Register, be sure to type an asterisk in the NUM column, identifying the transaction as a check to be printed.

■ Memorize transactions to dramatically lessen your check-writing work, because addresses and additional memos are recorded along with everything else. Press Ctrl-M to memorize a transaction or Ctrl-T to retrieve a memorized transaction.

■ Memorize related transactions—for instance, all loans, or all bills due on the 15th of the month—into transaction groups, which allow you to process many transactions at once, whenever they're due. Memorize each transaction individually; then press Ctrl-J. Name the group and select the transactions to be included. Several days in advance of the group's due date, Quicken will display a screen message reminding you to execute the group. When the group comes due, press Ctrl-J and select it to bring the grouped transactions into the Register and print them.

■ A transaction group can also consist of a single transaction. Use this technique for important payment deadlines that you don't want to miss—your mortgage, for example.

■ To refine settings related to printing checks, select Set Preferences from the Main Menu; then select Checks & Reports Settings. You can specify whether Quicken should print the second memo line and the category, indicate whether Quicken should alert you in case of duplicate check numbers, and change the default date formats, if you wish.

■ Printing checks painlessly involves five steps. First, be sure your printer is ready and the checks are loaded. Second, press Ctrl-P to display the Print Checks window and type **A** to print all checks or **S** to print either the ones you select from a list or the ones that precede a specified cut-off date. Third, enter the number of the first check and begin printing. Fourth, examine the printed checks. Fifth, if any checks need to be reprinted, enter the number of the first incorrectly printed check, tear up the bad checks, and reprint.

TERMS

■ A *transaction group* is a set of memorized transactions that Quicken can execute—in other words, enter into the Register and print—all at once on a specified date. You might wish to create a transaction group for all the bills to be paid on the first of the month, for example. When you set up a transaction group, you can specify the frequency of payments and the next payment date so Quicken can give you prior warnings when the group is coming due.

■ *Billminder* is a program supplied with Quicken that can serve as your bill paying alarm clock. When you start your computer, Billminder lets you know if any transaction groups will soon be due or if there are any checks to print. Billminder should be installed when you install Quicken; it loads through your AUTOEXEC.BAT file.

■ *Postdating* a transaction means entering it in the Register with a date later than the current date, and without a check number. When you're ready to print the check, enter an asterisk into the NUM column and the transaction will appear in the Write Checks screen as an unprinted check. People post-date checks to manage cash flow or to ensure that they earn the maximum possible interest on money earmarked for future bills.

IMPORTANT IDEAS

■ As you begin issuing checks in two distinct ways—writing them by hand away from your home or business and printing them with Quicken—you'll need to set up your numbering system to accommodate two sets of numbers. Estimate approximately how many checks of each type you'll use per year; then give yourself several years' leeway.

■ A check printed by Quicken can have more information on it than a check you write by hand. Including the mailing address on the check will save time, especially if you use envelopes with address windows. Checks printed by Quicken can also include a second memo line, which is useful for identifying account numbers or for other notes.

■ Transaction groups are powerful tools for reminding you about transactions that come due periodically. They are the next logical step beyond memorizing transactions. Using a transaction group, you can actually pay a large number of monthly bills all at once with one brief series of keystrokes. To get the most out of Quicken, look for every opportunity to create and use transaction groups.

■ Quicken can alert you either to the upcoming due date of a transaction group or to the presence of unprinted checks. When you start Quicken, you'll see a message on the Main Menu screen if a transaction group will be due soon or if there are unprinted checks. You can also depend on Billminder (installed with Quicken), to alert you to these things when you turn on your computer, whether or not you load Quicken.

4

Make Payments Electronically

PLAN AHEAD

DECISIONS

Should You Use Electronic Payments?

Let's face it: bill paying is an unpleasant chore. Most people open the bill, write a check by hand, stuff the envelope, hunt for a stamp, and trudge down to the nearest post office box to pay their bills. Even the most efficient people can't avoid investing between three and five minutes for every bill they pay. If you use Quicken and the Level 3 check printing method, you'll realize the benefits of capturing data on your personal computer, but you'll rarely cut a lot of time out of processing and mailing your routine bill payments; you still have to print them, stuff them, lick them, and mail them.

To save time both preparing your payments and capturing the data, consider paying your bills electronically using the CheckFree method built into Quicken 5. You'll probably need to invest more time up-front planning and experimenting, but later this investment will pay off handsomely by cutting the time you spend paying each bill to less than a minute.

The economics are reasonably straightforward: as of mid-1991, Check-Free charged an average of 45 cents per transaction for someone who makes 30 CheckFree transactions per month. This compares with about 40 cents per transaction for writing and mailing a normal Quicken check (11 cents for the check and 29 cents for the stamp). While electronic payments cost 5 cents more in this scenario, they typically save at least two minutes for each payment: if your time is worth more than $1.50 per hour, you're ahead using CheckFree. Furthermore, the interest on the extra float can mount up, as you'll discover in this level. At much higher volumes—50 or more payments per month—paying bills with CheckFree costs just about the same as printing paper checks.

When Should You Use Electronic Payments?

Almost any bill you pay can be handled through CheckFree—from a major bank credit card payment to a weekly charge for lawnmowing services. Any vendor ("merchant" in CheckFree parlance) to whom you write a check today can accept a CheckFree transaction. After all, CheckFree completes most transactions by printing and mailing a check from its Ohio processing center in much the same way you would with Quicken.

Given the processing and initial setup time necessary for each new merchant, however, CheckFree is best applied to situations in which you will be paying the same merchant more than once, and the payments will not be due immediately on demand. Continue to use hand-written checks when you go to the grocery store, for example, or when it's critical that the check be received within the next five business days (as in the case of late December charitable contributions, which you want to have credited in the current tax year).

Should You Use Both Printed and Electronic Checks?

Printed and electronic checks are not mutually exclusive within a given bank account; an account that is set up for CheckFree can also be used to print checks on an ad hoc basis. However, occasions for doing this should be rare, such as those end-of-year charitable contributions mentioned earlier. You're better off sticking to CheckFree, and handwriting checks for exceptions such as last-minute payments.

MATERIALS

Special Equipment: A Modem

To use CheckFree, your computer must be equipped with a modem and whatever wiring is necessary to connect your PC to the telephone lines. If you're traveling with a laptop or notebook computer and wish to transmit a CheckFree payment, you will probably need to carry a length of telephone wire that has the appropriate modular connectors on both ends.

CheckFree Start-Up Letter

You'll receive a start-up letter about two weeks after signing up with Check-Free (see "Sign Up with CheckFree" in this level). The first time you use CheckFree in Quicken, you should have on hand the three numbers Check-Free supplies in this letter: the access telephone number, your identification number (probably your social security number unless you have multiple CheckFree accounts), and your four-digit account number/security code.

You should also note in your start-up letter the maximum communications speed for the access telephone number supplied by CheckFree. Sometimes this number will be less than the top speed of your modem, the only consequence of which is that your modem will communicate more slowly than usual.

Bills

Choose a few "safe" bills for your first CheckFree payments, bills that have a due date at least two weeks away and no substantial penalties for late payment. In addition, you should chose bills owed to merchants with whom your credit standing is good. While most CheckFree startups go smoothly, it's best to start slowly and carefully when you're changing a process as fundamental as how you distribute your money.

Check the amounts you'll be paying. Are there outstanding payments that you've made, but have not yet been credited to your account? On the invoices, circle the amount you intend to pay; this will make things go more quickly when you're at your keyboard entering a stack of bills.

PRELIMINARIES

Complete Levels 1, 2, and 3

By now, you should have your own account and category structure set up and be comfortable recording transactions, reconciling bank statements, and obtaining standard reports. In addition, you should know how to memorize and split transactions.

It's also a good idea to read Level 3 if you haven't already. Several important concepts covered in that level—such as transaction groups—are equally applicable to electronic payments.

Sign Up with CheckFree

In your Quicken package, you'll find a new service form inviting you to sign up for CheckFree. If you don't have this form for some reason, call Check-Free's sales department at (800) 882-5280 and ask them to send you one. The service form requests five types of information:

■ *Computer configuration specifications (RAM and floppy disk size)*   This is largely irrelevant for those who use CheckFree with Quicken; if you've successfully installed Quicken, you have all the RAM and software necessary to run CheckFree.

■ *Personal information (name, address, and social security number)*   Check-Free uses your social security number as your account number. If you open a second CheckFree account, the company will assign you a second nine-digit identification number to use with the second account.

■ *Credit card information (account number and expiration date)*   This number will be used only when you overdraw your checking account with a CheckFree payment. In many cases, the merchant will receive the money before the overdraft is detected, because the money is actually drawn on CheckFree Corporation's bank account. CheckFree keeps your credit card information to ensure repayment in case you have insufficient funds in your bank account.

■ *A four-digit CheckFree account number/security code*   This is a number that you choose, similar to the Personal Identification Number (PIN) that you use with automated teller machines. Protect this number as carefully as you would any password or PIN.

■ *Bank account information and authorization*   You need to supply Check-Free with detailed information on the checking account you plan to use with

CheckFree. Most of the details of the account—such as account numbers and electronic codes required by the Federal Reserve System—actually appear on the face of a voided blank check, which you're asked to submit with the service form. You are also asked to sign a statement authorizing your bank to post your bill paying transactions from CheckFree to your bank account.

Send the service form to CheckFree using the envelope provided with your Quicken package. Don't forget to include a voided blank check. In about two weeks, you'll receive a start-up letter from CheckFree containing your account number and telephone numbers for accessing CheckFree.

Check Your Computer's Time and Date

Before starting Quicken, check and, if necessary, correct the system time and date on your computer. Quicken uses this information to schedule Check-Free payments. Any inaccuracies here may cause Quicken to be inaccurate in reporting how soon a bill can be paid.

To set the system date from the DOS system prompt, simply type **DATE**. If the displayed date is correct, press Enter. If not, type the new date (in the form 12-15-91), and then press Enter.

To set the system time, type **TIME**. To enter a new time, type it using a 24-hour clock (3:22 p.m. would be entered as 15:22) and then press Enter. If the time displayed is accurate, you can simply press Enter without changing it.

Turn On the Electronic Payments Option

Quicken hides most of the menu choices covering electronic payments until you inform the program that you will be using CheckFree to pay your bills. To set up for electronic payment, begin by choosing Set Preferences in Quicken's Main Menu; then choose Electronic Payment Settings. Quicken displays a window with two additional options: Modem Settings and Account Settings. You must specify both of these settings.

Modem Settings

Establish your modem settings by choosing Modem Settings. Quicken displays the Electronic Payment Settings window, shown in Figure 4.1.

Figure 4.1   **Electronic Payment Settings window**

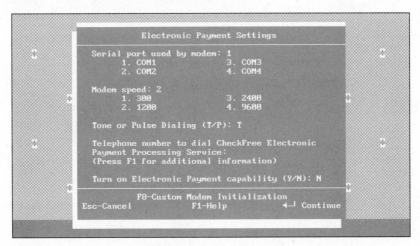

This window requires you to enter five types of information. To complete the settings in this window, follow these steps:

1. Specify the serial port number of your modem. If your modem is connected to COM1, press Enter to select it; otherwise, type the appropriate number and press Enter.

2. Indicate your modem speed by typing the appropriate number, then press Enter. Use your modem's maximum rated speed or the speed specified by your CheckFree start-up kit, whichever is lower.

Note. If you have a call waiting feature on your telephone service, you may want to disable it temporarily when you call CheckFree, so your transmissions won't be interrupted. In most areas, you can accomplish this by preceding the telephone number with the characters *70, (the comma signifies a one-second pause).

3. Enter your dialing method. Type **T** for touch-tone, or **P** for pulse or rotary, then press Enter.

4. Type the access number supplied by CheckFree, preceded by any extra digits you might need to dial to obtain an outside telephone line. For example, if you normally need to dial 9 to reach an outside line, type **9** followed by a comma (to indicate a pause); then press Enter.

5. Type **Y** (for Yes) in answer to the prompt "Turn on Electronic Payment capability?" Press Enter to leave the window.

Most modems in use today are Hayes-compatible and will therefore work with Quicken's communications module. In rare instances, a modem may require different initialization steps from those built into the software. Try Quicken with standard modem settings first; if you have trouble, return to the Electronic Payments Settings window and press F8 to open the Custom Modem Initialization window, shown in Figure 4.2. Your modem manual will list the special codes needed to initialize your particular brand of modem.

Figure 4.2   Custom Modem Initialization window

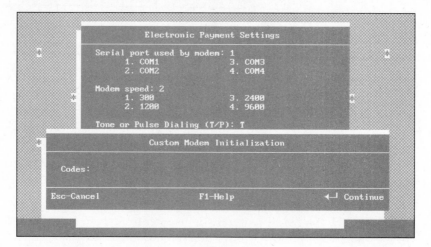

Account Settings

The final step before using CheckFree is setting up one of your Quicken bank accounts for electronic payment. You may use only existing bank accounts with CheckFree; if you're using a bank account that will be new to your Quicken file, you must create the account in your Quicken file before you set the parameters for electronic payment.

To complete the settings in the Automatic Settings window, do the following:

1. Choose Account Settings. (From the Main Menu, choose Set Preferences and Electronic Payment Settings; then choose Account Settings.)

2. Choose the bank account you wish to set up for electronic payment by highlighting it and pressing Enter. Then type **Y** and press Enter to confirm that you wish to set up the account for electronic payment. Quicken will display the Electronic Payment Account Settings window, shown in Figure 4.3.

Figure 4.3   **Electronic Payment Account Settings window**

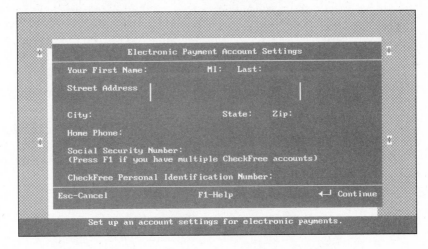

Note. If you try to enter an invalid zip code for the state you entered, Quicken will prevent you from doing so by displaying an error message.

Note. Quicken lets you enter your telephone number in any format (with area code first). After you press Enter, Quicken automatically converts it into the standard (NNN) NNN-NNNN format.

3. In the first nine blanks in the window, enter your name, address, and telephone number. This identifies you to CheckFree when you transmit payments.

4. In the social security number blank, enter either your social security number or, if you have more than one CheckFree account, the alternate nine-digit identifier CheckFree issues to you. To continue, press Enter.

5. Finally, enter the four-digit account number/security code you chose on your service form in the blank marked CheckFree Personal Identification Number and press Enter.

6. When the Set Up Account for Electronic Payment window appears, showing that the account you chose has been activated for electronic payments, press Escape until you return to Quicken's Main Menu.

Note. Electronic check forms have no address block, and contain only one Memory blank.

Once you've completed this setup process, you'll notice two differences in Quicken's behavior: first, on Quicken's pull-down menus several new menu items will appear representing special functions applicable only to electronic payments. Second, anytime you choose to write checks in your electronic bank account, Quicken will display an electronic check form rather than one designed for printed checks.

Avoid the Pitfalls of Electronic Payments

Any time you introduce a new intermediary into your bill paying routine, you're also creating new opportunities for error or misunderstanding. Computer bulletin boards buzz with war stories of missed payments, late charges, and damaged credit ratings, which the injured parties blame on electronic bill paying services. Further examination often reveals, however, that these problems spring from a user who is pushing too far, too fast with electronic transactions, leaving too little room for error, too early in the learning process.

If you follow these simple guidelines, you'll minimize the chances of problems and position yourself to harvest the full benefit of time savings that electronic payment offers:

- To test the waters, issue your first CheckFree payment to yourself. This is the quickest and safest way to detect problems in your account setup or in the way your financial institution handles Quicken transactions.

- Learn how Quicken handles your electronic payments. Even before payments leave your PC in the form of an electronic transmission, Quicken implements several procedures that allow Quicken and CheckFree to work together without mishaps.

- Understand how CheckFree processes payments. Don't be content to treat CheckFree as a black box; the more you know about how the program works, the more efficiently you can make it work for you.

- Remember that electronic payment practices are relatively new to the business world. Help persuade vendors to accept direct electronic payments. Even your newspaper carrier can set up electronic payments to a checking account, by simply filling out some paperwork and notifying the bank. Identify vendors who are slow to credit payments to your account. Talk to them—and to CheckFree—about solving the problem.

- As you add new merchants, double-check and update the vendor information you supply to the service. Many processing difficulties stem from errors in entering vendor names, phone numbers, addresses, or account numbers.

Note. Merchants are often slower to credit the first payment they receive from CheckFree than they are with later payments.

- Understand the importance of correctly assessing the amount of lead-time required to ensure payments will arrive on time. With new vendors, go slowly: specify your first payment to arrive about ten business days before it's actually due. Gradually decrease payment lead-times as you gain experience. It's likely that your merchants will also be learning how to handle these sorts of payments.

- Watch for changes in monthly payment amounts due. Don't be lulled into complacency by the convenience of monthly transaction groups.

- Report trouble promptly to CheckFree's customer service. User feedback is crucial to building an effective electronic-payment system.

The remainder of Level 4 will help you follow these simple guidelines and avoid the most common pitfalls of making payments electronically.

Make Your First Payment to Yourself

Before plunging into electronic payments with real vendors, it pays to experiment by writing and depositing your first check to yourself. This tactic serves a dual purpose: first, it assures that your CheckFree accounts are set up correctly; and second, it teaches you how Quicken handles electronic payments. Since the first month of CheckFree is free of all service charges, it won't cost you anything to follow this strategy.

Note. Don't worry about what it will cost you to write a check to yourself. The first month of CheckFree service is free.

Quicken is designed to make it easy for you to take advantage of Check-Free. Some of the features built into Quicken help you achieve peak efficiency when paying electronically, without compromising your promptness or your paying vendors too early. It's important to understand how Quicken handles these payments. Later in this level, you'll learn what happens after payment transmissions leave your computer—that is, how CheckFree executes your requests for payment.

Within ten days of transmitting a test payment to yourself, you'll be able to determine whether your account is set up correctly and whether your bank can handle CheckFree transactions smoothly. Moreover, you'll see first-hand how your payments will look when merchants receive them, which will help you communicate with vendors who are unfamiliar with this new form of payment.

Learn How Quicken Handles Electronic Transactions

Quicken records electronic transactions in a way very similar to the way it records checks to be printed. There are several important differences, however, in the way it handles electronic checks.

Note. Quicken calculates which days are business days. If you enter a check on a Saturday, Quicken will display the payment date for the following Friday, the fifth business day hence.

■ All checks must be postdated by at least five business days. This is to accommodate the maximum possible delay in interpreting, processing, and sending a payment once CheckFree receives your instructions.

■ Quicken maintains a database on the merchants you pay electronically. For every new merchant you want to include, you enter the merchant's name, address, telephone number, and your account or other identifying number, all of which CheckFree needs to ensure that it pays your bills consistently from month to month. When you add payees, Quicken transmits the new payee information to CheckFree along with your transactions. Changes to payee information and payee deletions are also transmitted to CheckFree.

■ New transactions go to CheckFree at the end of each Quicken session, no matter how many days or months the payment is postdated. Unlike printed checks, Quicken does not hold transactions for payment immediately before the due date. If you attempt to exit Quicken without initiating the transmission, Quicken will give you the warning shown below:

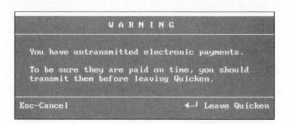

■ At the end of a transmission, Quicken receives from CheckFree a confirmation number for each transaction sent. This confirmation number uniquely identifies the transaction and comes in handy if you ever need to inquire about a payment.

At the end of a session, Quicken calls the CheckFree processing center in Columbus, Ohio (using local or toll free telephone lines) and sends a batch of payment instructions which are stored at CheckFree for later interpretation.

Enter the Transaction

Note. To remind yourself what the printed check form looks like, you can toggle between the electronic and printed form by repeatedly pressing F9.

A prominent change in Quicken's behavior that results from gearing up for electronic payment is the altered appearance of the Write Checks screen (see Figure 4.4).

Notice several important differences from the check image Quicken displays for printed check accounts. First, the default payment date is five business days from the present, rather than today's date. This forces you to allow adequate lead-time for CheckFree to pay the check. Second, there is no place for recording the merchant's address on the check, because you supply it separately. Finally, there is no room for a second memo line, because you provide account numbers when you supply information about the payee to Quicken.

To create an electronic payment to yourself,

1. Call up the Write Checks screen by pressing Ctrl-W.

Figure 4.4   **Write Checks screen for electronic payments**

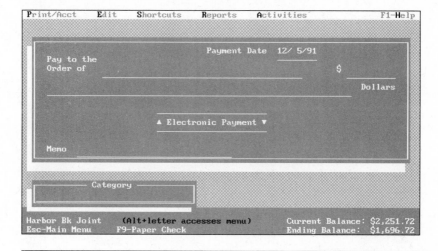

```
 Print/Acct    Edit    Shortcuts    Reports    Activities           F1-Help


                                    Payment Date  12/ 5/91
       Pay to the
       Order of  _____  $
                                                            _____
                                                              Dollars
       _____


                        ▲ Electronic Payment ▼


       Memo   _____



                    Category
       _____


  Harbor Bk Joint    (Alt+letter accesses menu)    Current Balance: $2,251.72
  Esc-Main Menu      F9-Paper Check                 Ending Balance:  $1,696.72
```

Note. Like other bank account transactions, CheckFree payments may be entered through either the Write Checks screen or the Register. You'll learn how to use the faster—albeit less intuitive—Register method later in this level.

2. Check that your electronic bank account is current: the account name should appear in the lower-left corner of the screen.

3. Type the date you want the payment to be made in the date blank. You cannot choose a date earlier than the one dictated by CheckFree's five business-day delay, but you can choose a later date. To receive your test payment as soon as possible, use the date Quicken shows.

4. Type your name in the "Pay to the Order of" blank. Quicken will respond with the following message, reporting that it does not recognize the electronic payee:

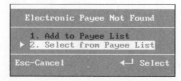

```
  Electronic Payee Not Found

    1. Add to Payee List
  ▶ 2. Select from Payee List

  Esc-Cancel              ◄┘ Select
```

This is not surprising, since you haven't yet entered any electronic merchants. To add your name as a new electronic payee, choose 1 (for Add to Payee List).

5. Your name is automatically transferred to the Set Up Electronic Payee window. Type your address and telephone number in the appropriate blanks. CheckFree requires an account number of at least two characters, which is meaningless in this case. Type whatever you wish; you can use up to 25 characters. The completed window should resemble Figure 4.5.

Figure 4.5   Set Up Electronic Payee window

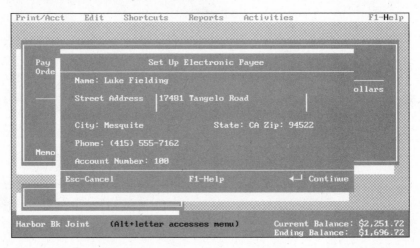

6. In the Write Checks screen, enter the amount you want to pay yourself—for example, $1.00. Quicken automatically fills in the written amount line.

7. Type a message to yourself in the memo field.

8. Categorize the transaction in an appropriate miscellaneous category. See Figure 4.6 for an example of a completed check screen.

9. Record the transaction by pressing Ctrl-Enter.

Of course, you don't actually execute the payment by merely recording it; you must still transmit the payment to CheckFree via telephone. Rather than sending your payments one at a time, Quicken stores a list of pending electronic payments for you to transmit as a group. If you press Ctrl-R to review the Register, you'll see the pending electronic transactions, as displayed in Figure 4.7. The >>>>> symbol in the check number column indicates a payment that has been entered but not yet sent to CheckFree.

Figure 4.6   **Completed electronic check screen**

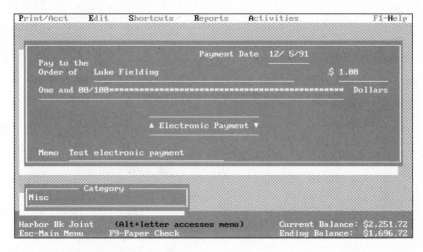

Figure 4.7   **Register with a pending electronic payment**

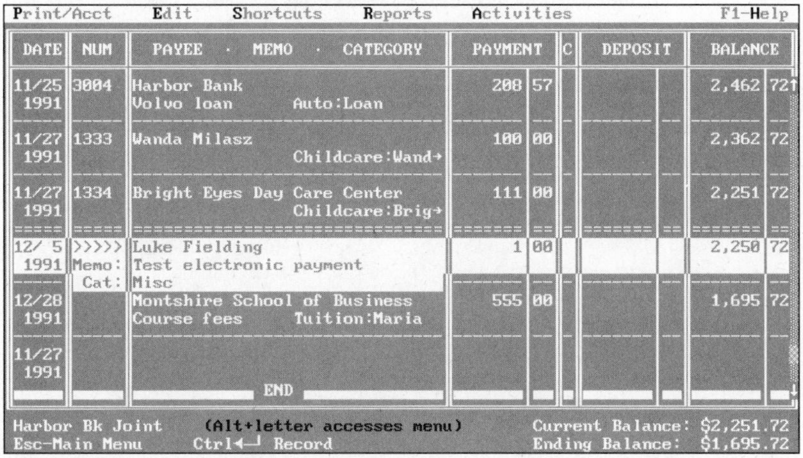

Preview the Transaction

You can preview electronic transactions before you transmit them. This is not only educational while you're learning about CheckFree; it's a good confirmation prior to starting a payment process that can be very difficult to derail. (Think of this precaution as making sure you've written the right amount on a check before you drop the envelope into the corner mailbox; you can't retrieve the payment once you've let it drop.)

To preview the list of pending electronic transactions, press Ctrl-I (for Initiate transmission) from the Register or Write Checks screen in your electronic account. Alternatively, you may choose Transmit Payments from the Print/Acct menu (Alt-P) on the Main Menu bar. Quicken informs you how many payments are pending by displaying the following message:

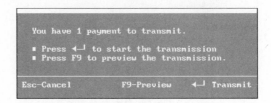

and offers to preview the transmissions for you.

Press F9 and you'll see the Preview Transmission to CheckFree window listing two pending transmissions as in Figure 4.8. In the top portion of the window, Quicken lists the actual payments—in this case, a $1.00 payment to yourself to be made five business days from now. In the bottom portion of the window, Quicken displays additions, deletions, and changes to the merchant list—in this case, an "Add Payee" transmission identifying you as a new electronic payee.

Figure 4.8   Preview Transmission to CheckFree window

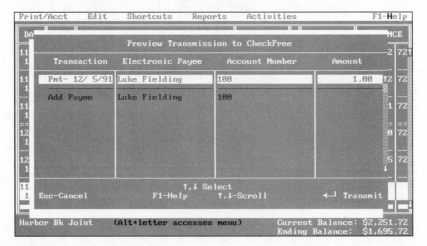

If everything looks good, go ahead and transmit the payment; if something is wrong with a pending transmission, press Escape. If the error is in the check, you can edit it in the Write Checks screen. If the payee list is inaccurate, correct it by pressing Ctrl-Y to see the electronic vendor list; then highlight the payee you need to change and press Ctrl-E to edit the entry.

In actual practice, you can certainly transmit without previewing. However, previewing is an easy step and an important safeguard to ensure that the payments you're sending are correct.

Transmit the Transaction

When you're ready to transmit, check to be sure your computer is connected to the modem and the modem is connected to a telephone line; then press Enter from the preview screen. (To transmit without previewing, press Ctrl-I as before, and press Enter immediately.)

Once you've instructed Quicken to begin a CheckFree transmission, your role is reduced to that of a spectator—unless something goes wrong. Quicken displays a series of messages describing its progress through the transmission: initializing the modem, dialing out, logging in, transferring payment data, receiving confirmation numbers, and so forth. If the transmission is successfully completed, Quicken displays the following message:

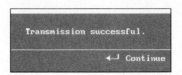

If an error occurs, don't give up too easily; the problem may be as simple as someone picking up an extension phone elsewhere in your home. Press Escape and then F1 to see if Quicken's help screens can give you a simple solution; then try transmitting the payment again. If the problem recurs at exactly the same point in the transmission, review the help screens more carefully; Quicken can help you diagnose the cause of most transmission errors, but in some cases Quicken won't be able to help, and you'll have to find the problem yourself.

After you've transmitted an electronic payment, the Register displays changes to show that the electronic payment has been made. Instead of the >>>>> symbol in the NUM column, you'll see E-PMT for the test payment.

Deposit the Transaction

If you've done everything correctly, you should receive a check in the mail—most likely drawn on your checking account—within a week. Figure 4.9 is a sample.

Figure 4.9   CheckFree check written to yourself

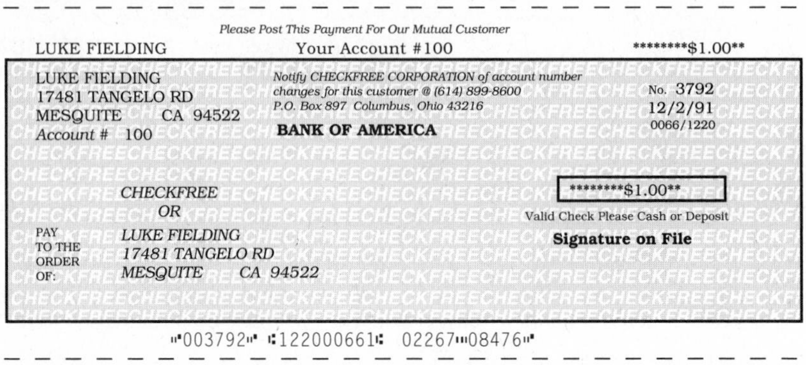

```
                          Please Post This Payment For Our Mutual Customer
      LUKE FIELDING            Your Account #100                    ********$1.00**

   LUKE FIELDING           Notify CHECKFREE CORPORATION of account number      No. 3792
   17481 TANGELO RD        changes for this customer @ (614) 899-8600           12/2/91
   MESQUITE    CA  94522   P.O. Box 897  Columbus, Ohio 43216                  0066/1220
   Account #  100          BANK OF AMERICA

      CHECKFREE                                              ********$1.00**
          OR                                              Valid Check Please Cash or Deposit
   PAY   LUKE FIELDING
   TO THE 17481 TANGELO RD                                 Signature on File
   ORDER
   OF:   MESQUITE      CA  94522

         ⑈003792⑈ ⑆122000661⑆ 02267⑈08476⑈
```

Before popping the champagne cork and declaring victory, however, remember that your bank has not yet been involved in the transaction. The true test of your CheckFree setup will come when the deposited check clears through your bank.

Deposit the check, if possible, to a bank other than the one you've chosen for your electronic payment account. This ensures that the check will go through the full check-clearing process, rather than taking a shortcut within the same bank. Some financial institutions, such as credit unions and money market mutual funds, have had problems handling initial CheckFree transactions; if you suspect trouble, call CheckFree right away. If you don't hear from either your bank or the deposit bank within five days, it's fair to assume that the deposit has been successful. Of course, the real certainty of success comes when you see the transaction recorded in black and white on your bank statement at the end of the month.

Learn How CheckFree Pays Your Bills

Although you don't have to know anything about how CheckFree works in order to use it, you'll almost certainly find some of this knowledge helpful. Learning how CheckFree handles different kinds of payments explains why CheckFree requires five days' lead-time for most transactions, deciphers the various ways CheckFree transactions appear on your monthly bank statements, and makes troubleshooting conversations with merchants or CheckFree much more efficient.

Figure 4.10 diagrams the process CheckFree uses to pay bills. When payment instructions arrive from your computer, CheckFree decides which of its three payment methods is best for any particular transaction, depending mainly on whether the specified merchant can process electronic payments.

After CheckFree pays the bill within the required time frame, the transaction moves through any necessary check-clearing processes and finally appears on your bank statement.

Before you continue, it will be helpful to understand the three types of dates that operate when you pay electronically through CheckFree. We'll describe them in reverse chronological order because the later dates determine the earlier ones. The three types of dates are

- *Due date*   This is the date your bill is due, found on your merchant's statement to you. For example, your current gas bill may have a due date of April 30. You want checks to arrive reliably on or before this date. If they arrive after, you may be liable for stiff penalties or finance charges, depending on the credit arrangements you have with the vendor.

- *Payment date*   You specify the date by which CheckFree should pay each bill. This date must be sufficiently in advance of the due date so the check has time to travel whatever course it takes from CheckFree in Ohio to the vendor's door and through the vendor's posting process. For example, the payment date for your gas bill might be April 18, around ten business days before the due date.

- *Transmit date*   This is the date you transmit the electronic payment to CheckFree. It must be sufficiently before the payment date so Quicken has time to process your payment instructions. You might transmit your gas bill payment on April 11, a week before you want CheckFree to pay the bill.

CheckFree Collects and Screens Incoming Payments

Every weekday evening around 9:00 p.m. (Eastern time), CheckFree's data center swings into action, processing all the transactions it received during the previous 24 hours. Computers compare user and merchant information against a large database, cross-referencing them to ensure that they can be accurately processed by the CheckFree system.

The system screens each new merchant against its consolidated database of every merchant it has ever paid. Most merchants who are new to an individual user are not new to CheckFree. In fact, a very large percentage of CheckFree's payments are to the same institutions: credit card companies, banks, utilities, department stores, and oil companies.

The system then consolidates individual payments which must be paid on the same day to the same merchant (American Express, for example) into a single payment. This, frankly, is how CheckFree makes its money. By consolidating as many as several dozen payments into a single transaction—which costs the same to send and post as each individual transaction would cost if sent separately—CheckFree realizes substantial economies of scale.

If CheckFree's computers don't recognize a new merchant, they call for human intervention. Since vendor consolidation is such a vital component of

Figure 4.10   CheckFree's bill payment process

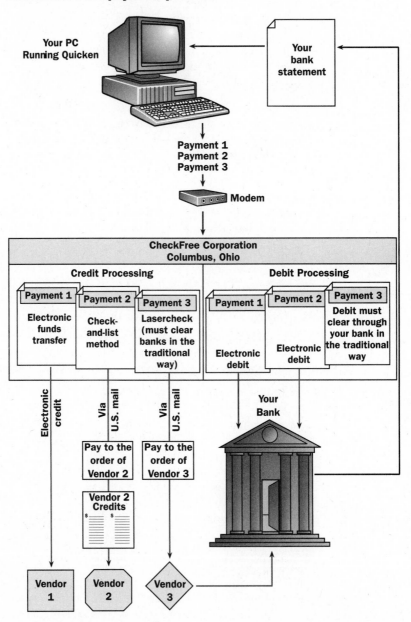

CheckFree Payment Processing

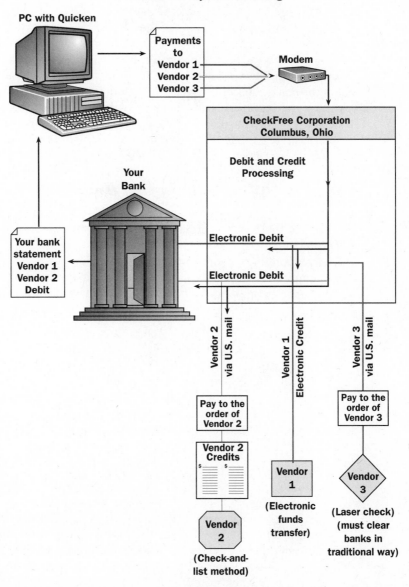

Note. In some cases, CheckFree makes special arrangements with a merchant to use a mailing address or other account information that differs from what you supply. This will be invisible to you and will not require changes to your merchant list.

CheckFree's economics, the company makes every effort—using the name, address, and telephone information you provide—to match new merchants to payees it already has established in its files. This is why it's so critically important that you provide an accurate address and telephone number when you set up an electronic payee in Quicken.

One other important aspect of the CheckFree system is detecting duplicate payments from the same person to the same vendor on the same day. These payments might result from a transmission that was inadvertently interrupted and then retransmitted. The good news is that you needn't worry about the consequences of CheckFree's computer receiving the same payment instruction twice. The bad news, however, is that even if you intend it, you can't send two payments on the same day with the same amount, account, and vendor. If you have reason to do this, either consolidate the payments into one or pay one of them a day early.

CheckFree Chooses a Payment Method

CheckFree's computers choose the best way to pay each merchant from three options. The method is determined by the company's past experience with the merchant and by the characteristics of your bank account. These three methods vary according to the medium used for payment. CheckFree decides upon some combination of electronic funds transfers and/or paper checks to debit your account and credit the vendor's. The three possible methods are

- *Electronic-electronic*   In an entirely electronic funds transfer, the payee's account is credited and your account is debited directly through the Federal Reserve System on the day that you specify. (CheckFree has also begun paying some merchants through MasterCard's electronic payments network.) This is CheckFree's preferred method, because it is the most accurate and precisely timed of the three. In fact, CheckFree would not require a lead-time of five business days if all payments were electronic-electronic. Unfortunately, this method currently accounts for only a third of CheckFree's transactions.

- *Electronic-paper*   In this type of transaction, only the debit to your account is processed electronically. If a vendor won't accept electronic payments but CheckFree has several payments to make to that vendor on the same day, it uses a second method called check-and-list. CheckFree adds up all the amounts due to a vendor on a particular day, writes one check for the total against its own bank account, and sends it, accompanied by a list of accounts and amounts, through the U.S. mail approximately three days before the payment date (see Figure 4.11 for a sample of such a payment). CheckFree then charges the users' bank accounts electronically (through the Federal Reserve System) on the specified payment dates. Ideally, this process spans four to five days, beginning when CheckFree receives your payment request and ending when the merchant receives the check.

Figure 4.11   Sample check-and-list payment

THE FACE OF THIS CHECK HAS A COLORED BACKGROUND-NOT A WHITE BACKGROUND

THIS CHECK IS A

BILL PAYMENT REMITTANCE FOR **ALL CUSTOMERS NOTED** ON THE **ATTACHED FORM**

IF FORM IS MISSING, CALL (614) 899-8600 IMMEDIATELY

CHECK NO.	01832200
SEQ NO.	04663

CHECKFREE CORPORATION
P.OL BOX 897
COLUMBUS, OHIO 43216

THE CHASE MANHATTAN BANK, NA
SYRACUSE, NEW YORK

50-937
―――
213

******1,547 DOLLARS AND 13   /100 CENTS

CHECK DATE	CHECK AMOUNT
04/23/91	***1547.13

TO THE   GOLDEN STATE TELEPHONE
ORDER   P.O. BOX 1000
OF: MARINA, CA 95641

REMITTANCE CHECK VOID IF NOT CASHED WITHIN 90 DAYS

AUTHORIZED SIGNATURE

---

*C*HECKFREE ®

CORPORATION――――
P.O. Box 897
Columbus, Ohio 43216

04/23/91   Page   1 of   3

BILL PAYMENT REMITTANCE

CheckFree, the nation's electronic payment system, is utilized by an increasing number of people across the nation to pay their bills. Our mutual customers, listed below, have authorized us to remit payments on their behalf.

Please help us increase accuracy and speed in crediting your accounts by informing us of any corrections to your remittance address or customer accounts receivable numbers. CheckFree can make it very easy for you to receive payment electronically. If you would like to receive these payments electronically, please call CheckFree Merchant Services at (614) 899-8600

GOLDEN STATE TELEPHONE
P.O. BOX 1000
MARINA, CA 95641

CTRL# 8757   CHECK#   1832200

ACCOUNT NUMBER	CUSTOMER NAME		AMOUNT	DATE
415 555-0180 406	**ELLIS RAOUL W** 82 TREVAND ROAD MENLO PARK	CA 94026	41.97	04/23/91
4155553390191	**EVANS CARSON L** 31 CIDER ROAD LAKETON	CA 95429	54.44	04/23/91
415-555-1278 329	**FAUTH MERITA R** 597 ARROW CT BELMONT	CA 94501	24.62	04/23/91
707 555-0456 473	**FERRO ANGELO** 9501 SCHOOL ST ROSEDALE	CA 95951	53.58	04/23/91
415-555-7162-812	**FIELDING LUKE R** 17481 TARGDO RD MESQUITE	CA 94522	166.98	04/23/91
	10 ITEMS PAGE TOTAL: CONTINUED ON NEXT PAGE		341.59	

Please direct any billing questions to CheckFree Merchant Services (614) 899-8600

■ *Paper-Paper*   In this method of payment, no credits or debits are performed electronically. CheckFree sends a laser-printed paper facsimile of
your personal check (a *laser check* in CheckFree parlance) directly to the
merchant by U.S. mail, just as though you had written the check yourself.
The signature blank lists the account holder's signature as "on file," as
shown in Figure 4.12. The merchant deposits a laser check like any other
check, and your account is debited when the check clears the bank.

Figure 4.12   Sample laser check

Please Post This Payment For Our Mutual Customer
RAYMOND X. BRANDYZE   Your Account #89-5000Y41-B2   ********$235.15**

RAYMOND X. BRANDYZE   *Notify CHECKFREE CORPORATION of account number*   No. 3793
118 VILLAGE ROAD   *changes for this customer @ (614) 899-8600*
CLIFF,   PA 15239   *P.O. Box 897 Columbus, Ohio 43216*   11/05/91
Account # 89-5000Y41-B2   **HILLSIDE BANK**   0066/1220

CHECKFREE   ********$235.15**
OR   Valid Check Please Cash or Deposit
PAY   *LANG'S DEPARTMENT STORES*   **Signature on File**
TO THE   *PROCESSING DEPARTMENT*
ORDER   *P O BOX 725004*
OF: *COLUMBUS   OH 43218*

⑈003793⑈ ⑉043000096⑉ 05773520⑈

Your Merchants Process the Payments

Imagine the first time a merchant receives a laser check from CheckFree.
The last 200 envelopes the vendor has opened have dutifully included the
customer's billing stub and are easy to identify and post. (Some stubs even
have magnetic or optical coding to speed the posting process.)

Now, along comes an odd duck: a laser-printed check with no bill stub
and no customer signature! All the necessary account information is there,
but in a form the merchant is unaccustomed to seeing. Many merchants side-
track these payments into an "exceptions handling" queue, which can delay
the posting of your account by several days, so it's essential that you build in
an extra cushion when you start paying a merchant with CheckFree. As merchants receive more CheckFree payments from you (and others), processing
these payments will become routine, and you'll be able to reduce lead-times
to more normal levels.

Your Bank Statement Arrives

When you begin using CheckFree, you'll also see some important differences in your bank statement. Electronic and check-and-list payments should appear on your checking account statement as detailed line items that give the vendor's name, as shown in Figure 4.13. You will, however, receive no canceled check for these payments.

In addition, you may find one or more laser checks in your stack of canceled checks. These unnumbered checks will probably be listed on your bank statement without payee names in the detail line, but with a generic bank description instead, such as "debit memo" or "debit transaction."

Start Paying Other Bills

Note. If you have more than one account at a single merchant (if you pay two telephone bills to the same telephone company, for example), see "When You Have More than One Account with a Merchant," later in Level 4, for special rules that apply to the name field.

Once you've become familiar with the basic workings of CheckFree, you'll want to start adding actual merchants. Again, start with low-risk payments in your first month, leaving plenty of extra time to credit your account.

Add New Merchants

You may add merchants to your electronic payee list at any time from the Register or Write Checks screen. For example, suppose you want to pay your Golden State Telephone bills electronically.

To set up this vendor as a new payee,

1. From the Register or Write Checks screen, press Ctrl-Y or select Electronic Payee List from the Shortcuts menu (Alt-S). Quicken displays the Electronic Payee list, shown in Figure 4.14.

2. Choose <Set Up a New Payee> from the Electronic Payee list to see the Set Up Electronic Payee window.

3. Type the name of the merchant (up to 28 characters) as you want it to appear on the check; in this case, you would type **Golden State Telephone Co.**

Note. If no phone number is listed (as is often the case with magazine subscription billings), try some other source— a phone book or directory assistance. As a last resort, call CheckFree customer service at (614) 899-7500; if they've had experience with the merchant, they can tell you what number to use.

4. Type the vendor's street address, city, state, and zip code, using the address on any return envelope included with your bill. This address is frequently different from the company's business offices. Using the correct address is critical to minimizing the time between your requesting a payment and its actually being credited to your account.

5. Enter the vendor's phone number. Although people often ignore the telephone number that appears on a bill, it plays a very important role when CheckFree matches your payee additions to those in its file. Consequently, Quicken will not allow you to leave this space blank. Look on the bill for a "billing inquiries" number or for the main phone number for the company.

Figure 4.13   CheckFree transactions on a bank statement

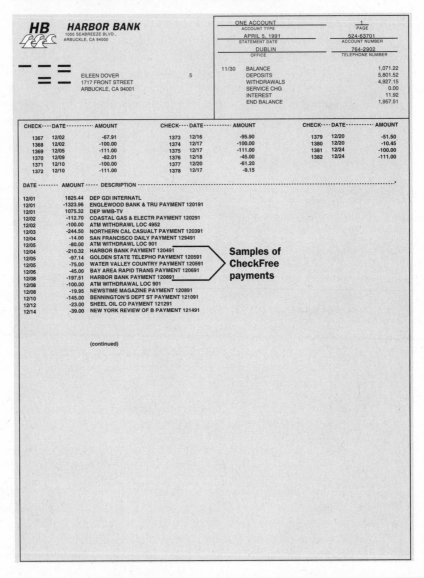

	HARBOR BANK		ONE ACCOUNT	1

HB   HARBOR BANK
1050 SEABREEZE BLVD.,
ARBUCKLE, CA 94000

		ONE ACCOUNT		1
		ACCOUNT TYPE		PAGE
		APRIL 5, 1991		524-63701
		STATEMENT DATE		ACCOUNT NUMBER
		DUBLIN		764-2902
		OFFICE		TELEPHONE NUMBER

EILEEN DOVER   5
1717 FRONT STREET
ARBUCKLE, CA 94001

11/30	BALANCE	1,071.22
	DEPOSITS	5,801.52
	WITHDRAWALS	4,927.15
	SERVICE CHG	0.00
	INTEREST	11.92
	END BALANCE	1,957.51

CHECK	DATE	AMOUNT	CHECK	DATE	AMOUNT	CHECK	DATE	AMOUNT
1367	12/02	-67.91	1373	12/16	-95.90	1379	12/20	-51.50
1368	12/02	-100.00	1374	12/17	-100.00	1380	12/20	-10.45
1369	12/05	-111.00	1375	12/17	-111.00	1381	12/24	-100.00
1370	12/09	-82.01	1376	12/18	-45.00	1382	12/24	-111.00
1371	12/10	-100.00	1377	12/20	-61.20			
1372	12/10	-111.00	1378	12/17	-9.15			

DATE	AMOUNT	DESCRIPTION
12/01	1825.44	DEP GDI INTERNATL
12/01	-1323.96	ENGLEWOOD BANK & TRU PAYMENT 120191
12/01	1075.32	DEP WMB-TV
12/02	-112.70	COASTAL GAS & ELECTR PAYMENT 120291
12/02	-100.00	ATM WITHDRAWL LOC 4952
12/03	-244.50	NORTHERN CAL CASUALT PAYMENT 120391
12/04	-14.00	SAN FRANCISCO DAILY PAYMENT 129491
12/05	-80.00	ATM WITHDRAWL LOC 901
12/04	-210.32	HARBOR BANK PAYMENT 120491
12/05	-97.14	GOLDEN STATE TELEPHO PAYMENT 120591
12/05	-75.00	WATER VALLEY COUNTRY PAYMENT 120591
12/06	-45.00	BAY AREA RAPID TRANS PAYMENT 120691
12/08	-197.51	HARBOR BANK PAYMENT 120891
12/08	-100.00	ATM WITHDRAWAL LOC 901
12/08	-19.95	NEWSTIME MAGAZINE PAYMENT 120891
12/10	-145.00	BENNINGTON'S DEPT ST PAYMENT 121091
12/12	-23.00	SHEEL OIL CO PAYMENT 121291
12/14	-39.00	NEW YORK REVIEW OF B PAYMENT 121491

Samples of CheckFree payments

(continued)

Figure 4.14   **Electronic Payee List screen**

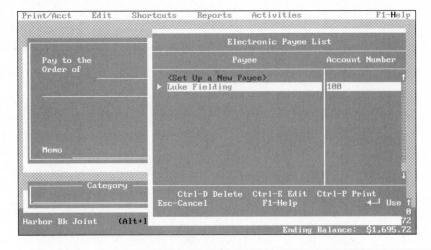

6. In the Account Number blank, enter a number from your bill that uniquely identifies you as a customer—your account, customer number, policy number, or loan number, for example—using up to 28 characters. If there is no such number, type your last name: CheckFree requires an entry in this field. *Don't* use the invoice number. The invoice number changes from bill to bill, and the number you type must remain constant. The completed window should resemble Figure 4.15.

7. Double-check the accuracy of your payee information—particularly the account number. Because your payments will arrive without billing stubs, the merchant must rely on proper account information to credit your account correctly. Finally, press Enter to leave the window.

When You Have More than One Account with a Merchant

Occasionally, you'll need to enter the same payee in your payee list more than once. For example, you might have an auto insurance policy as well as homeowner's policies for both your residence and vacation home with the same insurance company.

The second time you add the same merchant to your Electronic Payee list, Quicken will warn you that you're creating multiple payees with the same name (see Figure 4.16) and will prompt you for additional identifying information.

Type a short description such as "Volvo" or "Lake Tahoe"; Quicken will display this description in braces along with the payee's name, as shown in

Note. If, when you look for a unique identifying number on your bill, you find two numbers that are similar, pick one and identify it in the Account Number blank—type "Policy No." or "Client No.", before the digits for example. This will help ensure that your account is properly credited.

Note. You can go back and add additional identifying characters to the first duplicate payee as well. Highlight the first payee and press Ctrl-E; then type the extra characters, including the braces, after the name.

Figure 4.17. However, the additional description will not appear on the check issued by CheckFree. Since these additional characters must fit within the character limit in the Name field, you'll only have as much space for this extra notation as there are spaces remaining after the name.

Figure 4.15   Completed Set Up Electronic Payee window

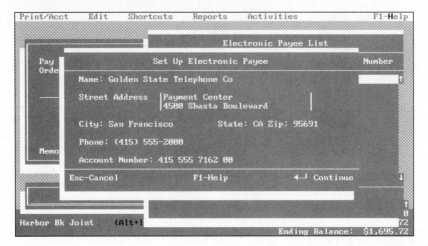

Figure 4.16   Multiple Electronic Payees with the Same Name window

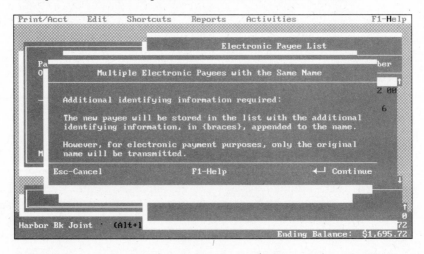

Figure 4.17   Duplicate payees in the Electronic Payee list

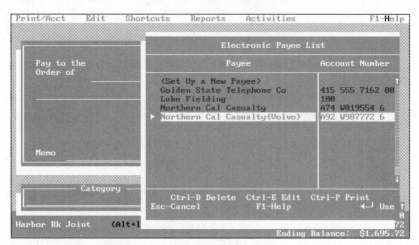

Maintain the Merchant List

You may edit or delete merchant information in your Electronic Payee list at any time. While viewing the Register or Write Checks screen of your electronic account, press Ctrl-Y to see the payee list; then highlight the payee you want to edit or delete, and press Ctrl-E (for Edit) or Ctrl-D (for Delete).

When you make changes, they are stored locally on your PC until the next time you transmit a payment to CheckFree for that particular merchant. After CheckFree receives the information, it updates its central payee file. If you try to delete a payee for whom there is an untransmitted electronic payment, Quicken will prevent you from doing so; you must transmit the payment before you can transmit instructions to delete the payee. (If you decide you don't want the payment to go through, you must delete the transaction from the Register or Write Checks screen. See "Write Transactions Through the Register.")

You might give yourself some practice and do CheckFree a favor by deleting your own name, which was transmitted to CheckFree when you sent the test payment to yourself.

To delete your own name,

1. From the Register or Write Checks screen of your electronic account, press Ctrl-Y to see the Electronic Payee list.

2. Highlight your name as the payee you want to delete.

3. Press Ctrl-D to delete your name, then press Enter to confirm the action.

4. Press Escape to leave the payee list. At the end of this session, when you transmit other electronic payments, instructions to delete your name from the CheckFree files will also be transmitted.

Write Transactions Through the Register

Note. After you type > into the NUM field, Quicken automatically changes the transaction date to the earliest possible date it can commit to an electronic payment—five business days later—and prevents you from entering an earlier date.

You'll find the quickest way to enter electronic transactions is to bypass the Write Checks screen and enter them directly into the Register. Enter them just as you would enter any other Register transaction, but beware of two exceptions: In the NUM field, type **>** to designate the payment as an untransmitted electronic transaction. As soon as you type >, the blank will change to the familiar >>>>> symbol. In the PAYEE field, type enough of the name to uniquely identify it in the Electronic Payee list, and press Enter. If you've successfully identified a single electronic payee, Quicken will automatically complete the payee's name. If not, the program will display the Electronic Payee Not Found message and allow you to choose from the payee list or add a new merchant to the list.

After you've finished entering all your electronic payment transactions in the Register, you can begin transmitting them to CheckFree by pressing Ctrl-I (for Initiate) or by selecting Transmit Payments from the Print/Acct menu (Alt-P). If you decide you don't want a payment to go through, delete it in the Register by pressing Ctrl-D.

Memorize Electronic Transactions

Although Quicken stores names, addresses, and account numbers of merchants in its Electronic Payee file, it does not store categories or category splits. That's where memorized transactions come in.

To create a memorized electronic transaction, first enter the information, including anything you want memorized into the Register or Write Checks screen. Be sure to place the >>>>> symbol in the NUM field, and to include any categorization split information—including percentage splits—you wish to apply later.

Press Ctrl-M to memorize the transaction, and Ctrl-T to recall it later on. For information on how to edit memorized transactions, review the section on memorized transactions in Level 3.

Adjust Your Payment Lead-Times

The first time you pay a merchant, you should transmit the payment at least ten business days before the due date listed on the bill, and set a payment date at least five business days before the due date. This will account for the processing time, the mailing time from CheckFree headquarters in Ohio to your merchant, and the time it takes to post your account.

You may, of course, continue to maintain this cushion on every payment. However, if you're concerned about cash flow or want to get every dollar of interest out of your cash, you don't always have to maintain a long lead-time on every account. Especially with large payments such as mortgage bills, shortening the lead-time will improve your cash position and save you money in the form of interest on the float.

As you begin using CheckFree, you'll find it's worth tracking the speed with which merchants credit your account. For this purpose, we've supplied another item for your Quicken Toolkit: a CheckFree Payment Performance Log. This tool will help you determine how much to reduce (or, in rare instances, increase) the lead-time for paying CheckFree merchants.

TOOLKIT   A CheckFree Payment Performance Log

| Merchant | Month 1 | | | Month 2 | | | Month 3 | | | Paid-to-Credit Lag (Days) | | | | Method |
	Due	Paid	Credit	Due	Paid	Credit	Due	Paid	Credit	Mo. 1	Mo. 2	Mo. 3	Avg	(PorE)
1.														
2.														
3.														
4.														
5.														
6.														
7.														
8.														
9.														
10.														
11.														
12.														
13.														
14.														
15.														
16.														
17.														
18.														
19.														
20.														
21.														
22.														
23.														
24.														
25.														
26.														
27.														
28.														
29.														
30.														
Example:														
Golden State Tel.	1/8	1/1	1/3	2/8	2/1	1/31	3/8	3/6	3/6	2	-1	0	0.3	P

To use the log,

1. In the far-left column, list the vendors to whom you make the largest average payments through CheckFree each month.

2. To the right, you'll see three groups of three columns each, each group representing three months of payments. In the Due column, write the due date of the next bill you'll pay with CheckFree. In the Paid column, write the payment date you'll use for CheckFree (remember that you'll need to enter and transmit the payment at least five business days in advance of the Paid date).

3. When you receive your next month's bill from any vendor on the list, find the date on which the vendor credited the payment, and write it in the Credit column. Repeat this step for each vendor as soon as you receive a statement.

4. Subtract the credit date from the paid date to obtain a paid-to-credit lag time. In some cases, the payment could be received and credited one or two days before the paid date; CheckFree may have paid the bill slightly before the payment date, and an efficient postal service might have delivered it immediately. In this case, the paid-to-credit lag time would be a negative number.

5. Finally, check your bank statement to find out what method CheckFree uses to pay that particular merchant. Electronic-electronic transactions are usually recognizable, because the credit date is always the same as the date on which the transaction appears in your account, and because the vendor's name is always listed. Check-and-list transactions also show the vendor's name, but the credit date is usually different than the payment date. Laser checks are distinguished by a laser check in your pile of returned checks. In the Method column, write E for an all-electronic payment or P for a merchant paid by printed check.

After the first two months, begin looking for patterns in the performance log. Several trends may appear:

- You may see that electronic payments are usually made precisely on the date they're requested. It's safe to begin specifying that these payments be made on the due date or the day before.

- You may find that printed checks are less predictable than electronic checks, because of postal delays and hand posting processes. If the lag time is zero to two days, you can begin reducing the cushion between payment date and due date.

■ You may observe that some merchants are very slow at posting the credit to your account. If the lag is consistently more than five days, it's worth calling the merchant to find out what's wrong.

Over time, you'll develop a feel for lead-times and an appropriate cushion will emerge. It's important to remember, though, that the penalties for making late payments can be quite severe, relative to the benefit of a few extra days' interest income. When in doubt, err on the side of extra time.

Reconcile CheckFree Payments

Reconcile your CheckFree payments along with your other bank account transactions, matching your bank statement to the Quicken Register. The significant difference with CheckFree is that there are no typographical errors to find; any mismatches indicate an error by your bank, by CheckFree, or by the Federal Reserve's electronic payments system. Later in Level 4, under "Act Quickly If Trouble Strikes," you'll find suggestions for dealing with such problems.

Payments

In the reconciliation register, you'll find all CheckFree electronic payments grouped with other unnumbered transactions and sorted by date. You reconcile these by matching date and amount to the transactions in your bank statement. As you match transactions, mark them as cleared (using the space-bar) just as you would mark a cleared check. (For a refresher on reconciling with Quicken, see Level 2.)

If you find a mismatch, contact CheckFree customer service immediately, using one of the methods described later in Level 4, under "Act Quickly If Trouble Strikes."

Service Charges

Your service charges for the CheckFree service will also appear as an electronic transaction in your bank statement. CheckFree currently charges $9.95 per month for the first 20 payments and $3.50 for each additional block of ten payments (or portion thereof) per month. CheckFree charges extra for various extended service options, including processing account changes, account history research, stopping payments on short notice, or providing legal documentation of CheckFree payments.

Treat these charges as you would your checking account fees, creating a new transaction for them in the Register and categorizing it under "Bank Charges" or another appropriate category.

Make Periodic Payments with CheckFree

If you need to pay the same amount to the same vendor every week, month, quarter, or year, consider setting up a transaction group to handle these periodic payments. Level 3 contains a thorough discussion of how to set up and execute transaction groups. When you use transaction groups for electronic payments, however, you may want to take advantage of another feature CheckFree offers.

CheckFree allows you to store up to twelve advance payments for every merchant. This means that you could transmit a full year's worth of car lease payments at one time, for example, and not have to worry about paying this bill till next year. Every month, CheckFree will send your payment just before the payment date. This feature costs nothing extra, and you can stop the advance payments just as you can any other payment, up to five business days before the payment date. (For more on this subject, see "Stop Payment," later in this level.) You should wait until you've established a comfortable payment lead-time with the vendor to set up these advance payments. You probably shouldn't use this method if the payment amount could change at all.

Suppose, for example, you have a monthly service contract with a house-cleaning service, Professional Polish Inc., for $75.00, due on the twelfth of each month. You might prefer to pay three monthly bills at a time, allowing you to deal with these payments quarterly rather than every month. To set this up,

1. In the Register or Write Checks screen, enter the first transaction. Enter the payment date for the next bill that is due—in this example, you might have a payment date of 12/5/91 for a bill due 12/12/91. Type **>** in the NUM column to show it's on electronic payment. If necessary, enter new payee information. Include any information that should be memorized, such as the category and amount. Record the transaction as usual by pressing Ctrl-Enter.

2. Memorize the transaction by pressing Ctrl-M.

3. Set up a new transaction group. First, press Ctrl-J; then select an unused group. Enter a name for the transaction group and the frequency of payment—in this case, monthly.

4. Enter the next scheduled payment. In this case, you've already entered the next bill into the Register, so the next scheduled payment would be the one after that, say, 1/5/92 for the bill due 1/12/92. Your screen should now resemble Figure 4.18.

5. When you press Enter to leave the window, Quicken asks you to indicate which of the memorized transactions you want to include in the transaction group. Press the spacebar to mark the transaction you just memorized.

Figure 4.18   Describe Group 3 screen

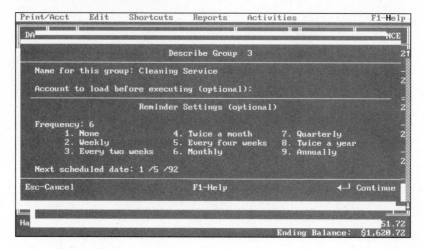

6. Execute the new transaction group as many times as you want to make advance payments—in this example, twice more, for a total of three payments to the cleaning service, as shown in Figure 4.19. Execute each transaction group by highlighting the name and pressing Enter. Confirm the date Quicken displays. When you return to the Register, you'll see the duplicate payments—with different dates at one month intervals.

7. Transmit the payments as usual. The transaction group will come due again when a fresh payment is required—in three months' time for the cleaning service. You can then execute the group three more times for another quarter's payments.

Act Quickly If Trouble Strikes

To make the system work you must monitor it and provide immediate feedback to CheckFree if you have problems. You can imagine the scale of customer service operations required to deal with merchants ranging in scale from American Express to the neighbor who trims your hedges. Almost everybody has a different way of billing, collecting, crediting your account, and making deposits.

The backbone of CheckFree's business is identifying and developing payment methods that work for every individual merchant it pays. The more information you can provide CheckFree, the better the system will work in the future.

Figure 4.19 **Periodic payment transactions in the Register**

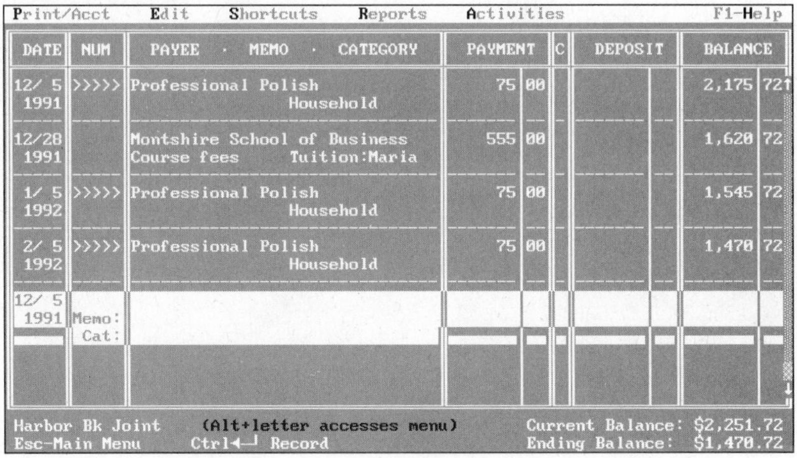

```
 Print/Acct    Edit     Shortcuts     Reports     Activities              F1-Help
╔════╦════╦═══════════════════════════════════╦═════════╦═╦═════════╦═════════╗
║DATE║NUM ║ PAYEE  ·  MEMO  ·  CATEGORY        ║ PAYMENT ║C║ DEPOSIT ║ BALANCE ║
╠════╬════╬═══════════════════════════════════╬═════════╬═╬═════════╬═════════╣
║12/ 5║>>>>>║Professional Polish               ║    75 00║ ║         ║2,175 721║
║1991║    ║              Household             ║         ║ ║         ║         ║
║12/28║    ║Montshire School of Business       ║   555 00║ ║         ║1,620 72 ║
║1991║    ║Course fees      Tuition:Maria     ║         ║ ║         ║         ║
║1/ 5║>>>>>║Professional Polish               ║    75 00║ ║         ║1,545 72 ║
║1992║    ║              Household             ║         ║ ║         ║         ║
║2/ 5║>>>>>║Professional Polish               ║    75 00║ ║         ║1,470 72 ║
║1992║    ║              Household             ║         ║ ║         ║         ║
║12/ 5║    ║                                   ║         ║ ║         ║         ║
║1991║Memo:║                                   ║         ║ ║         ║         ║
║    ║Cat:║                                   ║         ║ ║         ║         ║
║    ║    ║                                   ║         ║ ║         ║         ║
╚════╩════╩═══════════════════════════════════╩═════════╩═╩═════════╩═════════╝
 Harbor Bk Joint      (Alt+letter accesses menu)    Current Balance: $2,251.72
 Esc-Main Menu        Ctrl←┘ Record                 Ending Balance:  $1,470.72
```

Correspond with CheckFree

Because of the importance of hearing from customers, CheckFree's customer service department has instituted many channels of communication, ranging from prosaic to state-of-the-art. You'll get the most out of these channels if you diligently watch for problems and act quickly when they appear.

The first step in resolving an unposted payment is to call the merchant directly. Often, you'll find that the payment was posted to your account after the billing date, and that your account is current. If the payment has not been credited, obtain the name and telephone number of a contact in the merchant's credit department. You can use this information when you notify CheckFree.

If a payment you've already transmitted hasn't been received by the merchant, contact CheckFree directly. CheckFree prefers that you use the electronic mail capability built into Quicken—particularly when the inquiry is related to a specific transaction. When Quicken transmits the data, it includes the confirmation number of the transaction, which helps CheckFree trace any problems.

To send an electronic message to CheckFree,

1. In the Register, locate and highlight the transaction about which you'd like to inquire.

2. From the Edit menu (Alt-E), choose Electronic Payment Inquiry. Quicken will display a Payment Information screen (see Figure 4.20), containing data that will identify your transaction to a CheckFree troubleshooter.

Figure 4.20   Payment Information window

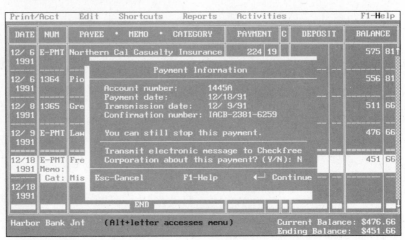

3. Confirm that you want to send an inquiry by typing **Y** at the prompt. Quicken will display the Transmit Inquiry about this payment to Check-Free window.

4. Type the number that applies to the type of inquiry you're making. Also indicate whether you've contacted the bank or the payee by typing **Y** after either or both of these statements.

5. Complete the message text if you need to supply other details. Quicken supplies the date, a salutation, and your name on the message form. There are only three lines for a message, so explain the problem succinctly, avoiding obscure abbreviations. If you have a contact name in the merchant's credit department, send it along, too. The transaction details that you saw a moment ago are transmitted along with your message, so you don't need to take up space with that information. Your screen should resemble Figure 4.21.

6. Press Ctrl-Enter to transmit the inquiry. Unlike electronic payments, Quicken does not wait to transmit until it collects a batch of inquiries; it acts immediately. Quicken also tells you that the transmission has been successful and that you should hear from CheckFree within five business days.

If the error appears to be at the merchant's end, CheckFree will provide proof-of-payment remittances to both you and your merchant. If the posting problem is the result of an error by CheckFree, its representatives will resolve the situation directly with the merchant, including payment of late fees up to fifty dollars.

Note. You may also transmit a free inquiry to CheckFree without referring to a specific payment. While in the Register or Write Checks screen, choose Send Electronic Mail from the Activities menu (Alt-A). Compose your message and press Ctrl-Enter to send it.

Figure 4.21   Transmit Inquiry about this payment to CheckFree window

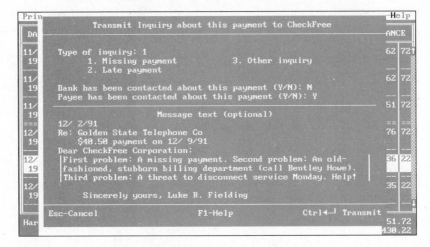

Note that Quicken's electronic mail system does not allow for responses from CheckFree. Their answer to your payment inquiry will come via the U.S. mail or, in rare instances, by telephone. However, in an emergency situation, this is sometimes not soon enough.

The best solution, of course, is not to let things like missing payments go until it's almost too late. In case a missing payment does slip by, though, CheckFree provides numerous alternatives for contacting its customer service representatives. Here are the available contact methods, in approximately decreasing order of urgency and expense:

Note. Unfortunately, the toll free number for CheckFree sales cannot be used to contact customer service.

- *Telephone*   Call CheckFree directly at (614) 899-7500. Current hours are Monday through Friday from 8:00 a.m. to 8:00 p.m. (except Wednesdays from 1:00 p.m. to 4:00 p.m.).

- *Fax*   CheckFree's facsimile number is (614) 899-7202.

- *MCI Mail*   Address your inquiries to the MCI Mail address: CheckFree.

- *CompuServe Mail*   Address your inquiries to CheckFree's EasyPlex mailbox: 72537,2156.

- *U.S. Mail*   Address mail to:

CheckFree Corporation
Attn: Customer Service Department
P.O. Box 897
Columbus, Ohio 43216-0897

Note. If you want to change one part of a payment, such as the amount or payment dates, the most efficient way to do so is to stop the previous transaction and then set up a new transaction.

Stop Payment

When you transmit your payment instructions to CheckFree, they are held until five business days before the payment date that you've specified. At any time before that date, you may cancel, or stop payment, on a CheckFree transaction.

To stop payment before the five-day period,

1. Go to the Register and highlight the transaction that you want to stop.

2. From the Edit menu (Alt-E), choose Transmit Stop Payment Request. If you're acting at least five business days in advance of the scheduled payment date, you'll see the Transmit Stop Payment Request window, shown in Figure 4.22.

Figure 4.22   Transmit Stop Payment Request window

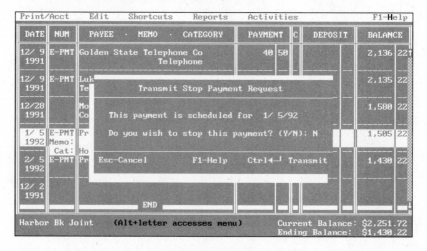

3. Confirm that you want to stop payment by typing **Y** and pressing Ctrl-Enter. Quicken will transmit your request immediately.

4. After Quicken voids the transaction, marks it as stopped, and clears it in your Register, Quicken inserts the confirmation number for the stop order in the memo field for the voided transaction.

If you've passed the five-day limit, Quicken will inform you that the payment can no longer be stopped. However, depending on the payment method, you still may not be too late. Call CheckFree immediately at (614) 899-7202. There is a special charge for stopping a payment on short notice: currently, it's about $15.

Protect Your System

One final word of caution about using electronic payments with Quicken: Once you've installed CheckFree on your PC, you've given your PC the ability to write valid checks—in any amount—on your bank account. Furthermore, the overdraft protection you granted to CheckFree by giving them your credit card number means that checks can be written over the cash balance in your checking account.

Obviously, you should take extra precautions to protect the security of your PC; not just your privacy is at stake—your money is, too.

To use Quicken's password protection capability to discourage unauthorized access to your account,

Note. Once you've entered a password, it will be impossible to use your Quicken file without it, so be sure to write your password down and store it in a secure place.

1. From the Main Menu, select Set Preferences and then Password Settings.

2. Select File Password from the menu. Quicken will display the Set Up Password window shown in Figure 4.23.

3. Type a password up to 16 characters long, including spaces, and then press Enter.

4. Type the password again to make sure you typed it correctly the first time, and press Enter.

Figure 4.23   Set Up Password window

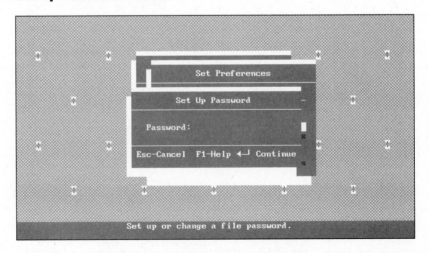

If you feel even higher security is warranted, you can do any of the following:

- Lock your computer when you're not using it.

- Use a commercial hard-disk locking program, which prevents access to certain directories and subdirectories of your hard disk, if no password is provided.

- Store your Quicken data on floppy disks rather than your hard disk, and lock up your floppies when you aren't using them.

Level 4 has been full of caveats and cautions. That's natural, because electronic payment methods are still developing and are not yet a routine part of the relationship among users, their merchants, and their banks. However, electronic payments offer tremendous opportunity to save money and time.

Simply stated, it's worth a little extra effort to understand them, to learn their capabilities and limitations, and to make sure appropriate safety nets are in place as you venture forth. Your money and credit rating are, after all, on the line.

LEVEL 4 BUILDING BLOCKS

TECHNIQUES AND PROCEDURES

■ Prepare Quicken for transmitting electronic payments by selecting Set Preferences from the Main Menu, then choosing Electronic Payment. Enter both modem and account settings.

■ Quicken stores payee names, addresses, phone numbers, and account numbers, so you can recall payee information quickly. When entering an electronic transaction, type the first few characters of the payee name; if you've typed enough to identify it fully, Quicken fills in the rest of the name for you when you press Ctrl-E. To enter new payees from the Register or Write Checks screen, press Ctrl-Y or choose Electronic Payee List from the Shortcuts menu (Alt-S). To edit a payee, highlight the payee's name and press Ctrl-E; to delete a payee, highlight the name and press Ctrl-D.

■ Each payee name must be unique. If you have two accounts with one merchant, Quicken lets you append a few distinguishing characters in braces to the merchant's name. These characters don't transmit with any transactions to that payee.

■ Double-check your pending transmission by previewing it: press Ctrl-I to initiate the transmission, and then press F9. You'll see pending payments plus any additions, edits, or deletions to your payee list. To transmit the previewed payment instructions, press Enter.

■ An interrupted transmission to CheckFree means you must retransmit the same group of payments. If CheckFree has already received part of the transmission, retransmitting may result in duplicate transactions. To prevent double payments, once a day CheckFree searches all transactions received and eliminates duplicates (same source, date, payee, and amount). For this reason, you shouldn't intentionally submit two identical payments on the same day.

■ If you make regular payments in the same amount to the same vendor, you can send several in advance to CheckFree at one time. CheckFree holds all advance payments until they are due. To simplify this procedure, memorize the first such regular transaction by pressing Ctrl-M, then create a transaction group including only that transaction by pressing Ctrl-J. When you're ready to send a batch of these payments, press Ctrl-J to execute the transaction group once for each advance payment you want to send. Quicken will adjust the payment date each time you execute the group.

■ If you fear a payment never occurred or was made incorrectly, and if the vendor can't verify the mistake, the easiest way to communicate with Check-Free is by sending an electronic message from Quicken. From the Edit menu, choose Electronic Payment Inquiry; provide a concise description of your problem, and then press Ctrl-Enter to transmit the message.

■ If you decide you need to stop payment on a check up to five business days before the payment date you specified, highlight the transaction and select Transmit Stop Payment Request from the Edit menu. If the bill has entered the five-day period, call CheckFree to see if the payment can be stopped; note that you may be assessed a stop-payment fee.

■ To establish password protection for your Quicken files, select Set Preferences from the Main Menu, and then select Password Settings. Next, select File Password, type a password of up to 16 characters, and press Enter. Be sure to write down the password and store the information in a safe place.

TERMS

■ The *due date* is the date your bill is due, which appears on your merchant's statement to you. You want checks to arrive on or before this date.

■ The *payment date* is the date on the check CheckFree issues, or the date an electronic funds transfer occurs. You specify this date when you create a transaction in Quicken. With inexperienced merchants, this date should be five business days before the due date.

■ The *transmit date* is the date you send the electronic payment to Check-Free. You should allow at least five business days between the transmit date and the payment date.

■ *Electronic-electronic* transfers, the type most profitable for CheckFree, occur when CheckFree debits your account and credits your vendor's account on the same day, all completely electronically. This is the fastest and most accurate method.

■ *Electronic-paper* transfers, also referred to as *check-and-list* transfers, occur when CheckFree groups all payments due to a single vendor on a single day, pays one check to the vendor, and itemizes the accounts and credits separately. CheckFree then debits your account electronically.

■ *Paper-paper* transfers, CheckFree's last resort, occur when CheckFree sends *laser checks* (that is, laser-printed) to your merchant. Debits and credits are made the traditional way, through the banks as the check clears.

IMPORTANT IDEAS

■ It's always worthwhile to set up a new system carefully—but with a new electronic payment system, it's crucial. Your good standing with merchants may hinge on whether you enter their names and addresses correctly as Quicken payees. Take extra time to hunt down the right phone numbers and to proofread the account number you type. CheckFree's existing merchant lists will help you avoid errors, but they can't help you if you mis-type the number that uniquely identifies you to the merchant.

■ In the beginning, transmit your payments to CheckFree around ten business days before their due dates, giving both CheckFree and the merchant five days to receive and handle the payment. Gradually decrease the time for vendors who process the payments faster than you've allowed. Merchants who are consistently slow may need personal contact on the matter; Check-Free may be able to help, too.

■ After you're signed up with CheckFree, leaving your personal computer unprotected is tantamount to leaving money lying around. Secure your computer with a password or a lock to prevent unauthorized payments of your funds.

■ Although this chapter offers many cautionary notes, working with a relatively new system for doing business can be exciting. You may need to give reluctant vendors a friendly nudge toward this new method—a simple phone call will probably do it—but this will be worth your time, especially if you have only a few holdovers to the printed or manual check routine.

5

Manage Sophisticated Transactions

PLAN AHEAD

Set Up Additional Accounts

Handle Common Cases

Tackle Special Purpose Categories

Track Your "Profit" Like a Business

Get More Out of Standard Reports

BUILDING BLOCKS

PLAN AHEAD

DECISIONS

How Much Sophistication Do You Need?

Quicken can account for your financial condition at almost any level of
detail. If you wish, you can use Quicken to track every penny of your cash
flow and net worth, just as a business would. In fact, though, individuals
rarely need that much information. In this level, you'll learn several ways to
add complexity selectively, by separating the components of income and
expense associated with many transactions to the degree that is appropriate
to your financial goals. For example, is it enough to merely categorize your
paycheck as Net Salary, or do your tax and financial planning needs dictate
that you track all the tax and savings plan deductions?

The benefit of detailed tracking is that it allows you to track the size and
trajectory of your net worth much more accurately. This is particularly important if you are seeking credit, if you are depending on Quicken to generate
accurate tax data, or if you are setting highly specific goals for your financial
growth.

The insight you gain from detailed tracking can be very rewarding, but
that insight has a price: Detailed tracking requires that you pay attention to a
larger number of accounts. Paycheck transactions can take several times
longer to enter, and on some loans, you'll have to keep track of complicated
amortization tables to get an accurate picture. As always, you should work
only as hard as necessary to accomplish your personal objectives.

Which Transactions Require Detailed Treatment?

If you need to track your assets more closely—for credit reporting purposes
or because you are planning your finances at a high level of sophistication,
for example—you should take a more detailed approach to certain transactions such as payroll, your mortgage, other loans, and partnership distribution. If you are depending on Quicken for tax information, you'll need to
add detail on tax refunds, dependent child care, and property contribution
transactions to the extent they apply.

You may want to get more specific on several other types of transactions,
too. If you're reimbursed for business expenses, you can set up categories to
recoup all you spend. Proper treatment of a medical expense category can
help you decide whether you've made the best decision on medical coverage.
You'll find techniques for all of these approaches described in this level.

MATERIALS

Paycheck Stubs

Your bank deposit records don't provide enough information for you to account for your paycheck accurately. Each paycheck actually represents several aggregate transactions: a salary or commission transaction on the plus side, and a series of tax and benefit withholding deductions on the minus side. To capture the full detail, you should have your paycheck stubs for the past month on hand. If you're entering data from previous months, it's best to have paycheck stubs for the entire period, but you can approximate your payroll deduction transactions even if you don't have every stub.

Mortgage Bill

Mortgage payments are composite transactions, too. Often they consist of an interest payment, a principal payment, and an escrow deposit to cover insurance and property tax obligations. Keep your mortgage bill close by during this session. If you don't have individual bills for the month, you'll learn how to estimate the interest/principal splits without them. If your mortgage bills don't show your escrow account balances, try to find your latest mortgage escrow account reconciliation statement, as well.

PRELIMINARIES

Complete Levels 1 and 2

By now, you should have set up your own account and category structure, and be comfortable with recording transactions, reconciling bank statements, and running standard reports. In addition, you should know how to memorize and split transactions. You don't need to know how to write checks and make electronic payments, since the techniques in Level 5 work equally well on historic records of manually written checks.

Review the Details of Your Mortgage and Other Loans

If you plan to apply detailed accounting methods to your mortgage and other loans—particularly fixed-payment loans that amortize the principal over the term of the loan—you'll want to refamiliarize yourself with the terms of those loans. Pay strict attention to the original principal amount, the duration, number of payments, interest rate, and any special provisions, such as balloon payments or interest-only periods. If a loan is reasonably conventional and you have the terms at hand, Quicken can save you considerable entry time by building and applying a detailed amortization schedule.

Set Up Additional Accounts

Not every transaction fits neatly into an expense or income category. There are two other types of transactions for which you should prepare your Quicken file:

- *Funds Transfers*   These transactions represent the movement of money from one account to another, such as a transfer from a checking account to a savings account or from a savings account to a brokerage account. You should set up in Quicken all the bank and investment accounts among which you'll be moving funds.

- *Asset Transfers*   These transactions represent the purchase or sale of assets (such as real estate or a certificate of deposit) or changes in what you owe to others (for example, a principal payment on a loan). Asset transfers can't be described as expenses because they merely represent the conversion of value from one form to another. As you begin setting up and monitoring asset and liability accounts, you'll develop an appreciation not only of your income and expense flow but also of the growth and distribution of your entire net worth.

Note. Because your asset and liability accounts are tracking only inflows and outflows, any Net Worth reports you run will be unreliable until you follow the complete asset setup procedures discussed in Level 9.

Set Up Investment Accounts

For the time being, we recommend you treat investment accounts (such as brokerage accounts and IRAs) just like bank accounts, tracking only the cash level in them. You may become much more ambitious after learning to track your investment account values on a daily basis in Level 8. For now, however, you'll rely on these accounts to capture the money transactions that may flow back and forth.

To set up an investment account,

1. Press Ctrl-A to see the Select Account to Use screen.

2. Press Home to highlight <New Account>, and then press Enter. The Set Up New Account window appears.

3. Type **6** to specify Investment Account, and press Enter.

4. Type a descriptive name, such as "Luke's IRA," and press Enter. Press Enter again to move past the prompt that asks whether this is a mutual fund (the answer should be no). Your screen should now resemble Figure 5.1.

5. Enter an optional description of the account, and press Enter to exit the window. Quicken places the new account name in the active accounts list. Press the PgDn key if necessary to see the new name.

Figure 5.1   **Set Up New Account window for an investment account**

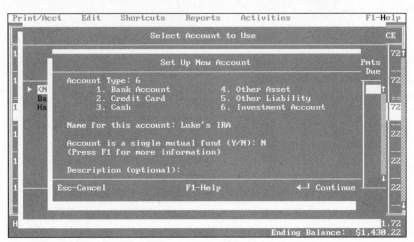

At this point, don't worry about selecting the account to view the invest-ment account register. In Level 8 you'll learn the procedure for entering investment account transactions, which differs from that for bank accounts. For now, the balances and activity of your investment accounts will simply reflect the related activity in your bank accounts.

Set Up Asset and Liability Accounts

There's a large gray area between clearcut expenses and asset transfers. For example, when you buy furniture, have you incurred an expense or have you actually increased an asset under the Home Furnishings category? Consider adopting this rule of thumb: Any item you would list on a net worth statement to a bank becomes an asset; everything else is an expense. In some cases, you'll want to be guided by tax considerations: permanent home improvements increase the tax base of your home, so you'll probably want to accumulate these improvements in an asset account called "Home Improvements."

For now, you should only bother with asset and liability accounts that will change due to transactions to and from bank accounts. You'll set up more asset and liability accounts to reflect your entire net worth profile in Level 9.

Here are three common accounts you may want to set up:

- *A savings plan or retirement account* (an asset account)   If you're making voluntary contributions to a company savings plan or retirement account, you will need to set up an account to record such deductions from your paycheck. Don't worry about the opening balance here; you will set it up correctly when you begin tracking your net worth in Level 9.

- *Home mortgage escrow account* (an asset account)   The escrow account is usually a savings account out of which your mortgage bank pays your property taxes and homeowner's insurance. Your mortgage statement will sometimes show the escrow balance, too. If yours doesn't, you may have to locate an escrow reconciliation statement, which the bank is required to send each January.

- *Home mortgage principal account* (a liability account)   The mortgage principal account represents the total you owe the bank. You can usually record this amount directly from a mortgage statement.

Set up asset and liability accounts in the same way you did bank and investment accounts: Press Ctrl-A to start, choose <New Account> to obtain the Set Up New Account window, and then type **4** (Other Asset) or **5** (Other Liability). Use the same time frame as you used for any accounts you set up in Levels 1 and 2, and enter the earliest starting value of these assets and liabilities within the time frame you choose (see Figure 5.2).

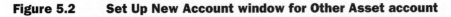

Figure 5.2   Set Up New Account window for Other Asset account

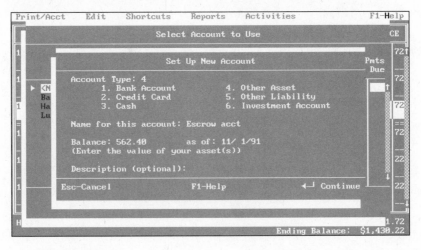

On the Set Up New Account window, you'll notice a credit card account type. Leave this alone for now, and continue to treat your credit card bills as split transactions. Later, you may want to set up your credit cards almost like bank accounts, entering transaction-by-transaction detail. Level 6 covers techniques for doing this.

Assign Quick Keys to Your Accounts

As your accounts increase in number and variety, you may find you need to switch between them frequently, to view recent transactions or check the closing balance or value. Quicken offers a simple and fast way to move between accounts. After you set up an account, you can assign a quick key to the account. You can then press the quick key for the account and Quicken instantly displays the register for that account.

To assign a quick key to an account,

1. Set up the account as usual.

2. In the Select Account to Use window, highlight the name of the account to which you want to assign a quick key, and press Ctrl-E (for Edit).

3. In the Edit Account Information window, next to quick key assignment, type a number from one to nine. For example, you might want to assign the number 1 to your main bank account. Press Enter to leave the window.

4. In the Select Account to Use window, the quick key column now displays the number you assigned, as shown in Figure 5.3.

Figure 5.3   **Select Account to Use window showing quick key assignment**

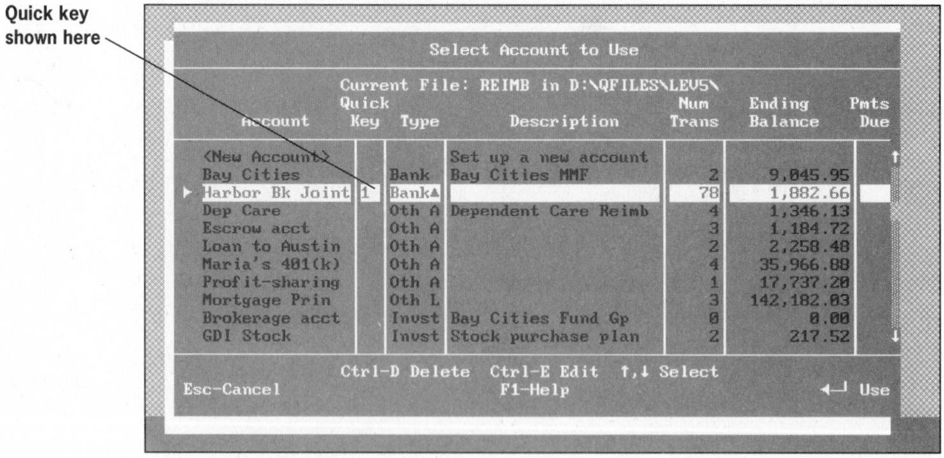

Quick key
shown here

```
                        Select Account to Use

            Current File: REIMB in D:\QFILES\LEU5\
                    Quick                              Num     Ending     Pmts
        Account      Key  Type      Description       Trans   Balance     Due

      <New Account>             Set up a new account
      Bay Cities          Bank  Bay Cities MMF          2      9,045.95
    ▶ Harbor Bk Joint 1  Bank▲                          78     1,882.66
      Dep Care           Oth A  Dependent Care Reimb     4      1,346.13
      Escrow acct        Oth A                           3      1,184.72
      Loan to Austin     Oth A                           2      2,258.48
      Maria's 401(k)     Oth A                           4     35,966.88
      Profit-sharing     Oth A                           1     17,737.20
      Mortgage Prin      Oth L                           3    142,182.03
      Brokerage acct     Invst Bay Cities Fund Gp        0          0.00
      GDI Stock          Invst Stock purchase plan       2        217.52

              Ctrl-D Delete   Ctrl-E Edit   ↑,↓ Select
   Esc-Cancel                     F1-Help                          ↵ Use
```

When you're working in another account, switch to this account by pressing Ctrl and the number you assigned—Ctrl-1 in this example. Consider assigning quick keys to the two or three accounts you use most frequently.

Get an Overview of Your Accounts

Before charging ahead, it's worthwhile to take one last look at the account structure of your file. Press Ctrl-A to view the account list. Have you included all the major asset and liability accounts into and out of which money flows in your financial life?

As an example, look at Table 5.1, which shows the account structure set up by Luke Fielding and Maria Lombardi, a professional couple with two children.

Table 5.1   Luke and Maria's Accounts

Assets	Liabilities
BANK ACCOUNTS	Mortgage
Harbor Bank joint account	School loan
Bay Cities Funds Group (money market)	Auto loan (Toyota)
Mortgage escrow account	Auto loan (Volvo)
INVESTMENT ACCOUNTS	
College Bank IRA (Luke)	
GDI Stock (company purchase plan)	
Bay Cities Fund Group (brokerage acct)	
Whitney Lewis (mutual fund)	
OTHER ASSETS	
401(k) (Maria)	
Profit-sharing (Maria's company)	
Loan to Austin Fielding	

Handle Common Cases

Most of the transactions you'll enter in Quicken will be very straightforward; they'll be checks categorized in a single expense account. Some transactions, however, require special treatment. Fortunately, most of these special cases follow one of the patterns discussed in the sections that follow.

Your Paycheck

Your paycheck is a fairly complex transaction. It consists of a salary amount that is higher than the check and several deductions that reduce the amount you actually receive. While every paycheck stub is different, they all contain similar information: a gross pay amount (sometimes divided into salary, bonus, and commissions); a series of tax and FICA (social security) deductions; some miscellaneous deductions (such as group health insurance or company health club fees); and perhaps an amount set aside for a salary deduction savings program (such as a 401k plan).

You should handle paychecks as split transactions. Most of the components will be allocated to income and expense categories. Others, such as savings plan contributions, should go into appropriate asset accounts.

For example, Luke Fielding's biweekly paycheck is $1,503.92. This net amount reflects his gross biweekly salary of $2,719.84 minus $180.99 in pretax adjustments (retirement and medical deduction) and $1,034.93 in a combination of benefit and tax deductions (including fees for a company fitness club and contributions to a company stock purchase plan). Luke records each deduction category on a separate line in a split transaction. He then records the stock purchase contributions and any other savings plans as transfers to Other Asset accounts to track the accumulated deposits. The other deductions are mainly expense categories. (Later in this level you'll learn a few useful techniques for handling some of these deductions.)

To enter your paycheck as a split transaction,

1. Open the Register and enter the date of the deposit, the name of your employer, and the check amount (the net pay that is credited to your checking account, *not* your gross salary) in the DEPOSIT column. Then press Ctrl-S to display the Split Transaction (Ctrl-S) window.

2. On the first line under Category, type **Salary** (or the appropriate category), then enter the gross salary amount over the net amount you entered in the Register. Your gross salary is almost always more than your net salary, so a negative number will appear on line 2, as in Figure 5.4. This is the total amount of the payroll deductions you'll be entering in the rest of this split transaction.

3. For each of the deductions and adjustments on your paycheck, enter the appropriate category or account; then type the amount to be deducted. You can have up to thirty elements in a split transaction.

4. When you finish, no uncategorized balance should remain, which indicates that you've successfully entered all the deductions listed on your paycheck. Press Ctrl-Enter once to return to the Register, and a second time to record the check.

Figure 5.5 shows Luke Fielding's paycheck stub and the completed Split Transaction window for his deposit transaction. The lines connect matching elements on the check stub in the window.

Paychecks are typically the most complex transactions you'll enter in Quicken. Yet they are reasonably consistent in structure from pay period to pay period. Therefore, you'll probably find it very helpful to memorize a

Note. If your paycheck is also consistent in amount, you would do well to memorize it with all the amounts filled in, editing any as necessary on those occasions when a deduction changes.

Figure 5.4   **Entering gross salary as a split transaction**

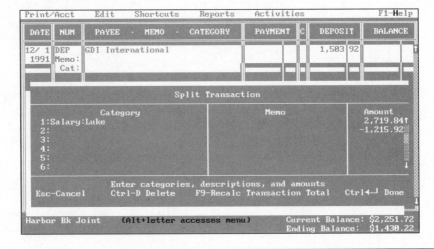

paycheck transaction with all the split categories and accounts in place, and the amount fields blank. When you memorize the transaction, specify that you want to memorize amounts by typing **A**. Figure 5.6 shows the Split Transaction window for this transaction.

Note. If you estimate your deductions using percentage splits, remember that some deductions, such as FICA and 401k contributions, may be capped. Don't forget to take these caps into account when and if you reach them.

If you want to save even more time, you can memorize your paycheck transaction using percentage splits rather than actual amounts. (The following procedure may result in imprecise year-end totals, so verify that the resulting calculations are correct if you are using your Quicken data for tax purposes.) Complete the Split Transaction window as described earlier, entering actual amounts from your paycheck. Press Ctrl-Enter to leave the Split Transaction window, then press Ctrl-M to memorize the transaction. Type **P** to indicate you want to memorize percentages. When you recall the memorized transaction, Quicken asks you to enter an amount from which to calculate the totals; enter your *net* pay. (To see the percentages themselves, press Ctrl-T to see the memorized transactions, highlight your paycheck transaction, and press Ctrl-E then Ctrl-S.)

Taxable Perquisites

You may receive additional taxable benefits from your employers. It's worthwhile to track these benefits for tax planning purposes and to ensure that there are no big surprises when you receive your W-2 at the end of the year. Some of these benefits, such as a car allowance, will be easy to identify and account for because they come in the form of a check. For these, simply set

Figure 5.5   Completed paycheck transaction and paycheck stub

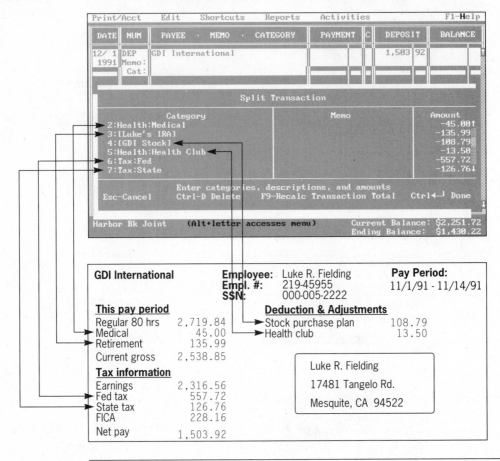

up a memorized deposit transaction (categorized as Car Allowance or Benefits) and record it in the Register each time you get a check.

Other benefits, such as taxable life insurance benefits, are more elusive because they don't involve the transfer of cash and are not consistently reported on your paycheck stubs. To be very accurate, you should enter offsetting splits in your paycheck transaction to reflect the taxable portion of company life insurance: one under Taxable Benefits (income) and the other under Life Insurance (expense). If this amount is not reported on each paycheck stub, you can divide last year's amount (reported on your W-2) by the number of pay periods, to determine a working approximation. The amount probably won't change much, so you may want to build this amount into your memorized paycheck transaction (see Figure 5.7).

Figure 5.6   **Format for memorized paycheck transactions**

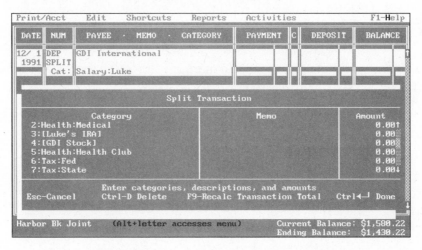

Figure 5.7   **Taxable noncash benefits in memorized paycheck transaction**

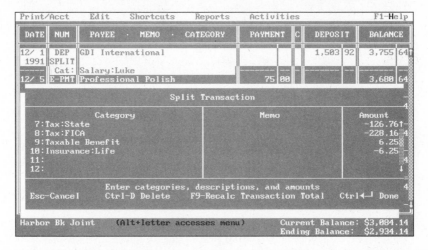

Your Mortgage

Another complicated but regular transaction is your mortgage payment. Although the amount of each payment is generally constant, the breakdown among principal, interest, and mortgage escrow amounts varies from month to month.

Monthly Payments

The trick to handling monthly payments is determining the split among principal, interest, and escrow. If you receive a comprehensive mortgage statement, the task is easy: the bank will tell you how to divide each month's transaction. Set up a memorized transaction which includes an expense category for mortgage interest, a liability account for the mortgage principal, and an asset account for your mortgage escrow. Figure 5.8 shows how a completed mortgage transaction split might look.

Figure 5.8   **Mortgage transaction split**

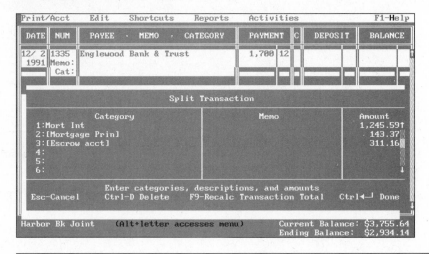

Automatic Loan Amortization

Note. Banks can use one of several formulae for calculating monthly payments on amortized loans. Quicken uses the most common such formula, but your mortgage bill may differ by a few pennies.

Quicken 5 also offers a tool for determining the interest/principal split—in other words, the amortization schedule—for a fixed mortgage transaction. Unfortunately, Quicken doesn't support variable-rate mortgage loans due to the complexity of these calculations. Quicken links amortized loans to memorized transactions. This way, the proper interest and principal amounts appear automatically in the split window for the transaction.

Suppose the original principal of a home mortgage was $155,000 and the 30-year fixed-rate loan was established at an interest rate of 10.25% in March 1984. With the loan now in its ninth year, the homeowner is interested in tracking the interest/principal split, especially since the deductible interest amount is declining. The amortization schedule attached to his mortgage payment transaction lets him see instantly what the split is.

You set up an amortized loan transaction as follows:

1. Enter into the Register the mortgage transaction you want to memorize. Use the Split Transaction window (Ctrl-S) to list amounts for principal, interest, and escrow, as described above under "Monthly Payments."

2. Memorize the transaction by pressing Ctrl-M. Press Enter to memorize amounts, not percentages.

3. Open the Memorized Transactions list (Ctrl-T), highlight the loan transaction you want to amortize, and press F9 to indicate that this is an amortized transaction. The Set Amortization Information window will appear.

4. Quicken places information from the memorized transaction into the window, filling in the payment amount, payee, categories for principal and interest, and the payment date next to "Date of first payment." You enter the interest rate, total years' term of the loan, and confirm the number of periods per year (Quicken guesses 12).

5. To complete the schedule window, list the date of the first payment (for example, March 1, 1984) and the number of payments made on the loan (in our example, 94, if you've just made the payment for December 1991). Your screen should resemble Figure 5.9.

Figure 5.9   **Set Amortization Schedule window**

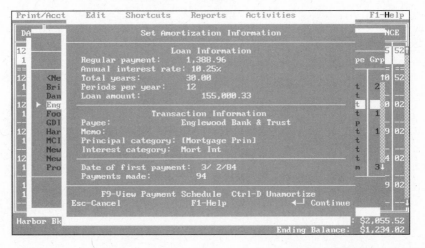

6. Press F9 to view the full amortization schedule for the loan, as shown in Figure 5.10. To obtain a printed copy of the amortization schedule, press Ctrl-P.

Figure 5.10   Payment Schedule for Amortizing Loans

```
 Print/Acct    Edit     Shortcuts    Reports    Activities        F1-Help
 DA                          Set Amortization Information                 NCE
12                                                                      5 52
 1                      Approximate Payment Schedule              pe Grp
==
12   <N      Date     Pmt    Principal      Interest      Balance     t0 52
 1   Br                                                              t  2
--   Da     8/ 2/91    90     138.58       1,250.38     146,248.25  ↑t
12 ▶ En     9/ 2/91    91     139.76       1,249.20     146,108.49   t   0 02
 1   Fo    10/ 2/91    92     140.95       1,248.01     145,967.54   t   1
--   GD    11/ 2/91    93     142.16       1,246.80     145,825.38   p
12   Ha  ▶ 12/ 2/91    94     143.37       1,245.59     145,682.01   t   9 02
 1   MC     1/ 2/92    95     144.60       1,244.36     145,537.41   t
--   Ne     2/ 2/92    96     145.83       1,243.13     145,391.58   t   4 02
12   Ne     3/ 2/92    97     147.08       1,241.88     145,244.50  ↓t
 1   Pr                                                              m   3↓
--             Ctrl-P Print  ↑,↓ Select
 1         Esc-Cancel             F1-Help           ←┘ Continue          9 02
 1
 Harbor Bk                                              : $2,055.52
                                          Ending Balance:  $1,234.02
```

Note. Should you later delete an amortized loan transaction, you must manually reset the Payments Left field for the loan.

7. When you record this memorized transaction in the Register, Quicken will automatically paste the proper interest and principal amounts into the appropriate lines of the transaction's split window. Other line items, such as escrow account contributions, will remain unchanged. Whenever you record an amortized transaction, Quicken will increase by one the Payments made entry in the Set Amortization window.

Early Principal Payments

Occasionally, you may feel that reducing the principal amount of your mortgage loan is your best possible investment. When this happens, the bank recomputes the amortization schedule (that is, the allocation between principal and interest) on the loan. Depending on the bank, this doesn't necessarily change the payment amount: the loan is merely paid off earlier. (Bank policies vary—some banks will make the change on request for adjustable-rate mortgages.)

If you make an early principal payment, you should add a second mortgage principal line to the split window for your mortgage transaction, as in Figure 5.11. Note in the memo field that this represents an early principal payment.

Figure 5.11   **Early principal payment in the Split Transaction window**

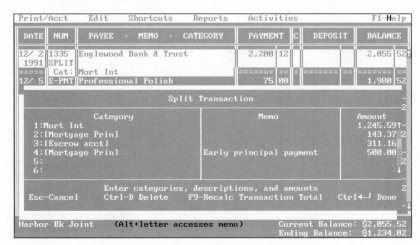

If your bank does adjust the amount of the mortgage payment, follow this procedure to adjust the Set Amortization window settings when the adjustment goes into effect:

1. Press Ctrl-T to see the list of memorized transactions.

2. Highlight the mortgage transaction, then press F9 to see the Set Amortization Information window.

3. Enter the new regular payment amount from your mortgage statement.

4. Press Ctrl-Enter to leave the window, and Escape to return to the Register.

Late Charges

In most cases, your bank grants you a grace period (typically 15 days) after the due date during which you may make your mortgage payment without penalty. If you make this payment after that date, the bank usually assesses a very stiff late charge, which often shows up on a later mortgage bill.

The only good news about the late charge is that it is often deductible as mortgage loan interest. When you pay a late charge as part of a regular mortgage payment, create an extra mortgage interest line in the payment's Split Transaction window (Ctrl-S), and annotate the line as a late charge, as in Figure 5.12. If you anticipate late charge payments to be frequent events (heaven forbid!), you may consider creating a subcategory under mortgage interest called "Late Charges"; this will help you understand how much your tardiness is actually costing you.

Figure 5.12   Late charge notation in the Split Transaction window

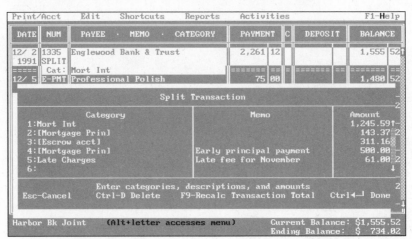

Mortgage Escrow Adjustments

If your mortgage loan carries an escrow account for property taxes and/or homeowner's insurance, you should have set up an Other Asset account to represent it. Each month, you allocate a portion of your mortgage payment as a transfer to this escrow account.

Periodically, you will receive tax and insurance bills which you will forward to the bank to be deducted from the mortgage escrow account. When you receive these bills, you should make an entry in the escrow account register to reflect the payment of these tax and insurance bills out of your escrow account.

To make an entry into your escrow account register, press Ctrl-A (for Account) and select the name of your escrow account from the list. You'll discover that Quicken maintains transaction registers for Other Asset accounts very similarly to the way it handles bank accounts. Enter a new transaction in the escrow account register, categorizing it in the appropriate tax or insurance category. Figure 5.13 shows the register screen for a typical mortgage escrow account.

Your Other Loans

Once you've mastered the basics of mortgage loans—splitting principal and interest, building amortization schedules, and handling early and late payments—you can apply them to almost any loan.

Note. At least once a year, you'll receive a reconciliation statement for your escrow account. It will list your insurance and tax payments, as well as interest earned on your account. You can reconcile this statement just as you reconcile a monthly bank statement.

Figure 5.13 **Mortgage Escrow Account register**

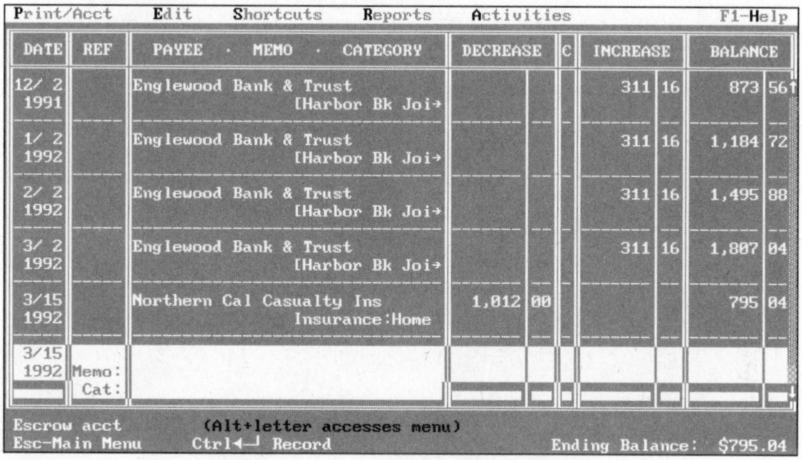

```
Print/Acct    Edit    Shortcuts    Reports    Activities              F1-Help
┌──────┬─────┬─────────────────────────────────┬──────────┬─┬─────────┬──────────┐
│ DATE │ REF │ PAYEE · MEMO · CATEGORY         │ DECREASE │C│ INCREASE│ BALANCE  │
├──────┼─────┼─────────────────────────────────┼──────────┼─┼─────────┼──────────┤
│12/ 2 │     │Englewood Bank & Trust           │          │ │  311 16 │  873 56↑ │
│1991  │     │            [Harbor Bk Joi→      │          │ │         │          │
│ 1/ 2 │     │Englewood Bank & Trust           │          │ │  311 16 │ 1,184 72 │
│1992  │     │            [Harbor Bk Joi→      │          │ │         │          │
│ 2/ 2 │     │Englewood Bank & Trust           │          │ │  311 16 │ 1,495 88 │
│1992  │     │            [Harbor Bk Joi→      │          │ │         │          │
│ 3/ 2 │     │Englewood Bank & Trust           │          │ │  311 16 │ 1,807 04 │
│1992  │     │            [Harbor Bk Joi→      │          │ │         │          │
│ 3/15 │     │Northern Cal Casualty Ins        │ 1,012 00 │ │         │   795 04 │
│1992  │     │            Insurance:Home       │          │ │         │          │
│ 3/15 │Memo:│                                 │          │ │         │          │
│1992  │Cat: │                                 │          │ │         │          │
└──────┴─────┴─────────────────────────────────┴──────────┴─┴─────────┴──────────┘
Escrow acct         (Alt+letter accesses menu)
Esc-Main Menu       Ctrl◄─┘ Record                     Ending Balance:  $795.04
```

Money You Owe

Always set up an Other Liability account first. That way, you'll have a place
to record the principal portion of each payment. Amortizing loans (such as
most car and boat loans) may be handled exactly the same as mortgage loans
(see the previous section).

Interest-only loans are even simpler: each payment is a single-category
transaction. You may set up the liability account if you wish, but this won't
be necessary until you either begin tracking your net worth or begin making
principal payments.

Don't forget that only certain types of interest payments are tax deductible, now that recent tax reform measures have been fully implemented.
You'll want to separate the tax-deductible interest expenses (such as mortgage and investment interest) from the ones that are not deductible (such as
personal and credit card interest) by designating deductible categories as tax-
related in the Edit Category window. To access this window, press Ctrl-C (for
the Category and Transfer list), select the category you want to edit, and
press Ctrl-E (for Edit).

Money Others Owe You

For loans you've made to others, follow the same procedures as for money
you owe, but make the amount of the loan an Other Asset account, and
assign the interest to an income category. For example, you may have made
a loan to a relative for capital funds for a new business. Record payments
you receive as a deposit transaction, split between the appropriate interest

income category (for interest payments) and loans receivable asset account (for principal payments). Figure 5.14 shows an example of such a transaction with the Other Asset account name shown in brackets.

Figure 5.14   Split Transaction window showing a loan payment

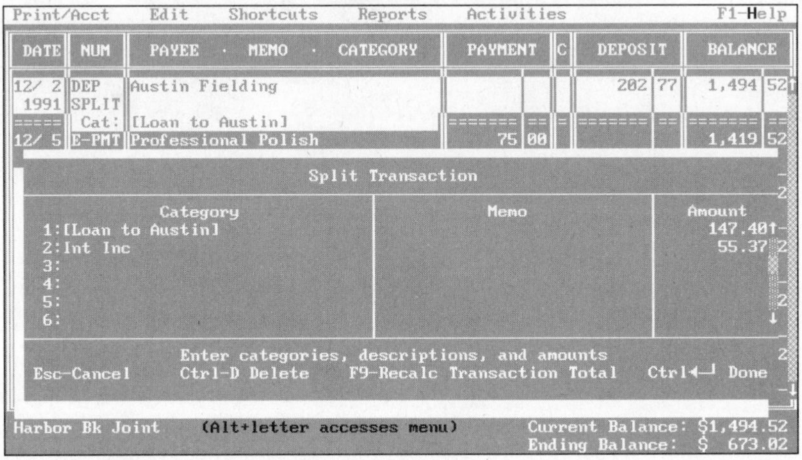

```
 Print/Acct    Edit    Shortcuts    Reports    Activities         F1-Help

 DATE  NUM   PAYEE  ·  MEMO  ·  CATEGORY    PAYMENT  C  DEPOSIT    BALANCE

12/ 2 DEP  Austin Fielding                            202 77    1,494 52
1991  SPLIT
===== Cat: [Loan to Austin]                ======= ==  ======= ==  ======= ==
12/ 5 E-PMT Professional Polish              75 00                 1,419 52

                          Split Transaction                              2

            Category                       Memo              Amount      2
       1:[Loan to Austin]                                    147.40
       2:Int Inc                                              55.37      2
       3:
       4:
       5:                                                                2
       6:                                                                ↓

                Enter categories, descriptions, and amounts             2
   Esc-Cancel    Ctrl-D Delete    F9-Recalc Transaction Total   Ctrl← Done

 Harbor Bk Joint    (Alt+letter accesses menu)     Current Balance: $1,494.52
                                                   Ending Balance:  $  673.02
```

Tax and Other Refunds

Sometimes, when you've overpaid an expense, you'll receive a refund check. A common instance is a tax refund, when you have overpaid your tax liability through withholding or estimated tax payments.

When you receive a refund check, it may be effective simply to credit the deposit against the original transaction. However, when you apply a refund credit that reflects a previous expense transaction, you may throw off the current month's budget.

For example, Susan Milner purchased a trellis and a set of outdoor furniture at a garden center in August for a total of $551.50, which she assigned to the Household category. Upon discovering defective workmanship in the furniture when she set it up, she returned it for a refund in September. She credited the refund check, which arrived in October, to the Household category for October rather than August. Because of its size, it canceled out all the other household expenses for October.

You must beware of such distortions under two circumstances: when the payment is in a tax-deductible category, and when you're using monthly expense data as a basis for budgeting for the following year. If necessary, you can eliminate such matching distortions from your documents by following this procedure.

1. Create an Other Asset account called "Refunds."

2. When recording the deposit of the refund check, categorize the deposit as a transfer from the Refunds account. This will result in a negative balance in that account.

3. Locate the transaction in which the overpayment occurred. Edit the transaction to make it a split transaction, categorizing the amount of the overpayment as a transfer to the "Refunds" asset account as shown in Figure 5.15. Your expenses for that month will now reflect the proper amount, and the Refunds asset account will balance out to zero.

Figure 5.15   **Editing an expense overpayment transaction**

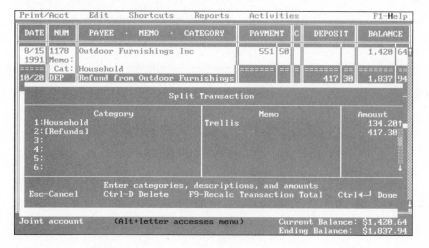

Tackle Special Purpose Categories

Some transactions aren't so straightforward as the ones described so far. Transactions that involve reimbursements, payroll deductions, and partnerships, for example, may require you to set up other Quicken accounts and adopt some special routines to track them.

Reimbursable Business Expenses

When you spend money that will later be reimbursed by your company, you are incurring reimbursable business expenses. Quicken helps you keep track

Note. Some of the reimbursable business expenses you claim—such as taxis, tolls, and so on—will result from cash expenditures rather than checks or credit card purchases. Unless you're careful to record these expenses and charge them against your Reimbursable category, over time you'll end up with a positive balance in this category.

of these expenses and the amount you receive from the company, so you can be sure you're being reimbursed for all the money you've spent.

Consider this example: Luke Fielding, who manages Executive Dining Services at his company's headquarters, is recognized by company executives as an expert in fine wines and is responsible for the company's wine stores. He takes occasional buying trips into the wine-making regions of California, Germany, and France at company expense. In theory, his travel expenses should be exactly offset by a series of deposits representing reimbursement checks from the company.

Luke's—and your—first instinct might be to treat expense reimbursements as an income category and business expenses as an expense category. That's not the best plan, though, because it doesn't take advantage of the opportunity to track how effectively you are recapturing business expenses through expense account reimbursements.

Instead, put your reimbursable business expenses and your expense account reimbursements into the same expense category, which you might call "Reimbursable" or "Reimb Business." As you incur business expenses, charge them against this category. As you deposit expense checks, record these amounts as deposits against the same category, as in Figure 5.16.

Figure 5.16   **Reimbursable business expense transactions in the Register**

```
 Print/Acct    Edit    Shortcuts    Reports   Activities              F1-Help
┌──────┬─────┬──────────────────────────────┬─────────┬─┬─────────┬──────────┐
│ DATE │ NUM │ PAYEE  ·  MEMO  ·  CATEGORY   │ PAYMENT │C│ DEPOSIT │ BALANCE  │
├──────┼─────┼──────────────────────────────┼─────────┼─┼─────────┼──────────┤
│12/18 │1352 │Wanda Milasz                  │  100 00 │ │         │ 3,031 67↑│
│ 1991 │     │          Childcare:Wand→     │         │ │         │          │
│12/20 │1353 │Green Bros Market             │   88 19 │ │         │ 2,943 48 │
│ 1991 │     │           Food:Groceries     │         │ │         │          │
│12/20 │1354 │Cities of the World Travel    │ 1,440 00│ │         │ 1,503 48 │
│ 1991 │     │France deposit  Reimb Business│         │ │         │          │
│12/22 │DEP  │GDI International             │         │ │  824 50 │ 2,327 98 │
│ 1991 │Memo:│Napa trip (11/91)             │         │ │         │          │
│      │Cat: │Reimb Business                │         │ │         │          │
│12/22 │     │Coastal Gas & Electric        │  161 60 │ │         │ 2,166 38 │
│ 1991 │     │             Utilities        │         │ │         │          │
│12/25 │     │Foothill Credit Union         │  196 65 │ │         │ 1,969 73 │
│ 1991 │     │Toyota loan       Auto:Loan   │         │ │         │          │
└──────┴─────┴──────────────────────────────┴─────────┴─┴─────────┴──────────┘
 Harbor Bk Joint    (Alt+letter accesses menu)     Current Balance: $2,166.38
 Esc-Main Menu    Ctrl◄┘ Record                     Ending Balance: $1,056.16
```

Over time, this category should total zero. You can check this by creating an Itemized Categories report and filtering the report for the single category Reimbursable, a procedure covered later in this level. If the category balance is negative, you're failing to put all your reimbursable expenses onto your expense account. If it's positive, you're probably overclaiming expenses.

Medical Expenses and Insurance

Like reimbursable business expenses, you should handle medical expenses and insurance payments through a single category. As you incur medical expenses, charge them against a Medical category; then, as you receive payments from your health insurance company, credit these deposits against the same category.

Note. Quicken can also help you determine if your medical expenses are above the limits allowed for deductability under U.S. tax law.

Periodically, create an Itemized Category report filtered for that category (as explained later in this level). Over time, any balance for the category should reflect the deductibles and exclusions your health insurance does not cover, plus any portion of your health insurance premiums which you yourself pay. If the net medical expense is very high over a period of time, you may want to consider extending your coverage or lowering your deductible. In any case, Quicken will help you measure the medical expense gap that is not covered by insurance. This—like any insight Quicken helps you attain—can drive a decision about the type of health care coverage you buy.

Dependent Care Expense Accounts

If you're participating in a tax-free dependent care reimbursement account offered by your company, Quicken can also help you track expenses and reimbursements, although this procedure varies slightly from reimbursable business or medical expenses.

The difference lies in two characteristics of these dependent care accounts: first, any expenses in excess of what the account can cover may be eligible for a dependent care tax credit on your income tax form; second, these funds are withheld from your paycheck on a pretax basis, so the IRS requires that any balance in the account at year's end be forfeited to Uncle Sam. It's critical to track these reimbursable expenses and the fund balance to make sure you're using all available funds in the account, especially if you think your expenses will come close to what you're withholding.

For example, a couple named Jim and Segonia Vickery have decided to withhold a total of $5,000 (the current maximum allowed by the IRS) from Segonia's paycheck to cover child care for their son, Benjamin. Before taxes, this amounts to $192.31 for each biweekly pay period. They estimate that total annual child care costs are $5,800, leaving $800 in unreimbursed dependent care costs for which they may be eligible for a tax credit.

By setting up an Other Assets account to track the reimbursement account, Jim and Segonia can ensure that they regularly submit canceled checks for reimbursement. In addition, by using a single category for all child care costs, they can get a category-specific report on the costs that are not reimbursed. The Vickerys can also be certain they're incurring expenses at the rate they anticipated, so that no money will be left in the fund at the end of the year.

To handle this type of account with Quicken,

1. Press Ctrl-A and select <New Account> to set up an Other Asset account to track the balance of your reimbursement account. Type **4** to indicate an Other Asset account, and give the account a descriptive name, such as "Dep Care." The account balance should be the amount already deducted from your paycheck this year (less any reimbursements you've already claimed), or $0.00, if this is a new account.

2. Set up a category for these expenses, such as Child Care or your care provider's name.

3. Split your paycheck transaction, and under Category, enter the account name in brackets, as in "[Dep Care]," to indicate a transfer. The amount you enter for that deduction will be credited to the Dep Care account. The Dep Care account balance increases with each paycheck.

4. After your monthly reconciliation, generate an Itemized Categories report for the month, which will organize transactions according to their categories. Use that report to locate the actual child care checks for which you should be reimbursed. Itemized Categories reports are introduced in Level 2.

5. Also at reconciliation time, check the balance of the Other Asset account to determine the available amount against which you can submit checks for reimbursement. Once you submit a claim, enter the total amount for reimbursement into the Other Assets account as a decrease and identify the item as "Submitted for Reimbursement," and enter the name of the current account—the dependent care account—in the Category field. When the check arrives, change that transaction to a transfer into the account where you deposited the check, as illustrated in Figure 5.17.

Note. Remember that you need only enter enough of the account name to uniquely identify it in the category field before you press Enter. When you enter an account name this way, you can omit the brackets; Quicken will supply them automatically.

Partnership Gains and Losses

Larry Milner is part of a limited partnership named the Goldberg-Fraeman Fund, and receives periodic distributions. These deposits are not always easy to categorize: Are they dividends, interest income, or capital transactions? Often, he finds that the correct answer is a blend of all three. If you are part of a partnership that doesn't report the exact composition of distributions as they occur, you'll probably have to wait until your K-1 partnership tax returns arrive early the following year to know precisely how to categorize partnership distributions.

Figure 5.17   **Dependent Care account register**

```
 Print/Acct     Edit    Shortcuts    Reports    Activities              F1-Help
┌──────┬─────┬────────────────────────────────┬─────────┬─┬─────────┬──────────┐
│ DATE │ REF │ PAYEE · MEMO · CATEGORY        │ DECREASE│C│ INCREASE│ BALANCE  │
├──────┼─────┼────────────────────────────────┼─────────┼─┼─────────┼──────────┤
│11/ 1 │     │Transfer                        │         │ │  192 31 │  344 81↑ │
│1991  │     │            [Joint Account]     │         │ │         │          │
├──────┼─────┼────────────────────────────────┼─────────┼─┼─────────┼──────────┤
│11/15 │     │Transfer                        │         │ │  192 31 │  537 12  │
│1991  │     │            [Joint Account]     │         │ │         │          │
├──────┼─────┼────────────────────────────────┼─────────┼─┼─────────┼──────────┤
│12/ 1 │     │Transfer                        │         │ │  192 31 │  729 43  │
│1991  │     │            [Joint Account]     │         │ │         │          │
├──────┼─────┼────────────────────────────────┼─────────┼─┼─────────┼──────────┤
│12/15 │     │Transfer                        │         │ │  192 31 │  921 74  │
│1991  │     │            [Joint Account]     │         │ │         │          │
├──────┼─────┼────────────────────────────────┼─────────┼─┼─────────┼──────────┤
│12/22 │     │Submitted for reimbursement     │  825 00 │ │         │   96 74  │
│1991  │     │            [Joint Account]     │         │ │         │          │
├──────┼─────┼────────────────────────────────┼─────────┼─┼─────────┼──────────┤
│12/22 │Memo:│                                │         │ │         │          │
│1991  │Cat :│                                │         │ │         │          │
└──────┴─────┴────────────────────────────────┴─────────┴─┴─────────┴──────────┘
 Dependent Care      (Alt+letter accesses menu)
 Esc-Main Menu      Ctrl←┘ Record                     Ending Balance:  $96.74
```

Because Larry is not given good classification data with the distribution check, he places these distribution deposits under an income category called "Partnership." This technique may completely serve your needs, too, and it's certainly the cleanest, simplest way to handle the situation. To the extent that Larry needs to account for the partnership distributions more accurately, he goes back and edits his partnership distribution transactions as follows when his partnership K-1 forms arrive:

1. Using the Find command (Ctrl-F), he locates the partnership distribution he wants to change.

2. He presses Ctrl-S to open a Split Transaction window for the transaction. The category Partnership is already inserted into the Split Transaction window.

3. Using the line items listed on the K-1, he substitutes the appropriate amounts and categories (such as interest income, interest expense, dividends, and capital gains realized) for the single Partnership Distributions line item in the window. You'll find an example in Figure 5.18.

4. He already created an asset account in the name of each partnership he owns. The opening balance of these accounts was the amount of his capital account, which can be either the amount invested or the size of the capital account as reported on the latest K-1. In editing his partnership distribution transactions, he makes sure to record changes in the capital accounts listed on the K-1 as increases (retained earnings) or decreases (return of capital) in the value of the Quicken partnership account.

Note. Obviously, you'll want to consult a tax advisor on how to actually apply these line items when you file your taxes. Your objective in Quicken should be to gain as accurate a picture of your financial situation as possible, and not to determine precisely how you should file your taxes.

Figure 5.18   **Split Transaction window with K-1 line items**

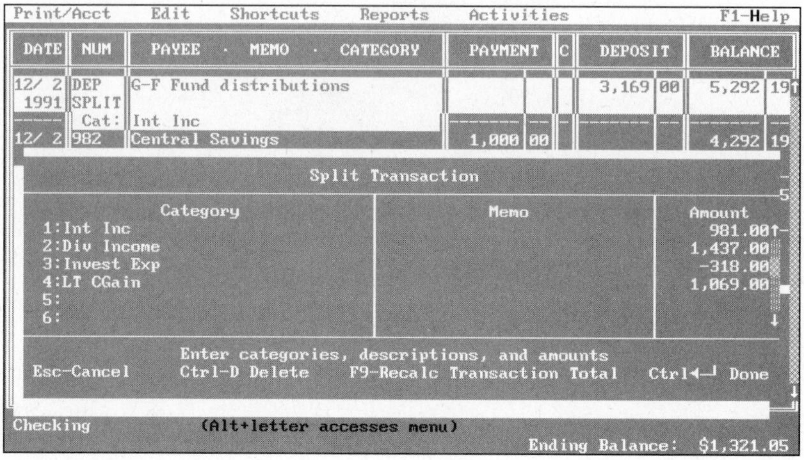

```
 Print/Acct     Edit     Shortcuts     Reports     Activities          F1-Help
┌──────┬─────┬──────────────────────────────────┬─────────┬──┬─────────┬──────────┐
│ DATE │ NUM │ PAYEE  ·  MEMO  ·  CATEGORY       │ PAYMENT │C │ DEPOSIT │ BALANCE  │
├──────┼─────┼──────────────────────────────────┼─────────┼──┼─────────┼──────────┤
│ 12/ 2│ DEP │ G-F Fund distributions           │         │  │ 3,169 00│ 5,292 19 │
│ 1991 │SPLIT│                                  │         │  │         │          │
│      │ Cat:│ Int Inc                          │         │  │         │          │
│ 12/ 2│ 982 │ Central Savings                  │ 1,000 00│  │         │ 4,292 19 │
└──────┴─────┴──────────────────────────────────┴─────────┴──┴─────────┴──────────┘
                           Split Transaction
              Category                    Memo              Amount
      1:Int Inc                                                981.00↑
      2:Div Income                                           1,437.00
      3:Invest Exp                                            -318.00
      4:LT CGain                                             1,069.00
      5:                                                             ↓
      6:
             Enter categories, descriptions, and amounts
  Esc-Cancel     Ctrl-D Delete     F9-Recalc Transaction Total    Ctrl⏎ Done

 Checking              (Alt+letter accesses menu)
                                          Ending Balance:  $1,321.05
```

Occasionally, you'll receive more than one partnership distribution in a single year. Since it's usually not possible to break each distribution separately into its component parts, the best alternative is to total all the deposits, calculating each categorized item as a percentage of the sum of those deposits (the percentages should add up to 100 percent), and then entering those percentages into the Split Transaction window for each partnership distribution deposit.

Charitable Contributions of Property

Note. This technique applies to any charitable contribution of property—clothing and household items as well. If you want to record these contributions, set up an Other Asset account for "Household Assets," containing a lump sum estimate of their worth; record contributions against this account.

If you give something you own to a charitable cause, you may be eligible for a charitable tax deduction. For example, Luke Fielding might decide to donate a good bottle of wine from his private cellar to a public television auction. Quicken's main function in this instance is to offer a reminder at tax preparation time of the date, amount, and circumstances of this contribution.

Luke's donation is the first transaction we've discussed that does not pass through a bank account. It is purely a transfer from his asset account (named Wine Cellar) to an expense category, such as Charity. He should have an account already created for the asset he's donating—then the transaction can be completed as follows:

1. Press Ctrl-A and select the Other Asset account (for example, Wine Cellar) from the list.

2. Create a new transaction with the payee being the name of the charity receiving the asset.

3. Choose the appropriate charitable contributions expense category, such as Charity (see Figure 5.19).

Figure 5.19 **Register entry for a charitable contribution of property**

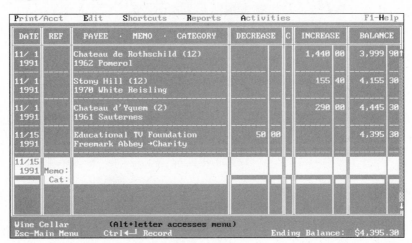

Use this technique to represent any expense that is paid for by liquidating an asset.

Track Your "Profit" Like a Business

While the Cash Flow report offers a useful picture of the rise and fall of your cash accounts, it can also give an incomplete answer to the question we all ask of ourselves: How well am I doing? This is because a well-managed personal portfolio minimizes changes in bank and cash accounts over time and builds assets such as investment accounts and home equity.

To find out how well you're doing, you can use the Profit and Loss (P&L) Statement. Although Quicken classifies this statement as a business, rather than a personal report, it can be extraordinarily useful for individuals.

The P&L Statement displays only income and expenses. The net difference between these two (your net income or "Total Income/Expense," as Quicken's reports refer to it) is the amount by which your net worth increased or decreased over the period being reported.

To obtain a P&L Statement,

1. From the Reports menu (Alt-R from the Register or Write Checks screen), select Business Reports (B) and then P&L Statement (S).

2. Enter an optional report title.

3. Adjust the range of months to represent the period for which you want to see a P&L Statement; then press Enter.

Quicken shows income categories first, sorted alphabetically, then lists expense categories, as in Figure 5.20.

Figure 5.20   Profit & Loss Statement

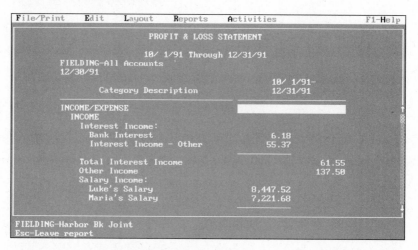

At the bottom of the report, Quicken shows all the transfers to and from each account in your file. Note that these are not net amounts: if you have transfers both into and out of an account, the transfers in are totaled and shown separately from the transfers out. The total transfers should balance out at zero.

Get More Out of Standard Reports

Quicken offers a rich array of customization options with which you can tailor your reports to your decision-making needs. We'll explore those options in Level 6; however, there are some techniques you can implement immediately to make the three standard reports we've discussed so far—Cash Flow, Itemized Categories, and Profit & Loss—even more helpful.

Delve for Transaction Details with QuickZoom

When you're viewing a summary report such as the Profit and Loss Statement, you may want to peek at the detail behind any given line item. This can be particularly useful if a summary amount looks suspiciously low or high. Alternatively, you might want to determine why a particular month's mortgage interest shows up as zero—did you miss a payment?

Previous versions of Quicken forced you to create another report in order to see this transaction-level detail. Quicken 5, however, gives you QuickZoom, a way to view instantly the transactions that underlie any summary income or expense line.

To use QuickZoom to delve into the transactions that make up an entry in a summary report,

1. View a summary report such as a P&L Statement (from the Reports menu, which you call by pressing Alt-R, select Business Reports and then P&L Statement). Across the top of the screen, you'll see the Reports menu bar.

2. A highlight bar appears in the Amount column of the report, which you can then move to the category into which you'd like to delve (see Figure 5.21).

Figure 5.21   Highlighted category in the Profit & Loss report

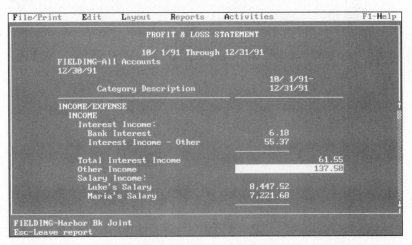

3. Once you've highlighted the category you'd like to explore, press Ctrl-Z (QuickZoom), or select QuickZoom from the File/Print menu (Alt-F). The detail transactions appear in a Transaction List window that overlays

Note. Quicken allows you to delve only into income and expense summary lines. If you try to delve into a transfer summary line, you'll be rebuffed.

the summary report (see Figure 5.22). Use the Up and Down Arrow keys to scroll through the transaction detail.

4. At this point, you can either return to the report by pressing Escape, or you can move to the Register to change or further examine a transaction. Move the highlight bar to the appropriate transaction and press F9; you'll find yourself in the Register, with the transaction highlighted. You won't, however, be able to return directly to the report from this point; you'll have to re-create the report.

Figure 5.22   Transaction List shown during QuickZoom

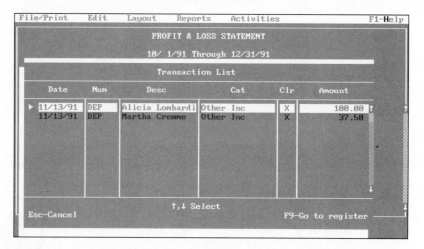

Set Up a Single Category Report

The Itemized Category report, which you first saw in Level 2, lists the transaction detail behind each category and subcategory, covering all transactions for a given time period. But sometimes you may want a report that focuses on only one category.

For example, earlier in this level we discussed techniques for tracking business expense reimbursements and medical expenses. If you've adopted those techniques, you now have some double-duty categories that track both income and expense transactions. To monitor your business expense reimbursements, you need a report that gives you a balance for only the Reimbursable category. To obtain this information, you can create a filtered Itemized Categories report.

To set up a single category report,

1. From the Reports menu (Alt-R), select Personal Reports and then Item-ized Categories.

2. Enter an optional report title.

3. Adjust the time period. For example, you might want to encompass the month in which you last incurred business expenses. Press Enter to see the full report.

4. From the Report menu bar, press Alt-E to see the Edit menu, and select Filter Transactions. The Filter Transactions window shown in Figure 5.23 appears.

Figure 5.23   Filter Transactions window

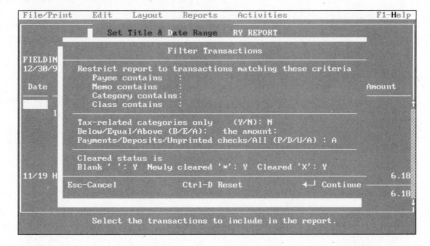

5. Specify the matching patterns Quicken should use to select transactions for the report. To filter a specific category, such as Reimbursable, type the category name in the "Category contains" field. Alternatively, you can press Ctrl-C to display the Category and Transfer list, and then choose the category from the list.

6. Leave the remaining settings as they are, and press Ctrl-Enter to display the filtered report (see Figure 5.24).

Figure 5.24   **Itemized Category report filtered by a category**

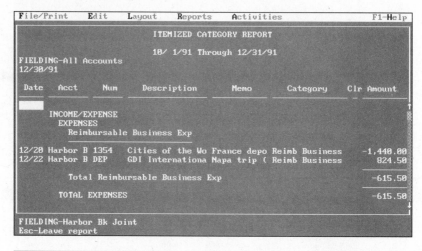

Compare Expenses from Different Time Periods

Often you'll need to compare income, expenses, and other Quicken information over a period of time. For example, you might want to find out how much more you spend on heating utilities during the winter than you do during the summer. When you first request a report, Quicken assumes you want to cover a single time period—from the beginning of the year to the present. You can change the columns to show the same information by month, by quarter, or by a variety of other time periods.

For example, with a Cash Flow report on your screen, filter it so it shows only transactions assigned to the Utilities: Gas & Electric category (from the Edit menu, choose Filter Transactions, and type the category name next to "Category contains"). Then from the Layout menu (Alt-L), choose Column Headings (H) and Month (M). Quicken will reformat the report, showing you summary data by month, as in Figure 5.25. Since the display is not wide enough to handle all 12 months, you can use your Right and Left Arrow keys to scroll around the screen.

Print Your Reports

Again, Level 6 covers printing in detail but if you're anxious to get a Quicken report on paper, press Ctrl-P (for Print) while the report you want is on the screen. From the Print Report window (Figure 5.26), type **1** to use the report printer you set up during installation. Make sure you've loaded and positioned the paper before you press Enter to start the process.

Figure 5.25   Summary data by month

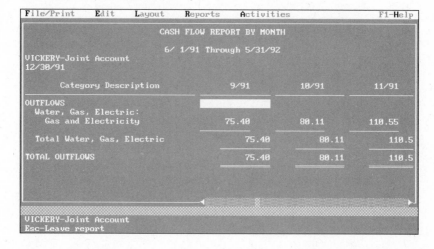

Figure 5.26   Print Report window

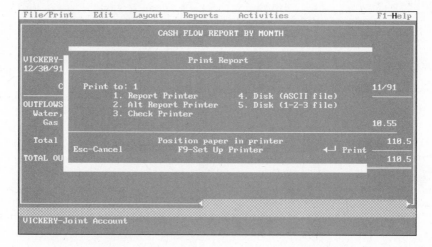

LEVEL 5 BUILDING BLOCKS

In Level 5, you explored ways to handle more sophisticated transactions, often involving transfers among other Quicken accounts.

TECHNIQUES AND PROCEDURES

■ Common but complex transactions—such as your salary or mortgage—work neatly with Quicken's category-account structure. Deal with the myriad deductions on a paycheck by splitting the transaction (press Ctrl-S). Categorize each deduction, so you can periodically check what you've paid into taxes or medical benefits, for example. For money automatically deposited into a company savings plan, first set up an Other Asset account; then record the deduction as a transfer to that account.

■ Tax and other refunds distort the size of particular expense categories for the month the refund is received. If you're worried about the effect this might have on your planning (for instance, if you're budgeting based on category totals), set up an Other Asset account called "Refunds Receivable" and treat the deposit as a transfer to that account. Also, split the original transaction to note the amount of the refund.

■ Standard reports, such as Cash Flow or Profit and Loss, can yield surprisingly rich detail if you use the QuickZoom (Alt-Z) command to delve into them. While in a report, move the cursor to the category you'd like to explore and press Enter. Quicken will show you the category details that produced the totals in the report.

■ Create a single category report by first setting up an Itemized Categories report and then selecting Filter Transactions from the Edit menu (Alt-E while viewing a report). Specify the category by which you want to filter.

TERMS

■ A *transfer* is a transaction amount deducted from one account and credited to another. A transfer might be a payment written from your checking account to your savings account, or a mortgage principal amount that reduces the balance in the account tracking what you owe on your home to the bank. Transfers help you maintain an accurate reflection of your net worth by charting how your assets change over time.

■ *Other Asset* and *Other Liability* accounts track what you own and what you owe, respectively. Other assets might be money owed to you, a valuable collection of baseball cards, or a piece of property. Other liabilities might be car or school loans.

■ *Investment accounts* help you track investments that fluctuate in price. You use investment accounts to monitor mutual funds, stocks, and bonds.

IMPORTANT IDEAS

■ Split and memorized transactions are powerful tools for helping you achieve the level of detail you expect from Quicken. If you decide to go beyond mere income and expense reporting to consider assets you're building, you can split transactions such as mortgage payments and paychecks to accurately reflect the complex details in your overall financial picture. Memorizing these transactions makes such fine-tuned tracking as easy as pressing a few keys.

■ Setting up accounts for all your assets and liabilities is also necessary if you want to obtain greater detail. Other Asset and Other Liability accounts are as easy to use as Bank accounts. Quicken's built-in amortization tables allow you to accurately include loan principal in your net worth assessments, and help you decide whether early principal payments are a good investment.

■ Lost or late reimbursements may be robbing you of cash to which you're entitled. Using categories to track reimbursable business expenses and funds received to cover them will help you reclaim cash as efficiently as possible. Tracking medical reimbursements will also give you a better understanding of whether your medical benefits are providing the coverage you need.

■ The flip side of putting information into Quicken is drawing information out in a form you can use to assess your finances, make decisions, and take action. Get a business-like view of your personal finances with the useful Profit and Loss report, and explore for the details in this and other reports to find out what's behind the summaries. Filter reports to isolate categories in the Itemized Categories report when a particular aspect of your money-management interests you.

2

Make Quicken Work for You

6

Apply More Advanced Tracking Methods

PLAN AHEAD

Manage Your Credit Cards

Manage Your Cash Expenditures

Use Classes for Richer Detail

Design a Suite of Reports

Set Up Personal Payroll and 1099 Accounts

BUILDING BLOCKS

PLAN AHEAD

DECISIONS

What Should You Track Other than Checking Accounts?

Keeping track of a financial picture would be much simpler if everyone worked entirely out of a checking account. In fact, that's the philosophy behind the all-in-one checking, savings, and investment accounts now being offered by some major banks and brokerage houses. However, it's impossible to capture all the significant detail of complex financial lives by simply recording all checks and bank deposits.

In addition to checking accounts, money commonly changes hands via credit cards, cash expenditures, and brokerage or other investment accounts. Level 8 is dedicated to investment accounts. In this level you'll discover several options for dealing with credit card and cash expenditures.

As we advised in earlier levels, you should only collect as much data as you can really use. Each additional credit card or cash account you create means more work for you, although it also increases the accuracy and richness of your data. You should decide up front, therefore, how much detail you want to collect and maintain in these accounts.

How Detailed Should You Be with Credit Cards?

To decide how much detail to accumulate on your credit cards, try this simple exercise: Take out your wallet and lay your credit cards on the table (pretty frightening, isn't it?). Separate the cards into three piles.

In pile one, place all the credit cards that are dedicated to a single purpose—that is, whose spending would fall predominantly into a single Quicken category—and which you intend to pay in full every month. This pile might contain oil company credit cards, clothing store charge cards, and company-issued business travel cards, as well as cards from rental car companies and airlines.

Piles two and three will be for more general-purpose credit cards (such as American Express, MasterCard, Visa, and Discover), and cards for general retail outlets such as department stores. Place in pile two those cards that you pay off in full each month but use for fewer than five transactions, which are generally distributed across three or fewer categories or which represent a very small percentage of your spending. These cards aren't worth tracking meticulously.

You'll note that the remaining cards—those in pile three—really function much like checking accounts, with many transactions distributed across many expense categories. These will probably be the cards you use frequently to make a variety of large and small purchases. This pile should also contain cards that you don't pay down to a zero balance each month.

Each pile demands a tracking method that garners a different level of detail. These methods are described later in this level. Only one of the three, the *Detail Method,* uses a special Quicken charge card account, designed solely to track charge card activity. The other two methods—*Summary* and *Partial Detail*—use your regular bank account, against which you probably write the checks to pay each credit card company. You should apply these methods to the piles of cards:

- Use the Summary method when you pay the monthly bills for pile one's single purpose, single category cards.

- Use the Partial Detail method for recording activity on pile two's multipurpose but less frequently used cards.

- For the multipurpose, general-use cards in pile three, use the Detail method; these are the only ones that merit special treatment. This method is also suitable for cards that carry a balance from month to month, because Quicken can track the money you owe over time, enabling you to account for this liability accurately.

How Detailed Should You Be with Cash?

Just as you did with credit cards, you should examine how much you rely on cash for the kinds of expenditures you might want to track. If you're like most people, you periodically trek down to an automatic teller machine or to the supermarket's service desk to replenish the cash in your wallet. Do you want to track how you spend this money?

In most cases, you won't want to bother tracking cash detail, and the Summary method in your regular bank account will suffice. However, if your personal style is such that you pay a large percentage of your expenses in cash, Quicken will misrepresent your spending patterns if it focuses solely on bank account activity. In this case (and in the case of business cash spending), you might want to apply the Detail method to your cash records.

Likewise, if you make charitable contributions in cash (for instance, the money you might put into the collection plate at church), you must record these transactions in Quicken to finish the year with accurate tax records. For these expenditures, you might want to apply the Partial Detail method described in this level.

Should You Use Classes As Well As Categories?

Categories provide a one-dimensional way of viewing your income and expenditures. They describe the dollars spent on either gas or clothing or some other category—but never more than one.

There are occasions, however, when you might want to view your income or spending in more than one way. For instance, you might categorize the electric bill on your vacation home under Utilities, but later decide to group all your vacation home expenditures together.

Quicken's classes provide an additional structure for categorizing your financial transactions. Once you apply classes, you can craft your reports to include or exclude specific classes, or even to organize different classes of information into various columns on a report. But each transaction (or portion of a split transaction) may be assigned to only one category and one class. Therefore, take care not to set up too many class schemes.

Now is the time to consider alternative ways you might want Quicken to save and report your transactions. Here are some suggestions for deciding whether to classify as well as categorize them:

- *Business versus personal*   If you have a small business with which you share your checking account, you may want to use classes to distinguish your business-related expenses from your personal expenses. This is a great way to separate out the information for Schedule C (Profit or Loss from Business) of your income tax return.

- *Real estate properties*   If you have investment real estate, you'll want to distinguish among different properties as you record expenses. This is not only useful in evaluating the return on your investment; it's also required when reporting your rental income and expenses for tax purposes.

- *Projects (or clients)*   Classes help segregate expenses related to a particular project—either business or home. For example, if you want to identify income and expenses related to two clients in your business, you can create a class designation for each client in addition to any categories you might assign.

- *Family members*   If you have a reason to keep track of the income or expenses related to a particular member of the family, classes are a useful way to accomplish this.

- *Tax status*   Quicken's categories can be designated as tax-related, but even so, their tax status may not always be so clear-cut. For example, you may receive interest from an investment in one year but be liable for taxes on that income in another. In this case, the transaction, though tax-related, is not subject to tax. You could add a "Tax-Free" class to any transaction which is classified in a tax-related category but which is, nonetheless, not tax related.

- *Automobiles*   Your car expenses may be spread across many different categories—insurance, gasoline, car repairs, and so on. By using class designators like Honda and Jaguar, you can instantly obtain reports on how much each vehicle is costing you to operate.

What Additional Reports Will You Need?

You should think of Quicken's standard reports—Cash Flow, Profit and Loss, Net Worth, and the like—as mere starting points toward defining the collection of reports you'll use for managing your personal finances. Quicken 5 makes it very easy to start with these standard reports and then begin adding variations—columns that represent months or quarters, or rows that summarize transactions by payee or class, for example.

To prepare for Level 6, look over the Gallery of Quicken Reports in Appendix D. Knowing that rows and columns can be customized, note any changes that might render the reports more useful to you.

MATERIALS

Credit Card Statements and Receipts

Collect the most recent credit card statements for all cards on which you'll be maintaining full or partial detail. To derive full benefit from your expense tracking, enter historical credit card data beginning in the same month you chose to start tracking your bank account.

You will obtain a more timely view of your credit situation if you enter transactions from charge receipts as you receive them, rather than waiting for credit card statements. If you choose this approach, save your credit card receipts so that you can enter them the same way you'd enter hand-written checks.

Cash Log

If you keep a log of major cash expenditures, you should have that on hand, too. If you plan to record full detail of your cash expenditures, consider starting a cash log. This level will describe how to begin logging cash expenses.

PRELIMINARIES

Complete Levels 1 and 2

All you need to start using advanced tracking and reporting methods is a basic knowledge of Quicken—the kind of knowledge of accounts, registers, categories, and basic reporting described in Levels 1 and 2. Knowing how to write checks, either on paper or electronically, is not necessary. Nor do you need to know how to handle the special accounting situations covered in Level 5.

Manage Your Credit Cards

In the Plan Ahead section for this level, you decided which of three methods—Summary, Detail, or Partial Detail—you'll use to account for each credit card. The Summary and Detail methods don't require you to set up separate credit card accounts. However, you will need to set up credit card accounts for each card that requires the Detail method.

Summary Method

For single-purpose credit cards that you pay off monthly, simply record the transaction in the bank account that you use to pay the credit card balance, and categorize it exactly the same as you would any other expense.

Although most of these transactions will be expenditures assigned to one category (such as Auto Fuel or Clothing), there are two circumstances under which you may want to split a transaction: if your bill reflects finance charges or if you want to record additional detail.

If your bill reflects a finance or service charge resulting from an overdue payment, you should place this charge in a Finance Charge or Personal Interest expense category. (Remember, credit card interest expense is no longer deductible from your taxes.) Figure 6.1 shows a split transaction accounting for a finance charge. (For a reminder on splitting transactions, see Level 2.)

Figure 6.1   Split transaction showing a finance charge (Summary method)

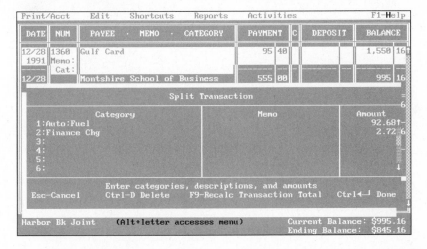

If you want to record additional detail on your charges—for example, if your gas card includes charges for an oil change as well as for gasoline—you may want to split the transaction into two categories: Auto Service and Auto Fuel. In general, though, you'll find that a single category is sufficient for these credit card bills.

Detail Method

When you choose to apply the Detail method, you'll record every credit card transaction just as you would checks in a bank account register. All of the category assignment functions work here exactly as they do in bank accounts. Figure 6.2 shows the register of a credit card account in which transactions are recorded using the Full Detail method.

Figure 6.2   **Credit Card Account register (Detail method)**

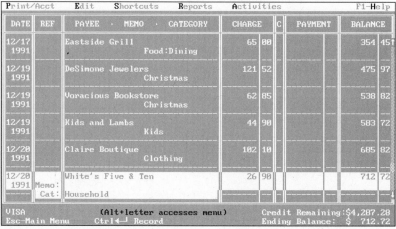

A credit card account is similar to a Quicken bank account. In particular, it has a register which resembles and acts very much like a bank account. However, before you set up your first credit card account, there are some major differences that are worth noting:

- Credit card accounts are liability accounts, while bank accounts are assets. More often than not, credit card accounts have a negative or zero balance.

- You cannot use the Write Checks screen from a credit card account.

- In a credit card account register, you record purchases in the CHARGE column and payments in the PAYMENT column.

- Quicken can report how much credit you have remaining if you enter your credit limit while setting up the account. When you view a credit card account register, Quicken indicates your available credit in the lower-right corner of the screen.

To set up a credit card account,

1. From the register of any account, press Ctrl-A (or choose Select Account from the Main Menu).

2. Choose <New Account>. Quicken displays the Set Up New Account window.

3. Type **2** for Credit Card, and type an account name, such as **Visa**.

4. Enter an opening balance for the account. If you tend to pay the balance in full each month, enter zero. If an unpaid balance remains from the previous month, enter that balance. Also enter the date of the last statement. A sample account setup is shown in Figure 6.3.

5. Enter an optional description for the account, and press Ctrl-Enter to leave the window.

Figure 6.3   Set Up New Account window for a credit card

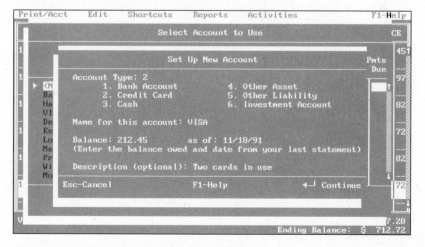

6. Quicken displays the Specify Credit Limit window. Here you can specify the credit limit for your account, which will enable Quicken to display your available credit on the Credit Card Register screen.

Note. Because Quicken combines payment and reconciliation, it's a good idea to handle payments on your credit card accounts separately from your other bills.

When a credit card bill comes due, Quicken enables you to pay it easily and to reconcile your credit card account at the same time. In fact, you can arrange for Quicken to issue a check or electronic payment from the appropriate bank account—just as though you had entered the check as a transaction in that bank account. To use this feature,

1. From the Activities menu, select Reconcile/Pay Credit Card.

2. In the Credit Card Statement Information window, enter information from your most recent account statement. Quicken asks for total charges and cash advances, payments and credits, the new balance, the statement opening and closing dates, and any assessed finance charges. When you finish, press Enter. Figure 6.4 shows an example.

Figure 6.4   **Credit Card Statement Information window**

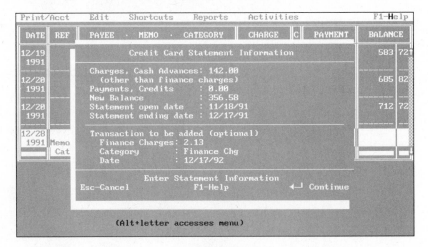

3. Quicken displays the Reconciliation Summary window, listing all uncleared transactions in the account. For each transaction that appears on your statement, highlight that transaction on the screen (assuming that you've been entering credit card transactions as they occur) and press Enter to clear it; Quicken places an X in the cleared (C) column. When you finish clearing transactions, the amount next to Difference in the lower part of the screen should be zero, indicating that your account balances with the credit card statement. Press Ctrl-F10 to continue.

4. Next, Quicken displays the Make Credit Card Payment window, shown in Figure 6.5. Quicken shows the outstanding balance on the account, and offers to begin the process of paying the bill. If you don't yet want to pay the bill, press Escape. If you do, type the name of the account out of which the bill should be paid (or press Ctrl-C to see a list of accounts). Next to "Computer check/Manual check/Electronic payment," type **M** if you want to hand-write a check, or **E** if you want Quicken to transmit a check electronically; otherwise, press Enter for Quicken to print the check. Press Enter to continue.

Figure 6.5   **Make Credit Card Payment window**

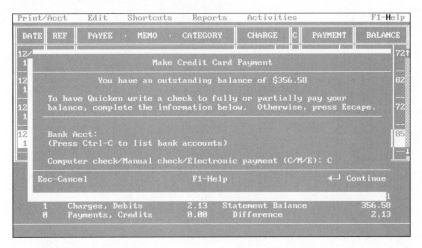

5. If you opted to have Quicken pay the bill, Quicken displays the Write Checks screen for the account you specified, with the unpaid balance for the credit card account already filled in. You merely complete the payee; the category already notes the credit card account as the transfer account. See Figure 6.6 for an example of a completed credit card payment check.

Partial Detail Method

When you choose the Partial Detail method, you want to capture some of the category detail of your credit card transactions without going to the trouble of setting up and maintaining an entirely new credit card account. To do this, record each credit card payment as a split transaction, logging only as much detail as you really need.

Figure 6.6   **Write Checks screen showing a credit card payment**

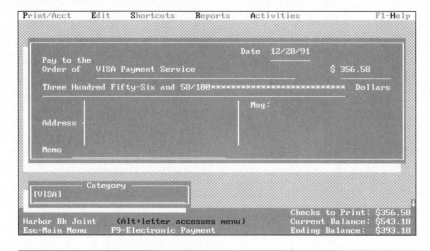

Note. Entering transaction detail on split transaction lines "hides" it in transaction reports summarized by payee. With the Partial Detail method, you sacrifice some vendor detail in reports organized by payee.

Note. While your cash flow may prevent you from paying your credit cards in full each month, it's rarely a good idea to make this a regular practice. Credit card interest is one of the most expensive forms of credit available.

For example, you might record a payment on your Sears credit card as follows:

1. Enter the credit card payment in the bank account register from which you will pay the bill. The payee is Sears, and the amount is the total bill.

2. Under category, choose Ctrl-S (for Split) to split the transaction into multiple categories.

3. In the Split Transaction window, record as much detail as you like on the 30 transaction split lines available—right down to 30 individual credit card purchases, if that amount of detail is crucial. The Amount column will always show the balance of transactions you haven't recorded in the last line.

4. When you've recorded all the detail you want and a balance still remains from transactions you haven't detailed, you should determine how you'll categorize the balance (a Miscellaneous category, if nothing else). Figure 6.7 shows a split transaction with a miscellaneous balance.

5. Return to the transaction by pressing Ctrl-Enter; then record the transaction by pressing Ctrl-Enter a second time.

Sometimes you may not pay the entire balance of your credit card bill, choosing instead to pay interest to the bank next month. If you do this, your credit card account will carry a negative balance, and a credit card liability will appear on all your net worth reports.

Figure 6.7   **Split transaction (Partial Detail method)**

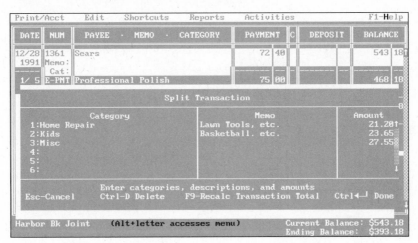

Manage Your Cash Expenditures

A separate Quicken cash account is rarely necessary—the Summary method adequately captures the character of most people's cash expenditures. The exceptions are people who pay many large expenses by cash or who need to track cash expenditures for tax or business reimbursement reasons. In these cases, you may want to use either the Detail or Partial Detail methods described later in this section. (The Plan Ahead section at the beginning of this level will help you choose an appropriate approach to account for cash expenditures.)

Summary Method

Dale Scott, whom you met in the preliminary chapter, "Laying the Groundwork for Your Financial Future," is an example of someone for whom the Summary method of cash management would work well. Dale uses cash for only a small percentage of his expenditures, and he doesn't need to track any individual cash transactions for tax or business purposes (he doesn't itemize his tax deductions). With the Summary method, he can estimate by percentage how his cash expenditures are distributed across his expense categories or, alternatively, he can assign 100 percent of his expenditures to a miscellaneous expense category.

The first step in using the Summary method is to develop a memorized transaction which estimates how your cash expenditures should be distributed. You can determine this estimate by keeping a log of your cash spending over the course of a month and noting how these amounts split among the expense categories you've set up in Quicken.

For example, if you spend about 30 percent of your cash on entertainment, 10 percent on lunches at work, 30 percent on restaurants, 20 percent on transportation, and 10 percent on miscellaneous small items, you should set up a memorized transaction to reflect this distribution, as follows:

Note. Remember that you can edit a memorized transaction to accommodate changes in your spending patterns. Find the memorized transaction by pressing Ctrl-T and choosing it from the list; then press Ctrl-E to edit the transaction.

1. Press Ctrl-T to call up the Memorized Transactions list, and choose <New Transaction> from the list.

2. Type **Cash Spending** in the Payee blank and enter 100 (for 100%) in the Payment column.

3. In the category field, use Ctrl-S to open the Split Transaction window. For each line in the window, enter the expense category (such as Entertainment) and the whole number representing the percentage of your cash spending in that category (30, rather than 30%). Figure 6.8 shows the breakdown of this example. If your cash spending is too insignificant to categorize, you may enter Miscellaneous in the category blank. Press Ctrl-Enter to leave the window.

Figure 6.8   **Split transaction for cash spending**

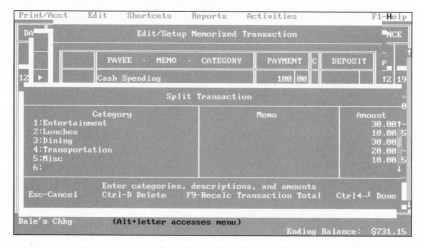

4. When you press Enter to leave the Edit/Setup Memorized Transaction window, Quicken asks if you want to memorize amounts or percentages. Type **P** and press Enter. In the Memorized Transactions list, the number in the Amount column has changed to Percent.

5. Leave the window by pressing Escape.

How you actually enter the summary transactions in your bank account depends on how you obtain the cash before you spend it. Most people obtain pocket money by one of four methods:

- Cashing checks drawn on a personal bank account

- Withdrawing money through an automated teller machine

- Depositing a paycheck (or other check) to a bank and asking for part of the deposit back in cash

- Cashing a paycheck (or other check) directly, without depositing it

Each of these requires the Summary method of cash tracking to be applied slightly differently.

When you cash a check drawn on your personal account, you must open your checking account register, type the date and check number, and recall the memorized cash spending transaction (Ctrl-T). Quicken displays the following message:

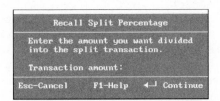

```
            Recall Split Percentage

   Enter the amount you want divided
   into the split transaction.

   Transaction amount:

 Esc-Cancel    F1-Help    ←┘ Continue
```

Type the amount of cash you received, and press Enter. If you now press Ctrl-S to see the split information, you'll see that the amount of the check has been automatically distributed among the categories you chose when you memorized the transaction. (See Figure 6.9 for an example.) Press Ctrl-Enter to record the check.

For automated teller withdrawals, again, recall the memorized cash spending transaction (Ctrl-T). Then enter the date, ATM in the NUM column, and the amount. Press Ctrl-Enter to record the transaction.

Enter deposits with cash back as two separate transactions: a deposit transaction followed immediately by a cash spending transaction dated on the same day. Note when it comes time to reconcile your account that your bank may report only a single transaction reflecting the net amount deposited, rather than separate deposit and withdrawal transactions.

When you cash checks without depositing them, dealing with them in Quicken can be tricky, since you must first generate an income transaction before you can record the money as spent. If you do this frequently, you may want to create a separate cash account and enter separate deposit and withdrawal transactions in the amount of the cashed check, using the memorized

Figure 6.9   **Split Cash transaction**

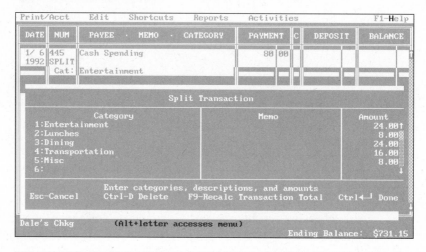

cash spending transaction for the withdrawal. If you do this occasionally, though, you might want to enter into your main bank account two "phantom" transactions—one a deposit and one a withdrawal—exactly balancing each other. Be sure when you do this that you mark both transactions as cleared (place an X in the C column) so you aren't confused when you reconcile your bank account statement at the end of the month. Figure 6.10 shows an example of how these paired transactions would look.

Detail Method

Larry Milner is an example of someone who might use the Detail method, given both his interest in closely tracking his spending against a budget and the amount of cash he requires in his daily life. The Detail method uses a Quicken cash account to track individual cash expenditures, allowing you to categorize each expenditure the same as you would any other transaction.

To use the Detail method, you should first create a cash account (press Ctrl-A and choose <New Account>, specifying cash account in the account type blank). For purposes of illustration, you can name this account "Cash on Hand."

Your cash account register resembles the register for bank accounts, with two exceptions: Instead of AMOUNT and DEPOSIT, the words SPEND and RECEIVE appear in the cash register, and the cleared (C) column does not appear.

To record an increase in your cash on hand—typically categorized as income or as a transfer from another account—enter it as a "receive"

Figure 6.10   Deposit and withdrawal transactions for a cash check

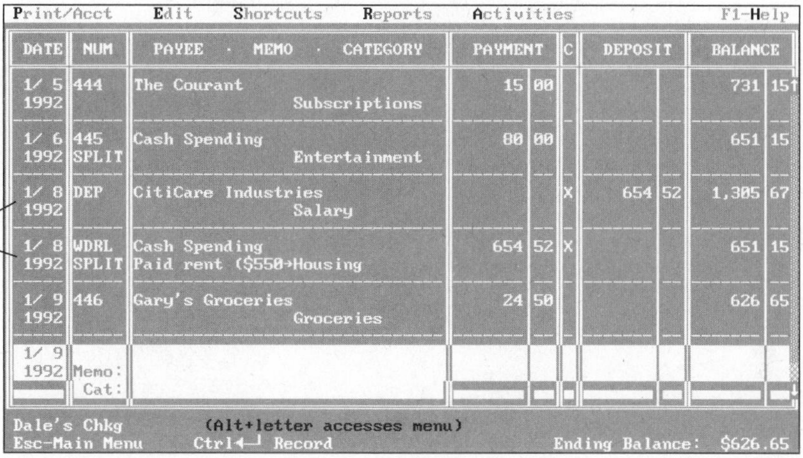

Transactions for an undeposited, cashed check

transaction. To record a decrease in cash on hand—an expense item—enter a "spend" transaction. Occasionally, you'll need to adjust your cash account balance to reflect what's really in your wallet; select Update Account Balance from the Activities menu to do this quickly, categorizing the adjustment as Miscellaneous.

Figure 6.11 shows a typical set of transactions that might appear in a cash account register.

Partial Detail Method

When you apply the Partial Detail method, you are tracking only those cash expenditures which are most important to record—for business or tax reasons. Luke Fielding might find the Partial Detail method useful to record his charitable donations and the miscellaneous cash expenses related to his fledgling consulting business; he has little need to be more detailed.

To apply the Partial Detail method, start by categorizing your cash withdrawals from your checking account. You can either classify them as Miscellaneous Expenses, or use the percentage estimation technique described earlier under the Summary method. When you need to record a specific cash expenditure, such as a cash contribution,

1. Choose a cash withdrawal transaction already in the register, on or near the date of the cash expenditure you want to record. If possible, choose a withdrawal larger than the cash expense you're recording.

2. Highlight that transaction, and open the Split Transaction window (Ctrl-S).

Figure 6.11   Cash Account register transactions

```
 Print/Acct    Edit    Shortcuts    Reports    Activities              F1-Help

  DATE  REF   PAYEE  ·  MEMO  ·  CATEGORY   SPEND       RECEIVE      BALANCE

  1/ 2        City Transit Authority        65 00                    135 00↑
  1992        Commuter rail t→Transportation

  1/ 2        Thriftway Stores              32 17                    102 83
  1992                       Groceries

  1/ 4        Pizza Galore                  12 40                     90 43
  1992                       Dining

  1/ 5        Diver Drugstores              21 19                     69 24
  1992                       Medical

  1/ 7        Consolidated Food Drive       15 00                     54 24
  1992                       Charity

  1/ 7        Sammi's                        8 50                     45 74
  1992 Memo:
       Cat: Dining

 Cash On Hand       (Alt+letter accesses menu)
 Esc-Main Menu      Ctrl←┘  Record                    Ending Balance:  $45.74
```

3. Enter the category, description, and amount for the cash expense in the first available line in the Split Transaction window.

4. Adjust any remaining items in the Split Transaction window so that their sum equals the amount of the transaction (Quicken displays the amount of the gap on the first blank line in the window). Press Ctrl-Enter to record the transaction. Figure 6.12 shows an example of a transaction recorded with this method.

When you produce both summary and transaction reports, your major cash expenditures will show up in the appropriate category.

Use Classes for Richer Detail

Note. It's not necessary to have pairs of classes—for example, Quicken doesn't require that you create a Personal class to parallel a Business one. If you create only one class, Quicken will display unclassified items under "Other" in your reports.

Classes add dimension to your category structure and offer powerful alternative views of your financial picture. A category is either income or expense; a class can encompass both. Classes can provide a slice of your expenses and income, narrowed to specific themes, activities, or topics—business versus personal, specific clients or projects, special events. The Plan Ahead section of this level describes in detail why you might want to use classes in addition to categories.

It's crucial to remember that classes supplement your category structure— they don't replace it. Every transaction may be assigned to both a category (such as Rental Income) and a class (Main Street Apartment). At different times, it may be useful to use the Rental Income category to generate a

Figure 6.12   Cash transaction (Partial Detail method)

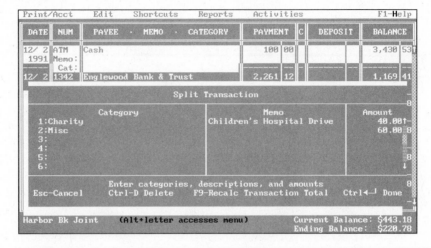

report on rental income from all your properties; at other times, you may want use the class structure to look at all of the income and expense categories associated with a single property.

To identify a class in the Category field, follow your category designation with a slash (/), and add the class name. In a rental income transaction for the Main Street apartment, the entry next to Category would be "Rental Income/Main Street Apartment." As with categories, you may set up classes in advance or as you enter transactions. When you enter a class name that Quicken doesn't recognize, the program will display the following message:

Note. If you enter both a category and a class name that are new to Quicken, you'll have a chance to add both to their appropriate lists, one after the other.

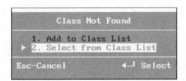

You then have an opportunity to choose an existing class name from a list or to add the class to the list.

Quicken also supports subclasses which allow you to group and subtotal several classes in a broader class. For example, if you have a Business class, you might have subclasses for the clients or projects you deal with. The syntax of subclasses is similar to that of subcategories: Enter subclasses by appending a colon (:) and the subclass name to the class name. There is a 31-character limit for the entire class/subclass phrase.

Quicken offers many of the same opportunities for viewing, editing, deleting, and printing the list of classes and subclasses that it offers for categories. For example:

- Press Ctrl-L to view the class list (see Figure 6.13).

Figure 6.13   Class List window

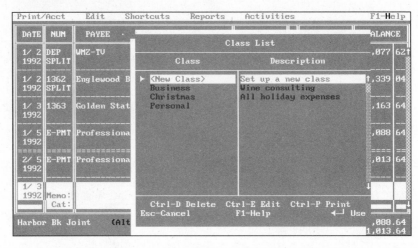

- Edit a class name or description by highlighting it and pressing Ctrl-E (for Edit).

- Delete a class by highlighting it and pressing Ctrl-D (for Delete).

- Print the class list by pressing Ctrl-P (for Print) while the class list is displayed.

Note. In order to determine the percentages by which business and personal use should be split, you should, of course, keep a detailed log in which you record whatever expense you're splitting.

You can use classes in conjunction with other Quicken features such as memorization to create some powerful shortcuts. Any expense that must, according to tax law, be split between business and personal use (car expenses, home office expenses, and so on) is fair game for a memorized class transaction. For example, 60 percent of Larry Milner's telephone expenses are attributable to business use and 40 percent to personal use. Larry created a set of memorized transactions that, when applied to any telephone expense, automatically splits that expense 60 percent to business and 40 percent to personal. Here's how you can do the same:

1. Press Ctrl-T to call up the Memorized Transactions list, and choose <New Transaction> from the list.

Note. If you want to memorize percentage splits for transactions that involve subcategories as well as categories and classes—such as Auto:Service or Auto:Fuel—you'll need to memorize a transaction for each subcategory in order to see the correct breakdown in your reports.

2. Type 100 (for 100%) under Payment.

3. In the category field of the new transaction, use Ctrl-S to open the Split Transaction window, and enter two category names, such as Telephone/-Business and Telephone/Personal.

4. After each of the category names, enter whole numbers representing the percentages in the AMOUNT column—60 and 40, for example. Press Ctrl-Enter when you're finished entering the list, and Ctrl-Enter again to leave the Edit/Setup Memorized Transaction window. Type **P** to memorize the percentages.

5. When you need to pay a telelphone expense, call up the Memorized Transactions list (Ctrl-T), choose the appropriate split transaction from the list, fill in the date, check number, payee, and amount, and press Ctrl-Enter to record the transaction. If you open the Split Transaction window (Ctrl-S), the amount will be allocated according to the percentages, as in Figure 6.14.

Figure 6.14 **Transaction splitting by percentage of business use**

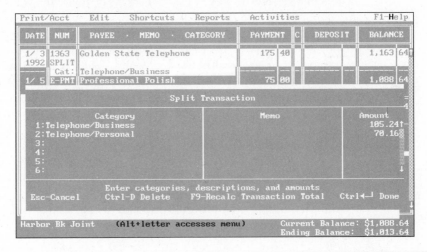

When you use this technique, you'll be accumulating information that's easily separable into business and personal use, using the customization features of Quicken's report generator.

Design a Suite of Reports

Quicken offers a good, basic set of reports that will probably fill many of your needs. However, once you've learned the full range of customization options offered by Quicken's report writer, you'll probably want to design and memorize a suite of reports that reflect the way you customarily look at your personal financial picture.

To graduate beyond standard reports, you must understand some basic principles of report design in Quicken: the basic types of reports, selecting the data set, changing a report's layout and display, and memorizing your work so you can apply the format repeatedly.

Understand What Type of Report You're Using

Quicken offers five general kinds of reports, each of which has different characteristics and presents different opportunities for customization. The report types are transaction reports, summary reports, account balance reports, budget reports, and specialized reports.

Transaction Reports

Transaction reports list all the individual transactions which meet a set of selection criteria that you specify. You can group and subtotal these transactions in a number of useful ways: by category, class, payee, account, or time period. Quicken's standard transaction reports are Itemized Categories, Investment Transactions, Tax Schedule, and Tax Summary. Transaction reports are useful for diagnosing ways to improve your financial picture ("How did I end up so overbudget on recreation this year?") or for documenting your financial picture in detail (as required for tax filings).

Summary Reports

In essence, summary reports list the subtotals of transaction reports without all the transaction detail. Therefore, you can build summary reports by category, class, payee, account, or even tax schedule. In addition, you can create column headings for your report that further divide your spending and income by time period, category, class, payee, or account. Quicken's standard summary reports are Cash Flow, Investment Income, P&L Statement, Payroll, Accounts Payable and Receivable, and Job/Project. Summary reports are the best way to obtain an overview of your income and expenses.

Account Balance Reports

While summary and transaction reports focus on movement of cash, income, and expenses over periods of time, account balance reports represent snapshots of your assets at particular points in time. Quicken's standard account balance reports are Net Worth, Balance Sheet, and Portfolio Value. Account balance reports are the most useful way to assess your assets. Use them in tandem with summary reports to give you a comprehensive overview of your financial situation.

Budget Reports

Budget reports are a special kind of summary report, though they have different customization options and limitations that are worth noting. You use them principally to compare your planned income and expense patterns to your actual experience. There are two kinds of budget reports: the standard Budget report and the Monthly Budget report.

Specialized Reports

Some reports have special formats that don't follow the summary, transaction, account balances, or budget report formats. Standard specialized reports include the Investment Performance, Capital Gains, and Missing Check reports. Many of the customization options available for the more common reports discussed previously are not available for the more specialized standard reports.

Select the Appropriate Data Set

The first element you may want to customize is the data set the report covers. Normally when you initiate a report, Quicken constructs one that covers every transaction in the current account over the range of dates you specify. You can change the data set by choosing Edit (Alt-E) while viewing any report and selecting an option from the pull-down menu. Through the Edit menu, Quicken gives you three ways to select which transactions your report will address:

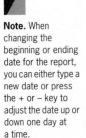

Note. When changing the beginning or ending date for the report, you can either type a new date or press the + or – key to adjust the date up or down one day at a time.

- Set Title or Date Range is a way of choosing the date ranges covered by the report. Every time you request a standard report from Quicken, you'll be asked to specify a date range for the report. You can change this range or the title of the report at any time by pressing Alt-E D (Edit menu, Date). Figure 6.15 shows the Set Title or Date Range window.

- Filter Transactions is a way of choosing only specific transactions that match a certain set of criteria—certain payees, memo contents, categories, or classes. For example, a report could show only transactions with the text "sport" somewhere in the payee field. You can even cut out amounts that are below a certain number. Figure 6.16 shows the Filter Transactions window that gives you these choices for most reports (there's a special form for investment reports). You can limit transactions using the filter window at any time you're viewing a report by pressing Alt-E F (Edit menu, Filter).

Figure 6.15   Set Title or Date Range window

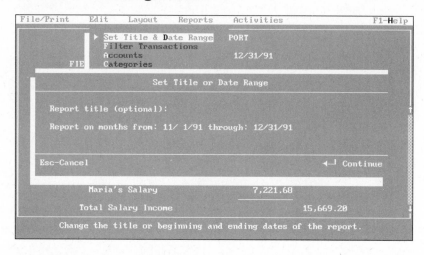

Figure 6.16   Filter Transactions window

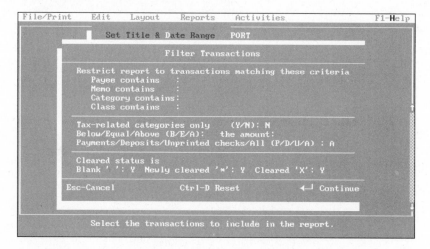

■ The Accounts, Categories, and Classes options also limit transactions covered in the report. In each case, you can choose to report on the current account, category, or class, on all of them, or on selected ones. You may specify or change these criteria at any time by pressing Alt-E (Edit menu), A (Accounts), C (Categories), or L (Classes), and then typing C (Current),

A (All), or S (Selected). If you ask to specify selected accounts, categories, or classes, you'll be presented with a list from which to choose (see Figure 6.17). Use the spacebar to make your selections.

Figure 6.17   Select Categories To Include window

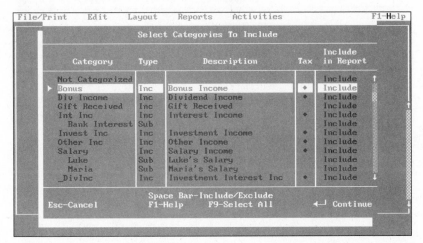

When you filter transactions, you'll have a chance to specify one or more criteria which will reduce the number of transactions or accounts that form the basis of the report. It's usually a good idea to press Ctrl-D (for Default) before you start specifying a filter, to ensure that no selection criteria carry over from a previous session. There are five ways you can apply a filter to a report:

■ *Phrase matching* In the Filter Transactions window (see Figure 6.16 above), you'll see four criteria fields for payee, memo, category, and class. In each of these fields, you can enter a full or partial text item that Quicken should look for in the payee, memo, category, or class fields. For example, you could tell Quicken to find any memo with the word "Anniversary" in the memo field. If you prefer, you can use the special match characters described in Table 6.1. One particularly useful match character is the tilde (~), which identifies matching transactions you want to *exclude* from your report. In the "Category contains" and "Class contains" fields, you can pop up lists of categories (Ctrl-C) or classes (Ctrl-L) and choose from the appropriate list.

Note. Quicken ignores distinctions between upper- and lowercase characters when it searches for transactions that match your selection criteria. It also ignores stray spaces before or after your entry.

Note. You can locate all the transactions which are not categorized by entering a tilde and two dots (~..) in the "Category contains" field. The tilde (~) means "exclude," while ".." represents any number of characters.

Table 6.1   **Match Characters to Select or Exclude Transactions for Reports**

Type	To Do This:	Examples:
anytext	Find the exact text, regardless of upper- or lowercase letters.	"State" finds "STATE," "state," "State"
anytext..	Find the text by itself or followed by other characters.	"Park.." finds "park," "Parkway"
..anytext	Find the text by itself or preceded by other characters.	"..day" finds "Day," "holiday," "Sunday"
~anytext	Exclude items consisting of only this text, but find items that have this text embedded within other characters.	"~auto" finds "Automobile," but not "Auto"
~..anytext..	Exclude any item that contains the text anywhere within it.	"~..Bank.." excludes any entry with "bank" in it, including "embankment"
..	Represent any entry or number of characters; serves as a wildcard for any number of characters within other characters.	".." finds any item
?	Represent a single character; serves as a wildcard for only one character within an entry.	"c?rd" finds "Card" and "cord"

Note. There is no corresponding way to report only categories that are not tax related. Entering N in the tax-related categories field causes all transactions to be considered.

- *Tax-related categories*   When you first created each category, you had a chance to designate it as tax-related. Type **Y** in the "Tax-related categories only" blank to report exclusively on those tax-related categories.

- *Dollar-amount cutoff*   Type a letter—**B** (Below), **E** (Equal), or **A** (Above)—and an amount to select only those transactions which meet a certain magnitude criterion. For example, if you're interested only in transactions that are greater than $500.00, type **A** for above, and then **500**.

- *Transaction type*   You can gather payments, deposits, unprinted checks, or all transactions by typing **P, D, U,** or **A** respectively.

- *Cleared status*   You may select transactions according to whether or not they have been cleared during reconciliation. The descriptions—Blank, Newly Cleared, and Cleared—refer to the C column in the Register. Blank transactions are those that have not been cleared during reconciliation. Newly cleared (*) transactions are those that have been marked as cleared in the Register, but for which the reconciliation process is not yet complete. Cleared transactions (X) are those that have been marked as cleared in a completed reconciliation process.

For example, Dale Scott wants to obtain a report containing all the checks he has written on his Twin City Bank account that are for more than $10.00 and are not made out to Cash. Figure 6.18 shows how he would specify the criteria for this report. Clearly, these combinations of selection criteria can be extremely powerful in crafting the specific reports you need.

Figure 6.18   **Filter Transactions window**

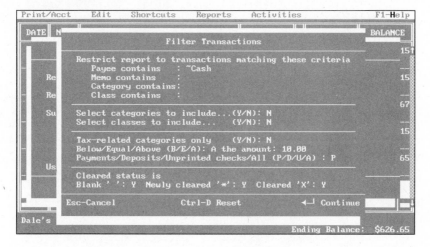

Investment reports offer slightly different possibilities for filtering (see Figure 6.19). Aside from a phrase-matching field for the Security name, the Filter Investment Transactions window also allows you to select from a list the security types and investment goals you want to include.

Change the Report's Layout and Display

Quicken also lets you control many aspects of how it displays reports—from the display of decimal places to how transactions are sorted to changing the rows, columns, groupings, and subtotals. In general, you can access the Layout and Display options by pressing Alt-L (Layout) while viewing any report. From the Layout pull-down menu (shown in Figure 6.20), you can choose from a wide variety of options which will change both the appearance and substance of your reports.

Quicken offers nine ways to change the appearance of its reports:

■ *Display cents*   Use the Hide/Show Cents switch (press Alt-L E) to omit fractions of dollars from your reports or to restore them. This is a useful way to narrow your columns when you're using many of them.

Figure 6.19   Filter Investment Transactions window

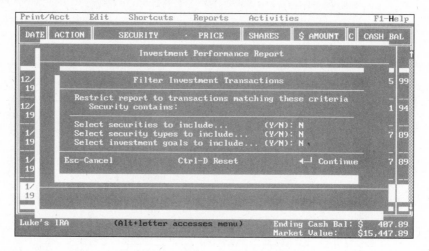

Figure 6.20   Layout menu

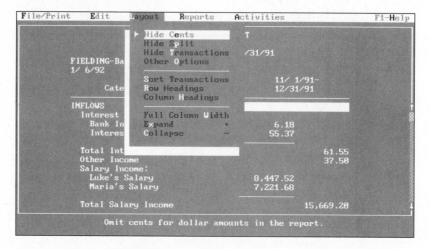

- *Display split transactions*   In transaction reports, use the Hide/Show Split switch (press Alt-L P) to include or omit the line-by-line information on split transactions assigned to multiple categories. For example, if rental car fees paid by credit card are always recorded in split transactions, this option will ensure that those transactions appear in transaction reports.

■ *Display transactions*   In transaction reports, the Hide/Show Transactions switch (press Alt-L T) is a way of omitting or displaying all the individual transaction line items. With this option, you can see only the dollar amounts for transactions that match the specified criteria.

■ *Add memo or category columns*   For transaction reports, the Show Memo/Category/Display both selection (under Other Options, press Alt-L O) lets you create one or two columns for the category or memo field, or for both.

■ *Display subcategories*   Using the Subcategory Display option (under Other Options, press Alt-L O), you can choose one of three ways to display subcategory or subclass information. When you select Normal, subcategories appear indented under their parent category or class. With the Suppressed option, you can eliminate subcategory or subclass information altogether (although the subcategory amounts will still be included in the parent category's amounts). With Reversed, you can reverse the parentage of subcategories, so that subcategories with identical names like Utilities:Nantucket and Telephone:Nantucket can be recast to group all the Nantucket expenses together.

Note. When you sort transactions, you can't dictate the sort order. Date and Check Number are always in ascending order, Amount lists highest amounts first, and Accounts are listed in alphabetical order.

■ *Sort transactions*   In transaction reports, you can use Sort Transactions (press Alt-L S) to change the order in which transactions are listed. By choosing from the pull-down menu, you may decide to sort your transaction reports by Account, Date, Check Number, or Amount.

■ *Change column width*   With the Column Width switch (press Alt-L W), you can expand or contract the text columns displayed in any report. For example, Full Column Width expands the Description column of a Transaction report from 18 characters to 36. In most cases, the width is doubled or halved as you toggle this switch.

Note. You can also collapse entire sections of a report by selecting either the heading or total line for those sections and issuing the Collapse command.

■ *Collapse detail*   Use the Collapse option (press Alt-L C) to suppress all the detail listed below a particular row heading of a summary, budget, or account balances report. For example, if the Entertainment category has several subcategories, you can collapse them under the Entertainment heading. Before you issue the Collapse command, use the cursor keys to highlight the row you want to collapse. When you issue the Collapse command, all the detail is summarized under what was once the total line; note that the totals don't change. See Figure 6.21 for an example of a report's appearance before and after implementing the Collapse option.

Note. If you use a mouse, you can collapse a summary line by pointing at the heading and double-clicking. Double-click on the item again to expand it.

■ *Expand*   Use the Expand command (press Alt-L E) to reverse the effects of the Collapse command and show the detail once again. Note that the Expand command cannot create detail; it can only reveal detail that has already been hidden by the Collapse command. To see transaction detail while you're viewing a summary report, use the QuickZoom (Ctrl-Z) command instead.

Figure 6.21   Report with row expanded (A) and collapsed (B)

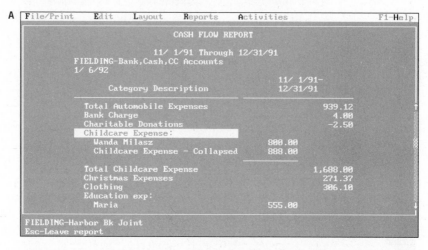

You can also use the Layout commands to change the substance of your reports in five ways:

- *Row headings*   In summary reports, the Row Headings option (press Alt-L R) changes the nature of the line items used to create the summary. Using the pull-down menu, you can choose to base your report on categories, classes, payees, or accounts. For example, it may be more useful to see an Income and Expenses report organized by class; use this option to display classes as row headings.

■ *Column headings*   Normally, summary and account balance reports list amounts in a single column, which covers the specific date or time period you chose when you first specified the report. You can use the Column Headings option (press Alt-L H) to create multiple columns for your report. These columns can represent either multiple sequential time periods or another dimension such as category, class, payee, account, or tax schedule. Figure 6.22 shows a portion of a summary report which uses categories as the row headings and uses a class-based column heading to separate business and unclassified (Other) expenses.

Figure 6.22   Summary Report

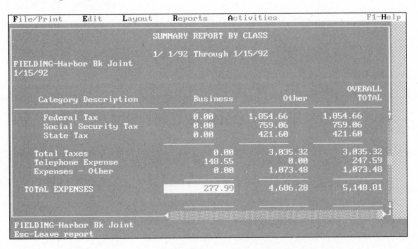

■ *Report organization*   Listed under Other Options (press Alt-L O), this option affects the way summary items in a report are grouped and subtotaled. For summary and budget reports, as well as transaction reports subtotaled by category, you can choose an Income and Expense approach (income, expense, and transfer items grouped separately) or a Cash Flow approach (inflows and outflows grouped together). For account balance reports, you can choose a Net Worth approach (net worth is the last item) or a Balance Sheet approach (assets and liabilities balance, and an equity line is placed in the liabilities section).

■ *Transfers*   Also listed under Other Options (press Alt-L O), this option allows you to decide whether to include or exclude transfers from all accounts in the file or to eliminate transfer transactions that cancel each other in the report.

■ *Include unrealized gains*   Also under Other Options (press Alt-L O), this option allows you to create temporary "phantom" transactions among your investment accounts—for reporting purposes only—which represent the paper-only gains and losses resulting from changes in the value of securities you own.

Explore Transaction Detail in Summary Reports

When you view summary reports on your computer screen, you'll probably have questions about the detail behind those summary lines (for example, "How could I possibly have spent that much on clothing last month?"). Quicken offers a way of digging behind the summary lines into the detail.

When you're viewing a summary report, use your cursor keys to highlight any amount about which you'd like more information. When you press Ctrl-Z (for QuickZoom), you'll see a Transaction List window (see Figure 6.23) showing all the transaction items that went into the summary amount you're exploring. Use the Up and Down Arrow keys to scroll through the list, and press Escape when you're ready to return to the summary report.

Figure 6.23   Transaction list for the QuickZoom

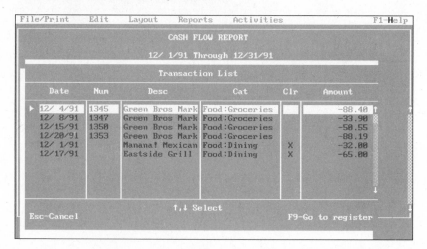

Note. If you need to use QuickZoom to go to the Register from a custom summary report, be sure you memorize your report (as described in the next section) to save all the custom settings; otherwise, you'll lose some of the work you invested in customizing your report.

The QuickZoom feature allows you to dig one level deeper for detail when you're in the Transaction List. If you highlight a particular transaction in the list and press F9, Quicken will take you directly into the register that generated the transaction. Use this second-level exploration with caution, however: when you move to the register level through QuickZoom, Quicken cannot find its way back into the report. You must re-create it.

Memorize Your Reports for Later Use

Once you've achieved the level of data selectivity and the layout you want, you should save the report format in case you want to use it again. Memorizing a report saves all the display settings, filters, column and row definitions, and sorts that you've chosen. It does *not,* however, memorize the date range or printer information.

> **Note.** If you enter a report title that duplicates one already in the Memorized Reports list, Quicken will overwrite the old report (although it will warn you first).

To memorize a report, press Ctrl-M (for Memorize) while viewing it. You'll be asked to enter a title for the report, which you'll use to select the memorized report later on.

To use a memorized report, in the Register press Alt-R M (Reports menu, Memorized Reports). Or, from the Quicken Main Menu, C then M (Create Reports, Memorized Reports). If you've memorized more than one report in the past, you'll see a Memorized Reports list (see Figure 6.24) from which you may highlight a title and press Enter. Quicken will ask you what date range you want to cover and will display your report.

Figure 6.24   **Memorized Reports list**

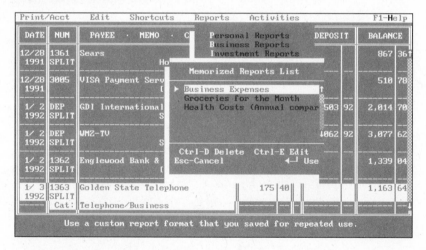

Use a custom report format that you saved for repeated use.

Print Your Reports

Intuit claims that Quicken can support any printer, and with the addition of PostScript-printer support in version 5, that's now true. At a minimum, Quicken can format your reports as straight 80-character-per-line text. On the most popular printers such as Hewlett-Packard LaserJet and Epson-compatible dot-matrix printers, however, Quicken can support a broader range of output formats such as compressed printing and wide columns. In addition, Quicken can "print" reports to a disk for later printing or for import into other software programs.

Any request to print a report begins with the display of that report on the screen. Once you've used the Report (Alt-R), Edit (Alt-E), and Layout (Alt-L) menus to display the report you'd like to see, you should press Ctrl-P to initiate the report printing process. Quicken will display the Print Report window (shown in Figure 6.25).

Figure 6.25   **Print Report window**

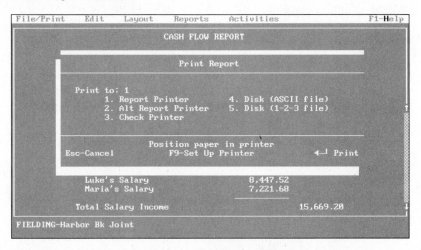

Quicken organizes its output options into two groups (three printer options and three disk options):

- When you installed Quicken, you were able to specify three different printers, though these options could represent three separate styles for the same printer. These are named the Report Printer option, the Alternate Report Printer option, and the Check Printer option. If you use only one printer, you might set the Report Printer option up for normal sized (12-characters-per-inch) print style, the Alternate Report Printer for compressed (17-characters-per-inch) print style, and the Check Printer for slightly enlarged (10-characters-per-inch) print style.

- Quicken also offers you the chance to output your report in one of three formats: ASCII (plain text) files, Lotus 1-2-3 (spreadsheet-readable) files, and tax files (to move information to tax preparation programs).

If you've forgotten which printer and style is associated with which printer, you need only press F9 and choose from a list which settings you want to examine. You'll see three overlapping windows, as shown in Figure 6.26.

Figure 6.26   Menu options for printer setup

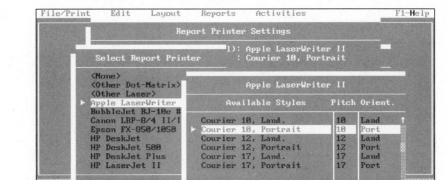

- The top window shows printer styles for the printer you specified for that option. Change the style by using the cursor keys to highlight the one you'd like.

- Press Escape to close the style window and display a list of available printers. Again, the current printer specification is highlighted. Change the printer by moving the cursor key and pressing Enter when you've found the right one.

- Press Escape again to see a settings sheet (see Figure 6.27) which gives you more complete control over the format for your printed report—the indentation, page length, number of characters per line, and whether the printer should pause between pages, for example. You can get even deeper into the process by manipulating the actual control codes that Quicken sends to the printer; press F8 to see these, but don't change anything until you've consulted the Quicken User Manual.

If your printer supports compressed type, it's a good idea to set up either your primary or alternate report printer to support a compressed style. This is because some of Quicken's reports are too wide to be printed on a printer that supports just 80 characters across the page.

If the report you want to print is too wide for a page, try these tips:

- Use a compressed printing style (such as, for example, 17-pitch type).

- Make sure that indent is set to 0, and that the characters per line is set at the maximum your printer will allow at the type size you've chosen (136 characters per inch at 17 pitch, for example).

Figure 6.27   Report Printer Settings window

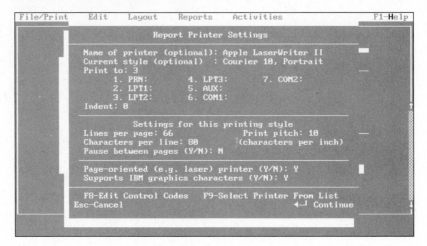

- If your computer supports landscape (sideways) printing, choose this option from the Printer Settings window.

- If you're printing a transaction report, avoid choosing Full Column Width from the Layout menu (press Alt-L W to turn this option on and off).

- If you can, reduce the number of columns you're trying to print across the top—either by filtering the report differently, restricting the date range, or changing the column subtotals.

If your report is still too wide, Quicken will still print it in vertical strips that you can tape together, side-by-side, to see your complete report.

When you print a report to a disk file, you're usually doing so either because you want to use it in another software program (such as a word processor, electronic-mail, spreadsheet, or a tax-preparation program) or to print it later. The format you choose depends on how you intend to use it later.

- Most word processors and electronic-mail programs can use text files, which in computer jargon are known as ASCII files. When you choose this option, you'll be asked for a DOS file name, the length of the page, and how many characters should appear on a line. In most cases, you should type 0 in the page length blank, which will ensure that your text file doesn't have any gaps in it. This option may also be used for files you want to print later, though most of the special, printer-specific formatting information will be lost if you print to a file, and then later send that file to a printer.

- The Lotus 1-2-3 format is designed especially to accommodate the import of report files into spreadsheet programs for later analysis or enhanced display. For more on how to use this option, see "Transfer Your Reports to a Spreadsheet" later in this level.

- The final disk-output option is used by several major tax-preparation packages for importing information from Quicken. We'll discuss this in more detail in Level 10 ("Plan, Organize, and Prepare Your Taxes"), but suffice it to say that when a tax-preparation package claims to support the import of information from Quicken, it is typically through printing to a tax file on disk.

Transfer Your Reports to a Spreadsheet

Note. When you specify a file name for transferring your report to Lotus 1-2-3, it's a good idea to also enter the path name you customarily use for your spreadsheet data files, such as C:\123DATA\REPORT-.PRN. This way, you'll be able to locate your Quicken report file easily while in your spreadsheet program.

Sometimes Quicken's built-in customization is not enough. For example, you may want to sort your expense items from largest to smallest instead of in alphabetical order as Quicken produces it. Alternatively, you may want to produce a report that compares this year's first quarter expenses with last year's, without any intervening detail. Or you may want to calculate the changes in an amount from one period to the next.

For this level of customization, the best approach is to transfer your Quicken report to a spreadsheet—a task which is very easy to accomplish:

1. Create a report in Quicken with all the information you want to transfer.

2. With the report showing on the screen, press Ctrl-P to print it. In the "Print to" blank in the Print Report window, type **5** for Disk (1-2-3 File); then press Enter and type a file name for the transfer file (such as REPORT). Quicken gives the file the extension .PRN.

3. Leave the report, exit Quicken, and start your spreadsheet program.

4. Use your spreadsheet's data import capability (/FIN, for File Import Numbers, in Lotus 1-2-3) to import the report transfer file.

5. Make whatever modifications you want to the report in your spreadsheet, including creating new calculated columns.

Note. If you plan to use your report in Microsoft Excel, you must rename the file (using the DOS Rename command) to give it the extension .CSV.

For an example of the kind of customized reports you can produce with a spreadsheet, look at Figure 6.28. It shows a spreadsheet report Larry Milner produced to show his fourth-quarter income and expenses for 1990 and 1991 and the dollar and percentage growth in each, sorted by the 1991 amounts. Larry produced this spreadsheet by creating a quarterly P&L Statement, exporting it to a spreadsheet, deleting the three irrelevant quarters between the two he wished to compare, creating two calculated columns to show dollar and percentage change, and sorting both the income and expenses by 1991 amounts in descending order.

Figure 6.28   Report showing comparison of fourth-quarter income and expenses

MILNER: QUARTERLY INCOME/EXPENSE COMPARISON

Category Description	1991 Q4	1990 Q4	ANNUAL CHANGE	%CHANGE
INCOME/EXPENSE				
INCOME				
Interest Income:				
Bank Interest	19.12	18.40	0.72	0.04
Interest Income - Other	132.44	155.37	(22.93)	(0.15)
Total Interest Income	151.56	173.77	(22.21)	(0.13)
Other Income	111.14	37.50	73.64	1.96
Salary Income:	52,247.90	41,982.81	10,265.09	0.24
Income - Other	1,971.98	1,885.40	86.58	0.05
TOTAL INCOME	54,482.58	44,079.48	10,403.10	0.24
EXPENSES				
Automobile Expenses:				
Auto Fuel	114.45	92.68	21.77	0.23
Auto Loan Payment	810.44	810.44	0.00	0.00
Auto Service	92.00	36.00	56.00	1.56
Total Automobile Expenses	1,016.89	939.12	77.77	0.08
Bank Charge	15.50	14.00	1.50	0.11
Charitable Donations	150.00	150.00	0.00	0.00
Christmas Expenses	1,140.40	1,271.37	(130.97)	(0.10)
Clothing	492.47	324.10	168.37	0.52
Entertainment	182.18	159.50	22.68	0.14
Finance Charge	0.00	4.85	(4.85)	(1.00)
Food:				
Dining Out	160.00	157.00	3.00	0.02
Groceries	714.82	601.60	113.22	0.19
Total Food	874.82	758.60	116.22	0.15
Gift Expenses	52.00	35.00	17.00	0.49
Health:				
Health Club	34.00	28.00	6.00	0.21
Medical & Dental	82.40	117.97	(35.57)	(0.30)
Total Health	116.40	145.97	(29.57)	(0.20)
Home Repair & Maint.	101.19	110.00	(8.81)	(0.08)
Household Misc. Exp	287.66	335.90	(48.24)	(0.14)
Insurance	244.50	244.50	0.00	0.00
Late Charges	0.00	20.00	(20.00)	(1.00)

Miscellaneous	62.50	128.55	(66.05)	(0.51)
Mortgage Interest Exp	6,271.51	6,484.95	(213.44)	(0.03)
Recreation Expense	110.00	105.00	5.00	0.05
Reimbursable Business Exp	544.55	615.50	(70.95)	(0.12)
Subscriptions	42.00	41.95	0.05	0.00
Taxes:				
Federal Tax	22,324.04	18,924.41	3,399.63	0.18
Social Security Tax	5,221.78	4,379.10	842.68	0.19
State Tax	8,277.10	6,912.47	1,364.63	0.20
	----------------	----------------	----------------	----------------
Total Taxes	35,822.92	30,215.98	5,606.94	0.19
Telephone Expense	118.87	112.80	6.07	0.05
Water, Gas, Electric	387.14	466.47	(79.33)	(0.17)
Expenses - Other	92.47	149.63	(57.16)	(0.38)
	----------------	----------------	----------------	----------------
TOTAL EXPENSES	48,125.97	42,833.74	5,292.23	0.12
	----------------	----------------	----------------	----------------
TOTAL INCOME/EXPENSE	6,356.61	1,245.74	5,110.87	4.10
	----------------	----------------	----------------	----------------

Set Up Personal Payroll and 1099 Accounts

When you pay someone who works for you—a child care professional or a gardener, for example—you're required by law to keep records, file forms, withhold taxes, and make payments to federal and, typically, state tax authorities. You must do this if the person works in or around your house and if you dictate factors such as pay, schedule, conduct, and appearance. If you pay $50 or more each quarter, you must make a social security contribution on behalf on your employee. If the compensation is greater than $1,000 per quarter, you're liable for unemployment contributions.

Maintaining the paperwork for such employees can be an enormous hassle. In many ways, you're keeping the same records that the payroll department of a large company keeps. Quicken can help make this sort of record keeping relatively painless.

There are two approaches to keeping payroll records: a manual and an automated method. As with so many choices, there is a tradeoff: the automated approach is quicker and less vulnerable to errors, but it requires the purchase of a separate add-on program called QuickPay, distributed by Intuit and priced at $49.95. The alternative is setting up all the accounts and reports on your own, calculating employee withholdings from tax tables, and entering the information manually into Quicken.

If your personal payroll needs are only temporary or are limited to one or two people who are paid the same amount every week, the manual method described in this section will suffice. If your needs are more complex, you are likely to save enough time using QuickPay to offset its price. Quick-Pay is described in more detail in Level 11, "Keep the Books for Your Small Business."

Manage Payroll Manually

There are seven general steps involved in the manual process of preparing Quicken to calculate payroll and make payments to employees:

1. Set up payroll categories and liability accounts.

2. Set up a memorized payroll transaction.

3. Calculate gross pay, withholding taxes, and other deductions.

4. Enter the data into Quicken.

5. Print payroll checks.

6. Complete tax reports.

7. Print checks for tax payments.

Prepare Quicken to Handle Payroll

Quicken uses expense categories and liability accounts to track all the deductions and payroll taxes associated with payroll transactions. The payroll categories represent expense items paid by the employer. The principal category is gross pay, but additional categories are necessary for taxes that employers pay over and above an employee's gross pay: Social Security, unemployment taxes, Medicare, and state disability contributions. The liability accounts represent items that are deducted from an employee's paycheck, and that an employer pays to the appropriate authority at another time. These include federal and state income taxes, employee FICA contributions, and so forth.

Note. A Quicken Assistant is a script that "plays back" a series of prerecorded keystrokes into Quicken, automating an otherwise tedious task.

Quicken offers an automated process, the Payroll Assistant, that will, in less than 20 seconds, establish a basic set of categories and accounts for handling payroll. This setup includes a new Payroll category with five subcategories and six new Other Liability accounts (see Table 6.2). You can run the Payroll Assistant from any Quicken file. To do so, press Escape repeatedly until you see the Quicken Main Menu; then type **T** and **P** (Use Tutorials/Assistants, followed by Create Payroll Support). Press Enter to begin the process, and supply your state's two-letter abbreviation.

Table 6.2   **Table of Payroll Categories and Accounts**

	Name	Type	Description
Category	Payroll	Expense	Payroll transaction
Subcategories	Comp FICA	Expense	Company FICA contribution
	Comp FUTA	Expense	Company FUTA contribution
	Comp MCARE	Expense	Company Medicare contribution
	Comp SUI	Expense	Company SUI contribution
	Gross	Expense	Compensation to employee
Accounts	Payroll-FICA	Other Liability	FICA contributions
	Payroll-FUTA	Other Liability	Federal unemployment tax
	Payroll-FWH	Other Liability	Federal income tax
	Payroll-MCARE	Other Liability	Medicare contrib.
	Payroll-SUI	Other Liability	State unemploy. tax
	Payroll-SWH*st*	Other Liability	State income tax

A payroll check is one of the most complicated split transactions you'll have occasion to write in Quicken. This is a place where the memorized transaction function *really* comes in handy.

When you're ready to create a memorized payroll transaction, press Ctrl-T (for Transaction List) to pop up a list of memorized transactions, and choose <New Transaction> from the list. When the blank Edit/Setup Memorized Transaction window appears, type a name such as Payroll for the memorized transaction and press Ctrl-S (for Split) to call the Split Transaction window. Especially if you use voucher checks, you should divide your split transaction entry into two sections—one for payroll deductions that should be printed on the check stub and one for those that should not.

Note. When you use voucher checks with split transactions, Quicken will print only the first 16 split-line items on the check stub. Start categories and notes that you don't want printed on the check on line 17 in the Split Transaction window.

Gross pay and employee payroll deductions should go on lines 1 through 16 as shown in Figure 6.29. These amounts will be printed on the check stub if you use voucher checks. Use the Memo column to enter the description of each category and account as you want it to appear on your employee's paycheck.

Additional taxes and benefits that the employer pays should be entered on lines 17 and below, as shown in Figure 6.30. Since you'll accumulate these amounts to be paid on a monthly, quarterly, or annual basis, they should be entered as paired transactions—each expense transaction offset by an equal and opposite liability transaction—to track the amounts.

Once you've set up the memorized payroll transaction structure, you can save it by pressing Ctrl-Enter. Tell Quicken to save amounts, and to memorize the transaction as a payment.

Figure 6.29   Gross pay and employee payroll deductions

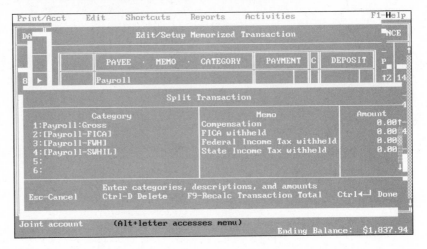

Figure 6.30   Taxes and benefits contributed by employer

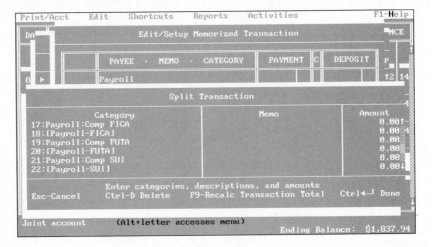

Issue Paychecks

For example, Larry Milner employs a housekeeper, Sara Greenfield, and a nanny, Leah Robinson. When it's time to pay them, he follows these steps:

1. Press Ctrl-T (for Transaction List) and choose the memorized payroll transaction from the list.

2. Type the paycheck date and employee's name—for example, Sara Greenfield—in the date and payee blanks.

3. Press Ctrl-S (for Split) to open the Split Transaction window.

4. Enter the gross pay amount on the first line—275.00, for example. This will be a positive number; all the following deductions and expenses will be negative numbers.

5. Using tax tables you can obtain from the federal and state governments, calculate the appropriate deductions and employer contributions for this pay period, taking into account the gross pay level, length of pay period, and exemptions claimed by the employee on Form W-4. For example, for this biweekly paycheck, Larry might withhold $27.00 in state income tax from Sara's paycheck, and contribute $17.00 for her unemployment insurance.

6. Enter the employee withholdings as negative numbers starting on line 2. The employer contributions should be entered as paired line items on lines 17 and higher—positive amounts for the employer expenses and negative amounts for the corresponding increases in your payroll liability accounts (see Figure 6.31).

Figure 6.31   Entry of employer contributions in Split Transaction window

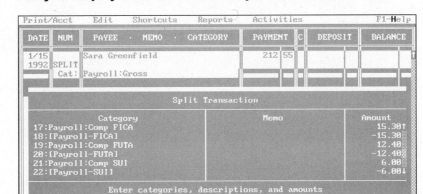

7. Press Ctrl-Enter to record the transaction.

If you pay the same amount every week, it's wise to memorize the entire transaction—complete with employee name and amounts. Then all you have to do at pay time is call up the memorized transaction, fill in the date, and print the check.

If you have several employees whose individual compensation is the same each pay period, you can set up a periodic transaction group (for example, weekly or monthly) and complete your entire payroll in just a couple of minutes.

As time passes, your payroll liability accounts will accumulate a series of transfer transactions which represent money you owe the government— either taxes you've withheld or payroll related contributions you're obligated to make on your employees' behalf. Figure 6.32 shows an excerpt from the Federal Income Tax liability account register for the housekeeper and nanny in Larry Milner's household. Larry created the final transaction, which reduces the account balance to zero, by writing a check from his main checking account to his bank (which collects withholding tax for the government), specifying the Payroll-FWH account in the category blank.

Figure 6.32   **Sample federal income tax liability account register**

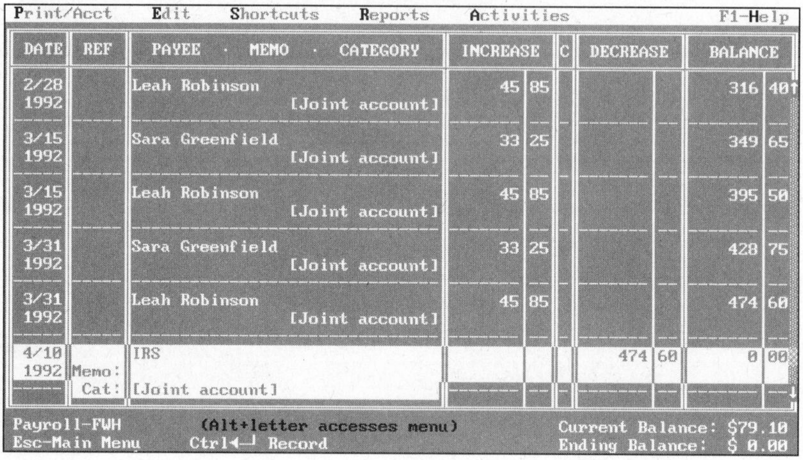

Complete Payroll Reports
As an employer, you're obligated to fill out four federal employment filings: Form W-2 (Wage and Tax Statement), Form W-3 (Transmittal of Income and Tax Statements), Form 940 (Federal Unemployment Tax), and Form 941 (Employer's Quarterly Return). In addition, you may need to complete some state tax forms.

While Quicken won't format the reports or fill them out for you, the standard Payroll report will generate the raw data you need to fill out the forms. The Payroll report is located under the Business Reports submenu, accessible by pressing Alt-R B Y (Reports menu, Business, Payroll) from any register or reports screen.

The standard Payroll report is merely a summary report, filtered (by phrase matching) to include only categories and accounts containing the word "Payroll," organized with payees (employees or bank payees) down the side and categories and accounts across the top. (For the standard report, see the Gallery of Quicken Reports in Appendix D.) Since we're dealing with personal payroll in this section and you have, therefore, only one or two employees, you may find this report more manageable if you rearrange it—using the Alt-L (for Layout) commands—to place payees as the row headings and categories as the column headings. Figure 6.33 shows the report that results from this transposition.

Figure 6.33   **Payroll report with adjusted layout**

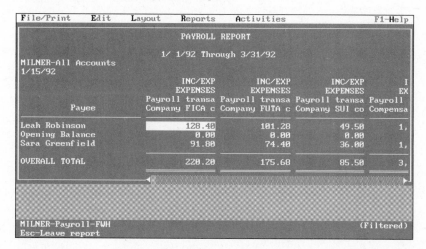

Most of the line items you need for your tax filings will be directly obtainable from the Payroll report. The Quicken manual contains a comprehensive table that maps line items from the Payroll report onto line items on the federal tax forms.

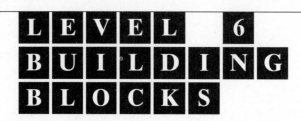

LEVEL 6 BUILDING BLOCKS

In Level 6, you learned techniques for managing credit cards and cash, integrating classes into your organizational structure, and reporting. You also saw how Quicken can help you manage a payroll.

TECHNIQUES AND PROCEDURES

■ Set up a credit card account by pressing Ctrl-A and typing **2** for Credit Card in the Set Up New Account window. Name the account, and enter the balance as of the last statement (or 0 if your account is paid in full), along with a date for that balance. Enter an optional description, and press Enter. Then enter the credit limit for the card, so Quicken can inform you of your remaining credit at any time.

■ Pay your credit card bill and reconcile your account in one simple procedure. When you're ready to pay the bill, press Alt-A R (Activities, Reconcile/Pay Credit Card). Enter the account summaries from your bill, and then mark which transactions in the account have appeared in your bill. Quicken will monitor those "cleared" transactions and let you know when the account balances with the statement. Then Quicken will tell you how much you owe (which should match your statement) and, if you wish, initiate the payment for you.

■ Set up a cash account by pressing Ctrl-A 3 for Cash in the Set Up New Account window. Name the account and enter the amount of cash you currently have on hand. Enter an optional description and press Enter.

■ Use classes to provide a structural level beyond categories for organizing your personal finances. To see a list of classes, press Ctrl-L. To add a new class, select <New Class> and type the class name. To classify a transaction, follow the category name with a slash (/) and type the class name, such as Telephone/Business. You can specify a subclass after a class by separating the two with a colon, as in Telephone/Business:Client1.

■ If a type of expense should always be split into classes by percentage, set up a memorized transaction to do this automatically. Press Ctrl-T to see the Memorized Transaction list, and select <New Transaction>. In the Category field, press Ctrl-S to see the Split Transaction window. Enter the category, class, and a whole number representing the percentage. Then enter the remainder of the split (also as a whole number). After you press Ctrl-Enter twice to leave the window, press P for Percentages and Enter to tell Quicken to memorize the percentages. When you use the memorized transaction (by pressing Ctrl-M and selecting it from the list), enter the total bill amount; Quicken will split it according to the percentages you entered.

■ You can customize the data on which a Quicken report is based with the options on the Edit menu (press Alt-E). The options let you manipulate the title and date range; specify the accounts, categories, and classes covered; and construct criteria to filter the data.

■ With options on the Layout menu (Alt-L), you can determine the report's appearance, including the column width, sorting, the display of cents, and so on. You can also change the substance of a report as influenced by its layout. Row or column headings can designate categories, classes, payees, or accounts. Column headings can also show multiple sequential time periods.

■ When viewing a report, use the QuickZoom option to delve into the details behind the report. Highlight any amount about which you'd like more information, and press Ctrl-Z. Quicken will display a Transaction List window showing all the transactions behind that amount.

■ When you've set up a report to your satisfaction, memorize it by pressing Ctrl-M and supplying a unique report title. To retrieve the report, press Alt-R M (Reports menu, Memorized Reports). Select the report you want from the list.

■ To set up your file to handle payroll transactions, use the Quicken Payroll Assistant. At the Main Menu, select Use Tutorials /Assistants; then select Create Payroll Support (type **T** and then **P**). Quicken will set up the five sub-categories and six Other Liability accounts required to track payroll.

■ Set up a single memorized transaction containing categories and liability accounts to represent the employee deductions (on lines 1 through 16 of the Split Transaction window) and employer contributions (on lines 17 and beyond) required for each paycheck. When payday comes, recall the transaction, and enter the date and the employee's name. In the Split Transaction window, enter the gross pay, and then specify the amount for each deduction and contribution. Every quarter, generate a standard Payroll report to determine the amounts you must pay to government agencies on the employee's behalf.

TERMS

- The *Summary method* for credit card and cash management allows you to categorize these expenses without treating individual purchases as single transactions. This method is suitable for tracking single-purpose credit cards that you pay in full each month. When you pay a credit card bill, simply categorize the amount under the category most appropriate for that card—Clothing for a department store credit card or Auto Fuel for a gas card. For cash purchases, estimate the percentage of your spending for various categories—transportation, dining out, entertainment, and so on. Then incorporate these percentages into a memorized split transaction that you implement each time you make a withdrawal from the automatic teller machine or otherwise obtain cash.

- The *Detail method* enables you to treat credit card and cash purchases exactly as you would checks—by recording them in dedicated accounts as categorized transactions. This method works well for multipurpose cards that often carry an unpaid balance. Set up separate Cash and Credit Card accounts, save your receipts, and enter them as usual.

- The *Partial Detail method* is a compromise that provides necessary detail without requiring you to set up individual cash and credit card accounts. Use this method for cards that have relatively little activity across only a few categories. With this method, you split transactions to isolate expenditures that you do want categorized explicitly; then you categorize the remaining balance using any percentages you set up earlier or simply under Miscellaneous.

- *Classes* add another dimension to your category structure. You can classify any transaction, whether expense or income, according to broad designations to more fully characterize your financial picture. For example, a Business class could identify all business expenses and income; a Christmas class could isolate all expenses related to this holiday, regardless of whether they're for food, gifts, or travel. If you run a business serving several clients, you could create a class for each. When you generate financial reports, classes dramatically increase the precision of summarized information.

- Quicken offers five types of reports. *Transaction* reports (including Itemized Categories, Investment Transactions, and Tax Summary reports) list all individual transactions that meet your selection criteria. *Summary* reports (such as Cash Flow, Investment Income, Payroll, Accounts Payable and Receivable, and Job/Project reports) give subtotals without transaction details. *Budget* reports are summary reports that compare your actual spending patterns to your plans. *Account Balance* reports (Net Worth, Balance Sheet, and Portfolio Value, for example) give you snapshots of your accounts at specific moments. *Specialized* reports (including Investment Performance,

Capital Gains, and Missing Checks) are unique reports that provide useful information unobtainable through the other reports.

IMPORTANT IDEAS

■ Classes are the next logical step in unraveling a tangle of financial information. Using classes, you can track the themes, activities, or events that influence your spending and income. Classes can help you to simplify tax reporting, summarize finances related to second homes or rental properties, budget for the financial needs of a child in college, or estimate future costs for vacations and special events. Learn how to manipulate Quicken's standard reports to highlight classes, so you realize their full benefit as a financial management tool.

■ The time you devote to creating reports will be well spent if you memorize them. Quicken's reporting capabilities are broad and thorough, allowing you to adjust the content, substantial layout, and appearance of reports. As you manage your finances, use these memorized reports to see with a few keystrokes the budget areas you're most concerned with, to determine the total payments from a client within a time period, or to obtain a comparison of spending between quarters or years. The more frequently you consult a certain report or the more complex it is, the more valuable it is to set it up carefully and memorize it.

■ The spending patterns of someone living in today's complex world can never be neatly pigeonholed, which is why split transactions are so useful. It pays to become accustomed to using them, especially in working with credit cards or cash, because these two areas can account for a large fraction of your expenses. The percentage split capability allows you to approximate your spending in various categories by entering percentages and then having Quicken allocate portions of your spending based on those percentages. This gives you a realistic picture of where your petty cash ends up.

DECISIONS

What Are You Trying to Accomplish?

"Budget" is one of those words that always seems to evoke a strong reaction—and rarely a positive one. It's not surprising that budgets have such bad press; in early work and home life, budgets are used most commonly as an excuse *not* to do something. Budgets can be used effectively only when they reflect your fiscal priorities, namely, when you use them to determine what kind of fixed obligations you can maintain, how much you intend to save, and with what emphasis you want to spend the rest.

The first decision you must make, then, is to approach budgeting in the right frame of mind: budgets are priority mechanisms, not straitjackets. They're a strategy for ensuring that you spend your money where you want to and alerting you when you drift off track.

How Detailed Should Your Budget Be?

Quicken is capable of budgeting your finances right down to a category and subcategory for each expenditure. Within each category and subcategory, you can enter a different budget for every month. Quicken also allows you to budget transfers among accounts: for example, monthly transfers to a savings account.

You face four decisions, therefore, on the level of detail you should apply to your budgeting:

- *Should you budget every category?*   To do a thorough job of planning your priorities, you should budget every line item. This affords you the best opportunity for starting the year with a balanced budget. However, if you wish only to monitor and control your spending on a small number of line items, you could certainly budget just those few.

- *Should you budget every subcategory as well?*   This will depend on how you've structured your categories and subcategories. If the subcategories you've set up reflect your budget planning, and if you foresee that subcategory variations will occur throughout the year and that they will be difficult to capture at the category level, then budgeting at the subcategory level will be useful. If you have few subcategories, category-level budgeting will suffice to give you a balanced budget and convey information about your financial priorities.

- *Should you create monthly budgets?*   Specific monthly amounts—as opposed to a monthly average gleaned from the annual amount—are useful only for significant expenses that arise at fairly predictable points in the year: tuition, homeowners' insurance, heating bills, and vacation expenses, for example. For everything else, you should be able to rely on monthly averages.

■ *Should you budget transfers?*　Two types of transfers will be important to consider: major planned asset purchases or sales (like buying a car or selling your house), and savings programs (like putting $500 into a brokerage account every month). Transfers among bank, cash, and credit card accounts (like moving cash from your joint checking account to a personal checking account) need not be budgeted.

Should You Zero-Base Your Budget?

In corporate circles, a popular debate among financial planners is whether you should budget based on last year's actual spending ("We should plan to increase spending on advertising by 8 percent but cut office supplies by 15 percent") or apply a technique called *zero-base budgeting*. When you zero-base a budget, you ignore last year's spending patterns and build your budget from the ground up, challenging every assumption about how you spend money.

Zero-base budgeting is an interesting and challenging exercise for personal financial planning. As a practical matter, though, if you're not prepared to radically change your lifestyle or don't face imminent financial crisis, you should work towards a budget based on predictable changes from last year's income and spending.

However, even if you base your budget on last year's spending, you'll probably find that a zero-based attitude toward certain discretionary expenses (such as dining out, recreation, clothing, travel, and entertainment) is healthy.

Do You Want to Start a Savings Plan?

We all have a goal to save toward: a new home, college for the children, a once-in-a-lifetime vacation, or financial security for our family. Yet saving for these goals doesn't come naturally: everyone tends to accelerate his or her spending when the bank account is full and to economize when cash is tight. It takes special initiative and discipline to put away a certain amount of money each year toward a long-term objective.

One of the greatest advantages of a Quicken budget is how it can support you in creating and implementing a personal savings plan. Developing a savings strategy lets you be certain there's room in your budget for salting some money away. And by letting yourself be reminded periodically of where you stand on your savings plan, you'll have the satisfaction of knowing you're achieving your savings goal.

Before you start the budgeting process, though, you should decide if you do want to adhere to a savings plan and how much you'd like to save. The amount to save hinges on three considerations: the cost of the items you're saving for (remember to take inflation into account); the length of the time over which you want to save; and after-tax returns on your savings. In Table 7.1, we have calculated the monthly savings amounts required to accumulate $5,000, $25,000, $100,000, $250,000, and $1,000,000 over time periods ranging from two to thirty years, assuming an after-tax return of 6 percent on your savings. You'll also find a spreadsheet model on ZiffNet for calculating your own version of this table, using different interest rate assumptions; see Appendix B for details.

Table 7.1   **Monthly Savings Required to Achieve Long-Term Goal (6 percent after-tax interest, rounded to nearest dollar)**

Goal	$5,000	$25,000	$100,000	$250,000	$1,000,000
2 years	$197	$985	$3,938	$9,845	$39,381
5 years	$72	$360	$1,439	$3,598	$14,391
10 years	$31	$154	$615	$1,539	$6,155
15 years	$17	$87	$349	$871	$3,485
20 years	$11	$55	$221	$551	$2,205
25 years	$7	$37	$148	$370	$1,479
30 years	$5	$26	$103	$257	$1,026

MATERIALS

Information on Last Year's Spending

Unless you're willing to start from scratch with a zero-based budgeting approach, you should gather as much information as possible about your spending last year. If you've already been using Quicken, the task is very easy. If not, you've got some work ahead of you.

In addition, you'll want to identify every item in your expenses that might vary from last year to this. For example, was there an interest rate adjustment which changed your mortgage payment at midyear? Have there been significant changes in the utility rates or your lawncutting fees? On some spending items (and income items too, for that matter), you'll find the rate you're paying at the close of the year more accurately predicts next year's expenses than a whole-year figure does.

List of Fixed Income and Obligations

Some items in your budget are fixed, and would take extraordinary effort to change. Your salary is probably fixed, for example; unless you change jobs, get a raise, or are self-employed in a business that fluctuates, you can predict quite precisely what your net salary will be. On the expense side, mortgage payments, other loan payments, taxes, insurance, school costs, and utilities are among the fixed obligations.

Identify the fixed income sources and expense obligations that you've built into the structure of your life. During the budgeting process, you may identify some changes you need to make here, but simply build the list for now.

PRELIMINARIES

Complete Levels 1 and 2

You will need a working knowledge of registers, categories, and reports to construct and use a Quicken budget. No other techniques are required.

Set Up a Complete Category Structure

Before you start creating a budget, you should have constructed a relatively stable category structure. The categories you set up in your initial sessions with Quicken usually undergo radical changes over the next few months, as you fit your expenses and income to them. It's a waste of time to enter a budget into an untested category structure. You'll probably want to have worked with Quicken for several months before you embark on the budgeting process, refining the category structure as you gain experience. At the very least, you should have had experience collecting data for several months, completing one or two full reconciliation cycles.

Adopt a Budgeting Process

You can take many approaches to building a budget. This guide describes one approach that is particularly tuned to Quicken 5's capabilities.

You should closely analyze the types of inflow and outflow that will appear in your budget. Inflows are generally represented by your income—salary, commissions, bonuses, investments, and other income. Expenses, however, are derived from a variety of sources. Although you don't have to enter each type into your budget as a group, you will need to treat them differently when it comes time to balance your budget. Your expenses may include

- *Fixed expenses*   These outlays won't change without a radical restructuring of your finances. Fixed expenses include obligations such as loan payments and taxes.

- *Operating expenses*   These are the costs of maintaining your home and keeping your family fed, clothed, healthy, and educated at the most basic level. These expenses may fluctuate over time, but it may take significant cutbacks in your style of living to decrease them.

- *Savings*   You commit this money to an investment or savings account, usually toward a specific objective. In a Quicken budget, a savings amount essentially represents a transfer of funds from your bank accounts to savings or investment accounts.

- *Discretionary expenses*   These expenses support the style and quality of your life. They might represent travel, recreation, gifts, entertainment, charitable contributions, club dues, subscriptions, and dining out. Asset purchases such as home improvements, a new car, boat, stereo or computer equipment are also discretionary expenses.

The budgeting process presented in this level follows these general steps:

1. Enter inflows and outflows into the budget.

2. Determine whether your budget balances—both overall and by month. If it's out of balance, follow the techniques recommended in this level to bring it into line.

3. Produce budget reports periodically to track your spending against your plans. Make adjustments as necessary—either to your spending or to the budget.

There are, of course, many different sequences by which you could assemble and track a budget. Whether you embrace our approach or not, you really ought to adopt a strategy for setting your priorities, explicitly addressing your savings goals, identifying the areas you're willing to cut back if necessary, and tracking your progress so you'll know when and where to adjust.

Enter Your Annual and Monthly Budgets

You manage your Quicken budget through the Budget screen, accessible through the Activities menu. From any register or report screen, press Alt-A B (Activities menu, Set Up Budgets). After a few moments, you'll see the screen shown in Figure 7.1.

Figure 7.1   **Quicken Budget screen**

```
 File    Edit    Layout    Activities                              F1-Help

         Category Description        Jan.     Feb.     Mar.     Apr.

INFLOWS
   Bonus Income                     [        ]    0        0        0
   Dividend                              0        0        0        0
   Gift Received                         0        0        0        0
   Interest Income:
      Bank Interest                      0        0        0        0
         Interest Income - Other         0        0        0        0

      Total Interest Income             0        0        0        0
   Investment Income                    0        0        0        0
   Investment Interest Inc              0        0        0        0
   Long Term Cap Gain Dist              0        0        0        0
   Other Income                         0        0        0        0

   Total Budget Inflows               0        0        0        0
   Total Budget Outflows              0        0        0        0
   Difference                         0        0        0        0

 FIELDING-Bank,Cash,CC Investme                              (Filtered)
```

Note. Quicken's budget capability has been greatly expanded in version 5. While it is possible to manage budgets using earlier versions, much of the discussion in this level applies only to the most recent one.

The Budget screen is laid out like a spreadsheet: months appear across the top and a list of categories appears on the left. Pressing the PgDn key displays more categories. The right-most column following December (which you can view by pressing the Right Arrow key) totals the monthly numbers for each category across the row. A three-line section at the bottom of the screen shows inflows, outflows, and the difference, which is your budgeted net cash flow for the month. Quicken's budgets are based on cash flow into and out of your main transaction accounts as a group—your bank, credit card, and cash accounts.

You'll also see a new menu bar across the top of the screen, offering File commands for saving and loading budget files, Edit commands that assist with data entry, Layout commands for choosing the time periods used for column headings, and Activities commands for moving to other Quicken activities.

Quicken budgets cover a single calendar year from January through December. If you plan your life on a time frame other than the calendar year, you can still use Quicken's budgeting facility, but you will have to accept that January will always appear as the first column and December as the last.

Set Up Appropriate Detail Level

While reading the Plan Ahead section, you should have made decisions about whether you'd be budgeting down to the subcategory level and whether you'd be budgeting account-to-account transfers, which are mostly devoted to building your savings plans. Before you go any further, you should program these decisions into Quicken.

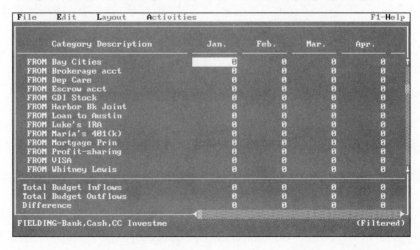

Note. Try to adhere to one method or the other. If you opt for subcategory budgeting after practicing category-only budgeting for awhile, the budget data you entered for parent categories will be ignored when you make the switch.

Quicken will budget at the subcategory level by default. To tell Quicken not to budget subcategories, press Alt-E S (Edit menu, Budget Subcats). Quicken will redisplay the budget screen without subcategories. To later revert to subcategory budgeting, you should press Alt-E S again.

Quicken does not budget transfers unless you tell it to. To prepare Quicken to handle budget transfers, press Alt-E T (Edit menu, Budget Transfers). You can use the same procedure to toggle between transfer-budgeting and category-only budgeting.

If you chose budgeting for subcategories and transfers, your budget screen will appear as follows: first, any subcategories will be displayed, slightly indented, with a total line for the category immediately following; second, at the end of the inflows section, Quicken will list your accounts, preceded by "FROM" (see Figure 7.2); similarly, your accounts will appear in the list at the end of outflows, preceded by "TO." You will plan and record transfers among different accounts in these fields.

Figure 7.2 **Budget screen showing transfer and subcategory settings**

File	Edit	Layout	Activities				F1-Help
Category Description			Jan.	Feb.	Mar.	Apr.	
FROM Bay Cities			0	0	0	0	
FROM Brokerage acct			0	0	0	0	
FROM Dep Care			0	0	0	0	
FROM Escrow acct			0	0	0	0	
FROM GDI Stock			0	0	0	0	
FROM Harbor Bk Joint			0	0	0	0	
FROM Loan to Austin			0	0	0	0	
FROM Luke's IRA			0	0	0	0	
FROM Maria's 401(k)			0	0	0	0	
FROM Mortgage Prin			0	0	0	0	
FROM Profit-sharing			0	0	0	0	
FROM VISA			0	0	0	0	
FROM Whitney Lewis			0	0	0	0	
Total Budget Inflows			0	0	0	0	
Total Budget Outflows			0	0	0	0	
Difference			0	0	0	0	
FIELDING-Bank,Cash,CC Investme						(Filtered)	

Zero the Budget Screen

Note. If you have any budget information you want to save, see the later section, "Maintain Multiple Budgets."

Unless you've set up budgets before, all of the amounts should be zero. If there are numbers leftover from prior activity, you may want to clear them so you can start with a clean slate. You could use the cursor keys to enter zero in each cell, but there is a much faster way:

1. Press Alt-L Y (Layout menu, Year) to collapse the budget screen into a single annual budget column, as shown in Figure 7.3.

Figure 7.3   Budget screen collapsed into a single annual budget column

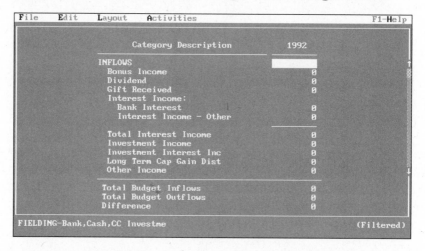

Note. To zero a field, you can also simply type zero over the existing entry. Be aware, however, that Quicken does not completelt erase a field when you start typing over it. Make sure you type over every digit with a zero or a blank.

2. Use the Down Arrow key to move down the budget column, checking to ensure that each number in the column is zero. If you find a nonzero amount, highlight it and press Ctrl-Backspace to clear the field. As soon as you move the cursor again, a zero will appear in the empty field.

3. Press Alt-L M (Layout menu, Month) to return the budget screen to a monthly column format. Zeros should appear in every cell, and the total budget inflows, outflows, and difference should also be zero.

Enter Your Income and Spending Amounts

Starting with your income and working toward fixed, operating, savings, and discretionary spending, you should begin constructing a budget. For every category, enter fresh numbers that represent your best guess of future spending in that category. When you start from scratch, you are approximating the zero-base budgeting process.

Note. Quicken calculates the budget totals based on the budget figures you enter for each category and month. You cannot edit these totals directly.

Note. If you've entered a number and want to repeat it in the field immediately below, press the Down Arrow key to move to the next field, and then type ' or ".

Note. When you enter budget amounts for income, be sure you're also budgeting appropriate amounts for income taxes, timed in a way that reflects withholding amounts, quarterly estimates, and filing payments that you expect to make.

Note. When you collapse monthly budgets to display them by quarter or for the whole year, Quicken retains monthly detail. As soon as you change a category amount at the annual or quarterly level, however, the monthly amounts are recalculated as averages and the monthly detail for the category is lost.

If you plan to base your budget on last year's spending, as described in the following section, you should first bring in the actual numbers from last year and then make specific category entries for this year. The incoming numbers will overwrite any data already in the budget screen.

As you enter them, your income and expense items will probably fall into one of five areas, each of which requires a slightly different approach:

- *Lump-sum amounts* These amounts occur in large groups once or twice a year. They include insurance payments, tuition bills, property taxes, and bonus income. Enter these amounts by using the cursor keys to highlight the appropriate category-and-month cell, and then typing the number.

- *Fixed monthly amounts* These amounts are the same or at least similar from month to month. They include mortgage and other loan payments, groceries, utility bills, newspaper subscriptions, and salary income. Enter these amounts by typing the monthly average into the January column, pressing Alt-E F (Edit menu, Fill Right) to copy that amount to the other eleven months of the year. Alternatively, you can collapse your budget to a single annual column by pressing Alt-L Y (Layout menu, Year). Now enter an annual budget. When you switch back to a monthly view by pressing Alt-L M (Layout menu, Month), Quicken will allocate your annual sum equally across all twelve months of the year.

- *Seasonal expenses* These expenses are higher during one particular time of year and lower in others. They include heating bills, electricity (if you air-condition your home or heat it with electricity), water bills (during droughts and summers), travel expenses (during vacation season), landscaping, and holiday expenses. The quickest way of entering these amounts will probably be to budget them on a quarterly basis by pressing Alt-L Q (Layout menu, Quarter). Each quarter's expenses will then be spread evenly by month within the quarter.

- *Variable monthly amounts* You need to budget these expenses explicitly every month, because they change in unique ways. Heating bills may fall into this category once you've gained a few seasons of experience in a particular house and climate. So too might your salary, if you run a business that fluctuates by season. Enter these numbers directly into each cell in the budget screen.

- *Consistent monthly expenses with predictable exceptions* These expenses are reasonably constant through most of the year, with the exception of one or two abnormally high months. For example, your telephone bill for a summer home may be $15 per month for most of the year, but jump to $50 for July and August. Enter these amounts by following the procedure for consistent monthly amounts described earlier; then overwrite the exceptional amounts in the appropriate columns.

Note. When you copy a previous year's actual numbers into your budget screen, those numbers will overwrite any budget data you've already entered.

Note. When you transfer actual data into a budget, the number of months covered must be equal, but not necessarily the months themselves.

Base Your Budget on Last Year's Spending

You can quickly devise a personal budget by basing next year's budget on the previous year's spending. This method is particularly useful if

- You didn't run into any cash flow problems last year

- You don't expect many significant changes in income and spending

- Last year's expenses were an accurate reflection of your financial priorities

You can use the actual income, expense, and transfer data from any number of months up to 12, applying them to an equal number of months in your budget. Alternatively, you can compute averages for up to 12 months and enter them into any single month column.

To load the budget screen with historical data,

1. While you're viewing the Budget screen (see Figure 7.1), press Alt-E A (Edit menu, AutoCreate). You'll see the Automatically Create Budgets window, shown in Figure 7.4. The date range will show January through December of the previous calendar year.

Figure 7.4   **Automatically Create Budgets window**

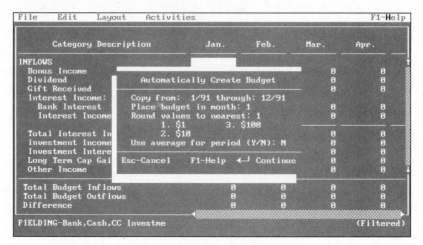

2. Change the range of source dates if you wish.

3. Enter the starting budget month in which you'd like Quicken to place your actual data. By default, Quicken places the data beginning in the January column.

4. Quicken automatically rounds figures to the nearest dollar; you may choose to round more coarsely by typing **2** or **3** next to "Round values to nearest."

5. If you want Quicken to calculate a monthly average for the period and enter the average in the starting budget month (as determined in step 3), type **Y** in the "Use average for period" blank.

6. Press Ctrl-Enter to actually initiate the transfer. Figure 7.5 shows a portion of Luke Fielding's actual budget.

Figure 7.5   **Section of a budget showing numbers from the previous year**

```
 File     Edit    Layout     Activities                           F1-Help

        Category Description        Jan.      Feb.      Mar.      Apr.

      Auto Fuel                      97        71        64        95
      Auto Loan Payment             405       405       405       405
      Auto Service                   25        25         0        80
      Automobile Expenses - Other     0         0         0         0

      Total Automobile Expenses     527       501       469       580
      Bank Charge                    10        10        10        10
      Charitable Donations            0        75       100       200
      Childcare Expense:
        Bright Eyes                 444       555       444       555
        Misc babysitting             50        50        50        50
        Wanda Milasz                400       500       400       500
        Childcare Expense - Other     0         0         0         0

      Total Budget Inflows        5,176     5,134     5,272     8,641
      Total Budget Outflows       4,926     4,343     5,828     5,802
      Difference                    250       791      -556     2,839

 FIELDING-Bank,Cash,CC Investme                            (Filtered)
```

Note. Fill Right (press Alt-E F) works on a single category row. Fill Columns (Alt-E R) takes the highlighted monthly column and replicates all its category and transfer line items to the remaining months of the year. Use these carefully; improperly applied, they overwrite valuable data.

In step 5 if you choose to transfer averages rather than actual monthly income and spending, remember that only one month will be set up in your Quicken budget with the average amounts. You must use Fill Right (Alt-E F) or Fill Columns (Alt-E C) to apply these averages to the other months.

Enter Savings and Other Transfers

If you're using Quicken budgets to support a savings plan or if you plan to make a major capital outlay such as for a car or home improvements, you should explicitly list these items when you build your budget. You will do this as you budget important transfers as well as your income and expense categories.

Note. Quicken divides your accounts into transaction accounts (Bank, Credit Card, and Cash) and long-term accounts (Investment, Other Asset, and Other Liability). Budgets are based on cash flow into and out of the transaction accounts; the long-term accounts are usually the targets of transfers from the transaction accounts.

If you haven't already done so, you should activate the Budget Transfers option by pressing Alt-E T.

When you turn Budget Transfers on, you'll see several new line items added to the end of the category list of both the inflows and outflows groups. These new items are designed to budget transfers to and from your Investment, Other Asset, and Other Liability accounts.

Figure 7.6 shows how Larry Milner makes use of these transfer items in building his monthly budget. He plans to put aside $2,000 per month in savings—$1,200 to a mutual fund investment account and $800 to a brokerage account. In addition, he deposits $600 of his paycheck into a company-sponsored 401(k) savings plan each month. He puts $415 of his monthly mortgage payment toward amortizing his mortgage loan. Finally, he plans to spend $22,500 in January to buy a new car and $5,000 on improvements to his home in March.

Figure 7.6   **Budget showing transfers for savings**

```
 File    Edit    Layout    Activities                          F1-Help

    Category Description        Jan.     Feb.     Mar.     Apr.

    Water                         75       75       75       75
    Water, Gas, Electric - Other   0        0        0        0

    Total Water, Gas, Electric   230      220      210      210
    TO Autos                  22,500        0        0        0
    TO Birscher                  800      800      800      800
    TO Checking                    0        0        0        0
    TO Mitsou 401(k)             600      600      600      600
    TO Money Market                0        0        0        0
    TO Mortgage Princ            415      415      415      415
    TO PlusOne MF              1,200    1,200    1,200    1,200
    TO Ridge Rd House              0        0    5,000        0

    Total Budget Inflows      39,550   17,050   18,106   17,050
    Total Budget Outflows     37,745   18,750   17,305   16,975
    Difference                 1,805   -1,700      801       75

 MILNER-Bank,Cash,CC Investment                        (Filtered)
```

Transaction groups (explained in Level 3) are valuable for reminding you to make deposits into savings accounts. If you regularly deposit the same amount, set up a transaction group to remind you of the payments and even issue checks.

Balance Your Budget

The toughest aspect of developing a budget is balancing it, as is apparent to anyone who follows the budget debates in Congress or a state legislature these days. Once you've entered your anticipated income and spending levels, as well as the major savings contributions and asset purchases you're planning, you'll want to determine whether your budget balances.

Unfortunately, Quicken's capability for doing this automatically is incomplete; you'll have to do some work by hand. The following is a step-by-step process for balancing your budget as painlessly as possible.

First, obtain a broad overview of your planned cash inflows and outflows. By viewing the whole year, you can determine whether your overall income, spending, and savings rates are realistic. To do this, collapse your budget screen to see most if not all of the year at once. A good summary for this purpose is the quarterly view (Alt-L Q, for Layout menu, Quarter), which displays your budget in four quarterly columns and a total column. The total column and the three summary lines, shown in Figure 7.7, tally your planned inflows and outflows for the year, as well as the difference between the two. If the difference is negative, you need to either cut expenses, increase your income, defer some asset purchases, or sell some assets to make ends meet. If the difference is significantly positive, you should probably plan to save more.

Figure 7.7   **Quarterly view of a budget**

```
 File    Edit    Layout    Activities                        F1-Help

    Category Description      Qtr 1    Qtr 2    Qtr 3    Qtr 4    T

 OUTFLOWS                                                            T
   Automobile Expenses:
     Auto Fuel                 120      120      120      120
     Auto Loan Payment       2,550    2,550    2,550    2,550
     Auto Service               60      140       60      140
     Automobile Expenses - Other  0        0        0        0

   Total Automobile Expenses  2,730    2,810    2,730    2,810
   Bank Charge                  45       45       45       45
   Charitable Donations        450      450      450      450
   Clothing                    750    1,000    1,000    1,000
   Dining Out                  375      375      375      375
   Dues                         50      100       75       75

 Total Budget Inflows       74,700   52,400   52,400   52,400    2
 Total Budget Outflows      73,515   51,581   53,341   51,936    2
 Difference                  1,185      819     -941      464

 MILNER-Bank,Cash,CC Investment                          (Filtered)
```

Second, identify those items to which you can make adjustments, starting with discretionary expenses. Always try to avoid decreasing your monthly savings or selling assets to finance shortfalls. Make adjustments to your overall spending to bring your annual inflows and outflows into line.

Next, look at the cash flow you can anticipate for each individual month. Expand your budget screen to a monthly view by pressing Alt-L M (Layout menu, Month), and starting with January, examine the difference line, which represents net cash flow (as shown in Figure 7.8). Unless you applied broad averages for all category items for every month, you'll probably observe large variations in cash flow from month to month. In months with a positive difference, you'll be accumulating cash; in those with a negative difference, you'll be spending more than you earn.

Figure 7.8   Budget showing monthly cash flow

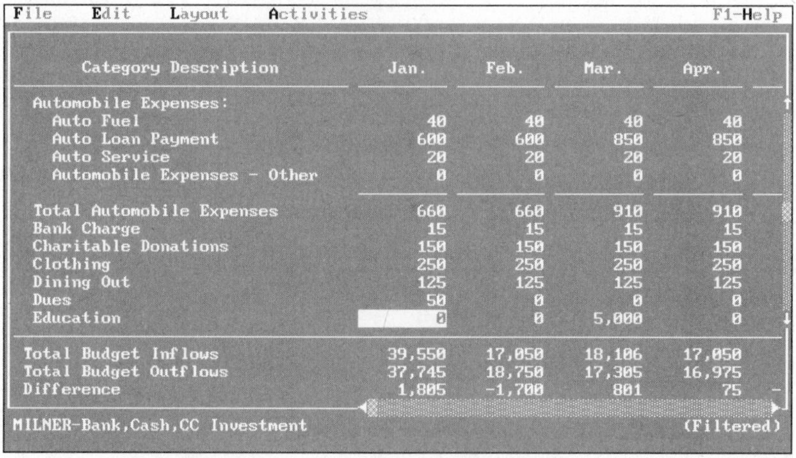

File Edit Layout Activities				F1-Help
Category Description	Jan.	Feb.	Mar.	Apr.
Automobile Expenses:				
Auto Fuel	40	40	40	40
Auto Loan Payment	600	600	850	850
Auto Service	20	20	20	20
Automobile Expenses – Other	0	0	0	0
Total Automobile Expenses	660	660	910	910
Bank Charge	15	15	15	15
Charitable Donations	150	150	150	150
Clothing	250	250	250	250
Dining Out	125	125	125	125
Dues	50	0	0	0
Education	0	0	5,000	0
Total Budget Inflows	39,550	17,050	18,106	17,050
Total Budget Outflows	37,745	18,750	17,305	16,975
Difference	1,805	-1,700	801	75
MILNER-Bank,Cash,CC Investment				(Filtered)

Now, calculate the cumulative cash flow—that is, your need for cash at any given point in the year. Regrettably, this requires a manual step, but one worth the effort. We've made it easier by providing a Toolkit, the Peak Cash-Needs Calculator, described later in this level. The Toolkit will help you quickly identify whether, at some point in the year, you will have a need for cash obscured in the annual budget overview. To understand how these cash needs can remain obscured, let's examine Larry Milner's budget. Table 7.2 shows his cumulative cash flow pattern.

If your cumulative planned outlays look like they will significantly out-pace your planned inflows at some point during the year, you might consider several ways of coping with it. For example, you could change your planned spending patterns (for example, defer the new car purchase a few months), change the timing—but not the total amount—of your savings plans, plan to temporarily dip into capital, or seek a temporary credit line to help you through the crunch. Make these changes to your monthly budget amounts until you reach a manageable cumulative sum.

Table 7.2　　**Cumulative Cash Flow for Larry Milner's Budget**

	This Month	Running Totals
Start of Year	—	400
January	3,656	4,056
February	1,087	5,143
March	-2,440	2,703
April	-3,215	-512
May	578	66
June	1,965	2,031
July	765	2,796
August	-2,510	286
September	2,420	2,706
October	1,638	4,344
November	-4,655	-311
December	2,153	1,842

Larry will experience cash crises in April and November.

If your cumulative planned inflows will run ahead of your spending, you may temporarily build up cash that you'll need later in the year. This is a good point at which to make investments that will mature in a short but well-defined amount of time, such as a bank CD or a treasury bill. Your Quicken budget will aid you in analyzing the most opportune moment to make such an investment, the best amount, and the date you'll need the cash back to cover planned spending.

Once you've made these adjustments, you should have a balanced annual budget in which you've made provisions to accommodate the peaks of your cash flow cycle.

TOOLKIT   A Peak Cash-Needs Calculator

	This Month	Cumulative
Start of Year	—	
January		
February		
March		
April		
May		
June		
July		
August		
September		
October		
November		
December		

My peak need for cash is $_____ in the month of _____.

My peak availability of cash is $_____ in the month of _____.

This Toolkit is designed to help you identify the months during which you will have excess cash and those when you may be cash poor. With this information, you can change to your planned inflows and outflows now, while you're looking ahead—instead of later, when an unanticipated shortfall could thwart some of your discretionary plans.

To use the Toolkit,

1. Determine the amount of cash available to you in January for the year that you're budgeting. You can estimate the cash available to you, or you can generate a standard Cash Flow report, specifying the entire previous year as the date range. To generate the Cash Flow report, press Alt-R P C (Report menu, Personal Reports, Cash Flow). Enter the net cash amount into the Toolkit in the cumulative column for the start of the year.

2. Referring to your completed budget screen, enter the difference for each month into the Toolkit, in the "this month" column next to the appropriate month heading.

3. Using the Quicken Calculator (Ctrl-O), subtract the difference for the current month from the previous month's cumulative number. Enter the result in the cumulative column for the current month. Repeat this for every month until the cumulative column is filled in.

4. Write the largest negative number below the chart and write the month name in the last one.

5. Write the largest positive number in the next blank beneath the chart and write the month name in the last one.

This Toolkit is also available as a 1-2-3 spreadsheet through ZiffNet. See Appendix B for information on how to obtain it.

Note. If none of the cumulative numbers is negative, this could mean that you are accumulating cash too rapidly, resulting in a large positive number at the end of the year. If this is the case, you should consider increasing your savings.

Manage Your Spending

With a finalized budget in hand, matching your spending to your budget limits makes sense—and Quicken makes it easy. Simply work into your maintenance routine a step involving a comparison of your expenses with your budget, giving yourself ample opportunity to put the brakes on your spending if need be.

Monitor Budget Reports

Quicken's standard budget reports allow you to closely monitor your income, spending, and savings performance against your budget guidelines. These reports present simple comparisons of your actual cash flow, your budgeted cash flow, and the difference over a given period of time up to one year.

Quicken offers two types of budget reports: the Budget report and the Monthly Budget report. There are subtle distinctions between the two.

The Budget report aggregates a designated period of time into a single actual spending column, a budget column, and a difference column. You create this report in the Register by pressing Alt-R U (Reports menu, Budget). A sample of this report appears in Figure 7.9. It shows your performance versus your budget on an income statement basis, grouping cash flows into income items, expense items, and transfers. Quicken includes all accounts in this report.

Figure 7.9 Standard Budget report

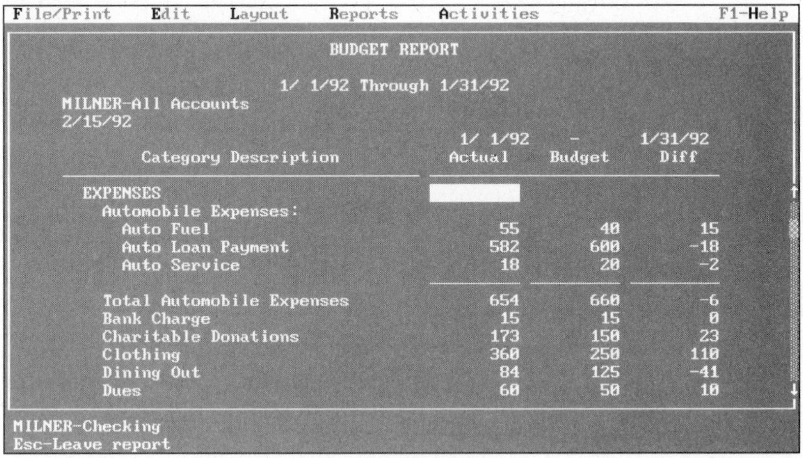
File/Print Edit Layout Reports Activities F1-Help

BUDGET REPORT

1/ 1/92 Through 1/31/92

MILNER-All Accounts
2/15/92

Category Description	1/ 1/92 Actual	- Budget	1/31/92 Diff
EXPENSES			
Automobile Expenses:			
Auto Fuel	55	40	15
Auto Loan Payment	582	600	-18
Auto Service	18	20	-2
Total Automobile Expenses	654	660	-6
Bank Charge	15	15	0
Charitable Donations	173	150	23
Clothing	360	250	110
Dining Out	84	125	-41
Dues	60	50	10

MILNER-Checking
Esc-Leave report

The Monthly Budget report displays three columns for each month covered in the date range of the report. You create this report by pressing Alt-R P B (Reports menu, Personal Reports, Monthly Budget). The report shows your performance versus your budget on a cash flow basis, grouping transfers into and out of your Investment, Other Asset, and Other Liability accounts into the appropriate inflow and outflow sections of the report. For each month, the report provides Actual, Budget, and Difference columns. The Monthly Budget report also provides a final set of columns on the far right, shown in Figure 7.10, which summarizes the months in the date range.

The Monthly Budget report most closely reflects the way you established your budget in the first place—on the basis of cash flow. The Budget report, with its profit-and-loss basis, more accurately reflects the effects of budgeted and actual performance on your total net worth.

Figure 7.10   Monthly Budget report showing summary data for a three-month period

```
File/Print    Edit    Layout    Reports    Activities            F1-Help

                        MONTHLY BUDGET REPORT

                      1/ 1/92 Through 3/31/92

 MILHOME-Checking Acct
 4/ 5/92
                                3/31/92     1/ 1/92      -      3/31/92
            Category Description    Diff      Actual    Budget    Diff

 Automobile Expenses:
     Auto Loan Payment             -257       2,037     2,050     -13
     Automobile Fuel                -12         113       120      -7
     Automobile Service             -20         170        60     110

 Total Automobile Expenses         -289       2,320     2,230      90
 Bank Charge                          0          45        45       0
 Charitable Donations              -25         375       450     -75
 Clothing                          126         671       750     -79
 Dining Out                        -35         270       375    -105
 Dues                                0          60        60       0
 Education                           0       5,000     5,000       0

 MILHOME-Checking Acct
 Esc-Leave report
```

Adjust Your Budget at Midyear

However carefully you plan your budget, some of your assumptions will prove inaccurate. Your bonus check will be bigger or smaller than you expected, interest rates will change, energy prices will soar or crash, and your children will almost inevitably eat more than you thought possible.

It's worth reviewing your budget periodically through the year to ensure that your previously well-balanced budget isn't leading you slowly into a cash flow bind. Certainly your reports will help alert you to imbalances so that you will know whether to apply the brakes or loosen your limits on your discretionary spending items. If fixed or operating expenses are coming in much higher than expected, you should probably rebudget the rest of the year.

For example, Luke Fielding decided to review his budget in June. His stocks had performed well during the first five months of the year, but higher than expected medical expenses had put him in a cash flow bind. He decided to rebudget the rest of the year. He saved his original budget (see "Maintain Multiple Budgets" later in this level) and then decided to create a new one with the first five months of the year reflecting his actual spending.

Luke used the AutoCreate command (Alt-E A, for Edit menu, Auto-Create) to transfer the first five months of actual spending data into the first five months of his new budget. He then proceeded to balance the rest of the year's budget, employing the same balancing techniques he used to set up the year's budget in the first place.

Note. If you're afraid of losing your original data when you adjust your budget, don't worry. The next section, "Maintain Multiple Budgets," will show you how to keep a copy of your original budget on hand

Maintain Multiple Budgets

Note. Your file will be saved using the Quicken Interchange Format (QIF) form, which can be read or produced by a few other financial management packages. Its principal purpose here, though, is to save budget scenarios for later use.

You may find it valuable to create and save several budgets for the year. These can reflect different scenarios than the original budget (what you might spend if you get a big bonus versus a low-bonus scenario), or they can reflect successive revisions of a budget.

Whatever the motivation, it's easy to save Quicken budgets into a file and to retrieve those budgets later on:

1. While you're viewing the Budget screen, press Alt-F E (File menu, Export Budget) to tell Quicken you'd like to save the budget that's currently being displayed.

2. Quicken will display the Save budget to file window (see Figure 7.11), asking you to name the budget file; enter up to eight characters, such as HIBONUS. Press Enter when you're finished, and Quicken will save your budget into a file.

Figure 7.11   **Save budget to file window**

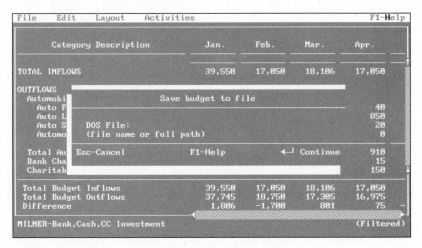

3. To retrieve a budget file you saved earlier, press Alt-F I (File menu, Import), and insert the name of the budget file you want to see. Remember that your current budget will be overwritten, so save it first if you're going to want it later.

Unlike other areas of Quicken, you can't get a list of saved budget files, so you need to keep track of the names you give budget files—an argument for simplicity. Try saving your budget files in a single subdirectory.

Wrap Up the Year

Often the most logical time to prepare an annual budget occurs around the beginning of the new year. If this is the case for you, it may also be a good time for you to consider using a few Quicken procedures to help you ring out the old year and ring in the new. These procedures are not merely budget specific—they affect all the accounts in your Quicken file.

Unlike traditional accounting packages and even most personal finance software, Quicken does not require a complicated close-out procedure at the end of the year. In fact, you have no obligation to do anything whatsoever at the end of the year; as long as you have room in memory and on your hard disk, you can continue accumulating Quicken transactions for as many years as you'd like.

Quicken does offer two procedures which you might consider running at the end of the year. You can find both of them by starting from the Main Menu (press Escape repeatedly to get there), and pressing P, F, and then Y (Set Preference, File Activities, Year End). The Year End window offers both procedures—archiving and starting a new year.

Archiving takes a snapshot of your entire current file and saves it in a separate archive file, leaving the current file intact. When you choose Archive, you'll be offered the Archive File window in which you choose a file name, a directory path (you may specify a floppy disk drive instead), and an as-of date for the archival snapshot (see Figure 7.12). When you press Ctrl-Enter, Quicken will make a copy of every transaction, account, and any other file information through the as-of date.

Note. While closing out accounts at the end of the year frees up disk space, it has the disadvantage of preventing you from readily making year-to-year comparisons or creating reports that span many years.

Note. If you're regularly backing up your accounts, as described in Level 1, you shouldn't need to use the archive function.

Figure 7.12   Archive File window

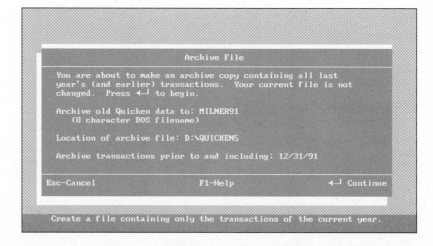

Starting a new year actually closes out old data before a certain date, saving only investment transactions and transactions that have not yet been cleared in a reconciliation step. The Start New Year window shown in Figure 7.13 asks you for a new file name, a location, and an as-of date. Your old data file is renamed with the new name, and a smaller file is created containing only the most recent transactions (those completed since the as-of date) as well as investment and uncleared transactions carried forward from the old file. This smaller file, which retains the name of your old data file, is now the selected file in which you'll work henceforth.

Figure 7.13   Start New Year window

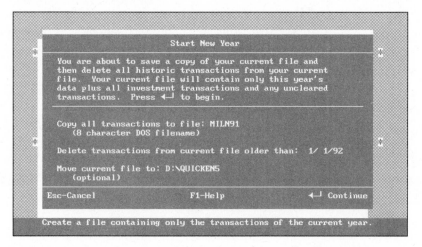

Each of these procedures produces a working file in which your new Quicken transactions will be recorded and an archival file containing old transactions. You should not need to make any changes in the archived file; therefore, it's a good idea to protect it with a password to make sure you don't record transactions in it by mistake.

To make a file *read-only* (that is, available for examination without your being able to record new transactions in it),

1. Start from the Main Menu, which you can reach by pressing Escape repeatedly.

2. Make sure the file you want to protect is the current file: press P F S (Set Preferences, File Activities, Select/Set Up File), and then choose the appropriate file. Press Escape to leave the Select Account to Use window.

3. Press Escape again to see the Set Preferences window (or from the Main Menu press P again). In the Set Preferences window, press W, then T (Password Settings, Transaction Password). You'll see the Password to Modify Existing Transactions window. Enter a password and type any distant date—such as 12/31/99—as in Figure 7.14. The date should easily encompass the transactions in the file, so all are protected.

Figure 7.14   **Password to Modify Existing Transactions window**

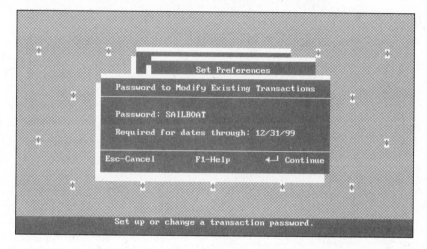

4. Press Ctrl-Enter, confirm the password, and you'll find that the archive file is now read-only. This will remain the case until you change the as-of date for the password (using the same procedure just outlined) to a very low date, such as 1/1/50.

LEVEL 7 BUILDING BLOCKS

TECHNIQUES AND PROCEDURES

■ Begin budgeting with Quicken by pressing Alt-A B (Activities menu, Set Up Budgets). If any figures remain in the budget screen from a previous budgeting session, collapse the budget into a single yearly column by pressing Alt-L Y (Layout menu, Year). Enter zeros next to each category, then fully expand the budget to see zeros across all rows by pressing Alt-L M (Layout menu, Month).

■ To budget only at the category level, from the budget screen press Alt-E S (Edit menu, Budget Subcats).

■ To include transfers to and from Quicken accounts—for example, should you want to establish a regular savings pattern—from the budget screen press Alt-E T (Edit menu, Budget Transfers). Quicken will list all accounts twice, once at the end of inflows, marked FROM (to signify transfers from those accounts into your cash flow), and again at the end of outflows, marked TO.

■ If you intend to follow the principles of zero-base budgeting, simply replace the zeros opposite the categories with figures for each month.

■ To enter consistent monthly amounts—for instance, if you always pay $75.00 per month for yard maintenance—enter the figure once in the first column; then press Alt-E F (Edit menu, Fill) to have Quicken copy the number across the row.

■ Collapsing the budget to display quarterly or yearly columns will speed up your budgeting. Collapse the budget to a quarterly scheme to enter amounts that vary by season. Collapse to a single annual column to form a budget based only on annual totals. Collapse or expand a budget by pressing Alt-L (Layout menu), then pressing Y (Year), Q (Quarter), or M (Month). If you've entered numbers into collapsed columns, when you expand the budget to a longer period Quicken will calculate an average based on the aggregate amount and distribute it across the columns.

■ Base your budget on actual spending and income data from the previous year by pressing Alt-E A (Edit menu, AutoCreate). Adjust the date range and indicate the budget month in which the actual data should begin appearing.

You can also opt to carry in only monthly averages based on the total from the period, rather than actual numbers. When you leave the settings window, Quicken brings the numbers into the budget screen, writing over any figures already there. Midyear, when you're adjusting your budget to match reality, you can bring actual numbers for only the first few months into the budget using this technique, and then adjust the remaining months' figures to comply.

■ See the Budget report by pressing Alt-R U (Reports menu, Budget). This report presents your spending and budget comparison in a profit-and-loss arrangement.

■ Obtain the Monthly Budget report by pressing Alt-R P B (Reports menu, Personal Reports, Monthly Budget). This report shows the spending, budget, and difference comparisons for each month, and a total comparison for the period you specified for the report.

■ Maintain several budgets by naming and saving each one. To save a budget, press Alt-F E (File menu, Export Budget). Specify a file name of eight characters or less, then specify the date range to be saved.

■ Close out the Quicken transactions of the previous year and maintain a file containing only the current year's transactions. From the Main Menu, press P F Y (Set Preferences, File Activities, Year End), and opt for archiving (which makes a copy of the entire file) or starting a new year (which isolates the old transaction into a separate file).

TERMS

■ *Zero-base budgeting* is a form of budgetary planning that requires you to start from scratch. Rather than basing an expense or income amount for a category on recent history, you base it on your current needs and circumstances. This forces you to assess and document your planned spending in detail without the luxury of relying on your previous patterns. You can zero-base a budget in Quicken simply by entering all numbers from scratch.

■ *Fixed expenses* are those that remain constant over time and are difficult to change. These include mortgage payments and taxes.

■ *Operating expenses* are the general costs of maintaining your home, your family, and yourself. These include clothing, food, education, care costs, and so on. Any flexibility in this category usually occurs through major decisions that affect your routines and priorities.

■ *Discretionary expenses* represent spending that, although nonessential, correlates directly to the quality of your life. The higher the amount of discretionary spending in your budget, the greater the flexibility this area allows when your budget is out of balance.

IMPORTANT IDEAS

■ As with all other areas of Quicken, the level of budgetary detail you track depends entirely on what kinds of decisions you want to make. At a minimum, use the category structure you've refined over time to help you develop a budget; don't intentionally skip categories during the budget process, or a report comparing spending with your budget will be incomplete. Specific monthly figures for each category usually provide the most effective tool for ongoing management of your finances, but averages may be sufficient.

■ Quicken can make it much easier to save money. As you plan and balance your budget, you should set up Quicken to budget transfers between accounts—so a certain amount every month, for example, is earmarked for a savings goal. The Totals column of the budget screen may also give you an encouraging sneak preview of how much you'll have accumulated at the end of the year with the savings plan you set up. As you progress through the year, Quicken can even remind you of savings payments due (through the use of transaction groups) and can issue the checks for you. Your periodic reports will show you at a glance whether you're ahead of or behind your scheduled savings plan.

■ Balancing the budget you've fashioned in Quicken is mainly a matter of creative thinking. Consider shifting the timing of major purchases, trimming back slightly (but not much) on your savings, or the obvious—cutting back on spending in discretionary categories. Also use the Toolkit in this level to determine cumulative cash flow. Quicken's budget provides instantaneous answers to your "what if" questions, so you can determine the right allocations to make your budget work.

Evaluate and Manage Your Investments

PLAN AHEAD

DECISIONS

What's Your Objective?

Like so many other aspects of applying Quicken, effective use of the investment account features requires that you consider exactly why you want to
track your investments. Your objectives will help determine when you start,
how much historical data you assemble, how often you update your prices,
and what reports you learn to use.

Two questions are worth asking yourself now:

■ Will Quicken be the principal tracking tool with which you evaluate and
manage an active (two to three trades per month) investment portfolio?

■ Will the data be used for tax purposes?

If you answer "yes" to the first question, you need to do three things:
first, enter complete information on when and for what amount you purchased each security in your portfolio; second, group similar investments
together by investment objective and security type; and third, download pricing data from an information service, rather than entering it from a newspaper. If you'll be using Quicken to monitor a less active portfolio or one that's
managed by someone else, historic data, groupings, and automated pricing
will be less important.

If you plan to use this data for tax purposes, you have three additional
tasks: first, record all transactions (purchases, sales, dividends, interest, and
so on) which have occurred this year, regardless of when you started your
Quicken bank account register; second, carefully determine and enter the
tax basis for each security, so that capital gains and losses will be reported
accurately; and third, pay close attention to how you enter transaction dates,
so long-term and short-term gains are correctly distinguished and year-end
transactions are reported in the proper tax year.

In this level, you'll learn techniques for identifying and entering historic
information which will help ensure that your valuations and capital gains
information are reliable.

Which Assets Should You Handle as Investment Accounts?

Investment accounts are assets that fluctuate in value over time. The obvious
candidates are stock, bond, and mutual funds portfolios. You can also use
investment accounts to manage other variably priced investments such as
precious metals and collectibles.

Some assets—like your home and car—also fluctuate in value over time,
but these are not necessarily appropriate for investment accounts because

precise values are not always obtainable. This also holds for money market mutual funds, which don't really fluctuate in price. Similarly, private limited partnerships aren't appropriate for investment accounts because prices aren't available and, in many cases, these partnerships may not be traded. In general, you should classify an asset into an investment account when

■ Its price varies frequently and unpredictably

■ The price is available through public or private sources

■ You anticipate buying or selling the asset (particularly when a purchase or sale is a taxable event)

Real estate and possessions such as cars, home furnishings, and equipment (such as your computer) should generally be classified as other assets. Money market mutual funds are best handled either as bank accounts (especially if you use the check-writing privileges many of them offer) or as other assets. Finally, private limited partnerships are usually better tracked as other assets.

In cases such as your Individual Retirement Account (IRA), you may have invested in Bank Certificates of Deposit or other assets that do not fluctuate in value. If you are considering changing your IRA to riskier securities whose prices do vary, you should set up your IRA as an investment account now.

How Should You Group Your Investments into Accounts?

The most basic investment unit in Quicken is a *security*—a single investment that has an identifiable value and price. This could be a stock for which the price per share and the number of shares you own drive the value of your investment, or a work of art to which you assign a price (for Quicken's purposes, this is also its value).

Quicken allows for grouping securities into accounts or collections of assets that are managed together. All the securities in one brokerage account would be an appropriate grouping. So, too, would the diverse holdings in an Individual Retirement or Keogh Account.

In general, you should group into an account securities which

■ You administer together as a portfolio unit (the proceeds from the sale of one security in the portfolio are used to buy other securities in the same portfolio)

■ Generate a consolidated account statement, such as a brokerage, trust account, or company savings plan statement

■ Are taxable in the same way to the same person

When you hold securities directly—private investments in a company that's recently gone public or shares you've received through a company stock purchase plan, for example—it's a good idea to start a separate Quicken account for each such security you own.

In cases such as brokerage or trust accounts, there will be either an uninvested cash balance or a margin loan amount associated with the account. Quicken accommodates these cash balances (positive for uninvested cash, negative for loans) in regular investment accounts.

Finally, you may be using one of the all-in-one money market, checking, and brokerage accounts offered by some of the large brokerage houses (Merrill Lynch's Cash Management Account or Fidelity's USA Account, for example). These accounts consolidate all transactions into a single statement and simplify transfers from one kind of investment to another. However, they are actually several separate accounts grouped together for reporting purposes. If you use one of these accounts for both checking and investment transactions, you should, for Quicken's purposes, treat the checking portion as a bank account and the investment portion as one or more investment accounts.

How Should You Handle Mutual Funds Investments?

Quicken actually offers two kinds of investment accounts: regular investment accounts and mutual fund accounts. But before you lump all your mutual funds into mutual fund accounts and everything else into investment accounts, you should understand the benefits and limitations of using Quicken's mutual fund designation.

A regular investment account and a mutual fund account differ in these ways:

■ A *regular investment account* may hold one or more securities and may maintain an optional cash balance. Its register displays the cash balance—a positive balance shows cash available to invest, while a negative balance shows money borrowed, frequently through a margin loan. Regular investment accounts are very flexible, since you may add and subtract securities and cash at will.

■ A *mutual fund investment account* is designed to hold a single security—specifically, a single mutual fund. It has no cash balance, so the register balance is expressed in terms of shares rather than dollars. A mutual fund investment account can simplify accounting procedures if you hold a single mutual fund over a sustained period of time—especially if you reinvest dividends or make periodic purchases, perhaps toward a long-term savings program.

Don't be confused by the names of these accounts. A regular investment account is more appropriate for holding a collection of mutual funds among which you freely switch your funds as market conditions change. Likewise, a mutual fund investment account can be used very appropriately to hold a single stock in which you're making periodic investments (such as through a company stock purchase program). The upshot is this: Use a regular investment account if you need a cash balance or if you need to track multiple securities in a single account. Otherwise, consider using a mutual fund investment account.

MATERIALS

Brokerage Statements

You'll want to pull out your latest brokerage account statement, which summarizes the composition, pricing, and value of your brokerage portfolios. If you will be tracking your IRA, company savings plans, or mutual fund portfolio as investment accounts, you'll also want to gather the most recent statements on these investments.

If you are using Quicken for tax purposes and starting after the first of the year, you should locate brokerage statements for the entire year. This will enable you to take full account of all the dividends, interest payments, and deductible investment interest you'll need to describe on your tax return.

Stock Acquisition Records

If you plan to use Quicken to track the performance of your investments from time of purchase to the present—and especially if you intend to use Quicken to calculate the taxable gains and losses which would be triggered by any sale—you'll want to track down the original purchase records for your investments: old brokerage statements, trade confirmations, stock option exercise receipts, company stock purchase plan statements, and the like. For each stock that you own, you should be able to identify the date it was purchased, the number of shares you bought, and the price per share and commission (or the total cost of the stock).

If you want Quicken to disclose the tax consequences of a potential sale of any investment in your portfolio, you should always record the tax-basis cost for each purchase. Scrutinize the more exotic transactions by which you acquired stock. For example, some employee stock options (incentive stock options) have a tax basis equal to the price of the option, while other types of options (nonqualified stock options) carry a tax basis equal to the market value of the stock at the time the option was exercised. In the latter case, the IRS taxes the increase in value between the exercise price and the market value at the time of exercise.

In some cases, you'll find that you acquired a security in several stages—at different prices and dates. These are called "tax lots." It's important that you account for these sequential purchases, for if you sell only part of your investment in a security with multiple tax lots, Quicken needs all the tax lot detail to report your capital gains liability correctly. Finding the tax basis often entails a fair amount of detective work. In this case, however, such detective work is required by law; tracking your investments in Quicken merely means that you'll find the information earlier than you otherwise would.

Finally, pay close attention to stock splits and, less commonly, stock dividends. Neither is a taxable event, but they do affect the tax basis of your shares. If you own 400 shares of a security now and you can only remember buying 200, chances are your stock has split two for one (or has declared a 100 percent stock dividend). Hence, your tax basis per share is only half what you originally paid for it. Since Quicken provides an easy way to enter stock splits and make appropriate tax-basis adjustments, you need only note that the split occurred. Try to determine when the split occurred through your broker or a stock reference guide. By recording the split date correctly, you insure that any historic market prices you enter will result in an accurate portrayal of your investment's market value over time.

Source of Current Stock Quotes

For portfolios of fewer than ten securities, a daily newspaper is a perfectly adequate source of pricing information. For New York and American Stock Exchange securities, use the closing price listed; for over-the-counter stocks, use the last trade or bid price.

For larger portfolios which you'll be pricing at least once a week, you may find that looking up prices and entering them by hand is an inefficient use of your time. Consider obtaining prices from an on-line information service. By using a script you can set up for your communications software, you'll find that updating a portfolio of hundreds of stocks can take less than three minutes and cost just a few dollars. To apply on-line updating to Quicken, you'll need to have your account number and password, your local telephone access numbers, appropriate communications software, and a list of the securities you want to price.

PRELIMINARIES

Complete Levels 1 and 2

To use Quicken as an investment portfolio tracking program, you need to know very little beyond the basics of Quicken's three R's: registers, reports, and reconciliation. You do not need to know how to write electronic or paper checks to use Quicken's investment account features.

List All Priced Assets for Tracking

Take the time to list on a sheet of paper all the securities you want to track, breaking them into appropriate account groupings. Check to see that you have acquisition histories, current prices, and split information for each security.

This is a good time, too, for you to gather the stock ticker symbols for each of the securities you're following. If they don't appear on your brokerage statements or trade confirmations, you can get them from your broker, a stock guide, or from most on-line services which provide security pricing information.

Open an On-Line Stock Quote Account

If you plan to update securities prices in your portfolio electronically, open an account with an on-line service that offers quotes. In this level you'll learn how to update your portfolio using CompuServe's stock quote service, which may be accessed either directly through CompuServe or through ZiffNet. Appendix B explains how to open a ZiffNet account through which you can access the full range of CompuServe's services.

Enter Your Portfolio

Assuming you already have investments, you'll first want to set up appropriate investment accounts and then fill in these accounts with your securities.

Set Up an Investment Account

Some of the steps in setting up an investment account are very similar to those required to create bank and other asset accounts. If you've already set up a brokerage account as part of your earlier work in Level 5, skip directly to the section called "Enter Securities in a Regular Investment Account."

To create a new investment account,

1. From the Register, press Ctrl-A to see the Select Account to Use screen. Or, from the Main Menu, choose Select Account.

2. Press Home to highlight <New Account> and press Enter. The Set Up New Account window shown in Figure 8.1 appears.

Figure 8.1   **Set Up New Account window**

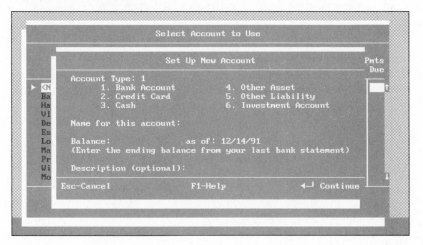

3. Type **6** to specify Investment account as the account type, and press Enter.

4. To name the account, type a descriptive name such as "Maria's Savings," and press Enter. If you're creating a mutual fund investment account, enter the name of the mutual fund.

5. If you are setting up the account for a single mutual fund, answer **Y** to the next question; otherwise, type **N**. Your screen should resemble Figure 8.2. The Plan Ahead section of this level contains information that will help you decide how to answer this question. Pressing F1 to see Quicken Help will provide additional information to help you decide whether this account should be a regular investment account or a mutual fund account.

Figure 8.2   **Set Up New Account window for investment accounts**

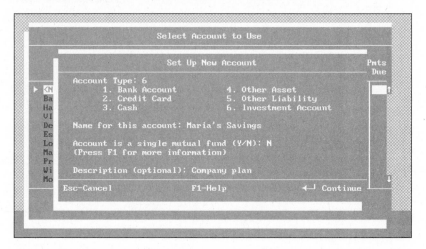

Note. Any description you enter for the account will appear in your net worth reports. If you don't enter a description, the reports will show the account name.

6. Enter an optional description for the account, and press Enter to exit the window. Quicken places the new account name in the list. Press the PgDn key, if necessary, to view it.

If you're creating a regular investment account, Quicken will return you to the Select Account to Use window, where your new investment account appears in the list. Now you may either set up another investment account or skip to the "Enter Securities in a Regular Investment Account" section of this level. If you're initializing a mutual fund account, read the next section to finish activating this type of account.

Specify Information for a Mutual Fund Account

Quicken will display the Set Up Mutual Fund Security window (see Figure 8.3) when you've completed the setup process for a new mutual fund account. The name you've chosen for your mutual fund is already entered (though you may change it later).

Figure 8.3   **Set Up Mutual Fund Security window**

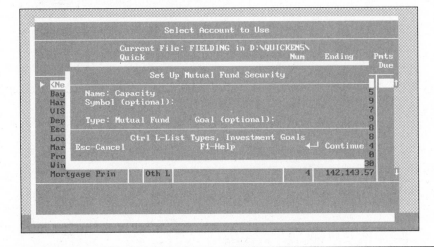

Note. Accurate entry of the ticker symbol is crucial to automatically updating your prices from an on-line service. Either upper- or lowercase characters may be used.

To complete the window,

1. Enter the ticker symbol, if you know it, for the mutual fund in this account. If it's not available on your statement or trade confirmation report, ask your mutual fund company to supply it, or consult an on-line information service.

2. In the Type field, Mutual Fund should appear if you specified this type in the Set Up New Account window. If you didn't, press Ctrl-L (for List) to see a list of types, and select Mutual Fund. (You can change the type later as you classify your investments into more sophisticated categories.)

3. In the Goal field, you may enter a classification by which you want this investment grouped: by risk (Speculative, Growth, Low-Risk, and so on) or by investment goal (College-Suzanne, Retirement Savings, and so forth). Later, you can use these goal classifications to compare performance and group securities for reports. Ctrl-L calls a list of options that are already entered into Quicken. You may also enter a new goal if you wish by selecting <Set Up New Goal> from the list and filling in the requested information.

Press Ctrl-Enter when you've finished entering information about the mutual fund. If this is the first investment account you've set up, Quicken will suggest that you review Chapter 18 in the *User Manual* before you begin to work with investments; press Enter to move past the message. Then choose the mutual fund account you've just created from the account list that's displayed. Use the cursor keys to highlight the account name and press Enter.

Since this is the first time you've used the mutual fund investment
account, Quicken will display the Create Opening Share Balance window
shown in Figure 8.4. This window offers valuable guidance regarding what
date and price information to use, depending on whether you'll be using
Quicken for tax purposes or to evaluate the performance of this investment
since you purchased it (see "What's Your Objective?" in the Plan Ahead section of this level).

Figure 8.4   **Create Opening Share Balance window**

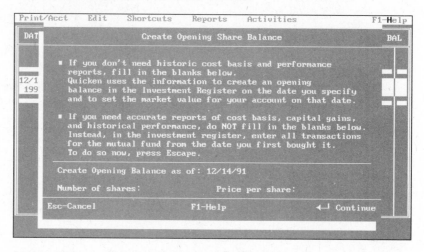

If you'll be entering historical information on your mutual fund purchases, necessary for accurate tax and performance assessment, press Escape
and skip to the next section, "Enter Securities in a Regular Investment
Account." Otherwise, fill in the blanks for an opening balance date, number
of shares you now own, and the share price as of the opening balance date.

When you press Enter to complete the window, Quicken will display the
register for your new mutual fund account, showing an opening balance
transaction and the current share balance for your account (see Figure 8.5).

Enter Securities in a Regular Investment Account

If you have not already selected your investment account as the current
account, do so now by pressing Ctrl-A (for Account), highlighting it in the
account list and pressing Enter. If this is the first time you've used a regular
investment account, you'll encounter the First Time Setup window, which
merely provides instructions on how to get started. Press Enter to remove
the message.

Examine, for a moment, the investment account register (Figure 8.6) that now appears. In many ways, it resembles the bank account register you've used in earlier levels of this guide. The resemblance, however, is more apparent than real.

Figure 8.5   Opening balance transaction for mutual fund investment account

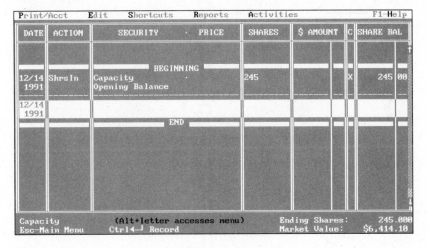

Figure 8.6   Regular investment account register

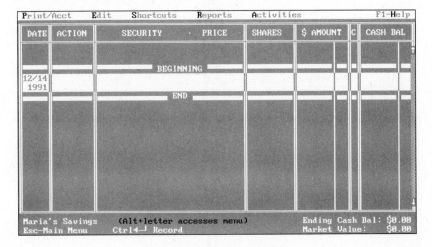

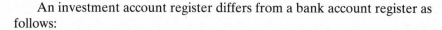

An investment account register differs from a bank account register as follows:

Note. A more limited number of actions may be applied to mutual fund investment accounts than to other investment accounts. These actions are listed and described in Table 8.2, in the "Mutual Funds" section under "Handle Special Situations," later in this level.

- While the first column, DATE, is the same, the second column is labeled ACTION rather than NUM. In this column, you will designate one of 25 types of investment transactions which you can record—various kinds of purchases, sales, transfers, capital gains distributions, dividends, reinvestments, and stock splits. Table 8.1 contains a complete list of the kinds of actions you may designate.

- The SECURITY * PRICE column actually contains room for three pieces of information: the name of the security to which the action is applied, the price per share (or other investment unit), and a memorandum.

- The SHARES column shows the number of shares affected by the action. For some actions (such as cash dividends), this column is blank.

- The $ AMOUNT column contains both the dollar amount of the transaction and, in some instances, ancillary information such as the commission or fee paid.

- The C column, as in the check register, identifies transactions that have been cleared during a reconciliation process.

Note. In a mutual fund investment account, the rightmost column will show a share balance rather than a cash balance.

- The CASH BAL column is used to track any cash or margin loan amounts that may be associated with your investment account. If you always transfer cash into or out of other accounts when you buy or sell securities or receive dividends, you will probably not be carrying a cash balance in your account. This would be the case, for example, if you were tracking the investment portion of an all-in-one money market brokerage account. However, most brokerage accounts contain a cash balance awaiting reinvestment, which typically results from collecting dividends and interest payments on the securities you have got on deposit in the brokerage account.

- At the lower-right corner, you'll see the ending cash balance and a summary of the current market value of the investment account. Remember, however, that the market value is only as good as the most recent pricing data you've entered for each security.

Table 8.1 **Investment Actions for Regular Investment Accounts**

	To record this transaction	Press Ctrl-L and select	Then select
Shares	Purchase shares with cash in account	Buy shares	Buy
	Purchase shares with cash transferred from another account	Buy shares	BuyX
	Sell shares and deposit cash in account	Sell shares	Sell
	Sell shares and deposit cash in another account	Sell shares	SellX
	Add shares to account	Add/Remove shares	ShrsIn
	Remove shares from account	Add/Remove shares	ShrsOut
	Record a stock split	Other transactions	StkSplit
Investment Income: Capital Gains Distributions	Receive cash from long-term capital gains distributions into account	Capital gains distr	CGLong
	Receive cash from long-term capital gains distributions and transfer it into another account	Capital gains distr	CGLongX
	Receive cash from short-term capital gains distribution into account	Capital gains distr	CGShort
	Receive cash from short-term capital gains distributions and transfer it to another account	Capital gains distr	CGShortX
Investment Income: Dividends	Receive cash from dividends into account	Dividend	Div
	Receive cash from dividends and transfer it into another account	Dividend	DivX
Investment Income: Interest	Receive cash from interest income into account	Interest	IntInc
Reinvesting Income	Reinvest income from dividends, interest, or income distributions in additional shares	Reinvest	ReinvDiv
	Reinvest income from long-term capital gains distributions in additional shares	Reinvest	ReinvLg
	Reinvest income from short-term capital gains distributions in additional shares	Reinvest	ReinvSh

Table 8.1   Investment Actions for Regular Investment Accounts (continued)

	To record this transaction	Press Ctrl-L and select	Then select
Miscellaneous	Pay interest on margin loans with cash in account	Interest	MargInt
	Pay for a miscellaneous expense with cash in account	Other transactions	MiscExp
	Receive cash from a return of capital	Other transactions	RtrnCap
	Set up a reminder of a pending transaction in the account	Other transactions	Reminder
	Transfer cash from another account into account	Transfer cash	XIn
	Transfer cash from account into another account	Transfer cash	XOut

Note. You navigate in an investment register with the same techniques you use to get around in a bank account register. This includes the quick find (Ctrl-F) and go to date (Ctrl-G) techniques described in Level 2.

The most important task you'll tackle in setting up your investment accounts is entering each security along with the appropriate information on when it was purchased and for what price. Remember, if you're using Quicken for tax purposes, you may want to enter each tax lot of a security separately. You'll learn how to do that later in this level, under "Multiple Purchase Lots."

Even if you have chosen to start using Quicken at mid-year, you will probably find it useful and relatively painless to record all your investment transactions—right back to the beginning of the year. If you choose to do so, you should first record the state of your portfolio as of December 31 of the prior year. Otherwise, record your portfolio composition as of the ending date of your most recent brokerage statement.

For each security investment you want to enter in the investment account, follow these steps:

1. In the DATE column, enter the date the investment was acquired (or, if historic information is not important, accept today's date). For example, if Maria Lombardi wanted to set up an account to track her company savings plan, she would enter the date that she enrolled in the plan: August 1989.

2. Type **ShrsIn** to tell Quicken that you want to record a stock transfer (including cost information) without changing the cash balance. You can type the first few letters of the action word and press Enter; Quicken will automatically complete the word for you. (You may also press Ctrl-L (for List), select Add/Remove Shares, and then select ShrsIn—Add Shares to Account—to perform this step.)

Note. You may own the same security—for example, stock in the same computer company—in several investment portfolios. After you first identify the security to Quicken, be sure to use the same security name in all other accounts, so Quicken can update the market value of the security in all accounts simultaneously.

3. Type the security's name in the SECURITY column. In Maria's case, this would be Carson 1st Equity (a mutual fund). If this is the first time you've identified this security to Quicken, the program will display the following message:

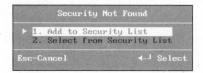

Select Add to Security List to add this security to Quicken's list. Next you'll see the Set Up Security window shown in Figure 8.7.

Figure 8.7   Set Up Security window

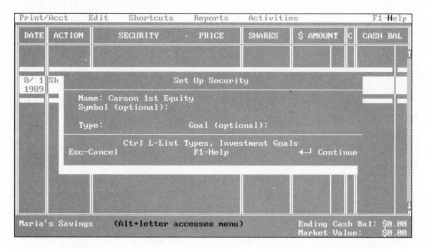

Note. If the type of investment you have is not listed in the Type list, select <Enter New Type> and specify the form of investment you have, such as coins or antiques. You can also indicate whether Quicken should display prices in decimal or fractional form.

4. In the Set Up Security window, Quicken displays the security name you entered. Edit the name if necessary, and then enter the ticker symbol. In the Type field, press Ctrl-L and select a type, such as Mutual Fund, from the list. Also enter a goal (such as College Fund or Growth) in the Goal field. (Alternatively, you can press Ctrl-L and select a goal from the list that appears.) When you have finished, press Enter to return to the investment register.

5. Type the price per share (or other investment unit) in the PRICE column. You may enter the price in either decimal or fractional form. In

Note. The stock exchanges have been discussing for some time reporting stock prices as "35.25" rather than "35¹/₄," and allowing the full range of decimal price values. Fortunately, Quicken can accommodate either format.

Note. While commissions on investments are not tax deductible in the year you make the investment, they are added to the cost basis on which you'll calculate your capital gain. With ShrsIn transactions, you include the commission in the amount you paid; with Buy and Sell transactions, Quicken can calculate the commission automatically.

Maria's example, Carson 1st Equity sold for $21.74 per share when she enrolled in the plan. If price per share is not relevant (such as for a real estate investment), type **1** in the PRICE column. (That way, you can use the SHARES entry as a proxy for your price; when multiplied by 1, the value will display correctly on your reports.) Since Quicken uses this information to maintain a historic price record on each security in the database, you should use the actual market price per share rather than the net price after commission. You'll enter the commission in a moment.

6. In the SHARES column, type the number of shares you own as of the date you entered. For example, Maria purchased 100 shares of Carson 1st Equity when she enrolled.

7. Under $ AMOUNT, you'll already see an amount calculated using your shares and price entries. Because of commissions, however, this is rarely the amount you actually paid. With a ShrsIn transaction, you should press Ctrl-Backspace to erase the calculated amount, and then enter the actual amount you paid, including commission. For example, if the commission to purchase $2,174 worth of shares of Carson 1st Equity was $130, Maria would enter $2,304.

8. Enter any short memorandum you wish—such as "MutuaLetter recommendation"—into the Memo field.

9. Press Ctrl-Enter when you're ready to record the transaction.

10. Repeat these steps for every security you want Quicken to track in this account, as well as for any shares you've purchased or sold since the ShrsIn transaction. If a stock has split or the company has declared a stock dividend, you'll need to enter a stock split or dividend transaction to ensure that Quicken has correct information on the tax basis per share. Refer to the section entitled "Stock Splits and Stock Dividends" later in this level for information on how to handle this kind of transaction.

11. When you've recorded all the securities you want to track, record any cash balance in this account—either as of last December 31st (if you're recording detail for the whole year) or as of the date of your last brokerage statement. Do this by selecting Adjust Balance from the Activities menu and indicating that you want to adjust the cash balance for the account. Then enter the appropriate amount and date in the Adjust Cash Balance window shown in Figure 8.8, and press Ctrl-Enter to record the entry.

By the time you're done with this account, Quicken will have all the historical information it needs to provide you with up-to-the-hour reports on portfolio value, potential capital gains and losses, and investment performance. All you have to do is add current pricing information.

Figure 8.8   Adjust Cash Balance window

```
 Print/Acct      Edit     Shortcuts     Reports     Activities            F1-Help

  DATE  ACTION        SECURITY    ·   PRICE    SHARES    $ AMOUNT  C  CASH BAL

  5/ 2 ShrsIn  Carson 1st Equity ·21.760     50          1,153 28         0 00↑
  1991

  8/ 1 ShrsIn              Adjust Cash Balance                 7          0 00
  1991

  8/ 2 ShrsIn     Cash balance for this account:              8          0 00
  1991

 11/ 1 ShrsIn     Adjust balance as of: 12/14/91              9          0 00
  1991

 11/ 2 ShrsIn   Esc-Cancel        F1-Help        ◄┘ Continue 7          0 00
  1991

 11/ 1
  1991
                                   END

 Maria's Savings    (Alt+letter accesses menu)    Ending Cash Bal: $      0.00
                                                  Market Value:    $20,108.50
```

Bring Your Market Values Up to Date

You can update the security prices in Quicken as often as you like, depending on how active an investor you are. Quicken maintains a complete history of every security you own, starting with prices on each day you bought shares. Every time you update a price, Quicken adds that price to its historic record. You'll find this record very useful in tracking the performance of your investment portfolio over time.

Note. While Quicken will accept price updates more than once a day, its historical price file will only save the latest price entered for any given day.

The downside, of course, is that each of these historical prices takes up space in your Quicken data file. Fortunately, Quicken is very efficient at storing historical prices; each price occupies only two bytes of space, but even at this small rate, a 100-stock portfolio updated daily for 250 days per year adds 50k of pricing data to your data files each year.

Note. The 15-minute delay is imposed by the stock exchanges to distinguish high-priced professional quote wires from lower-priced nonprofessional services.

Every time you prepare to make investment decisions supported by Quicken, you should first determine that you're working with the most current pricing data. The least expensive, most time consuming, and potentially least timely way to do this is using a newspaper. Your brokerage firm may offer a telephone quote line which gives you prices that are only 15 minutes old (your broker can give you up-to-the-minute quotes, but you may not wish to call him or her every time you sit down with Quicken). On-line services also offer 15-minute-old data, and in some cases you may save lots of time by automating the process of entering portfolio information into Quicken.

Enter Current Prices

To enter current prices into Quicken manually—for example, from newspaper listings or from a telephone quote line,

1. Open the register of the investment account whose securities you want to price (check the account label near the lower-left corner of the screen; if the appropriate account name is not showing, press Ctrl-A and choose the correct account from the list).

2. Press Ctrl-U (for Update), or select Update Prices from the Activities menu. The Update Prices and Market Value screen will appear, showing only the securities in the current account, as in Figure 8.9.

Figure 8.9   **Update Prices and Market Value screen for one account**

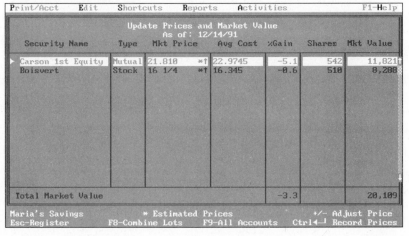

3. If you want to update the prices in all your investment accounts at once, rather than one account at a time, press F9. The label All accounts will appear near the lower-left corner of the window (see Figure 8.10). Update prices on all accounts at once if you're using a single reference such as a newspaper or on-line service. Use single account updating if you're entering prices from a brokerage statement.

4. Note the date displayed near the top of the window. It displays today's date by default. If you're using today's paper to update yesterday's prices, you'll want to change the "As of" date for these prices to yesterday's date. Press Ctrl-G (for Go to Date) and enter the date corresponding to the pricing data you're entering, then press Enter, and the "As of"

Note. Typing over a price entry does not erase the prior entry. If you type 102 over the preexisting 101$\frac{1}{2}$ without typing spaces over the $\frac{1}{2}$, you'll end up with the incorrect price 102$\frac{1}{2}$. To prevent this, press Ctrl-Backspace to erase the prior entry before you type a new one.

date at the top of the window will change. In the Go to Date window, you can also change the selected date by pressing Ctrl-Left Arrow to go to the previous day, and Ctrl-Right Arrow to go to the following day. When you change dates after updating prices, Quicken will confirm that it should record the prices before moving to the new date.

5. Using the arrow keys, highlight the security whose price you want to adjust. Quicken displays the most recent price it is aware of for this security (which, if you've just started, is the price you paid for the most recent lot purchase). Adjust the price either by typing over the current price or by repeatedly typing the gray + or – key to adjust the price up (+) or down (–) by one-eighth of a point at a time.

6. When you've finished updating all the prices, press Ctrl-Enter to record them.

Figure 8.10   **Update Prices and Market Value screen for all accounts**

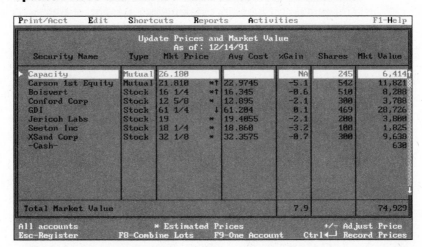

Take a moment to examine the Update Prices and Market Value screen (call it up again with Ctrl-U if you've already returned to the register). The screen contains several significant pieces of information:

■ The name of each security in the account (press F9 to toggle between a view of all securities and a view of the securities in the current account), in alphabetical order by security type

■ The type of security, which you entered when you first identified the security (all securities are grouped by type)

Note. If a price has not changed from an earlier session, the asterisk may remain. Enter an asterisk (*) in the price field to inform Quicken that a price has not changed. The price will reappear and will no longer be marked as an estimate.

- The market price of the security (the most recent price in the security's price history file)

- An asterisk (*) in the Mkt Price column if the price shown does not reflect an updated price for the "As of" date—in other words, the price should be regarded as an estimate for the date shown

- A tick symbol (either an up or down arrow) indicating the direction in which the displayed price has changed from the previous price in the security's history file

- The average cost per share for the security (net of commissions)

- The percent gain (positive) or loss (negative) in the security's value from its average cost per share to the current market price

- The total number of shares you own in either the selected account or in all accounts (depending on how you've set the F9 toggle)

- The market value of those shares (multiplying price per share times the number of shares—not taking into account, of course, the commission you'll pay when you sell)

- A cash line at the end of the securities list which identifies the cash balance from your investment account register as of the selected date

- A summary line near the bottom of the screen, summarizing the market value and percent gain for your entire portfolio

You'll find that the Update Prices and Market Value screen is not merely used to enter price data—it is also the easiest way to get a quick summary of your investment portfolio. At any time while you're working in the investment register, you can view this quick summary by pressing Ctrl-U.

Once you've entered your portfolio and brought its prices up to date, it's wise to check your Quicken securities list (names and share numbers) against your brokerage account statement. As a further test, you may also want to enter the market prices on your latest brokerage statement (make sure you use Ctrl-G to go to the appropriate date); if the market value on your Update Prices and Market Value screen matches the value your brokerage statement reports, you've done your job correctly.

Update Prices from an On-Line Service

For larger portfolios and frequent updates, you'll probably want to avoid tedium and minimize errors by updating your individual security prices automatically from an on-line information service. Because of stock exchange regulations, prices on most on-line information services are delayed by 15 minutes. Still, this serves the needs of most investors. (If you really require and can afford real-time quotes, you probably need more sophisticated tools than those Quicken offers.)

Although the specific steps to updating portfolio prices vary widely among the information services and communications software, the general steps for gathering data on prices are as follows:

1. Use the information service's stock price update capabilities to build a list of stock symbols and prices in one of the following formats:

   IBM,112.5

   "IBM",112.5

   "IBM","112.5"

   The only requirements are that the price and symbol must be on the same line, must be separated by commas, and must not contain any embedded spaces.

2. Using either the capture or file transfer capabilities of your communications program, get the formatted price list into a text file on your PC.

3. To import the prices into Quicken, display the Price screen and select Import Prices from the Print/Acct menu (Alt-P), or press Ctrl-I. Then enter the name of the text file containing the prices and the date of the imported prices in the Import Price Data window (Figure 8.11).

Figure 8.11   Import Price Data window

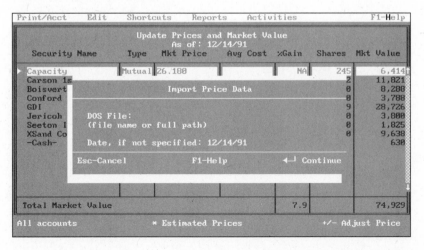

Depending on the communications program you're using, you may write a script to automate the process of logging onto the service, locating the security prices you need, formatting them, and transferring them to a file on your PC. We've provided a Toolkit in this section to help you complete this task on CompuServe or ZiffNet. Appendix B describes how you can use ZiffNet to download a ready-made CompuServe script for use with the Crosstalk communications program.

TOOLKIT A CompuServe Script for Downloading Current Stock Quotes

Maintaining stock quotes from CompuServe is relatively straightforward, but does require some extra steps the first time you download securities prices. These extra steps will help ensure that subsequent price updates are as automated as possible.

First Time Setup

To set up CompuServe for the most automated processing of your quote requests, you should build a text file with your instructions and ticker symbols and send the file electronically to CompuServe.

1. Make sure you have your CompuServe account number and password. If you don't have a CompuServe account, you may follow the procedures in Appendix B to obtain access to CompuServe through ZiffNet, the on-line information service for computer users from the publishers of *PC/Computing*, *PC Magazine*, and *PC Week*. You should also ensure that you're using communications software that supports error-checking file transfers (such as XMODEM or Kermit) and, preferably, a way of "recording" your keystrokes into a script you can use again and again.

2. On your PC, before you log onto CompuServe, create a text file named TICKERS, which will contain a list of the ticker symbols for the stocks you'll want to price, preceded by three lines of text which will instruct CompuServe to format and package the output in a way Quicken can understand. Your file should look something like this:

```
/ITEMS=1,5
/OPTIONS=6
/OUTPUT=STOX.TXT
IBM
MSFT
CPQ
```

and so on.

The first line (/ITEMS=1,5) instructs CompuServe to print only the ticker symbol and the most recent (or closing) price. The next line (/OPTIONS=6) instructs CompuServe to separate the ticker symbol and the price with a comma. The third line (/OUTPUT=STOX.TXT) instructs CompuServe to place the output in a file called STOX.TXT, rather than showing it on the screen. The remaining lines (IBM, MSFT, and CPQ) are ticker symbols for your stocks or mutual funds.

3. Log onto CompuServe or ZiffNet (all of CompuServe's services are available to ZiffNet customers through an electronic gateway). At any ! prompt, type **GO CIS:MQUOTE** to move to CompuServe's financial data area. Once you're there, follow this procedure:

CompuServe prompts:	You type:
MQuoteII!	**FILTRN**
Transfer Protocol (choices)!	(Type the number corresponding to the file transfer method supported by your communications program.)
Direction!	**2** (for Upload to CompuServe)
File Type!	**1** (for ASCII, or text file)
Enter the CompuServe File Name:	**TICKERS**
Please initiate your program to Send	(You should now follow your communications program's procedures for sending a file using the protocol you've chosen. Be sure you specify the correct location and filename for the TICKER file you created in Step 2. Press Enter when done. After the transfer is complete, some protocols require that you press Enter to complete the process.)
File transfer completed!	
MQuoteII!	(You're now ready to proceed to the next step.)

Download the Prices

The First Time Setup procedure created a file on CompuServe that contains the tickers and format information the service needs to process your request. Each time you need fresh pricing data for Quicken, use the following procedure to create a data file named STOX.TXT on your PC, ready for import into Quicken:

1. If you aren't already logged onto CompuServe or ZiffNet, do so now, and type **GO CIS:MQUOTE** at any ! prompt.

2. Follow this script:

CompuServe prompts:	You type:
MQuoteII!	**QQUOTE**
Issue:	**@TICKERS** (This is where you instruct CompuServe to use your ticker file.)

CompuServe prompts:	You type:
STOX.TXT already exists. (A)ppend, (S)upersede, or (R)e-enter file name?	**S** (This message will appear after you've used your TICKER file at least once. Type **S** to supersede your old STOX.TXT file. Your quotes will now reside in a file on CompuServe.)
Issue:	Enter (Pressing Enter will take you to the next menu.)
MQuoteII!	**FILTRN** (This will take you to the file transfer utility, to get your prices back to your PC.)
Protocol!	(Type the number appropriate to your communications software.)
Direction!	**1** (for Download from CompuServe)
File Type!	**1** (for ASCII, or text file)
Enter the CompuServe file name:	**STOX.TXT**
Please initiate your program to Receive.	(You should now initiate your communications program's procedure for receiving a file. Keep track of the directory and name you use for the file you create on your PC; you'll need this information for telling Quicken's Import Prices function where to find the prices file.)
File Transfer Completed!	
MQuoteII!	**OFF** (to log off, or you may issue any other CompuServe command)

Your prices file now resides on your PC in a form Quicken's Import Prices function can use. Once you've created the ticker file, this procedure should take no longer than two or three minutes. For even faster and easier operation, you should use your communication program's capability to "learn" your keystrokes in order to create a script.

One such script—for the popular Crosstalk communications program—is available through ZiffNet's software library. See Appendix B for instructions on how to download it for your use.

As your list of stock holdings changes, you'll want to modify your ticker file. The easiest way to do this is to maintain it on your own PC, editing it as necessary and using the upload procedures described in the First Time Setup section to transfer that file to CompuServe.

Note. Remember, every historic stock price entry you make takes up several bytes of memory. Storing large numbers of historic prices may limit the memory and disk space you can allocate to other purposes.

Record Price Histories

As you evaluate the performance of your stocks over time, you'll want to add more pricing data to the historic price file for each security. You can track this information daily, weekly, monthly, or quarterly—really at any interval you like.

Because entering historical prices can be so tiresome, it's a good idea to use an on-line information service to enter price histories. The steps for generating and importing these histories are the same as those described earlier in "Update Prices from an On-Line Service," with one exception: you should include the date as a third piece of information in each line of the price list. The acceptable formats are

IBM,112.5,11/30/91

"IBM",112.5,"11/30/91"

"IBM","112.5""11/30/91"

Here again, we've included a Toolkit script to help you update price histories from CompuServe or ZiffNet.

**TOOLKIT   A Script for Downloading Historic Prices
from CompuServe**

Once you've set up a ticker file for current stock prices (see the toolkit earlier in this level), it's relatively easy to obtain prices for your securities list for any day in the last ten years. To do so, follow this procedure:

1. Log onto CompuServe or ZiffNet, and type **GO CIS:MQUOTE** at any ! prompt.

2. Follow this script:

CompuServe prompts:	You type:
MQuoteII!	**DATA** (This invokes the historic data retrieval program.)
Data Types (choices)!	**1** (for Prices)
Output to TTY or filename:	**HSTOX.TXT** (the filename you'll use)
Issue:	**@TICKERS** (You'll see three error messages corresponding to the three special control lines in your ticker file. Ignore these messages.)
Issue: (D)aily, (W)eekly, (M)onthly?:	**D** (You'll only want one day's data.)
Starting date:	(Enter the date you'd like to price in MM/DD/Y format.)
Ending date:	(Enter the same date.)
Option:	**COMMAS**
Option:	(Press Enter)
Enter list of desired items!	1,5 (for ticker symbol and closing price)
Data requested is now stored in HSTOX.TXT	
Enter choice!	(Press Enter)
MQuoteII!	FILTRN (This will take you to the file transfer utility, to get your prices back to your PC.)
Protocol!	(Type the number appropriate to your communications software.)
Direction!	**1** (for Download from CompuServe)
File Type!	**1** (for ASCII, or text file)
Enter the CompuServe file name:	**HSTOX.TXT**
Please initiate your program to Receive.	(You should now initiate your communications program's procedure for receiving a file. Keep track of the directory and name you use for the file you create on your PC; you'll need this information for telling Quicken's Import Prices function where to find the prices file.)

CompuServe prompts:	**You type:**
File Transfer Completed!	
MQuoteII!	**OFF** (to log off, or you may issue any other CompuServe command)

Now, the file HSTOX.TXT is on your PC, ready to be imported to Quicken. Make sure, when you import these prices, that you specify the correct historic date for them.

Record Financial Transactions

Quicken's investment accounts are designed to accommodate a variety of transactions—25 in all for regular investment accounts. Mutual fund investment accounts have a more limited range of 12 transactions available. Most of these are variants of three general classifications: purchase and sale of securities; dividend and interest collections; and cash or stock transfers.

Buy and Sell Shares

There are two ways to buy a security: with cash from your brokerage account (Buy) or with a transfer from one of your bank accounts elsewhere in your Quicken files (BuyX). Likewise, there are two ways to sell a security: by retaining the proceeds in your brokerage account (Sell) or by transferring the money to another money account (SellX).

To record a buy or sell transaction,

Note. Two dates are associated with each stock trade: the trade date on which the agreement to buy or sell is struck and the settlement date, often five business days later, when money changes hands. Always record the trade date to ensure that your transaction will be reported in the correct tax year.

1. In the DATE column, enter the trade date.

2. Press Ctrl-L (for List) to see a list of actions. To buy a security, select Buy Shares, and then either Buy (for a purchase using the cash balance in the account) or BuyX (for a transfer of funds from another account). To sell a security, select Sell Shares, and then either Sell (when the resulting cash stays in the investment account) or SellX (when the proceeds are transferred to another Quicken account).

3. Enter the name of the security. If you type just enough characters to uniquely identify it and press Enter, Quicken will complete the name for you. Or, you can press Ctrl-Y to call up the security list and then select the name you want.

4. Enter the price at which you are buying or selling the security. You can enter it in fractional or decimal form.

5. Enter the number of shares of the security involved in the transaction.

6. In the $ AMOUNT column, enter the dollar amount involved in the transaction. If you include the commission in the number, Quicken will calculate the difference between the market value (shares multiplied by price) and the amount you entered and will display the difference in the Comm/Fee: field. Alternatively, you can explicitly enter the actual market value and then enter the commission for the transaction.

7. Press Ctrl-Enter to record the transaction. Figure 8.12 shows examples of buy-and-transfer transactions.

Figure 8.12   Buy-and-transfer transactions

DATE	ACTION	SECURITY	· PRICE	SHARES	$ AMOUNT	C	CASH BAL
1/ 1 1991	ShrsIn	Jericoh Labs	·19	200	3,881 08		0 00↑
4/ 2 1991	BuyX	Locke Ent	·17	100	1,758 00		0 00
5/31 1991	Sell	Conford Corp	·16 1/2	100	1,592 80		1,592 80
6/21 1991	Buy	Insight Fund	·13.375	100	1,417 75		175 05
7/15 1991	BuyX	Seeton Inc	·15	100	1,557 40		175 05
8/10 1991	SellX Memo: Account:	XSand Corp [Bay Cities]	·40	100 Comm/Fee: Xfer Amt:	3,917 60 82 40 3,917 60		175 05

Print/Acct   Edit   Shortcuts   Reports   Activities   F1-Help

Brokerage Acct   (Alt+letter accesses menu)   Ending Cash Bal: $ 175.05
Esc-Main Menu   Ctrl↵ Record   Market Value: $21,312.55

BuyX transactions

Record Dividends and Interest

Quicken's investment accounts not only record the receipt of dividend and interest payments; they also associate those payments with the security that generated them, making it easy to assess total return information (capital appreciation plus income) for any security you own.

Recording a dividend or interest income is very straightforward, with the action you specify depending on whether you retain the money in your account (Div and IntInc), reinvest it (ReinvDiv and ReinvInc), or transfer it to another account (DivX). If you're reinvesting, you'll need to enter the price per share at which you're reinvesting, and any applicable commission. If you don't enter a current price per share, Quicken alerts you that it's using the most recent price it has, which is now only an estimate.

For securities that pay a regular, reliable dividend or interest amount, you can save even more time by memorizing these transactions (as described in Level 2).

In some cases, your account will earn interest not from bonds or commercial notes in your portfolio but rather from the interest your brokerage firm pays on cash awaiting reinvestment. Consequently, Quicken doesn't require you to associate a security with every interest income transaction. To make these interest items easier to track, you might want to make up a new security priced at 1 and called "Cash Awaiting Inv." Then you can associate your general brokerage account interest with that phantom security.

When you invest more cash than you have in your brokerage account, you will trigger a margin loan. (Make sure you've made arrangements with

Note. Quicken does not provide a transfer action associated with interest income. To transfer the interest to a bank account, follow the interest income transaction with a transfer cash out transaction (XOut) in the same amount.

your broker well in advance!) This loan will show up as a negative cash balance in your investment account. Record the interest on this margin loan by using the IntExp (Interest Expense) action.

Transfer Cash or Stock

Whenever you transfer money to and from your brokerage account, you will generate a transaction with a cash in (XIn) or cash out (XOut) action.

When you specify a cash transfer action within an investment account, Quicken asks for the name of the account to or from which you're transferring the money. If the transfer is actually an income or expense transaction in the other account, you should specify one of two actions in the investment register: MiscInc (to record miscellaneous income) or MiscExp (to record miscellaneous expense). When you choose one of these two actions, Quicken asks you to choose an income or expense category for the transaction. For example, if you won $20,000 in the state lottery and decided to deposit the money into your brokerage account, you would record a MiscInc transaction and specify the category Lottery Win. This way, your personal income and cash flow statements would reflect the income properly.

You can generate these transactions automatically from within your bank account register when you write and categorize a check with the name of the investment account to which you're transferring the money. An XIn transaction will automatically appear in your investment account. Figure 8.13 shows both halves of a transfer—one transaction in your bank account register and a corresponding transaction in your investment account register.

When you first set up a Quicken investment account, you seed the account with securities using the ShrsIn action. This action (and its counterpart, ShrsOut) may be used to move securities from account to account. For example, you might close out a brokerage account that tracks a single stock and transfer that security to another account that tracks several securities. When you use ShrsIn and ShrsOut to move a security from one account to another, take special care that the date, shares, and price are identical in both the originating and the receiving account. This is one of the rare places in which Quicken does not provide automatically generated balancing transfer transactions.

You can use ShrsIn to record the receipt of shares by gift, bequest, or grant. Consult your tax advisor on the appropriate tax basis to use for the shares you've received. Using ShrsIn for this purpose means, however, that your income statement will not reflect the gift, bequest, or grant as income—the shares will merely materialize from thin air as an increase in your net worth. To reflect this income properly, you should record a miscellaneous income (MiscInc) transaction in the amount of the tax basis for the security, and then "buy" the security with a Buy transaction. This will have no net impact on your cash balance. Enter the correct tax basis into your investment records, and record the income properly.

Figure 8.13   Register entries for an investment account cash transfer

| Print/Acct | Edit | Shortcuts | Reports | Activities | | F1-Help |

DATE	NUM	PAYEE · MEMO · CATEGORY	PAYMENT	C	DEPOSIT	BALANCE
12/26 1991	1358	Bright Eyes Day Care Center Childcare:Brig→	111 00			1,690 16↑
12/26 1991	1359	Wanda Milasz Childcare:Wand→	100 00			1,590 16
12/28 1991	DEP	State Lottery Commission My lucky day! Lottery Win			20,000 00	21,590 16
12/28 1991	E-PMT Memo: Cat:	Bay Cities Fund Grp [Brokerage Acct]	20,000 00			1,590 16
12/28 1991	1360 SPLIT	Gulf Card Auto:Fuel	95 40			1,494 76
12/28 1991	1361 SPLIT	Sears Home Repair	72 40			1,422 36

Harbor Bk Joint   (Alt+letter accesses menu)   Current Balance: $ 510.78
Esc-Main Menu   Ctrl↵ Record   Ending Balance: $3,248.39

Funds transferred

| Print/Acct | Edit | Shortcuts | Reports | Activities | | F1-Help |

DATE	ACTION	SECURITY · PRICE	SHARES	$ AMOUNT	C	CASH BAL
5/31 1991	Sell	Conford Corp ·16 1/2	100	1,592 80		1,592 80↑
6/21 1991	Buy	Insight Fund ·13.375	100	1,417 75		175 05
7/15 1991	BuyX	Seeton Inc ·15	100	1,557 40		175 05
8/10 1991	SellX	XSand Corp ·40	100	3,917 60		175 05
12/28 1991	XIn Memo: Account:	Bay Cities Fund Gr· [Harbor Bk Joint]		20,000 00		20,175 05
12/31 1991						
		END				

Brokerage Acct   (Alt+letter accesses menu)   Ending Cash Bal: $20,175.05
Esc-Main Menu   Ctrl↵ Record   Market Value: $41,312.55

Handle Special Situations

Quicken is optimized for the most common kinds of investment transactions: buying and selling stock and collecting dividends and interest. Quicken's designers worked hard to make these and other investment actions as similar as possible to the bank account transactions with which you should now be familiar.

Not every investment transaction corresponds naturally to a check-and-register metaphor, however. You have to be creative about the ways you devise to record less common types of transactions—particularly listed options.

Mutual Funds

As discussed in this level's Plan Ahead section, Quicken is designed to accommodate mutual funds. You can manage these funds either as a group (in a regular investment account) or singly (in one or more mutual fund investment accounts).

If you choose to use a mutual fund investment account, there are 12 possible investment actions you can take (some regular investment account actions that pertain to cash in the account are irrelevant in a mutual fund account). Table 8.2 lists the actions you can initiate in a mutual fund investment account.

Keep these important considerations in mind when you work with mutual fund transactions:

Note. By identifying loads and sales charges as commissions, even if they're built into the purchase price, you will maintain consistency in the historic price file Quicken maintains for the security. Always enter the NAV as the price for your mutual fund.

- When you buy (or sell) mutual fund shares in a mutual fund account, be prepared to specify an account which the money will come from or go into. There is no cash balance in these accounts, so all purchases and sales are BuyX or SellX transactions.

- When you buy mutual fund shares, you will sometimes need to pay a "front-end load"—a commission that is built into the purchase price. Make sure you understand the difference between the Offer price (net of load) and the Net Asset Value price (NAV) (its real market value). To record the purchase of 1,000 shares of a 3 percent load mutual fund whose NAV is $10.00 and whose offer price is $10.30, enter the purchase of 1,000 shares at 10.00 and a dollar amount of $10,300. The load will automatically be listed as commission, as in Figure 8.14.

- Less commonly, there can be a "back-end load" added to the fund, so that the selling price is less than the NAV. Again, it's best to enter the NAV as the price of the shares, and the load as a commission.

Note. Long-term capital gains come from stocks that have been held in a portfolio for more than one year. At present, federal tax rates don't distinguish between long-term and short-term gains, but some states have different rates. In any case, federal tax forms require you to report both.

- Occasionally, you'll receive distributions from your mutual fund. In fact, funds are required to periodically turn over to their shareholders both the dividends they collect on their holdings and the capital gains they realize when they sell stocks in their portfolio. (A distribution will specify whether it covers dividends, long-term capital gains, or short-term capital gains.) You can usually specify whether you want to receive the proceeds in cash or use the money to buy more shares in the fund. Quicken offers nine actions to handle these distributions, depending on both the nature of the distribution and what you want to do with the money. Table 8.3 summarizes the actions you can specify for mutual fund distributions.

- If you choose to reinvest a distribution, you may be charged a front-end load on the new shares you purchase. In this case, identify the commission on the shares you obtain through reinvestment in exactly the same way you did when buying the original shares.

Table 8.2   **Investment Actions for Mutual Fund Investment Accounts**

	To record the following transaction	Press Ctrl-L and select	Then select
Shares	Purchase shares with cash transferred from another account	Buy shares	BuyX
	Sell shares and deposit cash in another account	Sell shares	SellX
	Add shares to account	Add/Remove shares	ShrsIn
	Remove shares from account	Add/Remove shares	ShrsOut
	Record a stock split	Other transactions	StkSplit
Investment Income: Capital Gains Distribution	Receive cash from long-term capital gains distributions and transfer it to another account	Capital gains distr	CGLongX
	Receive cash from short-term capital gains distributions and transfer it to another account	Capital gains distr	CGShortX
Investment Income: Dividends	Receive cash from dividends and transfer it to another account	Dividend	DivX
Reinvesting Income	Reinvest income from dividends, interest, or income distributions in additional shares	Reinvest	ReinvDiv
	Reinvest income from long-term capital gains distributions in additional shares	Reinvest	ReinvLg
	Reinvest income from short-term capital gains distributions in additional shares	Reinvest	ReinvSh
Miscellaneous	Set up a reminder of a pending transaction in the account	Other transactions	Reminder

Figure 8.14   Recording a front-end load in a mutual fund purchase

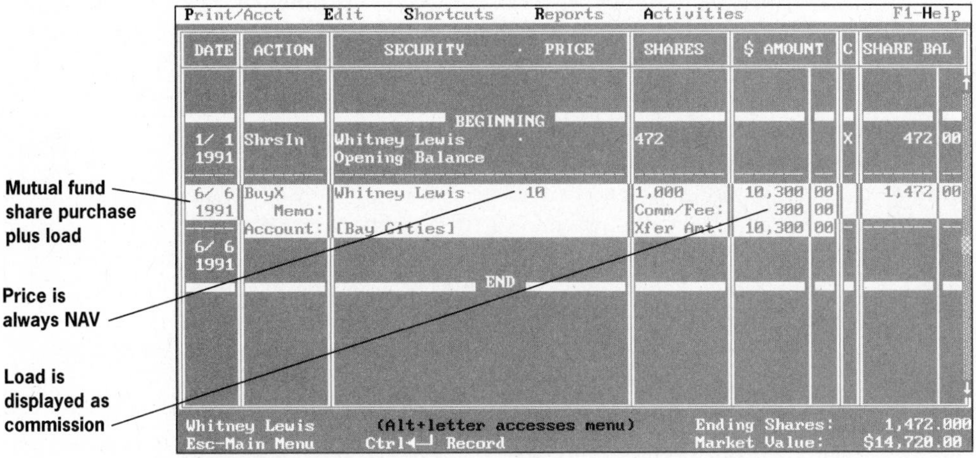

Mutual fund share purchase plus load

Price is always NAV

Load is displayed as commission

Table 8.3   Actions for Mutual Fund Distributions

	Reinvest	Keep Cash in Investment Account *	Transfer Cash to Bank Account
Dividend	ReinvDiv	Div	DivX
Long-Term Capital Gain	ReinvLg	CGLong	CGLongX
Short-Term Capital Gain	ReinvSh	CGShort	CGShortX

*Not available in mutual fund investment account because this type of account cannot maintain a cash balance.

■ While working in your bank account, you can take advantage of a very quick way of recording "buy" transactions in your mutual fund investment account without even leaving your bank account. Just record a check in your bank account, and put the name of the mutual fund in the category field. Quicken enters a BuyX transaction in your mutual fund account, and uses the most recent price to determine the number of shares. Use this technique with caution, however. Quicken is merely estimating the price based on recent history, so neither the price nor the number of shares may be correct—a fact that could wreak havoc at tax time.

Note. From the investor's viewpoint, a stock split is identical to a 100 percent stock dividend. Stock dividends are usually used to make minor (up to 50 percent) adjustments in the number of shares, while stock splits can double, triple, or even quadruple the number of shares outstanding.

Stock Splits and Stock Dividends

When the price of a company's stock gets so high that it's inconvenient for small investors to buy it in 100-share lots, the company may decide to declare a stock split or a stock dividend. After a two for one stock split, a shareholder still holds the same percentage of the company as before, but he or she holds twice as many shares, each of which has half its former value. Each stock split is announced in advance of the effective date; for Quicken's purposes, it's the effective date that's important.

It is vital that you record all stock splits, because Quicken adjusts the number of shares you own and the tax cost basis for each share in response to a split. For example, when you inform Quicken about a two for one split in a company's stock, Quicken doubles the number of shares you own in that company beginning with the effective date of the split and cuts by 50 percent the tax cost basis of each of that company's shares for any transaction recorded after the effective date of the split.

You should record the stock split in each account that includes any shares of that security, remembering to enter the same effective date for the split in each account. You must also change the stock price manually in the Update Prices and Market Value screen on the effective date of the split.

When you learn about a split (from a newspaper listing or your brokerage statement), record it in your investment account register as follows:

1. In the investment register, begin a new transaction by entering the effective date for the split.

2. In the ACTION column, press Ctrl-L and select Other Transactions and then StkSplit.

3. Enter the name of the security (either with Ctrl-Y or by typing a few characters and pressing Enter).

4. Enter the ratio of the split, as shown in Figure 8.15.

5. Press Ctrl-Enter to record the transaction.

6. Quicken displays the ratio for the stock split in the SHARES column. Finally, press Ctrl-U and change the stock price for the security that recently split; press Ctrl-Enter to record the new price.

In the case of a stock dividend, which is usually expressed as a percentage of the shares you own, you should also record it as a split. In entering the split ratio, add 1 to the decimal expression of the dividend percentage—for example, a 25 percent dividend should be expressed as a 1.25 to 1 split.

Sometimes, stock splits or stock dividends will create fractional shares; that is, you'll end up owning an odd .75 of a share. The company will usually buy these shares back as a courtesy. Brokerage firms often take care of this automatically. Clarify how your broker handles this, and enter an appropriate fractional-share Sell transaction.

Figure 8.15 **Stock split action in an investment account**

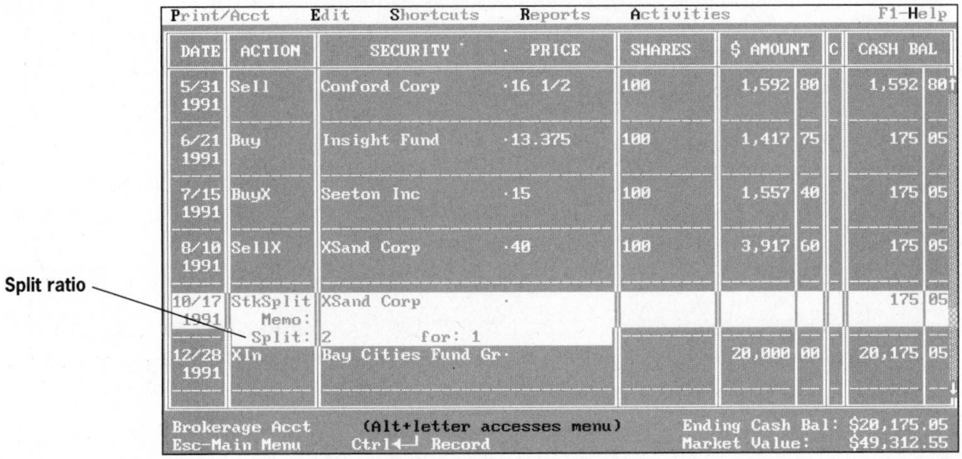

Split ratio

Multiple Purchase Lots

When you've bought a security at several times and several prices, you are said to be holding multiple lots of the security. When it comes time to sell some of the shares, there can be dramatically different tax consequences depending on which lot you actually sell.

For example, Larry Milner bought 100 shares of Seaver Research stock on each of four dates: on January 1 at 25, on April 1 at 28, on July 1 at 32, and on October 1 at 36. In December, with the price at 39, he decides it's time to sell 100 shares. He'll receive $3,900 when he sells (less the commission). His tax liability, though, depends on which lot he sells. If he sells his January stock, he'll be liable for a $1,400 capital gain; if he sells the October stock he's only stuck for a $300 gain—a significant difference!

Unfortunately, Quicken does not help you optimize your taxes. In fact, when you sell only a portion of the shares you own, previous versions of Quicken "sell" the tax lots you've owned the longest. As the previous example demonstrates, this is not always the best choice from a tax perspective. Fortunately, Quicken 5 corrects this deficiency, although its method for doing so can be awkward. If you want to be explicit about which tax lots are allocated to a specific sale, you can assign specific lot numbers to each stock purchase you've made. The following example assumes that you've already purchased one lot of a stock, and then decided to purchase additional lots now and in the future.

Follow these steps to allocate specific tax lots to a sale:

Note. Quicken's price screen sorts the securities in alphabetical and numeric order. If you use the date to code your purchase lots, you'll find that putting the year first and using a two-digit month identifier will keep your lots sorted in the correct date order.

Note. Be sure you combine the separate lots into a single line item on the screen before you enter the price. If you fail to do so, only the master security's price will be updated.

1. When you originally bought the security, you gave it a name, such as Seaver Res. We'll call this original lot of the security the "master" security. (If you plan in advance to purchase multiple lots of a security, first create a new security with the master name; this security will represent the first lot you purchase.) Remember that to create a new security, you press Ctrl-Y while working in an investment account, and choose <New Security> from the Security List.

2. When you purchase an additional lot, create a new security with a different name for that lot. Instead of just Seaver Res, for example, you might enter Seaver Res 91/04 to distinguish this security from the January 1991 lot. Use the same ticker symbol you used with the first lot.

3. Name any subsequent lots you buy using a consistent lot-designation scheme: Seaver Res 91/07, Seaver Res 91/10, and so on. Again, be sure to use the same ticker symbol; this symbol is the only way Quicken will know that the purchase lots actually represent the same stock.

4. When you go to the Update Prices and Market Value screen (Ctrl-U) to update prices, you'll see the lots listed separately, as in Figure 8.16. First combine the lots into a single item in the list by pressing F8. Quicken will show only the first (master) security and its price, and will display the combined total of all shares. Then update the price for the master security. When you press F8 again to see the separate lots, all prices will be updated.

5. When you decide to sell a particular purchase lot, simply specify the correct one by selecting it from the security list (Ctrl-Y). If you sell the original purchase lot before any of the others, Quicken will use the alphabetically first purchase lot in the list as the new master security.

Short Sales

A *short sale* is a bet that the value of a stock will decline over time. The investor sells stock that is lent to him by the brokerage firm. He must eventually cover the short position by buying stock to repay the brokerage firm's loan.

To enter a short sale, merely enter a Sell or SellX transaction and the amount you received in the exchange. Since you don't own the stock in this account, Quicken will flash a warning asking you to confirm that you're entering a short sale. Type **Y** in response to the warning. Short sales show up on the Update Prices and Market Value screen as negative share numbers with negative market values, signifying the amount you'll have to pay (at current market values) to settle your debt to the brokerage firm. In Figure 8.17, 300 shares of Conford Corp. are shown as short sales that have not yet been covered.

Figure 8.16   Separate lots in the Update Prices and Market Value display

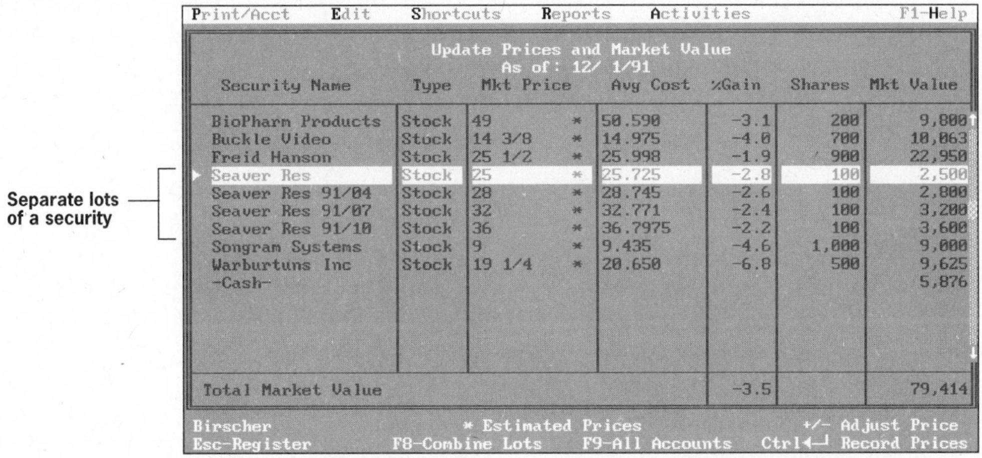

```
 Print/Acct    Edit    Shortcuts    Reports    Activities            F1-Help
┌────────────────────────────────────────────────────────────────────────┐
│                    Update Prices and Market Value                        │
│                         As of : 12/ 1/91                                 │
│         Security Name      Type   Mkt Price     Avg Cost  %Gain   Shares   Mkt Value │
│                                                                          │
│         BioPharm Products  Stock  49         *  50.590     -3.1     200     9,800 │
│         Buckle Video       Stock  14 3/8     *  14.975     -4.0     700    10,063 │
│         Freid Hanson       Stock  25 1/2     *  25.998     -1.9     900    22,950 │
│       ▶ Seaver Res         Stock  25         *  25.725     -2.8     100     2,500 │
│         Seaver Res 91/04   Stock  28         *  28.745     -2.6     100     2,800 │
│         Seaver Res 91/07   Stock  32         *  32.771     -2.4     100     3,200 │
│         Seaver Res 91/10   Stock  36         *  36.7975    -2.2     100     3,600 │
│         Songram Systems    Stock  9          *  9.435      -4.6   1,000     9,000 │
│         Warburtuns Inc     Stock  19 1/4     *  20.650     -6.8     500     9,625 │
│         -Cash-                                                            5,876 │
│                                                                          │
│                                                                          │
│         Total Market Value                                -3.5           79,414 │
│                                                                          │
│  Birscher                 * Estimated Prices             +/- Adjust Price │
│  Esc-Register      F8-Combine Lots     F9-All Accounts   Ctrl◄┘ Record Prices │
└────────────────────────────────────────────────────────────────────────┘
```

Separate lots of a security

Figure 8.17   Display of short sales in the Update Prices and Market Value screen

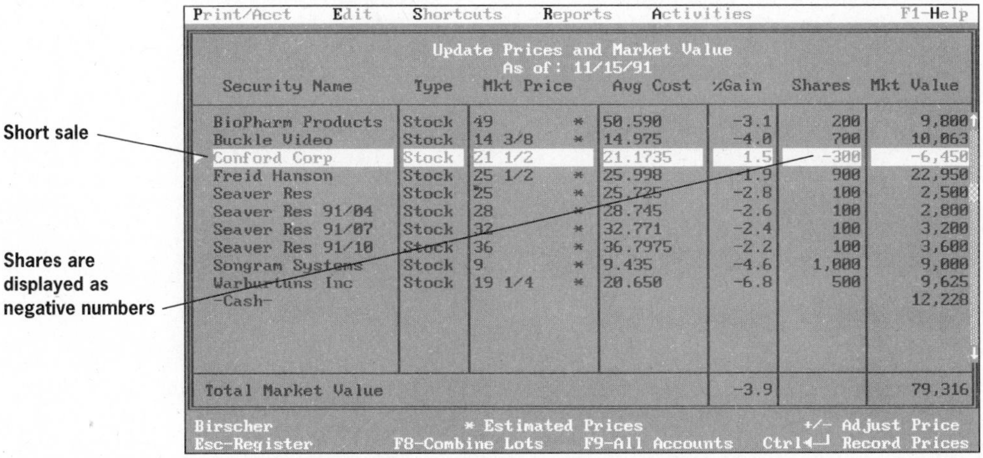

```
 Print/Acct    Edit    Shortcuts    Reports    Activities            F1-Help
┌────────────────────────────────────────────────────────────────────────┐
│                    Update Prices and Market Value                        │
│                         As of : 11/15/91                                 │
│         Security Name      Type   Mkt Price     Avg Cost  %Gain   Shares   Mkt Value │
│                                                                          │
│         BioPharm Products  Stock  49         *  50.590     -3.1     200     9,800 │
│         Buckle Video       Stock  14 3/8     *  14.975     -4.0     700    10,063 │
│       ▶ Conford Corp       Stock  21 1/2        21.1735    1.5     -300    -6,450 │
│         Freid Hanson       Stock  25 1/2     *  25.998     1.9      900    22,950 │
│         Seaver Res         Stock  25         *  25.725     -2.8     100     2,500 │
│         Seaver Res 91/04   Stock  28         *  28.745     -2.6     100     2,800 │
│         Seaver Res 91/07   Stock  32         *  32.771     -2.4     100     3,200 │
│         Seaver Res 91/10   Stock  36         *  36.7975    -2.2     100     3,600 │
│         Songram Systems    Stock  9          *  9.435      -4.6   1,000     9,000 │
│         Warburtuns Inc     Stock  19 1/4     *  20.650     -6.8     500     9,625 │
│         -Cash-                                                           12,228 │
│                                                                          │
│                                                                          │
│         Total Market Value                                -3.9           79,316 │
│                                                                          │
│  Birscher                 * Estimated Prices             +/- Adjust Price │
│  Esc-Register      F8-Combine Lots     F9-All Accounts   Ctrl◄┘ Record Prices │
└────────────────────────────────────────────────────────────────────────┘
```

Short sale

Shares are displayed as negative numbers

Listed Options

While Quicken isn't specifically designed to handle stock options, the investment register is flexible enough to accommodate most ordinary options transactions.

Calls

A *call option* is a contract to buy a specified number of shares of stock at a predetermined (striking) price on or before a certain date. You may either buy a call option or (usually if you already own the stock) write a call option for someone else to buy. Use the following techniques for recording your options.

Each option security is identified by three things: the company name, the striking price, and the expiration date. Therefore, each option should be recorded as a different security. Since Quicken only offers 12 characters of space for naming securities, you should develop a code for identifying your options. For example, MSFT CFeb@60 might describe a Microsoft Call at 60 dollars per share that expires in February. You would specify the type as Option.

When you buy a call, enter it as a Buy or BuyX transaction, typing the price of the option into the PRICE field and the number of shares you've optioned into the SHARES field. If the option expires and you don't buy the stock, close out the option in Quicken's register by entering a Sell transaction with a price of zero. If you exercise the option, the price of the option is rolled into the tax basis of what you pay for the stock. Unfortunately, Quicken doesn't offer a simple way to handle this.

For example, say Larry Milner bought a call option on MicroComp stock at a striking price of $50 per share, which would expire in April. To keep his tax and cash records straight, Larry would need to follow this procedure when he recorded the option exercise:

1. He would record the exercise as a Buy (not a BuyX) transaction, listing the actual security he was buying (not the encoded option name). To arrive at the price per share, he would add the price per share he paid for the option to the striking price. In the $ AMOUNT field, he would enter the total paid for the option plus the total paid to exercise the option. Quicken would calculate the commissions automatically.

2. Larry would cancel the exercised option by entering a Sell transaction (this time using the option security name) in exactly the amount he paid for the option.

3. If he transferred money into the investment account to pay for the stock (and normally would have used the BuyX action), Larry would complete the transfer by entering an XIn action. Figure 8.18 shows a set of transactions recording Larry's exercised call option.

Note. Remember that option contracts are written in blocks of 100 shares. Two option contracts represent an option to buy 200 shares. Newspaper and on-line price listings quote option prices at dollars per share.

Figure 8.18 **Investment account transactions for buying call options**

Transactions for an exercised call option

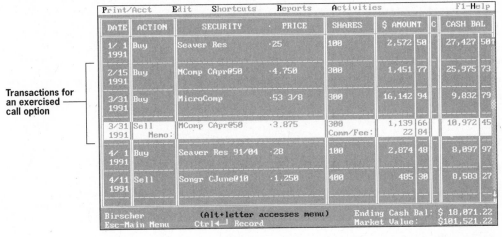

When you write a call option, you actually receive money from the buyer, so you would enter this exchange as a Sell or SellX transaction, showing the amount you receive. Quicken will ask you to verify that you're entering a short sale. Answer **Y**.

When a call option you've written expires, you must close out the contract by entering a Buy transaction for the contracted number of shares at a price of zero. However, suppose you wrote a call option to sell 400 shares of Songram Systems stock for $10 per share. If the buyer of the option exercised the right to purchase the stock, you would enter a Sell transaction for the stock in the normal manner, as shown in Figure 8.19. If the option expired unexercised, no further entries would be required; you would keep the stock and the money.

Puts

A *put option* is a contract to sell a specified number of shares of stock at a predetermined price on or before a certain date. As with call options, you may either write puts or buy puts. The Quicken entries you make follow the same logic as those you make for call options.

To buy a put, enter a Buy or BuyX transaction at the amount you paid. At the same time, you should enter a Sell transaction to close out the put on the expiration date; the amount should be zero. If you exercise the put, enter a Sell transaction for the stock at the striking (not market) price specified in the option contract, as shown in Figure 8.20.

Figure 8.19   Investment account transactions for writing call options

Transactions
for writing
a call option

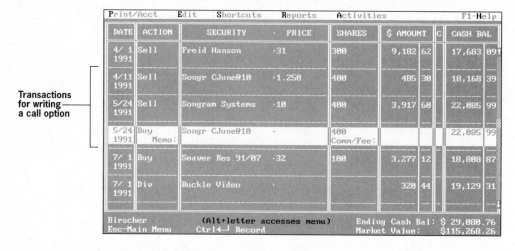

Figure 8.20   Investment account transactions for buying put options

Transactions
for buying a
put option

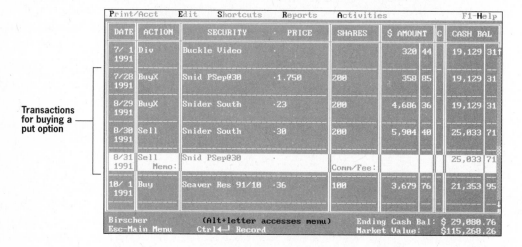

To write a put, enter a Sell or SellX transaction in the amount you received for the put (this will be flagged as a short transaction). If the put is not exercised, enter a Buy transaction for the put at a price of zero. If it is exercised, you need to enter a Buy or BuyX transaction for the stock, at a price that subtracts the original price you paid for the option from the striking price. You must also enter a Sell transaction of an amount equal to the price you paid for the stock less the amount you received when you wrote the put. You should then offset the original option transaction with an equivalent Buy transaction, as shown in Figure 8.21.

Figure 8.21   Investment account transactions for writing put options

Print/Acct	Edit	Shortcuts	Reports	Activities			F1-Help

DATE	ACTION	SECURITY	· PRICE	SHARES	$ AMOUNT	C	CASH BAL
10/ 1 1991	Buy	Seaver Res 91/10	·36	100	3,679 76		11,448 39
10/ 5 1991	Sell	Fgate PNov@40	·2.500	200	488 90		11,937 29
10/29 1991	Buy	Fargo & Fargate	·37 1/2	200	7,605 50		4,331 79
10/30 1991	Sell	Fargo & Fargate	·40	200	7,898 46		12,230 25
10/30 1991	Buy Memo:	Fgate PNov@40	·2.500	200 Comm/Fee:	511 10 11 10		11,719 15
11/15 1991	Sell	Conford Corp	·21 1/2	300	6,352 07		18,071 22

Transactions for writing a put option

Birscher	(Alt+letter accesses menu)	Ending Cash Bal: $ 18,071.22
Esc-Main Menu	Ctrl◄┘ Record	Market Value: $101,521.22

Although accounting for options in Quicken is tricky, it is certainly feasible. By following the procedures outlined here, you can properly account for the tax consequences of buying and writing both kinds of listed options.

Employee Stock Options

Employee stock options are much more straightforward than listed options. Your employer may grant you options to buy shares in the company at a specific price—typically the market price of the stock on the day the grant is made. The right to exercise these options "vests" over a period of several years.

Here is how Larry Milner accounted for his employee stock options: On July 1, 1989, Larry received an option grant from his company, Mitsou Corp., to purchase 15,000 shares at $30 per share, vesting annually over three years (5,000 shares each year). To account for his options in Quicken, Larry opened a regular investment account named Mitsou Options. For each of the three annual vesting dates, he entered two items: a reminder transaction to help him remember the vesting dates and a ShrsIn transaction for one-third of the 15,000 options (with a security name of Mitsou Optn@30), priced at zero and dated with the vesting date (see Figure 8.22). The zero price reflected the fact that the current market price equaled the exercise price, so the options carried no measurable value.

Note. Reminder transactions may be inserted in the investment register to jog your memory about upcoming events. When a reminder date arrives, Billminder will flash a message. To create a reminder transaction, simply specify a reminder action in the investment account register. If you don't wish to see the reminder, enter * in the C column or delete the reminder entirely.

Figure 8.22   **Setting up an investment account for employee stock options**

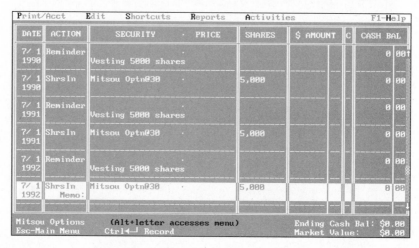

Note. The procedure described here is applicable to so-called Nonqualified Stock Option, by far the most common type of grant today. Incentive Stock Options must be handled in a way that reflects a tax basis different from the market value.

Note. In accounting for options, you sometimes need to enter into a transaction record a price per share that is different from the market price for those options. To keep these deviations from creating havoc with the price histories that Quicken keeps for each security, be sure you go back and update the price screen by pressing Ctrl-U and inserting the correct market price.

On July 1, 1990, 5,000 of Larry's options vested, with the company's stock price at 37. He decided not to exercise the options yet, but wanted to reflect their value in his investment and net worth reports. Therefore, he began updating the value of his Mitsou options by subtracting 30 (his option price) from the price of Mitsou's stock and entering the result (7) in the Update Prices and Market Value screen, as shown in Figure 8.23.

The most reliable way of valuing an employee option is to subtract the exercise price from the market price of the stock. Since Quicken provides no automated way to do this, the price must be updated periodically by hand.

By July 1, 1991, 10,000 of Larry's options had vested, and the company's stock price stood at 42. With the option market value up to date, Larry saw that he had $120,000 in vested value wrapped up in his employee option shares (option price of 30 subtracted from the current price of 42, times 10,000 shares). He decided that it was time to exercise those options, which meant paying $300,000 to the company and receiving $420,000 worth of stock in return.

To exercise his options, Larry entered a Buy transaction for 10,000 shares of the actual stock—Mitsou Corp—at $42, which would become the tax cost basis for the stock. To balance the books, two additional transactions were necessary: a $120,000 miscellaneous income (MiscInc) transaction to reflect the taxable income from the option windfall (categorized under a Misc Income category) and a $300,000 transfer from savings to cover the amount he had to pay to exercise the options. At the same time, he closed

out the options he'd exercised by entering a Sell transaction for 10,000
options at a price of zero. Finally, he pressed Ctrl-U to update prices with
the correct market value of the options (at 12). Figure 8.24 shows the register reflecting these actions.

Figure 8.23   Stock options in Update Prices and Market Value screen

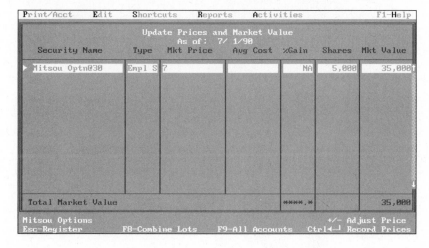

Figure 8.24   Register display of exercised stock options

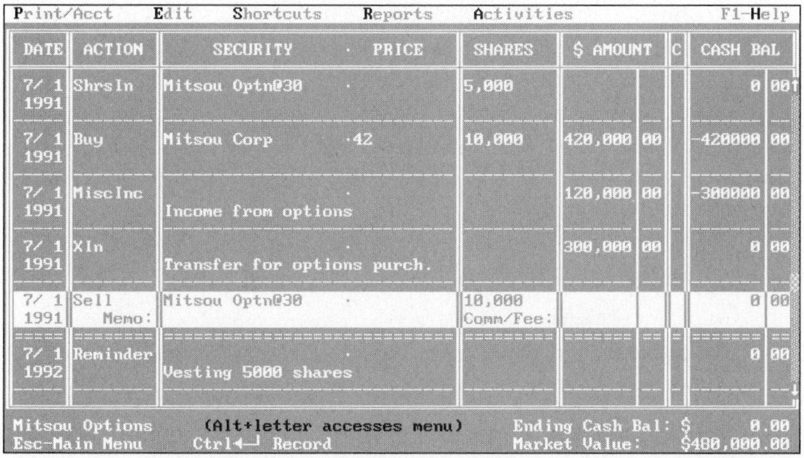

The tax basis for the 10,000 shares Larry owns is correctly set at $420,000, and his income (and tax) reports will show the $120,000 of ordinary income he's received as a result of the exercise. Figure 8.25 shows the market value of his portfolio on the Update Prices and Market Value screen.

Figure 8.25   Update Prices and Market Value screen

```
 Print/Acct    Edit    Shortcuts    Reports    Activities           F1-Help

                        Update Prices and Market Value
                              As of:  7/ 1/91
        Security Name       Type  Mkt Price    Avg Cost  %Gain   Shares  Mkt Value

▶ Mitsou Corp             Stock 42            42          0.0   10,000   420,000




















   Total Market Value                                    0.0            420,000

 Mitsou Options                                          +/- Adjust Price
 Esc-Register         F8-Combine Lots    F9-All Accounts  Ctrl◄┘ Record Prices
```

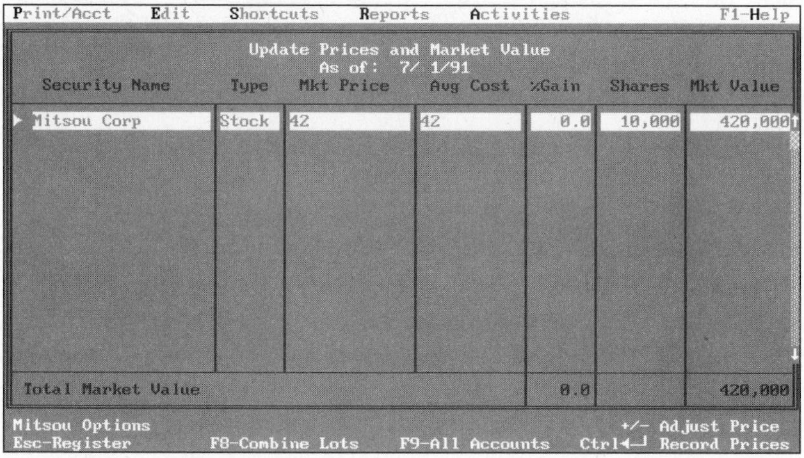

Bonds

Bonds are bought and sold in much the same way as stocks, except the income received is classified as interest income (IntInc) rather than dividends. Bonds are generally sold in principal amounts of $1,000, but are quoted at a par price of 100.

You'll want to enter a share number which is consistent with the way newspapers and on-line services quote prices. For bonds with $1,000 principal amounts, you should enter every bond as ten shares at $100 (or whatever the quoted price may be).

Limited Partnerships

Limited partnerships are tricky to account for in Quicken; however, investment accounts offer several types of transactions that help keep track of these investments:

- *Buy, BuyX*   Use these actions to record either purchases of public limited partnership shares or capital contributions to private limited partnerships. In the latter case, set the price at 1 and the number of shares as the amount of your contribution.

- *Sell, SellX*   Use these actions to record either sales of publicly traded shares or returns of capital for private limited partnerships.

- *MiscInc*   Use this action as a holding area for distributions you receive from a limited partnership until you have full detail on what the proper distribution should be among dividends, interest, capital gains, and return of capital.

- *Div, DivX, IntInc, CGShort, CGLong, RtrnCap*   If and when you have full detail on how to allocate a partnership distribution, you can use these actions to create a series of transactions which properly account for that distribution.

For more information on handling limited partnerships in Quicken, refer to Level 5.

Precious Metals

You can account for investments in gold, silver, platinum, or other precious metals, provided they are in a form that is not priced at a premium above the published price of the metals. To do so, use Buy and Sell actions in much the same way you would for stock. In the investment register, enter the number of ounces you buy or sell in the SHARES column and the market price of the metal under PRICE. Quicken will calculate the commission when you enter the dollar amount.

If your investment is in the form of precious metal coins that trade above the market price of the raw metal, either use the market price for that type of coin (if you have a price source readily available), or estimate the value based on the price of the rare metal. Consider, for example, a $20 gold coin that trades 10.2 percent higher than gold bullion.

To set up a precious metal coin account to track the rise and fall of the underlying metal price,

1. Enter a Buy (or ShrsIn) action, and name the security 20$Gold+10.2%. The number at the end of the name serves only to remind you that the number of ounces should be increased by this number before you multiply by the price of gold to obtain the approximate market value of your holdings.

2. In the Enter New Security window, enter **GOLD** as the symbol. This will enable all future valuations to be keyed to the price of gold.

3. For the number of shares, use the calculator (press Ctrl-O) to increase the number of ounces by 10.2 percent (multiply by 1.102). This will cause the estimated value of your gold coins to rise and fall with the price of gold.

4. When you sell coins, don't forget to increase the number of coins you sell by 10.2 percent again, before you enter a number in the SHARE column.

Note. For very high values, you may want to use multiples of one thousand or even—lucky you—one million. In this case, enter 1,000 or 1,000,000 in the number of shares and price in thousands or millions, as appropriate.

Collectibles

Collectibles such as works of art should be entered as separate securities, although you might group them together in a regular investment account called Art. In the BuyX transaction, use a share number of 1 and a purchase price of whatever you paid. As your collectibles appreciate in value, you may wish to update the prices by pressing Ctrl-U and entering the new value.

Other Priced Assets

There are two ways to handle other priced assets, depending on the character of the asset you're tracking:

- If the asset is one-of-a-kind (or a collection of one-of-a-kind items such as breeding horses), account for it in exactly the same manner as you account for collectibles: use a share number of 1, a price of whatever you paid, and update the price as you reappraise the value over time.

- If the asset is a collection of several items of like value, to and from which you frequently add and subtract items (such as a collection of porcelain figurines), you can create a security that embraces all the items as a class ("Porcelain Figurines," for example). Just enter the number of items in the SHARES column, and record their average value in the PRICE column.

Reconcile Your Brokerage Account

Many PC-based investment programs depend on you to enter purchase cost and other transaction data correctly, yet provide no second check on the accuracy of the data. This is one area where Quicken, by applying its check-register metaphor to investment accounts, stands head and shoulders above other personal finance software. If you use the reconciliation feature of your investment account register regularly, you can be quite confident that the tax-basis records of your securities will not be blemished by entry error.

The reconciliation process for a brokerage account is quite similar to the process described for regular bank accounts in Level 2. In fact, your brokerage statement is to investment account reconciliation what your checking account statement is to bank account reconciliation. Following the procedures outlined in Level 2, you should be able to successfully reconcile your investment accounts against statements from the various organizations that manage your investments.

Be aware of the following points when you are reconciling your investment accounts:

- At the start of reconciliation, when you enter the ending cash balance from your brokerage statement, be sure to subtract margin loan balances from the cash balance and include any money market fund balances in which your broker holds idle cash.

- In the Reconciliation register, actions that increase your cash balance (Sell, Div, IntInc, CGShort, CGLong, and so on) show up in the Amount field as positive numbers, and decreases to your cash balance (Buy, IntExp, MargInt, and so on) show up as negative numbers. Transactions that don't involve a change in cash in the investment account—such as BuyX, SellX, StkSplit, and ReinvDiv—show up as zero-amount transactions.

- When marking cleared items from your brokerage statement, be particularly vigilant on zero-amount items: the checks-and-balances system is weaker on these transactions, since you don't match the totals of these transactions to changes in cash.

- In bank account registers, you were able to edit items directly from within the Reconciliation register; with investment accounts, however, you have to return to the Investment Account register to make changes. Press F9 to toggle between the Reconciliation register and the Account register, and change the transactions you need to fix.

Troubleshoot Problems

Many of the troubleshooting techniques described in Level 2 also apply here. In addition, the following suggestions are relevant to reconciling brokerage statements:

- Double-check the ending cash balance on your brokerage statement. On some statements, it's easy to pick up an incorrect number. Make sure to locate all the places where your account keeps cash—money market funds, and so forth. Subtract all the margin loans you have outstanding. If margin loans are greater than cash, you should enter a negative number as the ending cash balance.

- Look for charges and fees against your brokerage account which may be buried in less than obvious places. Has an account fee been assessed? If so, enter a MiscExp transaction to account for the fee.

- Make sure you didn't enter a Buy or Sell action as a BuyX or SellX, or vice versa. While the purchase or sale information may be correctly recorded, its effect on cash would be wrong.

- If you recorded a stock split or stock dividend, check to see whether the split created fractional shares which your brokerage firm automatically sold. These should be recorded as Sell or SellX transactions.

Update Your Portfolio Values

As the final step in reconciliation, Quicken will take you to the Update Prices and Market Value screen where you'll be able to enter the market pricing information listed on your brokerage statement as of the statement ending date. Press Ctrl-G (for Go to Date), and enter the ending date of your statement. If you update your pricing information daily, especially from an on-line service, this step will probably be redundant. Nonetheless, it is an important final check on the integrity of your last month's data entries.

Print Reports That Every Investor Needs

Quicken's preformatted investment reports provide the basic information every investor needs to assess the value of his or her investments, to determine which capital gains have already been realized and which are still to be taken, and to compare how investments are performing relative to one another—both individually and in groups.

While working in an investment account's register, choose Reports from the Menu bar, and select Investment Reports from the Reports submenu. You'll see a list of the five standard reports Quicken offers: Portfolio Value, Investment Performance, Capital Gains, Investment Income, and Investment Transactions.

Quicken offers many ways to customize your investment reports. Some of these are report options, which you may select from a window that's displayed any time you request a standard report. Others are accessible by selecting Edit or Layout from the Report menu bar.

Follow these guidelines to decide which customizing options to use under various circumstances:

- In general, use the report options to enter a title for the report, to choose which subtotals to use, and to select the investment accounts that should be covered in the report.

- Use the Layout options to collapse detail in the report, to switch between income and cash flow basis accounting, to include or exclude transfers, to include or exclude unrealized capital gains, to display memoranda, to sort transactions, and to set the width of the report. You can display the Layout menu shown in Figure 8.26 by pressing Alt-L (Layout) when a report is displayed on the screen.

■ Use the Edit options to change the title and date range, to match specific transaction criteria, to set the accounts and classes to be included, and to set filters for the report. You can see the Edit menu shown in Figure 8.27 by pressing Alt-E (Edit) when a report is displayed on the screen.

If you use particular customization options frequently, you may want to memorize a report by displaying it and pressing Ctrl-M (for Memorize).

Figure 8.26   Layout menu

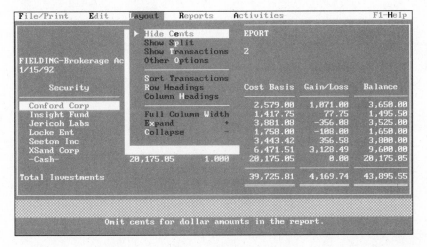

Figure 8.27   Edit menu

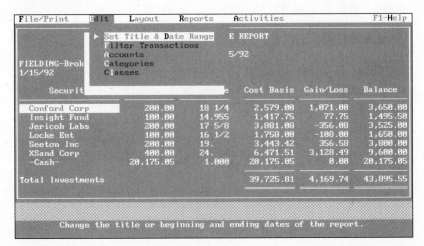

Portfolio Value Report

Whenever an investment account is current, you can get a quick snapshot of your investments—either for an individual account or for all accounts—by viewing the Update Prices and Market Value screen (press Ctrl-U).

For a different in-depth summary of your current portfolio—one that shows in dollars your cost basis and unrealized capital gains and losses—you may want to use the Portfolio Value report. When you request a Portfolio Value report, you'll be given the chance to specify a date for the valuation, to choose how you want to subtotal, and to define the scope of your report (current, all, or selected accounts). Figure 8.28 shows the options in the Portfolio Value Report screen.

Figure 8.28   Portfolio Value report options

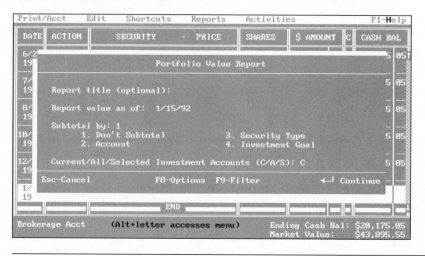

Use the Portfolio Value report to check your unrealized capital gains and losses at any time, as you look for selling opportunities. You can also use this report to assess the composition of your investments—how much diversity and balance you've achieved among types of securities or investment goals. Figure 8.29 shows how the Portfolio Value report appears on your screen, while Appendix D shows the report on paper.

Note. Quicken displays an asterisk (*) to designate that it does not have pricing information for a particular security on a particular day. In this event, Quicken uses the most recent price it has for the security.

Investment Performance Report

The Investment Performance report is a very different kind of report from those you'll see elsewhere in Quicken. It displays the average annual return of your investments over a specified period of time.

Figure 8.29   **Portfolio Value Report screen**

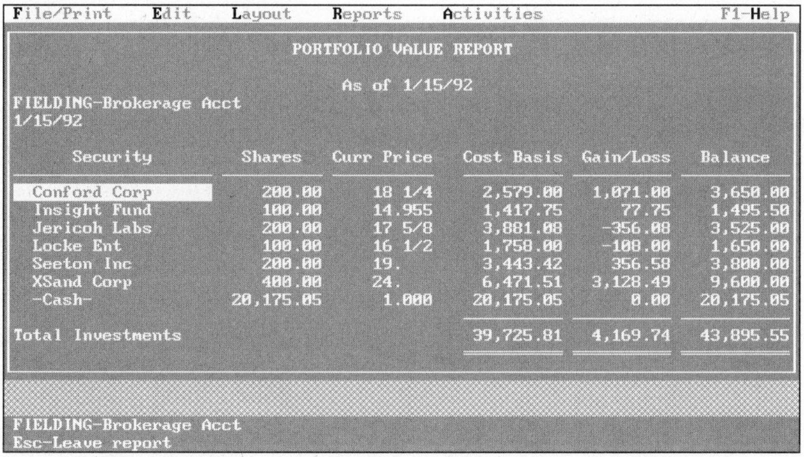

```
File/Print   Edit   Layout   Reports   Activities          F1-Help

                        PORTFOLIO VALUE REPORT

                           As of 1/15/92
 FIELDING-Brokerage Acct
 1/15/92

        Security        Shares    Curr Price   Cost Basis   Gain/Loss   Balance

     Conford Corp        200.00    18 1/4       2,579.00    1,071.00   3,650.00
     Insight Fund        100.00    14.955       1,417.75       77.75   1,495.50
     Jericoh Labs        200.00    17 5/8       3,881.00     -356.00   3,525.00
     Locke Ent           100.00    16 1/2       1,758.00     -108.00   1,650.00
     Seeton Inc          200.00    19.          3,443.42      356.58   3,800.00
     XSand Corp          400.00    24.          6,471.51    3,128.49   9,600.00
     -Cash-           20,175.05     1.000      20,175.05        0.00  20,175.05

 Total Investments                             39,725.81    4,169.74  43,895.55



 FIELDING-Brokerage Acct
 Esc-Leave report
```

Note. The performance reflected in the Investment Performance report is actually the internal rate of return (IRR) for the investments you select over the period you specify. The IRR is the discount rate at which the net present value of the investment's cash flows equals zero.

Quicken's performance calculations take into account not only the appreciation of the value of your holdings but also the income (dividends and interest, for example) that came from them and the expenses (such as margin interest and account fees) that went into them. In simple terms, a 9 percent average annual return on an investment means that your investment did as well as the same amount of money invested in a money market mutual fund that paid 9 percent interest.

These performance calculations are invaluable in assessing how effectively you've invested your money. The customization options for the report give you tremendous flexibility in checking different time periods to determine performance by time period, account, security, type, or goal. Figure 8.30 shows a sample of this report.

When requesting an Investment Performance report, it's important to remember several things:

- If you use very short time periods, you may see deceptively good (or bad) results. A movement of 1 percent in the value of a stock, not unusual over the course of a week, would be annualized to a return of 68 percent if you asked for performance over just that week. The longer the time frame you specify, the more confident you can be that you'll see a realistic annual performance.

- If your level of investment keeps changing—in other words, if you're constantly moving large amounts of cash into and out of an investment account—you may see some unusual performance results. For example, if all of 1992 is a bear market except April, and you just happen to park an extra $50,000 in your $25,000 investment account in April, you will look like a hero—not due to your stock-picking abilities, but to the fortunate timing of your cash flow.

Figure 8.30 **Investment Performance report**

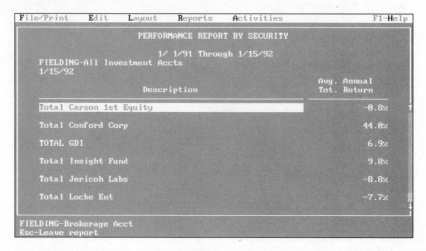

```
File/Print   Edit   Layout   Reports   Activities        F1-Help

              PERFORMANCE REPORT BY SECURITY
                 1/ 1/91 Through 1/15/92
    FIELDING-All Investment Accts
    1/15/92
                                              Avg. Annual
                    Description               Tot. Return
    Total Carson 1st Equity                       -0.8%
    Total Conford Corp                            44.0%
    TOTAL GDI                                      6.9%
    Total Insight Fund                             9.8%
    Total Jericoh Labs                            -8.8%
    Total Locke Ent                               -7.7%

    FIELDING-Brokerage Acct
    Esc-Leave report
```

■ Performance calculations are only as reliable as the pricing data you enter. If you update your prices quarterly but ask for performance by month, the resulting report will be unusable. Try to choose beginning and ending dates for your performance calculations for which you've entered up-to-date pricing information.

■ Finally, as advertising disclaimers announce, "Past performance is not a reliable indicator of future prospects for this investment." Enough said on that point.

Figure 8.31 shows a printed Investment Performance report for a $10,000 investment in IBM stock from April 1, 1989 to March 31, 1991, assessed quarterly.

Capital Gains Report

The Capital Gains report shows the gains and losses you've actually realized by selling your investments. It is designed not only to be a useful report but also to serve as Schedule D of your federal income tax return.

Quicken reports capital gains for the period you specify in the Capital Gains Report window shown in Figure 8.32. You can subtotal by time period, account, security, security type, or investment goal. Alternatively, you can divide your gains into short-term and long-term. The dividing line is set to a default of 365 days, which you can also change in this window.

Figure 8.31   Investment Performance report for IBM stock

```
                            IBM Stock Performance
                            4/ 1/89 Through 3/31/91
LOMBARDI-IBM Stock                                                   Page
1/15/92
                                                       Avg. Annual
                          Description                  Tot. Return

        TOTAL   4/ 1/89 -  6/30/89                        10.4%

        TOTAL   7/ 1/89 -  9/30/89                        -8.9%

        TOTAL  10/ 1/89 - 12/31/89                       -44.6%

        TOTAL   1/ 1/90 -  3/31/90                        62.6%

        TOTAL   4/ 1/90 -  6/30/90                        50.3%

        TOTAL   7/ 1/90 -  9/30/90                       -32.6%

        TOTAL  10/ 1/90 - 12/31/90                        27.0%

        TOTAL   1/ 1/91 -  3/31/91                         3.1%
```

Figure 8.32   Capital Gains report options

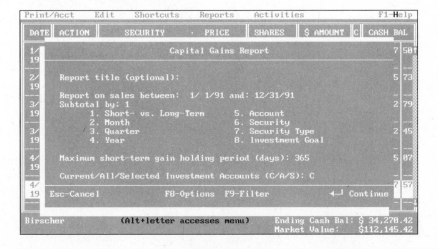

The default report format is designed to generate a report suitable for submission with Schedule D of your income tax return. Specifically, the IRS requires that you subtotal your gains as short-term and long-term. (You may need to adjust the date to cover the entire tax year.) The reporting of capital gains is limited to sales of securities in your accounts. Capital gains distributions from mutual funds and limited partnerships are reported separately in the Investment Income report.

Figure 8.33 shows a portion of a Capital Gains report set up for use with Schedule D.

Figure 8.33   Capital Gains report set up for use with Schedule D

```
 File/Print    Edit    Layout    Reports   Activities                F1-Help
                            CAPITAL GAINS REPORT
                         1/ 1/91 Through 12/31/91
 MILNER-Birscher
 1/15/92
      Security      Shares   Bought    Sold    Sales Price  Cost Basis  Gain/Loss
                    SHORT TERM
 MComp CApr@50        300   2/15/91  3/31/91     1,139.66    1,451.77    -312.11
 Freid Hanson        300   1/ 1/91  4/ 1/91     9,182.62    7,799.33   1,383.29
 Songram Syste       400   1/ 1/91  5/24/91     3,917.60    3,774.00     143.60
 Snider South        200   8/29/91  8/30/91     5,904.40    4,686.36   1,218.04
 Fargo & Farga       200  10/29/91 10/30/91     7,898.46    7,605.50     292.96
 Warburtuns In       200   1/ 1/91 11/15/91     5,507.04    4,130.00   1,377.04

              TOTAL SHORT TERM                 33,549.78   29,446.96   4,102.82

 MILNER-Birscher
 Esc-Leave report
```

Investment Income Report

An Investment Income report is, in essence, a profit and loss statement for your investment activities. On the income side, it shows dividends, interest, capital gains distributions, realized capital gains, and (optionally) unrealized capital gains. On the expense side, it shows investment interest and other costs you've detailed in your investment account.

The options for this report are straightforward: you can choose any time period, and subtotal by time period, account, security, or security group (see Figure 8.34). Many more formatting options become available after you display the report and select Layout from the Report menu bar. For example, this is where you would choose to include or exclude unrealized gains in the report (select Other Options from the Layout submenu).

You can use this report to assess the change in your net worth or total cash position that has resulted from your investment activity. You may also use it to gather information for Schedule B of your income tax return by carefully suppressing (using filters) tax-exempt securities, securities in accounts that need not be reported (like IRA or Keogh accounts), and unrealized gains and losses. Figure 8.35 shows an on-screen version of an Investment Income report.

Figure 8.34   Investment Income report options

Figure 8.35   Investment Income report

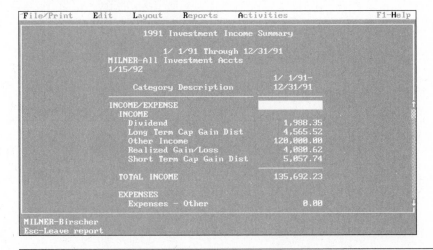

Investment Transactions Report

The Investment Transactions report provides a way to obtain complete detail on your investment transactions for a particular time period. This report shows the impact of each transaction on one of three things: cash, cost basis, or market value.

The report lists, in chronological order, each transaction in an account, including the action, security name, category (or Quicken account at the other end of a transfer of funds), price, shares, commission, and exchange of cash. As with other reports, you have several options for subtotaling the report to focus on individual securities or activity over a month or a quarter. Figure 8.36 shows a portion of an on-screen Investment Transactions report.

Figure 8.36 Investment Transactions report

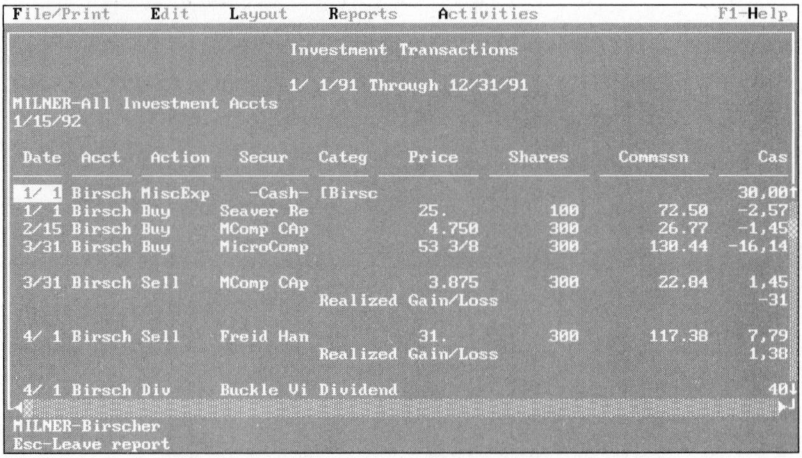
File/Print Edit Layout Reports Activities F1-Help

Investment Transactions

1/ 1/91 Through 12/31/91

MILNER-All Investment Accts

1/15/92

Date	Acct	Action	Secur	Categ	Price	Shares	Commssn	Cas
1/ 1	Birsch	MiscExp	-Cash-	[Birsc				30,00
1/ 1	Birsch	Buy	Seaver Re		25.	100	72.50	-2,57
2/15	Birsch	Buy	MComp CAp		4.750	300	26.77	-1,45
3/31	Birsch	Buy	MicroComp		53 3/8	300	130.44	-16,14
3/31	Birsch	Sell	MComp CAp		3.875	300	22.84	1,45
				Realized Gain/Loss				-31
4/ 1	Birsch	Sell	Freid Han		31.	300	117.38	7,79
				Realized Gain/Loss				1,38
4/ 1	Birsch	Div	Buckle Vi	Dividend				40

MILNER-Birscher

Esc-Leave report

Use a Spreadsheet for More Flexible Reporting

Quicken offers many options for customizing reports, but these options are designed to deal with bank, cash, credit card, asset, and liability accounts, rather than investment accounts. After you've worked with Quicken's investment accounts for a while, you may want to customize report formats in ways that Quicken will not allow.

One useful report, for example, is a view of unrealized capital gains and losses, sorted in order by the amount of gain or loss. This information can be helpful near the end of the year when you're seeking to balance your taxable gains and losses.

Note. In general, you'll find Quicken's investment capabilities less well developed than its other capabilities. This is a result of Quicken originally being designed for bank account transactions. The program's investment features were added six years after the first version shipped.

Unfortunately, the Quicken Transfer Utility—normally used to move data from Quicken to a spreadsheet—is of limited use for investment transactions. You're much better off creating a report in Quicken, printing the report to a file, importing it into your spreadsheet, and working with it there.

Here, for example, are the steps for creating a report of all your unrealized capital gains and losses, sorted by amount of gain or loss:

1. Generate a standard Portfolio Value report for your investment accounts. Specify no subtotals for your report.

2. With the report on the screen, select Print Report from the File/Print menu (Alt-F), or press Ctrl-P (for Print).

3. In the Print Report window, choose Disk (1-2-3 file) and press Enter. In the Print to Lotus File window, specify a name for the file, as shown in Figure 8.37. You needn't specify an extension; Quicken will give the resulting file a .PRN extension.

Figure 8.37   Print to Lotus File window

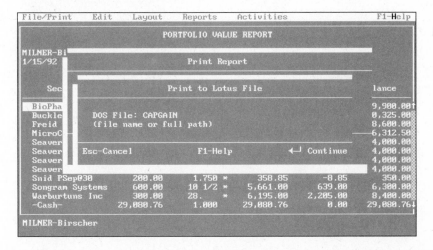

Note. Quicken's 1-2-3 file option does not literally produce a file in 1-2-3 format. The resulting file is, however, in a format 1-2-3 and most other spreadsheets can read easily. See Level 7 for more details on moving Quicken data to spreadsheets.

4. Leave the report and Quicken, and start Lotus 1-2-3 or a 1-2-3–compatible spreadsheet. If you're working in 1-2-3, make sure the cell pointer is in cell A1 (the upper-left cell), and then select the File Import Numbers command (type **/FIN**) to import the Portfolio Value report into your spreadsheet. (If you're working in another spreadsheet, enter the equivalent command to import the file.)

Note. If you have a ZiffNet or CompuServe on-line service account, blank spreadsheet formats are available with the correct column widths and numeric formats for this and many of Quicken's reports. See Appendix B for details on downloading these blank spreadsheets.

5. Adjust the widths of the spreadsheet columns by selecting Worksheet Column Set-Width (type **/WCS**). Adjust the format of the data by selecting Range Format (type **/RF**), choosing the format you want, and highlighting the cells that should have that format.

6. Using the spreadsheet's data sort functions, sort the body of the report by the data in the Gain/Loss column in descending order. In 1-2-3, select Data Sort (type **/DS**), then Data-Range (type **D**) and select the body of the report as the range to sort. Next, select Primary-Key (type **P**) and move to the Gain/Loss column. Specify descending order and select Go (type **G**) to execute the sort. The resulting spreadsheet should be similar to Figure 8.38.

Figure 8.38   Sorted report in Lotus 1-2-3

Milner: Gain/Loss Summary

Security	Shares	Curr Pric		Cost Basis	Gain/Loss	Balance
Freid Hanson	600	31	*	15,598.67	3,001.33	18,600.00
Warburtuns Inc	300	28	*	6,195.00	2,205.00	8,400.00
Seaver Res	100	40		2,572.50	1,427.50	4,000.00
Seaver Res 91/04	100	40		2,874.48	1,125.52	4,000.00
Seaver Res 91/07	100	40		3,277.12	722.88	4,000.00
Songram Systems	600	10.5	*	5,661.00	639.00	6,300.00
Seaver Res 91/10	100	40		3,679.76	320.24	4,000.00
MicroComp	300	54.375	*	16,142.94	169.56	16,312.50
-Cash-	29080.76	1		29,080.76	0.00	29,080.76
Snid PSep@30	200	1.75	*	358.85	(8.85)	350.00
Buckle Video	700	14.75	*	10,482.50	(157.50)	10,325.00
BioPharm Products	200	49.5	*	10,118.00	(218.00)	9,900.00
Total Investments				106,041.58	9,226.68	115,268.26

You can use this method to obtain all kinds of sorted investment reports, from ranked investment performance reports to portfolio reports sorted in order by the value of your holdings.

Measure Relative Investment Performance

Quicken's investment performance reports provide a very simple benchmark against which to monitor performance. If the average annual return displayed for your investments is greater than the interest you might have earned in a bank account or a money market fund, then you've done all right for yourself—but only relative to a bank account!

Two additional kinds of assessment are also important in judging which investments have paid off for you:

- Looking at your investments relative to each other—both individually and grouped by type and goal

- Looking at your investments' performance relative to other stocks in the market

Your principal tool for performing this assessment is Quicken's performance calculation. This, of course, you obtain by selecting the Investment Performance report option from the Investment Reports submenu under the Reports menu. Using the selection criteria offered by both the options screen and the Edit submenu on the Report menu bar, you can focus on the performance of particular stocks or groups of stocks over specific time periods.

Measure Performance by Goal and Type

You can look at performance for any of the classifications you chose for your investments—by goal or type, for example. To do so,

1. Select Investment Reports from the Reports menu (Alt-R). Then select Investment Performance.

2. In the Reports Settings window, enter **8** to tell Quicken to subtotal by investment goal.

3. Indicate that you want the report for all accounts, not just the current one. Figure 8.39 shows a sample report.

Figure 8.39   Printed report showing investment performance by goal

```
                       Investment Performance (by Goal)
                         1/ 1/91 Through 12/31/91
MILNER-All Investment Accts                                      Page 1
1/15/92
                                              Avg. Annual
                          Description          Tot. Return

       Total Growth                               10.6%

       Total High Risk                            32.9%

       Total Low Risk                             20.7%

       Total (No Goal)                             5.2%
```

Compare Your Performance with the Market

Occasionally, you'll find it useful to compare the performance of your investment against benchmarks other than securities or groups that are already in your portfolio. How have you done, for example, against the Dow Jones Industrial average or the Standard and Poor's 500 stock index? You shouldn't stick with strategies or investment advisors who consistently underperform the market, and Quicken can help you identify the culprits.

To properly assess benchmark performance against a market index, you must overcome two hurdles. First, Quicken is not designed to track the performance of these indices—or of any security you don't own, for that matter; you need to "force" these indices into Quicken in order to track them. Second, market indices don't take into account the *total return* (appreciation plus dividends) of the securities they represent; you must adjust the indices to correctly reflect the income they generate.

To do the former, create a new investment account that will hold "phantom" securities to represent each index or other benchmark that you want to consider. For example, you would take the following steps to create a benchmark S&P 500 index in Quicken:

Note. When you use this method, a new asset will appear in your Quicken accounts. Since this is a phantom asset created for tracking purposes only, you'll need to exclude it from reports of your net worth.

1. Create a new investment account called Market Indices. Set it up as a regular investment account.

2. Using the ShrsIn action, transfer into the account a new security called S&P 500, with the symbol SPX and a new type called Index. The price would be today's S&P 500 index price and the number of shares would be 100.

3. Periodically, you should update the price of the S&P 500 index by using the Update Prices and Market Value screen (Ctrl-U) to enter a new price for the index.

Steps 1 through 3 will give you a set of benchmarks that are of limited use unless you add historical prices and adjust for the dividend yield of the S&P 500. The easiest way to adjust for yield in the recent past and future is to enter dividend transactions to the index account every month which reflect the yield of the stocks in the index. The best way to adjust for yield in the more distant past is to enter historic prices that are adjusted for the dividend yield of the indexed stocks.

Note. If you have a ZiffNet or CompuServe on-line service account, you'll find a file containing yield-adjusted historic numbers for major market indices in a downloadable library, ready for import into Quicken; consult Appendix B for details.

You'll find the yield of major market index portfolios in the market data section of major investor publications such as *Barron's*. Armed with this data, you can complete your S&P 500 benchmark by continuing with these steps:

4. Enter the yield-adjusted monthly historic prices for the S&P 500 from Table 8.4. These prices are the index prices adjusted downward to reflect the yield between the listed date and July 31, 1991. (For example, the

Table 8.4   Actual and Yield-Adjusted Prices for Standard and Poors 500

Date	S&P 500 Stocks	Dividend Adjusted	Date	S&P 500 Stocks	Dividend Adjusted	Date	S&P 500 Stocks	Dividend Adjusted
31-Jan-81	129.55	84.93	31-Oct-84	167.49	132.12	31-Jul-88	272.02	245.56
28-Feb-81	131.27	86.41	30-Nov-84	163.58	129.52	31-Aug-88	261.52	236.81
31-Mar-81	136.00	89.88	31-Dec-84	167.24	132.92	30-Sep-88	271.91	246.96
30-Apr-81	132.81	88.12	31-Jan-85	179.63	143.30	31-Oct-88	278.97	254.12
31-May-81	132.59	88.33	28-Feb-85	181.18	145.04	30-Nov-88	273.70	250.08
30-Jun-81	131.21	87.77	31-Mar-85	180.66	145.14	31-Dec-88	277.72	254.51
31-Jul-81	130.92	87.94	30-Apr-85	179.83	144.99	31-Jan-89	297.47	273.41
31-Aug-81	122.79	82.83	31-May-85	189.55	153.37	28-Feb-89	288.86	266.29
30-Sep-81	116.18	78.73	30-Jun-85	191.85	155.76	31-Mar-89	294.87	272.65
31-Oct-81	121.89	82.98	31-Jul-85	190.92	155.53	30-Apr-89	309.64	287.15
30-Nov-81	126.35	86.40	31-Aug-85	188.63	154.20	31-May-89	320.52	298.10
31-Dec-81	122.55	84.18	30-Sep-85	182.08	149.38	30-Jun-89	317.98	296.57
31-Jan-82	120.40	83.11	31-Oct-85	189.82	156.27	31-Jul-89	346.08	323.66
28-Feb-82	113.11	78.46	30-Nov-85	202.17	166.99	31-Aug-89	351.45	329.56
31-Mar-82	111.96	78.06	31-Dec-85	211.28	175.07	30-Sep-89	349.15	328.29
30-Apr-82	116.44	81.57	31-Jan-86	211.78	176.03	31-Oct-89	340.36	320.88
31-May-82	111.88	78.76	28-Feb-86	226.92	189.19	30-Nov-89	345.99	327.09
30-Jun-82	109.61	77.55	31-Mar-86	238.90	199.75	31-Dec-89	353.40	335.07
31-Jul-82	107.09	76.16	30-Apr-86	235.52	197.48	31-Jan-90	329.08	312.87
31-Aug-82	119.51	85.36	31-May-86	247.35	207.99	31-Oct-87	251.79	221.23
30-Sep-82	120.42	86.40	30-Jun-86	250.84	211.50	30-Nov-87	230.30	202.99
31-Oct-82	133.71	96.34	31-Jul-86	236.12	199.66	31-Dec-87	247.08	218.45
30-Nov-82	138.54	100.38	31-Aug-86	252.93	214.47	31-Jan-88	257.07	227.96
31-Dec-82	140.64	102.31	30-Sep-86	231.22	196.61	29-Feb-88	267.82	238.19
31-Jan-83	145.30	106.11	31-Oct-86	243.98	208.06	31-Mar-88	258.89	230.91
28-Feb-83	148.06	108.55	30-Nov-86	249.22	213.13	30-Apr-88	261.33	233.78
31-Mar-83	152.96	112.56	31-Dec-86	242.17	207.68	31-May-88	262.16	235.26
30-Apr-83	164.42	121.43	31-Jan-87	274.08	235.65	28-Feb-90	331.89	316.40
31-May-83	162.39	120.35	28-Feb-87	284.20	244.96	31-Mar-90	339.94	324.96
30-Jun-83	168.11	125.03	31-Mar-87	291.70	252.03	30-Apr-90	330.80	317.07
31-Jul-83	162.56	121.32	30-Apr-87	288.36	249.75	31-May-90	361.23	347.16
31-Aug-83	164.40	123.13	31-May-87	290.10	251.88	30-Jun-90	358.02	345.00
30-Sep-83	166.07	124.81	30-Jun-87	304.00	264.59	31-Jul-90	356.15	344.28
31-Oct-83	163.55	123.35	31-Jul-87	318.66	277.99	31-Aug-90	322.56	312.80
30-Nov-83	166.40	125.94	31-Aug-87	329.80	288.35	30-Sep-90	306.05	297.73
31-Dec-83	164.93	125.27	30-Sep-87	321.83	282.02	31-Oct-90	304.00	296.63
31-Jan-84	163.41	124.54	31-Oct-87	251.79	221.23	30-Nov-90	322.22	315.35
29-Feb-84	157.06	120.15	30-Nov-87	230.30	202.99	31-Dec-90	330.22	324.15
31-Mar-84	159.18	122.24	31-Dec-87	247.08	218.45	31-Jan-91	343.93	338.50
30-Apr-84	160.05	123.37	31-Jan-88	257.07	227.96	28-Feb-91	367.07	362.23
31-May-84	150.55	116.49	29-Feb-88	267.82	238.19	31-Mar-91	375.22	371.26
30-Jun-84	153.18	119.00	31-Mar-88	258.89	230.91	30-Apr-91	375.35	372.38
31-Jul-84	150.66	117.51	30-Apr-88	261.33	233.78	31-May-91	389.83	387.79
31-Aug-84	166.68	130.49	31-May-88	262.16	235.26	30-Jun-91	371.16	370.20
30-Sep-84	166.10	130.53	30-Jun-88	273.50	246.15	31-Jul-91	387.81	387.81

unadjusted S&P 500 was 353.40 on December 31, 1989 and the average dividend yield of the indexed stocks was 3.4 percent between then and July 31, 1991. The adjusted price of 335.07 is the actual price divided by a yield adjustment of 1.0547.) To enter historic prices, call up the Update Prices and Market Value screen (Ctrl-U), highlight the index security, press Ctrl-H (for History), and enter the new price, as shown in Figure 8.40.

Figure 8.40   **Price History window for the S&P 500**

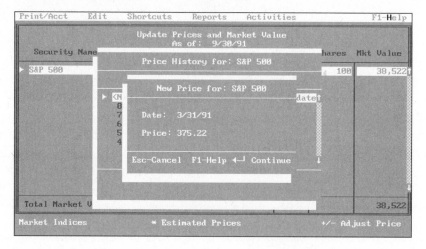

5. For more recent and future yield adjustments, you may enter dividend transactions representing the monthly yield into your benchmark index account. By doing so, you can continue entering published prices for the index without worrying about adjusting future prices explicitly to account for dividend yield.

For each month after July 31, 1991, create a dividend (Div) transaction for the S&P 500 index security. Divide the annual dividend yield by 12 and enter this number as the dividend amount for your index portfolio transaction. (If you don't have the exact yield, you can approximate with an average dividend yield, such as the one cited earlier.) Figure 8.41 shows a Market Index account register after a series of these transactions has been entered.

6. You can speed this process by memorizing the monthly yield transaction (Ctrl-M) and making it part of a monthly transaction group (Ctrl-J).

Once you've created these benchmarks, of course, you can compare against them the performance of any individual security, account, security type, or investment goal group over any period of time. Figure 8.42 shows, for example, the relative performance of Larry Milner's portfolio versus the S&P 500 from January 1 to December 31, 1990.

Figure 8.41   **Yield adjustments in Market Index Investment account**

```
 Print/Acct    Edit    Shortcuts    Reports    Activities              F1-Help
┌────┬──────┬─────────────┬────────┬────────┬──────────┬─┬──────────┐
│DATE│ACTION│   SECURITY  ·  PRICE │ SHARES │ $ AMOUNT │C│ CASH BAL │
├────┼──────┼─────────────┼────────┼────────┼──────────┼─┼──────────┤
│8/31│Div   │S&P 500      ·        │        │     1 09 │ │     1 09↑│
│1991│      │Yield adjustment      │        │          │ │          │
├────┼──────┼─────────────┼────────┼────────┼──────────┼─┼──────────┤
│9/30│Div   │S&P 500      ·        │        │     1 09 │ │     2 18 │
│1991│      │Yield adjustment      │        │          │ │          │
├────┼──────┼─────────────┼────────┼────────┼──────────┼─┼──────────┤
│10/31│Div  │S&P 500      ·        │        │     1 09 │ │     3 27 │
│1991│      │Yield adjustment      │        │          │ │          │
├────┼──────┼─────────────┼────────┼────────┼──────────┼─┼──────────┤
│11/30│Div  │S&P 500      ·        │        │     1 09 │ │     4 36 │
│1991│      │Yield adjustment      │        │          │ │          │
├────┼──────┼─────────────┼────────┼────────┼──────────┼─┼──────────┤
│11/30│      │             │        │        │          │ │          │
│1991│      │                      END                                │
└────┴──────┴──────────────────────────────────────────────────────┘
 Market Indices      (Alt+letter accesses menu)    Ending Cash Bal: $     4.36
 Esc-Main Menu       Ctrl◄─┘ Record                Market Value:    $38,526.36
```

Figure 8.42   **Comparing stock performance to a market index**

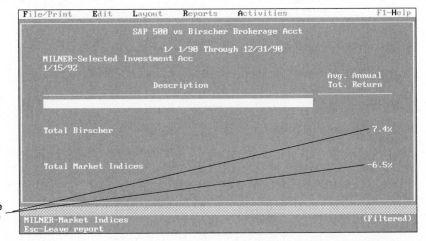

Portfolio outperformed the market by nearly 14 points

Build and Evaluate Hypothetical Portfolios

You can use the same kind of technique used to compare your investments with market indices to build and evaluate hypothetical investment portfolios. To do so, simply create a new investment account containing these securities, add to it the stocks you'd like to track, and make performance comparisons among them or with the investment portfolios you actually own.

You'll want to keep two suggestions in mind as you create and manage these hypothetical portfolios:

- Make sure you track all the income (dividends and interest) and splits associated with these securities; enter these transactions in your hypothetical brokerage account just as you would enter them into an actual account. Without these transactions, performance calculations will measure only the capital appreciation of the portfolio, not the total return.

- Take care to exclude these hypothetical portfolios from listings of your your assets, such as net worth statements. If you have many of these portfolios, you may wish to separate them from your personal accounts in a different Quicken file.

You need to be especially vigilant about maintaining hypothetical portfolios accurately, because you won't have brokerage statements against which to reconcile these accounts.

Analyze Your Commission Expenses

Quicken provides a way to enter and view commission expenses through the Register, but there is no way to summarize them in any of Quicken's investment reports. Especially if you use a full-service broker, it's a good idea to analyze your commission expenses to determine how much you're spending relative to the best discount brokerage rates available. If you're paying a premium for trading stocks, are you getting your money's worth in advice and service?

You'll need to use your spreadsheet to do this analysis. Here are some steps you can take to determine your commission expenses and estimate the premium you're paying above discount brokerage rates:

1. With the brokerage account that you want to analyze current, select Investment Reports from the Reports menu (Alt-R); then select Investment Transactions.

2. In the Investment Transactions Report window, enter the time period you want to analyze. Specify no subtotals for the report by typing **1** for Don't Subtotal. Don't exit the window yet.

3. Filter the report to include only buy and sell transactions: Press F9, and then, in the Filter Investment Transactions window that appears, move to "Select actions to include:" and type **Y** (for Yes). When you leave this window, Quicken displays another window in which you can specify that only buy and sell transactions should be included in the report. Press Enter as necessary to complete the settings in both windows and to create the report.

4. When the report appears on the screen, select Other Options from the Layout menu (Alt-L). In the Report Options window, leave the Report Organization setting on "Income and expense." Next to the Transfers field, type **2** to exclude all transfers. Also, make sure that the setting next to "Include unrealized gains" is N (for No). Press Enter to have Quicken generate the report with these new settings.

5. Print the report to a 1-2-3 (or equivalent) file: press Ctrl-P, or select Print Report from the File/Print menu (Alt-F). Then type **5** for Disk (1-2-3 file). Finally, type a file name, such as COMM.PRN, and press Enter.

6. Leave the report and Quicken, and start your spreadsheet program. In 1-2-3, use the File Import Numbers command to bring your report file into a blank spreadsheet. Before continuing, you may wish to delete any rows that are blank or that contain phrases such as "Realized Gain/Loss," to make your report easier to use. To do this, select 1-2-3's Worksheet Delete Row command. Also delete blank columns with Worksheet Delete Column.

7. Add headings for two new columns to the right of the existing columns: "Estimated Discount Commission" and "% Discount Commission" (abbreviate those names as you like). In the latter column, enter a formula that divides the estimated discount commission by the absolute value of the amount in the Cash column; then copy the formula down the column. (For now, the results will be 0.)

8. For a few of your buy and sell transactions, consult a commission table from one of the most aggressive discount brokerage firms to see what you would pay to trade each of these blocks of stock. Enter this amount in the Estimated Discount Commission column. In Table 8.5, you'll find a commission schedule for a discount brokerage firm in mid-1991.

9. Determine the average percentage commission for the transactions you chose, and apply that average percentage commission to the transactions you didn't explicitly look up.

10. Use the spreadsheet's @SUM function (or equivalent) to total both the commission and the estimated discount commission columns.

Note. The absolute value is required to change the sign for buy transactions, which result in a negative cash amount. You may obtain the absolute value of a number in cell F8 by entering the formula **@ABS(F8)**.

Note. If you know how to use your spreadsheet's built-in regression functions, you can apply regression to the number of shares and share price to obtain a more accurate approximation formula for discount commissions.

11. Subtract the estimated discount commission total from the commission total. The difference is the premium you're paying for the advice and service of your full-service broker.

Figure 8.43 shows a completed commission analysis spreadsheet.

Table 8.5   **1991 Commission Schedule for a Nationally Known Discount Brokerage Firm ***

Stocks

Transaction Size	Commission Rate
$0 - $2,500	$30 + 1.7% of principal
$2,500 - $6,250	$56 + 0.66% of principal
$6,250 - $20,000	$76 + 0.34% of principal
$20,000 - $50,000	$100 + 0.22% of principal
$50,000 - $500,000	$155 + 0.11% of principal
$500,000 +	$255 + 0.09% of principal

Options (with premiums of $.50 or under)

Number of Contracts	Commission Rate
0 - 49	$1.80 each + 1.5% of principal
50 - 149	$1.10 each + 1.8% of principal
150 - 499	$0.75 each + 2.0% of principal
500 - 1499	$0.60 each + 2.0% of principal
1500 +	$0.60 each + 1.5% of principal

Options (with premiums greater than $.50)

Dollar Amount	Commission Rate
$0 - $2,500	$29 + 1.6% of principal
$2,500 - $10,000	$49 + 0.8% of principal
$10,000 +	$99 + 0.3% of principal

Mutual Funds

Transaction Size	Commission
$0 - $15,000	0.6% of principal
$15,000 - $100,000	0.6% on first $15,000; 0.2% on amount over $15,000
$100,000 +	0.6% on first $15,000; 0.2% on amount between $15,000 and $100,000; 0.08% on amount over $100,000

* This table does not include overriding minimum and maximum fees or fees for very small or very large transactions.

Figure 8.43   Commission Analysis Spreadsheet

1991 COMMISSION COMPARISON

Date	Action	Security	Price	Shares	Commssn	Cash	Invest. Value	Est Disc Commssn	%Disc Commssn
1/ 1/91	Buy	Seaver Re	25	100	72.5	-2572.5	2572.5	69.50	0.0270
2/15/91	Buy	MComp C	4.75	300	26.77	-1451.77	1451.77	25.95	0.0179
3/31/91	Sell	MComp C	3.875	300	22.84	1451.77	-1451.77	22.20	0.0153
3/31/91	Buy	MicroCom	53.375	300	130.44	-16142.94	16142.9	125.14	0.0078
4/ 1/91	Buy	Seaver Re	28	100	74.48	-2874.48	2874.48	72.90	0.0254
4/ 1/91	Sell	Freid Han	31	300	117.38	7799.33	-7799.33	115.66	0.0148
4/11/91	Sell	Songr CJu	1.25	400	14.7	485.3	-485.3	14.33	0.0295
5/24/91	Sell	Songram	10	400	82.4	3774	-3774	80.05	0.0212
5/24/91	Buy	Songr CJu		400	14.7	-485.3	485.3	14.33	0.0295
7/ 1/91	Buy	Seaver Re	32	100	77.12	-3277.12	3277.12	59.64	0.0182
8/30/91	Sell	Snider So	30	200	95.6	4686.36	-4686.36	85.29	0.0182
10/ 1/91	Buy	Seaver Re	36	100	79.76	-3679.76	3679.76	66.97	0.0182
10/ 5/91	Sell	Fgate PNo	2.5	200	11.1	488.9	-488.9	8.90	0.0182
10/29/91	Buy	Fargo & F	37.5	200	125.5	-7605.5	7605.5	138.42	0.0182
10/30/91	Sell	Fargo & F	40	200	124.5	7605.5	-7605.5	138.42	0.0182
10/30/91	Buy	Fgate PNo	2.5	200	11.1	-488.9	488.9	8.90	0.0182
11/15/91	Sell	Conford C	21.5	300	117.93	6352.07	-6352.07	115.61	0.0182
11/15/91	Sell	Warburtun	28	200	92.96	4130	-4130	75.17	0.0182
12/28/91	Buy	Conford C	17	300	109.66	-6352.07	6352.07	115.61	0.0182

TOTAL 1/ 1/90 - 12/31/91   1401.44   -2428.78   8157.11   1352.98

TECHNIQUES AND PROCEDURES

■ Set up a new investment account by displaying the Select Account to Use screen (press Ctrl-A, or choose Select Account from the Main Menu). Highlight <New Account>; in the Set Up New Account window, type **6** for Investment Account. Enter a name, and indicate whether this is a mutual fund account. Enter an optional description; then press Enter to leave the window.

■ Many individual securities in our portfolios exist for a specific purpose—a college fund, retirement, or income. Quicken has built-in goals, or you can add your own. Assign a goal to a security when you define the security in the Set Up New Security window.

■ When entering an investment transaction into the register, you need to specify the date, security name, price per share, the number of shares, and either the commission or the total price including the commission. The first time you enter a particular security into the investment account register, you need to define that security for Quicken. In the Set Up Security window, enter the security name, symbol (if you want to update prices through an on-line service), type of security, and optional goal.

■ How you record many cash-related actions in an investment account depends on whether the cash originates in or will be deposited in the investment account, or will be transferred to or from another Quicken account. The codes for transfer actions end with X, as in BuyX (where you're buying shares with money transferred from another account) or DivX (where dividends you receive are automatically deposited in another account).

■ To update prices manually from sources such as the newspaper or telephone quote lines, press Ctrl-U to see the Update Prices and Market Value screen. The As Of date appears at the top of the screen, showing the date for which prices are displayed. Any prices that have not been updated for that date are noted by asterisks. To see prices or update for another date, press Ctrl-G and type the new date. Use the F9 key to toggle between a list of all securities and a list of only the securities in the current investment account.

■ An on-line information service such as CompuServe or ZiffNet is an efficient way to update prices for a busy portfolio. Through your on-line service, create a list of stock symbols and prices; then use your communications software to move the information into a text file on your PC. Next, import the file by pressing Ctrl-I (alternatively, select Read Prices from the Print/-Acct menu) and entering the file name and pricing date.

- Record stock splits using StkSplit, and type the ratio—for example, two for one—in the appropriate transaction fields in the register. Be sure to do this in every account in which you track that security. As a final step, enter the stock's new price in the Update Prices and Market Value screen, as of the effective date of the split.

- Quicken allows you to manage purchase and sale transaction in lots. To do this, use a different security name for each purchase lot, possibly encoded by the purchase date. Tie the related securities together by using the same stock symbol.

- To record listed options—puts and calls—that you buy or write, enter the option as a separate security with a name that reflects the option price and deadline, such as MSFT CFeb@60. Enter the option price and the number of shares as usual; then, depending on whether and when you exercise the option, you may need to enter a corresponding transaction to cancel the exercise option, plus a transaction to record the purchase or sale of the actual security.

- Handle employee stock options in a separate investment account. Assign a unique name to the options, and for each group of options that vests annually, enter a ShrsIn transaction dated with the vesting date and priced at zero. Also, enter a Reminder transaction dated with the vesting date, so Billminder can alert you as the date draws near. If you exercise the options, enter a Buy transaction and close out the vested option transaction that you exercised. In addition, you should record any funds that you transfer to cover the cost of exercising the options and record any income that results as miscellaneous income.

- Manage precious metals, collectibles, and similar investments in their own accounts. At the time of purchase, enter a share price of 1 and the purchase price that you paid; then be sure to update the market value (press Ctrl-U) whenever you reassess the asset's value.

- Quicken is exceptional for its ability to reconcile your investment accounts. Reconciling helps you detect any discrepancies among the myriad deposits, reinvestments, and commissions that populate these accounts. Use your brokerage statement as a basis for reconciling, and reconcile your investment accounts as regularly as you do your other accounts.

- Reports are the key to effectively tracking and evaluating your investment accounts. The many reports Quicken offers help with a variety of financial tasks, from simple chores such as tracking the performance of one security, to sophisticated efforts that ensure you're meeting your investment goals. To create a report, select Investment Reports from the Reports menu (Alt-R); then specify the type of report you want: Portfolio Value, Investment Performance, Capital Gains, Investment Income, or Investment Transaction.

TERMS

■ A *security* is a single investment with a value and, in most cases, a price per share. A security can be a stock, a bond, a certificate of deposit, shares in a mutual fund, an antique car, or a gold coin.

■ An *investment account* is the vehicle by which you keep track of any activity pertaining to one security or a collection of securities. In a regular investment account, you can track related securities—for example, all securities managed by a brokerage account, or all the works of art you own. A regular investment account may also have a cash balance. In a mutual fund investment account you can track a single mutual fund in which you own shares but which has no cash balance. Mutual fund investment accounts are also suitable for tracking a single stock, as for an employee stock purchase plan.

■ An *action* defines the type of transaction you're recording, such as purchase and sale of a security, dividends received, or interest paid on a margin loan. To see the available actions, move to the Action column and press Ctrl-L. There are few actions available for mutual fund investment accounts, because, unlike regular investment accounts, they do not maintain a cash balance; therefore, all cash-related transactions are transfers to and from other accounts.

IMPORTANT IDEAS

■ Investment accounts are designed for assets that fluctuate in price over time—stocks, bonds, mutual funds, even collectibles and precious metals. Assets that don't fluctuate, that don't have readily available prices, or that you don't anticipate buying or selling should be tracked in Other Asset accounts.

■ Group related assets into investment accounts when you want to track them as a collection instead of singly. Single accounts can track assets that logically belong together (for instance, stamps in a valuable collection), or securities that are managed by an organization, such as a brokerage firm or the administrators of a company's employee savings plan.

■ If you plan to use an on-line information service to update prices, be careful to enter the exact symbol for the security when first defining the security for Quicken. Quicken updates prices on the basis of symbols, not of security names.

■ Quicken's investment reports help you assemble information required by the IRS at tax time. If you plan to use Quicken in this way, set up your accounts to accommodate this practice from the start. Enter dividend and trade information for the entire calendar year, and memorize some useful reports that will mirror the information that will appear on various forms required by the IRS.

■ Be sure to enter the right date when entering transactions. When entering historical data, enter the acquisition date. When entering current data, enter the trade date, not the settlement date (when the money changed hands).

■ The Update Prices and Market Value screen is terrific for a quick assessment of how things stand with your investments, providing you update it whenever you take a look. The frequency with which you update prices depends on the relative activity of your portfolio, how independently you make trade decisions, and how often you plan to evaluate your portfolio's performance. Your reports will only be as accurate as the prices for the reporting period you've specified. Remember that each historic price occupies two bytes of space, which seems like a small amount until it's multiplied by dozens of prices incorporated every week.

Track Your Net Worth

PLAN AHEAD

DECISIONS

For Whom Are You Tracking Net Worth?

Before investing time in tracking net worth in Quicken, the first question you should address is who will be the principal recipient of the net worth information. Are you doing this for yourself alone or for others as well?

There are several reasons for tracking net worth for yourself. Most importantly, it can give you an excellent overview of the balance of your holdings. Are they sufficiently liquid? Are they comfortably distributed among real estate, retirement accounts, investments, and other assets? Does your portfolio include enough income producing assets? Are you over- or underleveraged? This overview can help you decide where to put new money as it comes in. It can help you decide which assets are salable in times of financial stress. Finally, it can help you develop a plan for increasing your net worth over time and tracking your progress toward that goal.

Tracking your net worth also becomes valuable when you are seeking credit or loans. Most loan applications—especially mortgage loans—require that you disclose your net worth in detail. If you maintain an unsecured credit line with a bank, you may be required periodically to submit a personal financial statement that includes a net worth report. A net worth statement is a vital reference point in any estate-planning discussion, and a current statement will be invaluable to your executor.

Decide which of these reasons are most relevant to you. These choices will affect how much detail you maintain, how you format your reports, and whether you use a spreadsheet in addition to Quicken for enhanced reporting and projections.

Do You Need Snapshots or Projections?

Quicken is very good at recording your financial history—that is, at taking financial "snapshots." By using a spreadsheet with Quicken, however, you can project the future course of your net worth, set goals for its growth, and determine the savings patterns and investment returns required to reach your goal.

For example, your Quicken net worth reports may show a net worth of $400,000 at age 45. If your goal is to retire a millionaire at age 65, using a spreadsheet in tandem with your Quicken accounts can help you plot a course towards realizing that ambition. (It can also help you see, using assumptions of future inflation, how little that million dollars will buy in twenty years.)

How Much Detail Do You Need?

Determining the degree of detail is largely a matter of how many accounts you maintain. Each account will be listed as a separate line item on your net worth statement. Investment accounts may be reported, at your option, as either a single summary line or a list of individual securities.

In general, you should keep as distinct accounts any assets you need or want to report separately. Early in this level, we'll offer an Asset and Liability Checklist to help you make sure you're accounting for everything.

Should You Track Cost or Value?

The most conservative way to compute your net worth is to record each asset at either its original cost or the current market value—whichever is lower (unless, of course, it's a marketable security with a published price). On the other hand, this conservative approach may distort your real worth— for example, if the home that cost $150,000 ten years ago is now worth $600,000. Your decision here depends on how you'll be using your net worth reports. Though a banker will appreciate conservatism, you should use the most current values in planning your estate.

Many people find the following approach helpful:

■ Record assets at their original cost unless there's a good reason to do otherwise.

■ In the case of assets that tend to wear out over time (such as automobiles or home furnishings), plan to decrease the value by entering a depreciation transaction of 5 to 33 percent a year, depending on the rate at which the asset wears out.

■ In the case of assets that appreciate over time (such as real estate, art, and jewelry), you may want to periodically adjust the value upward if it will cause a change of more than 5 to 10 percent in your net worth.

This level will help you handle each of these transactions appropriately.

MATERIALS

Appraisals of Your Assets

The principal materials you'll need are valuations of all the assets and liabilities you'll be tracking. This may involve digging out statements of the face value of your life insurance and loan statements, as well as estimating the total value of your automobiles, the furnishings in your home, or the equipment in your home office. The more closely you estimate these values, the more accurate your net worth report will be.

PRELIMINARIES

Complete Levels 1, 2, and 5

Beyond the registers, reports, and reconciliation basics of Levels 1 and 2, you should also know how to set up other asset and liability accounts, as discussed in Level 5. Level 5 also shows you how to record payroll, mortgage loan, and other complex transactions which affect balances in asset accounts as well as income and expense categories.

Complete Level 7 If You're Projecting Net Worth

Projecting net worth means using a spreadsheet, and that requires you to know the basic techniques for transferring Quicken data from your Quicken files to a spreadsheet. Level 7 discusses these techniques in detail.

Complete Level 8 If You Own Priced Investments

If you own stocks, bonds, mutual funds, precious metals, or other investments that vary in price, you should track these assets through investment accounts. Completing Level 8 will give you all the tools you need to represent your investments accurately in a net worth report.

Determine the Tax Basis for Improved Assets

Selling assets that appreciate over time may trigger a taxable capital gain. In some cases, calculating the gain is easy: simply subtract the purchase cost from the selling price. In other cases, such as a home that you're constantly improving, the cost basis is less clear-cut. This level will suggest techniques for tracking improvements to your home and other assets after you begin using Quicken. Now is a good time to recall and gather information about home improvements you made before you started using Quicken, so you have a complete record of your cost basis.

Enter Other Assets and Liabilities

The most challenging step in setting up the Quicken accounts you'll use to track your net worth is including *all* your assets and liabilities. To help in this process, we've provided another Toolkit, an Asset and Liability Checklist, which itemizes many of the assets and liabilities you might need to include. This Toolkit, located at the end of this section, also provides suggestions on how to determine the value of each of your asset and liability accounts.

To set up an Other Asset or Other Liability account,

1. Press Ctrl-A to see the Select Account to Use screen.

2. Press Home to highlight <New Account> and press Enter. The Set Up New Account window appears.

Note. If you plan to share your net worth statements with others, such as a bank or an estate planning advisor, remember to choose the descriptions you enter for your accounts carefully; these descriptions will appear on your net worth reports.

3. Press 4 or 5 to specify Other Asset or Other Liability account as the account type, and press Enter.

4. For the name of the account, type a descriptive name, such as "Lake Tahoe Hse," and press Enter.

5. Enter the account balance. For an Other Asset account, enter the value of the asset. For an Other Liability account, enter the amount of your liability. Change the date as necessary.

6. Enter an optional description for the account, and press Enter to leave the window. Quicken places the new account name in the list. Press PgDn if necessary to see it in the list.

Note. Other Asset and Other Liability accounts substitute the column headings DECREASE and INCREASE for the AMOUNT and DEPOSIT headings you're used to seeing in bank accounts.

In general, for Other Asset accounts, you should enter the original cost (if available) as the opening balance for the account. If you've made improvements which raise the cost basis for the asset, you might wish to enter one or more transactions describing these improvements. Enter dates for these transactions that roughly approximate the dates the improvements were made. When entering the category, use the name of the Other Asset account in which you're working; doing so will ensure that the cost of the improvements doesn't end up as an unclassified expense in your profit and loss statements.

The opening balance for the Other Liability account should be the current loan balance.

The following Toolkit provides a comprehensive list of the various assets and liabilities that may be part of your financial picture. For each asset or liability, the Toolkit notes the type of Quicken account you may need to set up (if you haven't already), and one or more sources of information on the cost or value of the item.

TOOLKIT   An Asset and Liability Checklist

Keeping in mind the level of detail you'll need for all your net worth reporting needs, review the following checklist for items that you may wish to include in your statements of net worth. For each relevant type of asset and liability, write an account name in the space provided. Use the finished list as a guide when you review your existing Quicken accounts in preparation for generating net worth reports.

Type of Asset or Liability	Quicken Account Type	Account Name	Source(s) of Valuation
Checking account	Bank	_____	Bank statement
Joint checking account	Bank	_____	Bank statement
Savings account	Bank	_____	Bank statement
Certificate of deposit	Other Asset	_____	Face value
Money market Account	Bank	_____	Account statement
Brokerage account	Investment	_____	Brokerage statement, daily quotes
Mutual fund account	Investment	_____	Mutual fund statement, daily quotes
Company savings plan	Investment or Other Asset	_____	Periodic statement of account
Individual retirement account	Investment or Other Asset	_____	Account statement, daily quotes
Precious metals	Investment	_____	Daily quotes
Principal residence	Other Asset	_____	Cost, recent appraisal, or cost adjusted for real estate inflation
Vacation home	Other Asset	_____	Cost, recent appraisal, or cost adjusted for real estate inflation

Type of Asset or Liability	Quicken Account Type	Account Name	Source(s) of Valuation
Investment real estate	Other Asset	_____	Cost, recent appraisal, or cost adjusted for real estate inflation
Home furnishings	Other Asset	_____	Cost, depreciated over 5 to 20 years
Art and antiques	Other Asset	_____	Cost or appraised value
Home office equipment	Other Asset	_____	Cost, depreciated over 3 to 5 years
Life insurance policy	Other Asset	_____	Cash value, from statement
Loans to others	Other Asset	_____	Original amount (interest only) or amortization table
Mortgage escrow account	Other Asset	_____	Escrow statement, monthly transfers
Tax refund receivable	Other Asset	_____	Tax return
Mortgage loan	Other Liability	_____	Mortgage statement, amortization table
Personal loan	Other Liability	_____	Original amount (interest only) or amortization table
Taxes payable	Other Liability	_____	Tax estimates, tax return

Address Common Situations

Depending on how accurate you need to be in tracking your net worth, you should consider taking advantage of several techniques for adjusting the value of your assets over time. Each of these techniques requires an investment of your time. With the exception of tracking real estate improvements (which every homeowner can use), you should apply these techniques only if you need an extraordinarily accurate picture of your net worth.

Note. Expenditures for ordinary maintenance and repair are neither tax deductible nor do they add to the tax basis for your home. Confer with your tax advisor if you're confused about how to classify expenditures.

Real Estate and Property Improvements

One of the most overlooked sources of personal income tax breaks is the effect home improvements can have on the tax you may owe when you sell your home. That's because the actual tax benefit is often realized long after the improvements are made and forgotten (especially because capital gains on principal residences are deferrable under many circumstances).

The IRS defines improvements as anything that adds to the value of your home or significantly prolongs its life. These are some of the expenditures that may qualify as improvements:

Alarm system	Kitchen improvements
Bathroom addition	Landscaping
Built-in bookcases	Lawn sprinkler system
Cabinetry	Paneling
Carpeting	Patio
Central air conditioning	Plumbing
Curtains	Roofing
Deck	Screens
Doors	Septic system
Driveway paving	Sidewalks
Earthquake retrofitting	Siding
Electrical outlets	Skylights
Fencing	Smoke detectors
Fireplaces and chimneys	Solar heating units
Flooring	Stairways
Furnace	Storm doors
Garage door opener	Swimming pool
Hot tub	Wall coverings
Insulation	Weather stripping

These costs are not directly deductible, but they may be used to adjust the cost basis of your home when you sell it (which, in turn, decreases the capital gain). Quicken makes it extremely easy to track such improvements and to maintain a complete and accurate record of the cost basis for any real estate you own.

Here is an example that shows how one family recorded the four most important kinds of transactions that relate to owning a home. This example illustrates how an Other Asset account (set up to track home improvements and changes in appraised value) and an Other Liabilities account (for monitoring mortgage principal) can help accurately record the sale of one home and the purchase of another. You might want to pattern your own transactions after the ones discussed here:

Note. A mortgage loan from a bank may also include funds for expenses that are not considered part of the new home's cost basis (prepaid interest, initial oil deliveries, and so forth). You can split the transaction between the new home's Other Asset account and regular expense categories to represent this situation.

- *Buying a new home*   When Luke and Maria bought their new home for $180,000 in June 1985, they created two new accounts. The first was an Other Asset account which they named "Sunset Lane Hse." When they wrote checks on their Harbor Bank checking account for the offer binder, deposit, and down payment, they categorized them as "Sunset Lane Hse." This generated the initial transactions in the Sunset Lane asset account. In addition, they started an Other Liability account to capture the mortgage loan from the bank. The first transaction they entered into this account was the loan principal, which they also categorized to the Sunset Lane house asset account. Along with other buying costs (mainly legal fees), these transactions in the Sunset Lane account, shown in Figure 9.1, constituted the home's cost basis.

Figure 9.1   Initial transactions in an Other Asset account for a home purchase

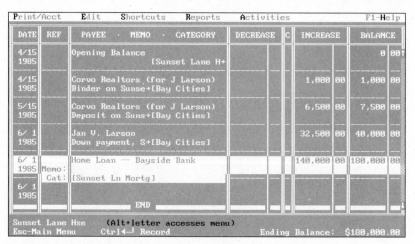

- *Making improvements*   As Luke and Maria made improvements to their home, they simply categorized expenses to the Sunset Lane asset account. This increased the balance of the Sunset Lane account over time, as shown in Figure 9.2. The memo field defines the purpose of each expenditure.

Figure 9.2   **Home improvements in the Other Asset account**

```
 Print/Acct    Edit    Shortcuts    Reports    Activities           F1-Help

 ┌────┬────┬──────────────────────────────────┬──────────┬─┬─────────┬─────────┐
 │DATE│REF │ PAYEE  ·  MEMO  ·  CATEGORY       │ DECREASE │C│ INCREASE│ BALANCE │
 ├────┼────┼──────────────────────────────────┼──────────┼─┼─────────┼─────────┤
 │2/27│    │Kiley Fencers/Landscapers          │          │ │4,550│00 │210,600│00↑│
 │1987│    │Backyard fence →[Harbor Bk Joi→   │          │ │     │   │       │   │
 │    │    │                                   │          │ │     │   │       │   │
 │7/14│    │Rooftree Builders                  │          │ │3,500│00 │214,100│00 │
 │1988│    │Family room exp→[Harbor Bk Joi→   │          │ │     │   │       │   │
 │    │    │                                   │          │ │     │   │       │   │
 │8/ 1│    │Rooftree Builders                  │          │ │4,000│00 │218,100│00 │
 │1988│    │Family room exp→[Harbor Bk Joi→   │          │ │     │   │       │   │
 │    │    │                                   │          │ │     │   │       │   │
 │3/15│    │Ralph & Sons Bricklayers           │          │ │1,900│00 │220,000│00 │
 │1989│    │Patio        [Harbor Bk Joi→      │          │ │     │   │       │   │
 ├────┼────┼──────────────────────────────────┼──────────┼─┼─────────┼─────────┤
 │3/15│Memo:│                                  │          │ │     │   │       │   │
 │1989│Cat :│                                  │          │ │     │   │       │   │
 │    │    │                                   │          │ │     │   │       │   │
 └────┴────┴──────────────────────────────────┴──────────┴─┴─────────┴─────────┘

 Sunset Lane Hse    (Alt+letter accesses menu)
 Esc-Main Menu      Ctrl◄─┘ Record              Ending Balance:  $220,000.00
```

Note. You can calculate the capital gains you've entered through value adjustment transactions by generating a transaction report to this account and applying a class filter to obtain only transactions in the unrealized class.

- *Adjusting for value increase*   When Luke applied for a bank credit line in 1990, he wanted to make sure that the full $325,000 appraised value of the house was reflected on the net worth statement he submitted. He entered a "value adjustment" transaction in the Sunset Lane account register which recorded an increase of $145,000 in the transaction, as shown in Figure 9.3. Under category, he entered "[Sunset Lane Hse]/Unrealized." Quicken will track the unrealized portion of the entry under a separate class for unrealized capital gains transactions.

- *Selling the house*   In January 1991, Luke and Maria sold the house for $400,000, less a brokerage commission of $24,000 and attorney fees of $3,500; they simultaneously purchased another home for $375,000. To represent this, Luke first entered a transaction in the Sunset Lane account which reversed the Value Adjustment transaction he'd entered the previous year, so he could determine the adjusted current cost basis for the house: $220,000. He also entered a decrease into the home mortgage liability account showing that the loan had been paid off. Then, in recording a deposit transaction for the sale price, he split the transaction: $220,000 to zero out the Sunset Lane account; $155,000 as Other Income; and the balance, $25,000, as Other Income to the Realized class, to track realized capital gains. Figure 9.4 shows the split transaction. He then set up a new Other Asset account for the new home, and transferred any down payment amount to that account as equity.

Figure 9.3   Home asset account showing a value adjustment

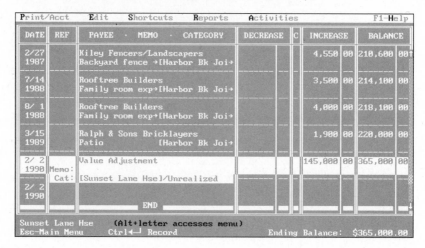

Figure 9.4   Split transaction for sale of house

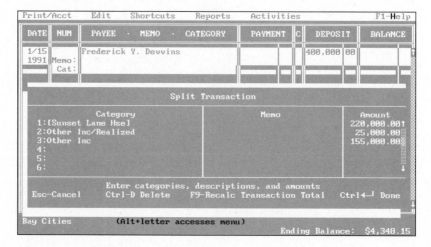

Other Appreciating Assets

Any appreciating asset, such as art or antiques, that is not tracked through an investment account may be handled in the same way as real estate, although improvements are rarely at issue. Here are some pointers to keep in mind:

- When you buy the asset, create a new Other Asset account.

- Periodically adjust the value of the asset (for net worth reporting purposes) by entering a value adjustment transaction, categorized as a transfer to the same account, with a class that designates an unrealized capital gain.

- When you sell the asset, reverse the accumulated value adjustments and generate a split transaction to zero out the asset account while categorizing the difference as realized capital gains income.

Depreciating Assets

If you have money invested in assets that wear out, such as a computer system for your home office, you might want to reflect the decrease in value of these assets over time.

For example, Larry Milner invested $12,000 in his computer system, a laser printer, a fax machine, and a fancy telephone for his home office. He estimated that these items lost about one-third of their value each year. Here's how Larry accounted for his home office equipment:

1. He set up an Other Asset account to represent these assets.

2. Every time he bought a new piece of home office equipment, he categorized the purchase as a transfer to his Home Office asset account.

3. At the end of each year, he entered a depreciation transaction. Using the Quicken calculator, he multiplied the account balance by 33 percent, entered it as a decrease in the account, and categorized it as a depreciation expense.

Note. These depreciation amounts are only approximations and will not meet IRS requirements for figuring depreciation tax reductions. Use IRS depreciation schedules for taxes.

While not as accurate as maintaining an item-by-item depreciation schedule, this method offers a reasonable approximation of the value decline in assets that have a limited life span. Using a 33 percent depreciation rate, you will find that an asset's value will decline to 10 percent of its original value in about six years. You may find that you need to increase the annual depreciation percentage for shorter-life assets and increase it for longer-life assets. Table 9.1 shows approximately how many years it will take to depreciate an asset to 10 percent of its original value for different depreciation rates.

Table 9.1   **Depreciation Approximation Percentages**

Annual percentage rate	Time to 10 percent residual value
10%	22 years
15%	15 years
20%	11 years
25%	8 years
30%	7 years
35%	6 years
40%	4 years
45%	3 years

Retirement Accounts

Retirement accounts vary greatly by type, from company savings plans to self-directed Individual Retirement Accounts. Each type must be treated slightly differently in Quicken. Remember these guidelines when deciding how to represent retirement accounts:

- The more precisely you can identify individually priced securities within a retirement account, the more appropriate it is to treat the retirement account as an investment account. A self-directed IRA is an investment account; a company-managed bond fund is best managed as an Other Asset account, which you update every time you receive a statement.

- If your company's contribution to your retirement account "vests" over time, you should report only the vested portion—that is, the portion you have a right to receive without working for the company any longer.

Retirement accounts occupy a very delicate position in any statement of net worth. On the one hand, they represent money that you've earned—a very real part of your net worth. On the other hand, most retirement accounts remain illiquid until you've passed retirement age, and many banks choose to ignore these accounts when assessing your personal financial status.

Measure Contingent Tax Liabilities

Even if your assets minus your liabilities add up to $1 million, you may not really be a millionaire. That's because when you start selling assets, Uncle Sam may come around to collect his due on the capital gains you realize from the sales. If you're going to include large unrealized gains in your statement of net worth, your net worth will be overstated by the amount of tax (the "contingent tax liability") that would be due if you sold your appreciated assets.

If you need precise reporting of contingent tax liabilities on capital gains, follow these steps to calculate and enter the amount:

1. Determine the amount of unrealized capital gains on your investment accounts by generating a Portfolio Value report on all your investment accounts.

2. If you've used the methods described earlier in this level to account for increases in the value of your home and other appreciating assets, you can total the capital gains you've entered through value adjustment transactions by generating a Transaction report to which you can apply a filter specifying only transactions with the class "Unrealized."

3. Use the Quicken calculator to add the unrealized capital gains from steps 1 and 2, and multiply them by your marginal tax rate.

4. In a liability account named "Contingent Tax Liability," enter a transaction to adjust the account balance to equal the liability you calculated in step 3. You may do this by selecting "Adjust Account Balances" from the Activities menu (Alt-A) and categorizing the adjustment transaction with the name of the Contingent Tax Liability account.

Note. Your marginal tax rate is the tax you pay on all additional income you receive. Don't forget to add state taxes to the federal tax rates to determine your marginal rate.

Enter Price Histories

Quicken's net worth report is very interesting when viewed at a single point in time; tracked at periodic intervals over time, it becomes exceptionally revealing. How quickly is your net worth increasing or decreasing? How is your mix of assets changing over time? These are questions that Quicken's net worth reporting can help answer.

Quicken will automatically accumulate the account balances and price adjustments which are necessary for showing how your net worth grows or shrinks over time. Entering information dating from your pre-Quicken days can be done with some difficulty; doing so accurately requires special care to ensure that you enter the correct prices and account balances for any date you choose to report.

To ensure you're reporting pre-Quicken assets and liabilities correctly, follow these guidelines:

■ Make sure that your opening balance transactions for the account predate the dates for which you will be reporting net worth.

Note. If you fail to enter an updated price for your reporting date, Quicken will choose from its price history file the most recent price prior to the date you choose for your report.

- Enter appropriate prices into the price history files of securities you owned as of each reporting date you plan to use. To do this, make one of your investment accounts current, then press Ctrl-G (for Go to Date) to select the reporting date you need. In the Price column, for every security displaying an asterisk (which indicates an estimated price for that date), enter the current price for the reporting date you specified.

- For other major assets that fluctuate in value, you may wish to enter value adjustment transactions into the appropriate asset account, as recommended earlier.

Print Reports for Yourself

Quicken's built-in net worth report provides a very serviceable snapshot of your net worth at any point in time. The advantage is that it's very easy to obtain; the disadvantage is that it organizes the information the way Quicken organizes its accounts—that is, by cash/bank accounts, other assets, investments, credit cards, and other liabilities. This may not be the way you group your assets and liabilities, and it's almost certainly not the way you want to display your net worth for a credit application.

You'll find the Net Worth report under Personal Reports on the Reports menu. The most basic report is one which lists all your account balances, grouped and subtotaled by account type, as shown in Figure 9.5. Quicken groups these further by assets and liabilities and subtracts one from the other to report your net worth.

Several characteristics of this report are worth noting:

- Quicken is slavish about classifying bank accounts as assets and credit cards as liabilities, even if you have negative balances in the account. This would happen if you had an overdraft in your bank account or a credit balance in your credit card account.

- Quicken normally displays both the account name and the long description you entered for the account. If there are redundancies between the two, you might see strange results like "Maria's IRA-Maria's Individual Retirement Acct."

- The Net Worth report does not consider any checks or other transactions that may be postdated beyond the As Of date of the report, even though these might technically be considered liabilities. For example, if you postdate to April 15th a $10,000 check to the Internal Revenue Service to cover taxes you owe on last year's income, that tax liability will not show up on any Net Worth report dated before April 15th.

Figure 9.5   Standard Net Worth report

```
                        NET WORTH REPORT
                        As of 12/31/91
SANDORI-All Accounts                                        Page 1
12/31/91
                                        12/31/91
                    Acct                Balance

        ASSETS
            Cash and Bank Accounts
                Bay Cities MMF               791.55
                Escrow                     1,752.00
                Misc Cash                     120.00
                Mutual One                 1,325.52

            Total Cash and Bank Accounts   3,989.07

            Other Assets
                Abby's 401(k)             31,532.80
                Abby's Profit             17,737.20
                Ardale Rd Home           414,200.00
                Loan to Barney               716.80
                Mutual One CD              4,217.00
                New home                   7,500.00

            Total Other Assets           475,903.80

            Investments
                Brokerage                 45,990.00
                Company Stock             34,027.50
                Ralph's IRA               34,020.00

            Total Investments            114,037.50

        TOTAL ASSETS                     593,930.37

        LIABILITIES
            Credit Cards
                Abby's MC                    320.22
                Gas Card                      55.45
                Joint AMEX                   391.55
                Ralph's VISA               1,860.41

            Total Credit Cards            2,627.63

            Other Liabilities
                Mortg principal          247,520.00
                School loan                5,156.00
                Toyota loan                6,505.10
                Volvo loan                 5,824.90

            Total Other Liabilities      265,006.00

        TOTAL LIABILITIES                267,633.63

        TOTAL NET WORTH                  326,296.74
```

- The default net worth report format includes unrealized capital gains—that is, the paper gains on stocks and other investments you haven't sold yet. In a moment, we'll explain how to turn this option off.

- By default, Quicken displays the balance of every asset and liability account you own—even the phantom investment index portfolios you might have created in Level 8. If you have accounts whose balances are inappropriate to include in a net worth report, you'll want to use Quicken's customization options to exclude them.

Altering Default Settings on Net Worth Reports

The customization options Quicken offers for your net worth reports are not as extensive as those offered for income- and expense-related reports. Still, you may find it helpful to make the following variations on your net worth report.

- Change the date or title of your net worth report by selecting Set Title & Date Range from the Edit menu (Alt-E) and typing a new title or date.

- Exclude accounts which are inappropriate to your report by selecting Accounts from the Edit menu (Alt-E). Choose Selected from the window that appears to see a list of all accounts. In the Select Accounts to Include window, a column entitled Include in Report shows whether an account is currently included. Highlight the account you want to exclude, then press the Spacebar twice to clear the column. Press Enter to leave the window.

- Decide whether the title should display only the shorthand account name, only the long description, or both. Choose Set Preferences from the Main Menu; then select Checks & Reports Settings. In the window that appears, next to item 7 ("In reports, print account Description/Name/Both"), type **N** for the account name only, **B** for both name and description, or accept D (the default setting) for just the description.

- Exclude unrealized capital gains from your investment accounts by selecting Other Options from the Layout (Alt-L) menu. Next to "Include unrealized gains," type **N** (for No).

- Change the format of the report to a "Balance Sheet" style—that is, one in which assets equal liabilities, and net worth is reported as equity—by selecting Other Options from the Layout menu (Alt-L) and choosing Balance Sheet format. Figure 9.6 shows a net worth report displayed as a balance sheet.

If you need to include the liabilities associated with postdated checks in your report, you should choose the Balance Sheet report from the Business Reports submenu rather than the Personal Net Worth report. The Gallery of Quicken Reports in Appendix D shows the difference between the two reports.

Print Reports for Your Bank

You will probably be more particular about how you present your net worth if you're preparing the report for a bank. There are two reasons for this:

- The bank may have a very different way of defining your assets than you do. For example, a bank might not allow you to count illiquid assets such as retirement accounts and vested pension fund balances in your net worth accounting.

- The bank may ask you to classify your assets and liabilities differently than Quicken does. For example, Figure 9.7 shows the Statement of Financial Condition on a typical mortgage application. Quicken doesn't conveniently group and subtotal your assets to conform to this format.

Figure 9.6   **Net Worth report in balance sheet format**

```
                         NET WORTH REPORT
                          As of 12/31/91
SANDORI-All Accounts                                      Page 1
12/31/91
                                          12/31/91
                        Acct              Balance

        ASSETS

            Cash and Bank Accounts
                Bay Cities MMF            791.55
                Escrow                  1,752.00
                Misc Cash                 120.00
                Mutual One             1,325.52

            Total Cash and Bank Accounts 3,989.07

            Other Assets
                Abby's 401(k)          31,532.80
                Abby's Profit          17,737.20
                Ardale Rd Home        414,200.00
                Loan to Barney            716.80
                Mutual One CD           4,217.00
                New home                7,500.00

            Total Other Assets        475,903.80

            Investments
                Brokerage              45,990.00
                Company Stock          34,027.50
                Ralph's IRA            34,020.00

            Total Investments         114,037.50

        TOTAL ASSETS                  593,930.37

        LIABILITIES & EQUITY

            LIABILITIES
                Credit Cards
                    Abby's MC            320.22
                    Gas Card              55.45
                    Joint AMEX           391.55
                    Ralph's VISA       1,860.41

                Total Credit Cards     2,627.63

                Other Liabilities
                    Mortg principal  247,520.00
                    School loan        5,156.00
                    Toyota loan        6,505.10
                    Volvo loan         5,824.90

                Total Other Liabilities 265,006.00

            TOTAL LIABILITIES         267,633.63

            EQUITY                    326,296.74

        TOTAL LIABILITIES & EQUITY    593,930.37
```

This is one of those times you may want to move beyond Quicken's capabilities to prepare good-looking reports. You can use the newer versions of Lotus 1-2-3, Microsoft Excel, and Borland Quattro Pro to prepare accurate, impressive financial statements in the format a lender requires. After all, in these conditions, a net worth statement is a selling document.

The approach you use to transfer and reformat your data for these reports depends on whether you need a one-time report or a periodic one. If preparing the report is a one-time event, follow these steps:

Note. The Disk (1-2-3 file) option works for any 1-2-3-compatible spreadsheet program that can import .PRN files.

1. Create a Net Worth report, and then print the file to a 1-2-3 file by selecting Print Report from the File/Print menu (Alt-F) or by pressing Ctrl-P (for Print). Type **5** for Disk (1-2-3 file), and enter a name for the file. Then press Enter.

2. Leave Quicken, start your spreadsheet program, and import the report into your spreadsheet using the File Import Numbers command or its equivalent.

3. In the spreadsheet, regroup and reformat the data by changing column widths, inserting or deleting rows, and moving rows of data. Figure 9.8 shows an example of a net worth statement that has been imported from Quicken, reformatted to comply with the Statement of Financial Condition in Figure 9.7, and made more attractive with the publishing features now available in spreadsheets.

Figure 9.7 **Mortgage lender's Statement of Financial Condition form**

This Statement and any applicable supporting schedules may be completed jointly by both married and unmarried co-borrowers if their assets and liabilities are sufficiently joined so that the Statement can be meaningfully and fairly presented on a combined basis; otherwise separate Statements and Schedules are required (FHLMC 65A/FNMA 1003A). If the co-borrower section was completed about a spouse, this statement and supporting schedules must be completed about that spouse also. ☐ Completed Jointly ☐ Not Completed Jointly

STATEMENT OF ASSETS AND LIABILITIES

Assets

Description	Cash or Market Value
Cash Deposit Toward Purchase Held By	$
Checking and Savings Accounts (Show Names of Institutions Account Numbers) Bank, S & L or Credit Union	
Addr.	
City	
Acct. No.	
Bank, S & L or Credit Union	
Addr.	
City	
Acct. No.	
Bank, S & L or Credit Union	
Addr.	
City	
Acct. No.	
Stocks and Bonds (No./Description)	
Life Insurance Net Cash Value Face Amount $	
Subtotal Liquid Assets	
Real Estate Owned (Enter Market Value from Schedule of Real Estate Owned)	
Vested Interest in Retirement Fund	
Net Worth of Business Owned (ATTACH FINANCIAL STATEMENT)	
Automobiles Owned (Make and Year)	
Furniture and Personal Property	
Other Assets (Itemize)	
Total Assets	A $

Liabilities and Pledged Assets

Indicated by (*) those liabilities or pledged assets which will be satisfied upon sale of real estate owned or upon refinancing of subject property.

Creditor's Name, Address and Account Number	Acct. Name if Not Borrower's	Mo. Pmt. and Mos. Left to Pay	Unpaid Balance
Installment Debts (Include "revolving" charge accounts) Co. Acct. No. Addr. City		$ Pmt./Mos. /	$
Co. Acct. No. Addr. City		/	
Co. Acct. No. Addr. City		/	
Co. Acct. No. Addr. City		/	
Co. Acct. No. Addr. City		/	
Other Debts including Stock Pledges		/	
Real Estate Loans Co. Acct. No. Addr. City		X	
Co. Acct. No. Addr. City		X	
Automobile Loans Co. Acct. No. Addr. City		/	
Co. Acct. No. Addr. City		/	
Alimony/Child Support/Separate Maintenance Payments Owed To		/	X
Total Monthly Payments			X
Net Worth (A minus B) $		Total Liabilities	B $

SCHEDULE OF REAL ESTATE OWNED (If Additional Properties Owned Attach Separate Schedule)

Address of Property (Indicate S if Sold, PS if Pending Sale or R if Rental being held for income)	▼	Type of Property	Present Market Value	Amount of Mortgages & Liens	Gross Rental Income	Mortgage Payments	Taxes, Ins., Maintenance and Misc.	Net Rental Income
			$	$	$	$	$	$
		TOTALS ►	$	$	$	$	$	$

If the report is one you'll have to submit again and again, such as an annual or quarterly statement of financialcondition, you may want to use the Quicken Transfer Utility (available separately from Intuit)to move information into a preformatted spreadsheet each time you prepare the report. The QTU allows you to embed codes in the first row or column of a spreadsheet that correspond to each line item in a net worth report. The Quicken Transfer Utility's documentation gives many examples of how to apply this technique.

Figure 9.8 **Net Worth report printed with a spreadsheet publishing program**

NET WORTH REPORT
Ralph and Abigail Sandori
As of 12/31/91

Account	Balance	Account	Balance
ASSETS		**LIABILITIES AND PLEDGED ASSETS**	
Cash deposit toward purchase held by:		**Installment Debts**	
Gerri Conway Realtors	$7,500.00	MasterCard	$320.22
Cash and Bank Accounts		9700 Franklin Plaza, Cleveland	
Bay Cities Group Money Market Fund	791.55	Acct no. 0000-0044-1111	
14 Center Plaza, San Francisco		The Gas Card	55.45
Acct no. 00-740055-B1		One Plaza Central, Houston	
Escrow-Tax/Insurance Acct	1,752.00	Acct no. 00005573-110	
Direct Credit Union		American Express Card	391.55
4500 Rice Blvd, Costa Mesa		18 Zenith Ave, New York	
Acct no. 5749182-5789		Acct no. 18972397-00	
Mutual One Joint Checking Account	1,325.52	VISA Card	1,860.41
1995 Corinth St, Berkeley		9970 3rd Ave, Seattle	
Acct no. 9958-389-3372		Acct no. 4024-0-1111	
Misc Cash	120.00	School loan, Mt Hope Credit Union	5,156.00
	--------	8545 San Lucas Rd, Bodega Bay	
Total Cash and Bank Accounts	$11,489.07	Acct no. 598783-279	--------
		Total Installment Debts	$7,783.63
Investments			
Bay Cities Brokerage Account	$45,990.00		
Company Stock Purchase Plan	34,027.50	**Real Estate Loans**	
	--------	Home Mortgage-Englewood CU	$247,520.00
Total Investments	$80,017.50	45 Simmons Ct, San Jose	
	--------	Acct no. BV97-40000-987	
Total Liquid Assets	$91,506.57	**Total Real Estate Loans**	$247,520.00
Other Assets		**Automobile Loans**	
401(k) fund (fully vested)	$31,532.80	Foothill Credit Union	$6,505.10
Profit-share account (fully vested)	17,737.20	19 Foothill Rd, Oakland	
Ardale Rd Home (primary residence)	414,200.00	Acct no. 1233-2108	
Loan to Barney York	716.80	College Bank	5,824.90
College Bank IRA	34,020.00	3701 33rd St NW, San Francisco	
Mutual One 5-year CD	4,217.00	Acct no. W20984-2793M	

Total Other Assets	$502,423.80	**Total Automobile Loans**	$12,330.00

TOTAL ASSETS	$593,930.37	**TOTAL LIABILITIES**	$267,633.63

		NET WORTH	$326,296.74

Determine Changes in Your Net Worth over Time

The longer you use Quicken, the more you'll learn from reports that show changes in your net worth over a period of time. Such reports are extremely useful in helping you discern trends in the size and composition of your wealth.

You can use Quicken alone to determine how your net worth has changed over time, or you may use Quicken in conjunction with a spreadsheet. Using only Quicken, you can see summaries of all the components of your net worth at two or more points in time, laid out in a multicolumn report. A quarterly report is an example of this.

To show your net worth at the end of each quarter during the past year,

1. Create the standard Net Worth report by selecting Personal Reports and Net Worth from the Reports menu (Alt-R).

2. From the Layout menu (Alt-L), select Column Headings and then Quarter.

3. If you want the report to display quarters from one or more previous calendar years in addition to this year, choose Set Title & Date Range from the Edit menu (Alt-E) and specify a new date range.

You may also use Quicken in conjunction with a spreadsheet to calculate a column that shows the changes in each line item from one date to the next. A particularly useful report, for example, is one that summarizes your net worth change year to year.

To generate this report,

1. Create the standard Net Worth report.

2. Choose Column Headings and Year from the Layout menu (Alt-L). Wait while Quicken redisplays the report.

3. From the Edit menu (Alt-E), choose Set Title & Date Range. Specify the date range so it encompasses a full year, 12/31 to 12/31, using the most recent complete calendar year. For example, if it were February 1992, the date range would be from 12/31/90 to 12/31/91. Quicken will generate a two-column report with your net worth detailed as of the end of each of the last two years.

4. Print the report to 1-2-3 spreadsheet format by selecting Print from the File/Print menu (Alt-F), or pressing Ctrl-P (for Print). Type 5 for Disk (1-2-3 file), and enter a name for the file to print to. Then press Enter.

5. Leave Quicken and start you spreadsheet program. Import the report into your spreadsheet using the File Import Numbers command or its equivalent. Change the column widths if necessary to view all of the imported data.

6. Create a new column entitled "Change in Net Worth," which subtracts the first year's account balances from the second year's. The result is the very useful report shown in Figure 9.9.

Figure 9.9   **Spreadsheet report showing changes in net worth components**

CHANGES IN NET WORTH DURING 1991

Acct	12/31/90 Balance	12/31/91 Balance	Change in Net Worth
ASSETS			
Cash and Bank Accounts			
Bay Cities MMF-Bay Cities Group	$12,455.12	$8,291.55	($4,163.57)
Escrow-Tax/Insurance Acct	0.00	1,752.00	1,752.00
Misc Cash	90.00	120.00	30.00
Mutual One-Mutual One Joint Acct	1,591.33	1,325.52	(265.81)
Total Cash and Bank Accounts	14,136.45	11,489.07	(2,647.38)
Other Assets			
Abby's 401(k)	24,802.88	31,532.80	6,729.92
Abby's Profit-Co. Profit Share	16,318.22	17,737.20	1,418.98
Ardale Rd Home	400,000.00	414,200.00	14,200.00
Loan to Barney	0.00	716.80	716.80
Mutual One CD-Mutual One CD 5 yr	3,879.64	4,217.00	337.36
Total Other Assets	459,200.74	468,403.80	9,203.06
Investments			
Brokerage-Bay Cities Brokerage	35,875.00	45,990.00	10,115.00
Company Stock-Stock Purch Plan	19,877.00	34,027.50	14,150.50
Ralph's IRA-College Bank IRA	26,474.00	34,020.00	7,546.00
Total Investments	82,226.00	114,037.50	31,811.50
TOTAL ASSETS	555,563.19	593,930.37	38,367.18
LIABILITIES			
Credit Cards			
Abby's MC-MasterCard	845.19	320.22	(524.97)
Gas Card	70.95	55.45	(15.50)
Joint AMEX-American Express	652.71	391.55	(261.16)
Ralph's VISA	2,221.75	1,860.41	(361.34)
Total Credit Cards	3,790.60	2,627.63	(1,162.97)
Other Liabilities			
Mortg principal-Home Mortgage	250,119.00	247,520.00	(2,599.00)
School loan	5,768.00	5,156.00	(612.00)
Toyota loan	8,109.48	6,505.10	(1,604.38)
Volvo loan	7,619.50	5,824.90	(1,794.60)
Total Other Liabilities	271,615.98	265,006.00	(6,609.98)
TOTAL LIABILITIES	275,406.58	267,633.63	(7,772.95)
OVERALL TOTAL	$280,156.61	$326,296.74	$46,140.13

Finally, you may use your spreadsheet's charting capabilities to plot the growth (or decline) of your wealth over time. Follow steps 1 through 5 in the previous example. In steps 2 and 3, you may wish to enter settings for a report that generates data for more points in time—either a quarterly or monthly report over a year, or several years, for example. This will result in a graph that contains more than two data points.

Once you've imported the information into your spreadsheet, you can use its graphics tools to specify the numbers in the Overall Total row for the y-axis and the dates across the top of the report as the x-axis. This will give you a simple bar chart that tracks your net worth. If you want to track one or two net worth components (such as cash and investments), you may want to convert the graph to a line chart and highlight the appropriate lines along with the total. This will yield the chart in Figure 9.10.

Remember that your net worth statements are only as accurate as your accounts are up-to-date. If you haven't been maintaining your account balances and entering the prices of your investment securities, your net worth reports will represent crude estimates, at best. On the other hand, if you're faithful about keeping your accounts up-to-date, you'll have at your fingertips a very powerful planning tool that will help you chart the progress you're making towards your financial dreams.

Figure 9.10   Spreadsheet-generated net worth time chart using Quicken data

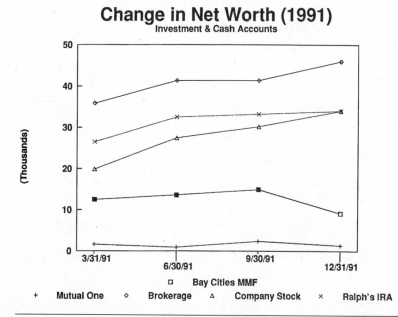

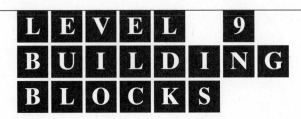

LEVEL 9 BUILDING BLOCKS

TECHNIQUES AND PROCEDURES

■ Create new Other Asset or Other Liability accounts by pressing Ctrl-A to see the Select Account to Use window, highlighting <New Account>, pressing Enter, and typing **4** (for Other Asset) or **5** (for Other Liability). Enter an account name, and if you prefer, an optional description (which will appear in your net worth reports). Press Enter to leave the window.

■ Home improvements (and their impact on the tax basis of your home) are easily tracked in an Other Asset account. The opening transaction in the account will be the loan amount and any cash you paid, together equaling the purchase price of your home plus any closing costs and legal fees. Whenever you spend money from another account on a home improvement, categorize it as a transfer to this asset account. If the home's appraised value changes, enter a value adjustment transaction to record the change, classifying the transaction under "Unrealized" to denote it as unrealized capital gains. When you sell the property, reverse any value adjustments with corresponding transactions, zero out the loan account, and split the deposit between the home asset account (to close it out) and the Realized class.

■ Other assets that appreciate in value can be tracked similarly. The opening transaction appears as the asset's cost; value adjustment transactions periodically reflect changes in valuation. Upon the asset's sale, a transaction would reverse the value adjustments, and a split transaction would zero out the account and apply the profit to realized capital gains.

■ Depreciation of an asset can be represented using an Other Assets account and the Quicken calculator. You can group related assets which depreciate at the same rate into a single account (the initial equipment purchase expenditures will be transfers to the account). Whenever you need to calculate the depreciation, use the calculator (Ctrl-O) to multiply the account balance by the depreciation percentage, and enter the result as a decrease in the account, categorized as Depreciation.

■ To print a standard Net Worth report, select the Reports menu (Alt-R) and then Personal Reports and Net Worth. Various options for customizing the standard report are available on the Edit menu (Alt-E) and the Layout menu (Alt-L), including suppressing accounts you don't want to have appear, excluding unrealized capital gains, and changing the reporting time period.

■ Transactions dated after the reporting date are not included in a standard Net Worth report, even though postdated transactions are a liability. The standard Balance Sheet report does show these as liabilities; view this report by selecting Business Reports and Balance Sheet from the Reports menu (Alt-R).

■ To import a Quicken file into a spreadsheet program, you can print to a file by pressing Ctrl-P, typing **5** for Disk (1-2-3 file), and specifying the file name. You then use your spreadsheet's import commands to bring the file into the program. Or use Quicken's Transfer Utility to move Quicken information to a preformatted spreadsheet embedded with codes that rearrange the data appropriately.

■ To see a report that illustrates changes in your net worth over specific time periods, modify the standard Net Worth report by selecting Column Headings from the Layout menu (Alt-L), and choosing another time period, such as Quarter, as the column heading. Then choose Set Title & Date Rate from the Edit menu (Alt-E) to expand the time period so several columns of net worth results are displayed.

TERMS

■ *Contingent tax liabilities* are taxes incurred when you sell assets for a profit—when you realize capital gains that were previously unrealized. If reporting contingent tax liabilities on capital gains is important, you can set up an Other Liability account to track them. Determine tax liabilities in your investment accounts using a Portfolio Value report. For Other Asset accounts, generate a Transaction report with a filter to show only transactions classified as Unrealized. Enter the totals into your Contingent Tax Liabilities account.

■ To *depreciate* an asset, you assign a value to the amount of the asset's useful life that has been used up during the last year, and deduct that amount from its current value. Some capital equipment, such as your personal computer or your car, will eventually wear out and need to be replaced. An item's useful life depends on the type of equipment and on how you expect to use it. Depreciating an asset gradually over the span of its useful life reflects its changing market value and position in your overall net worth.

■ The *Quicken Transfer Utility*, available separately, is a useful tool for creating custom reports in a Lotus 1-2-3 (or compatible) spreadsheet. You set up a preformatted spreadsheet that contains codes representing various

Quicken files, transactions, and balances. When you want to complete or update the spreadsheet, you use the Quicken Transfer Utility to quickly search your Quicken files for the required information and merge it into the spreadsheet.

IMPORTANT IDEAS

■ Quoting reliable sources for the cost or value of assets or liabilities is critical to accurately assessing your net worth. Take the time to unearth this information. Also, for assets such as your home for which improvements affect the tax cost basis, pull together information on expenditures that add to its value.

■ When you're ready to generate your net worth reports, be sure all prices and values are correct for your reporting date and are appropriate, given the purpose of the report. Investments should always be updated to reflect the current price. Your report can either reflect a conservative or a liberal estimate of your net worth, a decision which will affect whether you exclude or include value adjustments for appreciating assets.

■ Coupling Quicken with a spreadsheet program will lend polish and value to your net worth reports—from adding additional columns of calculated data, to printing reports using the sophisticated publishing features many spreadsheet programs now include.

Plan, Organize, and Complete Your Taxes

PLAN AHEAD

Optimize Your Categories for Tax Planning

Estimate Your Taxable Income

Make End-of-Year Decisions

Organize for Your Tax Preparer

Use Quicken Data with Tax Preparation Software

BUILDING BLOCKS

DECISIONS

What Kind of Tax Planning Do You Need?

If you itemize deductions and have a financial picture that is the least bit complex, you'll find that Quicken pays for itself at tax time. Quicken assists you in two major areas of personal taxes: tax planning and tax filing. Each year you use Quicken, you will be better organized, make better tax planning decisions, save money and/or time on tax preparation, and be better documented in the event of an IRS audit.

As you consider how you'll use Quicken for taxes, you should first ask yourself which of several planning tasks you'll use Quicken to accomplish:

■ *Estimate quarterly payments*   Estimated tax is a method of paying taxes on income not subject to withholding. This includes, for example, investment income (interest and dividends), capital gains, self-employment income, unemployment compensation, and alimony. If all of your income is subject to withholding, you probably don't need to worry about paying quarterly estimates.

You should check the current tax laws, but in recent years you've had to pay federal estimated tax if you expected owing at least $500 in taxes for the year and anticipated that your withholding and credits would be either less than you paid in taxes the previous year *or* 90 percent of the tax you expect to pay in the current year. Many states have similar requirements for state estimated tax payments.

Quicken can help with quarterly estimates in two ways: by helping you calculate your income and deductible expenses for this year and by reminding you what you paid in taxes last year.

■ *Calculate payroll tax deductions (W-4)*   The government allows some latitude in calculating how much money is withheld from your paycheck by your employer each pay period. Withholding too little subjects you to penalties if you don't also pay quarterly estimated taxes. Withholding too much is, in effect, giving Uncle Sam an interest-free loan till you get your tax refund.

Quicken can be a valuable aid in estimating your correct withholdings. Armed with this information, you can fill out your Form W-4 confident that the proper amount will be deducted from your paycheck.

■ *Make end-of-year decisions*   You can make myriad end-of-year decisions that directly affect how much you'll pay in taxes in any given year. Generally, these concern the way you time your income and deductible expenses, and the possible sale of assets that may have accumulated a capital gain or loss.

Quicken can guide you in identifying opportunities to optimize these year-end decisions; it can also help you measure their impact on your tax obligations.

■ *Plan cash flow*   Quicken can help you project how much cash you'll have available and when, so that quarterly or annual tax payments won't take you by surprise. If you expect to owe or receive back large amounts of cash on your taxes, you should consider using Quicken to help plan your cash availability.

Will You Prepare Your Taxes by Computer?

Tax preparation software has evolved so much in the last few years that it's now possible for most computer-savvy people to both prepare and electronically file their taxes by personal computer. In many cases, these programs can save you time and prevent errors. They can also help you discover tax savings which may have remained unrecognized or save you hefty professional fees.

Even if you employ a professional preparer, you will probably invest considerable time in assembling your tax information and organizing it the way an accountant might require it. Many people find that the same amount of effort can be redirected into entering the information into a PC-based tax preparation program. (Frankly, most tax preparers start by sending your data off to a service bureau to be entered into a software program hardly more sophisticated than the best PC tax packages.) If some of your tax data is already stored in Quicken, so much the better; the better tax preparation software supports electronic links with Quicken.

PC-based tax preparation is not for everyone by any means. Complex returns often demand judgment calls best made (or advised) by a seasoned professional who personally understands your individual situation. At the very least, tax preparation packages offer a superb way of organizing and estimating your tax liabilities—as well as a check against the results that a professional preparer calculates.

MATERIALS

Your Tax "Shoebox"

During the tax year—and especially during January immediately following the tax year—you should be accumulating a whole stack of tax documents: a W-2 from your employer; a Form 1099 from anyone who paid you interest, dividends, contract fees, or savings plan distributions; a K-1 from a limited partnership investment; and a mortgage summary statement from your bank. These documents, along with a year's worth of Quicken entries, form a data foundation for preparing your taxes. Whether you gather them in the proverbial shoebox or in a file folder, you should keep them close at hand as you plan and prepare your taxes.

Last Year's Tax Return

It's a good idea to save all your past tax returns, but last year's will be particularly critical. It can serve as a checklist to ensure that you haven't forgotten any income or deductions you've reported in the past. The figures on last year's return can help you in applying tests of reasonableness to this year's figures. Finally, last year's return may contain important carry-over numbers, such as passive losses that could not be fully exploited previously.

Your Tax Preparer's Organizer Forms

If you use a professional tax preparer, he or she will most likely give you a tax organizer or questionnaire that will help you organize your data. It's good to know what your preparer needs and what form it should be in—not merely for assembling the data, but also for building your Quicken category structure.

A PC-Based Tax Preparation Package

If you've decided to use a tax preparation package—whether it's for preparing your actual return or organizing your data—try to purchase it well in advance of when you'll need it. While the federal tax forms aren't even finalized until late in the fall, many tax packages issue "early bird" editions in November, which they automatically update (at no charge) when the forms and laws are finalized in early January.

In our experience, the most useful tax preparation package is Tax Cut from MECA Software. It combines an excellent collection of the forms you'll need with a very powerful "advisor" function, an expert system which questions you on the less straightforward areas of your tax return to help you decide what to report and how. As of late 1991, Tax Cut is available in two forms: Tax Cut EZ/A, for light tax filing requirements on Forms 1040EZ and 1040A; and Tax Cut 1040, for more complicated tax situations which require Form 1040 and its supplemental tax schedules. You should acquire Tax Cut EZ/A if: your income is from wages, interest, dividends, and unemployment compensation; your deductions are limited to Individual Retirement Account (IRA) contributions; and your credits are limited to child and dependent care expenses. Otherwise, use Tax Cut 1040.

PRELIMINARIES

Complete Levels 1, 2, and 5

Tax preparation and planning requires a basic working knowledge of Quicken and its category structures, but does not require you to use its full check-writing capability. To rely on Quicken's data for all your tax preparation activities, carefully read and adhere to the techniques for handling such common (but complicated) transactions as paychecks and mortgage payments.

Complete Level 7 for Accurate Tax Estimates

Many tax planning activities—particularly preparing quarterly tax estimates and optimizing your withholdings—are greatly enhanced when you maintain up-to-date budgets. Level 7 gives you all the skills to prepare and maintain an accurate budget which you can use for projecting your tax liabilities through the year.

Complete Level 8 if You Have Investments

If you plan to depend on Quicken for help managing your capital gains and losses, you should complete the investment section of this book, Level 8. Pay particular attention to accurately entering the cost basis and acquisition dates of the securities you own; these should to be reported individually on your tax return when you sell the stock.

Install Your Tax Program

Install and peruse Tax Cut or any other tax preparation program you plan to use. Get accustomed to using it, perhaps even by entering your tax data from last year. (Don't be alarmed if the tax calculation doesn't come out exactly as you filed it; year-to-year changes in tax laws and bracket amounts will inevitably mean you'll pay a different tax on the same income from one year to the next.)

Optimize Your Categories for Tax Planning

A stable and sensible category structure is essential for making the most of tax planning with Quicken. Even if you've been using your current category structure successfully for months, take the time to fine tune it to handle your tax planning.

Examine Your Category Structure

The most important thing you can do to prepare Quicken for tax applications is to review your category structure carefully. Your categories are the basis for both tax reports and any electronic transfers you use to move your data into automated tax preparation software.

Note. Classes are also perfectly suitable for tracking business income and expenses, provided you use them consistently.

You should check to make sure that each tax-related category is pure—that is, that it's not likely to gather nontax transactions. For example, if a category named Subscriptions contains both personal subscriptions (such as *Newsweek* and the *San Jose Mercury News*) and deductible business subscriptions (such as the *Wall Street Journal* and *Barron's*), it is useless as a tax category. You should, in this instance, create two subcategories to Subscriptions: a tax-related Subscriptions:Business subcategory and a nontax-related Subscriptions:Personal subcategory.

Also beware of categories which could contribute data to two or more different places on your tax return. For example, an Interest Expense category might collect mortgage interest, investment interest, personal interest, and interest on a small business loan. If you don't separate these expenses into separate categories or subcategories, you'll face much more work at tax preparation time.

To best analyze your category organization, we recommend sitting down with last year's tax return, looking at every expense or income line you filled out, and making sure there's a category collecting future data for each line item.

Assign Categories to Tax Schedules

Once you've made certain that you have pure and unambiguous tax categories in your category scheme, you can assign these categories to their corresponding tax schedules. This accomplishes two things: it produces an excellent tax transaction report at the end of the year, in which every transaction is sorted by the line items that appear on your tax returns; and it sets up your tax-related transactions in a format appropriate for an electronic transfer to Tax Cut and other tax preparation programs. Quicken maintains a comprehensive list of tax line items associated with 21 federal tax schedules and forms. In all, there are more than 200 such line items to which you may assign any of your Quicken categories.

Some of the standard home and business categories shipped with Quicken have already been assigned to tax schedules. For example, the standard category Charity is assigned to the cash charity contributions line item of Schedule A. To see this or any other category assignment, pop up the Category list by pressing Ctrl-C (for Categories) while displaying any register or the Write Checks screen, highlight a category, and press Ctrl-E (for Edit) to display the Edit Category window. The tax schedule information is displayed in the lower portion of the window (as in Figure 10.1), in the format *Schedule:Line Item*. If there is no schedule assigned to this category or subcategory, Quicken displays the legend <None> in the Tax Schedule blank.

Figure 10.1   Edit Category window showing a tax schedule

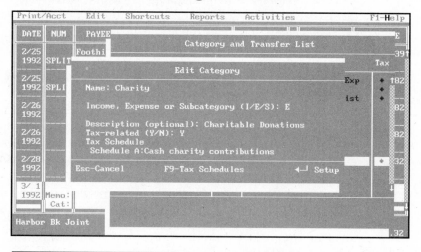

To change the tax schedule assignment or to create a new assignment, display the category's Edit Category window, and press F9. You'll see a list of common tax schedules (as in Figure 10.2), from the familiar Form 1040 and its accompanying Schedules A through F to other forms you might find useful, such as Form 2106 (Employee Business Expenses) and Form 2119 (Sale of Your Home).

Highlight one of these schedules and press Enter to see a list of specific line items to which any category can be linked (see Figure 10.3). Highlight the link you'd like to establish, and press Enter to create the link.

If later you want to break a category's tax schedule link without assigning it to a new tax schedule, display the category's Edit Category window, press F9, and move the cursor to <None>.

Note. If you've registered your copy of Quicken, you may obtain an updated Category list by calling Intuit at (800) 624-8742.

Every year, the federal government initiates changes that affect the list of tax schedules and line items to which you can link Quicken categories. For that reason, Intuit keeps this list in a separate disk file, which can be updated very easily. Table 10.1 shows the complete list of tax schedules and linkable line items as for late 1991. The order and abbreviations of the line items are shown as they appear in Quicken.

Figure 10.2   **Tax Schedule window**

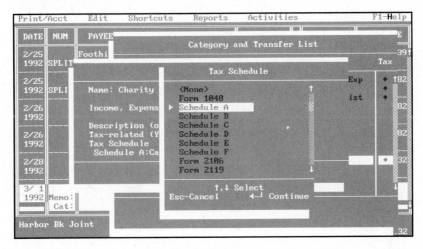

Figure 10.3   **Tax Line window for Schedule A**

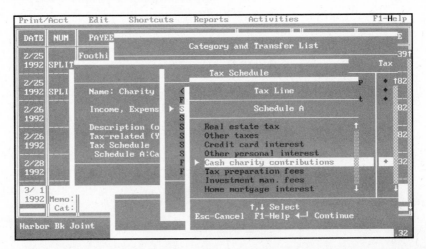

Table 10.1   **Quicken's Tax Schedule Structure**

IRS Form	Line Items Listed in Quicken	IRS Form	Line Items Listed in Quicken
Form 1040 (U.S. Individual Income Tax Return)	Other income—misc.	Schedule C (continued)	Supplies
	Sick pay or disab. pay		Other business expense
	Prizes, awards, gambling		Other business income
	State and local refunds		Advertising
	Alimony Received		Bad debts
	Unemployment comp		Car and truck expenses
	IRA contribs—deductible		Commissions and fees
	Keogh payments		Employee benefits progs.
	Alimony paid		Depletion
	Early withd penalty		Insurance (not health)
	Soc. Sec. income		Interest expense, mortgage
	Moving exp. reimb.		Interest expense, other
	Fed estimated tax		Office Expense
	Taxable fringe benefits		Pension and Profit Sharing
Schedule A (Itemized Deductions)	Subscriptions		Repairs and Maintenance
	Gambling losses		Taxes and licenses
	Medicine and Drugs		Travel
	Med. transport/lodging		Utilities
	State and local taxes		Description
	Real estate tax	Schedule D (Capital Gains and Losses)	Short term gain—security
	Other taxes		Short term gain—other
	Credit card interest		Long term gain—security
	Other personal interest		Long term gain—other
	Cash charity contributions	Schedule E (Supplemental Income and Loss)	Rents received
	Tax preparation fees		Royalties received
	Investment man. fees		Advertising
	Home mortgage interest		Auto and travel
	Points paid		Cleaning and maintenance
Schedule B (Interest and Dividend Income)	Dividend Income		Commissions
	Interest Income		Insurance
	US govt. interest		Legal and Professional
	State and mun. bond int.		Mortgage interest exp
	TE priv. act. bond int		Other interest expense
Schedule C (Profit or Loss from Business)	Spouse		Repairs
	Gross receipts		Supplies
	Meals and entertainment		Taxes
	Cost of goods sold		Utilities
	Returns and allowances		Wages paid
	Wages paid		Other expenses
	Legal and professional		Kind/Location of Property
	Rent on vehicles, mach, eq		
	Rent on other bus prop		

Table 10.1   **Quicken's Tax Schedule Structure (continued)**

IRS Form	Line Items Listed in Quicken	IRS Form	Line Items Listed in Quicken
Schedule F (Farm income and Expense)	Labor hired	**Form 2106** (continued)	Emp. meal exp reimb.
	Repairs and maintenance		Job seeking exp
	Interest expense—mort		Special clothing exp
	Interest Expense—other		Emp home office exp
	Rent—land, animals	**Form 2119** (Sale of Your Home)	Selling price of old home
	Rent—Veh., mach., equip.		Expense of sale
	Feed purchased		Basis of home sold
	Seed and plants purchased		Fixing-up expenses
	Fertilizers and lime		Cost of new home
	Supplies purchased		Date old home sold
	Breeding fees		Date moved into new home
	Vet fees and medicine	**Form 2441** (Credit for Child and Dependent Care Expenses)	Child care—day care
	Gasoline, fuel, oil		Child care—household
	Storage and warehousing		
	Taxes		
	Insurance (not health)	**Form 3903** (Moving Expenses)	Meals during moving
	Utilities		Meals househunting & temp
	Freight and trucking		Trans./store hshld goods
	Conservation expense		Travel and lodging
	Pension and profit shrg		Pre-moving expense
	Employee benefit prog.		Temp. living exp.
	Other farm expenses		Moving sale cost
	Chemicals		Moving purch. cost
	Custom hire (mach. work)	**Form 4684** (Casualties and Theft)	Basis of casualty prop
	Sales of livestock raised		Insurance/reimb
	Resales of livestock		FMV before casualty
	Coop. distributions		FMV after casualty
	Agric. pgm payments		Description of property
	CCC loans—election	**Form 4797** (Sale of Business Property)	LT dep. prop.—business
	CCC loans—forfeited		ST dep. prop.—business
	Crop ins. proceeds—recd		LT dep. prop.—res. rent.
	Crop ins. proceeds—defd		ST dep. prop.—res. rent.
	Other farm income	**Form 4952** (Investment Interest Expense Deduction)	Investment interest
	Cost livestock for resale		
	Principal Business/Prof.		
Form 2106 (Employee Business Expenses)	Education expense	**Form 6252** (Computation of Installment Sale Income)	Selling price
	Automobile exp.		Debt assumed by buyer
	Travel		Basis of property sold
	Local transportation		Depreciation allowed
	Other bus. exp.		Expenses of sale
	Meal and Entertain. exp.		Gross Profit Percentage
	Emp. expense reimb.		Payments recd this year

Table 10.1   **Quicken's Tax Schedule Structure (continued)**

IRS Form	Line Items Listed in Quicken	IRS Form	Line Items Listed in Quicken
Form 6252 (continued)	Payments recd prior years Description of property	**Schedule K-1** (continued)	Net sec 1231 gain/loss Partnership or S corp name
Form 8606 (Nondeductible IRA Contribution, IRA Basis, and Nontaxable IRA Distribution)	IRA value at end of year IRA contribs—nondeductible IRA basis at beg of year	**W-2** (Wage and Tax Statement)	Spouse Salary Federal Withholding FICA Local Withholding State Withholding Dependent Care Benefits Payer
Form 8815 (Exclusion of Interest From Series EE U.S. Savings Bonds Issued After 1989)	Qual. higher ed. expenses Nontaxable ed. benefits EE US svgs bonds proceeds Post-89 EE US savings bnd	**W-2P** (Statement for Recipients of Annunities, Pensions, Retired Pay, or IRA Payments)	Spouse Pensions and annuities—gross Pensions and annuities—taxable IRA distributions—gross IRA distributions—taxable
Schedule K-1 (Partner's or Shareholder's Share of Income, Credits and Deductions)	Spouse Ordinary income/loss Rental real est. inc/loss Other rental income/loss Interest income Dividends Net ST capital gain/loss Net LT capital gain/loss Guaranteed payments	**1099R** (Statement for Recipients of Total Distribution From Profit-Sharing, Retirement Plans, etc.)	Spouse Pension total dist—gross Pension total dist—taxable IRA total dist—gross IRA total dist—taxable

Estimate Your Taxable Income

Most of your tax planning activities with Quicken require you to make an estimate of your tax liability—sometimes before all the data are at hand. This affects three tasks in particular: preparing estimated tax filings, making sure the appropriate deductions are subtracted from your paycheck, and estimating how much cash you'll need to have on hand when you file your taxes.

Prepare Quarterly Tax Estimates

In the Plan Ahead section of this level, you had a chance to consider whether you'll need to make quarterly estimated income tax payments in addition to the amounts that are withheld from your paycheck. These payments are due on April 15 (for January through March), June 15th (for April and May), September 15th (for June through August), and January 15th (for September through December). Note that these aren't always three-month quarters—the second quarter is two months long and the fourth is four months long.

Note. If your estimated withholding taxes for the year are equal to or greater than the total amount you owed last year in taxes, you don't have to pay any additional estimated tax. Your withholdings and estimated tax payments only need to equal your previous year's taxes.

There are actually two methods for figuring your estimated tax: the full-year method and the annualized installment method. Each generates the information you need to complete the estimated tax worksheet contained in IRS Publication 505, *Tax Withholding and Estimated Tax*. The method you choose depends on whether your income is distributed evenly throughout the year. Quicken can help you prepare estimates using either method and can even help you decide which approach is best for you.

Estimate Taxes with the Full-Year Method

In the full-year method, you estimate your gross income, adjusted income, deductions, withholding taxes, and credits for the entire year. For each estimated tax payment, you then pay one-quarter of the amount you think you'll owe in excess of your payroll withholdings for the year. This method is useful if your income is relatively stable throughout the year.

The Quicken budget feature plays a large role as you estimate your income and deductible expenses for the year. You should first prepare a budget following the guidelines in Level 7. Then apply this method of estimating taxes:

1. After the end of each quarter, make sure your accounts are updated with the latest income and expense transaction information.

2. Update your annual budget with your actual spending and receipts this year to date. To do this, display the budget on the screen by choosing Set Up Budget from the Activities menu (press Alt-A B). With the budget on the screen, choose AutoCreate from the Edit menu (press Alt-E A). Enter the time period for the quarter you just completed, and then the month number for the first month of the quarter.

3. Create a standard budget report by selecting Budget from the Reports menu (press Alt-R U); then filter it to include only tax-related categories (press F9 to see the Filter Transactions window).

Using the filtered Budget report, you should have all the information you need to complete the estimated tax worksheet.

Estimate Taxes with the Annualized Installment Method

If you expect to have greater income in the latter part of the year, you may want to use the annualized installment method, which figures your tax only on your earnings and deductions up to a particular point in the year. As you can imagine, Quicken excels at showing and documenting your income and deductible expenses at any given point.

To use this method,

1. Make sure you've entered into Quicken all available information about your income and spending for the preceding quarter.

2. Display a Tax Summary report for the date range from the beginning of the year to the end of the quarter for which you're making an estimated payment.

This report gives you all the data you need to complete the Publication 505 worksheet for computing your annualized income installment.

Decide on W-4 Allowances

Note. Remember as your financial situation fluctuates that you may need to change the number of allowances you claim.

If you have other sources of income and you itemize deductions, you can save money and time by indicating the correct number of allowances on your Form W-4 at work. This is the filing that determines what percentage of your paycheck is withheld for the payment of federal and state income taxes.

If your itemized deductions are high, you shouldn't be surprised to find that you'll be claiming ten or more allowances—sometimes even twenty or more. Allowances are merely ways of matching your withholdings to your estimated taxes, not of informing the IRS how many blind people over the age of 65 live in your household.

Calculate your allowances using an up-to-date budget. Once you've done that, you can display a Budget report and filter it to include only tax-related transactions. From this filtered Budget report, pick out any items which are appropriate for your W-4 worksheet. The completed W-4 worksheet will guide you in deciding how many allowances to claim.

When you file more than ten allowances, your employer must send your W-4 to the IRS. Don't be alarmed by this; if you can back up your claim, you have nothing to worry about. Criminal penalties result from deliberate misfilings, not from honest mistakes.

Make End-of-Year Decisions

The second major area of activity for tax planning tends to happen in the last month of the year. Tax planning should be a year-round activity, and that's especially feasible with the foresight you can achieve with Quicken. Year-end scrambles are, however, a reality for anyone whose finances are complicated and who wants to pay only the taxes they're obligated to pay and no more.

As the end of the year approaches, you should be considering a number of ways to optimize your taxes. In general, these fall into three categories:

- Delaying or accelerating income or deductible expenses so that they are recognized in whichever year they'll be taxed at the lowest possible rate.

- Matching capital gain and loss transactions so that you won't pay unnecessary capital gains taxes, and you won't miss an opportunity to sell at a gain without being taxed (as is the case if there's an offsetting loss).

■ Avoiding penalties for underwithholding.

If you followed the methods described above for estimating your taxes and claiming the proper number of allowances on your Form W-4, you won't have to worry about the third category. It *is* important, however, to consider changing the timing of your income and deductions and to decide what gains and losses you should take this year.

Time Your Income and Deductions

Your thoughts about timing should be guided by two simple exercises:

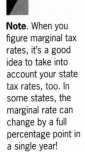

Note. When you figure marginal tax rates, it's a good idea to take into account your state tax rates, too. In some states, the marginal rate can change by a full percentage point in a single year!

■ First, you should estimate your taxable income and deductible expenses for the year. Follow the procedures outlined in the section on the full-year method for preparing estimated tax payments, and look up the tax you expect to owe from the tax tables in your Form 1040 or any appropriate tax guide.

■ Second, determine your marginal tax rate. This is the rate you'll pay on every extra dollar you earn (or will save on every extra dollar you deduct). Compare this rate with the marginal rate you expect for next year.

Marginal tax rates can change for two reasons: the tax law changes or your earning patterns are different. When the marginal tax rate for one year differs from the next, you should modify the timing of your income and deductible expenses.

For example, Luke Fielding and Maria Lombardi, the couple you met earlier in this guide, sold a vacation home in 1991 and took a capital gain. This raised their joint income for 1991 to $175,000 (even after deductions), which pushed them into a marginal federal tax bracket of 28%. In 1992, they expect their taxable income to be around $92,000, which would put them in a 33% bracket. Since their 1991 marginal bracket is five percentage points less than their 1992 bracket, it's in their interest to collect as much income as possible in 1991 (such as by taking other capital gains or pre-billing their freelance clients). This will also delay deductible expenses (Luke will contribute to the school fundraising drive after the first of the year); every dollar shifted in this way will go 5 percent further. Quicken eases this process by helping you estimate income and expenses, and by measuring the progress of your actions.

Time Your Investment Gains and Losses

The federal government allows us to deduct up to $3,000 in capital losses (net of capital gains) from ordinary income in any given year. If you have capital losses in excess of this, you must carry them over till future tax years.

Note. The $3,000 limit, like other tax-related numbers in this book, is subject to change as tax laws evolve. You should, of course, consult the most current tax instructions before you act.

Allowing a tax strategy to drive your investment strategy is comparable to letting the tail wag the dog. All other things being equal, though, it's better to take capital losses up to a total of $3,000 whenever you have the chance. If you have accumulated more than $3,000 in capital losses this year, you might consider selling enough investments in which you've accumulated gains to put you back below the $3,000 limit.

Two Quicken investment reports can help you with these decisions: the Capital Gains and Losses report and the Portfolio Value report. The Capital Gains and Losses report shows you the total gains and losses you've realized in your investment accounts so far this year. In considering where you stand on gains and losses, don't forget items that may not show up on this report, such as gains from the sale of a house or capital losses passed through in a limited partnership. The Portfolio Value report shows unrealized gains and losses—that is, gains and losses which would be available to you if you sold an investment.

If your objective is to deduct the $3,000 annual maximum and your Capital Gains and Losses report shows that you've realized $2,500 in capital gains so far this year, you should consult the Portfolio Value report to find $5,500 in unrealized losses. Again, don't do anything unwise from an investment point of view; your tax situation merely provides guidelines for your investments, not absolute direction.

Organize for Your Tax Preparer

The better prepared you are when you give or send information to your accountant, the more efficient he or she will be. This is where Quicken can pay for itself very easily. If you're the one who's doing the preparing, you'll still appreciate the time savings that a Quicken-organized tax file can offer.

Typically, a tax preparer provides a tax organizer, a booklet containing a set of forms and questionnaires designed for easy collection of the raw data for your return. This organizer essentially serves as a comprehensive checklist for all the potential opportunities to earn a tax deduction, as well as a way of guaranteeing that you've thought of all your possible sources of income.

The most important report you must complete for a tax organizer is the Tax Schedule report. Press Alt-R P S (Reports menu, Personal Reports, Tax Schedule). Quicken will display the Tax Schedule report, shown in Figure 10.4. This is a transaction report that shows every transaction in any category which you've linked to a tax schedule. Quicken subtotals all your transactions by tax schedule and, within each tax schedule, subtotals them further by line item. By and large, these items map quite neatly onto the forms in your tax organizer.

Figure 10.4   Tax Schedule report

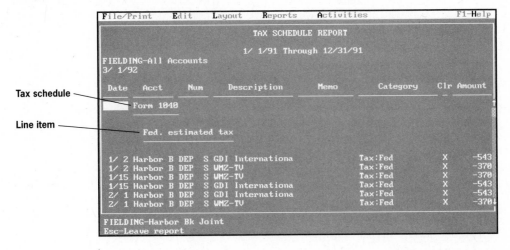

You should agree with your accountant on the best way to convey your data. One approach that works quite well is to cut up your Tax Schedule report and paperclip it to the appropriate page in your tax organizer, along with any documentation your accountant might need. It's also helpful to submit an entire copy of the Tax Schedule report tucked into the back of the tax organizer.

You should also print out a Capital Gains investment report and clip it to the appropriate page of your tax organizer. This report shows vital information which must be filed with your return, including the date you purchased each security, the selling date, purchase price, and selling price.

You should be selective about the documents you send with your tax organizer. In addition to the completed tax organizer, the Tax Schedule report, and the Capital Gains report, your accountant will need

- Your W-2 forms, supplied by your employer

- Any Form K-1 filings you may have received from a limited partnership

- A Profit and Loss report on any small business you've been running on your own

Use Quicken Data with Tax Preparation Software

A growing number of people are using their personal computer to actually prepare their income tax returns. For simple tax returns that don't require any judgment calls, this makes a lot of sense: especially if you use Quicken, you will already have completed most of the work by the time you are ready to hand your organized data over to an accountant. Since MECA's Tax Cut is our pick of the various tax preparation packages available today, we make it the focus for our discussion of linking Quicken data to automated tax preparation.

There are four ways you can organize and enter your data into Tax Cut: Forms, Shoebox, Interview, and Import. Your choice depends on personal style and preference:

- *Forms*   Many tax preparation packages present you with a menu of forms and, once you choose a form, they display a facsimile of it on the screen. You fill in the blanks, and the program does the math and transfers the information to other related forms. Figure 10.5 shows a Schedule A form ready to receive user input in Tax Cut. This option should be used by those who have a sophisticated knowledge of tax forms and who know exactly what goes where. Go to any Tax Cut form by choosing Forms from the Main Menu, Go to a Tax Form, and then selecting any form from the list that Tax Cut displays.

Figure 10.5   Tax Cut Schedule A form

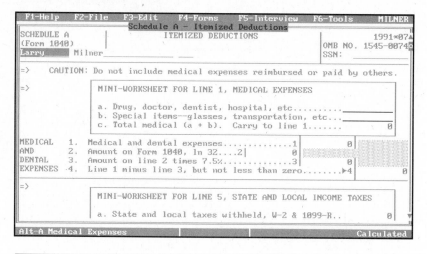

- *Shoebox*   Prior to Quicken, the most common way to organize tax information was to collect your W-2s, 1099s, tax receipts, and other documents in a file folder or even literally a shoebox. Tax Cut's Shoebox command determines what kind of document you'll be working with and takes you to the appropriate location on the correct form, where you can enter data from the document. Figure 10.6 shows the Tax Cut Shoebox menu for documents you might receive from your broker. Invoke Tax Cut's Shoebox command by choosing Forms from the Main Menu, and then Shoebox.

Figure 10.6   Tax Cut Shoebox menu

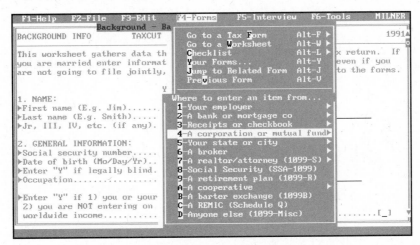

- *Interview*   Tax Cut simulates the questions a tax accountant would ask during a long planning session you might have before he or she started preparing your taxes. The program employs an expert system along with a dictionary of tax terms to aid you in making the easier judgment calls on how to file different elements of your income and deductible expenses. Figure 10.7 shows a portion of such an interview, which may be accessed by choosing Interview from the Tax Cut Main Menu.

- *Import*   If you've set up all your Quicken categories properly, you can import your Quicken data into Tax Cut directly. Tax Cut will automatically make entries in your tax returns consistent with your Tax Summary report. Figure 10.8 shows the menu sequence used for importing Quicken data: choose Tools from the Main Menu, then select Import, and finally choose Quicken from the list of compatible programs.

Whichever of these methods you use, Quicken can help you prepare for it. While the direct import approach should be the smoothest and least time consuming, you should know about several important caveats:

- The import capability stems from a standard agreement between Intuit and MECA, reached in barely enough time to include it in version 5.0 of

Quicken. Therefore, it is the least thoroughly tested portion of the product. For this reason, you should check every figure to make sure the transfer is correct.

Figure 10.7   Portion of a Tax Cut interview

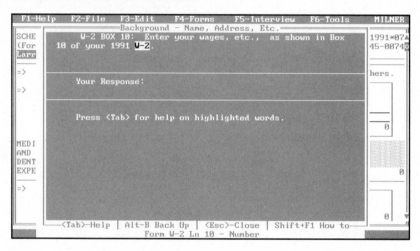

Figure 10.8   Tax Cut menus for importing Quicken data

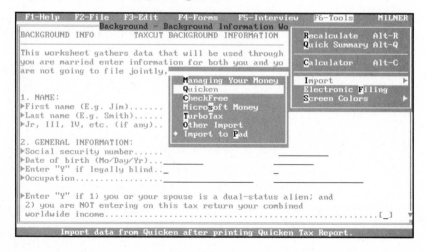

■ Tax Cut marks every imported transaction with an asterisk (*), which designates it as an estimated number. You should check each figure so marked—again, to ensure that the correct transfers have been made.

■ Even if the transfers from Quicken to Tax Cut are made correctly, they may not match the W-2s and 1099s you receive. If, for example, you paid $1,200 in mortgage interest on December 30, 1991, but your bank didn't post the payment until January 3, 1992, your bank will report $1,200 less interest to the IRS than your Quicken records show. To reduce confusion, go with the numbers filed with the government. If they differ from your Quicken records, however, you should take the time to understand why.

If you're nervous about using a PC-based tax preparation package, you might attempt an intermediate step instead. Try preparing your taxes using Tax Cut, and then ask your tax accountant to audit your return as the IRS might. This process will help identify any quirks in your tax situation which demand the help of a tax accountant. If an accountant doesn't turn up any discrepancies, you should consider relying even more heavily on tax preparation software next year.

In Level 10, you saw how you can use Quicken to help plan for and prepare your taxes.

TECHNIQUES AND PROCEDURES

■ You may need to modify your category structure to make it match the line items you complete on your tax forms. In the Category and Transfer list, create a new category by selecting <Add New Category> and defining it. Change a category name or its position in the hierarchy by highlighting it and pressing Ctrl-E; if necessary, type S for subcategory and then move the new subcategory into position under its new parent category.

■ To change the tax schedule with which a category is associated, press Ctrl-C to see the Category and Transfer list, then highlight the category and press Ctrl-E. Press F9 to see the list of tax schedules; highlight first the schedule and then the line item to be linked with that category.

■ Filter your reports for tax-related categories only to isolate tax data when you need to make decisions or meet with your tax preparer. After you press Alt-R (for Reports menu) and select the report you want, press F9 to see the Filter Transactions window. Type **Y** next to tax-related categories only.

■ To ready yourself for a session with your tax preparer, create a Tax Schedule report: on the Reports menu, select Personal (press P), and then Tax Schedule (press S). Other useful reports include the Capital Gains report and the Profit and Loss report, if you are completing a Schedule C for a small business.

TERMS

■ With the full-year method of determining your estimated taxes, first you estimate your gross income, adjusted income, deductions, withholding taxes, and credits for the entire year. Based on this, you then determine any tax liability beyond your withholding and pay one-quarter of this amount on each estimated tax due date. This is useful if your income doesn't fluctuate through the year.

■ The annualized installment method of determining your estimated taxes lets you base your estimate on only a portion of the year, if you expect your income to increase significantly after a certain point.

IMPORTANT IDEAS

■ As with many other techniques covered in this book, plunging into electronic preparation of your taxes becomes less daunting if you assemble the right tools and learn some techniques that will help you. Choose a tax preparation package and process that you and your preparer are comfortable with. Then become familiar with the other areas of Quicken that contribute to successful tax planning and preparation—category management, budgeting, and reporting, for example.

■ Quicken's strength as a decision-making tool becomes apparent when the end of the year approaches and you must assess your financial position with regard to final spending or investment decisions. Two particular reports come into play: the Capital Gains report and the Portfolio Value report. Check these reports far before the end of the year to prevent those anxious calls to your tax advisor and broker in December.

■ As critical as your tax return is, take nothing at face value. Take the time to verify that the Quicken data is correct after you move it to a tax preparation package.

Keep the Books for a Small Business

PLAN AHEAD

DECISIONS

Should Quicken Handle Your Basic Business Bookkeeping?

If you run a small business, Quicken may be capable of addressing your bookkeeping needs—at least during the early growth phases of your business. The objectives of Quicken's business bookkeeping applications are similar to those of personal bookkeeping: to assess how you're doing to enable you to make better decisions; to forecast cash requirements; and to support the reporting and filing of taxes. However, the demands of business bookkeeping must be a bit more stringent: more people are depending on your good decisions; the consequences of poor decisions can be dramatically negative; and every penny must be accounted for to satisfy the tax authorities.

Quicken can handle your small business books under three conditions:

■ *You have little or no inventory* Quicken is best suited to service businesses, in which inventory costs and holdings are relatively low and most accounting is done on a cash (rather than accrual) basis. In these businesses, most of the money you spend can be treated as an expense; when you receive it, it counts as income.

■ *Your accounts receivable are relatively simple* Businesses with either a rapidly increasing number of small accounts or an elaborate discount structure based on speed of payment will find that they quickly outgrow Quicken's capabilities.

■ *One person is responsible for maintaining your books* Quicken is not designed to be a multiuser system; it can't merge the work of several people working on separate computers.

Quicken is remarkably flexible at handling the needs of the small businesses that fit these criteria. If you doubt whether your business fits all of the above criteria or whether it will continue to do so for the next couple of years, you should do some serious thinking before you choose Quicken as your principal accounting system. Whether you use it to do your core bookkeeping or not, you'll find many uses for Quicken in any kind of business.

Will You Need to Split Personal and Business Expenses?

Especially in home-based businesses, you'll sometimes intermingle personal and business expenses. For example, your computer, car, home office, and telephone service may serve double duty as personal and business resources. Under other circumstances, you may find that your small business and personal affairs share one or more bank accounts.

If there is no intermingling of personal and business expenses or bank accounts, you should set up your business accounts as a totally separate Quicken file. This will eliminate any confusion or errors which can result from comingling funds. It will also make it much easier for you to report your business as a separate entity—with complete balance sheets and income statements.

If there is some sharing of expenses or bank accounts, however, you'll probably need to manage both your business and personal accounts from the same Quicken file, finding ways (through separate accounts, categories, or classes, for example) of distinguishing them.

Should You Use Payroll Software?

If you'll be using Quicken for a business with employees—especially if you'll be paying more than one or two people—you'll find that doing the payroll is quite a time-consuming task. You will not only need to calculate payroll deductions before issuing paychecks, but you must also fill out several different reports for federal and state tax authorities.

To lighten this burden, Intuit has introduced QuickPay, a software program specifically designed to speed the payroll preparation process and ensure its accuracy. Functionally, installing QuickPay is comparable to adding a set of payroll features into Quicken itself: you invoke payroll functions as part of the menus and function keys within Quicken.

If you need to make a payroll and saving time is a high priority, you should seriously consider using QuickPay to assist you in this task.

MATERIALS

Forms You'll Need to File

This level deals with a wide range of formal business applications for Quicken. Such applications are often designed to collect information for filling out forms, such as tax filings. As you begin to consider business applications for Quicken, think about the output you'll need to generate. Are there any forms you'll need to fill out based on the Quicken output? If so, what kinds of reports will you need?

It's always useful to organize your application around the results you need to obtain. If this involves forms to be filled out, you should examine them carefully to prevent leaving out anything vital from the application. For example, you should build a category structure for your application that maps closely onto the blanks you need to fill out on the form.

Business Records for Your Application

If you've been manually managing the information you're about to track with Quicken, gather together some samples of those manual records. Again, look for natural category structures or class groupings in your data. Early on, you could use data from your manual records to double-check your Quicken application to ensure that you get the same answers.

Chart of Accounts

Many businesses have a chart of accounts, which is basically a set of numbers organized into series corresponding to income categories, expense categories, bank and asset accounts, and liability accounts. Quicken does not require these numbers to maintain a category structure, of course, but you may want to retain these account numbers

■ *If you will later be required to roll your financial reports up into a larger parent corporation's books*   For example, you might be using Quicken to keep the books for a small subsidiary or branch office of a company, which requires that you submit reports with categories arranged in a very particular order and with each category preceded by a five-digit account code.

■ *If you report your categories not in alphabetical order (which is Quicken's normal mode) but in some other order*   In this case, you can use your chart of accounts in place of category names to force your reports to comply with a desired order.

■ *If you need, for some reason, to maintain consistency with previous reports*   If the ordering of your past reports was driven by the chart of accounts, then using the chart in Quicken is the best way to preserve that ordering and organization.

Recent Financial Statements

If you're applying Quicken to an ongoing business, it will be helpful to have a set of recent financial statements on hand—in particular, income statements and balance sheets.

QuickPay and Employer Information

If you plan to use the optional QuickPay payroll program, you should have purchased the software (see discussion of sources in Appendix B) and have it on hand, ready to be installed.

In addition, you'll need to assemble certain vital information about your company: its federal and state tax identification numbers; your federal unemployment tax (FUTA) rate; and notes on any other payroll deductions which might apply to your company (health insurance and other benefits, city tax, and so on).

Finally, you'll need to gather data on each employee: personal information such as address and Social Security number; the number of exemptions claimed on that employee's Form W-4; and each employee's year-to-date totals for earnings and taxes.

PRELIMINARIES

Review Levels 1, 2, and 3

Using Quicken to manage your business finance requires the same basic understanding of registers, reconciliation, and reports that personal financial applications require. This material is covered in Levels 1 and 2. Level 3 covers techniques for writing checks with Quicken, which will be useful if you use QuickPay to generate the payroll.

In addition, peruse Level 6 if you plan to set up cash and credit card accounts and Level 8 if you have business investments to track.

Obtain Voucher Checks for Your Business

Voucher checks will help you communicate more information to your payees than just the payee, amount, and a memo. For business-to-business vendors, you could print invoice numbers and amounts on the check stub and show that you've subtracted the 2 percent discount some businesses offer for quick payment. For paychecks, you can use the stub to display gross pay and deductions. (QuickPay uses the stub to show year-to-date totals for the employee, too.)

Bookkeeping for Your Small Business

Quicken is a fine bookkeeping program for small, simple businesses. The Plan Ahead section of this level describes several tests you might apply to your business to see if Quicken can handle it. Once you've decided you can use Quicken, you'll be ready to set up a chart of accounts and begin entering your business transactions in much the same way as your personal transactions.

Most business accounting packages (and manual accounting methods, for that matter) follow a method called *double-entry bookkeeping*. Under this method, every transaction has two parts: a credit to one account and an equal debit. This symmetry of credits and debits gives birth to the popular notion of "balancing the books."

One of the greatest advantages of using Quicken is that it maintains the balance and integrity of double-entry bookkeeping without the user even being aware of it. When you enter a deposit transaction, for example, Quicken automatically credits your bank account and issues a debit transaction that increases an income category.

One of the strongest arguments in favor of double-entry bookkeeping is that it greatly aids accuracy. By entering debits and credits separately and then checking that the entries balance, you can rest comfortably knowing that the transactions have been entered accurately. Quicken replaces this check-and-balance mechanism with another: the account reconciliation process. By checking your bank statement against the transactions you record, you can be just as certain as with the check-and-balance system.

Business accounting with Quicken differs from personal bookkeeping in several ways:

- You have less choice about what level of transaction detail to record. Every income and expense transaction has to be able to stand up to scrutiny by the tax authorities, and every material change in the company's affairs must be accounted for.

- For the same reason, every transaction must be assigned to either a category or another account. This is advisable but not mandatory in personal accounting; it's absolutely mandatory in business accounting. After all, it's through the category assignment process that Quicken quietly achieves the objectives of double-entry bookkeeping without the customary bother.

- At some point, the books for a business need to be closed for the year. In personal accounting, you can keep adding old transactions after the year's end. Businesses, however, need to report their profits and balance sheets reasonably soon after the close of the calendar (or fiscal) year. Late transactions must be handled differently when they appear after the books are closed for the year.

- It's important to track all your assets and liabilities. Every penny your business owns and owes must be traceable back to its point of origin.

- Your fixed assets—buildings and equipment, mainly—depreciate or are "used up" (at least in an accounting sense) over time. As depreciation occurs, you're required to take a depreciation expense against your income each year. While this is bad for your operating statement, it's great for your pocketbook because of the tax deduction it represents.

- Quicken will keep, on its own, a special account representing the owner's equity in the business. This is a number which represents initial investment in the business, plus the cumulative profits of the business, less any distributions (like dividends) which the owner has taken out of the business. On a balance sheet, this equity number is the difference between the company's assets and its liabilities.

The vast majority of techniques you developed for personal accounting apply to business bookkeeping as well. Your first step depends on whether you're using Quicken to support the startup of a business from scratch or you're transferring to Quicken the books of an ongoing concern.

Transfer the Books of a Going Concern

If you've been running a business—especially if you've been using an accountant to assist with the bookkeeping—you probably already have a chart of accounts. There are four kinds of accounts in most charts: assets, liabilities, income, and expenses. Asset and liability accounts directly correspond to accounts in Quicken. Income and expense accounts correspond to Quicken categories.

Note. In business bookkeeping, income and expense categories are conventionally referred to as "accounts." Don't be confused, since Quicken calls income and expense line items "categories."

Suppose you own a small graphic design company, and you are ready to enter your books into Quicken. Assuming you don't want to make any significant changes to the chart of accounts, you would start by transferring the chart directly into Quicken by

- Creating Asset and Liability accounts

- Setting up a category structure that reflects the organization of your chart of accounts

- Detecting hierarchies inherent in the chart of accounts and using categories and subcategories accordingly

- Adding classes to allow you to access information by chart or project

Create Asset and Liability Accounts

Note. If you plan to do the payroll with QuickPay, you'll set up liability accounts and categories for that purpose later in this level. Also, Level 7 details how you can use Quicken alone to handle very small payrolls; see that level for a discussion of accounts you can set up.

For each account in your chart, create an Asset or Liability account by pressing Ctrl-A (for Account) and choosing <Set Up a New Account> from the Account list that appears. If, for example, you received a bank loan to purchase some new computer layout equipment and software for the business, this loan would be recorded in an Other Liability account, and the value of the equipment would be listed in an Other Asset account. As the starting balance, you would use the account balance listed in your most recent balance sheet or trial balance.

Set Up a Category Structure

To create a category structure that reflects your chart of accounts,

1. In the register for any account in your business file, press Ctrl-C (for Category) and select <New Category> from the Category list.

2. Specify whether you're creating an Income or Expense category.

3. Enter the name of the category in the Category Name blank.

4. If you've been using account numbers, you may want to type them into the Description field. Figure 11.1 shows a sample category structure.

Figure 11.1   **Category structure reflecting a chart of accounts**

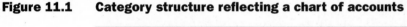

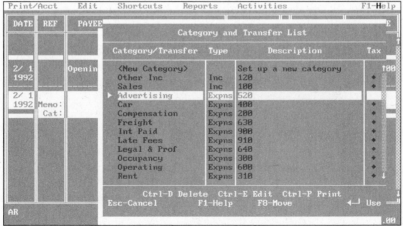

The Quicken manual suggests that you use the account numbers for category names, rather than the names themselves. However, doing so wastes the time you gain when you use autocompletion in assigning categories to transactions. If you must use account numbers, enter them in the Description field.

Detect Hierarchies in Your Chart of Accounts

Examine the chart of accounts for expenses that are actually arranged in hierarchies; for example, Rent and Utilities might fall under a parent category such as Occupancy. In a numbered chart of accounts, the numbering scheme often suggests this subcategory structure. In a five-digit chart of accounts, 40700 might represent Occupancy, while 40701 and 40702 represent Rent and Utilities subcategories, respectively. If you want to preserve any hierarchies, you may need to change some categories to subcategories.

To do this,

1. Call up the Category list (Ctrl-C).

2. Highlight the category you want to demote to a subcategory.

3. Press Ctrl-E (for Edit).

4. Next to "Income, Expense or Subcategory" type **S**, and press Ctrl-Enter.

5. Move the highlighted category name to the appropriate parent category and press Enter. Figure 11.2 shows a category structure with logical subcategories.

Figure 11.2   Logical subcategories

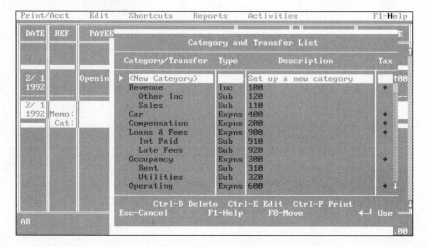

Add Classes to Your Accounts

Note. In the Class list, Quicken does not distinguish between classes and subclasses. You can designate any class as a subclass when entering a transaction simply by separating the two classes with a colon.

Consider adding classes to your business books, as well. Although this is rarely necessary in documenting the business for tax purposes, it often proves quite useful in supporting business decisions. Setting up classes allows you to create reports by client, project name, or type of project—to name just a few ways you could build classes. You can create classes on the fly as you need them, or in advance by pressing Ctrl-L (for Class) to see the Class list, selecting <New Class>, and entering the class name and description.

Double-Check Your Account Structure

To ensure that the balance sheet is correct, run a Balance Sheet report by pressing Alt-R B B (Reports menu, Business Reports, Balance Sheet). If you haven't created a separate file for your business, you'll need to create a custom version of the Balance Sheet report, filtering your transactions to include only a selected group of accounts—namely, the ones that relate to your business. The accounts should correctly fall under Assets and Liabilities, and the account balances should match those in your books.

Now you can skip ahead one section to the heading "Record Your Income and Expenses," where you'll begin the process of entering and recording the transactions for your business.

Start the Books for a New Business

Note. Level 2 suggests many additional income and expense categories which you may find useful for your business.

In the Plan Ahead section for this level, we weighed the pros and cons of maintaining your business records as a separate Quicken file. If you'll be using a separate file, you should create it by going to the Quicken Main Menu (press Escape repeatedly), pressing Ctrl-G (for Go to File), and choosing <Set Up File> from the Accounts list. Since you don't already have a chart of accounts, you should consider adopting the standard business categories listed in Table 11.1. Of course, you can add any other categories that make sense for you.

Suppose you're starting a video production company. After you've chosen or set up a file for your business, you should

- Create all the Asset and Liability accounts that relate to your business: your bank accounts, credit card accounts, fixed asset accounts, loan accounts, and any other assets and liabilities which apply to your business. Create these accounts by pressing Ctrl-A (for Account) and choosing <Set Up a New Account> from the Account list. If you already have balances in these accounts—for example, if you received some investment capital or if you have purchased some equipment—you should enter these balances when you initially set up these accounts.

- Create all the Income and Expense categories your business will need. If you started with standard business categories, you can augment them and change them as needed. Try to anticipate the specific information required by your business as you create the category structure: for example, what will you need to report to creditors, tax authorities, and shareholder/owners? What data will you need to support the decisions you'll be making in the business?

Table 11.1   Standard Business Categories in Quicken

Income Categories

Category Name	Description
Gr Sales	Gross Sales
Other Inc	Other Income
Rent Income	Rent Income

Expense Categories

Category Name	Description
Ads	Advertising
Car	Car & truck
Commission	Commissions
Freight	
Int Paid	Interest paid
L&P Fees	Legal & professional fees
Late Fees	Late payment fees
Office	Office expenses
Rent Paid	
Repairs	
Returns	Returns & allowances
Tax	
Travel	Travel expenses
Wages	Wages & job credits

- Classes allow you to examine your business from a different perspective—by product line, customer, or project, for example. You can create classes as you need them, or in advance by pressing Ctrl-L (for Class) to see the Class list, selecting <New Class>, and entering the class name and description.

Record Your Income and Expenses

Business bookkeeping, in contrast to personal accounting, absolutely requires that you assign every transaction to a category or designate it as a transfer to another account. This preserves the integrity of the invisible double-entry bookkeeping process which Quicken maintains.

If you haven't done so already, set Quicken's default settings to require that you assign each transaction to a category, and *never override this setting*. To set up mandatory categorization, go to the Quicken Main Menu (press Escape repeatedly), press P T (Set Preferences, Transaction Settings), and be sure "Require a category on transactions" is set to Y (yes).

From then on, recording transactions parallels closely the process of recording transactions in personal applications, as described in Levels 2 through 6 of this manual. The exceptions to this occur largely when the condition of the business changes but no cash actually changes hands. A common example of this is when a customer purchases a large order on credit, but won't actually forward the payment for 30 days. Deciding whether to track these noncash transactions determines the difference between cash-basis and accrual-basis accounting. Each of these methods places different demands on your business accounting process in Quicken.

Apply Cash-Basis Accounting Techniques

Cash-basis accounting is very simple. When you receive cash or deposit a check, you count it as income; when you write a check, you incur an expense. Your net profits are essentially the difference between the cash you receive and the cash you pay out.

Quicken is optimized for cash-basis accounting; it was designed principally for personal bookkeeping, and personal finance is largely cash-basis accounting. To use Quicken in operating a cash-basis business, simply set up one or two business checking accounts and assign every transaction to a category—it's as straightforward as that. The Asset and Liability accounts you set up earlier become useful in special situations, but you probably don't need to use them routinely.

Pay Your Bills

When you receive a bill, simply enter the transaction into your main bank account register as a postdated check, using the date you intend to pay the bill (see Figure 11.3). This will cause the expense to appear on your profit-and-loss statements only after the money actually changes hands, even though the amount is deducted from the running balance immediately. (Remember to adjust the date if your payment date changes.)

Note. If you're planning to use Quicken to actually write your checks, don't forget to type an asterisk (*) in the NUM field of the transaction, which signals that you expect Quicken to print a check at the appropriate time.

Figure 11.3 **Register showing bill to be paid**

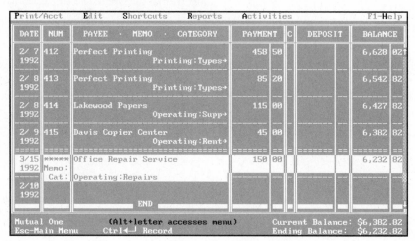

When you enter your payments, don't forget the timesavers built into Quicken's payment methods—particularly memorized transactions and transaction groups. These techniques can help you enter and forecast your periodic expenses even before you receive the bills. These techniques are described at length in Level 3.

When you write a business-to-business check, it's often important to include the invoice number or other reference information on the check. In some cases, you'll be paying several invoices at once; listing all the invoices on the check can help the payee credit your account properly. If you're using checks with stubs, you'll find the split transaction function effectively handles these multiple invoices, even when each invoice is categorized the same. Open the Split Transaction window (Ctrl-S) while you're entering a multiple-invoice transaction, and type each invoice number in the Memo column, followed by the appropriate amount, as shown in Figure 11.4. If you're taking the 2 percent discount frequently offered to business customers who pay within ten days, you can enter this number (and an explanation) in the Split Transaction window, too.

Finally, for purposes of its standard reports, Quicken considers every postdated check you enter to be an "Account Payable." To obtain an accurate picture of your accounts payable, you should enter all of your anticipated payments—whether or not you actually want Quicken to print the check. Of course, you can distinguish the checks you want Quicken to write by typing the asterisk (*) in the NUM field, otherwise, enter something under NUM or leave the field blank.

Figure 11.4   Split Transaction window with invoice notations

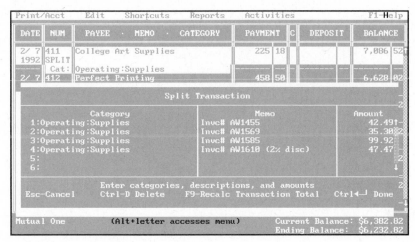

Issue Bills to Others

When you bill a customer under the cash accounting method, you won't be counting the revenue until you actually receive the money. However, you might want to use Quicken to help keep track of the unpaid invoices you issue.

Even under the cash accounting method, the best way to organize these accounts receivable is to set up a separate Other Asset Account for receivables in Quicken. Press Ctrl-A and select <Set Up New Account> from the Account list to do so.

When you issue an invoice, record it in the Accounts Receivable register (shown in Figure 11.5), using these guidelines:

- Date the transaction for the point at which you expect to receive the funds. Entering a realistic date here will help you with your cash flow projections.

- Place your invoice number in the REF field and your customer's name in the PAYEE field. Try to be consistent in entering the vendor's name in the PAYEE field; this will help you subtotal your receivables by customer later on. To achieve consistency, memorize the transactions of your repeat vendors. Level 2 contains complete information on how to create and use memorized transactions.

- When entering the amount of the invoices, be careful to record them in the INCREASE field; the software is designed to move your cursor first to the DECREASE field.

- Enter the date of the invoice in the MEMO field; this is important because you'll want a record of how long the invoice has been outstanding.

Note. Remember that classes may be used to group revenue by client, project, region, or any other categorization scheme you might choose. Level 6 offers complete information on establishing and using classes.

■ Categorize the transaction under the appropriate income category. If you are using classes or subcategories to track more detail, you should enter the appropriate subcategory or class now. Press Ctrl-Enter to record the transaction.

Figure 11.5   Accounts Receivable register

```
┌─────────────────────────────────────────────────────────────────────────────┐
│ Print/Acct    Edit    Shortcuts    Reports    Activities              F1-Help │
├──────┬──────┬──────────────────────────────┬──────────┬─┬──────────┬─────────┤
│ DATE │ REF  │ PAYEE · MEMO · CATEGORY      │ DECREASE │C│ INCREASE │ BALANCE │
├──────┼──────┼──────────────────────────────┼──────────┼─┼──────────┼─────────┤
│ 2/15 │B1442 │Rockland Dairy                │          │ │ 2,000 00 │10,475 00│
│ 1992 │      │12/15/92          Revenue:Sales/→      │ │          │         │
│      │      │                              │          │ │          │         │
│ 3/15 │B1444 │Cinematics                    │          │ │  550 00  │11,025 00│
│ 1992 │      │2/10/92                       │          │ │          │         │
│      │      │                              │          │ │          │         │
│ 3/15 │B1443 │Herbal Society                │          │ │ 1,500 00 │12,525 00│
│ 1992 │      │1/15/92           Revenue:Sales/→      │ │          │         │
│      │      │                              │          │ │          │         │
│ 4/ 1 │B1445 │Entre Interiors               │          │ │ 1,200 00 │13,725 00│
│ 1992 │Memo: │2/15/92                       │          │ │          │         │
│      │ Cat: │Revenue:Sales/Entre Int       │          │ │          │         │
│ 2/10 │      │                              │          │ │          │         │
│ 1992 │      │                              │          │ │          │         │
│      │      │            END               │          │ │          │         │
│      │      │                              │          │ │          │         │
├──────┴──────┴──────────────────────────────┴──────────┴─┴──────────┴─────────┤
│ AR                    (Alt+letter accesses menu)   Current Balance: $ 8,475.00│
│ Esc-Main Menu      Ctrl┘ Record                    Ending Balance:  $13,725.00│
└─────────────────────────────────────────────────────────────────────────────┘
```

Note. If you mistakenly press Enter before recalculating the transaction total with F9, Quicken will generate a new line in the Split Transaction window, which causes the transaction to add up to the amount in the register. You can correct this by finding the new amount, erasing it (Ctrl-Backspace), and pressing F9 before you do anything else.

When your customer pays a bill, open the Accounts Receivable register and find the transaction corresponding to the invoice the customer is paying. Use the Find (Ctrl-F) command to locate your transactions quickly. If your customer provides the invoice number with his payment, you can use the matching features to quickly locate the transaction that has a matching invoice number in the REF field. Once you've found it, follow this procedure to zero out the account receivable and complete the transaction:

1. Modify the date of the transaction to reflect the date your customer actually paid the bill.

2. Open a Split Transaction window for the transaction by pressing Ctrl-S. The category of the transaction appears on the first line of the window.

3. If the customer took a discount or credit, record it on the first available line in the Split Transaction window. Under CATEGORY, credits are typically assigned to the original income category and discounts to a separate discount category. However, you should follow the accounting procedures you've established for your business. Under AMOUNT, enter the discount or credit as a negative amount, but don't press Enter yet.

4. Press F9 to recalculate the transaction total. In the Register, the total displayed in the INCREASE column changes to reflect the credit or discount. Press Enter to move to the next line.

5. Enter the amount of the payment as a negative number in the next available category line. Under CATEGORY, enter the bank account name into which you're depositing the payment (see Figure 11.6). Before you press Enter, press F9 to recalculate the transaction total (which will be zero if the customer paid in full), and press Ctrl-Enter to close the window.

Figure 11.6   **Split Transaction window showing discount**

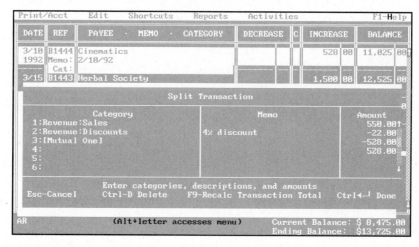

6. Finally, you should mark all fully paid invoices as cleared transactions by placing an asterisk (*) in the C (Cleared) field. This will facilitate the reporting of outstanding invoices later on.

The most critical disadvantage of this method is that it can, if you aren't careful, result in reporting income not yet received. Before you prepare profit-and-loss reports, you should check your Accounts Receivable register for old unpaid invoices. If you've passed the date you expected to be paid (and which you've entered in the Accounts Receivable register), you should re-estimate the date. If you don't, the unpaid invoice will be improperly counted as revenue.

Noncash Expenses

Even cash-basis businesses must handle some noncash expenses—in particular, depreciation. The section "Account for Depreciation," which appears later in this level, offers advice on accounting for business depreciation.

Note. Updating the Accounts Receivable register is especially important at the end of the fiscal year. If you don't update the dates of invoices that haven't yet been paid, you could end up paying taxes this year on income that shouldn't be recorded till next year.

Apply Accrual-Basis Accounting Techniques

Accrual-basis accounting is practiced when you want to measure every significant change in the company's business, whether or not it immediately involves cash. For example, when you're billed for a large expense, you might want to account for that expense immediately, rather than 30 (or 60 or 90) days later when you actually pay the bill. Likewise, when you sell something to a customer who will pay you over time, you may want to count the revenue as income when you deliver the goods, instead of when you actually receive the check.

The art of accrual accounting depends on matching the revenues you earn and the expenses you incur in earning them. And both of these must be matched, in turn, to the point at which you actually bill a customer.

Quicken is less adept at accrual-basis accounting than cash-basis accounting. Unlike many more feature-laden business accounting packages, Quicken does not offer formal software modules to handle accounts payable and accounts receivable. However, Quicken's structure of assets and liabilities does allow for simple accrual-basis accounting. As your business gets more complicated, though, you'll want to watch for signs that you're outgrowing Quicken's capabilities.

Accounts Payable

Your accountant will help you determine situations in which you should record a transaction as an expense prior to your actually paying a bill. Typically in an accrual-based business, this might happen at the end of a tax year; you might want to recognize as many expenses as possible to minimize taxes in that year, but take your time in actually paying the bills. Under these circumstances, you'll need an accounts payable account—an Other Liabilities account in Quicken's terms—to hold your expense transactions till you pay them.

When you receive a bill that you need to record as an account payable (and by no means will this include all your bills),

Note. Try to be consistent in entering the vendor's name in the PAYEE field. This will help when you create vendor reports later. To achieve consistency, memorize transactions for your repeat vendors. Level 2 contains complete information on how to create and use memorized transactions.

1. Open the Accounts Payable register (press Ctrl-A and choose from the Accounts list).

2. Enter the bill as a new transaction, recording the invoice number in the REF field and the amount in the INCREASE column. If the invoice number is longer than the REF field, try entering only the last few digits, or enter the invoice number in the MEMO field. Categorize the transaction in the appropriate expense category.

3. When you press Ctrl-Enter to record the transaction, Quicken will record the bill as an expense and will increase your liabilities by the same amount. Figure 11.7 shows an accounts payable register.

Figure 11.7   Accounts Payable register

Print/Acct	Edit	Shortcuts	Reports	Activities			F1-Help

DATE	REF	PAYEE · MEMO · CATEGORY	INCREASE	C	DECREASE	BALANCE
12/15 1991	1455X	Vista Film Rentals Rental/Vane As→	450 00			2,800 00↑
12/17 1991	1469X	Vista Film Rentals Rental/WAAS-FM	298 00			3,098 00
12/22 1991	4595	The Edwards Studio Rental/Wayland	3,000 00			6,098 00
12/30 1991	8C90	Vista Film Rentals Memo: Cat: Rental/Vane Assoc	870 00			6,968 00
2/10 1992		END				

AP   (Alt+letter accesses menu)
Esc-Main Menu   Ctrl←⏎ Record   Ending Balance: $6,968.00

When you write a check (or instruct Quicken to print a check or make an electronic payment), you should record the check as you would any payment. However, in the CATEGORY field you'll specify the name of your Accounts Payable account (as shown in Figure 11.8), not an expense category. Finally, you should go to your Accounts Payable register and mark the transactions you've paid as cleared (place an X in the C column). This will help you obtain complete reports of outstanding payables.

Figure 11.8   Register showing paid accounts payable (AP) transaction

Print/Acct	Edit	Shortcuts	Reports	Activities			F1-Help

DATE	NUM	PAYEE · MEMO · CATEGORY	PAYMENT	C	DEPOSIT	BALANCE
1/ 4 1992	406	Pro Typesetters Printing:Types→	85 00			11,315 00↑
1/ 5 1992	407	The Edwards Studio Memo: Cat: [AP]	3,000 00			8,315 00
1/18 1992	408	Brooks Bindery Printing:Bindi→	350 00			7,965 00
1/22 1992	409	Pro Typesetters Printing:Types→	331 30			7,633 70
2/ 1 1992	410	Kraemer Press Printing:Seps/→	322 00			7,311 70
2/ 7 1992	411 SPLIT	College Art Supplies Operating:Supp→	225 18			7,086 52

Transfer shows paid transaction

Mutual One   (Alt+letter accesses menu)   Current Balance: $6,382.82
Esc-Main Menu   Ctrl←⏎ Record   Ending Balance: $6,760.82

Accounts Receivable

The principles behind accounts payable and receivable are very similar for accrual-method companies. As in accounts payable, you'll be setting up a separate Quicken account for accounts receivable, but this time it will be an Other Asset account.

When you issue a bill,

1. Enter the details of the bill in the Accounts Receivable register. Type the amount of the bill in the INCREASE field.

2. Assign the transaction to the appropriate income category and, optionally, subcategory and class.

3. Press Ctrl-Enter to complete the transaction.

When you receive a payment, you should enter it in the Accounts Receivable register. Use the same customer name and reference numbers you used when you entered the original bill. The amount should be entered in the DECREASE field of the Receivables account, and the transaction should be marked as cleared by typing **X** in the C column. In the CATEGORY field, type the name of the bank account in which you're depositing the funds. Finally, return to the original bill transaction and mark it as a cleared transaction.

Account for Depreciation

Depreciation is a noncash expense—a charge against your earnings that represents the way your company's assets are "used up" over time. For a small business, depreciation primarily represents a tax deduction. In larger companies, it plays a much more visible role in helping to assess the operating performance of the business.

Large businesses keep two sets of books—one for taxes and one for financial reporting. The most significant difference between them is the depreciation schedules, which vary for tax and financial reporting purposes. Few small businesses keep two sets of books, because for them, the depreciation schedules dictated by tax authorities are perfectly adequate.

Assuming your accountant agrees, you should begin determining the depreciation charge appropriate for each fixed asset (property and equipment) owned by your company. Don't try to use Quicken for this unless you can count all your assets on your fingers—use a spreadsheet or get the number from your tax advisor or accountant.

Once you have the amount, you can enter an entire year's worth of depreciation into the appropriate register, using the memorized transaction (or transaction group) approach.

For each fixed asset that depreciates, you should know a monthly depreciation charge. Your net fixed assets are the difference between the amount you originally paid for the assets and the cumulative depreciation charges. Every depreciation charge is a decrease transaction in an Other Asset account, categorized in an appropriate depreciation expense category. There are three possible methods of handling these depreciation charges:

- *Individual depreciation accounts for every fixed asset account*   In this case, you make separate monthly depreciation entries into several depreciation Other Asset accounts. By matching Asset and Depreciation accounts, you'll be able to compare both the gross fixed asset value and the cumulative depreciation amounts on your balance sheet reports (see Figure 11.9).

Figure 11.9   Balance Sheet report

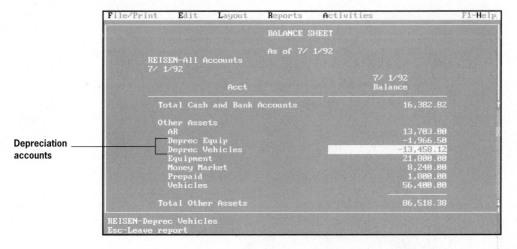

Depreciation accounts

- *A single depreciation account*   Using this method, you calculate depreciation each month and enter the number in a single account which holds all depreciation transactions (as in Figure 11.10). This method hides detail on individual depreciation account balances.

- *No separate depreciation account*   In this case, each depreciation transaction is made as a separate entry into the asset account to which it applies (see Figure 11.11). The running account balance is, therefore, the net value of the asset. You can identify the gross value and cumulative depreciation numbers by generating filtered summary reports.

Figure 11.10   Depreciation Account register

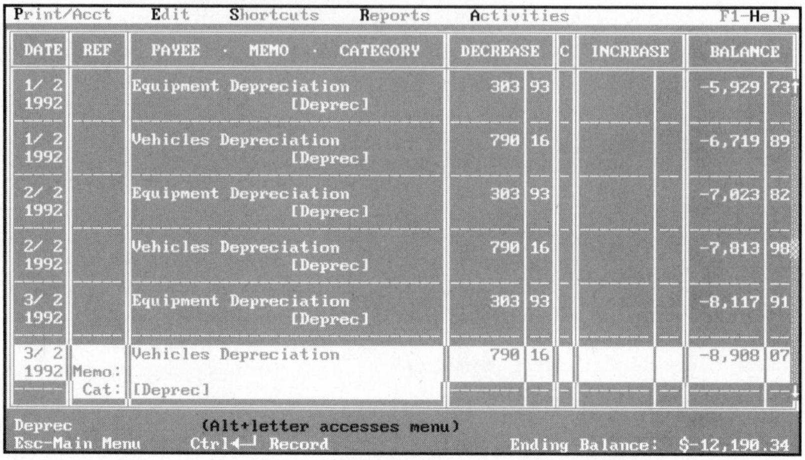

DATE	REF	PAYEE · MEMO · CATEGORY	DECREASE	C	INCREASE	BALANCE
1/ 2 1992		Equipment Depreciation [Deprec]	303 93			-5,929 73↑
1/ 2 1992		Vehicles Depreciation [Deprec]	790 16			-6,719 89
2/ 2 1992		Equipment Depreciation [Deprec]	303 93			-7,023 82
2/ 2 1992		Vehicles Depreciation [Deprec]	790 16			-7,813 98
3/ 2 1992		Equipment Depreciation [Deprec]	303 93			-8,117 91
3/ 2 1992	Memo: Cat:	Vehicles Depreciation [Deprec]	790 16			-8,908 07

```
Print/Acct    Edit    Shortcuts    Reports    Activities           F1-Help
Deprec                  (Alt+letter accesses menu)
Esc-Main Menu    Ctrl◄┘  Record              Ending Balance:  $-12,190.34
```

Figure 11.11   Depreciation transaction in an asset account

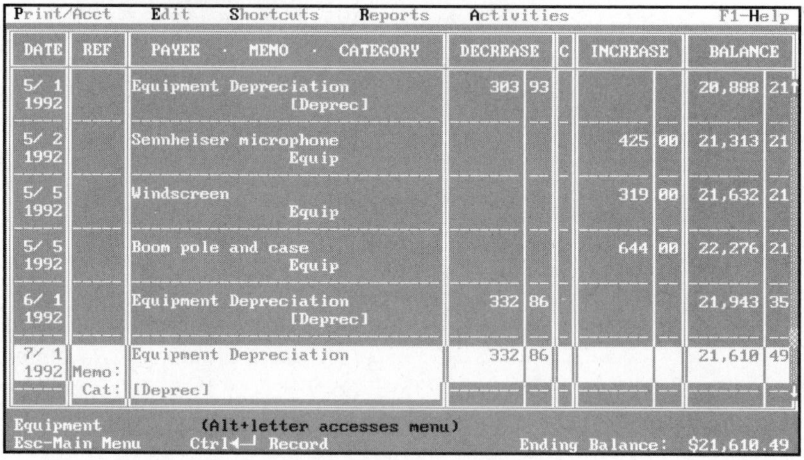

DATE	REF	PAYEE · MEMO · CATEGORY	DECREASE	C	INCREASE	BALANCE
5/ 1 1992		Equipment Depreciation [Deprec]	303 93			20,888 21↑
5/ 2 1992		Sennheiser microphone Equip			425 00	21,313 21
5/ 5 1992		Windscreen Equip			319 00	21,632 21
5/ 5 1992		Boom pole and case Equip			644 00	22,276 21
6/ 1 1992		Equipment Depreciation [Deprec]	332 86			21,943 35
7/ 1 1992	Memo: Cat:	Equipment Depreciation [Deprec]	332 86			21,610 49

```
Print/Acct    Edit    Shortcuts    Reports    Activities           F1-Help
Equipment               (Alt+letter accesses menu)
Esc-Main Menu    Ctrl◄┘  Record              Ending Balance:  $21,610.49
```

Meet the Payroll with QuickPay

Level 6 described a method for meeting very small payrolls at home—the kinds of situations that arise in paying domestic help. In very small businesses—those with one to three employees—the same techniques can apply.

As your business grows, however, you'll probably find that meeting the payroll stretches Quicken's capabilities to the limit. Recognizing this fact, Intuit is now marketing QuickPay, a software program that extends Quicken's ability to handle payroll administration and accounting.

QuickPay is a payroll system that automatically sets up payroll accounts, calculates wages, taxes, and other deductions, and creates Quicken checks with the appropriate payroll information on the stub. It also maintains a database of personnel information such as addresses, Social Security numbers, dates hired and released, and year-to-date information.

Prepare QuickPay for Your Business

To prepare QuickPay to manage the payroll for your business,

- Create a payroll category and account structure. When you pay an employee, you are actually making several complex transactions all on one check. Each paycheck has both expense components (such as gross salary and employer's Social Security contribution) and liability components (representing money you're deducting and holding on behalf of state and federal tax authorities). QuickPay requires that you set up categories and other liability accounts precisely to its specifications.

- Install the QuickPay files. This copies the appropriate program files and tax tables to your hard disk and creates a batch file for launching QuickPay.

- Enter your company and employee data. This will include company information such as tax ID numbers and unemployment tax rates, as well as employee information such as Social Security numbers, exemption claims, and year-to-date totals.

Once you've set up QuickPay as part of your collection of Quicken program and data files, you'll be able to access its features as integrated parts of Quicken.

Create a Payroll Account and Category Structure

Note. The Assistant feature is new to Quicken 5. With earlier versions, you have to create these categories and accounts manually.

For QuickPay to work properly, you must create several new categories and accounts to hold the payroll data. QuickPay does not set up these categories and accounts automatically; it depends on you to create them prior to starting to use QuickPay.

Fortunately, Quicken 5 offers an "Assistant" feature which makes this process almost automatic. From the Quicken Main Menu (press Escape repeatedly to get there), press T then P (Use Tutorials/Assistants, Create Payroll Support). Enter your state's two-letter abbreviation, and press Enter. When the Assistant is finished, it will have created a Payroll category with five subcategories, and six new Other Liabilities accounts.

If you have been using an earlier version of Quicken to administer your payroll, you'll need to change the names of your current accounts and categories to comply with QuickPay's requirements. Press Ctrl-C to see the Category list, find the category to change, and press Ctrl-E to edit it. If you need to demote a category to a subcategory, type **S** next to "Income, Expense or Subcategory," and press Ctrl-Enter. Then move the highlight to the appropriate parent category and press Enter.

Your payroll subcategories are designed to track payroll-related expenses that your company incurs. Table 11.2 lists the names of the payroll subcategories QuickPay requires (which are created automatically by the Payroll Assistant), along with an explanation of what these categories contain. All names for payroll deduction subcategories begin with the letters "Comp" (short for company); the custom portion of the name should not exceed nine characters. Use this table if you need to modify the category names.

Table 11.2   **Payroll-Related Categories**

What QuickPay Requires	What the Category Contains
Payroll:Gross	Gross compensation expense for your employees
Payroll:Comp FICA	Your company's contribution to the Social Security (FICA) system
Payroll:Comp FUTA	Your company's federal unemployment tax contribution
Payroll:Comp MCARE	Your company's contribution to Medicare
Payroll:Comp SUI	Your company's state unemployment (SUTA) contribution
Payroll:Comp SDI*	Your company's state disability insurance (SDI) contribution

*The SDI subcategory is not set up automatically by the Quicken Payroll Assistant. If you need it, you must set it up as a new subcategory.

Note. Remember that not all payroll deductions require expense categories—just those which are paid out of your company's coffers, as opposed to those being paid by the employee and merely held by you until due.

Next, you'll need to create any other expense subcategories unique to your company that may be important. For example, if your company matches employee contributions to a 401(k) savings plan, you should set up a subcategory to the Payroll category named Payroll:Comp 401K. Create these categories by pressing Ctrl-C to display the Category list, highlighting <New Category>, and pressing Enter. Don't forget to link these subcategories to the Payroll category.

As an employer, you are also obligated to collect payroll withholding tax deductions from your employees' paychecks and to later channel these amounts to the appropriate authorities. These withholdings accumulate, along with the money you owe on the company's payroll tax contributions, in a series of Other Liability accounts. Table 11.3 shows the accounts required by QuickPay, which again are created by the Payroll Assistant.

If you'll be making employee payroll deductions other than these, you should create additional Other Liabilities accounts now. For example, you may offer employees a payroll deduction program to facilitate contributions to a local charity such as the United Way. You'll collect these deductions in a Liability account, which could be named Payroll-UWay. To create this account, press Ctrl-A (for Account), and highlight <New Account> in the Account list.

Table 11.3   Payroll-Related Accounts

What QuickPay Requires	What the Account Contains
Payroll-FWH	Federal income tax withheld from your employees' paychecks
Payroll-SWH*st*	State income tax withheld from your employees' paychecks (*st* stands for your state's two-letter abbreviation—for example, Payroll-SWHNY for New York income tax)
Payroll-LWH*nn*[*]	Local income tax withheld from your employees' paychecks (*nn* stands for a two-digit local identifier; see Table 11.4 later in this level for a key)
Payroll-FICA	Social Security tax, both the portion withheld from your employees' paychecks and the company's contribution
Payroll-MCARE	Medicare tax, both employee withholdings and company contributions
Payroll-SDI[*]	State disability tax contributions paid by the company
Payroll-SUI	State unemployment tax contributions paid by the company
Payroll-FUTA	Federal unemployment tax contributions paid by the company

Note. While Quicken allows class names up to 15 characters long, QuickPay allows you to enter class names no longer than 11 characters in its employee database. In creating classes for payroll analysis purposes, remember to restrict class names to 11 characters.

[*]The Payroll-LWH*nn* and Payroll-SDI accounts are not set up automatically by the Quicken Payroll Assistant. If you need them, you must set them up as new accounts.

For larger businesses, you may want to create a structure of classes to help track your payroll expenses by type of employee (for example, by department or job level). To set up classes for use in entering new employee data, you should press Ctrl-L (for Class list), highlight <New Class> in the Class list, and press Enter.

If you're going to be starting QuickPay in the middle of the year, one final step remains. If you want to use Quicken's reports to summarize your payroll transactions with an eye towards helping you fill out your tax forms, you need to enter starting account balances for each employee in each Other Liability account. Follow this simple procedure to create starting balances for each employee:

1. Create a new bank account called Payroll YTD Adj. To do so, press Ctrl-A (for Account) and select <New Account> from the list. Enter an account balance of zero. When you're finished creating the account, select it to see the account register for the new account.

2. Create a memorized payroll transaction which contains a category split. Each payroll category and account will be represented on a separate line of the memorized transaction's Split Transaction window. To set this up, press Ctrl-T to view the Memorized Transaction list, highlight <New Transaction>, and press Enter. Then type the word **Payroll** in the PAYEE blank.

3. Press Ctrl-S (for Split) to call up the Split Transaction window, and, with the cursor on each successive blank line of the Category column, press Ctrl-C (for Category) and choose the next payroll category or account from the list. The order in which you enter these doesn't matter, and you don't need to enter amounts next to each category or account. Repeat this until all the categories and accounts are represented (as shown in Figure 11.12), and press Ctrl-Enter. Press Ctrl-Enter again to memorize the transaction, press A to memorize the split transaction amounts (as opposed to percentages), and then press 1 to memorize the transaction as a payment.

Figure 11.12   Split Transaction window

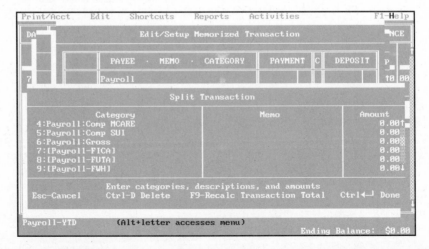

4. Now, with the Payroll YTD Adj Account register displayed, begin entering a new transaction by typing as much of the word Payroll as required to uniquely identify it among your other memorized transactions. Then press Ctrl-E to complete the entry and automatically recall the memorized transaction (this will bring in all the split account information).

5. With the cursor on the PAYEE field, press Ctrl-Backspace to clear it, and type an employee's name.

Note. Remember that split transaction entries without brackets are categories, and bracketed entries represent transfers to other accounts.

6. Press Ctrl-S (for Split) to open the Split Transaction window, and begin entering all the year-to-date expenses and deductions in the Amount column of the appropriate category or transfer lines. Enter the year-to-date expense totals as positive numbers, and the year-to-date liability totals as negative numbers. Figure 11.13 shows what the transaction should look like for one employee.

7. Press the F9 key to calculate a transaction total from your split transaction entries, and press Ctrl-Enter twice to record your transaction.

8. Repeat steps 4 through 7 for each employee whom you've paid this year.

9. Run a payroll report to check the accuracy of your entries. Press Alt-R B Y (Reports menu, Business Reports, Payroll Report). Name the report "YTD Balances." Customize the report with the Layout (Alt-L) menu, selecting Payee as the column heading and Category as the row heading. (Figure 11.14 shows a portion of the resulting report.) Compare the totals in the report with your own records; if you find errors, go to the appropriate employee transaction to make corrections as necessary.

10. Create a series of transactions, each of which summarizes all the payments you've made on a given payroll liability—for example, one transaction for the federal tax withholdings you have sent to the government, and another for the United Way payments you've made. You may use the payroll memorized transaction here, too, though you will be entering amounts only in the bracketed account transfer rows. Enter these payment summaries as positive amounts. Press F9 to calculate the transaction total, and Ctrl-Enter twice to record the transaction.

11. Finally, you'll need to zero out the Payroll YTD Adj account so it doesn't create any anomalies in your balance sheet or account balance reports. Note the account balance shown in the lower-right corner of the Register window. Then enter a final transaction entering that amount as an increase, categorized as a deposit into this account.

Your categories and accounts are now fully prepared for your first payroll session. Next you'll need to install the QuickPay software, and then enter the employee information on each person who works for your business.

Figure 11.13   Split Transaction window for one employee

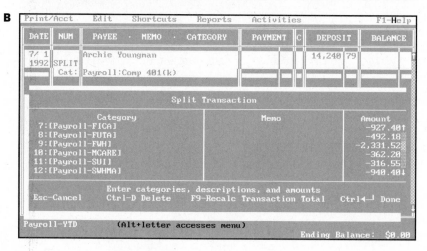

Install the QuickPay Files

When you install QuickPay into your Quicken directory, you're copying two
sets of files to your hard disk: four additional program files and a set of tax
tables from which your payroll deductions will be calculated. Most installations require that you insert the QuickPay disk into your floppy disk drive
and type **A:INSTALL** (or, if appropriate, **B:INSTALL**) from the DOS
prompt. Installation notes for more complicated situations are contained in
Appendix A.

Figure 11.14 YTD Balances report

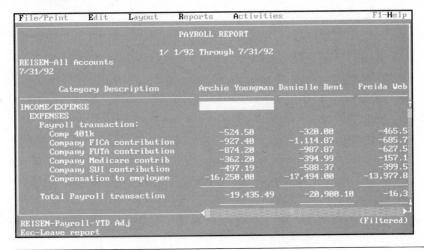

In addition to copying program files to your Quicken directory, the installation program creates a batch file for starting QuickPay. From now on, you should start Quicken by typing **QP** if you'll be using the payroll capabilities. You may start Quicken without QuickPay by typing **Q** as before.

Enter Your Company and Employee Data

The final preparatory step is to enter your company and employee data into QuickPay's database. Assuming you've started Quicken by typing **QP**, you should select the account from which you'll be writing your payroll checks and press Ctrl-W (for Write/Print Checks). At the bottom of the screen, you'll see a new option: F7 for payroll. Press the F7 key. The first time you do payroll you'll see the Set Up Company window. If you see the QuickPay Main Menu instead, press Ctrl-U (Set Up) to display the Set Up Company window (Figure 11.15).

Fill in the blanks as follows:

- *Company Name, Address, and Tax ID Numbers*   Enter this data for your information only. QuickPay doesn't print it on paychecks or reports.

- *Employee SUI, Employer SUI, and Employer FUTA Rates*   Enter the appropriate rates for state and federal unemployment taxes, expressed as a percentage of gross earnings (e.g., enter 1.25 for 1.25%).

- *Maximum Earnings$*   For all of the SUI and FUTA rates, enter the upper earnings limit to which the tax applies.

Figure 11.15   Set Up Company window

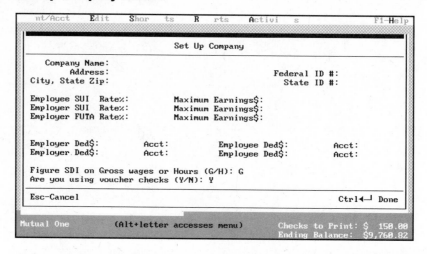

- *Employer Ded$* In these two blanks, you may define any extra contributions your company makes on each employee's behalf, such as profit sharing. You can enter either a percentage (e.g., 3.5%) or a flat amount for each pay period for each employee. Enter the unique portion of the appropriate account name (up to six characters) for this deduction in the Acct blank.

- *Employee Ded$* These two blanks function similarly to the Employer Ded$; use them to record the standard contributions each employee makes. Enter a percentage or a flat rate, and the unique portion of the appropriate account name.

- *Figure SDI on Gross Wages or Hours* Some states require that you base State Disability Insurance contributions on gross earnings (press G), while others base it on hours worked (press H).

- *Are you using voucher checks (Y/N)?* Press Y if you're using voucher checks. QuickPay will move the company's payroll contributions below line 16 in the Split Transaction window, so they don't print on your employees' check stubs.

Press Ctrl-Enter when you're finished entering your company data. You'll see the QuickPay Main Menu (as shown in Figure 11.16), which is designed to display a list of employees.

Quicken maintains a database of payroll-related information on each employee you'll be paying. To add a new employee, highlight <New Employee> on the QuickPay Main Menu list and press Enter. The Add New

Note. Some of these blanks may contain the same data for every employee. To create a template containing default values, highlight <New Employee> on the QuickPay Main Menu list, press Ctrl-E (for Edit), and fill in the data you want applied to everyone. Press Ctrl-Enter when you're done.

Employee window will appear. (See Figure 11.17 for a sample of the completed window.) Complete the form as follows:

■ *Full Name and Address* Enter this information exactly as you want it to appear on your employees' paychecks.

■ *Phone* This will not appear on the check.

Figure 11.16 QuickPay Main Menu

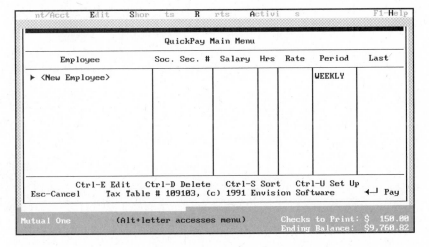

Figure 11.17 Completed Add New Employee window

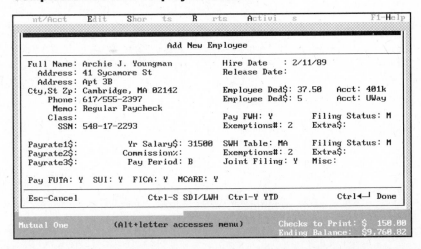

- *Memo*   This may contain any note (such as "Regular Paycheck") that you want to appear on each check.

- *Class*   If you're using Quicken classes to analyze payroll by department or job level, enter the class here.

- *SSN*   Enter the employee's Social Security number.

- *Payrate1$*   For an hourly employee, this should contain the hourly pay rate, expressed as dollars per unit of time (typically per hour). This blank should be empty for salaried employees.

- *Payrate2$ and Payrate3$*   These blanks may contain additional pay rates for overtime, night, or holiday work.

- *Yr Salary$*   For salaried employees, enter the annual salary.

- *Commission%* For employees on a simple commission plan (straight percentage of sales, for example), enter the percentage rate. You can combine this percentage with either the hourly or salary rate method for a base-plus-commission type of compensation plan.

- *Pay period*   Type **D** for daily, **W** for weekly, **B** for biweekly, **S** for semi-monthly, **M** for monthly, **Q** for quarterly, and **Y** for yearly.

Note. If your employees require more than two deductions to be recorded, you could try totaling the percentage deductions in one Employee Ded$ blank and the flat amounts in the other.

- *Pay FUTA, SUI, FICA, and MCARE*   Type **Y** if you're required to make an employer FUTA (federal unemployment tax), SUI (state unemployment insurance), FICA (Social Security), or Medicare contribution on behalf of this employee; otherwise, type **N**.

- *Hire Date and Release Date*   These dates are for your reference only and are not used by the software, except that QuickPay will not allow you to write a payroll check for an employee for whom a release date is entered.

- *Employee Ded$*   These two blanks hold extra deductions that apply to this employee only. Enter it as either a flat dollar amount or as a percentage, followed by the percent (%) sign. Enter the unique portion of the appropriate Payroll account to which this deduction should be transferred.

- *Pay FWH*   Enter Y if federal withholding tax should be subtracted from this employee's paycheck, or N in the rare case that it shouldn't.

- *Filing Status*   Used for calculating withholding tax rates; enter M for married, S for single, or H for head of household. This status is declared on Form W-4, Employee's Withholding Allowance Certificate.

- *Exemptions#*   Enter the number of exemptions the employee has claimed on his or her Form W-4.

Note. The QuickPay manual contains information specific to the tax laws of each state. You should consult the appendix on Tax Table Information as you enter your employee data—particularly as it relates to state withholding taxes.

■ *Extra$* If the employee has requested that additional tax be withheld, you should enter the requested dollar amount in this blank.

■ *SWH Table* Enter the state (two-letter abbreviation) for which an employee's withholding tax should be calculated.

■ *Filing Status* Enter the employee's marital status for state withholding purposes (see federal filing status entries above).

■ *Exemptions#* Enter the number of exemptions the employee claims for state tax purposes.

■ *Extra* If the employee has requested additional state tax withholdings, enter the appropriate amount here.

■ *Joint Filing* State tax rates for some states are affected by whether married employees will be filing joint returns with their spouses (type **Y**) or will be filing separately (type **N**).

■ *Misc* This extra blank is used by some states for additional tax parameters.

If your company and/or employees must pay State Disability Insurance premiums, you must press Ctrl-S while operating in the New Employee window, to see the Edit SDI/LWH window. Enter the appropriate percentage (e.g., 0.45 for 0.45%) under Employee and Employer SDI% and the maximum-dollar SDI deduction that can be paid by the employer or employee in any pay period (as in Figure 11.18).

Figure 11.18 **Edit SDI/LWH window**

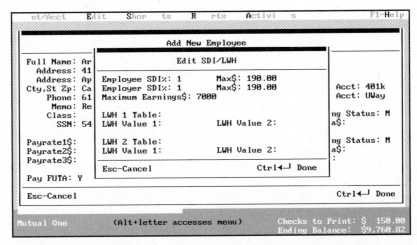

If your employees are subject to local tax deductions, you'll also need to enter appropriate local tax rates in the Edit SDI/LWH window (again, press Ctrl-S to see it). There are three LWH blanks to be filled out here: a table ID (which directs you to one of many local tax tables supplied with QuickPay) and two LWH Value blanks (which contain amounts that may vary from one employee to the next). Consult the QuickPay manual for the latest entries in these tables, but Table 11.4 shows the key to various local withholding tax tables supplied with an early version of QuickPay.

Table 11.4   **Key to Local Withholding Tax Tables in QuickPay**

Note. When entering the LWH ID, you must enter two digits. 01 is acceptable; 1 is not.

LWH Table ID	LWH Value 1	LWH Value 2
01: Dollar amount	Maximum dollar amount to be deducted over the entire year	Dollar amount to be deducted each pay period
02: Dollar amount times hours worked in the period	Maximum dollar amount to be deducted over the entire year	Dollar amount per hour to be deducted from each pay period
03: Percent of gross pay	Maximum dollar amount to be deducted over the entire year	Percentage to be deducted from gross pay (enter 1.5% as 1.5)
06: New York City resident	Blank	Blank
07: New York City nonresident	Blank	Blank
08: Yonkers resident	Blank	Blank. Resident
09: Yonkers nonresident	Blank	Blank
10: Michigan cities	Exemption amount in dollars	Percentage to be deducted from gross pay (enter 1.5% as 1.5)
11: Indiana counties	Blank	Percentage to be deducted from gross pay (enter 1.5% as 1.5)
12: Ohio school district tax	Blank	Percentage to be deducted from gross pay (enter 1.5% as 1.5)

Finally, if you begin using QuickPay sometime other than early January, you need to update the running year-to-date totals QuickPay maintains on each employee. There are two reasons to do this: first, to ensure that those withholding taxes (like FICA) and other obligations with a maximum cap are calculated correctly; and second, to ensure that year-to-date totals are printed correctly on your employees' paychecks. To enter year-to-date figures from the Add New Employee window for each employee, press Ctrl-Y (for Year-to-Date) and enter the appropriate numbers in the Edit Year to Date window (shown in Figure 11.19). Press Ctrl-Enter when you're done.

Figure 11.19   Completed Edit Year to Date window

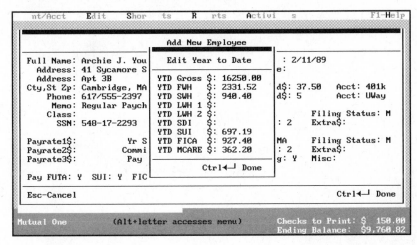

As you complete employee data forms, the QuickPay Main Menu will accumulate a list of employees, along with their Social Security numbers, salary, hours worked last pay period, pay rate, pay period, and last pay date. If you don't want salary and rate displayed, press Ctrl-P (for Protect) to hide them.

Compute and Issue Your Payroll

When it's time to issue the payroll, make sure you've started Quicken with the QP command (rather than just Q). Make sure too that your payroll bank account is selected (press Ctrl-A if you need to do so), and then press Ctrl-W to display the Write/Print Checks window.

Press F7 to invoke QuickPay. You'll see the QuickPay Main Menu, shown in Figure 11.20, which lists all of your employees. Highlight the one for whom you'd like to issue a paycheck, and press Enter. Now you'll see the Compute Payroll window into which you enter the information necessary to compute the paycheck. Figure 11.21 shows the completed Compute Payroll window.

Note. If you haven't started Quicken with the QP command, you'll find out soon enough. When Quicken displays the Write Checks screen, the F7-Payroll option will not show up at the bottom of the screen. Press Escape repeatedly to return to the Quicken Main Menu, and press E to exit Quicken. Then start again with the QP command.

Figure 11.20   QuickPay Main Menu

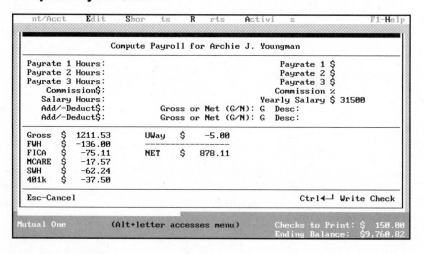

```
 nt/Acct    Edit    Shor    ts    R   rts   Activi   s              F1-Help

                          QuickPay Main Menu

        Employee          Soc. Sec. #  Salary  Hrs  Rate  Period   Last

     <New Employee>                                       WEEKLY
   ▸ Freida Weber         003-38-7737   36960               BIWEEKLY
     Daniele Bent         000-27-9711   29450               BIWEEKLY
     Craig Prendergast    595-00-4791   21400               BIWEEKLY
     Leon Rybarski        871-28-0000   33495               BIWEEKLY
     Simone Thibault      000-44-1289   38820               BIWEEKLY
     Archie J. Youngman   548-17-2293   31500               BIWEEKLY


         Ctrl-E Edit    Ctrl-D Delete    Ctrl-S Sort    Ctrl-U Set Up
   Esc-Cancel     Tax Table # 109103, (c) 1991 Envision Software      ↵ Pay

 Mutual One          (Alt+letter accesses menu)      Checks to Print: $  150.00
                                                     Ending Balance:  $9,760.82
```

Figure 11.21   Compute Payroll window

```
 nt/Acct    Edit    Shor    ts    R   rts   Activi   s              F1-Help

              Compute Payroll for Archie J. Youngman

   Payrate 1 Hours:                        Payrate 1 $
   Payrate 2 Hours:                        Payrate 2 $
   Payrate 3 Hours:                        Payrate 3 $
      Commission$:                         Commission %
      Salary Hours:                        Yearly Salary $ 31500
      Add/-Deduct$:          Gross or Net (G/N): G  Desc:
      Add/-Deduct$:          Gross or Net (G/N): G  Desc:

   Gross  $  1211.53     UWay  $    -5.00
   FWH    $  -136.00     -------------------
   FICA   $   -75.11     NET   $   878.11
   MCARE  $   -17.57
   SWH    $   -62.24
   401k   $   -37.50

   Esc-Cancel                             Ctrl↵ Write Check

 Mutual One          (Alt+letter accesses menu)      Checks to Print: $  150.00
                                                     Ending Balance:  $9,760.82
```

Actually, you are required to enter very little information in this window. For a salaried employee with no special changes to the weekly payroll, you need only press Ctrl-Enter and the check will be written automatically. For hourly employees you only need to enter the number of hours worked, and then press Ctrl-Enter.

Note. QuickPay retains all the information you entered in a payroll session from one pay period to the next. Don't forget to erase (with Ctrl-Backspace) any entries that don't carry over from the previous session; otherwise, you may find yourself paying someone a bonus twice!

The Computer Payroll screen can also accommodate many special situations. Here are some examples that illustrate the use of the other blanks in the Compute Payroll window:

- *Overtime*   If you've defined a second pay rate (Payrate2) for overtime hours, you should enter the number of overtime hours worked under Payrate 2 hours. The same technique should be applied to a third pay rate, which might be used for holidays or nights.

- *Commission*   If you've set up a commission plan percentage (5 percent of sales, for example), you should enter the number on which the commission is based in the Commission$ blank.

- *Bonus*   When you pay a bonus to an employee over and above the normal compensation, you should do so in the Add/-Deduct$ blank. Enter the amount in the blank, and type **G** to specify that you want it applied to gross wages. When you do so, the Add to Gross Wages window opens, which allows you to specify a category and subcategory (e.g., Payroll:Bonus) for the expense. You're also given the opportunity to exclude these extra earnings from the calculation of any of the major classes of withholdings (see Figure 11.22). Press Ctrl-Enter to complete the window. Finally, you can describe the adjustment (i.e., "Performance Bonus") in the Desc field of the Compute Payroll blank; this description will be printed on the employee's pay stub.

Figure 11.22   Add to Gross Wages window

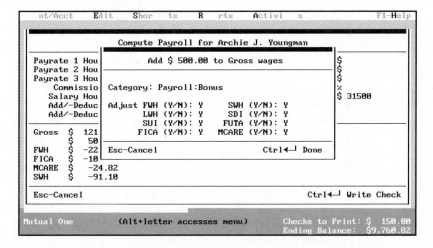

■ *Business Expense Reimbursements* Use the Add/-Deduct$ blank for these amounts, too. This time, however, you'll want to add the amount to net wages (since the reimbursements aren't subject to withholding and other payroll deductions). When you type **N** (Net wages), an Add to Net Wages window appears, asking you to specify an expense category for the additional money. Type the category (as in Figure 11.23); then press Ctrl-Enter.

Figure 11.23 Add to Net Wages window

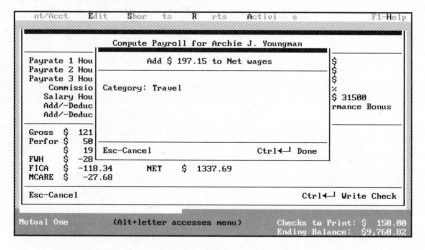

■ *Cash Drawer Shortages* If your employees are liable for shortages in the cash drawer for which they're responsible, you should enter this as a negative amount in the Add/-Deduct $ blank. In this case, the deduction should be against gross wages.

■ *Repayment of Payroll Advances* If you decide to give an employee a $200 advance against future earnings, you may write a check in Quicken as, in effect, a loan account called Payroll-Loan. On the next paycheck, you may deduct the loan amount from net pay by typing **-200** in the Add/-Deduct $ blank, specifying Net pay, and typing **[Payroll-Loan]** in the category blank.

■ *Tips* This is tricky: you're required as an employer to calculate withholding tax on tips an employee declares, but the employee has already received the money. You must use two Add/-Deduct lines for this transaction: one a positive dollar amount identified as gross pay (since tips are taxable), and the other a negative entry in the same amount, identified as net (since the employee already has the tip money).

After you press Ctrl-Enter to complete the Compute Payroll window, Quicken displays the Write Checks screen and proceeds to fill in the blanks of the check. In the Split Transaction window, Quicken enters each payroll category and account, along with the dollar amounts for each deduction and adjustment. If a category or account that you entered while completing the payroll information doesn't match any in Quicken's category or account lists, the paycheck process stops and Quicken displays the message:

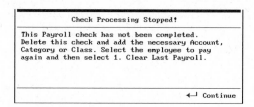

To correct the category or account, follow these steps:

1. Press Escape to remove the message, and again to close the Split transaction window (select Cancel Changes and Leave).

2. Then press Ctrl-D to delete the partially completed check.

3. To correct an account name, press Ctrl-A to see the list of accounts. Verify that the ones you created for QuickPay's use are correctly named.

4. Return to the QuickPay Main Menu by pressing F7.

5. To correct a category name, first verify that the categories you created for the payroll process are accurate; press Ctrl-C to see them, and edit any as necessary. If these are accurate, highlight the employee name in the QuickPay Main Menu associated with the paycheck you were generating, and press Ctrl-E (for Edit). Quicken displays the following message alerting you to the fact that the payroll for this person has already been initiated:

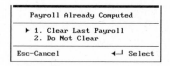

To verify that you want to clear the last payroll, highlight the first option and press Enter. Then double-check all the categories you entered for accuracy.

6. When you are finished, press Ctrl-Enter to reissue the paycheck s described earlier.

Quicken makes it easy to determine whether you've paid everyone by displaying the last pay date in the extreme-right column of the QuickPay Main Menu screen. Check this column to make sure you cover everyone who should be paid.

Before you actually print the checks, it's a good idea to examine each of them on the screen. Once you use Escape to leave the QuickPay Main Menu and return to the Write/Print Checks screen, you'll be able to scroll through each of the paychecks using the PgUp and PgDn keys. Within each check, you may view the component detail by pressing Ctrl-S to open the Split Transaction window. Figure 11.24 shows the first six lines of the Split Transaction window for a typical payroll check. Note that the description field, which will be printed on voucher checks, contains year-to-date totals in each of the employee deduction areas.

To print your payroll checks, press Escape to return to the Write Checks screen, and then press Ctrl-P. Make sure all the settings are correct (including the appropriate number for the check format), and press Ctrl-Enter.

Pay Your Tax Liabilities

Over time, you'll accumulate money from your payroll that you owe to various tax authorities, insurers, and other benefits suppliers. When you write a check to one of these organizations, you write it as you would any other Quicken check, but under Category, you should identify the transaction as a transfer from the appropriate Payroll Liability account.

In some cases, your bank will serve as an agent for the tax collections from several accounts. For example, you may want to write a single check to your bank, representing deposits of your federal income tax withholdings, your FICA contributions, and your Medicare deductions. Set this check up as a routine split transaction, specifying three different transfer accounts in the Category column, as in Figure 11.25.

Generate Reports and Complete Payroll Filings

When the time comes to file payroll reports to state or federal authorities, you should first print the standard Payroll report. Press Alt-R B Y (Reports menu, Business Reports, Payroll Report); then enter an optional title and specify the time period.

Both the Quicken and the QuickPay manuals contain detailed information on how to interpret this report data to correctly transfer summary information to your payroll tax forms. Consult these sources if you're the least bit confused regarding which Quicken numbers map to which tax return lines.

Figure 11.24   Split Transaction window for payroll check

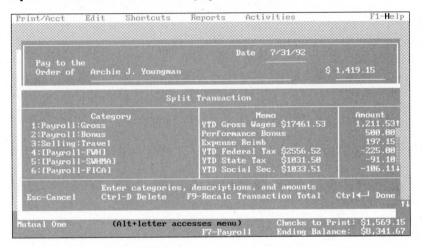

Figure 11.25   Split transaction for payroll liability payments

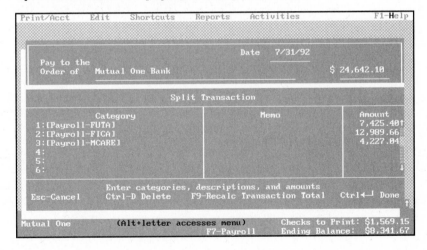

Maintain and Back Up Your QuickPay Database

Payroll is among the most crucial data to be regularly maintained and backed up. QuickPay provides a tremendous help in managing the complex information that meeting a payroll involves; it also makes it easy for you to update and archive the information.

Edit Employee Data

Every so often, as employees move, are promoted, or change their tax filing status, you'll find that you need to make changes to your QuickPay database. To change an employee's record from the QuickPay Main Menu, highlight the employee's name and press Ctrl-E (for Edit). Change the information as needed, and press Ctrl-Enter to record your changes.

Delete Employee Records

QuickPay also allows you to delete employees (not a good idea unless you've made an error—in entering data for them, not in hiring them). To do so, highlight the employees' names on the QuickPay Main Menu and press Ctrl-D (for Delete). You may also sort the employees by their first or last name by pressing Ctrl-S (for Sort).

Delete and Clear a Payroll Transaction

In case you make a mistake, QuickPay lets you clear the last transaction you made. To do this properly, you have to take two actions—one to reset QuickPay's payroll database and one to delete the transaction from Quicken's registers:

1. From the QuickPay Main Menu, highlight the employee whose payroll transaction you want to delete, and press Ctrl-C to clear it. This step clears the payroll transaction from QuickPay's database, resets the year-to-date figures in the employee records, and changes the last pay date display to its previous value.

2. Press Escape to leave QuickPay, and press Ctrl-R (for Register) to display the register for the account in which you're working. Find the errant transaction, highlight it, and press Ctrl-D (for Delete) to clear it from the register.

   You can only clear one payroll transaction in this manner—the most recent one. If you find you've made a mistake on an earlier transaction, you must manually adjust the year-to-date totals for the affected employee.

Backup Payroll Information

It's a good idea to back up your payroll information after every payroll. This is not something Quicken does automatically in its automated back-up

Note. With any luck, you'll never have to use your backup data, but if you do, you should make your Quicken directory current, insert your backup data disk, and type **COPY A:QUICKPAY.*** (or **COPY B:QUICKPAY.*** as appropriate).

routine. QuickPay offers a utility program, QPBACK, which the installation process places in your Quicken directory. When you start this utility by typing **QPBACK** from the DOS prompt (make sure you've made the directory where your Quicken files are stored current), you'll see the following message:

Type **2** to complete the operation.

Update Tax Tables

Tax rates—and therefore tax tables—are always changing, at both the federal and the state levels. For that reason, the tax tables built into your copy of QuickPay are likely to become obsolete unless you subscribe to the Tax Table Update Service offered by Intuit. Your first year of tax table updates is free when you register QuickPay.

Reset Totals to Start a New Year

Finally, you must remember to reset all the year-to-date deduction figures for all your employees at the beginning of the year. When you install Quick-Pay, you also install a separate utility which systematically reviews each employee's records and zeros out the year-to-date figures. From the DOS prompt in your Quicken directory, type **QPCLEAR**. Since it's impossible to reverse the process once you've cleared the year-to-date amounts, Quicken displays the following message, warning you that you're about to take a serious step:

If you're ready to start the new year, type **2** once, and then type **2** again when you are asked to confirm.

Use Quicken's Reports as Management Tools

Good business decisions require reliable information, and Quicken's reports are designed to give you solid information on the financial condition of your business. Quicken's reports can, for example, help you make the kinds of year-end decisions that characterize cash-basis businesses. Typically, these are tax-motivated decisions, such as asking a customer to wait till the beginning of the year to pay you or paying bills earlier than you otherwise would. It might make your Profit and Loss Reports look ugly, but you'll be grateful when the tax man cometh.

For accrual-method businesses, Quicken's variety of reports can help you manage cash flow as well as profit and loss; understanding the difference between these two can mean the difference between success and failure in managing an accrual-based business.

This section describes the Quicken reports most commonly used in managing businesses. Using Quicken's report customization features (Alt-E for Edit and Alt-L for Layout), you can position the rows and columns of almost any report to suit your information needs.

Remember: once you've found a report format that's useful to you, memorize that format by pressing Ctrl-M while the report is displayed on the screen. Supply a name, and then press Ctrl-Enter. When you're ready to recall that report, from the register press Alt-R M (Reports menu, Memorized Reports). Then select the name of the report you want to retrieve.

Profit and Loss

This is the most fundamental report for your business, designed to be a true representation of how much the value of your business has changed and why. To create a profit and loss statement for your business, press Alt-R B P (Reports menu, Business Reports, P&L Statement).

Cash Flow

For cash-basis businesses, cash flow and profit-and-loss are virtually identical. For accrual-method businesses, however, a cash flow report highlights some important differences. If your accounts receivable are slow to collect and you can't hold off your vendors any longer, you may run into a cash crunch that your profit-and-loss statement will simply not reflect. To create a cash flow statement for your business, press Alt-R B C (Reports menu, Business Reports, Cash Flow).

Accounts Payable (Cash Basis)

If you are using the cash-basis method of recording payables (that is, by post-dating register transactions), Quicken offers an accounts payable report that can be highly customized. The standard Accounts Payable report, however, highlights only those transactions which are set up as unprinted checks (that is, those which have an asterisk in the NUM column).

The standard Accounts Payable report is grouped by vendor, as shown in Figure 11.26. To create it, press Alt-R B P (Reports menu, Business Reports, AP by Vendor). Once you have the standard report on screen, you can introduce many variations, such as subtotaling transactions by week or category.

Figure 11.26   **Accounts Payable report for cash-basis business**

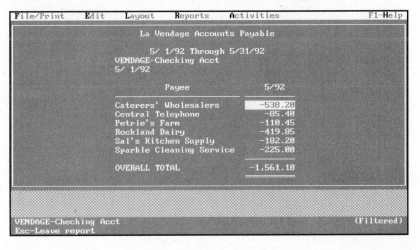

Accounts Payable (Accrual Basis)

Quicken's standard Accounts Payable report will not work for companies that use the accrual method, since the report depends on the entry of post-dated checks to identify accounts payable. Nonetheless, you can use Quicken's report writer to design two custom reports which provide vital accounts payable information. (For more information on customizing standard reports, see Level 6).

The first report provides a summary for a given time period, so you can see the most overdue bills. This is a summary report (press Alt-R S, for Reports menu, Summary), showing only data in your Accounts Payable account. Using the Layout menu (Alt-L), set up the report so payees (vendors) display in the row headings. With the Edit menu (Alt-E), filter the report to display only uncleared transactions—those that have not yet been paid.

The second report organizes your accounts payable by vendor. This is a transaction report (press Alt-R T, for Reports menu, Transaction Report), showing only data in your Accounts Payable account (see Figure 11.27). Using the Layout menu (Alt-L), subtotal by payee (vendor), and filter the report to display only uncleared transactions (using the Edit menu—press Alt-E).

Figure 11.27   Accounts Payable report for accrual-basis business

```
                        Accounts Payable by Vendor
                          12/15/91 Through 1/31/92
      REISEN-AP                                                   Page 1
      2/ 1/92

        Date     Num      Description      Memo      Category    Clr Amount

      1/20/92 332     Central Telephone            Operating:Telepho   -255.90
              Total Central Telephone Co                              -255.90

      1/16/92         Gerri Locke-Cooper           Contractor        -2,000.00
              Total Gerri Locke-Cooper                              -2,000.00

      1/24/92 776     Profetto Office Su           Operating:Supplie   -191.42
              Total Profetto Office Supply                           -191.42

      1/15/92 269     Rolland Broadcasti           Rental/WAAS-FM      -298.00
              Total Rolland Broadcasting                             -298.00

      1/18/92 4595    The Edwards Studio           Rental/Wayland    -3,000.00
              Total The Edwards Studio                             -3,000.00

      1/22/92 1901    Video Services               Equip            -1,975.00
              Total Video Services                                 -1,975.00

      12/22/91 8C90   Vista Film Rentals           Rental/Vane Assoc   -870.00
      1/15/92 1455X   Vista Film Rentals           Rental/Vane Assoc   -450.00
              Total Vista Film Rentals                             -1,320.00

              OVERALL TOTAL                                        -9,040.32
```

Accounts Receivable

Because cash-basis and accrual-basis companies should both create separate accounts receivable registers to record issued invoices, the reporting approach for both methods is very similar. You'll want to use Quicken's custom report-writing features to create reports that will help you look at receivables by age and by vendor. You might also want to see an entire history for a customer's payments.

To obtain a report showing receivables arranged by customer, use the standard Accounts Receivable by Customer report (press Alt-R B R, for Reports menu, Business Reports, A/R by Customer). The report displays customers as row headings and months as column headings, and includes an Overall Total column showing total receivables.

To customize the report so it shows only overdue accounts, edit the date range for the report (press Alt-E D, for Edit menu, Set Title & Date Range). Set the ending date to today's date minus the allowable days' payment terms.

To create a report that shows a customer's payment history, you must first enter an actual payment date into the Memo field of each invoice transaction in the Accounts Receivable register. Then create a transaction report with the date range encompassing all original invoices (press Alt-R T, for Reports menu, Transaction report), and subtotal the report by payee. The resulting report will show the original invoice date and the memo notation on the payment date.

Balance Sheet

A balance sheet is a statement of your company's assets, liabilities, and owner's equity (investment and accumulated profits or losses). This is the functional equivalent of the net worth statement you might have used in accounting for personal finances, with some slight degree of reorganization. To obtain a balance sheet for your business, press Alt-R B B (for Reports menu, Business Reports, Balance Sheet). Change the report date if necessary.

Remember that the information in your balance sheet is only as good as what you entered to begin with. Since owner's equity is a calculated number (obtained by subtracting liabilities from assets), there is no double-checking mechanism that ensures that your opening account balances were correct. When setting up your Asset and Liability accounts, be absolutely certain that you use the correct opening balances.

Job/Project

If you've used classes as a way of associating your revenue or expenses with particular projects or jobs, you'll want to apply these classes to some of the reports you create.

For example, the Job/Project report (press Alt-R B J, for Reports menu, Business Reports, Job/Project Report) can easily be modified to show revenue by project or by month (see Figure 11.28). To do this, you place classes in the row headings and months in the column headings, using settings on the Layout menu (Alt-L).

Figure 11.28   Job/Project report

```
 File/Print    Edit    Layout    Reports    Activities              F1-Help

                        Revenue by Client (Monthly)

                        1/ 1/92 Through 4/30/92
 REISEN-Mutual One
 5/ 1/92

        Class Description          1/92        2/92        3/92        4/92

 Cinematics                    4,000.00     8,000.00    2,472.00        0.00
 Entre Int                     1,754.00     2,500.00    2,937.00    1,705.00
 Herbal Soc                        0.00         0.00      595.00    1,842.00
 Rockland                        600.00        50.00    4,500.00    2,026.00
 Sergio's                     12,511.00     3,904.00      119.00        0.00
 Transactions - Other             0.00         0.00      528.00        0.00

 OVERALL TOTAL                18,865.00    14,454.00   11,151.00    5,573.00



 REISEN-Mutual One                                              (Filtered)
 Esc-Leave report
```

Establish a Budget for Your Business

There are no major differences between budgeting in your business and budgeting in your personal financial life. In both cases, you must forecast revenue; identify fixed, operating, and discretionary expenses; and balance the budget.

In a business, however, the stakes are often much higher. Fewer expenses will be counted as "discretionary" expenses in a business than in one's personal life. You'll find that curtailing expenses in response to an unanticipated change in financial condition is more difficult and painful in a business than in personal spending situations.

Apply the techniques discussed in Level 7 to budget your business and track its performance against your budget later. Use the reports faithfully and you'll know as much or more about your small business than most operating managers know about how their divisions are doing.

Forecast Business Cash Requirements

In any business—but particularly in a small one—it's crucial to be able to anticipate future cash needs. Especially if your revenue comes in waves (such as from monthly billings or quarterly catalogs), your cash balances will probably vary widely. Under these circumstances, it's important to look as far ahead as possible, anticipating the next time your cash cycle will hit bottom. By doing so, you'll avoid making decisions at the top of the cash cycle that you'll later regret when the tide shifts. You may want to look at cash on two levels: your annual cash needs and cash needs over the next month.

The annual view will help you determine whether your funding adequately supports the anticipated growth in the business and any natural seasonal cycles inherent in it. The Christmas tree business, for example, might hit its peak cash need in late November and its peak cash surplus in late December. If you were running this business, you'd want to avoid spending recklessly in January and make sure you had enough money to make it through November.

The short-term view helps you determine whether your anticipated receipts, expenditures, and bank balances are all consistent with each other over the next few weeks. This will help you decide whether to try to stretch your payables, call customers to try to accelerate receivables, or to put off discretionary spending you were considering.

You can accomplish annual cash flow forecasting quite effectively through the budget process, described in Level 7. This will identify the top and bottom of your cash cycle if your business fluctuates. As you go through this process, you may want to think creatively about how to smooth your cash cycle: If big annual insurance premiums are due at the time of year when cash is tightest, for example, can you work with your insurance agent to change the time of the year when you're billed?

Short-term cash flow forecasting is somewhat trickier and requires that you create "phantom" transactions that anticipate your major cash expenditures and receipts. Because of the work involved and the risk of making mistakes, we don't recommend that you use Quicken for short-term cash forecasting as a matter of routine. As you approach the bottom of your cash cycle, though, you'll find this technique very useful in helping you make decisions. To forecast your short-term cash flow,

1. For the time frame you're forecasting, enter any payments you expect to make; these will be postdated transactions in your regular bank account, dated for when you expect to make the payment.

2. Create an Other Asset account named Forecast. In this account, enter deposits you expect to receive over the time period.

Note. It is unwise to enter anticipated deposits in your regular bank account, because these will skew the account balances and may cause you to write bad checks.

3. Also in the Forecast account, enter as negative numbers any large expenditures which are distinct from vendor accounts payable. This might include the anticipated weekly payroll, payments to the government of withheld taxes, and large purchases.

4. Create a Cash Flow report for the time period that includes the Forecast account as well as your regular bank account (and any other accounts which might influence your cash position, such as Accounts Receivable).

5. Review this report periodically to see a short-term forecast. Be sure to keep the Forecast account updated by deleting any transactions that have been accounted for in other accounts.

LEVEL 11 BUILDING BLOCKS

In Level 11, you saw how Quicken can contribute to the financial management of a small business, including accounts payable, accounts receivable, and payroll.

TECHNIQUES AND PROCEDURES

■ For a cash-basis business, when bills arrive, enter payment as postdated transactions, using the date you expect to pay the bills.

■ Accounts payable transactions in an accrual-based business, which usually occur at the end of the year, can be tracked in an Other Liabilities account. When you actually pay the bill, enter the transaction in the account from which you want to pay it, and categorize it as a transfer from the Accounts Payable account. Remember to mark the accounts payable transaction as cleared.

■ Handle accounts receivable in accrual-based businesses by setting up an Other Asset account. Each payable bill should be entered as a transaction in the account; when the payment is received, enter a second transaction offsetting the first, and mark both transactions as cleared.

■ You can record depreciation in several ways. You may wish to have a separate depreciation account for every asset account or have a single depreciation account for all your assets. You could also record each depreciation transaction in the asset account to which it applies. The method you choose depends on how many assets you have, whether they fall into logical groupings for separate accounts, and the amount of detail you require.

■ To set up QuickPay to do your payroll, begin by invoking the Payroll Assistant (from the Main Menu, press T P, for Tutorials/Assistants, Create Payroll Support). Quicken will set up the accounts and categories required for payroll processing. It may be necessary to add or edit accounts or categories, according to the tables in this level and to the deductions unique to your business. Then install QuickPay and enter payroll information on your company in general and on individual employees.

■ If you plan to begin using QuickPay midyear and want Quicken to generate complete payroll data at year's end, take the time to record your year-to-date liabilities for each employee. Create a new bank account named Payroll-YTD Adj, and set up a split transaction containing all the payroll expense categories and accounts to serve as a template for entering each employee's year-to-date totals. Enter these employee totals, and run a Payroll report to verify the amount. Finally, record as single transactions any payments of withholding taxes you've made to government entities on behalf of your employees.

■ To compute and issue the payroll, from the Write Checks screen, press F7 to see the QuickPay Main Menu. One at a time, select each employee to be paid, and enter any information unique to this pay period in the Compute Payroll window. Press Ctrl-Enter to see QuickPay generate the check and the details on deductions and adjustments.

■ QuickPay can help you close out payroll accounts at the end of the year. At the DOS prompt in your Quicken directory, type **QPCLEAR**; then confirm your intention to clear the payroll files.

TERMS

■ With *cash-basis accounting*, all income and expenses are recorded at the time the cash arrives or departs. Checks deposited or cash received count as income; checks written count as expenses on the exact date they transpire. Personal financial management is a form of cash-basis accounting.

■ With *accrual-basis accounting*, you record transactions that have a significant impact on the business, regardless of whether they involve the actual exchange of cash. Orders for your goods may be recorded when they are placed, rather than when you deliver the goods; likewise, bills are recorded when received, not when paid.

■ *Depreciation* represents the useful life of any fixed asset, such as a building or a piece of equipment. Rather than deducting the entire—often significant—cost of such an asset in a single year, depreciation allows you to record the gradual decline in its value as an asset over as many years as you expect to use the item.

■ *QuickPay* is a program produced by Intuit that handles your payroll for you. When you install QuickPay, it becomes an "add-in" to Quicken—you see new QuickPay payroll options and prompts while you're working in Quicken. Once you set up employee and company payroll data, QuickPay efficiently manages the payroll of a modest number of employees.

IMPORTANT IDEAS

■ Although business bookkeeping differs from personal financial management in terms of the quantity and quality of information you must record, Quicken is readily adaptable to these more stringent requirements. The basics of financial management that you learned in this manual cross the boundaries between personal and business needs. Beyond these, Quicken has the capability of handling the special processes involved in business bookkeeping, including: following a chart of accounts; managing finances by job, project, or client; and closing the books at the year's end.

■ Consistency and organization are crucial to using Quicken efficiently in your small business. Use classes to represent clients or projects, so you can report on these items. Set up memorized transactions for vendor and client payments, to ensure that these are entered—and, therefore, reported—consistently.

■ At the end of the year, review your accounts, especially any containing accounts receivable transactions, to make sure that the right information is being included in the current year. Otherwise, you may find you are paying taxes on income that hasn't arrived yet.

Apply Quicken in Any Business Setting

PLAN AHEAD

DECISIONS

Which of Your Business Applications Are Suitable to Quicken?

As you discovered in the previous chapter, many people use Quicken for keeping the books for small businesses—as many as those who use it for personal finance. That's no great surprise—the software is both powerful and straightforward, and its capabilities adequately address the needs of less complex businesses.

What's more provocative is that you can and should use Quicken in any business, regardless of its size or complexity. Of course, we don't recommend keeping the books for General Motors on your PC. On the other hand, the individual managers at GM could find productive uses for Quicken on their desktops. They could productively run all manner of applications, from expense account monitoring to home-brewed ways of viewing their divisions' operating results in formats that are most meaningful to them.

Essentially, Quicken is a simple database, optimized for recording, classifying, and reporting financial transactions and results over varying lengths of time. Paired with a reasonably flexible report writer, it's perfect for many types of applications which have little or nothing to do with personal finance.

Whether you work in a small business or a large one, start thinking more broadly about how you can apply Quicken to your needs. Three general characteristics tend to distinguish an application suitable for Quicken:

■ The operation involves the accumulation of many numeric transactions (money, mileage, hours) over time which need to be added up and summarized in a flexible way.

■ These transactions easily lend themselves to being categorized in one or more meaningful ways, and periodic summaries by category and/or by time could be useful.

■ The transactions and summaries require no more precision than two decimal places.

Literally hundreds of business applications fit these criteria. This level will suggest several of them.

MATERIALS

Forms You'll Need to File

This level addresses a wide range of business applications for Quicken—both formal and informal. Even informal applications are often designed to collect information that is required for filling out forms: expense accounts, tax filings, petty cash reconciliations, and so on.

As you consider Quicken in light of potential business applications, think about the output you need to generate. For what forms will you need to rely on Quicken's output? What kinds of reports will you need?

You should always organize your application around the results you'll need to deliver. If this involves forms, have them on hand and examine them carefully to ensure that you don't inadvertently exclude anything important from the application. For example, you should build a category structure for your application that maps closely onto the blanks on the form.

Business Records for Your Application

If you've previously tracked information manually but now plan to rely on Quicken instead, gather some samples of those manual records. Again, look for natural category structures or class groupings in your data. You can also use data from your manual records to test your Quicken application by verifying that you get the same results.

PRELIMINARIES

Complete Levels 1, 2, and 6

To understand the business applications described in this level, you should have a basic knowledge of Quicken—registers, standard reports, establishing categories, and using split transactions—all the material covered in Levels 1 and 2. You should also have an understanding of classes and be familiar with customizing reports, as described in Level 6.

One of the applications in this level uses Quicken's budgeting feature, which you may wish to review in Level 7. Another application uses a regular investment account; however, only a cursory understanding of investment accounts, described in Level 8, is necessary to use that application.

Understand the Elements

Quicken can be used in any size business—small, medium, or large. That's a pretty bold statement to make about a software program designed for personal finance, but it's quite true. Quicken can be a secret weapon for all business managers.

Although it can't keep all the financial records for a large company, Quicken can create many ancillary reports to aid in decision making and can track whatever you manage in your part of the business. However, applying Quicken to any business requires that we view it in a different light than we have in the previous levels.

A database program and report writer, Quicken is optimized for a single purpose: recording, categorizing, and reporting financial transactions over particular spans of time. The metaphor it employs is a check register, which records a date, check number, payee, amount, category/class information, memo field, and a cleared flag associated with each transaction. These fields can apply just as easily to a number of other applications, as well:

- The DATE field is the principal way that Quicken sorts transactions. This field doesn't have to contain a transaction date, however; it can contain a due date, reminder date, birthdate, and so on.

- The NUM field should contain sequenced numbers—any numbers up to 999,999. Quicken can sort and report transactions by the numbers in this field. It can also contain letters, although it will not sort by them. Though designed for check numbers, this field can contain any sequenced numbers: ticker numbers, vouchers, purchase orders, and so forth.

- The PAYEE field should contain any name, word, or phrase that identifies the transaction. In building your business application, the entries in this field can refer to people, actions, company names—virtually any brief phrase that describes a particular entity or event.

Note. When you enter numbers in the millions, you need to do so without commas.

- The PAYMENT and DEPOSIT fields are actually the same data field with opposite signs; they associate a numeric amount with any transaction. Only one of these fields may be used in any transaction. They can contain numbers up to $9,999,999.99, with two decimal places of precision. You'll need to experiment to see which field you would use under which circumstances to get the sign right for your application. This may depend what your opening balance represents and whether you're increasing or decreasing it. For example, in a mileage log, you start with the present odometer reading and always add to it—all later transactions will appear in the positive column. With a budget log, however, you start with a budget target and subtract expenditures from it, so transactions are recorded as negatives.

- The CLEARED field is a simple on/off or true/false flag. You can use it to designate a completed task, to note when merchandise is received, or to record an expense item submitted on an expense account.

- The MEMO field contains notes on each transaction. It could play a central role in the design of the database if you plan, for example, to filter a report based on its contents.

- The CATEGORY field contains the information Quicken uses to group, subtotal, and summarize the transactions in reports. You can characterize a transaction in two ways at once: by category (and subcategory) and by class (and subclass). The amount may be distributed among many category-and-class combinations using the split transaction window. These categories and classes needn't necessarily be associated with expense and income; they can refer to people, projects, locations, or any other brief way of grouping and summarizing transactions.

Quicken is by no means a generalized database. It won't facilitate mailing lists or parts inventories, nor will it maintain customer complaint records. For these more general business applications, you'll want to rely on products like Paradox or dBASE. So many business applications fit into the check register metaphor, however, that Quicken can earn a place on every manager's workplace PC.

What follows is a sampler of interesting business applications to which you can apply Quicken. We encourage you to adapt these to your own purposes and use them as a springboard for devising more.

Expense Account Monitor

Maria Lombardi frequently travels for work, so she files expense account forms every week or two. Because she bills back some of her expenses to her firm's clients, she needs to file her expenses not only by type of expense (air fare, hotel, and meals), but also by client and project number.

As a Quicken user at home, Maria's instinct led her to turn to Quicken to build an expense account tracking application. Her categories corresponded to the types required by the company's expense account forms; she also created classes corresponding to each client and project number.

Maria had to decide whether to build this application as an entirely new and separate Quicken file or to integrate her expense account into her personal financial management process. The former method offered the advantage of being functional on her office desktop PC, and also allowed her to apply Quicken's reconciliation process to match reimbursements with expenditures. On the other hand, this same method required that she enter

Note. Quicken does not distinguish between classes and subclasses in the Class list. You can use any class in the list as a subclass by simply placing it after another class and separating them with a colon.

transactions twice—once as part of the expense accounting process and once when she enters the checks and charges in her personal accounts.

Because it would save so much time, Maria opted for the integrated approach and took three actions to modify her personal Quicken files to accommodate it:

■ First, she created a category called Business (with the description Reimbursable Business Exp) and subcategories corresponding to each of the types she needed to file as part of her expense account. Figure 12.1 shows how her category structure looked after she was finished.

Figure 12.1   **Category structure for expense account monitor**

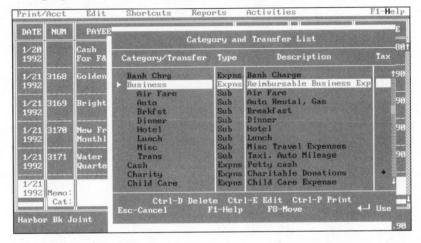

■ Second, she created classes for each of her clients (Ctrl-L) and subclasses under each client for the project numbers she'd be using (as in Figure 12.2).

■ Finally, she set up a separate cash account to track business cash expenses.

Note. If you plan to use categories, subcategories, classes, and subclasses, you should abbreviate the names so the combined number of characters in the Category field (including punctuation) does not exceed 31.

When she returns from each trip, Maria gathers the receipts and cash notes and enters the transactions in the appropriate registers: her credit card expenditures in her American Express account and her cash expenditures in the cash account. When she needs to record notes on business purpose and attendees for each meal expense, she either uses the MEMO field or, if she needs more space, enters notes into the Split Transaction window (even though the transaction amount doesn't need splitting). She categorizes each expense using the categories, subcategories, classes, and subclasses set up for her expense accounts. Figure 12.3 shows sample transactions from her credit card account.

Figure 12.2   Class structure for expense account monitor

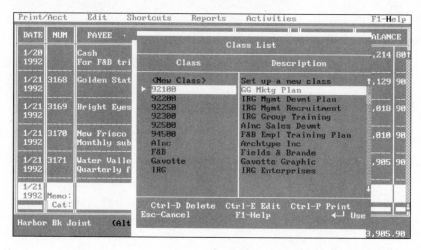

Figure 12.3   Credit card account transactions

DATE	REF	PAYEE · MEMO · CATEGORY	CHARGE		C	PAYMENT	BALANCE	
1/22 1992		American Airlines / Business:Air F→	172	67			172	67↑
1/25 1992		Riley's Wharf / Dinner with Ale→Business:Dinne→	75	00			247	67
1/26 1992	SPLIT	Wings Dining Room / Lunch, F&B staf→Business:Lunch→	61	00			308	67
1/26 1992		Cantina Frittata / Business:Dinne→	30	00			338	67
1/27 1992		AmericEast Hotel NYC / Business:Hotel→	425	10			763	77
1 /28 1992	Memo: / Cat:							

Amex
Esc-Main Menu   (Alt+letter accesses menu)   Ctrl↵ Record   Ending Balance: $763.77

Maria uses two types of memorized reports with her expense account application: an expense account transaction report and an expense account summary. The Expense Account Transaction report (press Alt-R T, for Reports menu, Transaction report) aids her in filling out expense reports. This filtered transaction report (F9) reveals the category Business and its subcategories with classes in the column headings; it is applied across all

Maria's accounts (see Figure 12.4). Each time she fills out an expense report, Maria runs this report for the date covered by her filing and uses it to complete the forms. She keeps the report and matches it against the reimbursement check she receives from the company.

Figure 12.4 **Expense Account Transaction report**

```
 File/Print    Edit    Layout    Reports    Activities              F1-Help

                         TRANSACTION REPORT

                     1/22/92 Through 1/29/92
 FIELDING-All Accounts
 2/ 5/92

  Date   Acct    Num    Description      Memo         Category     Clr Amount


  1/22 Amex              American Airline              Business:Air Far   -172.67
  1/25 Amex              Riley's Wharf    Dinner with  Business:Dinner/    -75.00
  1/26 Amex           S  Wings Dining Roo Andy Griswo  Business:Lunch/F    -61.00
  1/26 Amex              Cantina Frittata              Business:Dinner/    -30.00
  1/27 Amex              AmericEast Hotel              Business:Hotel/F   -425.10
  1/25 Cash Pur          Taxi fare        To airport   Business:Trans/F    -25.00
  1/25 Cash Pur          Taxi fare        To hotel     Business:Trans/F    -32.00
  1/25 Cash Pur          Housekeeping     Laundry      Business:Misc/F&     -3.00
  1/26 Cash Pur          Taxi fare        To hotel     Business:Trans/F    -10.00
  1/26 Cash Pur          Taxi fare        To F&B via   Business:Trans/F    -10.00
  1/26 Cash Pur          Rosie's                       Business:Brkfst/    -12.00

 FIELDING-Amex                                                  (Filtered)
 Esc-Leave report
```

"S" denotes a split transaction

The Expense Account Summary report (press Alt-R S, for Reports menu, Summary) gives Maria an overview of how her expense dollars were distributed. This is a summary report, filtered again to match the category Business and applied across all Maria's accounts. She memorized the report (Ctrl-M) in a format that places classes (clients and project codes) as column headings, and categories (expense types) as row headings, using settings on the Layout menu (Alt-L). A sample is shown in Figure 12.5.

Maria can instantly modify the summary report to show expenditures by month for each client (using Alt-E and Alt-L), as in Figure 12.6.

Finally, she can instantly obtain the detail behind any number in the report by using the cursor keys to highlight any cell, and then using the QuickZoom command (Ctrl-Z). Figure 12.7 shows a sample of such detail.

Automobile Mileage Log

When Dale Scott started his job as a commissioned sales representative, his car started doing double duty as personal and business transportation. That's when he started tracking both mileage and expenses associated with maintaining his car.

Figure 12.5   Expense Account Summary report

Category Description	Archtype Inc AInc Sales Dev	Archtype Inc TOTAL
INCOME/EXPENSE		
EXPENSES		
Reimbursable Business Exp:		
Air Fare	0.00	0.00
Breakfast	0.00	0.00
Dinner	0.00	0.00
Hotel	0.00	0.00
Lunch	0.00	0.00
Misc Travel Expenses	0.00	0.00
Taxi, Auto Mileage	12.50	12.50
Total Reimbursable Business Exp	12.50	12.50
TOTAL EXPENSES	12.50	12.50
TOTAL INCOME/EXPENSE	-12.50	-12.50

	Fields & Brand F&B Empl Train	Fields & Brand TOTAL	OVERALL TOTAL
	172.67	172.67	172.67
	23.00	23.00	23.00
	105.00	105.00	105.00
	425.10	425.10	425.10
	61.00	61.00	61.00
	3.00	3.00	3.00
	142.00	142.00	154.50
	931.77	931.77	944.27

Note. From the Quicken Main Menu, pressing Ctrl-G (Go to) will take you directly to the Select File menu, from which you can choose <Create New File>.

Keeping track of the expenses was easy, since Dale had already begun using Quicken to record all his spending. What was new to Dale, though, was maintaining the kind of mileage log required by the tax authorities to justify deducting the business portion of his car expenses.

Dale's friends advised him to buy a spreadsheet, but Dale suspected that that would be overkill. When he recognized the similarities between tracking and classifying mileage and tracking and classifying his spending, Dale decided to apply Quicken to the problem.

Wishing to avoid confusing mileage and money records, Dale started a new Quicken file for the mileage log. To do this, he moved to the Quicken Main Menu (by pressing Escape repeatedly to see it), and then he typed **T F** (Use Tutorials and Assistants, Create New File). He created a file called CARMILES containing no default categories. He then set up a cash account called Mileage and entered his current odometer reading as the starting balance of the account.

Figure 12.6   Expense Account Summary report by the month for each client

```
                              SUMMARY REPORT BY MONTH
                              12/ 1/91 Through 1/31/92
          FIELDING-All Accounts                                     Page 1
          2/10/92
                                                             OVERALL
                    Class Description      12/91      1/92    TOTAL

          Archtype Inc:
            AInc Sales Devmt              -895.70   -702.95  -1,598.65

          Total Archtype Inc             -895.70   -702.95  -1,598.65
          Fields & Brande:
            F&B Empl Training Plan           0.00   -931.77   -931.77

          Total Fields & Brande             0.00   -931.77   -931.77
          Gavotte Graphic:
            GG Mktg Plan                  -450.50   -677.61  -1,128.11

          Total Gavotte Graphic          -450.50   -677.61  -1,128.11
          IRG Enterprises:
            IRG Mgmt Recruitment          -58.00      0.00    -58.00

          Total IRG Enterprises           -58.00      0.00    -58.00

          OVERALL TOTAL                 -1,404.20 -2,312.33  -3,716.53
```

Figure 12.7   Transaction Detail window

```
 File/Print    Edit    Layout    Reports    Activities        F1-Help
                        SUMMARY REPORT BY MONTH
                        12/ 1/91 Through 1/31/92
F
                          Transaction List
                                                                    L
       Date     Num      Desc         Cat        Clr    Amount
    ▸ 1/22/92          American Airlin Business:Air F       -172.67 ↑
      1/25/92          Riley's Wharf   Business:Dinne        -75.00
      1/26/92    S 1338                Business:Lunch        -61.00
      1/26/92          Cantina Frittat Business:Dinne        -38.00 .65
      1/27/92          AmericEast Hote Business:Hotel       -425.10
      1/25/92          Taxi fare       Business:Trans        -25.00
      1/25/92          Taxi fare       Business:Trans        -32.00
      1/25/92          Housekeeping    Business:Misc/         -3.00 .77
      1/26/92          Taxi fare       Business:Trans        -10.00
      1/26/92          Taxi fare       Business:Trans        -10.00 ↓
                        ↑,↓ Select                                  .11
 Esc-Cancel                              F9-Go to register
                                                             tered)
```

Dale set up two income categories for the CARMILES file: Business and Personal. He also set up several subcategories under Business, representing the types of sales calls he makes (Prospect, Selling, Maintenance, Other). Later, he thought to set up classes representing his major accounts.

Dale keeps a paper log in his car in which he records the date, mileage, and business purpose of each business trip. Whenever he fires up his PC to enter his income and expenses into Quicken, he also transfers his mileage log into the CARMILES file, comparing the BALANCE column to the odometer to make sure he hasn't forgotten any trips. Figure 12.8 shows the register for Dale's Mileage account.

Figure 12.8   Mileage log

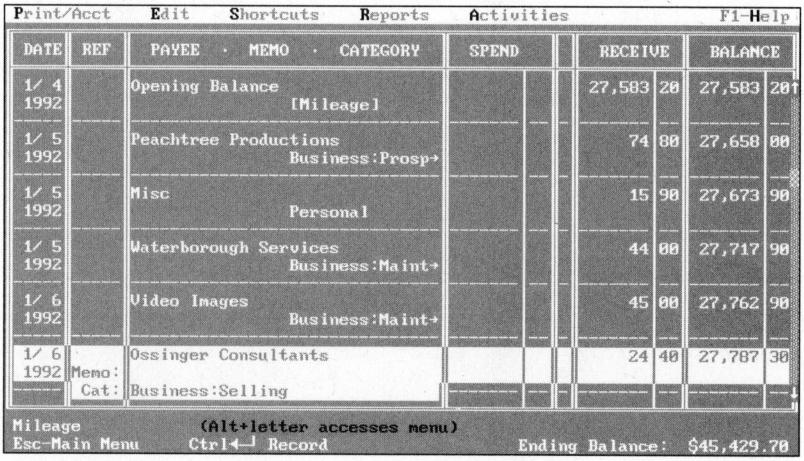

```
 Print/Acct    Edit    Shortcuts    Reports    Activities          F1-Help
┌──────┬─────┬─────────────────────────────────┬────────┬─────────┬──────────┐
│ DATE │ REF │ PAYEE  ·  MEMO  ·  CATEGORY      │ SPEND  │ RECEIVE │ BALANCE  │
├──────┼─────┼─────────────────────────────────┼────────┼─────────┼──────────┤
│ 1/ 4 │     │Opening Balance                  │        │27,583 20│27,583 20↑│
│ 1992 │     │             [Mileage]           │        │         │          │
│ 1/ 5 │     │Peachtree Productions            │        │   74 80 │27,658 00 │
│ 1992 │     │             Business:Prosp→     │        │         │          │
│ 1/ 5 │     │Misc                             │        │   15 90 │27,673 90 │
│ 1992 │     │             Personal            │        │         │          │
│ 1/ 5 │     │Waterborough Services            │        │   44 00 │27,717 90 │
│ 1992 │     │             Business:Maint→     │        │         │          │
│ 1/ 6 │     │Video Images                     │        │   45 00 │27,762 90 │
│ 1992 │     │             Business:Maint→     │        │         │          │
│ 1/ 6 │Memo:│Ossinger Consultants             │        │   24 40 │27,787 30 │
│ 1992 │ Cat:│Business:Selling                 │        │         │          │
└──────┴─────┴─────────────────────────────────┴────────┴─────────┴──────────┘
 Mileage                (Alt+letter accesses menu)
 Esc-Main Menu      Ctrl◄┘ Record                 Ending Balance:  $45,429.70
```

To fulfill the documentation requirements for his tax return at the end of the year, Dale created a Transaction report (Alt-R T, for Reports menu, Transaction report), listing each of his business-related car trips, by applying a filter (F9) to match only those transactions categorized as Business (see Figure 12.9).

In addition, Dale prepared an unfiltered summary report for the account showing his business and personal car mileage for the year (see Figure 12.10); he used this report and the Quicken Calculator (Ctrl-O) to determine the business-related percentage of his travel and therefore what percentage of his expenses were deductible.

Figure 12.9   Mileage Log Transaction report

```
 File/Print    Edit    Layout     Reports     Activities              F1-Help
                              TRANSACTION REPORT
                           1/ 1/92 Through 2/ 1/92
 CARMILES-Mileage
 2/ 5/92

  Date    Num      Description        Memo         Category      Clr  Amount

  1/ 5           Peachtree Productio              Business:Prospect     74.80
  1/ 5           Waterborough Servic              Business:Maintena     44.00
  1/ 6           Video Images                     Business:Maintena     45.00
  1/ 6           Ossinger Consultant              Business:Selling      24.40
  1/ 6           Burnham Productions              Business:Prospect     18.20
  1/11           Peachtree Productio              Business:Prospect     71.20
  1/11           Video Artisans                   Business:Selling      11.80
  1/11           Business Graphicals              Business:Prospect      8.80
  1/12           State University                 Business:Selling      74.30
  1/12           Burnham Productions              Business:Selling      18.40
  1/13           Waterborough Servic              Business:Maintena     38.30

 CARMILES-Mileage                                                   (Filtered)
 Esc-Leave report
```

Figure 12.10   Mileage Log Summary report

```
                              Car Mileage 1992
                          1/ 1/92 Through 12/31/92
   CARMILES-Mileage                                                  Page 1
   1/ 1/93
                                                1/ 1/92-
                    Category Description        12/31/92

                    INCOME/EXPENSE
                     INCOME
                       Business:
                         Maintenance         3,117.50
                         Other                 272.40
                         Prospect            4,410.50
                         Selling             5,970.80

                         Total Business                 13,771.20
                         Personal                        4,075.30

                     TOTAL INCOME                       17,846.50


                    TOTAL INCOME/EXPENSE                17,846.50

                    BALANCE FORWARD
                      Mileage                           27,583.20

                    TOTAL BALANCE FORWARD               27,583.20


                    OVERALL TOTAL                       45,429.70
```

Executive Information System

Larry Milner was upset when his company's MIS department told him that they couldn't create the reports he had requested for another three months. Larry wanted to take the monthly divisional operating statements he received each month and view the financial status of his division over different time periods, comparing them to last year's expenses and by product line. And now MIS was insisting it would take three man-months and $20,000 of programming to do the job.

As a Quicken user, Larry had an alternative. He installed Quicken on his assistant's PC and created a new file called COMPANY and a cash account named Op report with a starting balance of zero. He created a category structure which reflected the income and expense line items on the operating statements, and then set up classes which represented the different product lines on the reports.

Larry gave his assistant a year's worth of operating reports and asked him to enter transactions into the Op Report register corresponding to the monthly income and spending amounts listed on the operating reports for each product line. He also asked him to record the appropriate category and product line (class) for each transaction. Larry's assistant recorded income in the RECEIVE column and expenses in the SPEND column, as shown in Figure 12.11.

Figure 12.11   Op Report Account register

DATE	REF	PAYEE · MEMO · CATEGORY	SPEND		RECEIVE		BALANCE	
1/31 1991		Jan Revenue Product R Sales Revenue/→			41,644	00	101,535	00↑
1/31 1991		Jan Revenue Product T Sales Revenue/→			25,474	00	127,009	00
1/31 1991		Jan Salaries Product C Salaries/Produ→	13,212	00			113,797	00
1/31 1991		Jan Commissions Product C Commissions/Pr→	1,350	00			112,447	00
1/31 1991		Jan Selling Product C Selling/Produc→	1,840	00			110,607	00
1/31 1991	Memo: Cat:	Jan T&E Product C T&E/Product C	2,486	00			108,121	00

Print/Acct   Edit   Shortcuts   Reports   Activities   F1-Help

Op Report   (Alt+letter accesses menu)
Esc-Main Menu   Ctrl←┘ Record   Ending Balance: $106,275.00

Once these amounts were entered, a plethora of new report options became available. Larry could now group products, months, and line items together at will, without waiting for mainframe programmers to deliver the goods. His favorite monthly report was the Business Unit Profitability report, a standard Job/Project report (Alt-R B J, for Reports menu, Business reports, Job/Project report) which reported class (product line) in the columns, as in Figure 12.12.

The bottom line, though, was that with Quicken Larry had the flexibility of looking at his operating data from many angles—without a lot of professional programming. After using this system for awhile, Larry decided to enter his division's monthly budget into the application to obtain even more useful reports.

Figure 12.12   Business Unit Profitability report

```
                              JOB/PROJECT REPORT
                             1/ 1/92 Through 1/31/92
COMPANY-Op Report                                                      Page 1
2/10/92


  Category Description      Product C        Product H        Product R

INCOME/EXPENSE
  INCOME
    Sales Revenue           38,229.00        18,378.00        58,628.00

  TOTAL INCOME              38,229.00        18,378.00        58,628.00

  EXPENSES
    Capital Equip            2,100.00         3,005.00             0.00
    Commissions              2,600.00         1,010.00         4,800.00
    Equip Repair               850.00             0.00         1,730.00
    Postage                    220.00           375.00         1,700.00
    Salaries                14,900.00        13,100.00        21,450.00
    Selling                  7,400.00         3,010.00         8,590.00
    Shipping                 2,718.00         1,919.00         3,500.00
    T&E                      3,491.00         3,670.00         4,120.00
    Training                   350.00         5,450.00         1,835.00

  TOTAL EXPENSES            34,629.00        31,539.00        47,725.00


TOTAL INCOME/EXPENSE         3,600.00       -13,161.00        10,903.00


                                                             OVERALL
                                             Product T         TOTAL


                                            32,919.00       148,154.00

                                            32,919.00       148,154.00


                                               800.00         5,905.00
                                             2,900.00        11,310.00
                                               690.00         3,270.00
                                             1,400.00         3,695.00
                                            19,055.00        68,505.00
                                             2,080.00        21,080.00
                                             1,360.00         9,497.00
                                             3,305.00        14,586.00
                                               350.00         7,985.00

                                            31,940.00       145,833.00
```

Petty Cash Log

Susan Milner was given responsibility for the Petty Cash account of the branch office in which she worked. She needed to keep a detailed log of how the money was distributed and also wanted to know when she should ask for more cash from the finance department at headquarters. She decided to use Quicken to help with the task.

Susan installed Quicken on her office PC and created PETTYCSH, a new file with a single new cash account, Petty Cash. She set up a category structure consistent with her company's chart of accounts which included all those expense items for which she would be distributing petty cash: office supplies, postage and shipping, travel and entertainment, and miscellaneous expenses (she even put the chart of account numbers in the description fields of each category). She also added an income category for petty cash receipts to record deposits of petty cash from headquarters. (See the category structure in Figure 12.13.) Susan built in two classes—one for each of the business units which operated out of the branch office.

When she receives an infusion of petty cash from headquarters, Susan records a transaction as an INCREASE transaction under the Petty Cash Receipts category. She enters each expense with its chart of accounts designation (category) and business unit (class). Figure 12.14 shows the register for this account.

Figure 12.13   Petty cash category structure

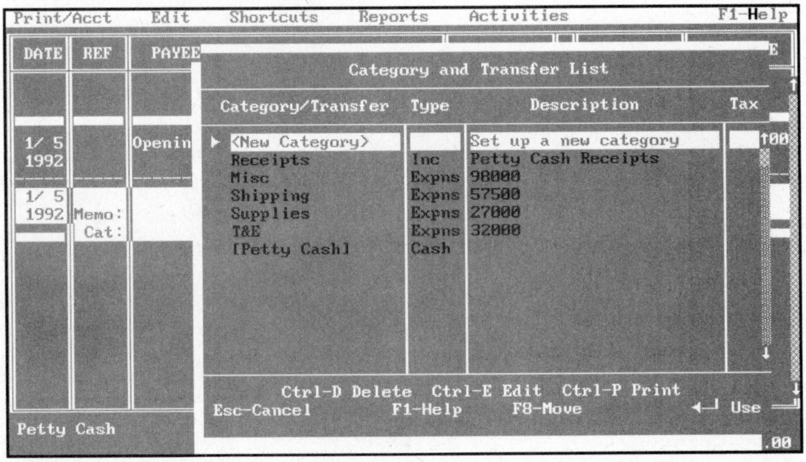

At the end of each month, Susan submits a standard transaction report (Alt-R T) on only the Petty Cash account, showing all petty cash transactions made during the month. Figure 12.15 shows this report.

Figure 12.14   Petty Cash register

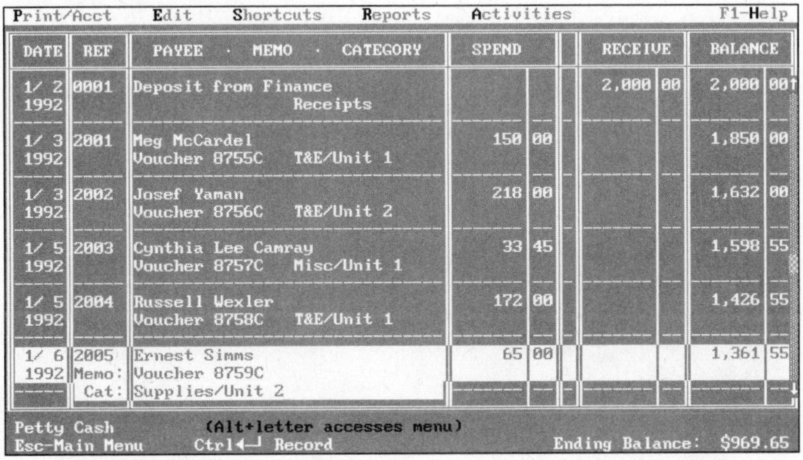

```
Print/Acct    Edit    Shortcuts    Reports    Activities              F1-Help
┌──────┬─────────────────────────────────┬──────────┬──────────┬──────────┐
│ DATE │ REF │ PAYEE · MEMO · CATEGORY   │  SPEND   │ RECEIVE  │ BALANCE  │
├──────┼─────┼───────────────────────────┼──────────┼──────────┼──────────┤
│ 1/ 2 │0001 │Deposit from Finance       │          │ 2,000 00 │ 2,000 00↑│
│ 1992 │     │            Receipts       │          │          │          │
│ 1/ 3 │2001 │Meg McCardel               │  150 00  │          │ 1,850 00 │
│ 1992 │     │Voucher 8755C   T&E/Unit 1 │          │          │          │
│ 1/ 3 │2002 │Josef Yaman                │  218 00  │          │ 1,632 00 │
│ 1992 │     │Voucher 8756C   T&E/Unit 2 │          │          │          │
│ 1/ 5 │2003 │Cynthia Lee Camray         │   33 45  │          │ 1,598 55 │
│ 1992 │     │Voucher 8757C   Misc/Unit 1│          │          │          │
│ 1/ 5 │2004 │Russell Wexler             │  172 00  │          │ 1,426 55 │
│ 1992 │     │Voucher 8758C   T&E/Unit 1 │          │          │          │
│ 1/ 6 │2005 │Ernest Simms               │   65 00  │          │ 1,361 55 │
│ 1992 │Memo:│Voucher 8759C              │          │          │          │
│      │ Cat:│Supplies/Unit 2            │          │          │          │
└──────┴─────┴───────────────────────────┴──────────┴──────────┴──────────┘
Petty Cash          (Alt+letter accesses menu)
Esc-Main Menu    Ctrl◄─┘ Record                      Ending Balance:  $969.65
```

Figure 12.15   Petty Cash Transaction report

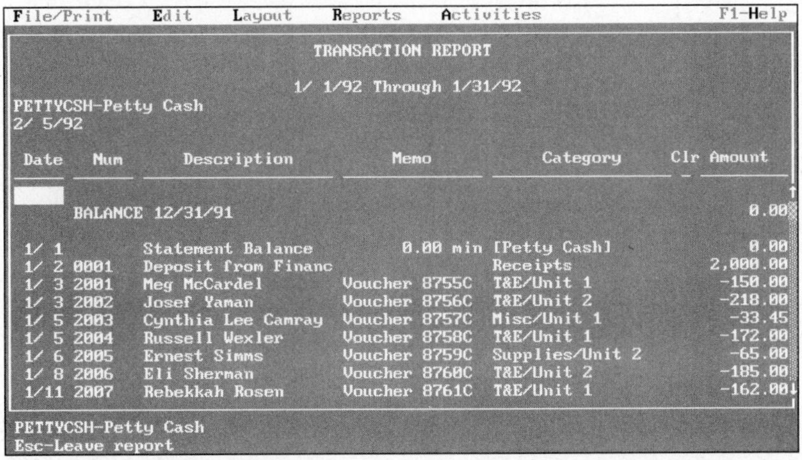

```
File/Print    Edit    Layout    Reports    Activities              F1-Help
                          TRANSACTION REPORT
                        1/ 1/92 Through 1/31/92
PETTYCSH-Petty Cash
2/ 5/92

Date   Num      Description       Memo          Category     Clr Amount

              BALANCE 12/31/91                                       0.00
1/ 1          Statement Balance   0.00 min  [Petty Cash]            0.00
1/ 2  0001    Deposit from Financ           Receipts           2,000.00
1/ 3  2001    Meg McCardel        Voucher 8755C  T&E/Unit 1     -150.00
1/ 3  2002    Josef Yaman         Voucher 8756C  T&E/Unit 2     -218.00
1/ 5  2003    Cynthia Lee Camray  Voucher 8757C  Misc/Unit 1     -33.45
1/ 5  2004    Russell Wexler      Voucher 8758C  T&E/Unit 1     -172.00
1/ 6  2005    Ernest Simms        Voucher 8759C  Supplies/Unit 2  -65.00
1/ 8  2006    Eli Sherman         Voucher 8760C  T&E/Unit 2     -185.00
1/11  2007    Rebekkah Rosen      Voucher 8761C  T&E/Unit 1     -162.00↓

PETTYCSH-Petty Cash
Esc-Leave report
```

In addition, Susan adapted the Standard Cash Flow report (Alt-R B C, for Reports menu, Business Reports, Cash Flow report) to display business units (classes) as column headings (see Figure 12.16). This summary report was then used by the accounting department to make the appropriate journal entries into the company's books.

Figure 12.16   **Cash Flow report showing petty cash by class**

```
 File/Print    Edit    Layout    Reports    Activities              F1-Help

                              Cash Flow Report
                          1/ 1/92 Through 1/31/92
 PETTYCSH-Petty Cash
 2/ 5/92
                                                                        OVE
 Category Description      Unit 1       Unit 2       Other              T

 INFLOWS
   Petty Cash Receipts      0.00         0.00      2,000.00          2,00

 TOTAL INFLOWS              0.00         0.00      2,000.00          2,00

 OUTFLOWS
   27000                    0.00        65.00         0.00             6
   32000                  484.00       403.00         0.00            88
   57500                    0.00        44.90         0.00             4
   98000                   33.45         0.00         0.00             3


 PETTYCSH-Petty Cash
 Esc-Leave report
```

Capital Budget and Purchase Order Monitor

Note. Quicken's budget reports allow for detailed budgeting by category only, not by class. If you'll be using both categories and classes, you should use the budget classifications you'll most frequently want to compare to actual spending as the categories.

Luke Fielding's company had been watching its cash flow very carefully and had instituted new guidelines for capital spending. Luke was given a capital spending budget that was detailed by type of equipment, project, and fiscal quarter. Luke was faced with a substantial tracking burden, since the capital budget would actually be spent with many dozens of purchase orders during the course of each quarter. The accounting department couldn't provide timely enough data to affect spending decisions, so Luke decided to set up a capital budget monitoring application in Quicken.

Luke created a new file called CAPITAL and a bank account called Cap Spending with an opening balance of zero. He also created a category structure corresponding to the project names and a class structure which reflected the equipment types.

At the beginning of the fiscal year, Luke located the budget screen while viewing the Capspend register by pressing Alt-A B (Activities menu, Set Up Budgets). He entered the quarterly, project-by-project budget amounts, as shown in Figure 12.17. He also entered into the register a deposit transaction representing the first quarter's total capital spending allotment.

Figure 12.17   Capital spending budget

Category Description	Jan.	Feb.	Mar.	Apr.	May	Ju
INFLOWS						
FROM Cap Spending-Cap	31,000	0	0	15,000	0	
TOTAL INFLOWS	31,000	0	0	15,000	0	
OUTFLOWS						
Project 18R	12,500	0	0	2,000	0	
Project 20H	2,000	0	0	3,500	0	
Project 22A	9,500	0	0	2,000	0	
Project 27B	7,000	0	0	7,500	0	
TO Cap Spending-Capit	0	0	0	0	0	
TOTAL OUTFLOWS	31,000	0	0	15,000	0	
Total Budget Inflows	31,000	0	0	15,000	0	
Total Budget Outflows	31,000	0	0	15,000	0	
Difference	0	0	0	0	0	

File   Edit   Layout   Activities   F1-Help

CAPITAL-Cap Spending

Whenever his business unit created a purchase order for a piece of equipment, Luke entered a transaction that described the P.O.—its date and number, an equipment description, and the project (category) and equipment type (class) appropriate to the purchase. When equipment arrived, Luke marked the C (cleared) column to indicate that the purchase request had been fulfilled. The BALANCE column gave a running total for all classes of purchases against the total figure for the quarter. Figure 12.18 shows the account register with fulfilled purchase orders marked as cleared.

At the start of the next quarter, Luke entered another deposit showing the capital budget for this period, against which he entered purchase order transactions. His company's finance department allowed him to roll over any budget balance from one quarter to the next, so he didn't zero out any balance from the previous quarter. However, any budget dollars unspent at the end of the fiscal year would be lost, at which point he will enter an equivalent debit transaction zeroing out the BALANCE column. He can then use the same register for the next fiscal year.

Luke used a number of different reports to track his capital spending against his budget. His principal report was the Budget report (Alt-R U, for Reports menu, Budget report), which showed year-to-date spending against the budget for each project, as shown in Figure 12.19. To see only the current quarter's results, he specified the quarter as the time period and modified the report to show quarters as column headings.

Luke also customized a transaction report to show only unfilled purchase orders. To do this, he filtered the transaction report (F9) to show only uncleared payment transactions, as in Figure 12.20.

Figure 12.18   Purchase orders listed in account register

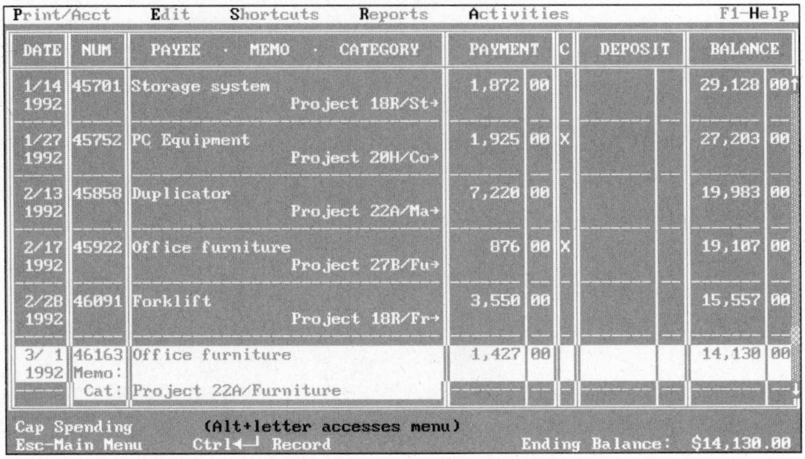

```
 Print/Acct    Edit    Shortcuts    Reports    Activities           F1-Help
┌──────┬──────┬──────────────────────────────┬─────────┬──┬─────────┬──────────┐
│ DATE │ NUM  │ PAYEE · MEMO · CATEGORY       │ PAYMENT │C │ DEPOSIT │ BALANCE  │
├──────┼──────┼──────────────────────────────┼─────────┼──┼─────────┼──────────┤
│ 1/14 │45701 │Storage system                 │ 1,872 00│  │         │ 29,128 00↑│
│ 1992 │      │            Project 18R/St→    │         │  │         │          │
│ 1/27 │45752 │PC Equipment                   │ 1,925 00│X │         │ 27,203 00│
│ 1992 │      │            Project 20H/Co→    │         │  │         │          │
│ 2/13 │45858 │Duplicator                     │ 7,220 00│  │         │ 19,983 00│
│ 1992 │      │            Project 22A/Ma→    │         │  │         │          │
│ 2/17 │45922 │Office furniture               │   876 00│X │         │ 19,107 00│
│ 1992 │      │            Project 27B/Fu→    │         │  │         │          │
│ 2/28 │46091 │Forklift                       │ 3,550 00│  │         │ 15,557 00│
│ 1992 │      │            Project 18R/Fr→    │         │  │         │          │
│ 3/ 1 │46163 │Office furniture               │ 1,427 00│  │         │ 14,130 00│
│ 1992 │Memo: │                               │         │  │         │          │
│      │ Cat: │Project 22A/Furniture          │         │  │         │          │
└──────┴──────┴──────────────────────────────┴─────────┴──┴─────────┴──────────┘
 Cap Spending         (Alt+letter accesses menu)
 Esc-Main Menu    Ctrl◄─┘ Record                   Ending Balance:  $14,130.00
```

Figure 12.19   Year-to-Date Budget report

```
 File/Print    Edit    Layout    Reports    Activities           F1-Help
                       Year-to-Date Budget Report

                    1/ 1/92 Through 3/ 1/92
              CAPITAL-Cap Spending
              3/ 1/92
                                      1/ 1/92    -       3/ 1/92
              Category Description    Actual     Budget  Diff

              INCOME/EXPENSE
                EXPENSES
                  Project 18R         5,422     12,500    -7,078
                  Project 20H         1,925      2,000       -75
                  Project 22A         8,647      9,500      -853
                  Project 27B           876      7,000    -6,124

                TOTAL EXPENSES       16,870     31,000   -14,130


                TOTAL INCOME/EXPENSE -16,870    -31,000    14,130

 CAPITAL-Cap Spending
 Esc-Leave report
```

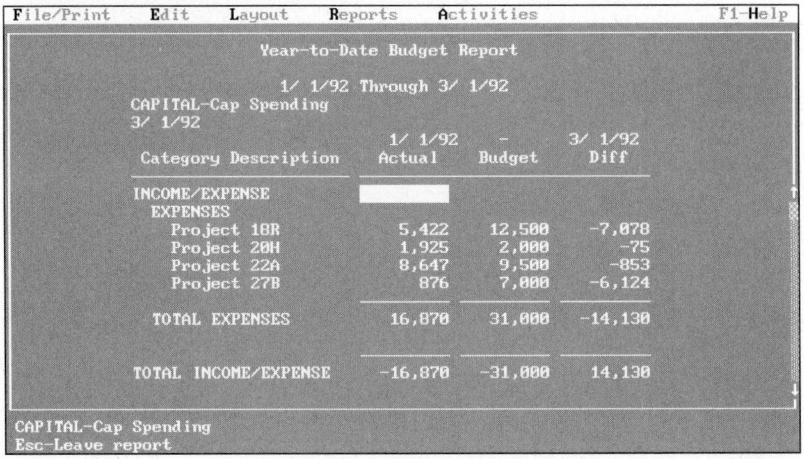

Figure 12.20 **Transaction report showing uncleared payment transactions**

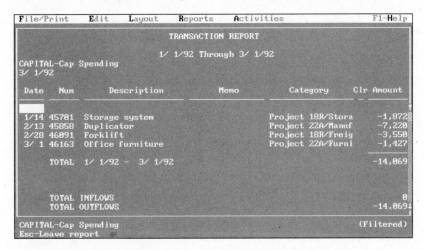

Employee Total Compensation Monitor

As general manager of a large division of a quickly growing company, Larry Milner had many employees who were benefitting from both incentive compensation and stock option plans in addition to their base salaries. Larry wasn't always certain what the effective total compensation for each employee was, especially regarding stock options. Although he wanted to preserve fairness across his management group and to stay within the bounds of reason in structuring the total compensation package for each employee, he didn't think he had all the information he needed to evaluate his compensation plans. Not surprisingly, Larry turned to Quicken for help in monitoring the total compensation of his management group.

To start building a total compensation monitoring application, Larry created a new file named COMPENS and a separate regular investment account for each manager whose compensation he wanted to track. For example, he opened an account named Bennett in which to gather compensation data on his operations manager, Paula Bennett.

The first transaction in a regular investment account must be a ShrsIn transaction (which adds shares to the account) or XIn transaction (which transfers cash into the account). To start Paula's account, Larry generated an XIn transaction in the amount of zero, transferred *from the same account,* entering **[Bennett]** in the Category field. This satisfied the requirement without actually transferring cash from another account.

Since he would be generating reports for time periods no shorter than quarters, Larry entered Paula's base salary for 1992 as four quarterly MiscInc

Note. Larry used investment accounts because he'd be tracking the value of options to his key employees. If no securities had been involved, he could have used a bank account instead.

(miscellaneous income) transactions, categorizing them under the expense category, Salary. He memorized the quarterly transaction to render this repetitious entry process painless. Larry remembered to include an estimate of the midyear salary increase he expected Paula to receive. He then repeated the process for the last couple of years' historic salary data.

Next, Larry entered the bonus he expected to give Paula at the end of the year—again, as a MiscInc transaction postdated to the end of the year. He noted in the Memo field that this was only an estimate and dated the estimate.

Finally, Larry entered ShrsIn transactions for each of the vesting dates of Paula's stock options—500 shares each quarter, representing the 2,000 options she'd been granted to vest in each of the next four years. For the security name, he used "Mitsou 9/91," for company stock options granted in September of 1991. For the stock symbol, he used MITS (the ticker symbol of the company). The option price granted to Paula was $35.

Whenever Paula exercised her options, Larry entered a Sell transaction for each set of options exercised, entering the market value on the day of exercise (as in Figure 12.21). This records as a capital gain the value Paula realized from exercising the option at a market value higher than the exercise price.

Figure 12.21   Register showing exercised options

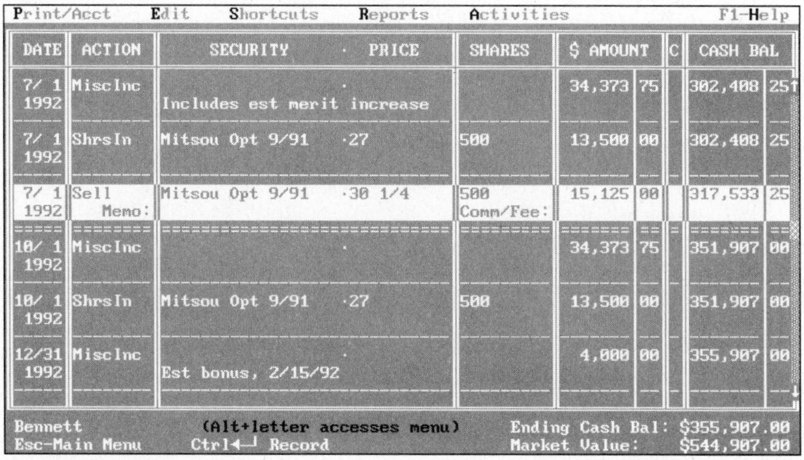

Larry employed several types of reports with this application. The one he most often referred to was a custom summary report (Alt-R S, for Reports menu, Summary) that he devised to see the annual compensation of all his managers (shown in Figure 12.22). This report displayed categories—salary, bonus, capital gains, and unrealized capital gains—as row headings and accounts (one for each employee) as column headings. He included unrealized capital gains by pressing Alt-L O (Layout menu, Other Options), then typing **Y** next to "Include unrealized gains." Before using this report, he updated the option price to reflect the stock's current value (Ctrl-U) and specified the entire calendar year as the time frame for the report.

Figure 12.22 Compensation Summary report

File/Print Edit Layout Reports Activities F1-Help

SUMMARY REPORT BY ACCOUNT
(Includes unrealized gains)
1/ 1/92 Through 12/31/92

COMPENS-All Accounts
7/ 2/92

Category Description	Bennett	Carrigan	Dali
INCOME/EXPENSE			
INCOME			
Bonus	4,000.00	3,500.00	3,000.00
Realized Gain/Loss	4,062.50	2,437.50	975.00
Salary	133,058.00	114,980.00	134,650.00
Unrealized Gain/Loss	2,437.50	2,437.50	4,387.50
TOTAL INCOME	143,558.00	123,355.00	143,012.50
EXPENSES			
Expenses - Other	0.00	0.00	0.00

COMPENS-Bennett
Esc-Leave report

Larry also used the Portfolio Value report (Alt-R I V, for Reports menu, Investment reports, Portfolio Value report), subtotaled by account (employee) to determine the value of each group of options still unexercised by his managers (as shown in Figure 12.23). He excluded cash from the report by filtering it; in the "Security contains" field of the Match Transactions window, he typed two periods (..), telling Quicken to include only transactions specifying a security.

Tickler File

Maria Lombardi needed to create a tickler file to remind her of important things to do, as well as birthdays and other special days. She remembered that Quicken has a reminder function built into its investment accounts. While it's no full-blown personal information manager, Quicken does offer convenient ways to organize reminders.

Figure 12.23   Portfolio Value report showing unexercised options

```
 File/Print    Edit    Layout    Reports    Activities           F1-Help
                    PORTFOLIO VALUE REPORT BY ACCOUNT
 COMPENS-All Investment Accts     As of 12/31/96
 7/ 2/92
                        * Estimated Prices

        Security      Shares   Curr Price   Cost Basis   Gain/Loss   Balance

 Bennett
   Mitsou Opt 9/9  7,000.00      27.    *  189,000.00       0.00   189,000.00

 Total Bennett                            189,000.00       0.00   189,000.00

 Carrigan
   Mitsou Opt 9/9  3,500.00      27.    *   94,500.00       0.00    94,500.00

 Total Carrigan                            94,500.00       0.00    94,500.00

 Dali

 COMPENS-Tsuyama                                                  (Filtered)
 Esc-Leave report
```

Note. A quick key is extremely useful with a reminder account, because it enables you to move instantly to an account without having to press Ctrl-A and highlight the file name. For information on setting up quick keys, see Level 6.

Note. You can dictate how much notice Quicken gives you in advance of due dates. At the Main Menu, type **P R** (Set Preferences, Automatic Reminder Settings).

For this application, Maria wasn't required to set up an entirely new file. Instead, she set up a new investment account called Reminder in her most frequently used Quicken file. When she wants to create a reminder, Maria makes sure she is working in the proper file, presses Ctrl-A (for Account), and chooses Reminder from the account list. She types the due date of the reminder and then Reminder in the Action column. The cursor moves immediately to the Memo field, where she describes the reminder (see Figure 12.24).

As the reminder due date approaches, a notification ("An investment reminder is due") flashes up on the initial screen beneath the Main Menu every time Maria starts Quicken (as in Figure 12.25). She added Billminder to the AUTOEXEC.BAT start-up file for her computer, so the same notice also appears every time she starts her PC. To see today's reminder, she can call up the register for the REMINDER account, and press Ctrl-G T (for Go to, Today), followed by the Enter key.

When she no longer wants to be reminded of something, Maria has two options. She can highlight a reminder transaction and press Ctrl-D (delete) to erase it or, if she wants to maintain a record of the reminder without seeing reminder notices related to it, she can enter an X in the C (cleared) column.

To obtain a list of pending reminders sorted by due date, Maria creates a custom transaction report, restricted to the Reminder account and excluding cleared items (Figure 12.26). To see the entire reminder text, she chooses the Full Column Width option from the Layout menu (Alt-L).

Figure 12.24 Reminder Account register

DATE	ACTION	SECURITY · PRICE	SHARES	$ AMOUNT	C	CASH BAL
2/18 1992	Reminder	· Frank's estimates ready			X	0 00↑
2/27 1992	Reminder	· Photo shoot for new brochure				0 00
3/ 1 1992	Reminder	· Presentation script due				0 00
3/ 8 1992	Reminder	· New savings elections due				0 00
3/15 1992	Reminder	· Closing on new house				0 00
4/26 1992	Reminder Memo:	Folks' 40th anniversary				0 00

```
Print/Acct    Edit    Shortcuts    Reports    Activities                F1-Help
```

```
Reminder            (Alt+letter accesses menu)      Ending Cash Bal: $0.00
Esc-Main Menu       Ctrl◄┘  Record                  Market Value:    $0.00
```

Figure 12.25 Investment reminder notice

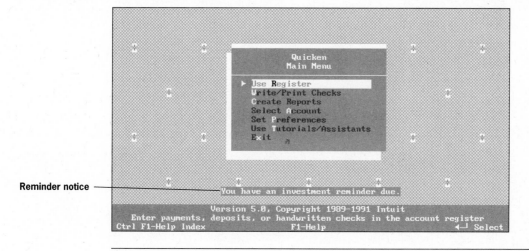

Reminder notice ————

```
                          Quicken
                          Main Menu

              ► Use Register
                Write/Print Checks
                Create Reports
                Select Account
                Set Preferences
                Use Tutorials/Assistants
                Exit
```

You have an investment reminder due.

```
            Version 5.0, Copyright 1989-1991 Intuit
  Enter payments, deposits, or handwritten checks in the account register
Ctrl F1-Help Index              F1-Help                      ◄┘ Select
```

Figure 12.26   Transaction report showing pending reminders

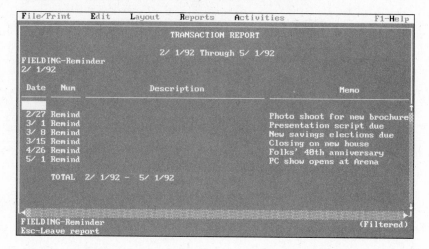

LEVEL 12 BUILDING BLOCKS

In Level 12, you've seen how Quicken lends itself to business applications that are unrelated to strict personal financial management.

IMPORTANT IDEAS

■ Clearly, Quicken is outstanding as a powerful yet flexible tool for personal financial management, but you can also be creative in how you apply the product. *Every* business setting is replete with many opportunities for you to use Quicken.

■ Earlier levels reinforced the techniques, procedures, and concepts that comprise Quicken. As you've seen in this level, the ways in which you can apply those building blocks—categories, classes, registers, accounts, files—have few limitations. If an application involves logs or accumulations of dated or numerical data, if it could benefit from categorization, and if it requires accuracy to only two decimal places, then it may be suitable for Quicken. Avid Quicken users usually become even more efficient by working unusual Quicken applications into their files and accounts.

■ Consider the applications covered in this book as springboards to your own tailored applications. The expense account monitor, mileage log, and petty cash log can be useful models for any routine record-keeping task. Three other sample applications—the executive information system, the capital budget and purchase order monitor, and the employee total compensation monitor—may require a larger investment of time and thought, but the payoff in useful reports and greater efficiency will pay off. Finally, the tickler file is a simple tool that draws on Quicken's ability to note time-sensitive transactions. Examine your business procedures and routines for similar activities that could benefit from Quicken.

■ All the applications described in this level rely on Quicken's useful array of reports to analyze the data you entered in formats compatible with your target use for the data. Whether you'll use the data to complete forms, track progress, or make decisions, reports are essential. It pays to understand techniques for customizing them, so that the data is organized sensibly, the time frame is accurate, and only relevant information is included.

APPENDIX A

Set Up Quicken for Your System

Appendix A supplies detailed information on how to install Quicken and configure it for your hardware. The installation of QuickPay is also covered.

Understand What Quicken Requires of Your Computer System

Prerequisites

Quicken requires that you have the following:

- An IBM PC, XT, AT, or PS/2 computer, or 100 percent compatible computer, with a hard disk or two floppy disk drives. We strongly recommend that you run Quicken from your hard disk. (If you are planning to install Quicken on floppy disks, one of the two disk drives must be a high-density 5 ¼" drive or 3 ½" drive.)

- DOS 2.0 or later.

- A minimum of 512k RAM under DOS 3.0 or later DOS versions (448k RAM for DOS 2.x).

- An 80-column monochrome or color monitor.

In addition, you may wish to have the following:

- A mouse and related software.

- A printer, for printing reports and checks. If you plan to print checks, you should not use a printer that requires thermal paper.

- A modem, if you plan to pay bills electronically through CheckFree or to download current stock price information from an on-line service such as CompuServe or ZiffNet.

- Quicken checks, if you plan to print checks. For information on ordering checks, see Appendix B.

Memory and Storage Consumption

The previous section listed the minimum memory and storage requirements for running Quicken on your system. Every time you create a transaction, category, class, security, or price, however, you'll be taking up more space both on your disks and in memory. So if your financial picture is at all complicated, you'll need a machine with more memory than the minimum requirement, and you should plan on Quicken's combined data and program files consuming up to two megabytes of your hard disk.

Here are some of the size constraints posed by Quicken's architecture, your disk capacity, and your machine's memory:

- *Transactions per file*   65,535 maximum, constrained by Quicken's internal architecture.

- *Transactions per account*   30,000 maximum, constrained by memory.

Note. To help you gauge the importance of these constraints, Intuit estimates that the typical home user generates between 200 and 1,000 transactions per year, while the typical small business generates between 300 and 3,000 transactions per year.

- *Saved transactions on floppy disks* Approximately 2,500 on a 360k (5 ¼ ", double-density) floppy, 9,000 on a 1.2Mb (5 ¼", high density) floppy, 5,000 on a 720k (3 1/2", double-density) floppy, and about 10,000 on a 1.4Mb (3 1/2", high density) floppy.

- *Transactions on hard-disk machines*   If you have a hard disk, the constraint you're more likely to encounter is Quicken's memory limitations. Quicken requires about 260k for its program files, plus 16 bytes per transaction, category, class, and so on. The space taken up by DOS, mouse drivers, and other memory-resident software is variable, so we can only offer a formula for estimating how much room you have. It is

$$T = \frac{(M - D - 260) \times 1024}{16}$$

where:

M is the memory installed in your machine;

D is the amount of memory consumed by DOS and any memory-resident programs you have running;

T is the approximate number of transactions that Quicken can handle;

260 is the amount of memory used by Quicken's core code;

1024 is a kilobyte of memory converted into bytes; and

16 is the average number of bytes taken up by a transaction.

- *Reports*   For some users, the tightest memory constraint is on the length and complexity of reports. In general, broader date ranges, more subtotals, and more transactions translate to more memory required to generate a report. If you run out of memory while building a report, you will see a warning message; you should respond by restricting the extent of the report.

Quicken does make limited use of extended memory if it's installed in your personal computer. This memory is used for reports, as well as for program overlays.

If you run out of memory using Quicken, you should try these techniques to free up memory:

- If you're using QuickPay, exit to DOS and start Quicken without it.

■ Exit to DOS and unload any memory-resident (pop-up) utilities you might have.

■ Copy your Quicken file to a new file by choosing Set Preferences from the Quicken Main Menu, then File Activities, and finally Copy File. When Quicken copies a file you've been using for awhile, it squeezes out unused storage that accumulates over time in the middle of a file.

■ Use the Year End procedures to summarize and eliminate old transactions from your file. From the Quicken Main Menu, choose Set Preferences, File Activities, and then Year End.

Install and Configure Quicken

The installation instructions are the same whether you're a first-time user of Quicken or you already have an earlier version of Quicken installed. Installing Quicken 5.0 over an earlier version does not affect your data files in any way.

After you begin the installation process and provide details about your equipment setup, Quicken accomplishes the installation process automatically. Quicken also modifies your CONFIG.SYS file to include the parameters BUFFERS=16 and FILES=12, if they aren't already present.

If you are a current user of an earlier version of Quicken, you may find it most convenient to install Quicken 5.0 in the directory containing your earlier version. Quicken looks for data files in the current directory; installing the new version over the old will allow Quicken 5.0 to find your data files in the usual place, and installation will not affect your files in any way. However, if you decide to install Quicken 5.0 in a new directory, you can specify the location of your data files by selecting Set Preferences from the Main Menu, and then File Activities and Set File Location. Enter the correct path for the data files.

Decisions to Make Before Running Install

Before running the install program, you should determine

■ *Where Quicken should install the program files*   If you're installing Quicken on your hard disk and you have a preference, you specify the subdirectory location where the program installs itself; if you don't care, Quicken creates a subdirectory called QUICKEN5 and installs itself there. If you're installing Quicken on one or more floppy disks, see "Install on a Floppy Disk System," below.

■ *The printer to specify*   Quicken needs to assign a primary and an alternate report printer and a printer for printing checks. The same printer can be used for all three. If you have two printers and wish to specify their uses, see "Printer Installations and Settings," later in this appendix.

- *Whether to install Billminder*   Billminder is a useful adjunct to Quicken that alerts you of Quicken transactions that are upcoming by flashing messages when you first turn on your computer. If you choose not to install Billminder, Quicken will still alert you of certain pending transactions when you start the program itself.

- *What style of menus you want to use*   Previous versions of Quicken used function key menus, in which you pressed a function key to see a Quicken menu and then typed a number representing an option on the menu's numbered list (see Figure A.1). More modern software programs comply with a standard called Systems Applications Architecture (SAA), which allows you to select menu options by pressing the Alt key and a designated letter (usually the first) of the menu option (see Figure A.2). Throughout this book we use the Alt key method. You are free to use either; see the section called "Further Tailoring," later in this appendix, for instructions on changing the menu style.

Figure A.1   Function key menus

Main menu items labeled with function keys

Pull-down menu items labeled with numbers or letters

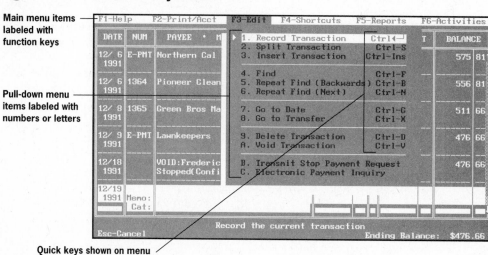

Quick keys shown on menu

Files Installed During the Installation Process

The Quicken program files installed on your hard disk are

- Q.EXE (the program itself)

- Q.HLP (the Help file)

- BILLMIND.EXE (Billminder, described later in this appendix)

Figure A.2   **Alt-key menus**

Alt key letter highlighted on menu bar

Submenu letter choice on menu bar

Quick key shown on menu

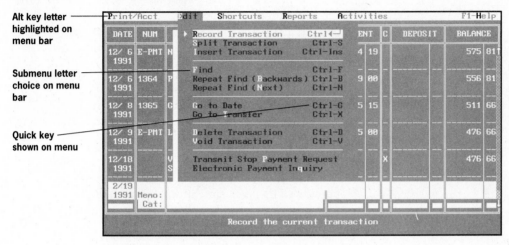

- QCHECKS.DOC (a blank checks order form in compressed format)
- PRINTER2.DAT (a predefined printer setup)
- HOME.QIF (the standard home categories)
- BUSINESS.QIF (the standard business categories)
- TAX.SCD (tax form information)

The following are data files used during the Quick Tour, an option available through First Time Setup:

- SAMPLE.QDI
- SAMPLE.QDT
- SAMPLE.QMT
- SAMPLE.QNX

Install on a Hard-Disk System

Before you start, make sure you have the necessary Quicken Install Disks (two 5 ¼" or one 3 ½"). To install Quicken 5.0,

1. Start your computer. The DOS prompt should be either C:> or D:>, showing the root directory of the hard-disk drive.

2. If you use 5 ¼" disks, insert Install Disk 1 in drive A. If you use 3 ½" disks, insert the Install Disk disk in drive A.

Note. If you need to install Quicken 5.0 from drive B, place the appropriate disk in drive B and specify that drive letter before the INSTALL command.

Note. You can always return to a previous dialog box and change the information you entered there by pressing Escape as many times as necessary.

Note. You cannot run Quicken from a low-density disk drive.

Note. You can always return to a previous dialog box and change the information you entered there by pressing Escape as many times as necessary.

3. Type **A:INSTALL** and press Enter.

4. The install program displays a series of dialog boxes, each of which asks a question about your equipment setup and preferences. Answer each question by typing the number next to the option you want, or by typing a full answer. To see more options in a list, press the Down Arrow key. Press Enter to continue to the next dialog box.

5. In the Drive and Directory dialog box, you specify the subdirectory location where Quicken should be installed. Quicken displays C:\QUICKEN5 as the default. If you are installing Quicken 5.0 over an earlier version, you may wish to specify the subdirectory of the earlier version, for example, C:\QUICKEN4, so the new program files replace the old ones. This does not affect your data files in any way.

6. When you've supplied all the necessary information, Quicken begins installing the program files.

7. When the installation is complete, store the original disks in a safe place.

Install on a Floppy Disk System

Before you start, assemble the following:

- Quicken Install Disks 1 and 2 (5 ¼"), or the Quicken Install Disk (3 ½").

- If you will run Quicken from a high-density disk drive (3 ½" or 5 ¼"), you will need one blank high-density formatted disk of the appropriate size to contain program files and data files. Label the disk "Installed Quicken Program."

To install Quicken 5.0 on a floppy disk,

1. Start your computer as usual with a system disk.

2. If you have one high-density disk drive, remove the disk and replace it with Install Disk 1 (5 ¼") or the Install Disk (3 ½"), depending on the type of drive you are using. Insert a blank, formatted high-density disk in drive B. (If drive A is your only high-density drive, you may insert the blank disk in drive A and the Install Disk in drive B.)

   If you have two high-density disk drives, insert Install Disk 1 (5 ¼") or the Quicken Install Disk (3 ½") in the other drive.

3. If necessary, change to the drive containing the original Quicken disk. Type **INSTALL** and press Enter.

4. The install program displays a series of boxes, each of which asks a question about your equipment setup and preferences. Answer each question by typing the number next to the option you want, or by typing a full

answer. To see more options in a list, press the Down Arrow key. Press Enter to continue to the next dialog box.

5. When you've supplied all the necessary information, Quicken begins installing the program files. Prompts tell you when to remove one disk and insert another. Be sure to insert the labeled program disks.

6. When installation is complete, store your original Quicken disks in a safe place.

Printer Installation and Settings

Quicken allows you to install three separate printers for generating hard copy of your checks and reports. It calls these printers the *check printer,* the *report printer,* and the *alternate report printer.*

Even if you don't have more than one printer, you can use these printer settings to specify the same printer with different printing styles. For example, you might want to use normal type for some reports and compressed type for others.

With Quicken 5.0, Intuit has added quite a bit of new printer support—new printer models and new styles. You can see the list of supported printer models and styles by going to the Quicken Main Menu (by pressing Escape repeatedly from anywhere in the program), pressing P (Set Preferences), and then pressing P again (this time for Printer Settings). Choose one of the three printer settings options and you'll then see a set of three overlapping windows: a Styles window (titled with the name of the printer you've previously selected, a Select Printer window, and a Printer Settings window), as shown in Figure A.3.

In the Styles window, you'll see a list of available styles for the particular printer you've chosen, the pitch (number of characters per inch), and the orientation of each style listed (portrait is vertically oriented; landscape is horizontally oriented).

Press Escape once, and you'll see a list of printers supported explicitly by Quicken. Use the cursor keys to scroll up and down through the list.

If a printer you use is not on this list, don't despair. Most printers emulate either an Epson FX-80, an IBM ProPrinter II, or an Apple LaserWriter (PostScript printer). Look in your printer manual to find out which type of emulation your printer supports. If all else fails, then choose <Other Dot-Matrix> or <Other Laser> from the list; in this event, however, you'll only have one printer to choose from. Alternatively, if you're familiar with the control codes for your printer (which are listed in your printer manual), you can read on to find out how to set up your printer exactly the way you want it.

Press Escape one more time and you'll reach the Printer Settings window for the option you selected. In this window, you can choose any new printer or printer style you'd like. Just type the name of a new printer or style into the appropriate blanks and fill in all the other appropriate fields. If you plan to change the control codes, press F8 and you'll see the Printer Control Codes window, where you can edit the control codes (Figure A.4).

Figure A.3 Windows containing printer settings

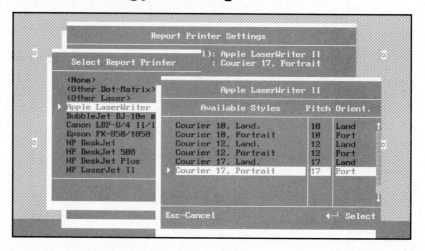

Figure A.4 Printer Control Codes window

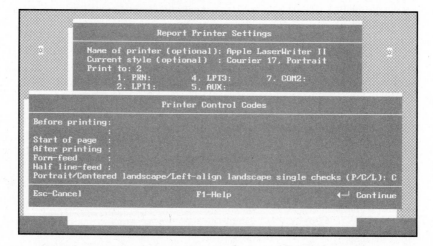

Setting printer control codes is less challenging than it appears. Each printer has a set of codes which tell it to do certain things, such as starting a new page, compressing print, selecting a certain font, choosing letter or draft quality, and so on. These codes are either letters and numbers or ASCII codes (which take the form of a number). To enter an ASCII code into the printer control codes window, precede it with a backslash (\). ASCII 24 would be entered, for example, as \24.

Use CheckFree with Your Modem

If you plan to use the CheckFree electronic checkwriting service from within Quicken, you'll need to specify settings for your modem within Quicken. Level 4 ("Make Payments Electronically") contains detailed information on how to do this. You can use any Hayes-compatible modem that transmits data at 300, 1,200, or 2,400 baud.

If you don't yet have a modem but need one, CheckFree Corporation sells a low-priced modem to its customers (recent price was $99.00). To order one, call CheckFree at (800) 882-5280.

Further Tailoring

Once you go through the automated setup procedure described in Level 1, "Get Started with Quicken," you'll be able to manipulate settings that affect your future Quicken environment and use. The settings described below are definable from the Quicken Main Menu, which you see after completing Quicken's setup procedure.

- *Color and Other Screen Settings*   Quicken provides a variety of color schemes for use with color monitors. To change the color,

   1. Select Set Preferences from the Quicken Main Menu.

   2. Select Screen Settings, and then Screen Colors.

   3. Choose the desired color setting, and press Enter. Press Escape several times to return to the Main Menu.

   Also in the Screen Settings area, Quicken allows you to display 43 lines on a screen, rather than the normal 25. When you set this option, you'll be able to see, for example, 14 transactions on a register screen, rather than the normal 6.

   Another screen setting is Monitor Display, which is designed for older CGA display monitors. If your monitor flashes a burst of distracting "snow" when it changes screens, you should use the Monitor Display settings to specify that you want a Screen Update Speed of Slow.

- *Menu Access*   This book uses the Alt key method of selecting menu options—you press the Alt key and type the first letter of a menu name to see the options on that menu. You may prefer to use the function key method, whereby each menu is assigned to a function key, and each option on a menu to a number; you press the function key and then type the number to invoke an option.

Quicken uses the Alt key method by default. To change it, choose Set Preferences from the Main Menu, Screen Settings, and then Menu Access. Type **1** to change to function key menus or **2** to change to Alt key menus. You must leave and restart Quicken in order for the change to take effect.

■ *Password Protection*　You can add a password to protect your files. To do this, choose Set Preferences from the Main Menu, then Password Settings. Select File Password or Transaction Password, depending on which password you want to create, then type the password you want.

If you forget your password, you'll need to supply some information to Intuit in order to unlock the file. First, choose Set Preferences from the Main Menu, then Password Settings. At the Password Settings menu, press Ctrl-Z. Quicken displays a Sequence number in the Forced Password Removal window; jot down this number, then call Intuit's Technical Support department at (415) 322-2800. They will give you an unlock code that you can enter to remove the password.

Creating and using passwords are also discussed in Level 4.

■ *Billminder Settings*　Billminder can remind you of pending transactions—checks to be printed or electronically transmitted, transaction groups due, and investments.

When you install Quicken, you can also opt to install Billminder on your hard disk. During the Billminder installation process, a line is added to your AUTOEXEC.BAT file to run Billminder whenever you start your computer. This line varies slightly depending on the version of DOS you are using and where you installed Quicken. For example, suppose you installed Quicken on your C drive in a directory called \QUICKEN5. For DOS 3.0 or above, the line would read

```
C:\QUICKEN5\BILLMIND C:\QUICKEN5
```

For DOS versions lower than 3.0, the line would read

```
BILLMIND C:\QUICKEN5
```

If you ever move your Quicken program files to another directory, you will need to edit the Billminder line in your AUTOEXEC.BAT file to reflect the program's new location so Billminder can find your files. Using a text editor, substitute the new file location for the old one.

Note. If you move your program files and then get an error message when Billminder runs, check to be sure that the Q.CFG file (which specifies the path to the program files) was also moved to the new location. Billminder uses this file as an indicator of the location of the Quicken program files.

You can also modify the Billminder line to pause after displaying the message and wait for you to press the Enter key before continuing. This is useful if your AUTOEXEC.BAT file executes other programs after the Billminder line. Using a text editor, add the phrase /P to the end of the Billminder line.

Once you install Billminder, you have to activate it from within Quicken. To turn on Billminder and specify how many days' advance notice Billminder gives you, choose Set Preferences from the Main Menu, then Automatic Reminder Settings. Enter the amount of advance notice you need, and type **Y** to invoke Billminder.

■ *Other Settings*   The other two choices on the Set Preferences screen—Transaction Settings and Checks & Reports Settings—present a whole series of options that help customize Quicken to your personal style. These options are discussed in detail in the various parts of Levels 2, 3, and 6 that cover transactions, checks, and reports.

Install on a Laptop Computer

You may use Quicken on a laptop computer. In fact, if you're a fairly mobile person, you'll probably find that airplane flights and train rides are an ideal time to exercise your Quicken routine.

Three things make laptop use somewhat different from desktop use. First, your screen will most likely be a monochrome display, and you should account for that in your settings. Second, if you use CheckFree to write checks electronically, you should know how to change the CheckFree telephone number quickly, to accommodate the different dialing sequences that may be necessary as you call CheckFree from hotel rooms or your office. Finally, if you use Quicken from two different machines, you need to develop a routine for synchronizing your desktop and laptop machines so that you are neither working with obsolete data files nor losing important information that you've entered.

Setting Quicken for your laptop's monochrome display is simple. From the Quicken Main Menu (press Escape repeatedly to get there), press P (Set Preferences) and then S (Screen Settings), followed by C (Screen Colors). The first choice you'll see on the screen is the Monochrome color set, which will work on any laptop computer. You can achieve a richer look with newer laptop computers which convert screen colors to various shades of grey. Experiment with different color sets if your laptop supports grey scales.

You can set the modem number for CheckFree through the Set Preferences function. This time, after pressing P (Set Preferences) at the Quicken Main Menu, press L (for Electronic Payment Settings) and M (Modem Settings). In this window, you'll see a blank for the telephone number you use to access CheckFree. Use the Tab key to move to this field and type over the current number, if you wish. To add an access number, such as 9, that you might use to get an outside line from a hotel or office, precede the Check-Free number with **9,** (the comma denotes a pause). Don't forget to change the number back before you next use CheckFree from home.

Using Quicken on two machines can be tricky. Every time you enter a transaction in Quicken, you are changing the database. Therefore, it's important that you always begin your session by working with the very latest copy of your data files, lest you miss the most recent changes. The best approach is to try to make all changes on one of your two machines, probably your laptop. The other machine might be used only for analysis and reports—functions that read the database without changing it. If you need to make changes on both machines, you should use a floppy-disk copy of the database to synchronize the files on both machines. The four files which you should be prepared to copy over are described in the section entitled "Understand Quicken's Filenames," later in this appendix.

Start Quicken from the Root Directory

When you install Quicken, the program places a batch file named Q.BAT in the root directory of your hard disk. This batch file lets you start Quicken from the root directory.

The drawback to this, however, is that Borland's Quattro Pro does the same thing. If you install Quattro Pro after you install Quicken, typing Q at the root directory will start Quattro Pro instead.

In this case, you should start Quicken from the directory in which it is installed. First, change directories (using the DOS CD command) to the QUICKEN5 directory (or whatever directory you specified when you installed Quicken). Then, when you type **Q**, Quicken will load.

Understand Quicken's Filenames

Each Quicken "file"—Quicken's term for a set of related accounts—is actually comprised of four individual files, each of which is necessary for you to use the data in Quicken. All four files have the same root name, usually your last name or the name of your business. The unique extensions define the purpose of the file.

The four files are

FILENAME.QDT	Contains the data
FILENAME.QNX	Contains the indexes to the data file
FILENAME.QMT	Contains the memorized items
FILENAME.QDI	Dictionary file; contains addresses of unprinted checks and descriptions of split transactions

Note. You can temporarily exit to DOS during a Quicken work session, without actually leaving Quicken, by choosing Use DOS from the Activities menu (Alt-A). When you're ready to return to Quicken, type **EXIT** at the DOS prompt.

If the index file (*.QNX) becomes unsynchronized with the data file (which may happen if you turn off your PC before leaving Quicken) or is accidentally erased, the next time you start Quicken it will automatically rebuild the index file. The other files are not dispensable; if they become lost or corrupted, you will need to rebuild the data yourself.

Use Quicken with a Mouse

Quicken 5.0 adds, for the first time, support for a Microsoft-compatible mouse or trackball with your computer. This can speed navigation and access to Quicken's commands.

Quicken automatically checks to see if you have a mouse installed on your personal computer as it starts each session. It does so by attempting to detect the presence of a mouse driver—the software that actually processes the mouse movements and commands.

Once it detects a compatible mouse, Quicken displays a cursor box on the screen that is different from the flashing cursor line that is associated with keyboard input. As you move the mouse on the desktop in front of you, the mouse cursor will move around the screen. As you click one of the mouse buttons, Quicken will act on your command. Most commands are issued with the left mouse button.

You don't have to use your mouse with Quicken; the keyboard still works exactly as it does without a mouse.

Menus

There are two types of menus in Quicken—menus that appear in a window (such as the Quicken Main Menu) and pull-down menus, which appear in a bar at the top of the screen.

To use a mouse with a menu in a window, simply use the mouse to move the cursor to the command you want and click the left mouse button.

A two-step process is required to select a command from a pull-down menu. Point to the choice you want on the menu bar and click the left mouse button. This displays the pull-down menu. Then point to the command from the pull-down menu and click again.

Cursor Positioning

In any account register, you may select (highlight) a transaction by moving the mouse cursor to that transaction and clicking. At the same time, the keyboard cursor will move to the spot in the transaction where you clicked, so you can begin typing at that position.

Hot Buttons

Along the bottom of the screen, you'll find "hot buttons," which describe functions you might want to use at any time in Quicken. These include Help,

Escape, and Record. The list changes as you move to different types of windows and screens in Quicken. To select one of these commands, point at it with the mouse and click the left mouse button.

Any selected transaction has hot buttons within it, too. Clicking on the Cat: label, for example, will open the Category and Transfer List window, from which you may use the mouse to select a new category. Clicking on the SPLIT label of a split transaction will display the Split Transaction window.

Scrolling and Choosing

On the extreme right-hand edge of most screens and list windows, a scroll bar will appear. This is a long strip with vertical arrows at either end and a colored bar in the middle. To move quickly through any list which is not fully displayed on a screen (such as a register or the Category and Transfer list), point to the arrow that points in the direction you'd like to scroll. Then click and hold the left mouse button until you find the place in the list you're looking for.

In the Register itself, you can also scroll by pointing to any transaction, holding down the left mouse button, and moving the mouse vertically or horizontally until you see the transaction you want to find.

To choose an item from a list, point at that item and double-click the left mouse button. For example, to categorize a transaction, you might first click on the Cat: label, use the scrolling arrows to find the category Medical, and double-click on the word Medical. Quicken inserts the category Medical into the appropriate field. (A single click merely highlights Medical.)

Other Mouse Tricks

Here are some other tips and tricks you'll find useful as you use a mouse with Quicken:

- The right button (or the middle button on a three-button mouse) always has the same effect as pressing Escape. Click it repeatedly to move to the Quicken Main Menu.

- If you have a three-button mouse, you can use the third button to get context-sensitive help.

- To increase a date by one day, point at the date field and click the left mouse button. To decrease it by one day, click the right (or middle on a three-button mouse) button.

- The calculator "keys" can't be worked with a mouse.

Use Quicken with Windows

Although Quicken 5.0 is not a Windows application, you can successfully run it under Windows. However, like most other DOS applications, Quicken does not run well in a window under 386 enhanced mode—specifically, the programs may freeze when you use your mouse. We advise running Quicken in full screen mode instead.

You may also run into another instance in which the similarity in program files names and start-up procedures between Quicken and Borland's Quattro confuses things. If you use Windows Setup to set up Quicken to run under Windows, it will assume that the Q.EXE file (Quicken's core program file) is a Quattro program file, and will set up Quicken under the name Quattro. To correct this, select the erroneous Quattro icon, move to the Windows Program Manager, and choose Properties from the File menu. Then rename the file to Quicken.

The Quicken Install Disk contains both a Quicken program information file (PIF) and a Quicken icon for Windows users.

Install QuickPay

If you'll be using Quicken to create and manage a small payroll—whether for your small business or for paying domestic help—you might want to consider installing the QuickPay add-in program marketed by Intuit. Level 11 contains a complete description of this product, along with guidance on whether it's appropriate to your situation.

This section describes how to install QuickPay on your system.

Additional Requirements

QuickPay demands two things of your personal computer system setup that Quicken itself doesn't:

- A hard disk. You can't run QuickPay with a floppy-only system.

- 82k of extra memory, above and beyond Quicken's requirements.

Note. If you have two copies of Quicken—for example, if you've installed a new version in a new directory without erasing the old version—there's a risk that QuickPay will find the incorrect directory.

Installation

The installation instructions are very straightforward:

1. Insert the QuickPay program disk into your A drive.

2. Type **A:INSTALL**, and then press Enter.

3. QuickPay's installation program will search your hard disk to find Quicken, and will display the directory where it first finds the program. If the location is correct, then type Enter; otherwise, you should type the directory where you want QuickPay installed, followed by Enter.

Within a minute or so, QuickPay will be installed on your hard disk and a new batch file—called QP.BAT—will be created in both your Quicken directory and your root directory.

The QuickPay program files installed on your hard disk are

- QUICKPAY.EXE (the program itself)

- QUICKPAY.DAT (tax tables, which are periodically updated)

- QPCLEAR.EXE (a utility which resets year-to-date figures at the end of the year)

- QPBACK.EXE (a utility for backing up your QuickPay information)

- QP.BAT (the batch file that loads both QuickPay and Quicken together)

QuickPay stores the payroll transactions it generates in the Quicken register with which it works. There are two data files it generates, however, containing information inappropriate for the register:

- QUICKPAY.SET (the information you enter about your company and its standard payroll deductions and procedures)

- QUICKPAY.TXT (the information you enter about each individual employee)

Startup

To start Quicken with QuickPay, you should simply type **QP**, and then press Enter. This works within either the root directory or the Quicken directory.

In some circumstances, you may not want to consume the extra 82k of memory which QuickPay demands. This might happen, for instance, if you are running complex reports. In these circumstances, you should start Quicken without QuickPay by simply pressing Q and then Enter. If you need QuickPay later during the session, you may exit Quicken and restart it by typing **QP**.

APPENDIX B

How to Obtain the Tools in This Guide

Quicken 5.0

Quicken 5.0 is available in most retail stores that carry software, including mass merchandisers and department stores that sell programs for PCs. In addition, direct-mail software outlets offer very attractive prices; check the listings in *PC/Computing* or most other computer magazines. Make sure, however, that you get the most current version of the software; you should not settle for Quicken 4.0.

If you prefer, you may obtain Quicken directly from Intuit. The company's order number is (800) 624-8742.

CheckFree

All the materials you need to sign up with CheckFree are contained in the Quicken box. If, for some reason, you don't have these materials, you can sign up directly with CheckFree Corporation by dialing (800) 882-5280. If you use either of these methods, the first month of service will be free of charge.

You will not need to buy the CheckFree software separately if you have Quicken, so call directly to sign up. Be sure to allow a couple of weeks for exchanging the paperwork that's necessary to set up your CheckFree account.

ZiffNet and CompuServe

Together, ZiffNet and CompuServe offer a comprehensive information service that will both support your financial information needs and offer a treasure trove of tips, techniques, and product information to help you use your PC more effectively.

One ZiffNet account will access both services. To join ZiffNet,

1. Call (800) 635-6225 to obtain the local access telephone number for ZiffNet in your geographic area (this is an automated touch-tone response number, available 24 hours a day).

2. Load your communications software and set its communications parameters to 7E1 (7 data bits, even parity, 1 stop bit).

3. Select the data transfer rate (bits per second or baud rate) that's appropriate for your modem: 300, 1,200, 2,400, or 9,600.

4. Have your modem dial the local ZiffNet number (obtained in step 1).

5. Respond to the prompts by entering the information below:

When you connect:	Ctrl-C
Host name:	**CIS**
User ID:	**177000,5555**
PASSWORD:	**ZIFF*NET**
Agreement number:	**QUICKEN**

6. ZiffNet will prompt you for your name and credit card number and will give you an account number and password that you can use immediately for ten days. Your new membership will be confirmed by mail.

Once you have your ZiffNet account, you can use it to obtain the templates and scripts designed for readers of this book, as well as thousands of other valuable utilities. After you've logged onto your account, type **GO ZNT:SOFTLIB** (which means "Go to the ZiffNet Software Library") and follow the instructions there on downloading programs to your PC.

All of the files associated with this book may be located on ZiffNet by executing a keyword search using the keyword QUICKEN.

TaxCut

TaxCut is available in most software retail stores or directly from its developer, MECA Software. The program is a seasonal item; it begins to appear around Thanksgiving each year and disappears from the shelves in late April (for obvious reasons).

TaxCut is available in two editions: TaxCut 1040 and TaxCut EZ/A. Level 10 discusses the differences between these two versions to help you decide which is appropriate.

In addition, TaxCut 1040 tends to come out in two sequential editions: an Early Bird edition, which hits the stores in the fall before the official tax forms are available, and a Final Edition, which comes out after the tax laws and forms are firm for the year. When you buy and register the Early Bird edition, you will automatically be mailed the Final Edition when it's available.

Finally, MECA Software also markets several versions of TaxCut which are appropriate for preparing state tax returns. To find out whether one addresses your state, you may ask MECA directly.

To order TaxCut directly from MECA, dial (800) 237-8400, ext. 232.

QuickPay

QuickPay is also distributed through retail stores and by direct mail, but is less widely distributed than Quicken itself. You may order QuickPay directly from Intuit by calling (800) 624-8742.

Quicken Transfer Utility

Unavailable through retail or direct mail outlets, this accessory can only be obtained through Intuit by calling (800) 624-8742.

Quicken Checks and Supplies

Intuit maintains a catalog of accessories and supplies designed for use with Quicken. These include custom checks and envelopes, deposit slips, endorsement and return address stamps, and forms leaders.

To obtain a catalog, call the Quicken order line at (800) 624-8742, Monday through Friday between 7 AM and 5 PM, Pacific Time.

Guide to Quick Keys in Quicken

This appendix lists the quick keys that can be used throughout Quicken, plus some of the special editing keys used to advance transaction numbers and dates, and to update security prices. Use this appendix to select the quick keys you should use to work as efficiently as possible.

The quick keys named in this appendix are organized according to the area of Quicken in which they work. For each quick key, you'll see a description and any menu commands that perform the equivalent function. If use of a quick key is restricted to a certain area of Quicken, this is noted in the description. When the letter for the quick key is reminiscent of a specific word (such as Ctrl-C for Category), the word is given in italics in the description.

Quick Keys in Account Registers and the Write Checks Screen

Quick Key	Description	Equivalent Menu Command
Ctrl-A	Select or set up a new *account*.	Press Alt-P A (Print/Acct menu, Select/Set Up Account)
Ctrl-B	Search *backwards* to find any previous transaction that matches criteria in the Find window (Ctrl-F).	Press Alt-E B (Edit menu, Repeat Find (Backwards))
Ctrl-C	Select or set up a *category*.	Press Alt-S C (Shortcuts menu, Categorize/Transfer)
Ctrl-C	Display account list to select an account for a transfer action (only in the Investment register).	Press Alt-S C (Shortcuts menu, Categorize/Transfer)
Ctrl-D	*Delete* the current transaction.	Press Alt-E D (Edit menu, Delete Transaction)
Ctrl-E	While entering a payee, type the first few characters of a memorized transaction payee, then press Ctrl-E for Quicken to automatically complete the entry. While working in a window such as the Set Up New Account window or Category and Transfer list, press Ctrl-E to *edit* the highlighted item (account, category, and so on).	None

Quick Key	Description	Equivalent Menu Command
Ctrl-Enter	Record the current transaction.	Press Alt-E R (Edit menu, Record Transaction)
Ctrl-F	To *find* a transaction, fill in the criteria, and then use Ctrl-B (for Backwards) or Ctrl-N (for Next) to find any previous or following transaction that matches the criteria.	Press Alt-E F (Edit menu, Find)
Ctrl-G	*Go to* transactions with or closest to a certain date.	Press Alt-E G (Edit menu, Go to Date)
Ctrl-I	*Initialize* the transfer of electronic payments.	Press Alt-P T (Print/Acct, Transmit Payments)
Ctrl-Ins	*Insert* a new transaction above the current transaction.	Press Alt-E I (Edit menu, Insert Transaction)
Ctrl-J	View the list of transaction groups.	Press Alt-S G (Shortcuts menu, Transaction Groups)
Ctrl-L	Select or set up a class.	Press Alt-S L (Shortcuts menu, Select/Set Up Class)
Ctrl-L	Select or set up an Investment action (Investment register only).	Press Alt-S A (Shortcuts menu, Select Action)
Ctrl-M	*Memorize* a transaction.	Press Alt-S M (Shortcuts menu, Memorize Transaction)
Ctrl-N	Find the *next* transaction that matches criteria in the Find window (Ctrl-F).	Press Alt-E N (Edit menu, Repeat Find Next)
Ctrl-O	See the Calculator.	Press Alt-A C (Activities menu, Calculator)
Ctrl-P	*Print* the Register or checks.	Press Alt-P P (Print/Acct menu, Print Register)
Ctrl-R	Display the *register* for the current account (not in register).	Press Alt-A R (Activities menu, Register)
Ctrl-S	*Split* the current transaction.	Press Alt-E S (Edit menu, Split Transaction)
Ctrl-T	Recall a memorized *transaction*.	Press Alt-S R (Shortcuts menu, Recall Transaction)

Quick Key	Description	Equivalent Menu Command
Ctrl-U	Display the *Update* Prices and Market Values screen (in the Investment register only).	Press Alt-A U (Activities menu, Update Prices)
Ctrl-V	*Void* the current transaction.	Press Alt-E V (Edit menu, Void Transaction)
Ctrl-W	Display the *Write Checks* screen for the current account (not in Write Checks screen or Investment register).	Press Alt-A W (Activities menu, Write Checks)
Ctrl-X	Go to the transfer for the current translation.	Press Alt-E T (Edit menu, Go to Transfer)
Ctrl-Y	Select or set up an electronic payee (only in accounts set up for electronic payments).	Press Alt-S P (Shortcuts menu, Electronic Payee list)
Ctrl-Y	Select or set up a security (Investment register only).	Press Alt-S S (Shortcuts menu, Security list)

Keys for Editing Dates in Account Registers and the Write Checks Screen

Editing Key	Description
+	Increase the date by one day.
–	Decrease the date by one day.
T	Enter today's date.
M	Enter first day of the current month.
H	Enter the last day of the current month ("H" represents the last letter in "month").
Y	Enter the first date of the current year.
R	Enter the last date of the current year ("R" represents to last letter of "year").
/	Move the cursor to the year portion of the date.

Keys for Editing Transaction Numbers in Account Registers

Editing Key	Description
+	In NUM column, increase number by one.
−	In NUM column, decrease number by one.

Quick Keys at the Main Menu

Quick Key	Description	Equivalent Menu Command
Ctrl-A	Select or set up an *account*.	Press A (Select Account)
Ctrl-B	*Backup* the current file.	Press P F B (Set Preferences, File Activities, Back Up File)
Ctrl-F	Start the *First Time Set Up* Assistant.	Press T S (Use Tutorials/Assistants, First Time Set Up)
Ctrl-G	*Go to* a file (displays Select/Set Up File window).	Press P F S (Set Preferences, File Activities, Select/Set Up File)
Ctrl-O	See the Calculator.	None from the Main Menu
Ctrl-R	Display the *register* for the current account.	Press R (Use Register)
Ctrl-W	Display the *Write Checks* screen for the current account.	Press W (Write/Print Checks)

Quick Keys for Working in the Reports Screen

Quick Key	Description	Equivalent Menu Command
Ctrl-M	*Memorize* the current report.	Press Alt-F M (File/Print menu, Memorize report)
Ctrl-O	See the Calculator.	Press Alt-A C (Activities menu, Calculator)
Ctrl-P	*Print* the report.	Press Alt-F P (File/Print menu, Print Report)
Ctrl-R	Displays the *register* for the current account (not in register).	Press Alt-A R (Activities menu, Register)
Ctrl-U	Return to Main Menu.	Press Escape several times

Quick Key	Description	Equivalent Menu Command
Ctrl-W	Display the *Write Checks* screen for the current account (not in Write Checks screen or Investment register).	Press Alt-A W (Activities menu, Write Checks)
Ctrl-Z	Use Quick*Zoom* to delve into the detail behind an item in a report.	Press Alt-F Z (File/Print menu, QuickZoom)
+	Collapse detail under a summary row into a single row.	None
–	Expand collapsed detail.	None

Quick Keys for Working in the Budget Screen

Quick Key	Description	Equivalent Menu Command
Ctrl-O	See the Calculator.	Press Alt-A C (Activities menu, Calculator)
Ctrl-P	*Print* the budget.	Press Alt-F P (File menu, Print Budgets)
Ctrl-R	Display the *Register* for the current account.	Press Alt-A R (Activities menu, Register)
Ctrl-U	Return to Main Menu.	Press Escape several times
Ctrl-W	Display the *Write Checks* screen for the current account (not in Write Checks screen or Investment register).	Press Alt-A W (Activities menu, Write Checks)
' or "	Repeat the amount from the previous column in the current column.	None

Quick Keys for Working in the Update Prices and Market Value Screen

Quick Key	Description	Equivalent Menu Command
Ctrl-A	Select or set up a new *account*.	Press Alt-P A (Print/Acct menu, Select/Set Up Account)

Quick Key	Description	Equivalent Menu Command
Ctrl-B or Ctrl-←	Display prices for the previous day (move *backwards*).	Press Alt-E P (Edit menu, Previous Day)
Ctrl-G	*Go to* a specific date (Quicken displays prices for that date).	Press Alt-E G (Edit menu, Go to Date)
Ctrl-H	Display the price *history* for the highlighted security.	Press Alt-S P (Shortcuts menu, Price History)
Ctrl-I	*Import* prices in a file downloaded from an on-line service.	Press Alt-P I (Print/Acct menu, Import Prices)
Ctrl-N or Ctrl-→	Display prices for the next day.	Press Alt-E N (Edit menu, Next Day)
Ctrl-P	*Print* the Market Value Summary as of the current date.	Press Alt-P P (Print/Acct menu, Print Summary)
Ctrl-PgDn	Display price for previous month.	None
Ctrl-PgUp	Display price for next month.	None
Ctrl-X	*Export* prices into a file.	Press Alt-P E (Print/Acct menu, Export Prices)
Ctrl-Y	Select or set up a security.	Press Alt-S S (Shortcuts menu, Security List)
+	Increase price of current security by $1/8$.	None
−	Decrease price of current security by $1/8$.	None
*	If price is unchanged, removes asterisk. If actual price (no asterisk) is displayed, returns to previous estimated price (asterisk displays, too).	None

APPENDIX D

A Gallery of Quicken Reports

This appendix provides a sample of each of Quicken's standard reports, along with descriptions of their uses. The samples are grouped according to type of report, as described in Level 6 of this guide. You should consult that section to become familiar with setting up standard reports and customizing them to your needs.

Summary Reports

Summary reports focus one level above the detail of transaction reports, sorting your transactions by category, class, account, payee, and so on to provide an overview of your spending.

The standard summary reports are the Profit and Loss Statement, the Cash Flow report, Income and Expenses report, Investment Income report, Payroll report, Accounts Payable (A/P) by Vendor report, Accounts Receivable (A/R) by Customer report, and the Job/Project report.

Figure D.1   **Standard summary report**

```
                      SUMMARY REPORT
                 5/ 1/92 Through 5/31/92

SCOTT-All Accounts                                      Page 1
6/15/92
                                        5/ 1/92-
              Category Description      5/31/92

      INCOME/EXPENSE
        INCOME
          Interest Income                     37.50
          Salary Income                    2,795.15

        TOTAL INCOME                        2,832.65

        EXPENSES
          Automobile Expenses:
            Service               37.50
            Fuel                  18.00
            Loan                 192.55

            Total Automobile Expenses        248.05
          Charity                             15.00
          Clothing                             0.00
          Entertainment:
            Dining                45.00
            Books/Music           72.80
            Theater               37.50

            Total Entertainment              155.30
          Federal Tax Withholding            515.44
          Groceries                          187.20
          Household                           45.00
          Insurance                          120.40
          Interest Expense                     2.00
          Recreation                          15.00
          Rent                               795.00
          Social Security Tax                197.81
          State Tax Withholding              194.25
          Transportation                      55.00
          Travel                             119.00
          Utilities:
            Electric              36.00
            Telephone             54.15

            Total Utilities                   90.15

        TOTAL EXPENSES                      2,754.60

      TOTAL INCOME/EXPENSE                     78.05
```

Profit and Loss Statement

The Profit and Loss Statement (which appears in the menu as P&L Statement) shows income and expenses. The Total Income/Expenses line at the bottom of the report shows the amount by which your net worth increased or decreased over the time period covered in the report.

Figure D.2 **Profit and Loss Statement**

```
                        PROFIT & LOSS STATEMENT
                       12/ 1/91 Through 12/31/91
FIELDING-All Accounts                                        Page 1
1/ 1/92
                                            12/ 1/91-
                     Category Description   12/31/91

           INCOME/EXPENSE
             INCOME
               Interest Income                     55.37
               Salary Income:
                 Luke's Salary         5,439.68
                 Maria's Salary        4,105.84

               Total Salary Income              9,545.52

             TOTAL INCOME                        9,600.89

             EXPENSES
               Automobile Expenses:
                 Auto Fuel               92.68
                 Auto Loan Payment      405.22

               Total Automobile Expenses          497.90
               Charitable Donations               -15.00
               Childcare Expense:
                 Bright Eyes            444.00
                 Wanda Milasz           400.00

               Total Childcare Expense            844.00
               Christmas Expenses                 184.37
               Clothing                           162.10
               Education exp:
                 Maria                  555.00

               Total Education exp                555.00
               Finance Charge                       4.85
               Food:
                 Dining Out              97.00
                 Groceries              261.04

               Total Food                         358.04
               Health:
                 Health Club             27.04
                 Medical & Dental       103.97

               Total Health                       131.01
               Home Repair & Maint.                21.20
               Household Misc. Exp                126.90
               Late Charges                        61.00
               Miscellaneous                       27.55
               Mortgage Interest Exp            1,245.59
               Reimbursable Business Exp          615.50
               Taxes:
                 Federal Tax          1,854.73
                 Social Security Tax    758.92
                 State Tax              421.58

               Total Taxes                       3,035.23
```

Figure D.2   Profit and Loss Statement (continued)

```
                         PROFIT & LOSS STATEMENT
                        12/ 1/91 Through 12/31/91
FIELDING-All Accounts                                               Page 2
1/ 1/92
                                                   12/ 1/91-
                      Category Description          12/31/91

              Telephone Expense                         40.50
              Toys, etc.                                68.55
              Water, Gas, Electric                     161.60
              Expenses - Other                           0.02

          TOTAL EXPENSES                             8,125.91


          TOTAL INCOME/EXPENSE                       1,474.98
```

Cash Flow

The Cash Flow report summarizes your income (inflows) and expenses (out-flows) by category for your bank, cash, and credit card accounts. At the end of the Inflows and Outflows sections, the report notes transfers to and from your other accounts. Although this report option is listed under both the Personal Reports and the Business Reports options, the two versions are identical.

Figure D.3   **Cash Flow report**

```
                        CASH FLOW REPORT
                   4/ 1/92 Through 6/30/92
    SCOTT-All Accounts                                      Page 1
    7/28/92
                                          4/ 1/92-
                   Category Description    6/30/92

         INFLOWS
            Interest Income                        110.32
            Salary Income                        8,385.45
            FROM Exeter Fund                        74.92

         TOTAL INFLOWS                            8,570.69

         OUTFLOWS
            Automobile Expenses:
               Service                55.02
               Fuel                   34.00
               Loan                  577.65

               Total Automobile Expenses           666.67
            Charity                                  85.00
            Clothing                                 65.00
            Entertainment:
               Dining                88.00
               Books/Music          110.00
               Theater               84.50

               Total Entertainment                 282.50
            Federal Tax Withholding               1,546.32
            Groceries                              561.60
            Household                               60.00
            Insurance                              240.80
            Interest Expense                         9.50
            Recreation                              55.00
            Rent                                  2,385.00
            Social Security Tax                    593.43
            State Tax Withholding                  582.75
            Transportation                         165.00
            Travel                                 224.00
            Utilities:
               Electric              98.00
               Telephone            155.45

               Total Utilities                     253.45
            TO Arch Money Mkt                      300.00

         TOTAL OUTFLOWS                           8,076.02


         OVERALL TOTAL                              494.67
```

Investment Income

The Investment Income report summarizes the income and expenses associated with all your investment accounts for a designated time period. It places investment income and expense categories as row headings, so you can see the distribution of your income and expenses across dividends, realized gains and losses, interest expense, and so on.

Figure D.4   **Investment Income report**

```
                       INVESTMENT INCOME REPORT
                         1/ 1/92 Through 3/31/92
JENKINS-Brokerage Acct                                          Page 1
4/ 1/92
                                              1/ 1/92-
                    Category Description        3/31/92

                    INCOME/EXPENSE
                      INCOME
                        Dividend                102.25
                        Realized Gain/Loss      656.52
                        Unrealized Gain/Loss  2,030.16

                    TOTAL INCOME               2,788.93

                      EXPENSES
                        Investment Interest Exp  65.45
                        Expenses - Other          0.00

                    TOTAL EXPENSES               65.45


                    TOTAL INCOME/EXPENSE       2,723.48
```

Payroll

The Payroll report summarizes employer payroll contributions you've made and liabilities you've incurred on behalf of your employees. Employee names are arranged as column headings, and the payroll categories and accounts (established when you run the Payroll Assistant, as described in Level 6) appear as row headings. The report summarizes all expenses and accounts according to the specified time period.

Figure D.5   **Payroll report**

```
                              PAYROLL REPORT
                         5/ 1/92 Through 5/31/92
VENDAGE-All Accounts                                                  Page 1
6/ 1/92
                                                          OVERALL
        Category Description   R Cellon   S Frasier   V Rowles    TOTAL

INCOME/EXPENSE
  EXPENSES
    Payroll:
       Comp 401k              15.79       46.05       12.37       74.21
       Comp FICA             120.79      140.91       94.63      356.34
       Comp FUTA              97.90      114.20       76.69      288.80
       Comp MCARE             47.37       55.26       37.11      139.74
       Comp SUI               63.16       73.68       49.48      186.32
       Gross              1,579.00    1,842.00    1,237.00    4,658.00

      Total Payroll       1,924.01    2,272.11    1,507.28    5,703.40

   TOTAL EXPENSES         1,924.01    2,272.11    1,507.28    5,703.40

TOTAL INCOME/EXPENSE     -1,924.01   -2,272.11   -1,507.28   -5,703.40

TRANSFERS
    TO Payroll-FICA        -120.79     -140.91      -94.63     -356.33
    TO Payroll-FUTA         -97.90     -114.20      -76.69     -288.79
    TO Payroll-FWH         -221.06     -257.88     -173.18     -652.12
    TO Payroll-MCARE        -94.74     -110.52      -74.22     -279.48
    TO Payroll-SUI          -63.16      -73.68      -49.48     -186.32
    TO Payroll-SWHNC        -78.95      -92.1       -61.85     -232.90
    TO Payroll-UWAY         -12.00      -18.00      -10.00      -40.00

TOTAL TRANSFERS           -688.60     -807.29     -540.05    -2,035.94

OVERALL TOTAL           -2,612.61   -3,079.40   -2,047.33    -7,739.34
```

Accounts Payable by Vendor

The Accounts Payable by Vendor report (shown on the menu as "A/P by Vendor") summarizes all unprinted checks in all your accounts according to payee, displaying the total amount of unprinted checks to that payee for the month in the second column. If you specify a date range of two or more months, it displays a column for each month.

Figure D.6   **Accounts Payable by Vendor report**

```
                           Accounts Payable by Vendor
                             12/15/91 Through 1/31/92
REISEN-AP                                                          Page 1
8/ 1/92

   Date      Num      Description       Memo      Category      Clr Amount

 1/20/92   332     Central Telephone            Operating:Telepho    -255.90
                 Total Central Telephone Co                          -255.90
 1/16/92           Gerri Locke-Cooper          Contractor         -2,000.00
                 Total Gerri Locke-Cooper                         -2,000.00
 1/24/92   776     Profetto Office Su           Operating:Supplie    -191.42
                 Total Profetto Office Supply                        -191.42
 1/15/92   269     Rolland Broadcasti           Rental/WAAS-FM       -298.00
                 Total Rolland Broadcasting                          -298.00
 1/18/92   4595    The Edwards Studio           Rental/Wayland     -3,000.00
                 Total The Edwards Studio                         -3,000.00
 1/22/92   1901    Video Services               Equip             -1,975.00
                 Total Video Services                             -1,975.00
12/22/91   8C90    Vista Film Rentals           Rental/Vane Assoc   -870.00
 1/15/92   1455X   Vista Film Rentals           Rental/Vane Assoc   -450.00
                 Total Vista Film Rentals                         -1,320.00
                 OVERALL TOTAL                                    -9,040.32
```

Accounts Receivable by Customer

The Accounts Receivable by Customer report (on the menu as "A/R by Customer") is most useful when you use a separate account to track individual unpaid invoices. Quicken looks for uncleared (in this context, unpaid) transactions in the selected accounts and summarizes the amount payable by each customer. The report lists each customer and the amount due for each month within the specified time period, providing an Overall Total column of receivables for each customer.

Figure D.7   Accounts Receivable by Customer report

```
                                A/R by Customer
                           2/ 1/92 Through 3/31/92
         REISEN-AR                                                      Page 1
         4/ 1/92
                                                            OVERALL
                    Class Description        2/92      3/92    TOTAL
               Entre Int                    995.00  1,200.00  2,195.00
               Herbal Soc                   450.00  1,500.00  1,950.00
               Rockland                   2,000.00    450.00  2,450.00
               Vane Assoc                 3,250.00    800.00  4,050.00
               Wayland                    1,545.00  2,225.00  3,770.00

               OVERALL TOTAL             8,240.00  6,175.00 14,415.00
```

Job/Project

If you use classes to organize transactions by job, project, or client, the Job/Project report can summarize income and expenses according to those classes. Classes—clients, for example—appear as column headings, and the income and expense categories appear as row headings.

Figure D.8   **Job/Project report**

```
                              JOB/PROJECT REPORT
                            5/ 1/92 Through 5/31/92
VENDAGE-All Accounts                                                Page 1
6/ 1/92
                                                                  OVERALL
       Category Description   Williams  Riley Inc Carmichael  Fortuna   TOTAL

INCOME/EXPENSE
  INCOME
    Revenue                   4,000.00  5,975.00  2,950.00  6,500.00  19,425.00

  TOTAL INCOME                4,000.00  5,975.00  2,950.00  6,500.00  19,425.00

  EXPENSES
    Beverage Costs              645.00  1,100.00    380.00  1,104.00   3,229.00
    Contract Labor              350.00    450.00    154.00    325.00   1,279.00
    Flowers/Decorations         250.00    400.00    220.00    676.00   1,546.00
    Desserts-Prepared           223.00    175.00    207.00    395.00   1,000.00
    Equipment                     0.00    325.00      0.00      0.00     325.00
    Food Costs:
      Ingredients               471.00   1050.00    551.00   1642.00    3714.00
      Prepared                  295.00    482.00    260.00    719.00    1756.00

      Total Food                766.00  1,532.00    811.00  2,361.00   5,470.00
    Laundry                      55.00     75.00     32.00     95.00     257.00
    Service Staff Fees          325.00    534.00    100.00    345.00   1,304.00
    Supplies                    525.00    250.00    180.00    312.00   1,267.00

  TOTAL EXPENSES              3,139.00  4,841.00  2,084.00  5,613.00  15,677.00

TOTAL INCOME/EXPENSE           861.00  1,134.00    866.00    887.00   3,748.00
```

Transaction Reports

The transaction report lists all the individual transactions for a current account. You can group and subtotal these transactions in a number of useful ways: by category, class, account, or time period. These reports provide the detail you often need to document or understand your financial position.

Standard transaction reports are the Itemized Categories report, Investment Transactions report, Tax Summary report, and Tax Schedule report.

Figure D.9   Standard Transaction report

```
                           TRANSACTION REPORT
                      12/ 1/91 Through 12/31/91
    FIELDING-Harbor Bk Joint                                   Page 1
    1/ 1/92

     Date    Num      Description        Memo        Category    Clr Amount


             BALANCE 11/30/91                                        977.69

    12/ 1 DEP  S WMZ-TV                            --SPLIT--      X  1,062.92
    12/ 1 DEP  S GDI International                 --SPLIT--      X  1,503.92
    12/ 1 1341   Community Health Pl              Health:Medical  X    -14.00
    12/ 2 ATM  S Cash                              --SPLIT--      X     40.00
    12/ 2 1342 S Englewood Bank & Tr               --SPLIT--      X -2,261.12
    12/ 2 DEP  S Austin Fielding                   --SPLIT--      X    202.77
    12/ 4 1343   Bright Eyes Day Car           Childcare:Bright E X   -111.00
    12/ 4 1344   Wanda Milasz                 Childcare:Wanda Mi  X   -100.00
    12/ 4 1345   Green Bros Market             Food:Groceries     X    -88.40
    12/ 5 E-PMT  Professional Polish          Household           X    -75.00
    12/ 5 1346 S Pioneer Cleaners               --SPLIT--         X    -85.00
    12/ 8 1347   Green Bros Market             Food:Groceries     X    -33.90
    12/ 9 E-PMT  Golden State Teleph           Telephone          X    -40.50
    12/11 1348   Bright Eyes Day Car           Childcare:Bright E X   -111.00
    12/11 1349   Wanda Milasz                 Childcare:Wanda Mi  X   -100.00
    12/15 DEP  S GDI International               --SPLIT--        X  1,503.92
    12/15 1350   Green Bros Market             Food:Groceries          -50.55
    12/15 DEP  S WMZ-TV                          --SPLIT--        X  1,062.92
    12/18 1351   Bright Eyes Day Car           Childcare:Bright E     -111.00
    12/18 1352   Wanda Milasz                 Childcare:Wanda Mi       -100.00
    12/20 1353   Green Bros Market             Food:Groceries          -88.19
    12/20 1354   Cities of the World France deposit Reimb Business  -1,440.00
    12/22 DEP    GDI International  Napa trip (11/ Reimb Business      824.50
    12/22 1355   Coastal Gas & Elect           Utilities             -161.60
    12/26 1356   Foothill Credit Uni Toyota loan Auto:Loan           -196.65
    12/26 1357   Harbor Bank      Volvo loan   Auto:Loan             -208.57
    12/26 1358   Bright Eyes Day Car           Childcare:Bright E     -111.00
    12/26 1359   Wanda Milasz                 Childcare:Wanda Mi      -100.00
    12/28 1360 S Gulf Card                       --SPLIT--            -95.40
    12/28        Montshire School of Course fees  Tuition:Maria      -555.00
    12/28 1361 S Sears                           --SPLIT--            -72.40
    12/28 3005   VISA Payment Servic           [VISA]                -356.58

          TOTAL 12/ 1/91 - 12/31/91                                 -465.91

          BALANCE 12/31/91                                           511.78


          TOTAL INFLOWS                                            6,200.95
          TOTAL OUTFLOWS                                          -6,666.86


          NET TOTAL                                                 -465.91
```

Itemized Category

When you need a complete listing of transactions from all your accounts for a given time period, generate an Itemized Category report. This report lists all transactions, grouping them by category and listing for each the date, number, description, memo, amount, and whether it's cleared.

Figure D.10   **Itemized Category report**

```
                         Itemized Category Report
                         11/20/91 Through 11/27/91
FIELDING-Harbor Bk Joint                                      Page 1
12/ 1/91

   Date   Num      Description          Memo        Category     Clr Amount


           INCOME/EXPENSE
             EXPENSES
               Automobile Expenses:


               Auto Loan Payment

   11/25 3003    Foothill Credit Unio Toyota loan  Auto:Loan        -196.65
   11/25 3004    Harbor Bank          Volvo loan   Auto:Loan        -208.57

                 Total Auto Loan Payment                            -405.22

               Auto Service

   11/20 3002    Hugh's Auto Service               Auto:Service      -36.00

                 Total Auto Service                                  -36.00

               Total Automobile Expenses                           -441.22

               Childcare Expense:


               Bright Eyes

   11/20 1332    Bright Eyes Day Care              Childcare:Bright -111.00
   11/27 1334    Bright Eyes Day Care              Childcare:Bright -111.00

                 Total Bright Eyes                                  -222.00

               Wanda Milasz

   11/20 1331    Wanda Milasz                      Childcare:Wanda M -100.00
   11/27 1333    Wanda Milasz                      Childcare:Wanda M -100.00

                 Total Wanda Milasz                                 -200.00

               Total Childcare Expense                             -422.00

               Recreation Expense

   11/20 3001    Water Valley Recreat Quarterly famil Recreation   -105.00

                 Total Recreation Expense                          -105.00

             TOTAL EXPENSES                                        -968.22

           TOTAL INCOME/EXPENSE                                    -968.22
```

Investment Transactions

The Investment Transactions report shows only transactions from your investment accounts for a designated time period. If you include only realized gains, the report shows the change in the cost basis of each security. If you include unrealized gains, the report shows the change in the market value.

The report arranges transactions by date and lists the following for each transaction: date, action, security, category, price, shares, commission, cash (the change in the account's cash balance that results from the transaction), the investment value (the change in either cost basis or market value), and the sum of the cash and investment value. Actions that involve several specific transactions (such as a reinvestment of dividends) are broken down into their component transactions.

Figure D.11   **Investment Transactions report**

```
                        INVESTMENT TRANSACTIONS REPORT
                          7/ 1/91 Through 12/31/91
        MILNER-Birscher                                              Page 1
        1/ 1/92

        Date  Action  Secur    Categ     Price    Shares  Commssn    Cash


              BALANCE  6/30/91                                     22,085.99

        7/ 1 Buy      Seaver Re            32.      100     77.12  -3,277.12
        7/ 1 Div      Buckle Vi Dividend                              320.44

        7/28 BuyX     Snid PSep           1.750     200      8.85    -358.85
                                [Money M                              358.85

        8/29 BuyX     Snider So            23.      200     86.36  -4,686.36
                                [Money M                            4,686.36

        8/30 Sell     Snider So            30.      200     95.60   4,686.36
                                Realized Gain/Loss                  1,218.04

        8/31 Sell     Snid PSep                                         0.00
        10/ 1 Buy     Seaver Re            36.      100     79.76  -3,679.76
        10/ 1 Div     Buckle Vi Dividend                              374.90
        10/ 5 Sell    Fgate PNo           2.500     200     11.10     488.90
        10/29 Buy     Fargo & F          37 1/2     200    105.50  -7,605.50

        10/30 Sell    Fargo & F            40.      200    101.54   7,605.50
                                Realized Gain/Loss                    292.96

        10/30 Buy     Fgate PNo           2.500     200     11.10    -488.90
                                Realized Gain/Loss                    -22.20

        11/15 Sell    Conford C          21 1/2     300     97.93   6,352.07

        11/15 Sell    Warburtun            28.      200     92.96   4,130.00
                                Realized Gain/Loss                  1,377.04

        12/28 Buy     Conford C            17.      300     89.66  -6,352.07
                                Realized Gain/Loss                  1,162.41


              TOTAL  7/ 1/91 - 12/31/91                             6,583.07

              BALANCE 12/31/91                                     28,669.06
```

Figure D.11   Investment Transactions report (continued)

```
                              INVESTMENT TRANSACTIONS REPORT
                                7/ 1/91 Through 12/31/91
        MILNER-Birscher                                                    Page 2
        1/ 1/92
          Invest.      Cash +
          Value        Invest.


        147,016.70    169,102.69

          3,277.12
                         320.44

            358.85
                         358.85

          4,686.36
                       4,686.36

         -4,686.36
                       1,218.04

              0.00
          3,679.76
                         374.90
           -488.90
          7,605.50

         -7,605.50
                         292.96

            488.90
                         -22.20

         -6,352.07

         -4,130.00
                       1,377.04

          6,352.07
                       1,162.41

          3,185.73      9,768.80

        150,202.43    178,871.49
```

Tax Summary

The Tax Summary report produces the same kinds of information as the one for itemized categories, but displays only tax-related data. Generate this report when you need a complete list of tax-related transactions from all your accounts for a specified time period.

Figure D.12   **Tax Summary report**

```
                            TAX SUMMARY REPORT
                         11/ 1/91 Through 12/31/91
      FIELDING-All Accounts                                          Page 1
      12/31/91

        Date   Acct     Num    Description    Memo      Category    Clr Amount


               INCOME/EXPENSE
                 EXPENSES
                   Charity-Charitable Donations

      11/15 Harbor B DEP  S WMZ-TV          United Way  Charity      X   -12.50
      12/ 1 Harbor B DEP  S WMZ-TV          United Way  Charity      X   -12.50
      12/ 2 Harbor B ATM  S Cash            Children's  Charity      X    40.00
      12/15 Harbor B DEP  S WMZ-TV          United Way  Charity      X   -12.50
      11/15 Wine Cel        Educational TV F Freemark Ab Charity         -50.00

               Total Charity-Charitable Donations                       -47.50

                   Mort Int-Mortgage Interest Exp

      11/ 2 Harbor B        S Englewood Bank &          Mort Int     X -1,239.36
      12/ 2 Harbor B 1342 S Englewood Bank &            Mort Int     X -1,245.59

               Total Mort Int-Mortgage Interest Exp                   -2,484.95

                   Tax-Taxes:


                     Fed-Federal Tax

      11/15 Harbor B DEP  S WMZ-TV                      Tax:Fed      X   -369.68
      12/ 1 Harbor B DEP  S WMZ-TV                      Tax:Fed      X   -369.68
      12/ 1 Harbor B DEP  S GDI Internationa            Tax:Fed      X   -557.72
      12/15 Harbor B DEP  S GDI Internationa            Tax:Fed      X   -557.65
      12/15 Harbor B DEP  S WMZ-TV                      Tax:Fed      X   -369.68

               Total Fed-Federal Tax                                  -2,224.41

                     FICA-Social Security Tax

      11/15 Harbor B DEP  S WMZ-TV                      Tax:FICA     X   -151.23
      12/ 1 Harbor B DEP  S WMZ-TV                      Tax:FICA     X   -151.23
      12/ 1 Harbor B DEP  S GDI Internationa            Tax:FICA     X   -228.16
      12/15 Harbor B DEP  S GDI Internationa            Tax:FICA     X   -228.30
      12/15 Harbor B DEP  S WMZ-TV                      Tax:FICA     X   -151.23

               Total FICA-Social Security Tax                          -910.15

                     State-State Tax

      11/15 Harbor B DEP  S WMZ-TV                      Tax:State    X    -84.02
      12/ 1 Harbor B DEP  S WMZ-TV                      Tax:State    X    -84.02
      12/ 1 Harbor B DEP  S GDI Internationa            Tax:State    X   -126.76
      12/15 Harbor B DEP  S GDI Internationa            Tax:State    X   -126.78
      12/15 Harbor B DEP  S WMZ-TV                      Tax:State    X    -84.02

               Total State-State Tax                                   -505.60
```

Figure D.12   Tax Summary report (continued)

```
                              TAX SUMMARY REPORT
                           11/ 1/91 Through 12/31/91
        FIELDING-All Accounts                                        Page 2
        12/31/91

         Date   Acct    Num    Description    Memo    Category    Clr Amount


                 Total Tax-Taxes                                   -3,640.16

               TOTAL EXPENSES                                      -6,172.61


               TOTAL INCOME/EXPENSE                                -6,172.61
```

Tax Schedule

Categories can be linked to tax schedule information to aid you in completing your tax returns. The Tax Schedule report lists transactions categorized according to the requirements of various tax schedules. Transactions are grouped first by tax schedule and then by line number on that schedule.

Figure D.13   **Tax Schedule report**

```
                          TAX SCHEDULE REPORT
                       11/ 1/91 Through 12/31/91
   FIELDING-All Accounts                                        Page 1
   12/31/91

     Date   Acct     Num    Description     Memo      Category      Clr Amount

            Form 1040

              Fed. estimated tax

     11/15 Harbor B DEP  S WMZ-TV                     Tax:Fed        X   -369.68
     12/ 1 Harbor B DEP  S WMZ-TV                     Tax:Fed        X   -369.68
     12/ 1 Harbor B DEP  S GDI Internationa           Tax:Fed        X   -557.72
     12/15 Harbor B DEP  S GDI Internationa           Tax:Fed        X   -557.65
     12/15 Harbor B DEP  S WMZ-TV                     Tax:Fed        X   -369.68

              Total Fed. estimated tax                              -2,224.41

              Total Form 1040                                       -2,224.41
              Schedule A


              Medicine and drugs

     12/ 1 Harbor B DEP  S GDI Internationa     Health:Medical X     -45.00
     12/ 1 Harbor B 1341    Community Health     Health:Medical X     -14.00
     12/15 Harbor B DEP  S GDI Internationa     Health:Medical X     -44.97

              Total Medicine and drugs                               -103.97
              State and local taxes

     11/15 Harbor B DEP  S WMZ-TV                     Tax:State       X    -84.02
     12/ 1 Harbor B DEP  S WMZ-TV                     Tax:State       X    -84.02
     12/ 1 Harbor B DEP  S GDI Internationa           Tax:State       X   -126.76
     12/15 Harbor B DEP  S GDI Internationa           Tax:State       X   -126.78
     12/15 Harbor B DEP  S WMZ-TV                     Tax:State       X    -84.02

              Total State and local taxes                           -505.60
              Cash charity contributions

     11/15 Harbor B DEP  S WMZ-TV        United Way Charity      X    -12.50
     12/ 1 Harbor B DEP  S WMZ-TV        United Way Charity      X    -12.50
     12/ 2 Harbor B ATM  S Cash          Children's Charity      X     40.00
     12/15 Harbor B DEP  S WMZ-TV        United Way Charity      X    -12.50
     11/15 Wine Cel         Educational TV F Freemark Ab Charity      -50.00

              Total Cash charity contributions                       -47.50
              Home mortgage interest

     11/ 2 Harbor B      S Englewood Bank &           Mort Int    X -1,239.36
     12/ 2 Harbor B 1342 S Englewood Bank &           Mort Int    X -1,245.59
```

Figure D.13   Tax Schedule report (continued)

```
                              TAX SCHEDULE REPORT
                           11/ 1/91 Through 12/31/91
        FIELDING-All Accounts                                        Page 2
        12/31/91

          Date   Acct    Num    Description    Memo    Category     Clr Amount

                  Total Home mortgage interest                         -2,484.95

                Total Schedule A                                       -3,142.02
                W-2


                  FICA


        11/15 Harbor B DEP  S WMZ-TV                    Tax:FICA    X   -151.23
        12/ 1 Harbor B DEP  S WMZ-TV                    Tax:FICA    X   -151.23
        12/ 1 Harbor B DEP  S GDI Internationa          Tax:FICA    X   -228.16
        12/15 Harbor B DEP  S GDI Internationa          Tax:FICA    X   -228.30
        12/15 Harbor B DEP  S WMZ-TV                    Tax:FICA    X   -151.23

                TOTAL FICA                                             -910.15

                TOTAL W-2                                              -910.15

                OVERALL TOTAL                                        -6,276.58
```

Account Balances Reports

The Account Balances report lets you see the value of your accounts at a particular point in time. Standard variations of this report are the Net Worth report, Balance Sheet report, and Portfolio Value report.

Figure D.14   Standard Account Balances report

```
                      ACCOUNT BALANCES REPORT
                          As of 1/1/92
FIELDING-All Accounts                                            Page 1
1/ 1/92
                                              1/ 1/92
                         Acct                 Balance

        ASSETS
          Cash and Bank Accounts
            Bay Cities-Bay Cities MMF          9,045.95
            Harbor Bk Joint                      511.78

          Total Cash and Bank Accounts        9,557.73

          Other Assets
            Dep Care-Dependent Care Reimb      1,346.13
            Escrow acct                        1,184.72
            Loan to Austin                     2,258.48
            Maria's 401(k)                    35,966.88
            Profit-sharing                    17,737.20
            Mesquite Lane Hse                305,400.00

          Total Other Assets                 363,893.41

          Investments
            GDI Stock-Stock purchase plan     22,972.45
            Luke's IRA                        15,828.97
            Brokerage Acct                     6,455.19
            Maria's Savings                   18,273.70
            Capacity Mutual Fund               1,090.14

          Total Investments                   64,620.45

        TOTAL ASSETS                         438,071.59

        LIABILITIES
          Credit Cards
            VISA                                 358.27
            MasterCard                           697.22

          Total Credit Cards                   1,055.49

          Other Liabilities
            Mortgage Prin                     142,182.03
            School Loan                         4,520.87

          Total Other Liabilities            146,702.90

        TOTAL LIABILITIES                     147,758.39

        TOTAL NET WORTH                       216,135.02
```

Net Worth

The Net Worth report provides a snapshot of your present net worth. It lists all your accounts and their balances, grouping bank, cash, other asset, and investment accounts under the heading Assets; and other liability and credit card accounts under the heading Liabilities. At the end of the report, an Overall Total list states your current net worth—the difference between your assets and liabilities.

Figure D.15 **Net Worth report**

```
                            NET WORTH REPORT
                             As of 12/31/91
SANDORI-All Accounts                                              Page 1
12/31/91
                                                   12/31/91
                          Acct                      Balance

          ASSETS
            Cash and Bank Accounts
              Bay Cities MMF-Bay Cities Group          791.55
              Escrow-Tax/Insurance Acct              1,752.00
              Misc Cash                                 120.00
              Mutual One-Mutual One Joint Acct        1,325.52

            Total Cash and Bank Accounts             3,989.07

            Other Assets
              Abby's 401(k)                          31,532.80
              Abby's Profit-Co. Profit Share         17,737.20
              Ardale Rd Home                        414,200.00
              Loan to Barney                            716.80
              Mutual One CD-Mutual One CD 5 yr         4,217.00
              New house                               7,500.00

            Total Other Assets                      475,903.80

            Investments
              Brokerage-Bay Cities Brokerage         45,990.00
              Company Stock-Stock Purch Plan         34,027.50
              Ralph's IRA-College Bank IRA           34,020.00

            Total Investments                       114,037.50

          TOTAL ASSETS                              593,930.37

          LIABILITIES
            Credit Cards
              Abby's MC-MasterCard                      320.22
              Gas Card                                   55.45
              Joint AMEX-American Express               391.55
              Ralph's VISA                            1,860.41

            Total Credit Cards                        2,627.63

            Other Liabilities
              Mortg principal-Home Mortgage         247,520.00
              School loan                              5,156.00
              Toyota loan                              6,505.10
              Volvo loan                               5,824.90

            Total Other Liabilities                 265,006.00

          TOTAL LIABILITIES                          267,633.63

          TOTAL NET WORTH                            326,296.74
```

Balance Sheet

The Balance Sheet report, like the Net Worth report, gives a view of your present financial situation. The Balance Sheet report groups assets (Bank, Cash, Other Asset, and Investment accounts) and liabilities (Credit Card and Other Liability accounts). The difference between assets and liabilities is your equity.

Figure D.16   **Balance Sheet report**

```
                            BALANCE SHEET
                            As of 4/ 1/92
        REISEN-All Accounts                                      Page 1
        4/ 1/92
                                              4/ 1/92
                           Acct                Balance

             ASSETS

                Cash and Bank Accounts
                   Money Mkt Acct                 45,251.22
                   Mutual One-Main checking account 4,923.60

                Total Cash and Bank Accounts       50,174.82

                Other Assets
                   AR-Accounts Receivable          23,440.00
                   Deprec                          -8,604.14
                   Equipment                       21,496.07
                   Prepaid                          1,800.00
                   Savings                          8,240.00
                   Vehicles                        23,400.00

                Total Other Assets                 69,771.93

             TOTAL ASSETS                         119,946.75

             LIABILITIES & EQUITY

                LIABILITIES
                   Other Liabilities
                      AP-Accounts Payable           8,390.32
                      Loans payable                17,150.00
                      Payroll-401k                      0.00
                      Payroll-FICA-FICA contributions 2,481.20
                      Payroll-FUTA-Fed unemployment tax 1,653.40
                      Payroll-FWH-Federal income tax  1,373.03
                      Payroll-MCARE-Medicare contrib. 2,357.22
                      Payroll-SDI                       0.00
                      Payroll-SUI-State unemploy. tax  760.66
                      Payroll-SWHMA-State income tax  1,089.78
                      Payroll-UWAY                    120.00

                   Total Other Liabilities         35,375.61

                TOTAL LIABILITIES                  35,375.61

                EQUITY                             84,571.14

             TOTAL LIABILITIES & EQUITY           119,946.75
```

Portfolio Value

When you track investments, it is helpful to obtain a snapshot of your portfolio's value on any given day. The Portfolio Value report provides this by listing all securities you currently own as row headings; under each, it lists the number of shares, price (based on the most recent price entered), cost basis, unrealized gain or loss, and the balance.

In the Current Price column, Quicken prints an asterisk (*) after any price that is estimated—that is, based on a price not entered specifically for the as of date of the report. In these cases, Quicken bases its valuation on the most recent price immediately prior to the as of date.

Figure D.17   **Portfolio Value report**

```
                        PORTFOLIO VALUE REPORT
                           As of 12/31/91
MILNER-Birscher                                              Page 1
12/31/91

        Security      Shares   Curr Price    Cost Basis  Gain/Loss   Balance

        AT&R            300.00    32 7/8        8,730.32   1,132.18    9,862.50
        BioPharm Product 200.00   49 1/2       10,118.00    -218.00    9,900.00
        Buckle Video    700.00    14 3/4       10,482.50    -157.50   10,325.00
        Del Elect       500.00     7 7/8 *      3,776.04     161.46    3,937.50
        Failure Grp   1,000.00     8 1/2 *      7,099.80   1,400.20    8,500.00
        Freid Hanson    600.00    31.          15,598.67   3,001.33   18,600.00
        GTE Corp        500.00    35.    *      17,133.80     366.20   17,500.00
        IBM             200.00   115 1/2 *      18,965.00   4,135.00   23,100.00
        MicroComp       300.00    54 3/8       16,142.94     169.56   16,312.50
        Oracle          400.00    10.    *      3,337.05     662.95    4,000.00
        Quantum         500.00    12.    *      6,598.10    -598.10    6,000.00
        Roto-Rooter     500.00    16 1/2 *      7,601.50     648.50    8,250.00
        Seaver Res      100.00    39.           2,572.50   1,327.50    3,900.00
        Seaver Res 91/04 100.00   39.           2,874.48   1,025.52    3,900.00
        Seaver Res 91/07 100.00   39.           3,277.12     622.88    3,900.00
        Seaver Res 91/10 100.00   39.           3,679.76     220.24    3,900.00
        Snid PSep@30    200.00     1.750          358.85      -8.85      350.00
        Songram Systems 600.00    10 1/2        5,661.00     639.00    6,300.00
        Warburtuns Inc  300.00    28.           6,195.00   2,205.00    8,400.00
        -Cash-       28,669.06     1.000       28,669.06       0.00   28,669.06

  Total Investments                           178,871.49  16,735.07  195,606.56
```

Budget Reports

Once you've set up a budget in Quicken, you'll want to know how your actual spending compares to it. Budget reports, like budgets, show the money flowing into and out of the associated bank account. They show any funds moving between accounts as transfers. There are two types of budget reports: the standard Budget report and the Monthly Budget report.

The standard Budget report compares actual to budgeted spending for any time period. Quicken totals all expenses (actual and budgeted) by category and also totals transfers to and from other accounts. The report then displays three columns for the specified time period, showing actual and budgeted spending, and the difference between them.

Figure D.18   Standard Budget report

```
                            BUDGET REPORT
                       1/ 1/92 Through 12/31/92
    SCOTT-All Accounts                                         Page 1
    1/ 5/93
                                   1/ 1/92      -     12/31/92
                                   Actual     Budget    Diff
            Category Description

        INFLOWS/OUTFLOWS
          INFLOWS
            Interest Income           395.14     360.00     35.14
            Salary Income          33,541.80  33,541.80      0.00
            FROM Exeter Fund           74.92       0.00     74.92

          TOTAL INFLOWS           33,936.94  33,901.80     35.14

          OUTFLOWS
            Automobile Expenses:
              Service                 418.00     300.00    118.00
              Fuel                    212.00     240.00    -28.00
              Loan                  1,950.60   1,950.60      0.00

            Total Automobile Expenses 2,580.60 2,490.60     90.00
            Charity                   285.00     300.00    -15.00
            Clothing                1,024.14   1,200.00   -175.86
            Entertainment:
              Dining                  425.00     400.00     25.00
              Books/Music             395.00     400.00     -5.00
              Theater                 510.00     450.00     60.00

            Total Entertainment     1,330.00   1,250.00     80.00
            Federal Tax Withholding 5,031.27   5,900.00   -868.73
            Groceries               1,742.45   1,800.00    -57.55
            Household                 284.50     300.00    -15.50
            Insurance               1,440.00   1,440.00      0.00
            Interest Expense           15.00      25.00    -10.00
            Recreation                318.00     200.00    118.00
            Rent                    9,900.00   9,540.00    360.00
            Social Security Tax     2,565.95   2,500.00     65.95
            State Tax Withholding   2,012.51   2,000.00     12.51
            Transportation            582.00     600.00    -18.00
            Travel                  1,019.00     900.00    119.00
            Utilities:
              Electric                432.00     480.00    -48.00
              Telephone               450.00     360.00     90.00

            Total Utilities           882.00     840.00     42.00
            TO Arch Money Mkt       2,800.00   2,400.00    400.00

          TOTAL OUTFLOWS          33,812.42  33,685.60   -273.18

        OVERALL TOTAL               124.52     216.20    308.32
```

Monthly Budget

The Monthly Budget report also shows projected versus actual spending, but calculates it on a monthly basis. If you specify more than one month as the time period, the report displays three columns for each month with a final set of three columns summarizing the months in the time period.

Figure D.19   Monthly Budget report

```
                            MONTHLY BUDGET REPORT
                           5/ 1/92 Through 5/31/92
            SCOTT-Bank,Cash,CC Accounts                                Page 1
            6/ 2/92
                                              5/ 1/92      -      5/31/92
                      Category Description    Actual    Budget     Diff

              INFLOWS/OUTFLOWS
                INFLOWS
                  Interest Income              37.50     30.00      7.50
                  Salary Income             2,795.15  2,795.15      0.00
                  FROM Exeter Fund             74.92      0.00     74.92

                TOTAL INFLOWS              2,832.65  2,825.15      7.50

                OUTFLOWS
                  Automobile Expenses:
                    Service                    37.50     25.00     12.50
                    Fuel                       18.00     20.00     -2.00
                    Loan                      192.55    192.55      0.00

                  Total Automobile Expenses   248.05    237.55     10.50
                  Charity                      15.00     25.00    -10.00
                  Clothing                      0.00    100.00   -100.00
                  Entertainment:
                    Dining                     45.00     50.00     -5.00
                    Books/Music                72.80     50.00     22.80
                    Theater                    37.50     60.00    -22.50

                  Total Entertainment         155.30    160.00     -4.70
                  Federal Tax Withholding     515.44    515.44      0.00
                  Groceries                   187.20    150.00     37.20
                  Household                    45.00     25.00     20.00
                  Insurance                   120.40    120.00      0.40
                  Interest Expense              2.00      0.00      2.00
                  Recreation                   15.00     25.00    -10.00
                  Rent                        795.00    795.00      0.00
                  Social Security Tax         197.81    200.00     -2.19
                  State Tax Withholding       194.25    200.00     -5.75
                  Transportation              55.00     50.00      5.00
                  Travel                      119.00     75.00     44.00
                  Utilities:
                    Electric                   36.00     40.00     -4.00
                    Telephone                  54.15     40.00     14.15

                  Total Utilities             90.15     80.00     10.15
                  TO Arch Money Mkt          300.00    300.00      0.00

                TOTAL OUTFLOWS             2,754.60  2,757.99     -3.39

              OVERALL TOTAL                   78.05     67.16     10.89
```

Specialized Reports

Other reports that have special uses include the Investment Performance report, Capital Gains report, and Missing Check report.

Investment Performance

The Investment Performance report shows the average annual total return in terms of the percentage change of a group of securities over a specified time period. The report calculates the return based on the changes in the market value of your securities, as well as on income you receive (for example, dividends and interest). If you don't subtotal the report, it generates a single number showing the performance for your entire portfolio as a whole. You can also subtotal by security, type, goal, and other options.

Figure D.20   Investment Performance report

```
                    PERFORMANCE REPORT BY SECURITY
                       9/ 1/91 Through 12/31/91
     MILNER-Birscher                                       Page 1
     12/31/91
                                               Avg. Annual
                         Description           Tot. Return
```

Description	Avg. Annual Tot. Return
TOTAL AT&R	22.1%
Total BioPharm Products	3.0%
Total Buckle Video	20.7%
Total Conford Corp	-82.0%
Total Del Elect	-55.6%
Total Failure Grp	18.6%
Total Fargo & Fargate	NA
Total Fgate PNov@40	91.2%
Total Freid Hanson	79.3%
Total GTE Corp	0.0%
TOTAL IBM	-32.0%
Total MicroComp	5.7%
Total Oracle	72.5%
Total Quantum	34.5%
Total Roto-Rooter	-12.9%
Total Seaver Res	278.2%
Total Seaver Res 91/04	169.4%
Total Seaver Res 91/07	80.7%
Total Seaver Res 91/10	26.2%
Total Songram Systems	15.7%
Total Warburtuns Inc	269.0%

Capital Gains

To see a report of the short- and long-term gains realized by selling securities during a specific time period, generate the Capital Gains report. The report relies on the information you've entered for the securities' purchase and sale dates, prices, and associated costs. This report can be used with a Schedule D tax form—just tell Quicken to subtotal the short-term and long-term gains, excluding any nontaxed accounts, such as IRAs.

Figure D.21   **Capital Gains report**

```
                           CAPITAL GAINS REPORT
                          1/ 1/91 Through 12/31/91
          MILNER-Birscher                                               Page 1
          12/31/91

              Security      Shares  Bought     Sold    Sales Price  Cost Basis  Gain/Loss

                        SHORT TERM

          MComp CApr@50       300  2/15/91   3/31/91    1,139.66     1,451.77     -312.11
          Snider South        200  8/29/91   8/30/91    5,904.40     4,686.36    1,218.04
          Snid PSep@30        200  7/28/91   8/31/91      350.00       358.85       -8.85
          Fargo & Farga       200 10/29/91 10/30/91     7,898.46     7,605.50      292.96


                        TOTAL SHORT TERM                15,292.52    14,102.48    1,190.04

                        LONG TERM

          Freid Hanson        300  1/ 1/90   4/ 1/91    9,182.62     7,799.33    1,383.29
          Songram Syste       400  1/ 1/90   5/24/91    3,917.60     3,774.00      143.60
          Warburtuns In       200  1/ 1/90  11/15/91    5,507.04     4,130.00    1,377.04


                        TOTAL LONG TERM                 18,607.26    15,703.33    2,903.93


                        OVERALL TOTAL                   33,899.78    29,805.81    4,093.97
```

Missing Check

When Quicken generates a Missing Check report, it lists all transactions in the current account, arranging them by check number. When it finds a gap in the check number sequence, it prints the number in sequence in the report, noting it as missing.

Figure D.22   **Missing Check report**

```
                          Missing Check Report
                        12/15/91 Through 1/15/92
FIELDING-Harbor Bk Joint                                        Page 1
1/16/92

   Date     Num     Description        Memo         Category      Clr  Amount


          Harbor Bk Joint

  12/15/91 1350    Green Bros Market                Food:Groceries      -50.55
  12/18/91 1351    Bright Eyes Day Ca               Childcare:Bright    -111.00
  12/18/91 1352    Wanda Milasz                     Childcare:Wanda M   -100.00
  12/20/91 1353    Green Bros Market                Food:Groceries      -88.19
  12/20/91 1354    Cities of the Worl France deposi Reimb Business    -1,440.00
  12/22/91 1355    Coastal Gas & Elec               Utilities           -161.60
  12/26/91 1356    Foothill Credit Un Toyota loan   Auto:Loan           -196.65
  12/26/91 1357    Harbor Bank        Volvo loan    Auto:Loan           -208.57
  12/26/91 1358    Bright Eyes Day Ca               Childcare:Bright    -111.00
  12/26/91 1359    Wanda Milasz                     Childcare:Wanda M   -100.00
  12/28/91 1360  S Gulf Card                        --SPLIT--           -95.40

              *** Missing Check 1361 to 1362 ***

  12/28/91 1363  S Sears                            --SPLIT--           -72.40
  1/ 2/92  1364  S Englewood Bank & T               --SPLIT--        -1,738.58
  1/ 3/92  1365  S Golden State Telep               --SPLIT--           -175.40

              *** Missing Check 1366  ***

  1/ 5/92  1367  S Gas Card                         --SPLIT--           -87.40
  1/10/92  1368  S MCI Telecommunicat               --SPLIT--           -72.19
  1/12/92  1369  S Hugh's Auto Servic               --SPLIT--           -142.50

              *** Missing Check 1370  ***

  1/15/92  1371  S Cash                             --SPLIT--           -30.00

              *** Missing Check 1372 to 3004 ***

  12/28/91 3005    VISA Payment Servi               [VISA]              -356.58
  12/28/91         Montshire School o Course fees   Tuition:Maria       -555.00
  1/15/92  DEP   S WMZ-TV                           --SPLIT--          1,062.92
  1/ 2/92  DEP   S WMZ-TV                           --SPLIT--          1,062.92
  12/15/91 DEP   S GDI International                --SPLIT--      X   1,503.92
  12/22/91 DEP     GDI International  Napa trip (11  Reimb Business      824.50
  12/15/91 DEP   S WMZ-TV                           --SPLIT--      X   1,062.92
  1/15/92  DEP   S GDI International                --SPLIT--          1,503.92
  1/ 2/92  DEPS    GDI International                --SPLIT--          1,503.92
  1/ 5/92  E-PMT   Professional Polis               Household           -75.00

          Total Harbor Bk Joint                                      2,557.01
```

INDEX

$10 REBATE! FROM CheckFree®

To receive your CheckFree rebate, do ONE of the following:

1. Purchase CheckFree software directly from CheckFree by completing the coupon below and mailing it to: Checkfree Corporation, Consumer Services, P.O. Box 897, Columbus, Ohio 43272-4320. You'll receive $10 off the suggested retail list price of CheckFree software ($29.95). So, you'll pay only $19.95. (Note: You don't need CheckFree software to use CheckFree with Quicken®.)

— OR —

2. Go to your local dealer and purchase Quicken or CheckFree. Then, complete and mail the coupon below, along with your Service Form (included in the software package) and a voided check. We'll credit $10 to your checking account.

Either way, you'll save $10. It's a limited-time offer. Offer expires 11/30/92.

CheckFree dealers include: Egghead Discount Software®, Electronics Boutique®, Babbages®, Waldensoftware®, Software Etc.®, CompUSA®, Radio Shack®, Best Buy®, Price Club®, Sam's Warehouse Club®, PC Connection®, MacConnection®, MicroWarehouse®, and MacWarehouse®.

Please note: Coupon cannot be mechanically reproduced or combined with any other offer. If your account cannot be credited electronically, a check will be sent to the address listed on your CheckFree Service Form. Limit one rebate per customer. Offer void where prohibited by law. Offer valid only in the United States. This offer provided solely by Checkfree Corporation. CheckFree® is a registered trademark of Checkfree Corporation. Quicken® is a registered trademark of Intuit Corporation. All other trademarks are the properties of their respective corporations.

YES, I WANT TO SAVE $10 ON CHECKFREE!

Name_____

Address_____

City_____State_____Zip_____

Phone Number (_____)_____ Social Security No._____

—— *Complete this section ONLY if you want to order CheckFree Software* ——

Software: ____ IBM ____ Mac   Disk Size: ____ 5 $1/4$" ____ 3 $1/2$"

Payment method: ____ Check for $19.95 enclosed ____ Bill to my credit card

Credit card: ____ MasterCard ____ Visa ____ American Express

Account #_____ Exp._____

Customer signature_____Date_____

Get PC/COMPUTING Now...and SAVE!

SPECIAL OFFER FOR READERS OF

GUIDE TO QUICKEN 5.0

SAVE
58%
on 12 Issues

SAVE
62%
on 24 Issues

FREE SOFTWARE! Get Our Utilities, Macros, and Secret Tips Online

PCComputing
WINDOWS SPECTACULAR!

HOT NEW PRODUCTS
Unleash the Power of Excel 3.0!
3X Laptops Take Windows on the Road

SMART STRATEGIES
Make Windows Soar on a 286
Build Your Own Programs—Fast!

AND MORE!
HP's Lightning Laser
IBM's First New/486

EXECUTIVE PHONE BOOK

Subscribe now and get a Free Disk!

You purchased *PC/COMPUTING GUIDE TO QUICKEN 5.0* with one thing in mind—to get *THE MOST* from your system. Now, to keep vital information coming throughout the year, order *PC/COMPUTING* —the indispensable resource that helps you work faster and smarter with your PC. 12 times a year, *PC/COMPUTING* delivers it all! Plus if you subscribe now you'll get The Executive Phone Book disk—your personal, on-line database that gives you instant access to your phone and fax numbers at the touch of a key—FREE with your paid subscription.

PC/COMPUTING delivers:
- Tips and techniques guaranteed to save you precious time and money.
- New product reviews to help you make smart, timely buying decisions.
- Fascinating features to inform you, intrigue you, and keep you one step ahead of the game.

Send in the SPECIAL SAVINGS CARD below:

- -

YES! I want to take advantage of this SPECIAL OFFER. Please rush me my Executive Phone Book disk and **PC/COMPUTING** for:

☐ One year (12 issues) only $14.97. I SAVE 58%
☐ Two years (24 issues) only $26.97. I SAVE 62%

Name_____
(please print)   8S3J3

Company_____

Address_____

City_____

State_____ Zip_____

☐ Payment enclosed.   ☐ Bill me later.

SAVE UP TO 62%

Please add $15 per year for postage outside the U.S., U.S. currency only. Canadian GST included. Please allow 30 days for delivery. Disk will be shipped upon payment.

GUARANTEE YOURSELF UP-TO-THE MINUTE PC INFORMATION. ORDER PC/COMPUTING TODAY!

FREE SOFTWARE! Get Our Utilities, Macros, and Secret Tips Online

PC Computing
WINDOWS SPECTACULAR!

HOT NEW PRODUCTS
Unleash the Power of Excel 3.0!
SX Laptops Take Windows on the Road

SMART STRATEGIES
Make Windows Soar on a 286
Build Your Own Programs—Fast!

AND MORE!
HP's Lightning Laser
IBM's First *Real* 486

SAVE 58%

when you order a one-year (12 issue) subscription.

SAVE 62%

when you order a two-year (24 issue) subscription.

MONEY-BACK GUARANTEE
If at any time you find that **PC/COMPUTING** does not provide you with the help and information you need, simply cancel your subscription for a *full refund* on all unmailed issues.

THIS IS A SPECIAL OFFER FOR GUIDE TO QUICKEN 5.0 READERS!

BUSINESS REPLY MAIL
FIRST CLASS MAIL   PERMIT NO. 66   BOULDER, CO

POSTAGE WILL BE PAID BY ADDRESSEE

P.O. Box 50253
Boulder, CO 80321-0253

NO POSTAGE
NECESSARY
IF MAILED
IN THE
UNITED STATES

Fold out for Quicken Maintenance Routine Toolkit

Quicken Maintenance Routine for 199__

May Week				June Week				July Week				August Week				September Week				October Week				November Week				December Week			
1	2	3	4	1	2	3	4	1	2	3	4	1	2	3	4	1	2	3	4	1	2	3	4	1	2	3	4	1	2	3	4

Done	Task	Frequency	January Week 1	2	3	4	February Week 1	2	3	4	March Week 1	2	3	4	April Week 1	2	3	4
	Enter your bills	W																
	Important bill #1:	M																
	Important bill #2:	M																
	Important bill #3:	M																
	Important bill #4:	M																
	Important bill #5:	M																
	Transmit payments to CheckFree	W																
	Enter paper checks & deposits	W																
	Enter pay stub data	W																
	Update investment portfolio prices	W																
	Enter investment transactions	W																
	Make weekly backup disk	W																
	Execute monthly transaction group	M																
	Reconcile bank account #1:	M																
	Reconcile bank account #2:	M																
	Reconcile bank account #3:	M																
	Reconcile brokerage account	M																
	Detail & pay credit card #1:	M																
	Detail & pay credit card #2:	M																
	Detail & pay credit card #3:	M																
	Detail & pay credit card #4:	M																
	Review expense reimbursements	M																
	Make monthly backup disk	M																
	Review tax reports for qtrly filings	Q																
	Review and revise annual budget	Q																
	Prepare quarterly payroll reports	Q																
	Review investment performance	Q																
	Gather tax information for returns	Y																
	Make year-end investment decisions	Y																
	Plan next year's annual budget	Y																
	Make annual backup disk	Y																
	Compress old data files, as required	Y